PUBLIC INTEREST LAWYERING

ASPEN ELECTIVE SERIES

PUBLIC INTEREST LAWYERING: A CONTEMPORARY PERSPECTIVE

Alan K. Chen
Associate Dean for Faculty Scholarship and Professor
University of Denver
Sturm School of Law

Scott L. Cummings
Professor of Law
UCLA School of Law

Wolters Kluwer
Law & Business

Printed in the United States of America.

1 2 3 4 5 6 7 8 9 0

ISBN 978-0-7355-7083-2

Library of Congress Cataloging-in-Publication Data

Chen, Alan.
  Public interest lawyering : a contemporary perspective / Alan K. Chen, Associate Dean for Faculty Scholarship and Professor University of Denver Sturm School of Law, Scott L. Cummings, Professor of Law, UCLA School of Law.
      pages cm.
  Includes bibliographical references and index.
  ISBN 978-0-7355-7083-2 (perfectbound : alk. paper)
  1. Public interest law—United States. 2. Practice of law—United States.
  I. Cummings, Scott L., 1969- author. II. Title.
KF299.P8C44 2013
344.73–dc23

                                                                        2012045863

About Wolters Kluwer Law & Business

Wolters Kluwer Law & Business is a leading global provider of intelligent information and digital solutions for legal and business professionals in key specialty areas, and respected educational resources for professors and law students. Wolters Kluwer Law & Business connects legal and business professionals as well as those in the education market with timely, specialized authoritative content and information-enabled solutions to support success through productivity, accuracy and mobility.

Serving customers worldwide, Wolters Kluwer Law & Business products include those under the Aspen Publishers, CCH, Kluwer Law International, Loislaw, Best Case, ftwilliam.com and MediRegs family of products.

CCH products have been a trusted resource since 1913, and are highly regarded resources for legal, securities, antitrust and trade regulation, government contracting, banking, pension, payroll, employment and labor, and healthcare reimbursement and compliance professionals.

Aspen Publishers products provide essential information to attorneys, business professionals and law students. Written by preeminent authorities, the product line offers analytical and practical information in a range of specialty practice areas from securities law and intellectual property to mergers and acquisitions and pension/benefits. Aspen's trusted legal education resources provide professors and students with high-quality, up-to-date and effective resources for successful instruction and study in all areas of the law.

Kluwer Law International products provide the global business community with reliable international legal information in English. Legal practitioners, corporate counsel and business executives around the world rely on Kluwer Law journals, looseleafs, books, and electronic products for comprehensive information in many areas of international legal practice.

Loislaw is a comprehensive online legal research product providing legal content to law firm practitioners of various specializations. Loislaw provides attorneys with the ability to quickly and efficiently find the necessary legal information they need, when and where they need it, by facilitating access to primary law as well as state-specific law, records, forms and treatises.

Best Case Solutions is the leading bankruptcy software product to the bankruptcy industry. It provides software and workflow tools to flawlessly streamline petition preparation and the electronic filing process, while timely incorporating ever-changing court requirements.

ftwilliam.com offers employee benefits professionals the highest quality plan documents (retirement, welfare and non-qualified) and government forms (5500/PBGC, 1099 and IRS) software at highly competitive prices.

MediRegs products provide integrated health care compliance content and software solutions for professionals in healthcare, higher education and life sciences, including professionals in accounting, law and consulting.

Wolters Kluwer Law & Business, a division of Wolters Kluwer, is headquartered in New York. Wolters Kluwer is a market-leading global information services company focused on professionals.

SUMMARY OF CONTENTS

TABLE OF CONTENTS

3   *POLITICAL IDEOLOGY AND PUBLIC INTEREST LAWYERING*

PART II. WHAT PUBLIC INTEREST LAWYERS DO

4 PRACTICE SITES FOR PUBLIC INTEREST LAWYERING

5 PUBLIC INTEREST ADVOCACY STRATEGIES

PART III. CONTEMPORARY CHALLENGES FOR PUBLIC INTEREST LAWYERING

7 LEGAL ETHICS IN THE PUBLIC INTEREST

PART IV. EPILOGUE

10 *NEW DIRECTIONS, ONGOING CHALLENGES*

ACKNOWLEDGMENTS

We gratefully acknowledge Richard Abel, Catherine Albiston, Anthony Alfieri, Sameer Ashar, Susan Carle, Christine Cimini, Jennifer Dieringer, Harris Freeman, Mark Hughes, Tamara Kuennen, Doug NeJaime, Julie Nice, Ascanio Piomelli, Nancy Polikoff, Deborah Rhode, Laura Rovner, Austin Sarat, Ann Scales, William Simon, Ann Southworth, Louise Trubek, Eli Wald, and Michael Wald, for their thoughtful comments and suggestions. In addition, we would like to thank several people who have been instrumental in getting this book into print: Lynn Churchill at Wolters Kluwer Law & Business, who advocated for and supported this book from its earliest stages; John Devins, our editor who has kept us on track and provided valuable advice and feedback; and Lisa Connery, who is principally responsible for the layout and appearance of the book and has demonstrated extraordinary patience with us throughout its final production stages.

Professor Chen: I would first like to thank Scott Cummings, who was the most enthusiastic supporter of this project long before he agreed to come on board as the co-author. I have learned an enormous amount from the breadth and depth of his knowledge in this vast and continually growing field. It has been an honor and pleasure to work with him.

I also would like to thank the following University of Denver law students who worked as research assistants on this book over the past several years: Angela Birky, Jared Briant, Katherine Dierking, Evan Grimes, Rhoda Hafiz, Robert Hamilton, Laurie Jaeckel, Kristin Krietemeyer, Emily Lyons, Petula McShiras, Sam Niebrugge, Jeffrey Pretty, Tanya Sevy, Kathyrn Stimson, Eliza Stoker, Emma Tetzlaff, Matthew Thompson, and Christine Thornton. As she has been throughout my career, University of Denver Faculty Services Liaison Diane Burkhardt was essential to much of the research necessary for this project and tirelessly hunted down sources that seemed impossible to find.

For a wide range of moral support and sustenance, I thank Steve Jankousky, Pamela Karlan, Martin Katz, Gregg Kvistad, Karen Lash, Teri Meehan, Kevin Swaney, Tom Unterwagner, and Robert Weisberg.

Finally, I would like to thank my late father, Ronald Chen and my mother, Emily Chen, for their unequivocal support and love, and Anne, Kit, Hannah, and Henry for allowing me the freedom and flexibility to devote a substantial portion of my life to completing this project.

Professor Cummings: My deepest gratitude goes to Alan Chen for having the vision to create this project, the generosity to invite me as his collaborator, and the perseverance to see it through. The book would not exist without his leadership and resolve. All of us who practice and study public interest law have him to thank for this enormously important contribution to the field.

I am also incredibly grateful to the students in UCLA's Epstein Program in Public Interest Law and Policy for their enduring inspiration, to Ana Jabkowski for her research assistance, to my colleagues—Rick Abel, Gary Blasi, David Binder, Devon Carbado, Joel Handler, Cathy Mayorkas, Hiroshi Motomura, Kathy Stone, and Noah Zatz—for making UCLA a special place for me to do this work, and to Ingrid, without whom none of this would be possible. I give special thanks to my mom and dad, for listening, and to Caroline and Audrey, for making me smile and giving me faith in the future.

Materials from the following books and articles appear with the kind permission of the copyright holders:

DAVID A. BINDER, PAUL BERGMAN, & SUSAN C. PRICE, LAWYERS AS COUNSELORS: A CLIENT-CENTERED APPROACH (1991). Reprinted with permission of Thomson Reuters.

CAUSE LAWYERS AND SOCIAL MOVEMENTS by Austin Sarat & Stuart A. Scheingold, eds. Copyright © 2006 by the Board of Trustees of Leland Stanford Jr. University. All rights reserved. Used with permission of Stanford University Press, www.sup.org

PRO BONO IN PRINCIPLE AND PRACTICE by Deborah L. Rhode. Copyright © 2005 by the Board of Trustees of Leland Stanford Jr. University. All rights reserved. Used with permission of Stanford University Press, www.sup.org

SOMETHING TO BELIEVE IN: POLITICS, PROFESSIONALISM, AND CAUSE LAWYERING by Stuart A. Scheingold & Austin Sarat. Copyright © 2004 by the Board of Trustees of Leland Stanford Jr. University. All rights reserved. Used with permission of Stanford University Press, www.sup.org

STONES OF HOPE: HOW AFRICAN ACTIVISTS RECLAIM HUMAN RIGHTS TO CHALLENGE GLOBAL POVERTY, edited by Lucie E. White and Jeremy Perelman. Copyright © 2011 by the Board of Trustees of Leland Stanford Jr. University. All rights reserved. Used with permission of Stanford University Press, www.sup.org

SUBURBAN SWEATSHOPS: THE FIGHT FOR IMMIGRANT RIGHTS by Jennifer Gordon, pp. 27, 68-69, 122, Cambridge, Mass.: The Belknap Press of Harvard University Press, Copyright © 2005 by Jennifer Gordon. Reprinted by permission of the publisher.

Scott L. Cummings, *Law in the Labor Movement's Challenge to Wal-Mart: A Case Study of the Inglewood Site Fight*, 95 CAL. L. REV. 1927 (2007), reprinted by permission of the California Law Review.

Scott L. Cummings & Deborah L. Rhode, *Public Interest Litigation: Insights from Theory and Practice*, 36 FORDHAM URB. L.J. 603, 609 (2009) was originally published as an article in the FORDHAM URBAN LAW JOURNAL.

Scott L. Cummings & Ann Southworth, *Between Profit and Principle: The Private Public Interest Firm, in* PRIVATE LAWYERS AND THE PUBLIC INTEREST: THE EVOLVING ROLE OF PRO BONO IN THE LEGAL PROFESSION 183 (Robert Granfield & Lynn Mather eds., 2009), reprinted by permission of Oxford University Press, Inc.

David Luban, *Taking Out the Adversary: The Assault on Progressive Public-Interest Lawyers*, 91 Cal. L. Rev. 209 (2003), reprinted by permission of the California Law Review.

Stephen Meili, *Cause Lawyers and Social Movements: A Comparative Perspective on Democratic Change in Argentina and Brazil, in* Cause Lawyering: Political Commitments and Professional Responsibilities 487 (Austin Sarat & Stuart Scheingold eds., 1998) , reprinted by permission of Oxford University Press, Inc.

Abbe Smith, *Can You Be a Good Person and a Good Prosecutor?*, 14 Geo. J. Legal Ethics 355 (2001). Reprinted with permission of the publisher, Georgetown Journal of Legal Ethics © 2001.

Kim Taylor-Thompson, *Individual Actor v. Institutional Player: Alternating Visions of the Public Defender*, 84 Geo. L.J. 2419 (1996). Reprinted with permission of the publisher, Georgetown Law Journal © 1996.

Karen Tokarz, Nancy L. Cook, Susan Brooks & Brenda Bratton Blom, *Conversations on "Community Lawyering": The Newest (Oldest) Wave in Clinical Legal Education*, 28 J.L. & Pol'y 359 (2008) was originally published in the Journal of Law & Policy.

Neta Ziv, *Cause Lawyers, Clients, and the State: Congress as a Forum for Cause Lawyering during the Enactment of the Americans with Disabilities Act, in* Cause Lawyering and the State in a Global Era 211 (Austin Sarat & Stuart Scheingold eds., 2001), reprinted by permission of Oxford University Press, Inc.

WHO PUBLIC INTEREST LAWYERS ARE

CHAPTER 1

DEFINING PUBLIC INTEREST LAWYERING

> After decades of pro bono practice, no one yet has a sharp or clean definition of public interest law.
>
> Patricia M. Wald (former judge, United States Court of Appeals for the District of Columbia Circuit), *Whose Public Interest Is It Anyway?: Advice for Altruistic Young Lawyers*, 47 ME. L. REV. 3, 5 (1995).

I. INTRODUCTION

This book is about the practice, pitfalls, and possibilities of *public interest lawyering*. In it, we examine which lawyers do it and why, the successes they have achieved, and the challenges they face. To do so requires that we first define the subject of analysis. This, it turns out, is no easy task. Indeed, what exactly it means to be a "public interest lawyer" or engage in "public interest lawyering" is a question that has generated debate and disagreement since the very beginning of the public interest law movement nearly a half-century ago. The discussion has focused on whether it is possible to adequately define lawyering in the "public interest," and if so, precisely what that definition is. Many attempts at definition have been made, and an equal number have foundered, leaving some scholars to jettison the concept altogether as hopelessly indeterminate. STUART A. SCHEINGOLD & AUSTIN SARAT, SOMETHING TO BELIEVE IN: POLITICS, PROFESSIONALISM, AND CAUSE LAWYERING 5-6 (2004). This chapter confronts public interest law's definitional problem as a threshold matter. What it reveals is that the concept of public interest lawyering is deeply contested. *See* Ann Southworth, *Conservative Lawyers and the Contest over the Meaning of "Public Interest Law,"* 52 UCLA L. REV. 1223, 1236-37 (2005) [hereinafter, Southworth, *Conservative Lawyers*]. Our goal is to clarify the terms of the debate and offer a means for analyzing it. In the end, we conclude that no definition is unassailable; all raise boundary questions and pose tradeoffs. We adopt the term *public interest lawyering* precisely because it has framed the boundary questions since the movement's inception and does so in a rubric that is both historically grounded and consistent with the term-of-art that contemporary American practitioners generally adopt. As we will see in Chapter 9, the term is also a vector of change — and controversy — around the world. *See generally* Scott L. Cummings & Louise G. Trubek, *Globalizing Public Interest Law*, 13 UCLA J. Int'l L. & Foreign Aff. 1 (2008).

Despite the disagreement over terminology, there long have been lawyers who have devoted their careers to promoting some version of the public good through their representation of individual clients, the pursuit of specific causes, or both. *See* Robert W. Gordon, *Are Lawyers Friends of Democracy?*, *in* The Paradox of Professionalism: Lawyers and the Possibility of Justice 31, 38-39 (Scott L. Cummings ed., 2011). These lawyers have played critical roles in defending and extending American democratic institutions, providing access to justice for those unable to afford it, and advancing the causes of marginalized groups unable to influence politics by other means. Richard L. Abel, Politics by Other Means: Law in the Struggle Against Apartheid, 1980-1994 (1995); Deborah L. Rhode, Access to Justice (2004); Laura Beth Nielsen & Catherine R. Albiston, *The Organization of Public Interest Practice: 1975-2004*, 84 N.C. L. Rev. 1591, 1595-96 (2006). They have made significant contributions to foundational struggles over poverty and civil rights, thus embodying the highest ideals of a profession that aspires to serve the public good. Martha F. Davis, Brutal Need: Lawyers and the Welfare Rights Movement, 1960-1973 (1993); Mark V. Tushnet, The NAACP's Legal Strategy Against Segregated Education, 1925-1950 (2d ed. 2004). Although they are a relatively small fraction of the total lawyer population, public interest lawyers have had a disproportionate role in making good on the profession's promise of "equal justice under law." The most prominent of these lawyers have become national icons who represent the highest aspirations of the legal profession. There are many notable examples, which include: Thurgood Marshall, and other lawyers for the NAACP Legal Defense and Education Fund, Inc. (LDF) during the civil rights movement; Clarence Darrow, famous for his pro bono representation of unpopular and controversial clients, such as the 1925 defense of John Scopes against the charge of illegally teaching human evolution in Tennessee schools; Reginald Heber Smith, a lawyer in a private Boston law firm in the early 1900s, who first called the profession's attention to the severely unmet legal needs of the poor; and Ruth Bader Ginsburg, who, before she was a U.S. Supreme Court Justice, was a leading women's rights lawyer for the American Civil Liberties Union (ACLU) in the 1970s.

As we will see throughout this book, public interest lawyering extends far beyond these canonical cases to encompass a broad range of advocacy techniques (not just litigation) across various practice sites (not just nonprofit organizations) undertaken by different types of lawyers with distinct goals. This book is about these public interest lawyers and their efforts to create what they envision to be a better world. It seeks to understand their professional heritage, their personal choices, their most ambitious aspirations, and the practical limits on their achievements. It also seeks to present a picture of their day-to-day practice: the financial choices they face, the ethical problems they confront, and the strategies they deploy. In the end, we aim to present a comprehensive picture of contemporary public interest lawyering, assessing what it has attained so far and what the future holds.

Before we do, we begin with a preliminary, yet important, inquiry: What precisely do we mean by public interest lawyering? Does it represent a distinctive model of advocacy that contrasts with conventional lawyering? Does it encompass particular motivations? Does it refer to a specific set of clients or causes? The goal of this chapter is to provide a framework for thinking about the aspects of public interest lawyering that are most central to the concept and those that are more peripheral, while focusing on the always contested boundary cases and suggesting how the definitional debate has real world lawyering consequences. Ultimately, these materials point to an understanding of public interest law as a terrain upon which competing social interests do battle in order to define the very meaning of a just society.

II. TERMINOLOGY: WHAT'S IN A NAME?

At bottom, all lawyering affects the rules that guide our behavior as members of society. Every time lawyers act on behalf of clients to enforce, evade, reinterpret, distinguish, modify, repeal, or comply with law, they influence the basic terms of social interaction in ways that shape our collective experience of freedom and fairness. This is true whether we are talking about a plaintiff's lawyer representing an employee in a wrongful termination case, an in-house lawyer counseling her company on legal compliance, or a solo practitioner advising his client on forming a small business venture.

A threshold question, therefore, is what separates these acts of day-to-day lawyering designed to advance client interests from *lawyering that aspires to make society better*. Of course, framing the question in this way reveals the heart of the problem: one person's vision of a just society will be another's vision of a society gone wrong. And there are so many visions — all deeply contested — that choosing among them is ultimately an exercise in political judgment. How we make that judgment will, in the end, determine what counts as lawyering *in the public interest*.

For at least the last century, lawyers have sought to deploy their legal skill to advance the interests of certain types of individual clients or social groups: legal aid lawyers from the early twentieth century who dispensed free legal services to aid the urban poor, so-called country lawyers who provided professional charity to help their less fortunate neighbors, and activist lawyers who defended war protesters, labor organizers, and racial minorities suffering discrimination. Jerold S. Auerbach, Unequal Justice: Lawyers and Social Change in Modern America 15 (1976); Joel F. Handler et al., Lawyers and the Pursuit of Legal Rights 18-19, 22-24 (1978) [hereinafter, Handler et al., The Pursuit of Legal Rights].

Yet it was not until the 1960s that the term "public interest law" was coined in a self-conscious effort to describe a nascent movement to use legal advocacy, primarily litigation, to advance a political agenda associated primarily with the protection and expansion of rights for racial minorities, the poor, women, and other disadvantaged groups, while also seeking to protect collective goods, like a clean environment. Louise G. Trubek, *Public Interest Law: Facing the Problems of Maturity*, 33 U. ARK. LITTLE ROCK L. REV. 417, 417-20 (2011); *see also* Deborah L. Rhode, *Public Interest Law: The Movement at Midlife*, 60 STAN. L. REV. 2027, 2032 (2008). At the outset of the U.S. public interest law movement, its definition was sometimes couched in the language of market failure. In a classic study from the 1970s, public interest law was defined as "activity that (1) is undertaken by an organization in the *voluntary sector*; (2) provides *fuller representation* of underrepresented interests (would *produce external benefits* if successful); and (3) involves the *use of law instruments*, primarily litigation." Burton A. Weisbrod, *Conceptual Perspective on the Public Interest: An Economic Analysis*, *in* PUBLIC INTEREST LAW: AN ECONOMIC AND INSTITUTIONAL ANALYSIS 22 (Burton A. Weisbrod, Joel F. Handler & Neil K. Komesar et al. eds., 1978) [hereinafter, Weisbrod, *Conceptual Perspective*] (emphasis added). This study drew upon economic analysis to elaborate the concept of "external benefits," which was grounded in efficiency — putting productive resources "to their most 'valuable' uses" — and equity — ensuring that the distribution of the resulting goods and services was fair. *Id.* at 4-5. The central claim was that public interest law was activity that "if it is successful, will bring about significant external gross benefits to some persons; that is, the activity provides more complete representation for some interest that is underrepresented in the sense that the interest has not been fully transmitted through either the private market or governmental channels." *Id.* at 20.

It was this notion of "underrepresentation" that informed other definitional efforts. For the program officers at the Ford Foundation, who designed and executed the funding initiative that launched the field in the 1970s, public interest law was "the representation of the underrepresented in American society." Gordon Harrison & Sanford M. Jaffe, *Public Interest Law Firms: New Voices for New Constituencies*, 58 ABA J. 459, 459 (1972). This definition included the provision of legal services to "poor or otherwise deprived individuals who are unable to hire counsel," as well as legal actions in the defense of "broad collective interests" — such as on behalf of "consumer protection and environmental quality" — "for the benefit of large classes of people" who could not individually afford the cost of mounting lawsuits and who could not easily organize collectively to advance their political interests. *Id.* One observer, writing about public interest law at the end of the 1980s, articulated a similar position:

> Public interest law is the name given to efforts to *provide legal representation to interests that historically have been unrepresented or underrepresented* in the legal process. Philosophically, public interest law rests on the assumption that many significant segments of society are not adequately represented in the courts, Congress, or the administrative agencies, because they are either too poor or too diffuse to obtain legal representation in the marketplace.

NAN ARON, LIBERTY AND JUSTICE FOR ALL: PUBLIC INTEREST LAW IN THE 1980s AND BEYOND 3 (1989) (emphasis added).

The classic definition, rooted in underrepresentation, came under attack from two directions. Beginning in the 1970s, and gaining momentum in the 1980s, the emergent conservative movement took issue with both the efficiency and equity rationales for public interest law. Southworth, *Conservative*

Lawyers, supra, at 1248-49. In terms of efficiency, conservatives argued that it was not obvious that regulation benefitted society at large, rather than simply making distributional choices. *Id*. at 1249. Thus, environmental regulation could have the effect of reducing jobs, or consumer regulation might increase prices. Without aggregating individual preferences for a clean environment and jobs, for consumer safety and low prices, it was not clear *ex ante* what the optimal social welfare function was. The concept of equity was indeterminate as well. What qualified as an underrepresented group? Conservatives argued that the concept of underrepresentation was politically contingent and changed over time. Whether or not one agreed with the conservative framing, it highlighted a fundamental tension in equity conceptions of public interest law: on contested issues of public policy, one group's benefit could be construed as another's burden.

As conservatives challenged the meaning of public interest law from the right, critics on the left challenged its practice — and offered new theories to supplant what many viewed as the outmoded and politically ineffective model of litigation-centered reform embodied in the conventional definition of public interest law. Beginning in the 1980s, new theories emerged with an impressive array of labels: community lawyering, critical lawyering, facilitative lawyering, political lawyering, progressive lawyering, rebellious lawyering, third dimensional lawyering, law and organizing, and legal pragmatism — to name some of the most prominent. Although these theories varied considerably, they shared the concern that rights-based efforts, by themselves, were inadequate to the task of radical social transformation. All of these efforts rested upon a liberal discomfort with lawyer-led strategies that undercut genuine participatory democracy and risked inflicting a double-marginalization on clients: disempowered first by society and then by the very lawyers who purported to act on their behalf.

Despite all the critiques of its political and conceptual coherence, the use of "public interest law" as a label for a distinctive form of lawyering has shown great resilience. Although it is unavoidably contested, public interest law remains the term of choice for U.S. practitioners, and has taken root in emerging democracies around the world. It retains its power not because there is an Archimedean point by which we may judge the public interest across the divisions of politics and culture, but rather precisely because it claims a higher political ground, asserts a vision (or multiple visions) of the good society, and frames the definitional question in historically grounded and institutionally specific terms. In the end, the term "public interest lawyering" has continuing resonance because the contest over its meaning reveals the important political choices at stake. A label at the center of so much fighting must be worth fighting for.

This book uses the term "public interest lawyering" to refer to a broad and contested range of activities that includes legal advocacy focused on the representation of individuals shut out of the private market for legal services as well as lawyering to advance the collective interests of defined groups or constituencies (both liberal and conservative). Because there are no value neutral boundaries, what ultimately qualifies as public interest law turns on how one identifies the relevant criteria and values them in relation to one's conception of a just society. It is therefore useful to start by breaking down and examining in more depth the criteria considered most important in defining *what counts* as public interest lawyering. We conclude by exploring how the definition of public interest law can have tangible consequences by influencing the meaning of professional identity and the scope of professional regulation, while also determining eligibility for certain types of subsidies and programs.

III. CRITERIA: WHAT COUNTS?

Today, people use the term "public interest" law as a gloss for a wide range of sometimes contradictory lawyering categories. Some people define "public interest" law as lawyering for the poor. Some define it as "cause" lawyering. Others think of it as lawyering specifically with a left wing or politically progressive agenda. Still others define the term as encompassing jobs in the public and nonprofit sectors. This last definition equates "public interest" law with law practiced in organizational forms in which lawyers do not take fees for their legal services from their clients.

Susan D. Carle, *Re-Valuing Lawyering for Middle-Income Clients,*
70 FORDHAM L. REV. 719, 729-30 (2001).

A. EXERCISE: WHO IS A PUBLIC INTEREST LAWYER?

Before examining specific criteria, it is useful to think about your own perceptions of what constitutes public interest law. Consider the following narratives of lawyers in a range of settings about their commitment to the public good. Which ones would you classify as public interest lawyers? Why? For those who you do not consider to be public interest lawyers, what are your reasons?

Larry Ryan, Partner, Whitney & Phillips (250-person private law firm): I graduated from law school about 15 years ago. When I was in school, I participated in a lot of "leftie" organizations, such as the public interest society, which did some poverty work in the clinic. I enjoyed that and I still consider myself to be interested in using law for good things. Since I joined the firm, I've done a couple of pro bono matters helping battered women get protective orders. Still, my main work is products liability defense for large pharmaceutical companies, and I enjoy it a lot. It is intellectually stimulating, professionally rewarding, and I make a very good living. But I also feel like I'm doing good for society. The way I see my work is that there are an awful lot of frivolous lawsuits against drug manufacturers. I view my role as vigorously defending the companies when the suits have little or no merit. In that way, I help keep my clients' costs down so that they can use that money for innovation—like finding a cure for serious illnesses. Also, I see my work as helping to maintain lower drug prices for poor consumers. I see my firm's work lobbying on behalf of tort reform in the same light.

Bonnie McCarthy, Staff Attorney, Stop Abortion Rights Now (SARN): My faith is extremely important to me and has been a huge part of my life. When I went to law school, it seemed like most of the other students were not only not religious, but also even disdained religion, as if an intelligent person couldn't have faith. When I graduated, I went to work for a medium-sized law firm doing insurance defense, but the work wasn't satisfying. I made a lot of money, but I didn't really connect with my clients at all. I felt morally at sea. Then I got this job, and I do fulfilling work to stop the practice of abortion. While I respect those in the movement who carry out lawless acts to stop abortion, I prefer to use the legal system. I really see myself in the mold of someone like Thurgood Marshall, using the legal system to help those whom the law doesn't even recognize as people. I lobby for strict abortion regulations in the state legislature in order to protect unborn lives. I engage in litigation in abortion cases, including helping states to defend laws such as the partial-birth abortion ban.

Stephanie Wilson, County Prosecutor, Drug Crime Unit (major urban area): I went to law school to make a difference and to give back to my community. As an African-American woman from a low-income neighborhood, I have seen the devastation that drugs can visit on a community. The American criminal justice system may not be perfect, but it is the best tool we have to protect children in the poor neighborhoods of our big cities. I regard myself as making communities safer, one drug dealer at a time, and the fewer dealers on the street, the better our communities become. I do feel conflicted about the fact that most of the defendants in my cases are young, African-American men, many of whom have suffered from lack of opportunities, discrimination, and sometimes even abuse. But I also believe that we have to help the next generation avoid the trap of drugs and violence. So prosecuting drug crimes is a way I can use my legal skills to accomplish at least some change until the day comes—if it ever does—when we see more money funneled into communities for drug treatment and education programs.

Adam Lefkowitz, Community Political Activist: I was a union organizer before I went to law school. I guess organizing is just in my blood. I am not practicing law in the conventional manner. I spend most of my time doing grassroots organizing of community action groups to advocate for fair wages and decent and safe workplace conditions for the working class. Ultimately, my goal is to accomplish real change for people who live in these communities. Though I don't use my legal analysis and advocacy skills in the same way as courtroom lawyers, the law as a discipline still strengthens my ability to do policy analysis and political action. While I admire those lawyers who go into the courtroom to advance social causes, I don't really think they do much good in the long run. Anyway, many of them are totally disconnected from their clients. They're just pushing a cause and using clients as figureheads. I really know, and work side by side with, my "clients." I've even been thrown in jail with them a few times during direct actions. I think I have a better understanding of their needs and the real issues that face them. My organizing work is fulfilling in ways that putting on a suit and arguing against the bad guys in court could never be.

Sylvia Manzanares, Staff Attorney, Environmental Protection Agency, Region 8 Compliance Assurance and Enforcement Division: Although those in the public interest community sometimes look at the government as their adversary, the government and its lawyers can also do good things that would not happen if we relied only on private enforcement. At the EPA, I use my legal training to monitor corporate compliance with clean air and water standards. I go to court when necessary to enforce federal environmental regulations. This activity is essential to maintaining a clean and healthy environment. I know that some people think working for the government is a kind of cop-out because it's not the same as being on television like all the Sierra Club lawyers, but I think I am actually more effective in my own way by ensuring environmental health in our region. Plus, I earn a little more than most lawyers who work for nonprofit environmental organizations.

Frederick Gates, Legal Aid Staff lawyer: I grew up in an affluent, white, suburban community and had all the benefits that my clients will never have. My parents instilled in me strong values about helping those who are less fortunate than we are and that has stuck with me. As I grew up, I always knew I wanted to work in the trenches as a legal aid lawyer. I remember thinking how meaningful it would be. I was inspired when I saw Robert Redford in the film *The Candidate*. He plays the son of a former governor, and when you first see him he is a legal aid lawyer representing migrant workers in central California. His sleeves are rolled up and he is hard at work and is totally devoted to his clients. I thought to myself, "That's what I want to do with my life." I don't make much money, but for me it's all about helping others. I do receive some financial support from my family, which helps a lot.

Think about these examples as you read the next section, which explores different criteria commonly associated with public interest lawyering. It begins by considering whether public interest law can be defined by reference to the *clients, constituencies,* and *causes* for which lawyers advocate. Can lawyers be classified as acting in the public interest by virtue of whom or what they represent? The section then turns to consider the importance of individual *motivation* as a criterion informing the definition of public interest lawyering, asking whether being driven by altruism, moral or political commitment, or a desire to change the status quo makes one a public interest lawyer. Third, the section explores *institutional* factors: how important is where lawyers work and the type of work they do in defining them as public interest lawyers?

As you read the following materials, consider which criteria for defining public interest lawyering are most useful. Which lawyers do they include? Which do they exclude? How do they match your own definition of public interest lawyering?

B. CLIENTS, CONSTITUENCIES, AND CAUSES

1. Which "Public's" Interest?

The literal meaning of public interest lawyering is lawyering that advances the public's interest as well as (or perhaps instead of) the client's private interests. It therefore rests, in the first instance, on a crucial public-private distinction. Consider the following definition:

> A decision is said to serve *special interests* if it furthers the ends of some part of the public at the expense of the ends of the larger public. It is said to be in the *public interest* if it serves the ends of the whole public rather than those of some sector of the public.

Martin Meyerson & Edward C. Banfield, Politics, Planning, and the Public Interest: The Case of Public Housing in Chicago 322 (1955) (emphasis added). The question we immediately confront is whether this public-private distinction does any analytical work to help us understand what makes public interest lawyering special. Is this distinction between special interests and the public interest persuasive? Why or why not? Can you think of any action that genuinely "serves the ends of the whole public"?

The authors of the classic 1970s study of public interest law referred to earlier proposed a "Public Interest Ratio" to measure the relationship of external benefits created by an organization's work (inuring to members of the public outside the group's membership) to the total benefits (including those accruing solely to the membership):

> If all benefits are reaped by members of the group, external benefits are zero, and the ratio will be zero. In that case, the group can be said to be a pure "private interest" group, and its behavior can be explained in terms of the usual self-interest models. By contrast, the closer the value of the ratio is to unity — that is, the greater the value of external relative to internal net benefits — the more we might be justified in calling the group a public interest group, or the activity a public interest activity.

Weisbrod, *Conceptual Perspective, supra,* at 21. Is this formula useful? In applying it, how would one measure the benefits produced by a public interest law organization's activities?

The key question posed by this approach is what constitutes an external benefit — and, by extension, the public interest. The work of many lawyers has the potential for producing externalities, positive and negative, beyond the immediate result obtained by a particular client. For instance, an attorney's successful representation of Company A in a patent infringement suit may, in the long run, facilitate more innovation by that company and others, though the immediate goal is to protect A's economic interests. A lawyer representing the alleged infringer advances the interests of her client, but also may argue that she is promoting a broader public interest in having valuable products available to more people at lower prices. This example underscores the definitional dilemma. Because the public is comprised of competing groups with conflicting normative views regarding what is best for society as a whole, the notion of the "public interest" becomes an ideological battlefield on which groups compete for political influence by casting their claims in the language of the public good — and by labeling their adversaries as "special interests." For example, one group might view extensive government regulation of handguns as benefitting all of the public, while another group might believe just the opposite. From this vantage point, groups advocating on behalf of the public interest might be most accurately described as asserting a political claim that *their* vision of the public good should be adopted by society at large.

2. The Representation Rationale

Because of the indeterminate meaning of the "public interest," the effort to define public interest law as a category of practice has often been anchored to the types of clients lawyers represent and the causes they pursue. As we suggested earlier, a key concept is whether a particular group or cause is adequately represented — either through the existing private market for legal services or in the realm of democratic politics. Public interest legal representation is said to make up for deficient representation in the marketplace or political arena.

The market-based justification for public interest law begins with the unfairness of a legal system in which economic status determines one's ability to access services. Those with great financial resources will never want for legal representation because the economic market will always attract sufficient legal talent to satisfy their needs. A well-known New Yorker cartoon by J.B. Handelsman illustrates this point, showing a lawyer quipping to his client, "You have a pretty good case, Mr. Pitkin. How much justice can you afford?" Indeed, the interests of large corporations and other well-resourced segments of society always will be more than adequately represented — equipped with the best lawyers money can buy.

But, as we discuss in more detail in Chapter 7, many people go without representation in a pure market-based legal services system. Legal Services Corporation, Documenting the Justice Gap in America: The Current Unmet Civil Legal Needs of Low-Income Americans 17 (2009). This is, in part, a result of the structure of the market for legal services, which is artificially limited by entry barriers (such as the bar examination) and dominated by private lawyers. Clara N. Carson, The Lawyer Statistical Report: The U.S. Legal Profession in 2000 28 (2004) (noting that, as of 2000, 74 percent of lawyers worked in private practice). As a result, the U.S. legal profession serves less than 30 percent of the legal needs of the poor. Peter A. Joy, *The Law School Clinic as a Model Ethical Law Office*, 30 Wm. Mitchell L. Rev. 35, 47 & n.54 (2003); *see generally* Rhode, Access to Justice, *supra*. Those who have limited financial means are less likely to be able to afford legal services for most types of legal problems, criminal or civil. Even those in the substantial middle class of American society would likely struggle to finance any sort of significant legal dispute. Joy, *supra*, at 47 n.54.

One approach to the definitional issue is therefore to say that public interest lawyers are those who serve the needs of clients who would not otherwise receive legal counsel or would receive insufficient legal counsel. Nan Aron's statement in the previous section articulates this position, as does the following definition by the Council for Public Interest Law, the trade group of public interest firms originally funded by the Ford Foundation in the 1970s:

> Public interest law is the name that has recently been given to efforts to provide legal representation to previously unrepresented groups and interests. Such efforts have been undertaken in recognition that the ordinary marketplace for legal services fails to provide such services to significant segments of the population and to significant interests. Such groups and interests include the poor, environmentalists, consumers, racial and ethnic minorities, and others.

Council for Public Interest Law, Balancing the Scales of Justice: Financing Public Interest Law in America: A Report 6-7 (1976). Note that the Council refers to "previously unrepresented groups and interests." What happens when public interest lawyers begin to represent those groups and interests? Does that representation undercut the justification for associating those groups with the "public interest"? How far back should we go to determine if a group has been "previously unrepresented"?

David Luban offers a slightly different market-based definition of public interest law:

> By "public-interest law," I do not mean "law practiced on behalf of the public interest." That usage would make the phrase completely tendentious, because people disagree fundamentally over what the public interest is. Those on opposite ends of the political spectrum are likely to insist that they are practicing law in the public interest but their counterparts on the other side are not. I think that one should instead look for less loaded criteria. As I use the term, a public-interest lawyer is a lawyer for whom making money is not the primary purpose for taking a case — or, to put it in different terms, a lawyer who would like to take the case pro bono if it were feasible to do so. This minimalist definition aims to capture common-sense usage. An additional criterion, different from and not always consistent with the minimalist one, is that public-interest lawyers represent interests that would not otherwise be represented in the legal system. Though different, the two criteria are connected, because most lawyers would not take on pro bono cases from clients who can afford paid counsel, even if it were economically feasible to do so. Thus, cases that meet the first criterion (the lawyer would like to take the case pro bono) will typically meet the second criterion as well (the client would not otherwise be represented in the legal system). These criteria, rough as they are, avoid begging political questions. They include public interest law on the right as well as the left, and they include lawyers delivering routine legal services to low income clients . . . as well as lawyers representing causes. The second criterion does rule out self-styled "public interest" organizations that are really front groups for well-funded corporate interests that think it bad public relations to operate under their own flag. Some might see this structure as an anticonservative bias built into the definition. But I think not calling front groups for well-represented parties "public-interest lawyers" simply eliminates the basic functional difference between public-interest lawyers and lawyers for paying clients.

David Luban, *Taking Out the Adversary: The Assault on Progressive Public-Interest Lawyers*, 91 Cal. L. Rev. 209, 210 n.1 (2003). What do you think of Luban's definition? Does it address the concerns with using the phrase "public interest" to define this type of law practice? Does it include lawyers who work in private firms that enforce antidiscrimination law by bringing cases on behalf of women and minorities under contingency fee or fee-shifting arrangements? Before he became President, Barack Obama worked for Miner, Barnhill & Galland, a civil rights firm in Chicago, which among other things represents plaintiffs in important race discrimination lawsuits challenging violations of voting rights laws. Would he have been considered a public interest lawyer under Luban's definition?

Luban's definition is consistent with an *access* orientation to public interest law: free legal services should be provided to those unable to afford them. Under this view, lawyers who provide legal representation for those in lower socioeconomic groups would clearly qualify as public interest lawyers. But how are consumers and those interested in protecting the environment unable to secure legal representation? Because those two groups can conceivably cut across socioeconomic lines and include people who are wealthy, does the market-based rationale apply to lawyers who work on these issues?

Proponents of the market-based definition point out that legal interests are not always unrepresented in the legal process solely because the clients lack financial resources. Sometimes the interests of disparate citizens may go unrepresented because the benefit to each individual is small and the transaction costs of organizing and seeking representation outweigh the individual benefit. This sort of inefficiency was a driving force behind the adoption of the class action litigation device. *See* Barbara Allen Babcock et al., Civil Procedure: Cases and Problems 941 (3d ed. 2006). Do you think this collective action problem justifies labeling environmental or consumer lawyers as public interest lawyers? Does the existence of mechanisms to aggregate claims and shift fees, which create financial incentives for private attorneys to take on some of these claims, affect your judgment?

What about groups unable to secure representation because their views or conduct are morally repugnant? Here are some groups whose interests are probably under- or unrepresented in the American legal system: Nazis, pedophiles, terrorists, and serial killers.[1] Should attorneys representing these groups be classified as public interest lawyers?

Does a definition of public interest law that hinges on access to the legal system imply that substantive outcomes are irrelevant? Does it mean that there is no political content to public interest law? Consider the following commentary on this point:

> Because of the increasing variety of organizations that claim its status, public interest law has defined itself so as not to exclude organizations based on substantive legal programs. The diversity of substantive claims made by today's public interest law organizations and the tensions that result from the march of such a diverse group under one banner has generally required that public interest law define itself in procedural, representation-based terms. . . .

---

1. That is not to say that individual members of these groups necessarily lack representation in cases when they are charged with crimes. In that context, they may receive a legal defense from a public defender or court-appointed attorney.

In this way, the language of modern public interest law has become the language of procedural justice as articulated by [the philosopher John] Rawls. Presumably, the "public interest" is something to which everyone in a pluralistic society can reasonably agree. This is an application of Rawls' theory of the "overlapping consensus." Because this overlapping consensus cannot rely on any comprehensive religious, philosophical, or moral doctrines, modern public interest law does not permit religious, philosophical, or moral ideas to define what it is or does. Public interest law's insistence on a procedural and value-neutral identity—that of merely assuring representation—embodies the Rawlsian notion of the priority of the right over the good.

This was not the definition of justice for the National Civil Liberties Bureau [predecessor of the ACLU] or the Civil Rights Movement. . . . The Reverend King's movement represented a particular community with a particular substantive vision of the good whose cause was articulated as a moral and religious imperative. Modern public interest law faces an identity crisis as it seeks to reconcile the substantive visions of its predecessor organizations with the extirpation of visionary language from its modern "justice as procedure" rhetoric.

One public interest commentator attempts to solve this crisis of identity by recasting the substantive agendas of predecessor organizations in procedural justice terms. "Both [the NAACP and the ACLU] used the legal process to clarify and protect the rights of minorities—blacks and persons deprived of civil liberties—who would not otherwise have had adequate representation in the legal process." This assertion—that African-Americans and other politically unpopular groups would have gone without representation but for the NAACP and the ACLU—is a crucial one. In modern public interest law rhetoric, it is essential that these groups otherwise go without representation, because without this need the ACLU and NAACP might be seen as endorsing the substantive views of their clients or, worse, claiming that their clients' victories would enhance the common good. Modern public interest law, unlike its predecessors, denies the substantive good to be achieved by the victory of its clients.

David R. Esquivel, Note, *The Identity Crisis in Public Interest Law*, 46 Duke L.J. 327, 341-43 (1996). Do you agree with Esquivel's argument that the procedural approach to thinking about public interest lawyering leads to a morally neutral definition that diminishes the importance of the substantive issues these groups are addressing? Is the procedural definition too narrow? Can public interest lawyering be viewed more broadly, as encompassing the idea of access not only to the justice system in the context of litigation, but also to other institutions of change, such as the political process? Could the ends sought through such a process then be viewed as "substantive," thus addressing some of Esquivel's concerns?

As these questions suggest, the representation rationale for public interest law may also relate to *political*, not just legal, representation. One reason for this is that public interest lawyering emerged during a period when the United States was gradually reducing formal barriers to participation in the political process, but members of many groups had yet to achieve political power, even in proportion to their numbers, because of the effects of historical—and persistent—discrimination. That is, it was not just that minority groups were unable for financial reasons to secure legal counsel. It was that lawyers needed to represent these individuals and groups because the latter could not pursue social change through ordinary political channels because of limits on their political power. Lee Epstein, Conservatives in Court 9 (1985).

In perhaps the most famous example, the NAACP LDF's legal work on behalf of African Americans was deemed necessary because the white majority population in the early to mid-twentieth century did not support racial integration and the eradication of Jim Crow laws. Although formal barriers to political participation, at least in terms of voting, were wiped out by the ratification of the Fifteenth Amendment, African Americans represented both a numerical minority and a relatively powerless group because of discrimination against them and state voting laws designed to limit their participation. In a similar way, political dissidents, such as Socialists or Communists, have been unlikely to exercise much political power in the world of ordinary partisan politics. When their speech is restricted by the major political parties, going to court is an alternative — and perhaps the only viable — approach to advance their interests.

In a decision recognizing that legal advocacy is protected activity under the First Amendment, the Supreme Court acknowledged the political role of litigation:

> In the context of NAACP objectives, litigation is not a technique of resolving private differences; it is a means for achieving the lawful objectives of equality of treatment by all government, federal, state and local, for the members of the Negro community in this country. It is thus a form of political expression. Groups which find themselves unable to achieve their objectives through the ballot frequently turn to the courts. Just as it was true of the opponents of New Deal legislation during the 1930's, for example, no less is it true of the Negro minority today. And under the conditions of modern government, litigation may well be the sole practicable avenue open to a minority to petition for redress of grievances.

NAACP v. Button, 371 U.S. 415, 429-30 (1963).

This perspective resonates with a familiar doctrine from constitutional law. One justification for judicial enforcement of the federal Constitution against other branches of government suggests that such enforcement is most justifiable when the courts are intervening where the political process has broken down. *See, e.g., United States v. Carolene Prods. Co.*, 304 U.S. 144, 152 n.4 (1944) (stating in dicta that more stringent judicial review might be permissible to correct government "prejudice against discrete and insular minorities," which "may be a special condition, which tends seriously to curtail the operation of those political processes ordinarily to be relied upon to protect minorities, and which may call for a correspondingly more searching judicial inquiry."). As discussed below, some conservatives have criticized this aspect of progressive public interest lawyering. They have claimed, among other things, that lawyers who work to change the law through litigation are elitists seeking a second bite at the apple, bypassing the democratic political process and going to court where they have failed to gain majoritarian support for their values. *See* David Luban, Lawyers and Justice: An Ethical Study 303 (1988) (summarizing these arguments).

The political representation rationale, along with its market-based counterpart, supports a vision of public interest lawyering predicated on procedural fairness. It shows great faith in the adversary system of justice, as it relies on the assumption that if everyone's interests were equally represented in the legal and political arenas, outcomes would be fair (or at least fairer). However, it raises a number of questions.

Chief among them is how to know which groups are politically underrepresented and what the relevant time frame is for assessing their political power. Does underrepresentation have to be ongoing or is it sufficient that it occurred sometime in the past? Are environmentalists still underrepresented? What about the interests of workers? Does it matter *why* a group is underrepresented? For some groups, like undocumented immigrants, there may be costs to organizing because members may suffer retaliation if they raise their profiles. Consumers of collective goods like the environment may have insufficient incentives to act collectively because they believe that they can benefit from the work of others (the classic "free rider" problem).

What happens when there are multiple groups laying claim to underrepresentation whose interests are in conflict? When the interests of underrepresented groups clash, can we still categorize all of the attorneys on both sides of disputes as public interest lawyers? Labor unions, which traditionally have supported strong civil rights laws, have sometimes backed legal restrictions on immigration because they have viewed immigrant labor as a source of competition for domestic jobs. *See* Kevin R. Johnson, *Civil Rights and Immigration: Challenges for the Latino Community in the Twenty-First Century*, 8 LA RAZA L.J. 42, 58 (1995). Similarly, civil liberties organizations such as the ACLU, which staunchly support abortion rights, also have asserted the free speech rights of anti-abortion protestors. *See* Brief as Amicus Curiae of American Civil Liberties Union Supporting Petitioners at 6, *Hill v. Colorado*, 530 U.S. 703 (2000). Whose interests are more underrepresented: criminal defendants or crime victims? Environmentalists (backed by powerful groups like the Natural Resources Defense Council and Sierra Club) or small business owners? Minorities who benefitted from affirmative action or poor whites who received no preferences? Civil libertarians or defenders of religious rights? Are these the right comparisons to draw?

The following commentary revisits the classic definition of public interest law (referenced at the beginning of this chapter) as providing "fuller representation to underrepresented interests," which was proposed in the 1970s by Joel Handler, Burton Weisbrod, and Neil Komesar.

SCOTT L. CUMMINGS, *THE PURSUIT OF LEGAL RIGHTS—AND BEYOND*

59 UCLA L. Rev. 506, 522-25 (2012)

[W]e may fairly ask whether the original definition of public interest law propounded by Handler and others, perhaps lacking the courage of its progressive political convictions, has lead to a conceptual dead end—or whether it still offers a meaningful foundation for understanding the field. As the critiques of public interest law have made clear, it is not possible to define "external benefits" or "underrepresentation" in an absolute sense that is applicable across different contexts and over time. But this does not necessarily lead to the extreme relativistic point—that the "public interest" in public interest law is simply in the eye of the beholder — that some conservative critiques of public interest law would suggest. In this vein, it is worth recalling that a key force behind the early mobilization of conservative public interest law organizations was the Chamber of Commerce, which — urged on by soon-to-be-Justice Louis Powell — sought to counter the rising influence of liberal groups in court by promoting conservative counterparts that would appropriate the form and label of public interest law. The manipulation of terms for the advantage of powerful groups does not mean that such terms apply equally by virtue of mere invocation. Rather, it should cause us to scrutinize the labels more carefully.

Toward this end, building on Handler's definition might lead us to reframe the core element of contemporary public interest law in terms of *relative disadvantage*. Public interest law, as a category of practice, would thus be used to describe legal activities that advance the interests and causes of constituencies that are disadvantaged in the private market or the political process *relative to more powerful social actors*. Disadvantage, in this sense, relates to the resources (money, expertise, social capital) that a constituency may mobilize to advance individual or collective group interests. I draw attention to the relative nature of a constituency's disadvantage since disadvantage is, at bottom, deeply situational — shaped by power inequality between rival constituencies. This framing suggests that it is possible to identify the constituencies served by different organizations, in different cases, and then to assess the power differential between them. It does not claim that this calculation is easy — or even always possible. But it does point toward a metric — power — that can provide a basis for distinguishing which among competing causes might legitimately lay claim to the public interest.

The first type of disadvantage is basic market inequality, in which individuals, despite suffering a legal harm, are blocked from legal redress because they are too poor to pay for a lawyer (and there are no viable contingency or fee-shifting arrangements available). Public interest law responds to this type of disadvantage by providing no-cost or low-cost services to expand the entry of the poor into the legal system on an individual, case-by-case basis. Call this the *access dimension* of public interest law. Note that this dimension is the least controversial because it tracks the procedural justification for public interest law — facilitating representation as a means of achieving the equal opportunity to present claims — rather than advancing a substantive conception of the good by preferring some types of claims over others.

Market inequality maps onto, although it is not always coextensive with, forms of political inequality as well, which leads to the second (and more controversial) type of disadvantage: that of social groups or constituencies hindered in advancing collective interests through political channels. Several forms of such structural disadvantage continue to exist, despite important social gains, including disadvantage based on poverty, minority status, discrimination, and impediments to collective action. Members of disadvantaged groups have historically used American-style public interest law, particularly court-based litigation, to leverage policy gains that could not be effectively achieved through majoritarian politics. Thus, in the U.S. context, classic areas of public interest litigation have included welfare rights litigation on behalf of the poor, civil rights litigation on behalf of communities of color, and environmental and consumer litigation on behalf of those diffuse interests. Call this the *policy dimension* of public interest law.

A key feature of these types of public interest law activities is that, unlike standard access lawyering, they are oriented toward the enforcement and reform of laws and institutions that affect broad social groups. Accordingly, they inevitably clash with adversaries who hold different policy views: civil libertarians versus defenders of religious rights; environmentalists versus developers; consumer advocates versus business interests. Groups on both sides of these policy disputes deploy law to advance their aims. Which is public interest law? Focusing on relative disadvantage would frame the policy dimension of public interest law as encompassing advocacy on behalf of constituencies who seek to mobilize law to make up for their relative lack of political power to move policy in legislative arenas. This calculus would require looking at the nature and depth of a group's disadvantage vis-à-vis those against whom that group seeks to mobilize. This, in turn, would require attending to deeply entrenched and persistent forms of inequality based on poverty, race, national origin, gender, sexual identity, and other grounds. It would, on the other side of the political equation, lead us to ask whether proponents of public interest law legitimately pursue policy change on behalf of the less powerful — or whether they cynically invoke the banner of dispossession to mask the reality of privilege.

From this vantage point, public interest law would as a general matter include groups seeking to use legal means to challenge corporate or governmental policies and practices. This definition would encompass activities on both sides of the political spectrum that legitimately advance disadvantaged interests, but exclude lawyering on behalf of existing structures of power. It does not, in the end, suggest that all claims asserted by less powerful groups necessarily advance a normative conception of the public interest to which all segments of society should subscribe. Rather, it asserts that the public interest is served when constituencies that genuinely face greater barriers to influencing political decisionmaking because of their less powerful status gain meaningful avenues to assert their claims through law.

Building on Handler's definition in this way does not avoid the boundary questions that inevitably and inescapably arise. To the contrary, it asks hard political questions. Where should we locate certain plaintiff-side lawyers, who might use law on behalf of individuals (accident victims, consumers, or investors) to challenge systematic practices by corporate actors (insurance companies, product manufacturers, or corporate insiders) but who do so in the pursuit of private enrichment instead of political reform? Or how should we think about libertarian groups that might select cases on behalf of sympathetic and relatively disadvantaged groups as a means to build deregulatory precedent designed to advance a broader pro-business agenda that redounds to the benefit of powerful corporate financial patrons? Similar questions might be posed about some Religious Right organizations, which use the backing of politically influential Christian-denominated churches in the pursuit of a wider role for religion in public life (which may, in turn, curtail the rights of religious minorities or religiously disfavored groups, like gays and lesbians). Or we might ask how to define government lawyers, who may, in some instances, mobilize the power of the state to validate the repression of minority groups while, in others, might use their resources to advance minority interests? No definition of public interest law can definitively answer these questions based on neutral principles — but that does not mean that the questions should cease to be asked. And, indeed, to the extent that the liberal vanguard of public interest law has retreated from the definitional project, the questions are being asked — and answered — by their adversaries.

Is this reframing around relative disadvantage or power useful? Is it too facile to equate lawyering in the public interest just with lawyers who purport to represent the less powerful? Those with power could themselves use it to advance the public good. And lawyers for power holders could guide them along this path. This notion is consistent with the ideal of the "people's lawyer" associated with prominent Progressive era lawyer and Supreme Court Justice Louis Brandeis — someone who sought to be the "lawyer for the situation," counseling powerful corporate clients on solutions that would not just advance their private interest but also uphold the broader public interest. Clyde Spillenger, *Elusive Advocate: Reconsidering Brandeis as People's Lawyer*, 105 YALE L.J. 1445, 1472, 1502 & n.194 (1996). In another version of this idea, consider the following statement from a well-known liberal federal judge (and former legal aid lawyer):

> I firmly believe that a prosecutor who wisely and fairly uses his or her power to forego prosecuting someone when the interest of justice so requires furthers the public interest just as much as a public defender who, from the trenches, defends the criminally-accused indigent. A partner in a major law firm who works to ensure that his or her corporate clients treat their employees in a non-discriminatory manner, or that his or her clients take the high road even as they pursue the bottom line (for example, consider Enron or Worldcom) furthers the public interest just as much as the plaintiffs' lawyer who sues the corporation for discrimination or the government lawyer who charges the corporate executive with fraud and malfeasance.

Hon. Thelton Henderson, *Social Change, Judicial Activism, and the Public Interest Lawyer*, 12 WASH. U. J.L. & POL'Y 33, 35 (2003). Do you agree with Judge Henderson's broader conception of pursuing public interest law? Why or why not? Do any of the definitions discussed in this section make sense to you? If you were a government official or in charge of philanthropic giving at a foundation, would any of these definitions help you decide what types of law practice are worthy of being subsidized as advancing the public interest?

3. Operationalizing the Definition

In private practice, the decision about which cases to take is generally a business one. Clients who are solvent, can afford the law firm's hourly rates, and can pay bills regularly are likely to be taken on, assuming that the firm has sufficient staffing for the job and no conflicts of interest bar the firm from representation. Other reasons exist for law firms to turn down clients besides the profitability of the work. A law firm might, for public relations purposes, decline to represent an unpopular client, or a client that will make the firm's other clients uncomfortable by association. *See, e.g.*, Monroe Freedman, *Must You Be the Devil's Advocate?*, LEGAL TIMES, Aug. 19, 1993, at 19 (describing a Sullivan & Cromwell lawyer's refusal to accept a court appointment to represent a suspected terrorist in the 1992 World Trade Center bombing). Furthermore, law firms sometimes will not accept clients whose cases would require the firm to take a position that could be disadvantageous to its work for other clients in other cases. These are known as "positional" or "issue" conflicts. *See* NATHAN M. CRYSTAL, PROFESSIONAL RESPONSIBILITY: PROBLEMS OF PRACTICE AND THE PROFESSION 274-76 (3d ed. 2004); John S. Dzienkowski, *Positional Conflicts of Interest*, 71 TEX. L. REV. 457, 460 (1993). It is conceivable that a law firm might take a high profile pro bono case to enhance its stature in the legal community and the public eye, but even that decision may be related to generating future paying clients.

One way of distinguishing public interest lawyers from the rest of the bar, then, is by the factors they use to select clients and cases. As Robert Rabin observed:

> The distinctive element . . . is the criterion of case selection. The attorney who selects clients principally on the basis of whether representation would involve working on socially desirable cases is a lawyer engaged in law reform practice. Conversely, where the market is the principal, though not necessarily exclusive, determinant of docket priorities, the legal activity [does not constitute law reform practice].

Robert L. Rabin, *Lawyers for Social Change: Perspectives on Public Interest Law*, 28 STAN. L. REV. 207, 209 n.8 (1976).

In its early years, the Center for Law and Social Policy (CLASP), one of the organizations that pioneered public interest law, used the following guidelines to select cases:

(1) an important public interest is involved;
(2) the individuals and groups involved do not have the financial resources to retain and compensate competent counsel for the matter involved;
(3) no other legal institution is likely to provide effective representation;
(4) the area of the law has not been adequately explored;
(5) opportunities for innovation are present;
(6) the subject matter is one in which the staff of the Center has competence;
(7) the activity is one in which there is substantial room for participation by students at the Center;
(8) the resources of the Center required are commensurate with the gains likely to be achieved.

Charles R. Halpern & John M. Cunningham, *Reflections on the New Public Interest Law: Theory and Practice at the Center for Law and Social Policy*, 59 GEO. L.J. 1095, 1106 (1971).

Compare that to the case selection criteria used by the Public Citizen Litigation Group:

- Is the case likely to have significance beyond the parties involved? Would the substantive outcome of the case, if we win, matter? Is it important to a fairer process or a better world?
- Is the area central to the interests of the Litigation Group or some piece of Public Citizen or its allied public interest groups?
- Do we have a chance of winning?
- Will the cost of carrying on the litigation be within our means?
- Is anyone else likely to do the case, so we do not have to?
- Is there something we would rather do with our limited resources that this would prevent?
- Does the case involve an issue of such moral outrage that none of the above matter much?

BARBARA HINKSON CRAIG, COURTING CHANGE: THE STORY OF THE PUBLIC CITIZEN LITIGATION GROUP 43 (2004).

Given our discussion of the indeterminate meaning of the public interest and the contested nature of underrepresentation, do you think these criteria usefully guide client selection? Or are they simply a way for lawyers to exercise judgments about what types of cases are the most politically important to them? If so, what is the purpose of having criteria at all? Which, if any, of these concerns would be relevant to a lawyer representing clients in a private firm?

C. MOTIVATION

The representation rationale attempts to justify public interest law by reference to external facts — the degree to which particular groups or interests are underrepresented in the market or in politics. The limits of this approach, as we have seen, are that (1) there is no agreed-upon metric of underrepresentation, and (2) groups asserting underrepresented status have conflicting visions of what type of society fuller representation will produce.

This fundamental disagreement about the meaning of public interest law has produced alternative definitional efforts rooted not in the external world of political and economic inequality, but in the internal world of lawyer motivation. The most influential scholarly alternative is the concept of "cause lawyering," defined by Stuart Scheingold and Austin Sarat as follows: "At its core, cause lawyering is about using legal skills to pursue ends and ideals that transcend client service — be those ideals social, cultural, political, economic, or, indeed, legal." SCHEINGOLD & SARAT, SOMETHING TO BELIEVE IN, *supra*, at 3. The cause lawyering concept seeks to distinguish legal advocacy on the basis of lawyer *motivation* rather than a particular conception of the good society or a specific political agenda: "political or moral commitment [is] an essential and distinguishing feature of cause lawyering." *Id.*

This section explores the importance of motivation to public interest lawyering. In particular, we look at three types of motivation: altruism, moral or political commitment to a specific cause, and a desire to change the status quo. As we will see, these categories of motivation are not neatly separable and the very concept of motivation poses its own challenges as a vehicle for defining public interest lawyering. But the drive to do good is a key factor distinguishing what we think of as public interest lawyering from traditional notions of client-centered lawyering, in which lawyers' normative commitments are not supposed to matter (and which we discuss in more detail in Chapter 5). Moreover, understanding lawyers' motives for undertaking public interest work is important for reasons beyond defining this sector of the legal profession. From a systemic perspective, if the legal profession's goal is to increase the legal resources for public interest work, designing effective initiatives to encourage lawyers to devote more time and energy to such work is dependent on understanding the reasons underlying their professional choices.

1. Altruism

Altruism can be a key motivation of public interest lawyers, who seek to use their legal skills to benefit others (clients and society at large), in contrast to more conventional views of lawyering, which center on the advancement of client interests. Carrie Menkel-Meadow, *The Causes of Cause Lawyering: Toward an Understanding of the Motivation and Commitment of Social Justice Lawyers*, in Cause Lawyering: Political Commitments and Professional Responsibilities 31, 37 (Austin Sarat & Stuart Scheingold eds., 1998). In its purist form, altruism is the "unselfish regard for the welfare of others." Deborah L. Rhode, *Pro Bono in Principle and in Practice*, 53 J. Legal Educ. 413, 414 (2003) [hereinafter, Rhode, *Pro Bono*]. Yet altruistic behavior is rarely ever pure. Even public interest lawyers need to earn a living. Does that mean that they are something less than altruistic — or that we should understand altruism in different terms? Of course, public interest lawyers tend to earn less on average than their for-profit counterparts — a difference that economists might call the opportunity cost of engaging in a public interest law career. Does the fact that public interest lawyers make less money make them more altruistic?

Scholars in many disciplines have examined the underpinnings of altruistic behavior and have concluded that the concept of altruism is itself a complex one. As Deborah Rhode has observed, "Some branches of moral philosophy, joined by the rational choice school of economics, generally deny the possibility of wholly disinterested actions." Rhode, *Pro Bono*, *supra*, at 415. There are several complexities here. First, few human actions are compelled by a single motive. Even if altruism drives a lawyer, it would be difficult to trace the sole source of her actions to this motive alone. Second, lawyers who engage in public interest practice may receive nonpecuniary benefits from their altruism. That is, altruistic behavior is never completely altruistic — motives are generally "mixed." Menkel-Meadow, *supra*, at 37-42. As Rhode further observes:

> In describing the influences on altruism, researchers generally distinguish between intrinsic and extrinsic factors. Intrinsic factors include the personal characteristics, values, and attitudes that motivate decisions to help others. Extrinsic factors involve the social rewards, reinforcement, costs, and other contextual dynamics that affect charitable assistance. These factors are, of course, related. Individual motivations can be understood only in the context of larger forces that shape personal commitments and group identity.

Rhode, *Pro Bono*, *supra*, at 418. Recall David Luban's definition of a public interest lawyer, quoted above, as someone "for whom making money is not the primary purpose for taking a case." How is it possible to know when that is true?

Along these lines, consider the following reflection from a well-respected lawyer who is both a former federal judge and public interest lawyer. In addressing a group of law students, she asked them to look within themselves to honestly assess their reasons for desiring careers in public interest law:

> [W]hat is the source of my altruism? Is it really concern for others or a thin disguise for other less laudable motives — a good resume (useful for those with political or judicial ambitions) or an opportunity to feel good about myself and superior, even controlling, toward those I serve without pay, a welcome contrast to some to the irritating demands of a paying client[?]

Wald, *supra*, at 4.

As this suggests, public interest lawyers, while acting altruistically to pursue the interests of others or a larger cause, may also be motivated by important intrinsic benefits or "psychic income" that brings great satisfaction to them. Note, *The New Public Interest Lawyers*, 79 Yale L.J. 1069, 1117 (1970). These benefits may include enhanced feelings of social worth, as well as feelings of greater control over both the substance of one's work and one's lifestyle. Neil K. Komesar & Burton A. Weisbrod, *The Public Interest Law Firm: A Behavioral Analysis, in* Public Interest Law: An Economic and Institutional Analysis, *supra*, at 80, 87-88. Overall, these benefits may outweigh the downsides of low pay and other resource constraints associated with public interest practice. Empirical studies have tended to support this conclusion. One study from the 1990s found higher job satisfaction among public interest lawyers than among private firm lawyers (though the highest job satisfaction was among law professors). Kenneth G. Dau-Schmidt & Kaushik Mukhopadhaya, *The Fruits of Our Labors: An Empirical Study of the Distribution of Income and Job Satisfaction Across the Legal Profession*, 49 J. Legal Educ. 342, 346 (1999). More recently, the first wave of the *After the JD* study — a nationally representative longitudinal study of lawyers admitted to practice in 2000 — found a similar pattern, with public interest, legal services, and public defense lawyers expressing relatively high levels of satisfaction with the substance and social value of their work, in contrast to their big firm counterparts. Ronit Dinovitzer et al., After the JD: First Results of a National Study of Legal Careers 50 tbl. 6.2 (2004).

Public interest practice can also provide concrete career benefits. The 1970s public interest law study referenced earlier suggested that those who begin their careers in public interest law might enhance their subsequent career prospects in other sectors (government, teaching, and private practice) because of the notoriety that can come with high profile public interest work. Komesar & Weisbrod, *supra*, at 87-88. Another early study of public interest lawyers suggested that some of them viewed other external factors, such as "publicity, hobnobbing with Congressmen, [and] meeting celebrities" as adding value to their work. Note, *supra*, 79 Yale L.J. at 1140-41. Further research has documented how some lawyers use the professional capital accumulated through various forms of public interest practice to enhance their career trajectories in law firms, and in the wider world of government and politics. Yves Dezalay & Bryant G. Garth, *Constructing Law Out of Power: Investing in Human Rights as an Alternative Political Strategy, in* Cause Lawyering and the State in a Global Era 354, 354-55 (Austin Sarat & Stuart Scheingold eds., 2001);

David B. Wilkins, *Doing Well by Doing Good? The Role of Public Service in the Careers of Black Corporate Lawyers*, 41 HOUS. L. REV. 1, 21-22 (2004).

Extrinsic benefits may not just serve as rewards that public interest lawyers reap from practice, but may also nudge lawyers to engage in public interest work in the first instance. The way that public interest law opportunities are structured can affect lawyer motivation to select those opportunities among other options. Specifically, if the opportunity costs of public interest jobs are reduced, the jobs themselves may become more attractive. This is the rationale behind Loan Assistance Repayment Programs (LRAPs), which reduce the debt burden (and thereby increase effective take-home-pay) for public interest lawyers. Fellowship programs also operate to overcome the financial deficits of public interest law by conferring the nonpecuniary benefits of professional status and prestige. Once lawyers begin public interest practice, there is some evidence that they are more likely to continue. The 1970s public interest law study, for instance, found that "Legal Services lawyers who left their jobs went disproportionately into government, other jobs outside of private practice (but not commercial establishments), or public interest jobs; or, if they went into private practice, they did more and a different kind of pro bono work or had lower-status practices." HANDLER ET AL., THE PURSUIT OF LEGAL RIGHTS, *supra*, at 181.

The use of extrinsic rewards to encourage altruistic behavior can also be seen in other contexts. Notably, law firms that factor pro bono service into billable hour requirements and promotion decisions are generally more likely to see higher rates of pro bono participation, since the cost of pro bono service (in terms of time away from billable cases) is reduced. DEBORAH L. RHODE, PRO BONO IN PRINCIPLE AND IN PRACTICE: PUBLIC SERVICE AND THE PROFESSIONS 139-40 (2005). But does the lure of extrinsic benefits undermine the altruistic foundations of public interest lawyering? As Deborah Rhode puts it: "if law firms give full billable hour credit for unpaid public service, or law schools give academic credit for such work, does that undercut its moral foundations?" Rhode, *Pro Bono*, *supra*, 416. Thomas Hilbink, reflecting on the role of altruism among cause lawyers, has this response:

> [T]he idea that the presence of (professional or pecuniary) self-interest as a motivating factor might remove one's work from the category of cause lawyering altogether is firmly laid to rest [by the literature]. To conclude otherwise would require cause lawyers to be ascetics in every way, not even deriving pleasure from helping others. Thus, the line between cause lawyering and noncause lawyering lies somewhere near the fulcrum between pure altruism and pure self-interest.

Thomas M. Hilbink, *You Know the Type . . . : Categories of Cause Lawyering*, 29 LAW & SOC. INQUIRY 657, 670 (2004); *see also* Rhode, *Pro Bono*, *supra*, at 416 ("[I]t is desirable to encourage actions taken primarily out of concern for others, but . . . pure selflessness is an unrealistic ideal.").

Why are you interested in public interest law? Would you consider yourself to be motivated by altruism? By self-interest? By a mix of the two? Do you think it matters? How?

2. Moral or Political Commitment

Another way of understanding the role of motivation in public interest lawyering is to distinguish lawyers who pursue their practices because of a conscious moral or political commitment to a particular cause. Such lawyers are motivated by something other than simply representing clients in a professionally competent manner. As Scheingold and Sarat have written, "cause" lawyering "conveys a determination to take sides in political and moral struggle." SCHEINGOLD & SARAT, SOMETHING TO BELIEVE IN, *supra*, at 5. They argue that legal work constitutes cause lawyering only if it is carried out with the intent of pursuing such causes. *Id.* at 3; *see also* Ann Southworth, *Professional Identity and Political Commitment Among Lawyers for Conservative Causes, in* THE WORLDS CAUSE LAWYERS MAKE: STRUCTURE AND AGENCY IN LEGAL PRACTICE 83, 85-86 (Austin Sarat & Stuart Scheingold eds., 2005) (arguing that cause lawyering entails "[a] self conscious commitment to the cause"). Thus, a lawyer might go to work for a nonprofit immigrant rights organization because she believes U.S. immigration policy is regressive and inhumane, and she wants to use her practice to improve the basic living conditions for immigrant workers and their families. This would distinguish her from a lawyer who opens a private immigration law practice because he views this as an opportunity to pursue a new and profitable client market.

Of course, the line between lawyering for clients and for causes is a blurry one. Although cause lawyering attempts to avoid the definitional ambiguities of public interest law — which Scheingold and Sarat call a "notoriously slippery concept" — the concept itself raises its own tensions. SCHEINGOLD & SARAT, SOMETHING TO BELIEVE IN, *supra*, at 5. A key issue is just how ample the notion of "cause" is. Hilbink, *supra*, at 669. For example, in recent years, plaintiffs' lawyers have begun filing mass tort cases against tobacco companies, gun manufacturers, and other large corporations, and have pursued these cases both for pecuniary gain and also expressly for social policy reasons. As one commentator suggests:

> [T]he multiple motivations of mass tort lawyers may suggest a redefinition of "public interest" lawyering. Among lawyers and law students, public interest law practice connotes low pay. If mass tort lawyers use the rhetoric of public interest to describe their work, should that lead to rethinking accepted notions of public interest practice?

See Howard M. Erichson, *Doing Good, Doing Well*, 57 VAND. L. REV. 2087, 2091 (2004). Would mass tort lawyers qualify as public interest lawyers under David Luban's definition above?

If motivation is a key element in defining public interest lawyering, how would you characterize the following lawyers:

Example 1: Ann is a lawyer at the ACLU where she is constantly on the lookout for cases to vindicate the First Amendment right to freedom of speech. When she finds a potential client, she makes it clear that the ACLU litigates cases to judgment — in other words, she is not interested in settling, but rather wants to get law on the books. She admits to having little interest in the details of her clients' situations, caring instead about what their cases stand for.

Example 2: Bishop is a lawyer at Parker & Dolan, where he represents a large tobacco company against health-related lawsuits. He says that, although he does not smoke himself, he believes that it is a matter of individual choice and that the plaintiffs are not entitled to recover against the tobacco company for their own voluntary smoking. He believes that the company is right to protect itself against the suits, which he views as shakedowns by greedy plaintiffs' attorneys.

Example 3: Cecilia is a lawyer at legal aid who took the job because she believes that everyone is entitled to access to justice, irrespective of whether they have money to pay. She regularly represents poor clients filing for bankruptcy, which she personally finds morally repugnant, but she believes that they deserve zealous representation like everyone else.

Example 4: Dominik is a lawyer at a big law firm where he represents a range of different corporate clients on general litigation matters. He steadfastly disclaims any interest in whether the clients are "right or wrong." But he believes that by representing whatever client comes to him, he serves an important social function by bringing disputes into the judicial arena where they can be resolved in a civil and nonjudgmental way by the courts. He believes that by being a lawyer, he validates the authority of law and legal institutions, which are hallmarks of a functioning democracy.

Are any of these lawyers "cause lawyers"? Are all of them? If so, does the concept become the exception that swallows the rule? What *isn't* cause lawyering? How much does it matter, as Sarat and Scheingold suggest, that lawyers are taking sides in political struggle? What types of struggle matter?

In light of the boundary issues raised by the focus on motivation, some scholars writing in the cause lawyering tradition have reframed its meaning. Consider the following definition:

> Cause lawyering is any activity that seeks to *use law-related means* or seeks to change laws or regulations *to achieve greater social justice* — both for particular individuals (drawing on individualistic "helping" orientations) and for disadvantaged groups. [Essentially, it is] *lawyering for the good.*

Menkel-Meadow, *The Causes of Cause Lawyering, supra,* at 37 (emphasis added). Does this modify the definition of cause lawyering offered by Scheingold and Sarat? How? Menkel-Meadow speaks of "social justice" and doing "good." Are these categories self-evident or meaningful? How? Is Menkel-Meadow's definition different from the definitions of public interest lawyering that are focused on underrepresentation?

Focusing on commitment to a cause as the *sine qua non* of public interest lawyering may have important, unintended consequences for actual legal practice. As Erichson has suggested, "The danger of the prevailing conception of public interest practice [as primarily what lawyers do for little or no pay] is that by excluding so much, it may undermine a sense of commitment to the public interest in the everyday work that lawyers do." Erichson, *supra,* at 2091; *see also* Russell G. Pearce, *Lawyers as America's Governing Class: The Formation and Dissolution of the Original Understanding of the American Lawyer's Role*, 8 U. Chi. L. Sch. Roundtable 381, 417-19 (2001). In other words, distinguishing two sectors of the legal profession, defined largely by level of financial compensation, may suggest to lawyers with more lucrative practices that they need not concern themselves with the social good because that is not their role. Pearce, *supra*, at 418. A more expansive definition of public interest work might encourage private, profit-making lawyers to think about their practices in a broader context and to consider their role as professionals in contributing to the public good. That result, however, need not necessarily flow from such a broader definition. As Erichson observes:

> [T]here is reason to be skeptical that redefining the conception of public interest lawyering would alter lawyer conduct to any significant degree. Given the strength of self-serving bias as a cognitive matter, combined with lawyers' extraordinary ability to take moral refuge in the adversary system and the principle of moral nonaccountability, lawyers are likely to see the public good in their own work and unlikely to rethink basic commitments.

Erichson, *supra*, at 2092. Do you agree? Does focusing on commitment to causes shift the discussion away from the political legitimacy of the cause itself and the group that advocates on its behalf? Should groups that promote deregulation and are supported by corporations that benefit from the legal positions espoused be placed in the same category as groups that promote regulation to benefit the poor? If yes, then does the label "cause lawyer" extend to any lawyer whose work is animated by any personal or political conviction — no matter who it ultimately serves? If not, then does cause lawyering have to rely on an implicit political theory of the good society that it purports to reject as a basis of defining legal advocacy?

Ethical issues also may arise from redefining public interest lawyering to reflect lawyers' moral or political motivations. This may occur because the lawyer has a broader social agenda she is trying to pursue that extends beyond the interests of her immediate client.

> To the extent mass tort plaintiffs' lawyers are motivated by policy objectives such as improving product safety, fostering corporate responsibility or, for that matter, by any considerations other than maximizing their clients' recovery, do lawyer-client conflicts of interest arise? A conflict arises if a lawyer's commitment to social change objectives constrains the lawyer's ability or willingness to pursue the client's goals.

Id. at 2102. Do you think this poses a conflict? We will return to the ethical dimensions of this type of lawyering in Chapter 7.

3. Seeking to Change the Status Quo

From a motivational perspective, public interest lawyering may also be associated with a lawyer's pursuit of change to the status quo. Sarat and Scheingold emphasize this aspect in describing cause lawyering as that "directed at altering some aspect of the social, economic, and political status quo." Austin Sarat & Stuart Scheingold, *Cause Lawyering and the Reproduction of Professional Authority: An Introduction, in* Cause Lawyering: Political Commitments

AND PROFESSIONAL RESPONSIBILITIES 3, 4 (Austin Sarat & Stuart Scheingold eds., 1998). Another scholar similarly suggests that cause lawyers "apply their professional skills in the service of a cause other than—or greater than—the interest of the client in order to transform some aspect of the status quo." Lisa Hajjar, *From the Fight for Legal Rights to the Promotion of Human Rights: Israeli and Palestinian Cause Lawyers in the Trenches of Globalization, in* CAUSE LAWYERING AND THE STATE IN A GLOBAL ERA 68, 68 (Austin Sarat & Stuart Scheingold eds., 2001). In contrast, conventional lawyers "tailor their practices to accommodate or benefit the client within the prevailing arrangements of power." *Id.* But what does it mean to work toward changing the status quo, and how does that differ from arguing your client's claim within the current power structure?

Is "changing the status quo" an ideologically neutral criterion, or is it really just code for liberals who wish to reform our society? Thomas Hilbink raises this baseline question:

> What constitutes the status quo or prevailing distributions of power? Does U.S. affirmative action policy constitute the "status quo"? If so, are recent efforts by right-wing lawyers to eradicate affirmative action in higher education challenges to the prevailing power distribution? Or does such lawyering represent an attempt to maintain persistent racial inequality in the United States?

Hilbink, *supra*, at 660. Similarly, consider the abortion debate. The Supreme Court continues to recognize that the Constitution forbids governmental prohibition of a woman's right to choose to terminate a pregnancy before the fetus becomes viable. *Roe v. Wade*, 410 U.S. 113, 154 (1973). On the other hand, the Court has become increasingly tolerant of laws that regulate abortion in ways that make it more difficult for a woman to obtain an abortion, so long as the state does not prohibit it altogether or impose an undue burden on a woman's right to choose an abortion. *Planned Parenthood of Southeastern Pennsylvania v. Casey*, 505 U.S. 833, 874 (1992) (plurality opinion). Suppose one lawyer works for an organization advocating the overruling of *Roe v. Wade*. What about another lawyer who is part of a nonprofit organization that works vigorously to sustain *Roe*, while lobbying federal and state legislatures to relax what she views as burdensome regulations that limit women's access to abortion, but do not violate the *Casey* standard? What constitutes the status quo here and does it affect whom we view as engaged in public interest lawyering?

These questions force us to ask what the political and temporal baselines of the "status quo" are and whether it is meaningful to associate status quo challenges with public interest law. Conventional legal practice often, if not always, involves seeking changes to the status quo. A lawyer may seek judicial enforcement of a contract that is not presently being performed. A tort plaintiff may request compensation for unpaid expenses related to injuries resulting from a tortfeasor's negligence. Of course, one could also conceive of the lawyers' jobs in these cases as *restoring* the status quo ante (making the existing contract work; making the plaintiff whole). But a plaintiff who initiates litigation is almost always trying to change the status quo in the sense that she wants a court to enforce her rights. Conversely, many types of law practice that people would recognize as public interest lawyering, such as legal services attorneys representing indigent clients and environmental lawyers trying to get the government to enforce its own pollution standards, arguably are not involved in seeking changes to the status quo. Are they engaged in public interest lawyering even if not seeking such change? Or could you characterize their activities as social change oriented? Consider Hilbink's perspective on these questions:

> The work done by some poverty lawyers . . . appears to benefit the client within what Hajjar calls "the prevailing arrangements of power." The cause, as delineated by such lawyering, aims not to challenge the system but to help individuals get the best outcome they can within that system. However, the work of [such] lawyers . . . can be reframed as a cause dedicated to "improving the condition of some identifiable portion of the low income community and other disadvantaged citizens." Even if this involves no more than fulfilling unmet legal need, of balancing the scales of justice — a procedural rather than a substantive goal — it can still be characterized as a cause that challenges the status quo of the lives of the individuals represented. . . .
>
> Yet even in cases . . . where the values of the cause hew to the expressed ideals of the state, lawyers' actions in support of so-called mainstream values can constitute cause lawyering. This is because in a reality where "lawyers hold the state to its promises," lawyering serves not simply to uphold the status quo — where such promises are regularly and systematically ignored or neglected — but rather to force the state to a new place where rights are honored or, at the very least, recognized. The actual status quo, after all, does not look like the promise it pretends to have fulfilled. In this light, proceduralist lawyering constitutes a deviant strain by pursuing the ends of the rule of law because the state does not in practice support such ends.

Hilbink, *supra*, at 669. Does challenging the status quo offer a good basis upon which to rest public interest law? How do you think it compares to the representation rationale? To cause lawyering?

D. INSTITUTIONAL CRITERIA: PRACTICE SITE AND ADVOCACY APPROACH

Are public interest lawyers defined by where they work and what they do?

1. Practice Site

From the early era of public interest law, the movement was associated with lawyering in nonprofit organizations, whose very purpose it was to produce external benefits beyond the groups' membership. *See* Weisbrod, *Conceptual Perspective, supra*, at 20-21 (focusing on public interest lawyering in the voluntary sector). This was, in part, a function of the available funding. In the era before robust fee-shifting laws, foundation funding to nonprofit, charitable organizations was seen as the financial model upon which the movement would build — following the Ford Foundation's lead in seeding the first public interest law organizations in the 1970s. *See* Trubek, *Public Interest Law, supra*, at 417-18. In fact, lawyers associated with nonprofit groups sometimes viewed private lawyers with suspicion as too beholden to the bottom line to engage in transformative practice. Louise Trubek & M. Elizabeth Kransberger, *Critical*

Lawyers: Social Justice and the Structures of Private Practice, in Cause Lawyering: Political Commitments and Professional Responsibilities, *supra,* at 201, 202.

This suspicion may still linger. One might think that attorneys who work in a for-profit enterprise, whether it is a law firm or a business, cannot be public interest lawyers because they are ultimately pursuing their self-interest in the form of monetary gain. A recent empirical study distinguishes what it calls "Public Interest Law Organizations" (PILOs) from private law firms:

> PILOs differ from private law firms in that their primary goals focus on social justice or social change through law reform, rather than profit. Despite the legal profession's commitment to and recognition of the need for pro bono services, law practice in the private sector is profit driven. For lawyers in solo and small firm practice, large private law firms, and the corporate context, empirical studies show that the practice of law is a business that must be organized to ensure economic survival. PILOs are different precisely because the economic imperative is secondary to the organization's purposes. To be sure, PILOs must have sources of income to pay salaries and operating expenses, but they are not driven by the same profit motive as firms in private law practice. Rather than being controlled by the profit motive, however, PILOs may be constrained by restrictions that accompany funding from the federal government.
>
> PILOs must engage in extensive fundraising activities to fund litigation costs. This diverts significant time and energy from other objectives. Dependence on charitable funding may undercut PILO lawyers' professional independence, as they must be sensitive to the wishes and agendas of those that fund their work.

Nielsen & Albiston, *supra,* at 1596-97.[2]

As detailed in later chapters, it is true that a number of the most prominent public interest organizations have been nonprofit enterprises. However, lawyers across different types of practice sites, some in the private sector, associate themselves with public interest law.[3] How much weight should we place on organizational affiliation in deciding what counts as public interest lawyering? In addition to nonprofit advocacy groups, there are important government agencies at the federal, state, and local level through which attorneys may advance the public good. Lawyers employed by private law firms may contribute substantial numbers of hours of pro bono work to nonprofit groups and causes, and firms may even devote some of their attorneys' time to public interest work. Scott L. Cummings, *The Politics of Pro Bono*, 52 UCLA L. Rev. 1, 4-7 (2004). Moreover, social change may occur through coalitions of organizations, public and private, for-profit and not. Even nonprofit organizations may work in collaboration with networks of lawyers from private firms to accomplish their goals.

---

2. Although the authors of this study limit their examination to PILOs, they do not argue that public interest lawyering cannot be done by lawyers in private firms. *Id.* at 1602 n.52.

3. We consider practice sites more extensively in Chapter 4.

Is focusing on the structure and objectives of organizations helpful in defining public interest lawyering? Or is it too limiting? Should we think of public interest lawyering as an activity within the exclusive domain of a particular type of lawyer in a specific setting (the full-time staff attorney at a nonprofit public interest group) or as an activity that can (and should) be done by different types of lawyers in different locations (public or private) with different degrees of effort (full-time versus part-time) and motivation? Look back at the Exercise at the beginning of this chapter. Does *where* those lawyers work influence your perception of whether they are engaged in public interest lawyering?

2. Legal Skill

Does public interest lawyering presume the use of certain types of tactics and skills? Nonlawyers routinely engage in meaningful and effective advocacy for marginalized groups. Schoolteachers, social workers, health care professionals, and countless others do work that enriches and improves our society on a daily basis. Of course, what public interest lawyers do is often no better (or no worse) than what other socially committed professionals do, but it is distinguished by how they do it: applying special skills learned through a professional education in law.

The definition of public interest law activity from the Handler, Weisbrod and Komesar study includes as one of its three essential components that the conduct involve "the use of law instruments, primarily litigation." Weisbrod, *Conceptual Perspective, supra,* at 22. Indeed, any basic definition of lawyering would likely include the use of skills such as legal research, fact investigation, negotiation, client counseling; litigation skills such as brief writing, deposition taking, and trial and appellate argument; and transactional skills, such as drafting documents for the creation of nonprofit organizations or laying the legal groundwork for community economic development. As we will explore in greater detail in Chapter 5, lawyers may employ a number of different lawyering strategies to achieve social change. Not all of these activities, however, may depend on professional legal training. For example, is a lawyer's work organizing the constituent group she represents for political action or protest a type of public interest lawyering? What about lobbying or other types of legislative advocacy work? Or what about a lawyer who decides to hold a press conference at a low-income housing project to highlight a landlord's inattentiveness to basic maintenance and safety concerns? Are these activities public interest lawyering?

IV. APPLICATION: WHY DOES THE DEFINITION MATTER?

Although it has engaged scholars in many different fields, the debate over the definition of public interest lawyering is not purely an academic one. Tangible consequences flow from how we define public interest lawyering, and how lawyers and organizations engaged in such activity define themselves. First, how public interest law is defined affects how society views the legal profession and its relation to the public good. Specifically, how public interest law is understood may affect the nature and scope of professional regulation — both for public interest lawyers and the profession at large. Second, the definition of public interest law may affect how it is funded. In terms of organizational support, one of the most important structural mechanisms facilitating the existence of public interest law groups is the Internal Revenue Code, which provides substantial tax benefits to qualified charitable organizations. How the Code defines such organizations — and how other funders do as well — significantly influences their financial viability. In terms of individual lawyer support, many law schools now have LRAPs that help law graduates to pay their student loans if they pursue employment that serves the public interest. Defining which types of employment qualify for such programs presents important challenges for law schools. The final part of this chapter explores how the definition of public interest law matters in these contexts.

A. PROFESSIONAL ROLE

What is the significance of defining a distinct segment within the profession as "public interest law"? If the profession defines certain lawyers as public interest lawyers and others as "regular" lawyers, it may influence professional regulatory standards or measures of performance. For example, public interest lawyers may be held to a different standard than other practicing lawyers in soliciting clients in cases of social significance. Moreover, as Chapter 7 discusses in more detail, there may be other regulatory implications, particularly around conflicts of interests and fees.

Is it important for the legitimacy of the profession that a public interest law sector exist? Scholars define a profession as an occupational field whose members use specialized knowledge obtained through intellectual training tailored to the field. *See, e.g.*, Richard A. Posner, *Professionalisms*, 40 ARIZ. L. REV. 1, 2 (1998). Because members of a profession possess specialized knowledge, they are in a position to make decisions for lay people who must trust the professionals and have no independent way of evaluating the quality of their services. STEPHEN GILLERS, REGULATION OF LAWYERS: PROBLEMS OF LAW AND ETHICS 9 (7th ed. 2005). To protect consumers from abuse, professions typically self-regulate through a code of professional conduct; and to distinguish themselves from mere commerce, professions usually mandate that their members use their expertise to serve the public interest. The issue is how professionals fulfill their public interest obligation.

Consider the following observation by Sarat and Scheingold:

> Legal professions everywhere both need and at the same time are threatened by cause lawyering. They need lawyers who commit themselves and their legal skills to furthering a vision of the good society because this "moral activism" puts a humane face on lawyering and provides an appealing alternative to the value-neutral, "hired-gun" imagery that often dogs the legal profession.

AUSTIN SARAT & STUART SCHEINGOLD, *Cause Lawyering and the Reproduction of Professional Authority: An Introduction, in* CAUSE LAWYERING: POLITICAL COMMITMENTS

AND PROFESSIONAL RESPONSIBILITIES, *supra*, at 3, 3. What does this observation suggest? How is the profession potentially "threatened" by cause lawyering? Are the benefits Sarat and Scheingold refer to merely a form of public relations for the legal profession? A salve to the multitude of jokes about lawyers' lack of honesty and unethical behavior? Or is there something more significant about how these lawyers affect or even transform the profession itself?

In contrast, as we suggested above, some commentators have criticized the effort to cabin public interest lawyers off from the rest of the profession. The relegation of the pursuit of justice to a particular subset of lawyers might suggest, for example, that justice is not the responsibility of *all* members of the bar, undermining in some respects the idea that part of what defines a profession is that its members have a responsibility to serve the broader public interest. *See, e.g.*, Robert W. Gordon, *Portrait of a Profession in Paralysis*, 54 STAN. L. REV. 1427, 1443-44, 1454 (2002) ("The devolution of the public role onto separate corps of officials and other specialists cannot substitute for its performance by private lawyers."). Along these lines, consider the following observation:

> One of the basic ideals of the legal profession is that of public service. While the very need for the public interest firm stems from the failure of the bar to conform to that ideal, the public interest firm may end in killing it. For example, the mere existence of legal aid has allowed many attorneys who previously did free work to now refer that work to legal aid and, with a clear conscience, focus on paying clients. . . . The danger with the assertion that there are two kinds of legal practice — public interest and private interest — is that the public interest law firm may become the institutionalized conscience of the bar. For the traditional practitioner, justice may become, even more than it is today, "someone else's" problem.

Kenney Hegland, *Beyond Enthusiasm and Commitment*, 13 ARIZ. L. REV. 805, 808 (1971). Does the creation of "public interest law" make private lawyers think that serving the public good is "someone else's problem"?

B. FUNDING

1. Organizational

All charitable organizations, including public interest law organizations, rely in part on qualifying as tax-exempt institutions under the federal tax code. As a practical matter, therefore, public interest organizations that sustain themselves on charitable donations must be careful to engage in activities that conform to those permitted for their particular category of tax-exemption so that they may pursue their missions. There are multiple categories of tax-exempt status under the Internal Revenue Code. Section 501(c)(3) grants tax exemptions to:

> Corporations, and any community chest, fund, or foundation, organized and operated exclusively for religious, charitable, scientific, testing for public safety, literary, or educational purposes, or to foster national or international amateur sports competition . . . , or for the prevention of cruelty to children or

animals, no part of the net earnings of which inures to the benefit of any private shareholder or individual, no substantial part of the activities of which is carrying on propaganda, or otherwise attempting to influence legislation (except as otherwise provided . . .), and which does not participate in, or intervene in (including the publishing or distributing of statements), any political campaign on behalf of any candidate for public office."

26 U.S.C. §501(c)(3) (2006). Section 501(c)(4) grants exemptions to "Civic leagues or organizations not organized for profit but operated exclusively for the promotion of social welfare, . . . and the net earnings of which are devoted exclusively to charitable, educational, or recreational purposes." 26 U.S.C. §501(c)(4) (2006).

Federal tax law offers two distinct benefits for qualifying charitable organizations. First, both §501(c)(3) and §501(c)(4) organizations are exempt from paying taxes on their own income. Probably more significantly, the government provides additional support to §501(c)(3) organizations by permitting individuals who donate to them to deduct their contributions from their own taxable income. *See* 26 U.S.C. §170(c); *see also* Oliver A. Houck, *With Charity for All*, 93 YALE L.J. 1415, 1428 (1984) ("For the majority of public charities, the exemptions from income tax afforded under section 501(c)(3) are not nearly so important as these deductions available under section 170 to their donors."). However, §501(c)(4) organizations have greater freedom to engage in political lobbying than groups formed under §501(c)(3) organizations, which may do some lobbying as long as such work is not a "substantial part" of their activities. *Regan v. Taxation With Representation of Washington*, 461 U.S. 540, 543 (1983).

As a policy matter, does it make sense for federal law to allow tax deductions for donations that subsidize some types of public interest lawyering, such as law reform litigation, but not other types, such as lobbying and partisan political action? Why or why not? May the federal government choose which groups to provide tax benefits to in order to subsidize those groups' missions? Would there be any concerns about the government having such discretion?

What about other constraints imposed on public interest law groups that have to conform to federal tax standards? In 1983, the Supreme Court decided a case involving a constitutional challenge to the federal tax law brought by Taxation With Representation (TWR), an organization that was denied §501(c)(3) status because it proposed to engage in legislative advocacy for tax reform. *Regan*, 461 U.S. at 541-42. TWR claimed that Congress's decision to forbid deductions for donors to groups that engaged in substantial lobbying activity violated its speech rights under the First Amendment. *Id.* at 542. TWR argued that this was an unconstitutional condition — the denial of a government benefit to a party because it exercised a constitutional right. *Id.* at 545. The Court rejected TWR's claim, concluding that Congress's action did not infringe on their speech rights, but was a valid exercise of a discretionary decision not to subsidize lobbying by nonprofit organizations. *Id. Regan* therefore upholds the federal government's discretion to subsidize law reform activity, but not political activity, even if the two are directed at the same substantive goals. Do you agree with its conclusion? How would the rule affect your decision about what type of public interest organization to work in or create? What tradeoffs are involved in choosing not to be associated with a §501(c)(3) group?

The manner in which public interest groups organize their activities is also relevant to their financing. As discussed in Chapter 5, public interest lawyers and organizations can accomplish their goals through a variety of strategies, including litigation and traditional political activity. Public interest groups organized under §501(c)(3) must carefully monitor their activities to ensure that they are not engaged in "substantial" lobbying activity, since such activity can ultimately affect their eligibility for charitable tax-exemption and, thus, their financial viability. Alternatively, groups can organize under §501(c)(4) if they want to emphasize lobbying, but this may reduce the amount they raise through charitable donations.

The stakes can be high. The Internal Revenue Service (IRS) sometimes investigates and even rescinds tax-exempt status for organizations that are suspected of engaging in prohibited political activity. Sometimes when this occurs, there are suspicions that the IRS's actions are themselves motivated by partisan considerations. In a well-known instance of this, in 1966 the IRS ruled that donations to the Sierra Club were no longer tax-deductible after the Club took out full-page newspaper advertisements urging protection of the Grand Canyon. Houck, *supra*, at 1436. More recently, the IRS audited the NAACP after its president, Julian Bond, gave a speech criticizing President Bush before the 2004 election, though it ultimately allowed the NAACP to retain its tax-exempt status. Michael Janofsky, *Citing Speech, I.R.S. Decides to Investigate N.A.A.C.P.*, N.Y. Times, Oct. 24, 2004, at A12; *N.A.A.C.P. Cleared of Tax Violation*, N.Y. Times, Sept. 1, 1996, at A14. Nonetheless, the distinction between educational activity or public interest law reform activity and political action has held up over time, and organizations now typically divide themselves into two distinct branches, a §501(c)(3) organization to carry out law reform work and a §501(c)(4) organization that undertakes traditional political work.

Sometimes it is not self-evident that even a public interest organization that confines its activities to legal work would necessarily qualify for the exemption under §501(c)(3). That section requires that a group must be organized exclusively for the purpose of "religious, charitable, scientific, testing for public safety, literary, or educational activities," none of which explicitly encompass litigation or other legal work. 26 U.S.C. §501(c)(3) (2006). Older, more established organizations qualified for exemptions on the ground that they served "educational purposes," even if those purposes were sometimes furthered through litigation. Houck, *supra*, at 1446 & n.134. In 1970, however, just as many new public interest law organizations were applying for tax-exempt status, the IRS announced that it was suspending the granting of exemptions to such firms while it studied its own standards. *Id.* at 1444. The announcement prompted outcry from members of Congress, the organized bar, and public interest law groups, and after a little more than a month, the IRS reversed its position and stated that it would again issue exemptions to public interest law organizations. *Id.* at 1445-46.

The IRS later clarified its view of the tax status of public interest law organizations in its official rulings. IRS Revenue Ruling 75-74 concludes that "[a] public interest law firm that provides representation in cases it selects as having significant public interest and for which representation by traditional private law firms is not economically feasible is operated exclusively for charitable purposes and qualifies for exemption under section 501(c)(3) of the Code." The ruling elaborates on this understanding as follows:

> Organizations meeting the [IRS procedural] guidelines . . . are recognized as charities because they provide a service which is of benefit to the community as a whole. They provide legal representation on issues of significant public interest where such representation is not ordinarily provided by traditional private law firms. In this way, the courts and administrative agencies are afforded the opportunity to review issues of significant public interest and to identify and adjudicate that interest.
>
> Charitability rests not upon the particular positions advocated by the firm, but upon the provision of a facility for the resolution of issues of broad public importance. . . .
>
> Charitability is also dependent upon the fact that the service provided by public interest law firms is distinguishable from that which is commercially available.

REV. RUL. 75-74, 1975-1 C.B. 152.

Which of the criteria for distinguishing public interest lawyering from other types of lawyering (discussed earlier in this chapter) are germane to the IRS's definition of what qualifies as public interest law? Does the IRS's definition make sense to you? What does it exclude?

2. Individual

As a response to the impediment that heavy debt burdens impose on law school graduates, many law schools have created LRAPs — and the federal government has recently created a national program as well. These programs allow qualified students to borrow money to pay off their student loans and, often, forgive those loans if the students remain in qualifying employment for a minimum period. They are designed to promote public interest law careers (and are discussed in more detail in Chapter 8). Those who design and administer LRAPs have to make choices about what types of employment qualify a student for assistance. These important questions are often discussed by law school administrators and students as they establish new LRAP programs or modify existing ones. In turn, the law schools' definitions can effectively shape the pool of lawyers who can afford to pursue careers in public interest, and thus present another tangible context in which the definition of public interest lawyering is meaningful.

Most LRAP programs start with a basic definition of "qualifying" or "eligible" employment. Some schools refer directly to the IRS standards discussed in the previous section. Others focus on the type of work and the fulfillment of otherwise unmet legal needs. The University of Pacific McGeorge School of Law, for example, defines qualifying public interest work as follows:

> To be eligible to receive LRAP grants, graduates must be licensed attorneys employed on a full-time basis in law-related capacities in non-profit

organizations whose primary purpose is rendering representation on public interest issues to persons or organizations who could not otherwise obtain like services. Attorneys employed in government agencies are considered eligible; however, judicial clerks are not.

Program Eligibility, Loan Repayment Assistance Program, University of Pacific McGeorge School of Law, http://www.mcgeorge.edu/Financial_Aid/Loan_ Repayment_Assistance_Program_%28LRAP%29/Program_Eligibility.htm (last visited Aug. 11, 2012).

Many law schools' LRAP programs include government employment of various types within the definition of qualifying employment. Read the terms of the University of Georgia's LRAP program:

> A person is employed in the field of public interest law within the meaning of this charter if the employment requires a Juris Doctor degree and the person is employed to do legal work by (1) an organization described in subsection 501(c)(3) or 501(c)(4) of the Internal Revenue Code, (2) a local, state or federal government entity, including the military, or (3) a private practice where the practice is limited (or substantially limited) to clients comparable to those served by government supported and non-profit legal services organizations. The Law School will determine whether or not a particular job meets these qualifications. A judicial clerkship is not employment in the field of public interest law.

University of Georgia School of Law, Downs' Loan Repayment Assistance Program Charter, Section 2(b), http://www.law.uga.edu/downs-loan-repayment-assistance-program-charter (last visited Aug. 7, 2012).

For a very broad definition of qualifying employment, consider the most recent version of Stanford Law School's LRAP requirements:

> [T]he Program mandates that employment be (a) law-related, (b) public interest in spirit and content; (c) at least part-time (defined as .5 FTE pursuant to the employer's personnel policies) and (d) must be a paid position. "Law-related" means that the position must substantially utilize the legal training and skills of the graduate. "Public interest" work is defined as: (1) work for an organization qualifying for tax exemption under Internal Revenue Code §501(c)(3) or 501(c)(4) or 501(c)(5); or (2) work for a governmental unit, which includes federal, state, or local government (work performed for a foreign government may also qualify, but is subject to approval by the LRAP Committee); or (3) work for private employers (including self-employment or contract employment), at least fifty percent of which involves providing legal services on a *pro bono*, reduced, or court-awarded fee basis to persons or organizations that would otherwise not be able to obtain comparable services. In the case of private public interest employment, eligibility shall be determined by the LRAP Committee on a case-by-case basis dependent upon the participant's ability to verify the nature of his or her work and the percentage performed on a pro bono, reduced, or court-awarded fee basis.

Stanford Law School, Miles and Nancy Rubin Loan Repayment Assistance Program, Section A(1)-(3), http://www.law.stanford.edu/sites/default/files/page/132012/doc/slspublic/LRAP_2012_brochure.pdf (last visited Aug. 7, 2012). Stanford's program also permits students who take judicial clerkships to qualify for LRAP if they take public interest positions immediately following their clerkships, and for some students who go into clinical law teaching to qualify as well. *Id.* Why do you suppose Stanford's program includes even those working for private employers? Are the criteria for determining LRAP eligibility for private sector attorneys useful? How do you think the committee should exercise its authority to determine private sector eligibility on a case-by-case basis?

In contrast to the others considered so far, Yale Law School has a loan assistance program that is tied purely to income, not to the type of practice.

> COAP [Career Options Assistance Program] is open to all Yale Law School graduates. Graduates may join the Program at any time within ten years of graduation.
>   Eligibility is based upon the graduate's income and debt level, not the type of employment. Examples of employment areas from which we expect to draw participants include, but are not limited to, (1) local, state, and federal government, (2) private not-for-profit public interest law practice, (3) low wage private law practice, (4) non-legal not-for-profit organizations serving the public interest, and (5) academic jobs. The political or ideological orientation of the graduate, employer or work is not a factor in determining eligibility. . . .

Yale Law School, Career Options Assistance Program 2010, http://www.law .yale.edu/documents/pdf/Financial_Aid/COAP_10-14.pdf (last visited Aug. 7, 2012).

What types of legal needs might Yale's program support that other schools' LRAP programs do not? Overall, what do you think explains the differences among these programmatic definitions? Do you think it is fair that the definitions vary? The recently enacted federal loan assistance program (discussed in Chapter 8) promises loan forgiveness after a specified period for graduates employed by a government organization, nonprofit §501(c)(3) group, or other nonprofit organization (not a labor union or partisan political group) engaged in designated types of public service. Should that be the standard that all schools follow?

EXERCISE

Suppose that you are the director of a large philanthropic foundation that was established to support different types of social justice organizations. Your board of directors has decided to prioritize funding to organizations that use lawyers to accomplish social change on behalf of undocumented immigrants. The following organizations have submitted grant proposals to your foundation:

1. A nonprofit organization that seeks to hire lawyers to represent undocumented workers in class action impact litigation cases seeking enforcement of claims for unpaid wages under federal and state law.
2. A large private law firm that wants to use the funds to establish an in-house pro bono center focusing on the rights of undocumented immigrants and to train its associates to provide legal representation

to undocumented immigrants in obtaining basic social services, such as education, housing, and health care from local governments.

3. A state agency that wishes to increase the resources devoted to investigating and enforcing (through staff attorneys) wage claims on behalf of undocumented immigrant workers who perform labor for which their employers do not pay the promised compensation.

4. A small private law firm, located in an urban area where a large number of undocumented immigrants reside, that wants to create a specialized practice representing such persons in a wide variety of cases, including immigration work, wage claims, and family law matters, using a sliding scale fee structure that charges clients on the basis of their ability to pay.

5. A nonprofit workers center that wishes to organize undocumented immigrants to engage in protest and other direct action tactics to draw negative publicity to employers who fail to pay promised wages and public officials who fail to take action to regulate such employers.

Which of these groups do you think qualify as public interest law organizations? Which would you fund? Why?

CHAPTER 2

AMERICAN PUBLIC INTEREST LAWYERING: FROM PAST TO PRESENT

I. INTRODUCTION

This chapter provides a historical overview of public interest lawyering in American society, showing the trajectory of public interest practice from its incipient post-colonial expressions to the present state of the field. What it reveals is a dynamic set of institutions and practices that have deep historical roots in promoting the basic rule of law, but also have responded to and been shaped by crucial social and political ferment of the times—from the American Revolution of the eighteenth century to the civil rights revolution of the twentieth. In addition, as we will see, public interest lawyering has also been critically influenced by its relationship to the organized bar (sometimes hostile and sometimes supportive), and its location within the broader legal system, which has grown in complexity and expanded to cover a broader range of social disputes.

These materials chart the historical continuities of the public interest law movement, but also examine important moments of disjuncture and change. They highlight different (but by no means all) components of this history to provide a context for understanding key themes in contemporary public interest lawyering explored in later chapters—such as the historical divide between the legal aid model of dispensing individual legal services to the poor and more reform-oriented and transformative legal strategies. It also explores the degree to which public interest lawyering is the product of individual agency or a response to structural forces embedded in particular political and social contexts.

As you study these materials, can you think of individual lawyers, organizations, or movements that have inspired you to want to pursue a career in public interest law? What is it about these people, groups, or events that have motivated you?

II. THE ANTECEDENTS OF PUBLIC INTEREST LAWYERING: FROM REVOLUTION TO CIVIL WAR

While there was no distinct field of public interest practice in the early period of American history, the legal profession as a whole played a significant role in public life. In the following passage, Robert Gordon describes the public face of the early American legal profession.

> America in the early republic faced a vacuum of law, governance, and leadership authority. After the Revolution it turned out that the new states, the new nation, and the new economy required more regular and sustained attention to governance than part-time legislators and juries could provide. America did not have, and did not want, a powerful career civil service. Lawyers stepped forward to fill the vacuum. They had the credentials and the legitimacy because they had articulated the grievances of the Revolution in legal terms; they had drafted the new Federal and State Constitutions, and gradually got them accepted as legal texts subject to lawyers' arguments and judges' interpretations. Lawyers made law and legal discourse and legal procedures into primary modes of governance and dispute-settlement in the new nation. They dominated high offices, state and federal, elective and appointive; and (after early experiments with lay judges) achieved a complete monopoly of the upper judiciary—whose professional quality was fairly high, especially considering how little they were paid. Nearly all successful lawyers moved regularly in and out of politics and public service. By the 1830s Tocqueville was calling lawyers the American "aristocracy"—more legitimate than a gentry class because they were an aristocracy of merit.

Robert W. Gordon, *Portrait of a Profession in Paralysis*, 54 STAN. L. REV. 1427, 1440 (2002).

Despite their prominence in shaping the early republic, lawyers in this period were not engaged in the type of public interest lawyering we are familiar with today. Note that Gordon's description focuses on the establishment of the basic institutions of legal governance. In this period, the legal profession paid greater attention to building the foundational elements of the emerging legal system than on pursuing social reform through law. This reflects a natural progression; there must be a functioning system of law before a movement to reform law can emerge. Moreover, there must be a role for law that is, at least partly, independent from the political system—law must operate as an autonomous check on political power in order for it to be attractive and useful to those seeking reform. Accordingly, we may view the emergence of "public interest law" as a particular stage in the evolution of liberal democratic societies with a strong role for an independent judiciary (you may compare the distinct role of law in autocratic societies when we turn to the globalization of public interest law in Chapter 9).

Gordon's overview also highlights a particular type of early republican lawyer: the so-called lawyer-aristocrat or lawyer-statesman, who was generally part of the urban professional elite that periodically moved into government to take positions of power. *See* STUART A. SCHEINGOLD & AUSTIN SARAT, SOMETHING TO BELIEVE IN: POLITICS, PROFESSIONALISM, AND CAUSE LAWYERING 31 (2004); *see also* ANTHONY T. KRONMAN, THE LOST LAWYER: FAILING IDEALS OF THE LEGAL PROFESSION

(1993). In addition to these lawyers were the small-town practitioners—Abraham Lincoln being the archetype—who "served civic professionalism simply by being available to most citizens," playing a "peacemaker" role in the community. SCHEINGOLD & SARAT, *supra*, at 32. During the post-Revolutionary era, these two visions of lawyers existed in what historian Jerold Auerbach called "fragile synthesis." JEROLD S. AUERBACH, UNEQUAL JUSTICE: LAWYERS AND SOCIAL CHANGE IN MODERN AMERICA 16 (1976).

Yet, as Scheingold and Sarat point out, they were not the type of public interest lawyers we think of today, but merely their antecedents. SCHEINGOLD & SARAT, *supra*, at 32. There was none of the infrastructure of public interest law that now exists. Early American lawyers were constrained by limited resources and personnel to focus on fulfilling run-of-the-mill legal needs for those who could afford counsel. Other barriers to legal reform in the early republic also limited lawyers' roles. First, a legal culture that condoned slavery, and forbade women and people of color to vote or run for elected office, own property, or otherwise fully participate as citizens in a democratic society was deeply inhospitable to expansive rights claims. Second, many issues that would now be considered ripe for responses by public interest lawyers, such as labor conditions and environmentalism, would not be recognized as wider societal problems until the industrialization of the American economy at the end of the nineteenth century. Third, while an important component of modern public interest lawyering has involved the enforcement of federal constitutional and statutory rights, few enforceable individual rights were recognized before the Civil War. Substantively, the individual rights provisions of the Constitution were enforceable against only the federal government. *Barron v. City of Baltimore*, 32 U.S. (7 Pet.) 243, 250-51 (1833). Even as to the federal government, no cause of action existed for enforcing such rights, aside from cases brought under the Takings Clause; constitutional rights were therefore available only in a defensive posture. This period, of course, long preceded the New Deal, and accordingly there were also few, if any, federal statutory or regulatory frameworks for the protection of rights. While individual states had their own constitutions that could be enforced in state courts, federal limitations on the conduct of state and local public officials did not exist until after the Civil War. The ratification of the Fourteenth Amendment in 1868 created rights of due process and equal protection directly restricting the states. U.S. CONST. amend. XIV, §1. The later development of the Incorporation Doctrine extended the protections of the Bill of Rights, on a case-by-case basis, to state and local governments. ERWIN CHEMERINSKY, CONSTITUTIONAL LAW: PRINCIPLES AND POLICIES 503-05 (3d ed. 2006).

Not only were there few federal rights to enforce before the Civil War, but also there was no vehicle for enforcing them. Even after the ratification of the Fourteenth Amendment, there was no affirmative means to enforce due process and equal protection rights until Congress enacted the omnibus federal civil rights act (now known as 42 U.S.C. §1983) in 1871. To the extent that any federal statutory rights existed, those too were unenforceable, as Congress did not establish general federal question jurisdiction in the federal courts until 1875.

Additionally, until 1876 no civil legal services were provided to poor people. Likewise, the first public defender system was not introduced until 1913. Barbara Allen Babcock, *Inventing the Public Defender*, 43 AM. CRIM. L. REV. 1267, 1274 (2006). Although the private bar performed pro bono work on an ad hoc basis, the modern concept of pro bono work as an integral professional obligation was not an important part of legal culture until the second half of the twentieth century. Scott L. Cummings, *The Politics of Pro Bono*, 52 UCLA L. REV. 1, 4-5 (2004).

Although "public interest law" as such did not exist in the colonial and post-Revolutionary era, we can nonetheless find examples of individual lawyers using their professional training to pursue justice. As the following discussion of the period leading up to the Civil War suggests, such examples were powered by some of the most contentious social issues of the time: the scope of British royal power, the right of the accused to counsel, and the legality of slavery. In these examples, we may discern the outlines of practices and themes that would later become associated with the public interest law movement: the use of lawsuits to challenge the reach of governmental power, access to justice for poor or unpopular clients, and the mobilization of law to advance social movements.

A. EARLY "IMPACT" LAWSUITS: JAMES OTIS AND THE WRITS OF ASSISTANCE CASES

As Robert Gordon notes, lawyers in the Revolutionary period were "articulate spokesmen for the basic principle of republican government, self-rule by the People," viewing themselves as "playing the classical Ciceronian role of fearlessly independent spokesmen for republican liberty against tyranny, usually played out in defending individuals against encroachments on liberty." Robert W. Gordon, *Are Lawyers Friends of Democracy?*, *in* THE PARADOX OF PROFESSIONALISM: LAWYERS AND THE POSSIBILITY OF JUSTICE 31, 36 (Scott L. Cummings ed., 2011). One of these "encroachments" often cited as a root cause of the American Revolution was the British Crown's issuance and enforcement of general writs of assistance — legal warrants that permitted British customs officials to enter private property and engage in open-ended searches without any particular cause. Under British law, writs expired six months after the death of the sovereign who authorized them, and after King George II died in 1760, American colonists tried to legally prohibit the issuance of new writs of assistance. JACOB W. LANDYNSKI, SEARCH AND SEIZURE AND THE SUPREME COURT: A STUDY IN CONSTITUTIONAL INTERPRETATION 33 (1966). The British government sought to hire attorney James Otis as Advocate General for the Crown to defend the writs of assistance. *Id.* Otis rejected the King's charge, opting instead to represent a group of Boston merchants in a court challenge attacking the validity of the writs. *Id.*

In 1761, the case came before Lieutenant Governor Thomas Hutchinson. *Id.* The laws regarding writs of assistance provided no standards governing their issuance. *Id.* at 32. While this could have been a sufficient ground for challenging them, Otis attacked their legitimacy more broadly. He denounced the writs, calling them "the worst instrument of arbitrary power, the most destructive of English liberty and the fundamental principles of law, that was ever found in an English law-book." *Id.* at 34 (quoting Otis). He also argued: "This writ is against the fundamental principles of law, the privilege of house. A man who is quiet is as secure in his house as a prince in his castle, notwithstanding all his debts and civil procedures of any kind." *Id.* In sum, Otis argued that only special warrants—rather than general ones—were legal, and that Parliament's authorization of general writs was against the Magna Carta and fundamental principles of English law. *Id.* By most accounts, Otis was an eloquent and passionate advocate against the reauthorization of the writs. *Id.* at 34-35, 37. Ultimately, however, he lost the case, as the British government decided to reauthorize their issuance. *Id.* at 35.

Might we think of Otis as a sort of prototypical public interest lawyer? Although he was a private lawyer for hire, his advocacy sought to provide "external benefits" throughout the republic by barring the King's expansive power of search and seizure. How effective was he? He lost the Writs of Assistance cases. Yet his efforts to invalidate the writs of assistance brought the issue of the British government's authority to the public's attention, which was one of the events leading to the American Revolution. *Id.* at 37. Students of criminal procedure will recognize that Otis's arguments about the potential abuse of authority ultimately led to the terms of the Fourth Amendment, which requires that warrants issued to authorize government searches must "particularly describ[e] the place to be searched, and the persons or things to be seized." U.S. CONST. amend. IV; *see also* LANDYNSKI, *supra*, at 38.

B. INCIPIENT ACCESS TO JUSTICE: JOHN ADAMS AND THE BOSTON MASSACRE DEFENDANTS

Early American history is marked by an event commonly known as the "Boston Massacre," in which British soldiers posted in front of the Boston Custom House in 1770 shot and killed five local citizens. HILLER B. ZOBEL, THE BOSTON MASSACRE 184, 189, 198-99 (1970). The incident is viewed as an important catalyst of the American Revolution. According to some accounts of the events leading up to the shooting, the crowd was taunting and throwing objects at the soldiers. *Id.* at 196. A witness stated that after a British soldier was struck in the head with a club, the soldier yelled "fire" and shooting began. *Id.* at 198. Shortly thereafter, Thomas Preston, the British commanding officer at the scene, ordered the soldiers to stop firing. *Id.* at 200.

Following the shooting, Preston and the other soldiers were arrested and criminally charged by local governing authorities. They were unable to secure legal counsel for their defense, most likely because of the unpopularity of the cause. 3 LEGAL PAPERS OF JOHN ADAMS 6 (L.H. Butterfield et al. eds., 1965). John Adams, a local lawyer who would later become the nation's second President, agreed to represent Captain Preston, and thereafter took on the British soldiers' case as well. *Id.* In the context of the times, it is difficult to conceive of a lawyer agreeing to represent more unpopular clients. Adams apparently viewed his role as essential to the system of liberty that he and others envisioned. In his own words:

> Council ought to be the very last thing that an accused Person should want in a free Country. . . . Persons whose Lives were at Stake ought to have the Council they preferred: . . . [T]his would be as important a Cause as ever was tryed in any Court or Country of the World: and that every Lawyer must hold himself responsible not only to his Country, but to the highest and most infallible of all Trybunals for the Part he should Act.

LEGAL PAPERS, *supra*, at 6 (quoting Adams's diary).

Adams mounted what must, in hindsight, be viewed as a successful defense, with all defendants acquitted of murder, although two soldiers were found guilty of manslaughter. *Id.* at 24-31. At Captain Preston's trial, the jury found sufficient doubt that Preston had ordered the soldiers to shoot. *Id.* at 22-23. In the separate trial of the soldiers, Adams successfully argued that they had been provoked by the hostile crowd. *Id.* at 26-27. The latter was, from a strategic standpoint, no simple task, since the jury was made up of local residents unlikely to be sympathetic to the soldiers. *Id.* at 27.

Adams's defense of the British soldiers in these cases was highly controversial at the time. In 1815, he wrote that "[t]o this hour . . . my conduct . . . is remembered, and is alleged against me to prove I am an enemy to my country, and always have been." *Id.* at 33. Presumably, he risked his physical safety and his reputation and career because of his choice to represent the defendants. Despite this adversity, he later reflected on his representation in these cases as "one of the most gallant, generous, manly and disinterested actions of my whole life, and one of the best pieces of service I ever rendered my country." DAVID MCCULLOUGH, JOHN ADAMS 68 (2001).

Although Adams's professional conduct in this case can be viewed as facilitating his belief in a free society that protected human liberty, his high profile representation could have yielded other benefits to him. While he claimed that he "lost more than half his practice" as a result of the public's negative reaction to his defense of the soldiers, *id.* at 67, his reputation as an orator and attorney was enhanced by his performance at the trial. Witnesses described Adams's closing argument in the soldiers' trial as a "virtuoso performance," calling him "the finest speaker they have ever heard." *Id.* at 67, 69. Moreover, Adams went on to become a steadfast critic of British occupation. The Massacre trial provided him with an opportunity to take a stand against this practice, while still vigorously representing his clients. Though he placed blame primarily on the mob for inciting the soldiers to fire upon the crowd, he also condemned the soldiers as "the strongest Proofs of the Danger of Standing Armies." JOHN ADAMS, DIARY AND AUTOBIOGRAPHY OF JOHN ADAMS, Mar. 5, 1773 (L.H. Butterfield ed., 1961). Perhaps he gained credibility from this defense for his later public opposition to British occupation. In any event, John Adams was one of the first lawyers in America history to take on an unpopular cause to promote broader public good.

Think back to Chapter 1's discussion of the definition of public interest law. Was John Adams's representation of the British officers in the "public interest"? If Adams's motives were to advance his own political career and generate business for his private law practice, would your conclusion be the same? What if those motives contributed to his decision to take these cases, but he was also compelled by his sense of justice?

C. LAW AS A SOCIAL MOVEMENT STRATEGY: LAWYERING FOR ABOLITION

From the early years of the republic, there existed a strong network of antislavery organizations, which often used litigation and other law-related tactics both to protect individual slaves or freed African-American persons and to accomplish the broader social goal of abolition. During the era following the American Revolution, antislavery activists began organizing abolitionist societies focused on promoting manumission and protecting free blacks. *See* WILLIAM M. WIECEK, THE SOURCES OF ANTISLAVERY CONSTITUTIONALISM IN AMERICA, 1760-1848 84 (1977). These societies played a role in the movement to end slavery in the northern states, while also convincing some southern slaveholders to free individual slaves. *Id.* at 86, 90-91.

Early abolition societies "converted what had been principally a religio-moral impulse into a secular legal activity." *Id.* at 88. The early abolition effort was marked by at least three distinct characteristics. First, it focused on reform at the state, rather than federal, level. *Id.* at 85. Second, antislavery societies emphasized gradualistic efforts toward abolition rather than seeking immediate and universal emancipation of slaves. *Id.* Finally, early abolition efforts relied principally on legal, as opposed to political, action. While they did engage in some political lobbying, abolitionists' primary emphasis was on conventional lawyering activities such as litigation, counseling, monitoring slave registries, and compiling statutes. *Id.*

The work of these organizations showed the sophisticated relationship between legal strategy and overall movement aims. The lawyers working toward abolition were closely affiliated with abolitionist societies. The societies were "intensely litigious" and "skirted the edges of barratry and maintenance." *Id.* at 86. The older societies retained officers known as "Counsellors" who, among other things, provided legal representation and counseling to African Americans in lawsuits seeking their freedom; served as a resource on state laws and constitutional provisions pertaining to emancipation, the slave trade, kidnapping, and the rights of free blacks; and in states with gradual emancipation statutes, ensured that manumissions were properly recorded. *Id.* at 86-87. One of the leading societies to use legal tactics in the early movement against slavery was the Pennsylvania Abolitionist Society (PAS). RICHARD S. NEWMAN, TRANSFORMATION OF AMERICAN ABOLITIONISM 60 (2002). PAS had a dedicated group of lawyers who "represented literally thousands of African Americans seeking legal aid during the early republic." *Id.* Rather than bring "test cases" to trial, PAS attorneys "worked on the margins, using loopholes, technicalities, and narrow legal opinions to liberate African Americans on a case-by-case basis." *Id.* at 61. This strategy was typical of the gradualism of the early abolitionist movement. PAS also succeeded in part because it developed close ties with the African-American community. *Id.* at 66-69.

During the 1830s, the antislavery bar became more ideological and the development of militant abolitionism "produced an impulse to use litigation as a dramatic forum for ideology." ROBERT M. COVER, JUSTICE ACCUSED: ANTISLAVERY AND THE JUDICIAL PROCESS 160-61 (1975). The movement to abolish slavery became more aggressive and a "well-defined group of men" began bringing test cases to assert the unconstitutionality and immorality of slavery. *Id.* at 161. Antislavery attorneys used a variety of tools, including positivist and natural law, to argue the unconstitutionality and illegality of slavery. Most of these lawyers worked for free or reduced compensation. *Id.* They were largely ideological and many espoused a radical form of constitutionalism. *See* WIECEK, *supra*, at 257.

The companion cases of *State v. Post* and *State v. Van Beuren*, 20 N.J.L. 368 (1845), brought before the New Jersey Supreme Court by antislavery attorney Alvan Stewart on behalf of the New Jersey State Anti-Slavery Society (NJSASS), are an important illustration of this shift in tactics. Daniel R. Ernst, *Legal Positivism, Abolitionist Litigation, and the New Jersey Slave Case of 1845, in* ABOLITIONISM AND AMERICAN LAW 103, 103-06 (John R. McKivigan ed., 1999). NJSASS was committed to the task of bringing an antislavery legal challenge before the state supreme court. *Id.* at 109. Although unsuccessful, Stewart's argument was "equally notable for its strained attempt to find a basis in positive law for the antislavery cause" and the attention it brought to the issue of emancipation in New Jersey. *Id.* at 131. Lawyers such as Stewart attacked the institution of slavery using a variety of federal constitutional theories and arguments based on natural law and morality. *See, e.g.,* COVER, *supra*, at 163; ABOLITIONISM AND AMERICAN LAW, *supra*, at xv (1999). An important component of their strategy involved fugitive slave litigation, in which they made technical legal arguments that escaped slaves need not be returned to their owners. A substantial part of this approach was to argue for a strong view of states' rights, suggesting that states had the freedom to adopt procedural protections for fugitive slaves when their owners tried to recapture them. COVER, *supra*, at 161-63. For example, lawyers advocated for state laws requiring owners to use peaceful legal means rather than physical violence to recover slaves and for the fugitive slaves' right to jury trials in cases brought to recover them. *Id.* at 162-63.

This account of the abolition movement highlights competing strategies of gradualism and more aggressive forms of litigation. Earlier abolition attorneys tried to break down the slavery system by attrition, helping to free individual slaves and maintain their freedom. Later in the movement, lawyers worked for universal emancipation through legal decree. Think about the conditions that may have led lawyers to choose between these different approaches. As you study the materials in the forthcoming chapters, compare the abolitionist lawyers' approaches to the strategies that later public interest lawyers would adopt.

―――――――――

As these examples reveal, potent forms of lawyering for different causes were alive and well from the earliest stages of this nation's founding. Yet they generally involved individual efforts by courageous lawyers who staked their professional reputations on principle. The institutional structure of public interest law, marked by independent organizations with affiliated lawyers dedicated to the advancement of specific causes—although presaged by the abolitionist lawyers—would await the cataclysm of the Civil War, as the country sorted out the legacy of that "peculiar institution" in the context of political ferment, economic transformation, and the rupture of war.

III. THE INSTITUTIONAL FOUNDATIONS OF PUBLIC INTEREST LAW: FROM THE PROGRESSIVE TO POSTWAR ERA

The dawn of the twentieth century witnessed dramatic changes in the American political economy that spawned new social issues—and elicited innovative, and foundational, legal responses. The promise of post–Civil War Reconstruction gave way to the reality of Jim Crow; domestic peace ceded to world war; and the Industrial Revolution spawned economic dislocation and the Great Depression. These transformations occurred against the backdrop of dramatic changes in American governance, particularly the greater concentration of power in federal government, the "explosion" of legal regulation, and the increased stature and authority of the federal courts. LAWRENCE M. FRIEDMAN, A HISTORY OF AMERICAN LAW 503-37 (3d ed. 2005). It was in this context that the institutional foundations of public interest law were built.

A. EARLY PUBLIC INTEREST ORGANIZATIONS

Two national membership organizations most often associated with the emergence of law reform campaigns in the twentieth century are the National Association for the Advancement of Colored People (NAACP) and the American Civil Liberties Union (ACLU).

1. Civil Rights

Beginning in the 1880s, a group of African-American leaders, taking the mantle from their abolitionist forebears, established a number of important groups designed to advance the cause of racial justice during the post-Reconstruction period. SUSAN D. CARLE, INVENTING CIVIL RIGHTS LAWYERING: NATIONAL ORGANIZING FOR RACIAL JUSTICE, 1880-1910 (forthcoming 2013). These included groups with a range of strategic approaches and political ideologies, from radical to accommodationist, which all aspired to create permanent institutions to promote racial equality. *Id.* One of these groups, the Niagara Movement, was formed in 1905 by W.E.B. Dubois to challenge Booker T. Washington's more moderate platform by promoting a national agenda of civil rights and economic justice. *Id.*

Four years later, Dubois, along with other African-American leaders and white organizers concerned with racial justice issues (specifically, the increase in incidents of white violence against blacks), formed the NAACP. MARK V. TUSHNET, THE NAACP'S LEGAL STRATEGY AGAINST SEGREGATED EDUCATION, 1925-1950 1 (1987). Of all the iconic stories of public interest law, the history of the NAACP—and, later, its Legal Defense and Educational Fund (LDF)—is probably the most familiar and extensively researched. *See, e.g.,* TOMIKO BROWN-NAGIN, COURAGE TO DISSENT: ATLANTA AND THE LONG HISTORY OF THE CIVIL RIGHTS MOVEMENT (2011); RISA L. GOLUBOFF, THE LOST PROMISE OF CIVIL RIGHTS (2007); MICHAEL J. KLARMAN, FROM JIM CROW TO CIVIL RIGHTS: THE SUPREME COURT AND THE STRUGGLE FOR RACIAL EQUALITY (2004); RICHARD KLUGER, SIMPLE JUSTICE: THE HISTORY OF BROWN V. BOARD OF EDUCATION AND BLACK AMERICA'S STRUGGLE FOR EQUALITY (1975); GERALD N. ROSENBERG, THE HOLLOW HOPE: CAN COURTS BRING ABOUT SOCIAL CHANGE? (1991); TUSHNET, *supra.* It continues to resonate as the archetypal story of the political rewards and risks of mobilizing law for justice, against which the subsequent history of public interest law has been judged. The NAACP's shadow, therefore, still looms large.

The backdrop to the NAACP's development was the Supreme Court's decision in *Plessy v. Ferguson*, 163 U.S. 537, 550-51 (1896), which upheld laws requiring that providers of public accommodations, such as railroads, establish separate facilities for white persons and people of color. *Plessy* essentially endorsed the Southern states' adoption and enforcement of Jim Crow laws, which mandated the strict separation of races in virtually all walks of public and private life. *Plessy* ensured that the formal segregationist policies of state and local governments were immune from challenges under the Fourteenth Amendment's Equal Protection Clause so long as they required that the separate public and private facilities for whites and African Americans were roughly "equal."

In the late 1920s, a private foundation called the Garland Fund issued a grant to the NAACP to implement comprehensive litigation "campaigns to enforce the Constitutional rights of African-Americans in the South." Leland B. Ware, *Setting the Stage for Brown: The Development and Implementation of the NAACP's School Desegregation Campaign, 1930-1950*, 52 MERCER L. REV. 631, 638-39 (2001). The NAACP placed attorney Nathan Margold in charge of developing an overall strategy. *Id.* at 639. Margold produced a study confirming that despite *Plessy*'s separate but equal requirement, Southern states provided facilities for African Americans that were far inferior to those provided for white persons. *Id.* at 639-40. As an example, an African-American train passenger at the time of *Plessy* described the "colored" railroad cars as "[s]carcely fit for a dog to ride in." KLARMAN, *supra*, at 43. The Margold Report concluded that it would be too burdensome and inefficient to challenge the inequality of facilities across the nation in piecemeal fashion, arguing instead for a comprehensive attack on segregation. Ware, *supra*, at 640-41; TUSHNET, *supra*, at 25-28. However, Charles Hamilton Houston, former dean of the Howard University Law School, who succeeded Margold as the head of the NAACP's legal team, initially opted for smaller steps. Under his direction, the NAACP first developed a strategy to test *Plessy*'s staying power by filing individual equal protection suits challenging the actual inequalities between facilities provided to whites and those provided to persons of color. Ware, *supra*, at 635, 641-42.[1] He did so in part because he did not believe the Supreme Court was yet ready to revisit *Plessy*. *Id.* Eventually, these cases yielded important Supreme Court decisions invalidating many types of Jim Crow laws, particularly in higher education. *See, e.g., McLaurin v. Okla. State Regents for Higher Educ.*, 339 U.S. 637, 639-40, 642 (1950) (striking down a state university system that admitted an African-American student, but forbade him to use the same classrooms, libraries, cafeterias, and other facilities as white students); *Sweatt v. Painter*, 339 U.S. 629, 632-34, 636 (1950) (declaring the University of Texas's legal education system unconstitutional because the African-American public law school was substantially inferior to the white law school); *Missouri ex rel. Gaines v. Canada*, 305 U.S. 337, 352 (1938) (invalidating a state university system that, instead of establishing a law school for African Americans, sent those students to a black law school in another state). Much of this work was carried out by the LDF, which NAACP officials created in 1940 because the NAACP could not maintain tax-exempt status due to its lobbying activities. JACK GREENBERG, CRUSADERS IN THE COURTS: HOW A DEDICATED BAND OF LAWYERS FOUGHT FOR THE CIVIL RIGHTS REVOLUTION 19 (1994); TUSHNET, *supra*, at 100-01.[2]

The strategy in these cases was not, in fact, to have courts declare every Jim Crow law in the country unconstitutional on a case-by-case basis. Indeed, the limited resources available for plaintiffs' lawyers in these cases made such a goal impracticable. Rather, the lawyers' strategy was to eventually make it economically impossible for state and local governments to maintain segregated facilities across the board, and to educate courts, and specifically, the Supreme Court, about the actual inequalities on the ground in states with Jim Crow laws. Robert L. Carter, *A Tribute to Justice Thurgood Marshall*, 105 HARV. L. REV. 33, 36-37 (1991). Thus, the organization's approach embraced a gradualist strategy to undermine *Plessy* from the inside, and eventually dismantle racial segregation by changing controlling precedent. The strategy reached its culminating success in *Brown v. Bd. of Educ. of Topeka*, 347 U.S. 483, 495 (1954), in which the Court overruled *Plessy* in holding that segregated public schools were unconstitutional. In many respects, *Brown* represents the paradigm of public interest lawyering—a model that set the stage for the deep investment in the "public interest law movement" that would follow in its aftermath. Yet the limits of what *Brown* accomplished also formed the basis of important critiques of public interest law that we will examine in later chapters.

---

1. This approach had also been articulated by one of the NAACP's chief officers, Walter White, in an earlier memorandum to the Garland Fund. TUSHNET, *supra*, at 13-14.

2. The two groups continued to work together until the late 1950s, when the Internal Revenue Service began to question the LDF's tax-exempt status and its close affiliation with the NAACP. GREENBERG, *supra*, at 222-23. In 1957, the groups formally split and had a completely different set of board members and officers. *Id.* While the tax-exemption issue precipitated this formal separation, continuing disputes over direction and leadership had independently caused rifts between the two organizations. *Id.* at 478-86.

2. Civil Liberties

By the time the United States entered World War I in 1917, substantial opposition to the war effort and the related military draft had already developed. Antiwar activists formed organizations to oppose the war and to provide support for conscientious objectors to the draft. That opposition intensified as the country's role in the war grew, but the federal government did not look favorably upon public protest during wartime. By 1920, a group concerned with the government's expanding efforts to limit expression opposed to the war formed the National Civil Liberties Bureau, which would later become the American Civil Liberties Union (ACLU). SAMUEL WALKER, IN DEFENSE OF AMERICAN LIBERTIES: A HISTORY OF THE ACLU 46-47 (1990). Led by a pacifist political activist and social worker named Roger Baldwin, the ACLU split off from other antiwar groups that were more hesitant to aggressively support civil liberties during the war because of their concern that such advocacy might undermine their other antiwar efforts. *Id.* at 20-21; *see also* GEOFFREY R. STONE, PERILOUS TIMES: FREE SPEECH IN WARTIME FROM THE SEDITION ACT OF 1798 TO THE WAR ON TERRORISM 183 (2004).

Although the conventional historical account suggests that free speech law first developed as a direct outgrowth of the ACLU's efforts to challenge the enforcement of the Espionage Act of 1917, free speech doctrine existed and began to develop before the war, and was advanced by the Free Speech League. David M. Rabban, *The Free Speech League, the ACLU, and Changing Conceptions of Free Speech in American History*, 45 STAN. L. REV. 47, 48-49 (1992). Still, the ACLU emerged as the principal defender of civil liberties at least in part because of its high profile involvement in the fight against repression of political speech during this period.

Unlike the NAACP, the ACLU's agenda was not to represent the interests of a particular constituency (though it did take on a number of free speech cases for labor organizers and persons perceived as "radicals"). During its formative years following the end of World War I, from 1920 to 1924, the ACLU addressed a wide range of civil liberties issues, including the rights of labor organizers to hold meetings, issues stemming from the war (such as mail censorship, amnesty for political prisoners, and state sedition laws), and free speech rights in public schools. WALKER, *supra*, at 54-60. Even at this early stage, the group started employing a variety of legal tactics, including litigation, legislative advocacy, and public education (including educating public officials) on legal issues. *Id.* This period also saw early tests of the ACLU's commitment to free speech without regard to the speaker's political viewpoint. Though the ACLU advocated racial justice, it also publicly opposed restrictions on Ku Klux Klan meetings, on anti-Semitic articles published by industrialist Henry Ford's newspaper, and on exhibition of D.W. Griffith's racist film, *Birth of a Nation* (an issue that placed the ACLU in opposition to the NAACP). *Id.* at 61-62. During this period, the ACLU also struggled because of its association with the Communist Party, whose members it frequently represented. The Party's tactics and positions, particularly its intolerance for free expression, were not always embraced by the ACLU's representatives. *Id.* at 63-64. By and large, however, while this period saw sporadic activity by the ACLU, it yielded few civil liberties successes.

It was not until 1925 that the ACLU first started to gain momentum and develop both credibility and influence. Perhaps the most notable event raising the ACLU's national profile was the famous Scopes "monkey" trial, in which ACLU volunteer attorney, Clarence Darrow, represented a Tennessee school-teacher who was prosecuted for violating state law by teaching evolution in a public school. The case centered on issues of academic freedom and tolerance for diverse religious viewpoints. *Id.* at 72-76. Though Scopes was convicted, his conviction was overturned on appeal on a technical ground. *Scopes v. State*, 289 S.W. 363, 367 (Tenn. 1927). As Samuel Walker has written, the case was important because the ACLU was seen for the first time as defending "a cause with which the national press and its readers could identify. That is, they had little interest in the rights of Communists but saw science and education as the key to progress." WALKER, *supra*, at 73. Indeed, the ACLU raised enough money from the American Academy for the Advancement of Science to cover the expense of the trial. *Id.* at 75-76.

At the same time, the ACLU began to gain attention for bringing important cases to the Supreme Court. In *Gitlow v. New York*, 268 U.S. 652 (1925), the group represented a Communist Party founder who was convicted under a New York criminal syndicalism law for publishing a pamphlet that advocated revolution in a general way, but did not call people to imminent illegal action. WALKER, *supra*, at 79. The ACLU asserted that the abstract teaching of an idea is constitutionally protected by the First Amendment, and that the Constitution's free speech guarantees were applicable to states through the Due Process Clause of the Fourteenth Amendment. *Id.* Although the Court ultimately upheld Gitlow's conviction, for the first time it accepted the idea that the concept of due process encompassed free speech rights, and that the First Amendment applied to state and local laws. 268 U.S. at 666, 672. Although this statement was contained in dicta, *Gitlow* has long stood for the idea that the Due Process Clause "incorporates" the First Amendment. CHEMERINSKY, *supra*, at 499.

Building on this early success, in the late 1920s and early 1930s the ACLU expanded its role in protecting civil liberties. It fought government censorship of literature, materials relating to sex education and birth control, and erotic materials as part of its free speech mission. WALKER, *supra*, at 82-86. Over some dissent, Roger Baldwin then called for the organization to expand its influence into other areas, such as racial equality for African Americans and Native Americans, police misconduct, immigrants' rights, and compulsory military education in schools. *Id.* at 86. His most vocal opponent was board member (and later Supreme Court Justice) Felix Frankfurter, who argued that expansion of the ACLU's mission would dilute its concerns about more central civil liberties issues, *id.* at 87, a debate that continues in current ACLU leadership circles. In the following decades, the ACLU's docket grew to include cases raising civil liberties concerns with the expansion of government power during the New Deal, the persecution of minority religious groups like the Jehovah's Witnesses, and wartime governmental abuses, such as the internment of Japanese Americans in camps during World War II. WALKER, *supra*, at 95-149. Although the group defended suspected Communists and Communist sympathizers during the beginnings of the Red Scare, it became ensnared in internal controversy about its affiliation with and representation of Communists, which caused it to take inconsistent positions during the Cold War period — purging Communists after a 1940 ban, but later relaxing its standards in 1954, a move that provoked the departure of the hard line anti-Communist bloc. *Id.* at 127-32, 208-11.

As the ACLU emphasized different substantive issues, important organizational changes were occurring as well. In the 1920s, lawyers played a relatively small role in the ACLU leadership, in part because litigation was yet to become an important feature of the organization's mission. *Id.* at 69. Indeed, there was a dispute among the ACLU leadership about the propriety of seeking social change through the courts. ACLU founder Roger Baldwin was skeptical that the courts would ever take a central role in protecting civil liberties. *Id.* at 81. Frankfurter believed that it was inappropriate for courts to play such a role, preferring the legislative process as a vehicle for protecting civil liberties both because it was more democratic and more sustainable in the long run. *Id.* But other lawyers in the leadership believed the Supreme Court should and would step in to protect civil liberties interests. *Id.* Those volunteer attorneys, especially Walter Pollak, Walter Nelles, and Morris Ernst, began what would eventually become the ACLU's extensive Supreme Court litigation program. *Id.* The ACLU hired its first permanent staff attorney in 1941. *Id.* at 111. As the organization evolved, it turned increasingly to litigation precisely because it often represented politically unpopular minority groups. Emily Zackin, *Popular Constitutionalism's Hard When You're Not Very Popular: Why The ACLU Turned to Courts*, 42 Law & Soc'y Rev. 367 (2008).

What are the common themes leading to the emergence of these two major public interest lawyering organizations? Important differences?

B. THE PRIVATE BAR

In 1905, Louis Brandeis, a prominent lawyer in private practice, made an influential address at Harvard in which he argued that elite American lawyers had "allowed themselves to become adjuncts of great corporations and . . . neglected their obligation to use their powers for the protection of the people." Louis D. Brandeis, *The Opportunity in the Law*, 39 Am. L. Rev. 555, 559 (1905). His address conveyed the message that lawyers could work for the public good in two distinct ways. First, they could engage in law reform practice to make the law better; second, they could counsel their private clients to help them be more sensitive to the societal implications of their conduct, and encourage them to act in ways that would not harm the public interest. David Luban, Lawyers and Justice: An Ethical Study 171 (1988). Brandeis and other reformers during the Progressive era took these ideas seriously, and engaged in a substantial amount of legal work directed at what they perceived to be the broader public good. Brandeis himself frequently did pro bono work where he viewed the issues in a case as having a public impact. Clyde Spillenger, *Elusive Advocate: Reconsidering Brandeis as People's Lawyer*, 105 Yale L.J.

1445, 1448 (1996). He viewed the lawyer's role as not only participating in pro bono cases, but also counseling his paying clients to conduct themselves in a manner that promoted the public good. David Luban, *The Noblesse Oblige Tradition in the Practice of Law*, 41 VAND. L. REV. 717, 721 (1988). In the late 1800s, Brandeis engaged in efforts to prevent the monopolization of public transportation and gas companies in Boston, David W. Levy, *Brandeis, the Reformer*, 45 BRANDEIS L.J. 711, 714-15 (2007), and to reform and regulate the insurance industry, PHILIPPA STRUM, LOUIS D. BRANDEIS: JUSTICE FOR THE PEOPLE 75-78 (1984).

One of Brandeis's most significant roles was as general counsel for the National Consumers' League (NCL), a coalition originally formed by women's groups at the turn of the twentieth century to lobby for laws to improve conditions and wages for female employees. LEE EPSTEIN, CONSERVATIVES IN COURT 6 (1985). As the political scientist Clement Vose reported in an early study, the NCL was one of the first organizations to use litigation systemically to achieve social change. Clement E. Vose, *National Consumers' League and the Brandeis Brief*, 1 MIDWEST J. POL. SCI. 267, 276-90 (1957). While the NCL initially engaged in legislative work, it turned to the courts to defend constitutional attacks against much of the progressive regulation it had successfully lobbied to have adopted. EPSTEIN, *supra*, at 6. One impediment to its role in court was that it was the responsibility of government lawyers, usually state attorneys general, to defend state laws. *Id.* The NCL found the state governments' legal representation in these cases to be wanting, and beginning with *Muller v. Oregon*, 208 U.S. 412 (1908), a case challenging the constitutionality of a law capping the number of hours women could work, Brandeis persuaded the officials of many states to permit the NCL to defend these laws in court. *Id.* This unorthodox strategy led to a great deal of control on Brandeis's part. Indeed, Brandeis (who served without salary) and the NCL did not appear on the briefs for the states, though Brandeis negotiated complete control and coordination of the litigation as part of the terms of his representation. *Id.*[3] The other, more well-known, aspect of this litigation was Brandeis's insistence that leaders of the labor movement collect statistical information about the harmfulness of the labor practices (such as long working days for women) and his incorporation of this data in his briefs, now widely known as "Brandeis briefs." *Id.* This approach informed the work of later groups, like LDF, which famously used social scientific studies on the harmful impact of segregation as part of its litigation culminating in *Brown v. Board of Education.*

What are the important differences between the approach that Brandeis took and the strategies undertaken by the major public interest law groups that arose during the Progressive era (NAACP and ACLU)? What challenges might he have faced that the other groups did not? What advantages did he have that the other groups did not?

Brandeis embodied the paragon of elite professionalism, leveraging the moral authority of his status to serve as "lawyer for the situation"—guiding

---

3. Some have observed, however, that in this unusual, hybrid role as a private lawyer representing the state, Brandeis took on an influential role in shaping the public agenda without being accountable by virtue of being in any official public position. *See, e.g.,* Spillenger, *supra*, at 1456.

his corporate clients to make decisions consonant with (his version of) the public interest. There were other models of civic engagement, however, practiced by the majority of lawyers who fell outside this elite category.

> At the lower echelons of the profession, public service was conceptualized as a form of charity to the poor, which was generally provided through court appointment or professional courtesy. . . . On the civil side, state laws regarding civil appointments were . . . spare. Federal courts did not have a procedure for requesting counsel for *in forma pauperis* litigants until 1892, and even then it was restricted to poor people with meritorious claims. The system of appointments, which relied on state coercion rather than professional volunteerism, rested on the notion that lawyers were officers of the court and therefore integral to the administration of justice. Lawyers who accepted appointments therefore demonstrated the profession's commitment to standards of fairness while underscoring the centrality of client service — court-appointed attorneys owed the same duty of zealous representation to their indigent clients as to those who paid a fee.
>
> Outside of the system of court appointments, public service meant simply being "available" to the community. This notion of professional courtesy was exemplified in the prototypical "country lawyer" who would do what he could to help his neighbors. It was also embodied in the professional code of ethics, which exhorted lawyers to give "special and kindly consideration" to "reasonable requests of brother lawyers, and of their widows and orphans without ample means," providing them services for a reduced fee or "even none at all." In contrast to the system of appointments, this form of service to the poor was voluntary, performed through the enactment of individual instances of professional charity.

Cummings, *The Politics of Pro Bono, supra*, at 10-11. How does the professional service of the "country lawyer" compare with that of Brandeis? Which do you think was more important? More professionally legitimate?

Another element of public interest work performed by the private bar came from union-side labor law firms, which, along with in-house union lawyers, played an important role in the labor movement. Among other things, labor lawyers facilitated union organizing and represented unions in suits brought by employers to enjoin a wide range of labor activity. *See generally* WILLIAM E. FORBATH, LAW AND THE SHAPING OF THE AMERICAN LABOR MOVEMENT (1991); Jennifer Gordon, *A Movement in the Wake of New Law: The United Farm Workers and the California Agricultural Relations Act, in* CAUSE LAWYERS AND SOCIAL MOVEMENTS (Austin Sarat & Stuart A. Scheingold eds., 2006).

C. THE LEGAL AID MOVEMENT

The turn of the nineteenth century brought changes that moved the provision of legal services to the poor from the informal system of individual private lawyers dispensing professional charity to a more formalized system of organized legal aid offices. These changes included the influx of Southern and Eastern European immigrants to urban centers, which drew attention to the needs of the urban poor, and the increasing professionalization of the organized bar, which began to develop an infrastructure to address those needs. The provision of basic civil legal services to those who could not afford them was an issue that concerned the legal profession as early as the late 1800s. Preceded by the short-lived Freedman's Bureau, the first legal aid office was established in New York in 1876. Christine N. Cimini, *Legal Aid/Legal Services*, in 2 POVERTY IN THE UNITED STATES: AN ENCYCLOPEDIA OF HISTORY, POLITICS, AND POLICY 434 (Gwendolyn Mink & Alice O'Connor eds., 2004); William P. Quigley, *The Demise of Law Reform and the Triumph of Legal Aid: Congress and the Legal Services Corporation from the 1960's to the 1990's*, 17 ST. LOUIS U. PUB. L. REV. 241, 243-44 (1998). It was established to "render legal aid and assistance, gratuitously, to those of German birth, who may appear worthy thereof, but who from poverty are unable to procure it." AUERBACH, *supra*, at 53 (quoting the New York Legal Aid Society statement of purpose); *see also* SUSAN E. LAWRENCE, THE POOR IN COURT: THE LEGAL SERVICES PROGRAM AND SUPREME COURT DECISION MAKING 18 (1990). Charged with this duty, the office became a general provider of legal services to persons without the means to hire a private attorney. Cimini, *supra*, at 434. Legal aid expanded modestly during the next few years, with legal aid societies opening in Chicago in 1886 and four other cities by the turn of the century. AUERBACH, *supra*, at 53.

At that time, legal aid societies were funded exclusively by private donations, and operated independently of one another, with little or no coordination with other legal aid offices. Cimini, *supra*, at 434. Beginning in the 1900s, when private funding became more scarce, legal aid societies pursued affiliations with existing charitable organizations or sought local government funding to help finance their activities. *Id.* at 434-35. A national movement to establish a legal aid system was spurred by the 1919 publication of JUSTICE AND THE POOR by Reginald Heber Smith, a Boston law firm partner who served as general counsel to Boston's Legal Aid Society. MARTHA F. DAVIS, BRUTAL NEED: LAWYERS AND THE WELFARE RIGHTS MOVEMENT, 1960-1973 16 (1993). The book reported the results of a survey Smith conducted for the Carnegie Foundation on the state of legal services for the poor. *Id.* He concluded that the American justice system was unfairly dependent on the resources of the parties involved, imposing substantial injustice on the poor. *Id.* Moreover, in addition to calling for lawyers to represent poor people, Smith argued for legal aid organizations to pursue more systemic legal reform. *Id.*

Smith's book attracted interest from the mainstream bar, including the ABA, which established a committee to study legal aid in 1921. Cimini, *supra*, at 435. Such recognition was an important step, as there had been substantial early resistance from the private bar, which was concerned that a government-established legal aid network would reduce demand for the services of private lawyers. DAVIS, *supra*, at 15 (1993); Cimini, *supra*, at 435. Following the publication of JUSTICE AND THE POOR, the organized bar took on a greater role in funding legal aid, which grew from 40 legal aid societies in 1919 to 70 in 1947. JOEL F. HANDLER ET AL., LAWYERS AND THE PURSUIT OF LEGAL RIGHTS 19 (1978). Yet many lawyers at the lower echelon of practice continued to resist legal aid as a financial threat. In the same way that calls for a nationalized health care system have led to concerns about "socialized medicine," the legal aid movement met some resistance because of the concern that a nationalized legal aid system would represent a move toward socialized legal services.

Davis, *supra*, at 19; Handler et al., *supra*, at 19. The organized bar's resistance began to give way in the face of a proposed state funded and regulated legal aid system modeled on England's Legal Aid and Advice Scheme of 1950. Davis, *supra*, at 19. Rather than submit to state control, the bar redoubled its effort to fund and expand legal aid under its auspices.

By the 1960s, legal aid societies existed in nearly every major city. *See* Alan W. Houseman, *Legal Aid History, in* Poverty Law Manual for the New Lawyer 18, 18 (Nat'l Ctr. on Poverty Law ed., 2002). However, bar support continued to be only a small portion of the total legal aid budget—by one estimate, only 10 percent as late as the 1960s—and thus legal aid was primarily supported by charitable contributions from individuals, foundations, and local businesses. Richard L. Abel, *Law Without Politics: Legal Aid Under Advanced Capitalism*, 32 UCLA L. Rev. 474, 502 & n.163 (1985); Cummings, *The Politics of Pro Bono*, *supra*, at 12. As a result, "[c]ontroversial clients were generally avoided, cases that could generate fees were rejected, and client income eligibility was maintained at levels acceptable to private attorneys competing for lower-income clients. . . . Legal aid lawyers abjured reform-oriented advocacy and instead concentrated on resolving minor individual pursuits." *Id*. at 12-13. This model of traditional legal aid, built in the first half of the twentieth century as a vehicle for individual client service, would be profoundly influenced by the broader movements for progressive social transformation beginning to sweep through the nation.

IV. THE RIGHTS REVOLUTION AND THE MAKING OF MODERN PUBLIC INTEREST LAW

By the midpoint of the 1900s, the basic organizational outlines of the modern public interest law system were established. The legal arms of the early public interest law groups—the NAACP and ACLU—continued to be major forces in the American legal system, and their success began to spawn counterparts in other fields. As the private bar grew and became more diverse, the ethos and extent of pro bono service also began to expand; there were, in addition, examples of "radical" private sector lawyers whose work for political dissidents or unions aligned them with progressive social movements of the time. And the infrastructure of legal aid had grown into a national network of staffed offices catering to the legal needs of the urban poor.

Midcentury proved to be a watershed moment for public interest lawyering. There were two major forces at play—and modern public interest law emerged at their intersection. One was the expanding power of the federal government, which created new opportunities for lawyering that sought to leverage that power to benefit marginalized groups or causes. The New Deal of the 1930s had created the infrastructure of the modern welfare state, providing new benefits and protections to the poor that could be enforced in court; the civil rights movement would result in seminal new protections—such as the Civil Rights Act of 1964—that would further reinforce the federal government as the protector of minority groups against harmful state and private action. Important federal administrative agencies, such as the Environmental Protection Agency, began to take shape and gain power, offering lawyers a new venue to promote their causes by shaping the nature of federal rulemaking. Louise G. Trubek, *Crossing Boundaries: Legal Education and the Challenge of the "New Public Interest Law,"* 2005 Wis. L. Rev. 455, 459. And, perhaps most significantly, the changing composition and role of the federal courts invited lawyers to assert rights as a means to reshape fundamental social relations. At the apex of the federal judiciary, the Warren Court signaled its intent to extend and reshape rights across a variety of legal domains — particularly in the areas of discrimination and due process — in order to promote greater equality and protections for individual liberty. And the power of the federal government was mobilized to help support the enforcement of those rights, as was the case with the Kennedy Administration's Civil Rights Division in the Department of Justice. The Rights Revolution was upon the country. *See* Mark Tushnet, *The Rights Revolution in the Twentieth Century, in* 3 The Cambridge History of Law in America: The Twentieth Century and After (1920-) 377, 377 (Michael Grossberg & Christopher Tomlins eds., 2008). Public interest law was one of its causes (in that public interest lawyers brought many suits that created new rights) and an important consequence (in that successful rights claiming motivated new and greater organizational investments in public interest law groups).

The other major force emanated from the streets in the form of mass movements, which demanded a voice for the multifaceted and idealistic New Left. The civil rights movement, the political mobilization against the United States's involvement in Vietnam's civil war, the growth of the environmental movement, and the development and diversification of the women's movement were catalytic events that powered new transformative social visions — and sought to harness the power of law to realize their goals. For a brief period, New Left demands met with a receptive federal government to create "public interest law" as both a set of institutions and an ideal of social change.

We may understand the modern history of public interest law in the second half of the twentieth century as a story about the culmination of this ideal — and the subsequent reaction to it. It is thus a story about the fragile alliance between the federal government and public interest law, and the consequences of its unraveling, both in terms of institution building and political backlash. Thus, we may identify the period from *Brown v. Board* through the 1970s as one that coincided with the zenith of public interest law as a liberal political and institutional project, marked by the creation of new organizations and rights strategies largely (though never exclusively) mobilizing litigation to push the federal government toward reform. The period that followed is characterized by federal retrenchment and political backlash, resulting in the decline of the federal government as the protector of liberal rights claims, and the rise of a powerful conservative countermovement, which includes conservative public interest law as an important component. Thus, the historical trajectory of public interest lawyering is toward *greater diversification* — both in terms of the political nature of the organizations (multiple types of liberal and conservative groups) and the means they use to achieve their goals (beyond federal litigation to encompass other strategies).

A. LEGAL SERVICES FOR THE POOR

While efforts to provide free legal services to the poor in civil and criminal cases trace back to the turn of the century, the modern architecture of civil legal aid and public defense did not develop until the 1960s. For criminal representation, the turning point was the Supreme Court's decision in *Gideon v. Wainwright*, 372 U.S. 335, 342-43 (1963), holding that criminal defendants were entitled to representation by an attorney for all felony charges. For civil representation, the watershed event was the establishment of the federal legal services program in 1965.

1. Criminal Representation: The Public Defender System

Until the early twentieth century, criminal defendants who could not afford legal counsel could only hope to retain a volunteer lawyer or, in some jurisdictions, receive appointment of a private lawyer by the court. The first publicized call for government-funded public defense was by lawyer and suffragist Clara Shortridge Foltz at the 1893 Congress of Jurisprudence and Law Reform, a meeting associated with the Chicago World's Fair. Babcock, *supra*, at 1270-71. She argued that "[f]or every public prosecutor there should be a public defender chosen in the same way and paid out of the same fund." *Id.* at 1271 (citing text of speech). Though the recognition of a constitutional right to a criminal defense lawyer was decades away, Foltz maintained that public defenders would serve an important role in the criminal justice system. *Id.* at 1271-72. Foltz, who had substantial experience representing criminal defendants in the West, saw criminal defendants with limited financial resources as having a choice between sacrificing their economic futures or declaring indigence in order to gain a court-appointed attorney, who would often be inexperienced and lack sufficient resources to properly investigate the case. *Id.* at 1271. Foltz spent much of her life advocating for the creation of public defender systems and introducing legislation in various jurisdictions to accomplish this goal. *Id.* at 1273-74.

Despite the efforts of Foltz and others like her, support for public defense in the first half of the twentieth century was sporadic. In 1913, during the heart of the Progressive era, the City of Los Angeles created the first official public defender program. *Id.* at 1274. In the ensuing period, due to progressive support for the concept, a number of state legislatures introduced bills to create public defender offices. *Id.* Yet funds were limited and the idea itself remained controversial. A key dispute developed regarding the proper goal of public defenders and appointed defense counsel. One school of thought suggested that these defense lawyers ought to provide a defense comparable to that available to private defendants who could afford their own lawyers. Another camp argued that the government should provide defense counsel only to ensure minimal due process — protecting innocent defendants from wrongful conviction and helping maintain a generally fair system. *Id.* at 1268.

The status of defender programs began to change in the 1960s. First, the Ford Foundation began investing significant resources to increase the number and quality of defender programs with its 1963 National Defender Project. HANDLER, ET AL., *supra*, at 39. This effort, combined with the impetus to state and local government efforts provided by *Gideon*, led to a significant increase in programs over the ensuing decade.

> In 1961, defender programs existed in only 3% of the counties of the nation and served only about one-quarter of the population; by 1973, 650 defender programs were providing services in 28% of all United States counties, reaching two-thirds of the population. In addition, 16 states [had] organized and funded defender services at the state level.

Id.

Change took place at the federal level as well. Before 1965, the bar was the main source of counsel for indigent defendants in federal criminal cases. John J. Cleary, *Federal Defender Services: Serving the System or the Client?*, 58 LAW & CONTEMP. PROBS. 65, 67 (1995). Federal courts would often appoint private attorneys who were inexperienced and/or unwilling to serve, and no system existed to pay the attorneys or their expenses. *Id.* A report commissioned by Attorney General Robert F. Kennedy recommended a payment system for appointed counsel as well as the creation of a federal public defender system. *Id.* In 1964, Congress passed a law providing some funding for federal indigent criminal defense, and in 1971, Congress established two distinct entities to provide criminal defense: a full-fledged federal defender service and a community defender organization to provide neighborhood-based defense services. *Id.* at 67-68.

Since then, the number of public defender programs has increased. But concerns about the quality of defender services persist — and have even grown stronger. The key problem is inadequate resources and enormous caseloads, which can undercut the ability of even the best lawyers to provide an adequate defense. *See* AMERICAN BAR ASSOCIATION STANDING COMMITTEE ON LEGAL AID & INDIGENT DEFENDANTS, *GIDEON'S* BROKEN PROMISE: AMERICA'S CONTINUING QUEST FOR EQUAL JUSTICE 7-28 (2004). In response to the contemporary crisis in public defense, some public defenders' offices have begun to take action to address the substantial problems produced by drastically reduced financial resources and alarmingly high caseloads. The crisis makes it extraordinarily difficult for public defenders in many jurisdictions to adequately investigate their cases and challenge the government's charges by going to trial. Erik Eckholm, *Citing Workload, Public Lawyers Reject New Cases*, N.Y. TIMES, Nov. 9, 2008, at A1. Concerned about the impact of these resource issues on both their clients' constitutional right to counsel and their own ethical duties to competently represent clients, some offices have simply refused to take on new cases, while others have actually filed lawsuits to seek relief. *Id.* Some of the suits have been successful, with one in Florida resulting in a ruling that the Miami-Dade County public defenders' office could turn down the cases of defendants charged with lower-level felonies so that they could provide adequate representation to clients facing more serious charges. *Id.* Another suit in Kentucky yielded a ruling allowing public defenders to decline cases they could not handle ethically because of their workload. *Id.* Similarly, in Missouri, a state oversight commission granted the public defenders' offices permission to turn down misdemeanor cases and other lower-level charges that would not likely lead to imprisonment for convicted defendants. *Id.*

Why do you suppose that despite the existence of a federal constitutional right to a criminal defense attorney, at least in felony cases, and a widespread public defender structure, there continues to be a substantial crisis in basic criminal representation for the poor throughout the United States? Are there other systemic approaches to criminal defense that might respond to these deficiencies?

2. Civil Representation: The Federal Legal Services Program

The U.S. system of legal aid has followed a similar trajectory—from governmental support to governmental restriction. In the early 1960s, the Ford Foundation provided funding for several experimental projects in low-income areas of major urban cities to provide consumer, medical, educational, and legal services. Cimini, *supra*, at 435. These projects would foreshadow "the recurring battles over funding, politics, and independence of the legal aid/legal services movement." *Id.* One project, in New Haven, Connecticut, was shut down after its founding lawyer, Jean Cahn, became involved in a controversial criminal case. *Id.*

Yet the Ford projects also created a national model that shaped President Lyndon Johnson's War on Poverty, which was implemented by the newly established Office of Economic Opportunity. Davis, *supra*, at 32. In 1965, the OEO established a national legal services program, which authorized funding for indigent civil legal representation through local programs across the country. *Id.* at 32-34. In 1967, the program was providing more than $40 million to around 300 legal aid offices. *Id.* at 34; Earl Johnson, Jr., Justice and Reform: The Formative Years of the OEO Legal Services Program 71 (1974).

From its inception, the federal legal services program generated tension between those who viewed it as an institution whose primary goal should be addressing the specific legal problems of individual clients and those who envisioned it as a vehicle for social change. *See* Edgar S. Cahn & Jean C. Cahn, *The War on Poverty: A Civilian Perspective*, 73 Yale L.J. 1317, 1346 (1964). Early legal services lawyers took on issues of economic inequality, including affirmative claims to compel employers to pay wages to their workers. Jack Katz, Poor People's Lawyers in Transition 7 (1982). Yet they generally focused on individual dispute resolution rather than pursuing an affirmative antipoverty agenda. *Id.* In the 1960s, the legal services program — powered by the example of civil rights lawyering—began to systematically pursue social reform. In this era, legal services offices sought social change in at least two distinct ways. *Id.* First, building on the traditional legal aid model, legal services lawyers aimed to provide balance in the legal system so that previously unrepresented clients could enforce and protect their rights. Second, legal services lawyers also took on broader law reform cases challenging the structural foundations of poverty. Cimini, *supra*, at 436. These law reform efforts were supported by "backup centers," which were funded out of the federal legal services budget to provide assistance to local offices. *Id.* In one measure of their impact, the Supreme Court from 1967 to 1972 decided 136 cases filed by legal services attorneys, 73 of which changed the law in ways that advanced the interests of poor people. *Id.*

In response to these early achievements, however, some policymakers began to question whether it was appropriate for the federal government to subsidize poverty law, which was viewed by critics as ideologically driven and requiring the government to fund litigation against itself. Deborah M. Weissman, *Law as Largess: Shifting Paradigms of Law for the Poor*, 44 Wm. & Mary L. Rev. 737, 754-55 (2002). Conservative critics questioned the structure of the federal legal services program, and in 1974 Congress enacted a law creating the Legal Services Corporation (LSC). *Id.* at 755-56. Although the establishment of LSC as a separate entity insulated it to some degree from Executive influence, it also signaled a shift toward greater restrictions. *Id.* In response to criticisms of impact cases, the federal government cut funding for backup centers and imposed new limits on the type of work that federally funded legal services lawyers could perform. Alan W. Houseman & Linda E. Perle, Securing Equal Justice for All: A Brief History of Civil Legal Assistance in the United States 20-22 (2007).

Over the past 30 years, LSC has continued to sit at the center of controversy. Because there is no constitutional right to counsel in civil cases, *Lassiter v. Dep't of Soc. Servs.*, 452 U.S. 18, 25-27 (1981), policy makers arguably have greater discretion to limit the scope of legal aid lawyers' activities. President Reagan sought to abolish LSC and succeeded in curtailing its funding. *See generally* Luban, Lawyers and Justice, *supra*, at 298-302. In 1996, President Clinton bowed to Congressional Republicans by signing an act that both substantially decreased legal services funding and restricted its lawyers' activities in the most significant manner to date. Omnibus Consolidated Rescissions and Appropriations Act of 1996, Pub. L. No. 104-134 §§501-509, 110 Stat. 1321, 1321-50 to 1321-59 (1996) (OCRAA). A summary of the scope of these changes follows:

> LSC just barely survived the call for its total elimination, but not without suffering a crippling loss of funds. Program funding was reduced by thirty percent and resulted in dramatic reductions in staff and office closings. Aside from the loss of funding, new restrictions added new burdens on programs. Certain classes of clients were eliminated from eligibility for legal services, including prisoners (those already convicted as well as pretrial detainees), many categories of immigrants, and public housing residents alleged to have been involved in criminal drug activity. Those who remained eligible were limited in the types of legal issues which could be addressed on their behalf. Congress added to the list of prohibited substantive legal issues and forbade LSC-funded attorneys from engaging in any advocacy that challenged the constitutionality of state or federal welfare statutes or regulations in any forum.
>
> Moreover, the legal tools and strategies available to pursue permissible representation were severely circumscribed. Class actions, characterized by opponents as "the sexier lawsuits," were prohibited. Congress prohibited LSC lawyers from representing anyone who might have been provided with "unsolicited advice" to protect their rights by obtaining counsel or taking legal action. LSC lawyers were prohibited from lobbying legislative and administrative rule-making bodies. They were also denied the right to seek state or federal statutorily authorized attorney's fees from adverse parties. This thwarted the ability of LSC clients to enforce statutory rights, to deter against repeated wrongdoing, and deprived LSC programs of the opportunity to obtain

additional revenue for program work. These restrictions distorted the traditional attorney-client relationship; they required disclosure of information
related to the identity of legal services clients as well as the substance of
their cases, neither of which is permitted in private attorney-client relations.

Weissman, *supra*, at 765-66.

In recent years, the continuing justice gap for the poor has generated
interest in exploring alternative ways of delivering services and new theories
for expanding representation, including the "Civil Gideon" movement, which
seeks to advance a right to legal representation in at least some types of civil
cases. We return to these contemporary efforts in Chapter 7. For now, as you
reflect on the history of the legal services program, how would you assess its
success? Do you think that its founders were right to focus on reform efforts or
was that a political miscalculation in light of the program's dependence on
government funding? Are there other methods of delivering legal services to
the poor that might be more effective? Why do you think that there is not
greater support for universal legal representation in the form of a "Civil Gideon" or otherwise?

B. THE EMERGENCE OF LIBERAL PUBLIC INTEREST LAW

1. Movements

In addition to civil rights and civil liberties, many other important social
movements shaped the liberal wing of the public interest law field in the
second half of the twentieth century. This section highlights three important
movements — women's rights, environmentalism, and consumer rights — as
illustrative cases of movements whose efforts to leverage law to create change
led to the development of important public interest law organizations and
strategies on the political left.

a. WOMEN'S RIGHTS

The suffrage movement was a seminal part of the broader struggle for
women's rights in the United States. Indeed, a major part of the history of
women in public life arises out of the battle, first, to include women in the
Reconstruction era constitutional amendments, and later, to ratify the Nineteenth Amendment in 1920. Moreover, though the suffrage movement initially divided over support for the Fifteenth Amendment (because it did not
enfranchise women), an independent women's law activist movement
emerged that maintained "an extensive law reform agenda that included
but did not privilege suffrage, and . . . maintained relationships with both of
the main, oppositional suffrage camps." Gwen Hoerr Jordan, *Agents of (Incremental) Change: From Myra Bradwell to Hillary Clinton*, 9 Nev. L.J. 580 (2009). It is
also important to understand that while the suffragist cause stands alone as a
social movement, the women's law reform movement focused on other battles
for women's equality that were closely related to the right to vote. As Barbara
Babcock has observed, "Like voting, practicing law involved an unambiguous
passage into the public sphere. That is why the cause of women lawyers was

totally joined with the larger woman's movement, why all women lawyers wanted suffrage, and why many actively campaigned for it." Barbara Allen Babcock, Book Review, 50 STAN. L. REV. 1689, 1696 (1998) (reviewing VIRGINIA DRACHMAN, SISTERS IN LAW: WOMEN LAWYERS IN MODERN AMERICAN HISTORY (1998)).

In his work on identity-based social movements, William Eskridge frames the twentieth-century women's movement in the context of three major efforts on behalf of women's rights. William N. Eskridge, Jr., *Some Effects of Identity-Based Social Movements on Constitutional Law in the Twentieth Century*, 100 MICH. L. REV. 2062, 2115 (2002) [hereinafter, Eskridge, *Effects*]. First, the women's movement addressed the underenforcement of laws protecting women from sexual assault and other physical harm. *Id.* Second, it focused on laws protecting women and their families from harmful conditions in the workplace, though this was controversial among feminists because of its paternalistic nature. *Id.* at 2115-16. Third, the movement addressed morality-based laws, such as those prohibiting abortion and limiting access to birth control, which restricted women's freedom to control their own bodies and impeded their opportunities to pursue professional and public lives. *Id.* at 2117-24.

In 1961, President Kennedy formed a Commission on the Status of Women. Much of the groundwork for the legal theory expanding equal protection analysis was laid out in a memorandum by Pauli Murray, an African-American civil rights lawyer. *Id.* at 2128-29.

> Murray's arguments found their way into the congressional debates over the addition of "sex discrimination" to the jobs title of the Kennedy Administration's civil rights bill. . . . Murray and other feminists supported [the addition] and ensured that it was preserved in the final statute. The EEOC, however, refused to make sex discrimination a priority in its enforcement of the new law, a stance that drew strong protests. When officials ignored their complaints at a 1966 conference on women's status, Murray, Betty Friedan, and other feminists stormed out in protest and founded the National Organization for Women ("NOW"). As Friedan later recalled, "it only took a few of us to get together to ignite the spark" that grassroots feminist consciousness raising had already created, "and it spread like a nuclear chain reaction." In its statement of purpose, NOW went beyond the ambivalent agenda of the President's Commission and demanded not just formal equality for women, but also a dismantling of the separate spheres ideology. Women should not only have all the (public) economic and social opportunities as men, but men should also share in the (private) responsibilities of home and childrearing. In 1967, NOW set out an ambitious national agenda, including serious enforcement of the Equal Pay Act and Title VII by the EEOC and the courts; adoption of the ERA; and repeal of abortion laws. As Cynthia Harrison has argued, NOW's agenda reflected the first coherent feminist philosophy of the century, one that combined an updated politics of protection with a new politics of recognition: childbearing should be separated from both sexual intimacy and from child-rearing; both mothers and fathers are responsible for family as well as work.
>
> Like the NAACP, NOW established a Legal Defense and Education Fund to litigate issues of women's equality. In 1971, the ACLU established its Women's Rights Project, headed by Professor Ruth Bader Ginsburg. Representing a new generation of litigators, Ginsburg followed [women's rights pioneer Dorothy] Kenyon and Murray in pressing the Court to rule that women have all the same

legal rights and duties as men. These lawyers filed constitutional challenges to statutory sex discriminations, and state and federal judges found many of the challenged policies unconstitutional. . . .

Id. at 2129-31; *see also* Nadine Strossen, *The American Civil Liberties Union and Women's Rights*, 66 N.Y.U. L. Rev. 1940 (1991).

In addition to national advocacy groups such as the NOW Legal Defense and Education Fund (now known as Legal Momentum) and the ACLU, decentralized efforts to secure women's rights emerged as well. For example, a group of lawyers founded the Washington, D.C. Feminist Law Collective in 1976. Modeled on other law collectives discussed below, this group sought to form a law practice that explicitly incorporated its political goals not only into its legal work, but also into the way that members lived their professional and personal lives.

A central goal of many advocates in the women's right movement during the 1970s was the ratification of the Equal Rights Amendment (ERA) to the U.S. Constitution. At a time when the Supreme Court had not yet recognized a heightened standard of review for government discrimination on the basis of gender, activists supported an amendment providing that "[e]quality of rights under the law shall not be denied or abridged by the United States or by any state on account of sex." Although equal rights amendments had been introduced in Congress as early as 1923, support for such a measure reached its height in 1972, when Congress enacted it by a wide margin. Jane J. Mansbridge, Why We Lost the ERA 8-12 (1986). Securing state ratification, however, was a bigger challenge. Ultimately, the amendment was ratified by only 35 of the 38 states necessary to become part of the Constitution. *Id.* at 1. At the beginning, progressives were divided in their support for the ERA. Some women's groups in the early twentieth century opposed efforts to ratify the ERA because they feared it would undermine efforts to secure legislative reform to protect women's rights. Eskridge, *Effects*, *supra*, at 2125. Unions and other labor groups were opposed because they feared that if the ERA were ratified, it would be used to invalidate much of the Progressive era legislation protecting women in the workplace, which they had fought so hard to enact. Mansbridge, *supra*, at 8-9. Progressive support began to solidify in the 1970s, but an increasingly effective conservative opposition movement led by Phyllis Schlafly created sufficient doubt about the amendment that it was never ratified. *Id.* at 110-16.

Although this might have been a significant setback for the women's movement, advocates for women's rights were more successful in pursuing equal rights in other contexts. Even before Congress enacted the ERA, it had passed strong legislation to prohibit discrimination against women in the workplace with measures such as the Equal Pay Act of 1963 and Title VII of the 1964 Civil Rights Act. 29 U.S.C. §206(d) (2006); 42 U.S.C. §2000e (2006). As the women's movement progressed into the later twentieth century, there emerged a new emphasis on challenging laws enacted on the assumption that women were less fit than men to serve various public functions (sitting on juries, running for office, working in a wide range of employment settings). Eskridge, *Effects*, *supra*, at 2126-27. Women's advocates gravitated toward litigation attempting to expand the Supreme Court's interpretation of the

Fourteenth Amendment's Equal Protection Clause to protect women in the same way it was read to protect racial minorities and toward legislative efforts to add women as a protected class under civil rights statutes. *Id.* at 2126-30. These efforts ultimately culminated in new equal protection precedent requiring greater judicial scrutiny of laws overtly discriminating against women. *Craig v. Boren*, 429 U.S. 190, 197 (1976). Indeed, Reva Siegel argues that the political dynamic surrounding the ERA's proposal and defeat may have laid the groundwork for shaping the emergence of stronger constitutional protection against gender discrimination. Reva B. Siegel, *Constitutional Culture, Social Movement Conflict and Constitutional Change: The Case of the De Facto ERA*, 94 CAL. L. REV. 1323 (2006).

Building on these efforts, women's rights advocates won additional laws prohibiting employment discrimination on the basis of pregnancy and programs to support women's advancement in education, employment and other settings; they also worked to limit the anti-abortion movement's drive to increase government regulation of abortion and overrule *Roe v. Wade*. These successes were the product of organized political and legal advocacy. For example, the legislative campaign to pursue the federal Pregnancy Discrimination Act was led by a coalition of women's groups, including the ACLU, the National Organization for Women, and the Pennsylvania Commission on Women. *Feminist Leaders Plan Coalition for Law Aiding Pregnant Women*, N.Y. TIMES, Dec. 15, 1976, at 40. The campaign also reached out to labor and civil rights groups as well, with the ACLU coordinating a legislative strategy meeting including representatives from 50 different organizations. Deborah Dinner, *The Costs of Reproduction: History and the Legal Construction of Sex Equality*, 46 HARV. C.R.-C.L. L. REV. 415, 469-70 (2011). Through its Reproductive Freedom Project, in conjunction with its state affiliates, the ACLU was able to monitor state legislation restricting women's access to abortion and coordinate a national strategy on reproductive rights. Strossen, *supra*, at 1956-57.

As the women's movement progressed, however, like other social change movements it became even more diverse and complex. For example, different schools of feminist thought led to conflicts within the women's movement in specific cases. An oversimplified characterization of two of these schools is that one involved a quest for equal treatment under the law (by the government, employers, and others) without regard to gender. Another school of "difference" feminists argued that formal legal equality often yields inequality both because of past discrimination against women and because real differences between genders sometimes require accommodations that ultimately enhance equality. This debate manifested itself in *California Federal Savings & Loan Ass'n v. Guerra*, 479 U.S. 272 (1997). In that case, an employer challenged a state law requiring employers to provide female employees with up to four months of unpaid leave for disabilities relating to birth and pregnancy on the ground that the state law violated the federal Pregnancy Discrimination Act, which requires equal treatment of pregnant and non-pregnant workers. *Id.* at 274-79. Difference feminists argued in *Guerra* that though the law provided unequal treatment based on gender, that difference was justified as a way of overcoming the disadvantages women suffer in the employment context because of their child-bearing capacity. Brief for Coalition for Reproductive

Equality in the Workplace et al. as Amici Curiae in Support of Neither Party at 17, *Cal. Fed. Sav. & Loan Ass'n v. Guerra*, 479 U.S. 272 (1997) (No. 85-494). Equal treatment feminists contended that the state law impaired women's interests by endorsing the differential treatment of pregnant workers, which could lead to re-adoption of provisions that discriminated against such workers on the ground that pregnancy is a sui generis condition. Brief Amici Curiae of National Organization for Women, NOW Legal Defense and Education Fund; National Bar Ass'n, Women Lawyers' Division, Washington Area Chapter; National Women's Law Center; Women's Law Project; and Women's Legal Defense Fund in Support of Neither Party, *Cal. Fed. Sav. & Loan Ass'n v. Guerra*, 479 U.S. 272 (1997) at 17. For a thoughtful summary of these different approaches, see Joan Williams, *Do Women Need Special Treatment? Do Feminists Need Equality?*, 9 J. CONTEMP. LEGAL ISSUES 279 (1998).

As this debate suggests, one recurring issue with any identity-based social movement is uniformity of interest. Groups whose members have strong affinities and common interests are never monolithic. Thus, while the women's movement has generally advocated for broad rights of access to abortion, not all women share that view. As the previous material illustrates, even feminists who generally agree may split on their view of specific issues. This raises questions about the identity of a particular movement, and may cause tensions and even splits within coalitions that form that movement. How much of this type of conflict is related to how far along a movement is in its evolution? Is uniformity of interest (or at least something closer to uniformity) more likely to be present when a group is seeking the most basic rights, such as voting and freedom from physical harm, and less likely after basic advances have been established? These tensions and conflicts create difficult challenges for lawyers associated with movements, who must sometimes take sides in internal movement debates (as in *Guerra*) or identify mechanisms to discern which position best represents the broader community's interest.

b. ENVIRONMENTALISM

In 1892, a group of 182 naturalists who valued the natural beauty of the Western United States formed the Sierra Club

> [t]o explore, enjoy and render accessible the mountain regions of the Pacific Coast; to publish authentic information concerning them; to enlist the support and cooperation of the people and government in preserving the forests and other natural features of the Sierra Nevada Mountains; to take, acquire, purchase, hold, sell and convey real and personal property, and to mortgage or pledge the same for the purpose of securing any indebtedness which the corporation may incur, and to make and enter into any and all obligations, contracts and agreements concerning or relating to the business or affairs of the corporation or the management of its property.

Sierra Club, Articles of Incorporation (Original Version), June 4, 1892, *available at*: http://www.sierraclub.org/policy/articles/articles-all.aspx (last visited Aug. 7, 2012); *see also* Michael P. Cohen, The History of the Sierra Club: 1892-1970, Chapter 4 (1988), http://www.sierraclub.org/history/origins/default.aspx (last visited Aug. 7, 2012). The Club's first president was John Muir, a highly regarded preservationist and writer. The Sierra Club was not initially formed strictly as a social change organization. In its original incarnation, the Sierra Club was a membership organization devoted to scheduling outings to enjoy and observe the natural environment on the Sierra Mountain range, as well as encouraging government action to preserve the environment. Robert Gottlieb, Forcing the Spring: The Transformation of the American Environmental Movement 56 (2005). While other organizations, such as the Wilderness Society, the National Wildlife Federation, and the National Audubon Society, were also devoted to protecting the environment, the Sierra Club emerged as the first national organization to pursue an environmental agenda through legal action.

From the time of its creation through the early 1970s, the Sierra Club emphasized lobbying and organizing efforts on behalf of numerous environmental causes, including the creation of a national parks system and the designation of specific areas as national parks; the protection of redwood and sequoia trees; the enactment of the first major federal environmental legislation, the Wilderness Act and the National Environmental Policy Act; and halting the damming of many natural lakes, most famously in the Hetch Hetchy Valley in California. *History of Accomplishments*, The Sierra Club, http://www.sierraclub.org/history/downloads/SCtimeline.pdf (last visited Aug. 7, 2012).

Although it established a committee to advise it on legally related matters and built a network of volunteer lawyers who sometimes filed amicus curiae briefs on its behalf, the Sierra Club initially did not have an affirmative litigation program. Tom Turner, Wild by Law: The Sierra Club Legal Defense Fund and the Places It Has Saved 5, 13 (1990); Robert L. Rabin, *Lawyers for Social Change: Perspectives on Public Interest Law*, 28 Stan. L. Rev. 207, 257 & n.161 (1976). In fact, before the advent of the Sierra Club and other groups, lawsuits to protect the environment were conceived of as common law nuisance suits and had arisen in a number of different jurisdictions around the country. These cases were typically episodic and reacted to localized concerns.

> Environmental litigation . . . began with ordinary, law-abiding Americans who had never opposed anything in their lives suddenly faced with the destruction of their neighborhoods for interstate highways. Small groups of determined residents organized in Boston, Chicago, Washington, New Orleans, San Francisco, and San Antonio went to court to defend their downtowns, their homes, and their parks.

Oliver Houck, *Unfinished Stories*, 73 U. Colo. L. Rev. 867, 896-97 (2002).

One barrier to concerted efforts to draw environmental disputes into the federal courts was the doctrine of standing. Article III of the Constitution limits the judicial power of the United States to cases or controversies within the defined subject matter jurisdiction of the federal courts. U.S. Const. art. III. While many environmental cases arise under federal law, they must be brought by a party who has a personal stake in the case: someone who has been injured by the defendant's conduct. *Lujan v. Defenders of Wildlife*, 504 U.S. 555, 560-61 (1992). Before the 1960s, standing in federal litigation had typically been limited to those who had been physically or financially harmed. In 1965, the Second Circuit held that persons with an "aesthetic, conservational, or recreational" interest with which a defendant's conduct interfered had standing to bring a case in federal court. *Scenic Hudson Pres. Conference v. Fed. Power Comm'n*, 354 F.2d 608, 615-18 (2d Cir. 1965).

In the mid-1960s, the Sierra Club opposed the U.S. Forest Service's plan to open up the Mineral King Valley in the south Sierras for the construction and operation of an alpine ski resort. TURNER, *supra*, at 9. The principal figure interested in developing the area was the Walt Disney Corporation (an ironic twist, since Walt Disney had been awarded a lifetime Sierra Club membership for his company's production of wildlife films). *Id.* at 3. Though the Sierra Club tried to block federal approval for the development, by the end of 1967 all the federal agencies involved in the plan had granted permission to move forward. *Id.* at 13. The Sierra Club asked lawyers working for a small conservation organization to research possible legal theories for a lawsuit to block Disney's development of Mineral King. *Id.* Leaders of the Sierra Club's legal committee approved the ideas developed by these young lawyers, and the Sierra Club decided to move forward with the litigation, brought by attorneys at a private law firm. *Id.* at 16. The focus of the lawsuit became the Sierra Club's standing to assert its environmental claims. Eventually, the U.S. Supreme Court ruled that the Club did not have standing because the complaint had failed to allege that it or any of its members actually used the Mineral King valley. *Sierra Club v. Morton*, 405 U.S. 727, 735, 741 (1972). However, in dicta, the Court's opinion acknowledged what environmental activists had hoped: that aesthetic, conservational, or recreational harm to a plaintiff would, in the proper circumstances and with the appropriate factual grounding, constitute injury in fact that would provide such a plaintiff with Article III standing. *Id.* at 734. The Court also indicated that the decision did not preclude the Sierra Club from amending its complaint upon remand. *Id.* at 735 n.8.

While the decision was technically a loss for the Sierra Club, it is widely regarded as having been a major step in opening the federal courthouse doors to environmental groups to advance their causes. The concept of environmental harm as an Article III injury was one key to the expansion of conservation litigation, along with what would soon be the expansion of federal statutory causes of action for environmentalists, including so-called citizen-suit provisions granting statutory standing to those potentially harmed by violations of federal environmental standards. In later cases, the Supreme Court imposed more stringent standing requirements, especially in environmental litigation, *see, e.g., Lujan*, 504 U.S. at 560-61, thus arguably undercutting the effectiveness of litigation as a tool for environmental groups. *But cf.* Ann E. Carlson, *Standing for the Environment*, 45 UCLA L. REV. 931, 932-36 (1998) (arguing that tighter standing rules will compel environmental litigators to draft allegations and introduce evidence more strongly identifying the human impact of environmental harms, thus providing a more compelling case that will benefit the social movement as well as the litigants in individual cases).

In 1971, during the course of the Mineral King litigation, Don Harris and Fred Fisher, two volunteer attorneys affiliated with the Sierra Club's legal committee, formed the Sierra Club Legal Defense Fund (SCLDF) to pursue litigation to protect the environment. TURNER, *supra*, at 19. They had received a $98,000 start-up grant from the Ford Foundation for SCLDF (now known as Earthjustice). *Id.* SCLDF was formed independently of the Sierra Club to establish a litigation arm that would also qualify for tax-deductible contributions, a status the Club had lost a few years earlier. *Id.* SCLDF hired Jim Moorman, an attorney who had undertaken some major environmental litigation with the Center for Law and Social Policy (CLASP), to be its first executive director. *Id.* at 18-19.[4] On remand from the Supreme Court, SCLDF represented the Sierra Club in the Mineral King litigation, amending its allegations to detail the direct impact the development would have on the Club and its members, and adding a claim under the newly enacted National Environmental Policy Act, which required the government to produce an environmental impact statement. *Id.* at 21. The litigation never proceeded to trial, but instead played out in the policy and political arenas until the pursuit of the ski area development lost steam. *Id.* at 21, 23.

SCLDF was not the first organization to form around the idea of using litigation as a tool to advance environmental concerns. In 1967, the Environmental Defense Fund (EDF) was established by lawyers and scientists concerned with the environmental hazards associated with the use of the chemical pesticide DDT. GOTTLIEB, *supra*, at 1896. A few years later, several Yale law students and some lawyers from a large New York corporate law firm, who had acted as pro bono counsel in a lawsuit concerning a controversial power plant along the Hudson River, received Ford Foundation funding to create the Natural Resources Defense Council (NRDC). *Id.* at 140-42. As the NRDC's co-founder, Gus Speth, recalled, "it just occurred to me that there really should be an NAACP Legal Defense Fund for the environment" (*quoted in* PHILIP SHABECOFF, A FIERCE GREEN FIRE: THE AMERICAN ENVIRONMENTAL MOVEMENT 108 (rev. ed. 2003)).

Others took on environmental activism not through litigation, but by attempting to reach the mainstream public through awareness and education programs. These events shaped the beginnings of the modern environmental movement as well. In 1962, marine biologist Rachel Carson published *Silent Spring*, a book calling attention to the environmental impact and dangers to public health associated with unrestricted use of chemical pesticides. GOTTLIEB, *supra*, at 121. The book received national attention, and though it was assailed by pesticide industry officials, its impact was irreversible. Another successful attempt at environmental public outreach was Earth Day. Originally conceived of by U.S. Senator Gaylord Nelson, the first Earth Day was modeled on the teach-ins against the Vietnam War that activists routinely carried out. SHABECOFF, *supra*, at 106. The event, which involved local teach-ins about the environment across the nation, was designed in part to garner attention from a broader public audience beyond those already involved in the

---

4. While Moorman was with CLASP before joining SCLDF, he also filed cases to force the government to forbid the use of chemical pesticides and to impose barriers to the construction of the Alaska oil pipeline. TURNER, *supra*, at 18.

environmental movement. GOTTLIEB, *supra*, at 148-49. Indeed, the event's national coordinator, a bright, young Harvard graduate student named Denis Hayes, reported that he wanted the event to avoid the more confrontational style associated with other social movements on the left. *Id.* at 150. Moreover, there was a concerted effort to enhance the public salience of environmental issues by connecting environmental hazards to human health. SHABECOFF, *supra*, at 105, 109. The first Earth Day, held on April 22, 1970, was a tremendous success, attracting broad media and public attention. GOTTLIEB, *supra*, at 157. Although many of the older conservation groups did not play an active role in Earth Day, the resulting surge in public attention to environmental issues benefited them in the form of substantially increased membership rolls. SHABECOFF, *supra*, at 112.

Greater public awareness of the impact of development, timber harvesting, pesticide use, industrial and automobile pollution of the air and water, and other hazards to the environment helped expand the members and allies of environmental organizations. Increased public attention to environmental harm also placed pressure on elected officials to formulate policies responsive to these concerns. In the 1960s and 1970s, the federal government adopted numerous laws to regulate the increasing environmental hazards to air, water, land, and species caused by the mass industrialization of American society.

Like other movements, the environmental movement has diversified since its early phase. Traditional environmentalism has been challenged by advocates of the environmental justice movement, who have argued that mainstream environmental groups have not paid sufficient attention to disproportionate environmental harms suffered by poor and minority communities, and that current environmental and civil rights laws are not adequate to address the problems that lie at the intersection of race, poverty, and the environment. *See* Luke W. Cole, *Structural Racism, Structural Pollution and the Need for a New Paradigm*, 20 WASH. U. J.L. & POL'Y 265 (2006); Luke W. Cole, *Empowerment as the Key to Environmental Protection: The Need for Environmental Poverty Law*, 19 ECOLOGY L.Q. 619 (1992).

c. CONSUMER RIGHTS

Consumer activist Ralph Nader began his career as a young lawyer attempting to call the nation's attention to automobile safety. Almost single-handedly, Nader led a campaign against the American automobile industry, accusing it of keeping costs down by cutting corners that made cars unnecessarily dangerous. In 1965, expanding on an article about auto safety published in THE NATION, Nader published his first book, *Unsafe at Any Speed: The Designed-in Dangers of the American Automobile*, an indictment of the automobile industry in general, and of General Motors and its popular sports car, the Corvair, in particular. BARBARA HINKSON CRAIG, COURTING CHANGE: THE STORY OF THE PUBLIC CITIZEN LITIGATION GROUP 3-4 (2004). While it received some national attention, Nader's book might not have had a major policy impact had it not been for the fact that General Motors reportedly hired a private detective to snoop into Nader's personal life, hoping to find some embarrassing information that it could use to discredit Nader (Nader eventually sued General Motors for invasion of privacy and received a considerable judgment, which he reportedly used to further finance his social causes). *Id.* at 5-6. The exposure of the conduct of General Motors, coupled with the fact that they did not find much of anything to use against Nader, catapulted Nader and his cause into the national spotlight. *Id.* These events are largely credited with leading to the first serious federal regulation of automobile safety, the National Traffic and Motor Vehicle Safety Act, and Nader would continue to pursue this issue in the following years. *Id.* at 6-7.

These incidents also established Nader, whose lifestyle has been reported to be extraordinarily ascetic, as an almost mythical figure in American progressive politics. This gave him both credibility and a platform to expand his social agenda to address a wide range of problems he associated with a nation predominantly controlled by large corporations. Nader's vision of social change involved organizing ordinary citizens to become active in protecting their own interests, and arming them, and policymakers, with research and information about various safety, environmental, and other issues that could be used to both stir citizens into action and influence policymakers to adopt and enforce regulations to protect citizens' interests. *Id.* at 7-9, 13-16.

> Nader's *modus operandi* was to call a press conference to detail harm being done and to furnish exhaustive statistical and technological evidence of abuses knowingly perpetrated by an industry. To follow up on the diagnosis, he would lay out a specific remedial plan. Then he campaigned to force action. He was the rational analyst, the policy innovator and the policy promoter rolled into one. His approach was a sharp contrast to the "expose-and-run" tactic of most investigative journalists. Even the people's representatives in Congress more typically played the game of exposé for media visibility, not for lawmaking or corrective oversight of the executive branch. Indeed, as Nader would soon learn, even when Congress actually passed a law, it needed constant oversight to ensure it was implemented in the public interest. And, as he was learning from the auto safety issue, getting the government bureaucrats to implement Congress' promises effectively, even when they were reasonably clear, was more than a full-time job.

Id. at 8.

Another component of Nader's success was that the national attention he received for his activism helped him recruit many lawyers, dubbed "Nader's Raiders," to join him in Washington to pursue his agenda. *Id.* at 27. He was highly successful in drawing activist lawyers to his organizations, and creating an infrastructure for his network of issue-specific policy centers. Nader was responsible for the formation of numerous organizations with distinct missions to protect the interests of various consumer and citizen constituencies. The first organization Nader founded was the Center for the Study of Responsive Law, formed in 1969. *Id.* at 9, 13. The Center was designed to enhance the accountability of agencies that formally were charged with regulating corporate interests to protect consumers from harm.

> The Center's actions are directed toward making corporations and regulatory agencies give greater weight in their decision-making to the consumer interest. To that end, the Center investigates corporate and agency activity, publishes reports to embarrass officials and shock the public, badgers administrative agency personnel, and at times seeks relief in the courts.

Note, *The New Public Interest Lawyers*, 79 Y ALE L.J. 1069, 1103 (1970). Thus, the focus of the Center's activities was on increasing corporate and government accountability through research and dissemination of the findings of that research to educate the public. C RAIG, *supra*, at 18-19; *see also* J OEL F. H ANDLER, S OCIAL M OVEMENTS AND THE L EGAL S YSTEM: A T HEORY OF L AW R EFORM AND S OCIAL C HANGE 216 (1978).

With the help of Nader lieutenants Joan Claybrook and Sidney Wolfe, Nader's network of organizations expanded to include the Health Research Group, the Center for Auto Safety, and the Public Interest Research Group. *Id.* at 7, 14, 18-22. In 1971, Nader formed Public Citizen, an umbrella organization to oversee many of the different groups he had been influential in forming. C RAIG, *supra*, at 22. The groups have changed over time, but the issues addressed under this umbrella have included auto safety, food and drug safety, energy policy, congressional accountability, and public health. Because of the nature of Nader's social change strategy, much of the work of his organizations took place in the context of federal regulatory agencies. A pathbreaking political science work, Theodore Lowi's T HE E ND OF L IBERALISM (1969), suggested that many social reforms had largely been undermined by the failure of government to enforce its own laws. This was the product of powerful, organized interest groups becoming so involved with the regulatory process that the agencies became captured by the interests of those they were assigned to regulate. C RAIG, *supra*, at 28. From the intellectual foundation of Lowi's work emerged a pragmatic and strategic response.

> [P]ublic agencies were most often captives of the businesses they purportedly regulated, or were no longer interested in vigorously pursuing their legislative mandates, or both. If the government agency could not be trusted to represent the public interest, someone else would have to do so. . . . [P]articipation in agency deliberations by submitting evidence and testimony generally turned out to be not enough. Litigation was the hammer necessary to get an agency to listen to the little voices of the public interest groups over the din of the powerful. As Nader had quickly discovered from this first Raiders' efforts, public interest participation required public interest litigation.

Id. Thus, while Nader's work had focused on lobbying and advocacy with policymakers, Public Citizen formed the Public Citizen Litigation Group in 1972 to pursue the organization's agenda through court cases as well. *Id.* at 22. Nader hired an assistant U.S. Attorney named Alan Morrison as the group's first director, and it has become an important component of the Nader network, complementing the more policy-oriented approaches of its partners. *Id.* at 22, 33.

As you reflect on these movement histories, what common features do you identify? What differences do you see? In each case, how did social movements feed into and inform the development of public interest law organizations — and vice versa? How much do you think that the emergence and development of public interest law organizations in these areas owe their existence and success to charismatic and talented leaders (like Ralph Nader)? What role do you think is played by broader political and economic changes that create structural opportunities for movement organizations to emerge?

2. Institutionalization

As the previous section suggests, as public interest practice evolved in the second half of the twentieth century, it became institutionalized across a range of practice settings. Public interest organizations continued to proliferate, evolve, and diversify, while the private sector developed new forms of public interest practice in addition to pro bono service.

a. THE NONPROFIT SECTOR: EVOLUTION, INNOVATION, AND DIVERSIFICATION

Many of the organizations discussed in this chapter evolved in a similar pattern. They started off devoted to pursuing specific causes, recruited volunteer lawyers to assist with the legal aspects of such work, and then created an in-house legal department to represent the group's interests in judicial, administrative, legislative, or other legal settings. Over time, these groups grew in size and saw their missions evolve to respond to both internal staff interest and external demands. The ACLU and LDF illustrate these trends.

During the 1960s and 1970s, the ACLU pursued a broad civil liberties agenda that led it to advocate for strong separation of church and state; the expansion of the rights of persons suspected of and charged with crimes; racial equality and civil rights for women, gays and lesbians, students, and persons with developmental disabilities; and the expansion of the right of privacy, including the right to an abortion. WALKER, *supra*, at 217-320. Throughout this period, the organization also continued to advance its core mission, free speech, through cases related to the antiwar and civil rights causes. *Id.* at 240-42; 279-92. From a tactical standpoint, by the late 1960s, ACLU lawyers had moved from mainly filing amicus briefs in cases to taking on direct representation of clients for the purpose of protecting civil liberties. *Id.* at 262, 285. Much of this period coincided with the tenure of the Warren Court, which was more (though certainly not always) open to entertaining theories about constitutional civil liberties than past courts. Toward the end of this period, in 1977, a major controversy arose when the Illinois affiliate provided legal representation to a group of Nazi protestors who petitioned to hold a march in Skokie, Illinois, a location where numerous survivors of the Holocaust lived. *Id.* at 323-40. The controversial nature of this case, even for many ACLU supporters, caused some people to drop their memberships and resign from the organization. *Id.* at 327. Though its influence has ebbed and flowed, the ACLU has built itself into a national organization with more than half a million members, numerous state affiliate offices (many of them with their own full time legal staffs), a national legal office and several national project offices that work on different subject matter specialties under the broad umbrella of civil liberties. It has achieved numerous litigation successes in the federal and state courts. *ACLU History*, ACLU, http:/www.aclu.org/aclu-history (last visited June 29, 2012). The organization also approaches the protection of civil liberties through legislative work at the federal and state level, and through efforts to promote public education about civil liberties. *Id.*

In the post-civil rights period, the NAACP LDF emerged from its focus on dismantling Jim Crow laws to address other racial justice issues—such as racial disparities in the criminal justice system, particularly in the administration of the death penalty and in sentencing and incarceration. *History*, NAACP Legal Defense Fund, http://naacpldf.org/history (last visited Aug. 11, 2012). Its related work on educational access for minority communities and "dismantling" the school-to-prison pipeline has been an equally important part of its contemporary mission. *Id.* LDF has continued deploying traditional litigation strategies—for instance, seeking enforcement of the federal Voting Rights Act and defending affirmative action programs—while also expanding its strategic initiatives to include community organizing, educational reports to influence government officials and the general public, and national legislative work through its Washington, D.C. office. The NAACP Legal Defense and Education Fund, Inc., 2009-2012 Annual Report, at http://www.naacpldf.org/files/publications/2009-2010%20LDF%20Annual% 20Report.pdf (last visited Aug. 11, 2012).

As we have seen, in addition to the evolution of these pioneering organizations, the late 1960s and 1970s saw the creation and expansion of innovative new "public interest law firms" growing out of progressive movements and based on the ACLU and LDF model of deploying law for social reform. Rabin, *Lawyers for Social Change, supra,* at 224, 232-33. Formed as nonprofit entities, these firms set out to engage in law reform in the pursuit of a range of social causes. *Id.* at 232-36. At the outset, many of these organizations were spurred by grants from the Ford Foundation. Craig, *supra,* at 27. Among these groups were CLASP, the Center for Law in the Public Interest (CLIPI), the Mexican American Legal Defense Fund (MALDEF), the environmental groups SCLDF, EDF, and NRDC, and Public Advocates. Rabin, *Lawyers for Social Change, supra,* at 228-29, 228 n.65; *see also* Louise G. Trubek, *Public Interest Law: Facing the Problems of Maturity,* 33 U. Ark. Little Rock L. Rev. 417, 418-20 (2011). Some of the groups, such as SCLDF and EDF, were devoted to a single cause and thus more closely resembled the model established by the NAACP LDF.

Other groups, such as CLASP, CLIPI, and Public Advocates, organized themselves as broader public interest law firms, with lawyers specializing in different areas of practice and focusing on specific types of law reform and social policy. Many of these public interest law firms were formed with the explicit goal of representing "underrepresented interests" that we explored in the last chapter. One example was CLASP, the creation of which was motivated by many of the same factors that produced the Nader organizations. As described by Charles Halpern, one of the CLASP's founders, public interest law firms were a reaction to the fact that the conduct of corporations was driven primarily by the profit motive, without sufficient consideration of the social impact of their actions, such as environmental harm, risks to public safety, and fair treatment of their employees. Charles R. Halpern & John M. Cunningham, *Reflections on the New Public Interest Law: Theory and Practice at the Center for Law and Social Policy,* 59 Geo. L.J. 1095, 1096 (1971). At the same time, public agencies responsible for regulating these corporations were similarly unresponsive to the public interest. *Id.* at 1097. Firms such as CLASP, run by lawyers independent of government or corporate control, were created to promote public participation in the regulatory process. Lawyers in these public interest firms would "use their special knowledge and skill to help citizen groups formulate and clarify their objectives, and to suggest appropriate techniques by which to work for these objectives." *Id.* at 1102.

> The idea of the Center was worked out through dialogue with a broad range of lawyers and legal educators. The dialogue centered not only on the need for new legal institutions to represent citizen interests but also on the excessive abstractness and narrowness of legal education. Thus, in its final form the Center had two primary goals: to provide legal representation to previously unrepresented groups in the federal administrative process; and to experiment with new forms of legal education involving intensive clinical experience and concentration on the public policy aspects of the law. In addition, the Center has tried to developed [sic] a more flexible and humane institutional style of legal practice. The Center's goals have proven to be, as they were intended, closely interrelated. In twice-weekly seminars with students and staff, the Center attorneys and students have developed novel legal theories and have gained a dimension of awareness and self-criticism they could not have had otherwise.

Id. at 1103-04. Substantively, CLASP devoted itself to three areas of practice: environmental protection, consumer affairs, and the health problems of the poor. *Id.* at 1105.

The creation of CLASP and other groups in the first wave of public interest law transformed the field. By the 1980s, the nonprofit public interest law sector had grown and diversified to include a broad range of organizations that varied by size, location, substantive focus, legal strategy, and other characteristics. "Up to 1969, there were only twenty-three public interest law centers, staffed by fewer than fifty full-time attorneys. By the end of 1975, the number of centers had increased to 108, with almost 600 staff attorneys. In 1984, there were 158 groups employing a total of 906 lawyers." NAN ARON, LIBERTY AND JUSTICE FOR ALL: PUBLIC INTEREST LAW IN THE 1980S AND BEYOND 27 (1989). The median size of all groups was four attorneys, although there were some groups like the ACLU, LDF, and NRDC with much larger offices. *Id.* at 33. Most of the groups were headquartered in the Northeast, with about a quarter located in the West. *Id.* at 31. Of the groups, 15 percent served the poor, 13 percent were multi-issue, 10 percent focused on civil rights/civil liberties, another 10 percent were women's rights groups, 9 percent focused on disability issues, environmental and children's rights groups each were 8 percent of the total, and 4 percent worked on prisoners' issues. *Id.* "About three-quarters supplemented their litigation with other forms of legal advocacy and legislative activities. Almost two-thirds represented or advised individuals, and an equal proportion engaged in community organizing or public education work." *Id.* at 32. Funding came primarily from foundation grants (24 percent), individual contributions (20 percent), and membership dues (11 percent). *Id.* at 41.

How do you explain the growth and diversification of public interest law during this early period? What are the tradeoffs of creating a range of groups with different missions and strategies? As you reflect on the types of groups described in this section, what do you think are the advantages and disadvantages of focusing on one issue (like LDF) as opposed to a broader range of concerns (like CLASP)? What are the tradeoffs of being associated with a non-legal partner (like the NAACP or NOW) as opposed to operating as a freestanding legal organization?

b. THE PRIVATE SECTOR: LAW COLLECTIVES AND RADICAL LAWYERS

One of the most important developments over the past half-century has been the changing role that the private sector has played in the public interest law field. A key change has been the increasingly organized system for delivering pro bono services, which has been anchored primarily (though not exclusively) in large law firms. A fuller discussion of this important development is reserved for Chapter 4's exploration of practice sites. Here, we highlight other institutional trends occurring outside of the nonprofit domain that influenced the practice and scope of public interest law during and after the civil rights era: the development of people's law collectives and the rise of "radical lawyering" within private firm settings.

Based on radical political principles, such as Marxism or feminism (as discussed above in relation to the D.C. Feminist Law Collective) and devoted to the redistribution of wealth and power in the United States, law collectives developed in different communities across the country. *See* Paul Harris, *Law Collectives as Power Bases*, 2 NEW DIRECTIONS IN LEGAL SERVICES 164 (1976); Paul Harris, *The San Francisco Community Law Collective*, 7 LAW & POL'Y 19 (1985) [hereinafter, Harris, *San Francisco*]. Often closely linked to the National Lawyers Guild (NLG) these collectives attempted to integrate the political goals of their members with the practice of public interest law. A significant part of the philosophy was to create a non-hierarchical setting in which to practice law, with the goal of treating all members of the collective equally in terms of salary and decision making and not elevating lawyers to a higher professional status. Harris, *San Francisco, supra*, at 19. The D.C. Feminist Law Collective's statement of purpose explains some of these goals.

> One of the goals of our collective is the formation of a radical institution in which we do not split our lives between workplace and political effort. Another goal is to unify our personal lives and our work through the strong commitment we have to each other's private concerns. The collective has recognized, for example, the need for schedule flexibility to accommodate our child care responsibilities.
>
> We hope that the collective will offer a model for alternatives that involve basic structural change through redistribution of control over economics and politics. We realize, of course, that merely creating a small business does not protect or separate us from a repressive system. Our goal, however, is to create our own supportive structure while fighting the oppression around us.
>
> A collective is defined by its sharing of growth, process, and power. The issue of hierarchy is central. We chose not to impose a hierarchical structure on an effort which is feminist in philosophy. Each member shares in making decisions, solving problems, and resolving conflict. For example, the collective will

decide where to allocate our resources for low fee cases; at the same time, the collective determines the distribution of income by considering each woman's particular needs. We have bi-weekly meetings to discuss these and other issues, in an effort to continually analyze our work politically.

WASHINGTON, D.C. FEMINIST LAW COLLECTIVE STATEMENT OF PURPOSE (September 1976) (copy on file with authors).

Another important goal of collectives was demystifying the law to make it more accessible to those whose interests it could protect, thereby putting more power into the hands of clients and community groups. Harris, *San Francisco, supra*, at 19-20. Some collectives sought to serve as in-house counsel for community organizations engaged in social change. This approach was "based on the conviction that organizations of people struggling for change are more important to the revolutionary process than test cases dreamed up in lawyers' offices." *Id.* at 24. Although they do not constitute a substantial part of contemporary public interest practice, a number of law collectives continue to operate to this day, such as the People's Law Office in Chicago. Home Page, PEOPLE'S LAW OFFICE, http://peopleslawoffice.com (last visited June 29, 2012).

Outside of law collectives, radical lawyers used private practice to advance different causes. From the early days of the public interest law movement, there were private firms established by lawyers who had been active in progressive movements. Arthur Kinoy and William Kunstler, two charismatic and energetic progressive lawyers, formed Kunstler, Kunstler & Kinoy, a private law firm that was intended to carry on the individual work they had engaged in during the civil rights movement. ARTHUR KINOY, RIGHTS ON TRIAL: THE ODYSSEY OF A PEOPLE'S LAWYER 211 (1983). Kinoy and Kunstler would later found the Center for Constitutional Rights, a nonprofit civil liberties organization that is still actively engaged in public interest law. Center for Constitutional Rights, Mission and History, at http://ccrjustice.org/missionhistory (last visited Aug. 12, 2012). Kinoy and Kunstler were also closely associated with the NLG, an organization that supported a more radical form of lawyering for clients and causes. As Thomas Hilbink observes, "A willingness to transgress norms of the profession was a key aspect of radical lawyering in the 1960s and 1970s. . . . National Lawyers Guild attorneys involved in the civil rights movement were 'more supportive of demonstrations and sit-ins, less legalistic, and less interested in whether they antagonized the local power structure.'" Thomas M. Hilbink, *You Know the Type . . . : Categories of Cause Lawyering*, 29 LAW & SOC. INQUIRY 657, 670 (2004). As this suggests, radical lawyers—in contrast with some of their more traditional counterparts—were interested in using law as a means to advance movements and build power. Thus, they took on affirmative cases with movement implications but also engaged in defensive legal practice to protect the rights of protestors and other dissidents subject to criminal prosecution. Unlike nonprofit lawyers, who relied on philanthropy to fund their activities, radical lawyers also had to figure out how to do cause-oriented work while also paying the bills. Over time, they experimented with different models—some (like the tobacco lawyers profiled below) relying on contingent fee cases and others developing different models based on fee-shifting statutes and other mechanisms for subsidizing cause work.

C. THE RISE OF CONSERVATIVE PUBLIC INTEREST LAW

Although the ideological differences among public interest lawyers are treated more fully in Chapter 3, it is important here to mark the organizational development of conservative public interest law beginning in the 1970s. As we will see, conservative groups have both responded to and shaped the changing political environment, mobilizing legal resources to advance diverse issues, including economic deregulation, libertarianism, gun rights, and a greater role for religion in public life. Ann Southworth, *Conservative Lawyers and the Contest over the Meaning of "Public Interest Law,"* 52 UCLA L. Rev. 1223, 1241-44, 1262 (2005). In so doing, they have succeeded in contesting liberal public interest claims in specific cases and in reshaping the legal and political terrain in ways that have imposed structural impediments to liberal public interest lawyering.

V. THE NEXT WAVE

The previous section provided an overview of the institutional origins of the public interest law field. As it suggested, following the path forged by the seminal efforts of LDF and other early groups, public interest law expanded and became more diverse beginning in the late 1960s and accelerating into the 1970s and beyond. Since the first wave, the public interest movement has promoted the rights of a broad range of racial and ethnic groups and other constituencies, including children, the elderly, gays and lesbians, disabled persons, veterans, and immigrants—among others. In this section, we highlight some features of the field's ongoing development in both the nonprofit and for-profit domains. We begin by reviewing three movements that have come of age in the post-civil rights period (though have earlier roots) and have left distinctive marks on the nonprofit public interest sector: disability rights; lesbian, gay, bisexual, and transgender (LGBT) rights; and immigrant rights. Like our earlier discussion, these profiles are meant to illustrate developments in the field and are neither comprehensive nor exclusive of other key legal movements that have influenced public interest law's growth. We then describe the trajectory of U.S. tobacco litigation as one example of how some plaintiffs' law firms have built case portfolios designed to affect important social issues—thus advancing a version of public interest law reform. The chapter concludes with an overview of important contemporary issues that we will explore throughout the remainder of the book.

A. POST-CIVIL RIGHTS LEGAL MOVEMENTS

1. Disability Rights

In the United States, the modern disability rights movement emerged in the early 1970s as an effort to reshape society's attitudes toward individuals with disabilities. Samuel R. Bagenstos, *Justice Ginsburg and the Judicial Role in Expanding "We The People": The Disability Rights Cases*, 104 Colum. L. Rev. 49, 50

(2004). Early views of disabled people generally reflected the "medical/charity model, which . . . viewed people with disabilities as objects of pity, philanthropy, and paternalistic rehabilitation." Sande L. Buhai, *In the Meantime: State Protection of Disability Civil Rights*, 37 Loy. L.A. L. Rev. 1065, 1075-76 (2004); *see also* Laura L. Rovner, *Perpetuating Stigma: Client Identity in Disability Rights Litigation*, 2001 Utah L. Rev. 247, 271. Society often viewed individuals with disabilities as lesser persons to be cared for or "fixed" through medicine, rehabilitation or training. Bagenstos, *supra*, at 51; Buhai, *supra*, at 1077. "The result [of these patronizing attitudes] was the exclusion of people with disabilities from the community through such devices as institutionalization, denial of education, and refusal to permit participation in core civic activities." Bagenstos, *supra*, at 51.

The disability rights movement challenged the medical/charity paradigm of disability by employing a social or civil rights model. Under this new model:

> [P]eople with disabilities were not inherently different from those without disabilities in any substantive way. Instead, society had unnecessarily constructed a world that made disabilities relevant. . . . Society, not the large minority who had difficulties with stairs, had created the barriers. Problems people with disabilities faced were thus reframed as the result of societal attitudes and discrimination, not the inevitable consequences of the disabilities themselves.

Buhai, *supra*, at 1077; *see also* Rovner, *supra*, at 268.

The disability rights movement engaged in a mix of tactics including litigation, legislative lobbying, and direct action to seek changes in how the law treated the disabled. Bagenstos, *supra*, at 51. These efforts were modeled on the strategies of other civil rights movements, but have had to adjust to the fact that the legal concerns of persons with disabilities are not uniform because their disabilities vary widely. Kathi J. Pugh, *Introduction*, 27 A.B.A. Hum. Rts. Mag. 2, 2 (2000).

The most noteworthy legal development in the disability rights movement has been Congress's adoption of the Americans with Disabilities Act (ADA) in 1990. While other laws protecting the rights of persons with disabilities were in place before 1990, the ADA was comprehensive and wide ranging in its reform of civil rights law. Nonetheless, its effectiveness in promoting equality for the disabled is subject to some dispute. *Compare* Peter David Blanck, *Employment Integration, Economic Opportunity, and the Americans with Disabilities Act: Empirical Study from 1990-1993*, 79 Iowa L. Rev. 853, 854 (1994) (concluding that "[t]he ADA has played a significant role in enhancing labor force participation of persons with disabilities and in reducing dependence on government entitlement programs") *with* Samuel R. Bagenstos, *The Americans With Disabilities Act as Welfare Reform*, 44 Wm. & Mary L. Rev. 921, 923 (2003) (arguing that "ADA plaintiffs are among the least successful classes of litigants in the federal courts — with a rate of (non)success that is second in futility only to that of prisoner plaintiffs."); *see also* Samuel R. Bagenstos, Law and the Contradictions of the Disability Rights Movement 3 (2009) (suggesting that lack of success under the ADA may be the result of the significant diversity of interests among different constituencies within the disability rights movement); *but see* Michael Ashley Stein, Michael E. Waterstone & David B. Wilkins, *Cause*

Lawyering for People with Disabilities, 123 HARV. L. REV. 1658, 1660-61 (2010) (reviewing Bagenstos's book and arguing that the lack of significant success may be attributable to the fact that disability rights cause lawyers have not played a major role in any of the ADA cases heard by the Supreme Court).

A recent study drawing on interviews with disability rights lawyers reveals a complex and nuanced picture. Michael E. Waterstone, Michael Ashley Stein & David B. Wilkins, *Disability Cause Lawyers*, 53 WM. & MARY L. REV. 1287 (2012). It suggests that contemporary disability rights advocacy has been hampered by narrow Supreme Court interpretations of the ADA. Faced with this impediment, disability rights lawyers have taken a pragmatic approach to their work that employs a combination of lower court litigation, strategic coordination with other advocacy groups, regulatory and legislative advocacy, and mobilization to address the needs of the disabled. *Id.* at 1338-42.

> [T]hese lawyers focused their efforts on implementing some parts of the ADA rather than endeavoring to create new legal rights. By focusing on public services and accommodation suits whose settlements and verdicts redound to the national community of persons with disabilities, disability cause lawyers have made significant progress towards achieving the social integration envisioned by disability rights advocates . . . and contained in the ADA. This progress has moved social integration close to the point where citizens, disabled or not, are able to equally access opportunities and participate in society. Disability cause lawyers have enabled this social transformation by enforcing statutory rights in the shadow of the Supreme Court.

Id. at 1357-58.

2. Lesbian, Gay, Bisexual, and Transgender (LGBT) Rights

As with other identity-based social movements, the LGBT rights movement began with a struggle to protect gays and lesbians from discrimination in different domains of public and private life. A foundational element of state discrimination against gays and lesbians was the enforcement of laws regulating sexuality and gender noncomformity.

> Although states criminalized sodomy and municipalities made cross-dressing a minor crime before 1900, "homosexual sodomy" and "homosexuality" were not objects of state regulation until the early twentieth century. But once the state focused on "homosexuals and sex perverts," it did so with a vengeance. At the height of America's anti-homosexual terror, the half-generation after World War II, the state not only hunted and jailed "homosexuals" for cross-dressing and having sex with one another, but kicked them out of the civil service, closed their bars and hangouts, seized novels and journals about their "perversion," censored movies that mentioned the crime that dared not speak its name, deported them, and locked them in hospitals where they were electroshocked, castrated, and otherwise tortured.

Eskridge, *Effects, supra*, at 2159-60.

From the end of World War II until the 1960s, a nascent movement began to challenge state laws that oppressed gays and lesbians. *Id.* at 2160. In the 1950s, early organizational efforts were led by groups such as the Mattachine Society and the Daughters of Bilitis, which formed communities of support and informed their memberships of legal and social developments. Elvia R. Arriola, *Faeries, Marimachas, Queens, and Lezzies: The Construction of Homosexuality Before the 1969 Stonewall Riots*, COLUM. J. GENDER & L. 33, 33, 69-70 (1995). By the 1960s and 1970s, this movement grew substantially, as did the range of legal challenges on behalf of gays and lesbians. Organizations and individuals challenged civil service laws excluding gays and lesbians from public employment, continued to fight laws regulating private sexuality, protested and litigated to stop police harassment, and advocated for changes to various aspects of family law that precluded gays and lesbians from marrying and maintaining relationships with children through custody, visitation, and adoption. Eskridge, *Effects, supra*, at 2169-79. The 1969 Stonewall Riots — an act of resistance to police harassment of gays, lesbians, and transgender people in New York City — also occurred during this period, promoting greater public awareness of gay and lesbian rights as well as generating more support for legal advocacy for the gay community. Arriola, *supra*, at 33, 76-77. Stonewall signaled the transformation of earlier efforts to protect LGBT rights into "a gay liberation movement populated by tens of thousands of lesbians, gay men, and bisexuals who formed hundreds of new organizations demanding radical changes in the way gay people are treated by the state." William N. Eskridge, Jr., *Channeling: Identity-Based Social Movements and Public Law*, 150 U. PA. L. REV. 419, 457 (2001).

In the period after Stonewall, civil rights groups — including the Lambda Legal Defense and Education Fund, Inc., ACLU LGBT Project, National Center for Lesbian Rights, and Gay & Lesbian Advocates & Defenders (GLAD) — were formed and began engaging in extensive law reform actions on behalf of the gay and lesbian community. Eskridge, *Effects, supra*, at 2174. Over the past 25 years, the LGBT rights movement has expanded and evolved. It has continued to contest state-sponsored discrimination, particularly in the context of military service; won the invalidation of state anti-sodomy laws, *Lawrence v. Texas*, 539 U.S. 558, 578 (2003) (overruling *Bowers v. Hardwick*, 478 U.S. 186 (1986)); battled a strong counter-movement from religious and other social conservatives pushing a "traditional family values" agenda; and continued to fight for recognition of marriage equality, domestic partnership, and other liberties associated with the private lives of LGBT people. Eskridge, *Effects, supra*, at 2179-92. Much of this work has been done by lawyers and legal organizations devoted to social reform.

3. Immigrant Rights

The development of an organizational sector dedicated to enforcing the rights of immigrants has been an important aspect of public interest law during the past quarter century of rapid and changing migration patterns. The 1980s witnessed scores of refugees fleeing political oppression and seeking asylum in the United States under federal immigration law. Scott L. Cummings, *The Internationalization of Public Interest Law*, 57 DUKE L.J. 891, 908-10 (2008). The 1990s brought more attention to economic dislocation, rather than political repression, as a driver of immigration, particularly from Latin America, and saw an increasing number of undocumented workers entering the country. *Id.*

at 912-13. The increase in undocumented immigration, combined with an anti-immigrant backlash associated with the War on Terror, produced new legal vulnerabilities and challenges for immigrant communities. These changes "have redefined immigrant advocacy, transforming it from an ancillary part of civil rights and poverty law practice into a distinctive field." *Id*. at 908.

The main battleground for immigration law in the 1980s centered on immigrants' claims for asylum under the federal Refugee Act of 1980, which expanded the legal standard for asylum to those who could prove a "well-founded fear of persecution" in their home countries. *See* Refugee Act of 1980, Pub. L. No. 96-212, §201(a) 94 Stat. 102, 102-03 (1980) (codified as amended at 8 U.S.C. §1101(a)(42) (2012)). Though on its face this provision was politically neutral, the United States applied the asylum standard along political lines:

> Whereas U.S. opposition to the governing socialist party in Nicaragua meant that asylum claims from that country generally succeeded, the situation was different for those fleeing El Salvador and Guatemala, where U.S. support for military dictators made it reluctant to grant asylum to refugees from those countries—and thus concede persecution committed by U.S.-backed right-wing regimes.

Cummings, *The Internationalization of Public Interest Law*, *supra*, at 909-10. These practices mobilized the immigrant rights bar in two ways. First, lawyers moved to extend representation to refugees. At first, this came through legal aid offices funded by the Legal Services Corporation, but Congress soon foreclosed LSC representation of persons seeking asylum. *Id*. at 910, 914. As a result, an alternative non-LSC funded bar emerged.

> A key part of this new structure grew out of the Sanctuary Movement, in which churches were turned into sanctuaries for refugees denied legal entrance. In dioceses with large refugee populations, local Catholic church leaders also supported the establishment of legal programs to meet the needs of refugees, some of which were eventually consolidated into the Catholic Legal Immigration Network, Inc. (CLINIC) in 1988.

Id. at 910. The direct service needs of the immigrant refugee community were also met by grassroots organizations, the creation of pro bono asylum law projects, and law school clinics devoted to asylum work. *Id*. at 910-11. At the same time, some immigrant rights lawyers working on asylum issues pursued law reform. Groups such as the Immigrant Legal Resource Center in San Francisco and the ACLU pursued broader impact cases to ensure that the federal government complied with statutory and constitutional restrictions and applied the same legal standard to refugees from different countries without regard to its support for or antipathy toward those countries' policies and leaders. *Id*. at 912.

The combination of increasingly harsh U.S. immigration policy and post-Cold War economic dislocation changed the nature of migration—and the immigrant rights response to it. In 1986, Congress enacted the Immigration Reform and Control Act (IRCA), which simultaneously granted amnesty to undocumented immigrants who were in the United States and sought to deter new entrants by strengthening border security and imposing sanctions on employers who hired undocumented workers. *Id.* at 913. At the same time, the United States liberalized its trade policies with México. *Id.* at 912-13. The confluence of a robust U.S. economy and economic dislocation in México resulted in a large influx of those seeking economic opportunity, many of whom were undocumented. *Id.* at 913. IRCA's enactment also had other, unforeseen effects on migration patterns. Because of tighter security along the U.S.-Mexican border, immigration of undocumented workers was redirected to other regions, causing settlement patterns to spread throughout the United States. *Id.*

> Those who made it across the border began to stay longer, increasing their dependence on steady employment, which reinforced the movement out of seasonal agricultural work into the urban low-wage sector. Employers began to impose the costs of IRCA compliance on workers by lowering wages, contracting out work to subcontractors with lower labor standards, and engaging in more informal work transactions. Undocumented immigrant workers, whose precarious legal status made them loathe to contest mistreatment, experienced heightened insecurity as part of a second-tier labor system. In this environment, a dominant question for lawyers representing immigrants became how to afford legal protection to a class of people defined by their illegality. The workplace — where baseline protections existed — emerged as a central arena of legal struggle.

Id. at 913-14.

Undocumented worker representation was shaped by two events. *Id.* at 914. First, Congress extended its ban on LSC-funded lawyers to prohibit them from representing undocumented persons even if they did so using non-LSC funds. *Id.* Accordingly, the immigrant rights bar had to establish new, independent nonprofit offices to do legal work on behalf of undocumented workers. *Id.* Second, in 2002, the Supreme Court decided *Hoffman Plastic Compounds, Inc. v. NLRB*, 535 U.S. 137 (2002), which held that undocumented workers could not recover traditional labor remedies, such as back pay, when their employers illegally fired them for engaging in union organizing. Cummings, *The Internationalization of Public Interest Law*, *supra*, at 914. The decision jeopardized the already vulnerable position of undocumented employees in the workplace, but at the same time resulted in greater collaboration between organized labor and immigrant rights groups. *Id.* "It is against this backdrop that lawyers began to forge a network of non-LSC groups, grassroots worker centers, impact organizations, and law school clinical programs dedicated to protecting the rights of undocumented immigrant workers." *Id.*; *see also* Saru Jayaraman & Immanuel Ness, *Models of Worker Organizing, in* The New Urban Immigrant Workforce 71 (Sarumathi Jayaraman & Immanuel Ness eds., 2005). Grassroots organizations such as the National Day Laborer Organizing Network also emerged to facilitate the political and legal mobilization of immigrant workers. Cummings, *The Internationalization of Public Interest Law*, *supra*, at 916-17.

While issues surrounding undocumented immigration continue to be polarizing, they have also fed into a broader hostility toward immigrants irrespective of legal status. This has been reflected in efforts to limit access to public benefits for all immigrants, who on average have lower incomes and higher poverty rates than the general public. *Id.* at 923. California's Proposition 187 was a key event in this regard, generating a forceful public interest response. *Id.* at 923-24. Enacted in 1994 through the popular initiative process, Proposition 187 barred undocumented immigrants in California from access to public social services, nonemergency health care, and schools. Several immigrant rights organizations, such as the Center for Human Rights and Constitutional Law, the Immigrant Legal Resource Center, the National Immigration Law Center, the Asian Pacific American Legal Center, MALDEF, and the ACLU, brought consolidated federal suits that resulted in the invalidation of parts of the measure. *Id.* at 924. But the conflict over resource-restricting laws such as these continues in other jurisdictions.

Legal resources were also marshaled in response to efforts to deny means-tested public benefits to legal immigrants as well as undocumented persons. *Id.* A critical example of this was the 1996 federal welfare reform law, which denied legal immigrants disability benefits and food stamps and authorized states to enact similar provisions banning them from receiving welfare and Medicaid. In reaction to such measures, the Open Society Institute invested $50 million to create the Emma Lazarus fund devoted to promoting immigrant naturalization and engaging in public advocacy to restore eligibility for public benefits for immigrants. *Id.* at 924-25. These funds helped support both direct legal services work and impact litigation to address these policy concerns. *Id.* at 924.

Nonetheless, limits on immigrant representation continued to constrain this work.

> [P]olicymakers and funders deemed some groups within the immigrant community as more deserving of support than others. The outlines of a hierarchy of immigrant eligibility emerged most visibly within the federal legal services program, where after the 1996 restrictions a complex system of representation arose to assist immigrants who could demonstrate either *claims to legal status* or *claims to victimhood.* . . . Those with legitimate claims to legal status — naturalized citizens, lawful permanent residents, and those petitioning to obtain lawful permanent residence — continued to remain eligible under rules in place since the early 1980s. Those without legal status could nonetheless qualify for services under a series of modifications to the eligibility requirements that reflected sympathy for immigrants whose illegal status was a product of victimization — or made them more vulnerable to it [such as victims of domestic violence and human trafficking, torture victims, asylum seekers, and juveniles in the dependency and delinquent systems].

Limits on immigrant representation were not confined to LSC-funded offices. *Id.* at 926-27. A similar emphasis on "deserving" immigrants was also visible in some non-LSC groups and law school immigrant rights clinical programs.

More recently, immigrant rights lawyers have confronted new challenges. The September 11 terrorist attacks provoked repressive governmental policies directed at immigrants. *See* Kevin R. Johnson, *Protecting National Security*

Through More Liberal Admission of Immigrants, 2007 U. Cʜɪ. Lᴇɢᴀʟ F. 157 (2007). Among the reactions to the attacks were: a federal policy requiring primarily Arab and Muslim noncitizens to report to and register with federal immigration authorities; enforcement of these requirements through arrests, detentions, and deportations; and calls for increasing border security. *Id.* at 168-70. Though some of these policies have been discontinued, their impact on large segments of the immigrant population was significant. In addition, federal and state governments have increasingly transformed immigration law from a primarily administrative regime to a punitive, criminal law system. *See* Stephen H. Legomsky, *The New Path of Immigration Law: Asymmetric Incorporation of Criminal Justice Norms*, 64 Wᴀsʜ. & Lᴇᴇ L. Rᴇᴠ. 469 (2007). At the federal level, this has occurred through increasing the criminalization of immigration law violations, imposing immigration consequences for criminal convictions, and employing criminal law enforcement strategies and personnel to enforce immigration provisions. *Id* at 476-500. While this criminal regime has been imported to advance immigration policy, the rights of due process and other procedural protections routinely available to criminal defendants are not afforded to those charged with violating immigration laws. *Id.* at 524. Moreover, such policies raise serious concerns about racial profiling that may affect both noncitizens and citizens.

At the nonfederal level, states such as Arizona have attempted to impose criminal penalties for immigration violations and to use state and local police to enforce immigration law. In *Arizona v. United States*, __ U.S. __, 132 S. Ct. 2492, 2503, 2505 (2012), the Court invalidated state laws making it a misdemeanor to fail to comply with federal alien registration requirements or for undocumented persons to seek or engage in work. It also held that federal law preempted an Arizona law allowing law enforcement officers to engage in warrantless arrests of persons whom they had probable cause to believe had committed an offense that could require their removal from the United States. *Id.* at 2507. However, it rejected, for now, a challenge to that part of Arizona's law that authorizes law enforcement officials who have made a lawful stop, detention, or arrest to verify the detainee's immigration status. *Id.* at 2510. The proliferation of these punitive local approaches to immigration enforcement poses the next set of challenges to the contemporary immigrant rights movement.

B. THE ROLE OF THE PLAINTIFFS' BAR

One popular image of plaintiffs' lawyers is that they are ambulance chasers who provide legal representation for injured clients, but rake in a substantial amount of the settlement or jury verdict for themselves. These images are caricatures and have at times been promoted by corporate interests seeking to limit their exposure to lawsuits under the banner of tort reform. *See* Wɪʟʟɪᴀᴍ Hᴀʟᴛoᴍ & Mɪᴄʜᴀᴇʟ McCᴀɴɴ, Dɪsᴛoʀᴛɪɴɢ ᴛʜᴇ Lᴀᴡ: Poʟɪᴛɪᴄs, Mᴇᴅɪᴀ, ᴀɴᴅ ᴛʜᴇ Lɪᴛɪɢᴀᴛɪoɴ Cʀɪsɪs (2004). It is true that plaintiffs' firms are for-profit enterprises and that some individual attorneys in this area of practice can earn substantial amounts of money. However, many plaintiffs' lawyers think of themselves as working in the public interest, defending the "little guy" against corporations, and taking on cases to enforce plaintiffs' rights in a wide range of public interest law areas, such as civil rights, employment discrimination, housing discrimination, and environmental law. *See* Scott L. Cummings & Ann Southworth, *Between Profit and Principle: The Private Public Interest Firm, in* PRIVATE LAWYERS AND THE PUBLIC INTEREST: THE EVOLVING ROLE OF PRO BONO IN THE LEGAL PROFESSION 183 (Robert Granfield & Lynn Mather eds., 2009). We explore this type of practice in more detail in Chapter 4.

Since the early days of the public interest law movement, there have been some plaintiffs' lawyers who see their litigation as advancing a version of the public good. Over time, this style of practice has been facilitated by the advent of fee-shifting statutes and contingency fee arrangements. This section highlights one prominent — and controversial — area in which the plaintiffs' tort bar has attempted to engage in social reform through litigation as a window into broader public interest trends within the private bar.

Over the past two decades, plaintiffs' lawyers (in collaboration with some state attorneys general) mounted a successful litigation campaign to hold tobacco companies accountable for harms done to individuals and society from the sale of tobacco products. While much of this work was undertaken in cases that had the potential to, or did, yield profits for the attorneys, in some ways the litigation campaign resembled the efforts of other public interest law groups. First, the tobacco litigation lawyers have sought monetary damages for their clients, but also have a broader social goal of either reducing or eliminating the harm caused by use of these products. John J. Zefutie, Jr., Comment, *From Butts to Big Macs — Can the Big Tobacco Litigation and Nation-Wide Settlement with States' Attorneys General Serve as a Model for Attacking the Fast Food Industry?*, 34 SETON HALL L. REV. 1383, 1383-84, 1394-97 (2004). Second, the movement is arguably a reaction to the lack of responsiveness of political institutions to the public health problems associated with tobacco. Peter D. Jacobson & Soheil Soliman, *Litigation as a Public Health Policy: Theory or Reality?*, 30 J.L. MED. & ETHICS 224, 225-26 (2002).

Tobacco litigation originated in the 1950s. Early suits were brought on behalf of smokers who had developed lung cancer and sought recovery from tobacco companies under basic tort theories, such as negligence, deceit, and breach of warranty. Zefutie, *supra*, at 1387. These cases were unsuccessful because there was insufficient scientific evidence that smoking caused cancer. *Id.* From the early 1980s to 1990s, after causation was well established, lawsuits failed for the most part because the tobacco companies argued that persons who smoked in the face of the health evidence had assumed the risk of harm. *Id.* at 1388. It was not until the mid-1990s that lawyers representing plaintiffs suffering from the health effects of tobacco use were able to make headway. In part, this was a product of an organized effort by the plaintiffs' personal injury bar to invest a substantial portion of the funds they had earned in other tort litigation to finance a major class action lawsuit against tobacco companies and recruit some of the nation's top trial lawyers to take on the case. Peter Pringle, *The Chronicles of Tobacco: An Account of the Forces That Brought the Tobacco Industry to the Negotiating Table*, 25 WM. MITCHELL L. REV. 387, 389

(1999). This initial effort ultimately failed when the Fifth Circuit Court of Appeals reversed a federal trial court's grant of class certification in *Castano v. American Tobacco Co.*, 84 F.3d 734, 752 (5th Cir. 1996). This setback forced the tobacco plaintiffs' lawyers to reconsider their strategy, filing cases in state courts instead. Zefutie, *supra*, at 1391. But the state court suits, too, initially met with limited success.

The most recent wave of tobacco litigation was initiated by several states' attorneys general who filed suits on behalf of their states against tobacco companies to recover Medicare costs for treatment of persons with tobacco-related diseases. *Id.* at 1392. As part of their strategy, the states hired lawyers from the plaintiffs' personal injury bar to bring these cases. *Id.* at 1393. The alliance of the states, with their resources, and plaintiffs' lawyers, with their expertise, created a formidable adversary for large tobacco companies. In addition, in the context of state suits to recover Medicare costs, the tobacco companies' arguments about individual smoker assumption of risk were not relevant. Jacobson & Soliman, *supra*, at 229. The Medicare litigation also led to the disclosure of many documents during discovery showing that the tobacco industry had misled the general public regarding the health effects of tobacco. *Id.* In turn, these documents were used in private actions by tobacco users against tobacco companies, leading to greater success in that arena. *Id.* Ultimately, the Medicare litigation led to a $243 billion Master Settlement Agreement (MSA), as well as promises from tobacco companies to limit their advertising and provide funds for public education to discourage smoking. *Id.* at 228-29. Although the MSA has been regarded as a major success, there are numerous critics of the use of litigation to effectuate this type of social change, as well as critics of the states' actual implementation of the settlement. *See, e.g.*, W. Kip Viscusi, Smoke-Filled Rooms: A Postmortem on the Tobacco Deal (2002) (arguing that traditional government regulation is more transparent and ensures greater government accountability than restrictions imposed through tort litigation); Arthur B. LaFrance, *Tobacco Litigation: Smoke, Mirrors and Public Policy*, 26 Am. J.L. & Med. 187, 193 (2000) (claiming that tort litigation is not a useful vehicle for developing health policy); Robert L. Rabin, *The Tobacco Litigation: A Tentative Assessment*, 51 DePaul L. Rev. 331, 341 (2001) (describing how some states spent funds from the MSA settlement on programs not related to tobacco).

Questions about the relative success of the tobacco litigation are important, as some lawyers have turned to tort litigation to address other public health issues, such as suits against gun manufacturers to seek liability for the harm caused by firearms and cases against fast food companies because of the health effects of diets with high levels of fat, salt, and cholesterol. Zefutie, *supra*, at 1411; *see also* Stephanie Strom, *Lawyers from Suits Against Big Tobacco Target Food Makers*, N.Y. Times, Aug. 18, 2012, at A1. The degree to which such strategies reflect a genuine public interest mission or an attempt to win more lucrative cases is an ongoing issue that underscores the complexities of practicing public interest law in a private for-profit setting.

Do you think the tobacco lawyers described above should be considered public interest lawyers?

C. THE CONTEMPORARY PUBLIC INTEREST LAW FIELD

More than 40 years after its founding, public interest law occupies a radically different place within the profession. No longer in "fragile alliance" with the organized bar, public interest law in the United States now enjoys the status of a stable, distinct, and strongly supported occupational category within the legal profession. From an organizational perspective, the field has shown impressive expansion. Although direct historical comparisons are not possible, the available data points to significant growth in both the number and size of public interest law groups over the movement's lifespan. Using data collected in 1975, Joel Handler and his colleagues identified 576 lawyer positions in 86 public interest law organizations nationwide (excluding legal aid organizations), yielding an average of approximately seven attorneys per group. Joel F. Handler, Betsy Ginsberg & Arthur Snow, *The Public Interest Law Industry*, in PUBLIC INTEREST LAW: AN ECONOMIC AND INSTITUTIONAL ANALYSIS 42, 51 (Burton A. Weisbrod et al. eds., 1978). In addition, by 1972 there were approximately 2,660 legal aid staff attorneys. JOHNSON, *supra*, at 188. Taken together, these public interest lawyers were approximately 0.8 percent of the total bar at the time. According to Laura Beth Nielsen and Catherine Albiston's 2004 survey data, there were slightly more than one thousand public interest law organizations (including legal aid organizations) with an average of 13 lawyers per group, for an estimated total of 13,715 attorneys in the field—approximately 1.3 percent of the total bar. Laura Beth Nielsen & Catherine R. Albiston, *The Organization of Public Interest Practice: 1975-2004*, 84 N.C. L. REV. 1591, 1618-19, 1618 n.85 (2006). Although the 1975 and 2004 data are not directly comparable—and it is clear that public interest lawyers remain a tiny fraction of the overall bar—it does seem likely that significant growth has occurred, with these figures suggesting that the size of the public interest sector relative to the total bar grew by about two-thirds during this period. And this figure does not include public interest lawyers working in other sites, such as government, small firms, or clinical programs.

Consider the following perspectives on the state of contemporary public interest law. In the first, Nielsen and Albiston summarize the results of their national survey of public interest law organizations (PILOs). In the second, Rhode discusses some lessons from her research on a smaller subset of the nation's most prominent public interest law groups.

> We have indeed seen very significant changes in the field of PILOs. In a sense, the field has "matured." It now consists of larger organizations, paralleling organizational growth in the legal profession more generally. Like other sectors of sophisticated law practice, the PIL sector has witnessed trends toward leveraging lawyer talent with the efforts of non-lawyers. It has also become more diverse as the causes served by PILOs have become more diverse.
>
> But these trends also embody many of the tensions in public interest law that have been present for many years and remain unresolved. . . . [I]t appears that there now are two PIL industries — publicly-funded and privately-funded. On the one hand, we now see PILOs that receive a large amount of their funding from the LSC and other government agencies, largely provide direct services, and are statutorily prohibited from engaging in many law reform

activities. As a result, this sector of the field has grown, but also has become increasingly constrained.

Despite the increasing size of some organizations that rely heavily on federal and state funding, these organizations fall far short of delivering anything approaching an adequate level of civil representation to the poor. For example, using census data to estimate the number of people eligible to receive legal services from LSC-funded organizations (those who live in households with incomes less than 125% of the federal poverty rate), recent research demonstrates that the client to legal aid attorney ratio for those living in poverty is 1:6,861, while for Americans overall, the ratio of private lawyers to individuals is 1:525. Thus, lawyers who work in LSC-funded organizations attempt to meet an enormous potential legal need with resources far inferior to those available to private clients. Moreover, public funding comes at a price. These lawyers face significant demands at a time when government constraints on LSC organizations restrict their ability to leverage limited resources into sweeping legal reform through class actions or social change litigation.

In sharp contrast to the publicly-funded sector, we see a sector of privately-funded organizations that, while often smaller in budget and size, are free to pursue law reform activities as they please. Because this sector retains the professional autonomy to pursue social change through law, it may be a much more potent force for systemic change than the larger LSC-funded organizations despite significantly smaller budgets. Unlike the early period of PIL activity, this sector is now populated by conservative as well as liberal groups, by groups concerned with interests of the middle class, the wealthy, and the socially powerful, as well as the poor and socially disadvantaged. . . .

Our study demonstrates that PILOs have grown the most in sectors supported by government funding, where lawyers primarily representing people in poverty are most constrained in efforts at systemic change. The privately-funded sector of PILOs remains a context where lawyers can seek to have maximum impact on social policy through law, yet liberal groups no longer have a monopoly in this sector. Private power has realized that it too can lay claim to the mantle of "public interest."

Nielsen & Albiston, *supra*, at 1619-21.

Deborah Rhode's study of prominent public interest law groups concludes with the following assessment of the movement's achievements:

When assessing the achievements of public interest law in their field, participants in this study identified contributions along multiple dimensions. Some leaders emphasized the effect on individual lives. Brian Wolfman, litigation director of Public Citizen, noted the thousands of deaths and serious injuries prevented through litigation securing greater governmental accountability on health and safety issues. Heads of criminal justice organizations stressed the lives saved, the defendants exonerated, and the injustices reduced as the result of legal challenges and broader reform efforts in the indigent defense system. For disability rights leaders, the measures of success included increases in access to facilities, services, and opportunities that materially improved the quality of individual lives.

Other leaders stressed landmark legislation and legal decisions that have protected fundamental rights, established crucial principles, and safeguarded the environment. Providing checks on arbitrary or overreaching actions by judicial and governmental officials has also been critical. In fields that have emerged over the last quarter century, such as women's rights, environmental preservation, gay and lesbian rights, disability law, and information technology, public interest organizations have helped develop the central frameworks in which law and policy have evolved. As a consequence, the institutional landscape of many public and private sector organizations has been transformed. Commonly cited examples include racial integration of schools, workplaces, and the military, work/family innovations in employment, and environmentally responsive policies for corporations and regulatory agencies.

Many leaders also stressed more intangible but equally crucial advances in public awareness, social attitudes, and client empowerment. Their organizations' litigation and policy work, along with similar efforts documented in other studies, has helped to raise awareness, legitimate goals, mobilize support, attract funding, and gain leverage in dispute resolution and policy settings. The result is that Americans have a much greater understanding of problems affecting children and low-income and minority communities; of errors plaguing the American criminal justice system; of international human rights abuses; of the extent of environmental challenges; and of the concerns posed by new technologies. Many traditionally disempowered constituencies, and the groups that represent them, have gained greater respect and legitimacy. Poor communities have a voice in more of the decisions that affect them, and many grassroots organizations have increased their capacity to influence public policy.

Deborah L. Rhode, *Public Interest Law: The Movement at Midlife*, 60 STAN. L. REV. 2027, 2040-42 (2008).

How do you think the field of public interest law has changed from the earlier years of the movement? How has it stayed the same? Does Rhode's description of the "movement at midlife" make you think that public interest lawyers have achieved the goals they set 40 years ago? How does her description compare to Nielsen and Albiston's cautious tone about the limitations on groups promoting access to justice for the poor? After reviewing the materials in this chapter, would you say that the public interest law has been a "success"? In what ways? Have there been failures, missed opportunities, or other shortcomings?

QUESTIONS

1. You have now reviewed accounts of many prominent public interest law movements. Pick one of these histories and discuss the following: What causes public interest law to emerge as a tool to advance a particular cause? What factors influence the particular form public interest organizations and advocacy strategies take? Explain what historical events or circumstances were important to the development of this area of public interest lawyering. Describe how the absence of this historical context might have affected the success of this realm of public interest lawyering.

2. Consider the following quote, from Richard Ayres, one of the founders of the Natural Resources Defense Council:

> [I]n the 1960s "there was a whole series of issues which people my age saw as part of one seamless web of need for social change — ending the war, a better

criminal justice system, dealing with poverty and protecting the environment, which was a newly emerging or reemerging issue at the time."

SHABECOFF, *supra*, at 107. How much does the political environment affect the support and shape of public interest law? What do you think someone would say about the issues influencing contemporary advocacy?

3. What do you think the legacy of the public interest law movement is? What have been its most important achievements? In what ways has it not lived up to its aspirations? Why? What do you think public interest lawyers should do to meet some of the challenges you read about in this chapter?

CHAPTER 3

POLITICAL IDEOLOGY AND PUBLIC INTEREST LAWYERING

Public interest groups have been tagged "liberal" because they were originally identified with causes generally regarded as such. Today, public interest law can no longer be thought of as a monolithic movement dedicated to any one political agenda. It is practiced by organizations that span the ideological spectrum. Groups calling themselves public interest law firms . . . have become increasingly visible and active in pushing a conservative program.

NAN ARON, LIBERTY AND JUSTICE FOR ALL: PUBLIC INTEREST LAW
IN THE 1980s AND BEYOND 4 (1989).

The term "public interest" has been used throughout history to justify everything from democracy to totalitarianism.

BURTON A. WEISBROD, JOEL F. HANDLER & NEIL K. KOMESAR, PUBLIC
INTEREST LAW: AN ECONOMIC AND INSTITUTIONAL ANALYSIS 26 (1978).

I. INTRODUCTION

Public interest lawyering is commonly associated with liberal or progressive social movements. *See* Oliver A. Houck, *With Charity for All*, 93 YALE L.J. 1415, 1455 (1984); Ann Southworth, *Conservative Lawyers and the Contest over the Meaning of "Public Interest Law*," 52 UCLA L. REV. 1223, 1224 (2005) [hereinafter, Southworth, *Conservative Lawyers*]. This is because, as we saw last chapter, the public interest law movement was initially developed as a strategy to advance liberal rights claims. Yet, public interest lawyering for conservative causes has been going on nearly as long as its progressive counterpart, though it has generally received less attention — until recently. *See, e.g.*, STEVEN M. TELES, THE RISE OF THE CONSERVATIVE LEGAL MOVEMENT: THE BATTLE OF CONTROL OF THE LAW (2008); ANN SOUTHWORTH, LAWYERS OF THE RIGHT: PROFESSIONALIZING THE CONSERVATIVE COALITION (2008); Ann Southworth, *Professional Identity and Political*

Commitment Among Lawyers for Conservative Causes, in THE WORLDS CAUSE LAWYERS MAKE: STRUCTURE AND AGENCY IN LEGAL PRACTICE 83 (Austin Sarat & Stuart A. Scheingold eds., 2005) [hereinafter Southworth, *Identity and Commitment*]; John P. Heinz, Anthony Paik & Ann Southworth, *Lawyers for Conservative Causes: Clients, Ideology, and Social Distance*, 37 LAW & SOC'Y REV. 5 (2003) [hereinafter Heinz et al., *Lawyers for Conservative Causes*]. As a result, the precise meaning of the "public interest" has become politically contested, resting to some degree on the ideological perspective of the lawyers claiming to act in its behalf. We now see lawyers with a wide range of political views—liberal democratic, libertarian, evangelical, and radical left—all staking claims as public interest lawyers. STUART A. SCHEINGOLD & AUSTIN SARAT, SOMETHING TO BELIEVE IN: POLITICS, PROFESSIONALISM, AND CAUSE LAWYERING 107-22 (2004). We also see, in turn, ideological opponents contesting those claims and attacking the very basis upon which advocates make them. This chapter is about the struggle over the use of public interest law to advance ideologically diverse—and oppositional—causes.

The chapter maps the range of ideological views that lawyers claim to promote in the public interest. Although we discuss diversity on the left, we focus primarily on the conservative public interest law movement, showing that it (like its liberal counterpart) is far from monolithic, instead encompassing diverse and sometimes conflicting views, coexisting (sometimes uneasily) under the conservative banner. One question raised by this material, which echoes our definitional discussion in Chapter 1, is whether only certain political values are consonant with public interest lawyering or whether any political agenda may be advanced under the banner of public interest law. The chapter ends by looking at a consequence of the struggle over the ideological boundaries of public interest lawyering: political attacks against public interest lawyers (on both sides of the ideological spectrum) designed to limit their impact.

II. A NOTE ON IDEOLOGICAL TAXONOMY

In our daily lives, in the popular press, and even in academic literature, the terms "liberal" or "progressive" and "conservative" often get tossed about with a general understanding of what they represent, but without specific definitions. Liberals or progressives, for example, are likely to be in favor of issues such as women's equality, generally, and choice regarding abortion in particular; some forms of affirmative action; LGBT rights; strong environmental protection; an expansive reading of the Constitution's provisions guaranteeing individual rights, such as free speech and due process; government-funded social welfare to protect the poor; labor unions and workers' rights, government regulation of working conditions and consumer safety; and the rights of persons accused of crimes. They are generally thought of as sharing a set of values about the proper roles of government institutions, typically favoring an active role for the political branches of government as well as judicial intervention in support of minority rights and government regulation.

Conservatives, on the other hand, are generally associated with values that directly conflict with those of liberals. Some observers break down conservative thought into several subcategories, and (as with liberals) these values are not always compatible. For example, social conservatives are likely to favor values such as the legal protection of fetal life; the preservation of the traditional family structure, including heterosexual marriage; Christian religiosity and a central role for religion in public life; race-neutral government policies; and strong law enforcement and the protection of crime victims' rights. *See, e.g.*, Richard H. Fallon, Jr., *The "Conservative" Paths of the Rehnquist Court's Federalism Decisions*, 69 U. Chi. L. Rev. 429 (2002). Business conservatives, on the other hand, may support limits on the government regulation of the environment, consumer rights, and labor, which might impose costs on business firms, but be supportive of more expansive immigration policies that coincide with business interests (policies generally opposed by social conservatives). *See id.* at 447. Libertarian conservatives tend to believe in freedom from government interference with a wide range of private behavior, including gun regulation and limitations on use of private property. Libertarian conservatives may share the views of progressives who are passionate civil libertarians. But they are more distrustful of government in other areas than their liberal counterparts. Indeed libertarians tend to mistrust government at all levels, believe in a laissez-faire approach to most business practices (and on this issue align with business conservatives), and disfavor a strong judicial role in social regulation. While these different aspects of conservativism are diverse, they are often linked, both in reality and in the academic literature. Fallon, *supra*, at 447-48. In Ann Southworth's study of the rise of conservative public interest law firms, she describes conservativism as a connection of "various ideological strands of the uneasy but successful coalition of libertarians, business conservatives, and social conservatives that comprise the conservative social movement." Southworth, *Conservative Lawyers*, *supra*, at 1228 n.21.

These labels serve only as a starting point. Because they are generalizations, they break down in many different contexts. For example, it may be difficult to use this set of factors to categorize an institution such as the ACLU, which advocates for civil liberties, and most specifically freedom of conscience and speech. The ACLU, which most people associate with liberal values, has sometimes called itself "the most conservative organization in America" in that it promotes first principle constitutional values that protect individuals' autonomy from the state. *Print Advertisement*, ACLU, *available at* http://www.aclu.org/files/images/asset_upload_file672_27085.pdf (last visited July 14, 2012). In this way, it resembles (and is often aligned with) libertarian conservatism. In addition, while progressive groups generally favor strong government intervention in social causes, the ACLU's mission causes it to mistrust government in virtually all settings, with the important exception of its endorsement of strong judicial intervention to prevent political actors from infringing on civil liberties. Likewise, the ACLU sometimes finds itself in alliance with conservative organizations whose values it does not share in substance, but whose civil liberties might be at risk. In a recent Supreme Court case, for example, the ACLU joined forces with evangelical Christian groups in support of the free speech rights of high school students. *See Morse v. Frederick*, 551 U.S. 393, 398, 409-10 (2007) (upholding school board suspension of high school student who displayed a banner with the words "Bong Hits 4 Jesus" at a school-sanctioned public event). The ACLU represented the student, while multiple conservative groups such as the Alliance Defense Fund, the Christian Legal Society, and the American Center for Law & Justice submitted amicus curiae briefs on the student's behalf. *Id.* at 395; *see* Brief for Alliance Defense Fund as Amicus Curiae Supporting Respondent, *Morse v. Frederick*, 551 U.S. 393 (2007) (No. 06-278); Brief for American Center for Law and Justice as Amicus Curiae Supporting Respondent, *Morse v. Frederick*, 551 U.S. 393 (2007) (No. 06-278); Brief for Christian Legal Society as Amicus Curiae Supporting Respondent, *Morse v. Frederick*, 551 U.S. 393 (2007) (No. 06-278).

Other areas, too, blur traditional ideological lines. Protection of religious freedom, for example, can sometimes cut across conservative and liberal beliefs, at least in cases where the government directly infringes on minority religious practices or speech. However, ideological splits may emerge when the government defends its actions with the purpose of remaining neutral toward religious beliefs to avoid violating the First Amendment's Establishment Clause, which forbids state conduct that favors one religion over others or embraces religion and disfavors non-adherents. Environmental protection is also not a cause that is necessarily owned by the political left or right. *See also* Houck, *supra*, at 1455 n.166 (arguing that while environmental protection is associated with the left, many conservatives were strong proponents of such causes at the outset of the environmental movement).

III. PUBLIC INTEREST LAWYERING ON THE LEFT

The American political left has long been characterized by deep divisions both with respect to goals and tactics. The ideas and debates are familiar: the Old (i.e., class-oriented) Left versus the New (i.e., identity-oriented) Left, mainstream culture versus counterculture, the NAACP versus SNCC, organized labor versus immigrant rights, incrementalism versus revolution, civil disobedience versus "by any means necessary" — the list could go on. These same divisions are evident in the field of progressive public interest lawyering, which is marked by substantive conflict among lawyers about diverse political and legal goals, and more process-oriented conflict over the relationship between lawyers, clients, and causes. This latter conflict, which goes to the heart of the question over the appropriate role of public interest lawyers (to win legal victories, spur political victories, or empower clients?), will be treated in more detail in Chapters 5 and 6. For now, it is important to note that because of their broader commitment to notions of robust democracy, progressive public interest lawyers tend to experience more anxiety over the degree to which they set social change agendas and exclude clients from decision making, than do their conservative counterparts.

A key (though often blurry) historical and contemporary distinction is between those public interest lawyers who accept the existing social structure and seek to ensure that its benefits are fairly distributed, and those who question fundamental social arrangements and seek their transformation. Along these lines, Scheingold and Sarat describe an important divide between "liberal democratic cause lawyers" who see their mission as the "preservation and extension" of constitutional rights and more radical left lawyers — "social and emancipatory democrats" — who push for the realization of economic and social rights (health care, education, housing, secure employment) and, more transformatively, a radically participatory, egalitarian society. SCHEINGOLD & SARAT, *supra*, at 103-04. The paradigmatic example of this distinction is the contrast between ACLU lawyers — the quintessential constitutional rights enforcers — and radical community-based lawyers, who seek to use law to build political power (through organizing and other means) in order to destabilize the status quo and redistribute political and economic resources.

Even among similar types of liberal organizations, there are instances in which liberal lawyers find themselves on opposite sides of important public issues in "intra-ideological" splits. Consider the following two examples. In *Hill v. Colorado*, 530 U.S. 703, 707 (2000), the Supreme Court upheld the constitutionality of a Colorado statute that forbade protestors located near a health care facility from knowingly approaching within eight feet of persons, without their consent, for the purpose of displaying a sign, distributing a handbill or leaflet, or engaging in oral protest, counseling, or education. Several progressive groups, including the AFL-CIO, the ACLU, and People for the Ethical Treatment of Animals, were concerned with comparable restrictions on other protestors and filed amicus curiae briefs on behalf of the abortion protestors. Brief for the American Civil Liberties Union as Amicus Curiae Supporting Petitioners, *Hill v. Colorado*, 530 U.S. 703 (2000) (No. 98-1856); Brief for the American Federation of Labor and Congress of Industrial Organization as Amicus Curiae Supporting Petitioners, *Hill v. Colorado*, 530 U.S. 703 (2000) (No. 98-1856); Brief for People for the Ethical Treatment of Animals as Amicus Curiae Supporting Petitioners, *Hill v. Colorado*, 530 U.S. 703 (2000) (No. 98-1856). In defense of the restrictions, other liberal organizations such as the National Abortion and Reproductive Rights Action League, National Abortion Federation, and NOW Legal Defense and Education Fund, Inc., filed an amicus brief. Brief for National Abortion and Reproductive Rights Action League et al. as Amici Curiae Supporting Respondents, *Hill v. Colorado*, 530 U.S. 703 (2000) (No. 98-1856).

In *Hurley v. Irish-American Gay, Lesbian, and Bisexual Group of Boston,* 515 U.S. 557, 559-64 (1995), the Court heard an appeal from a state court decision holding that a private organization's exclusion of a gay group from participation in a St. Patrick's Day Parade for which that organization held a permit violated the state's public accommodations law by discriminating on the basis of sexual orientation. The Court reversed, holding that the private organization had a First Amendment right of expression that allowed it to exclude groups that represented views that were not consistent with its "message." *Id.* at 566. In that case, the Anti-Defamation League filed a brief on behalf of the gay groups, while the ACLU filed an amicus brief supporting the private organization's First Amendment rights of association. Brief for the Anti-Defamation League Supporting Respondents, *Hurley v. Irish-American*

Gay, Lesbian, and Bisexual Group of Boston, Inc., 515 U.S. 557 (1995) (No. 94-749); Brief for the American Civil Liberties Union as Amicus Curiae Supporting Petitioners, *Hurley v. Irish-American Gay, Lesbian, and Bisexual Group of Boston, Inc.*, 515 U.S. 557 (1995) (No. 94-749).

Other contexts exist in which progressive groups find themselves opposed to one another. Attorneys who identify as public interest lawyers line up on opposite sides of these cases to advocate for their own vision of good. What other examples of ideological conflicts on the left can you think of? In them, can either side make a superior claim to be acting in the public interest? If not, can lawyers on both sides of such disputes equally claim to be public interest lawyers? Is this even the right question?

IV. PUBLIC INTEREST LAWYERING ON THE RIGHT

Although academic interest in studying conservative public interest lawyering is relatively new, researchers have noted that several influential conservative groups began using litigation as a tool for social change and employing test case strategies as early as the late nineteenth and early twentieth century. LEE EPSTEIN, CONSERVATIVES IN COURT 16 (1985); Southworth, *Conservative Lawyers*, *supra*, at 1224 n.2. This section looks at the development of conservative public interest lawyering, mapping its continuities and points of conflict.

A. FIRST-WAVE CONSERVATIVE PUBLIC INTEREST LAWYERING

In a comprehensive study, Lee Epstein breaks conservative groups into three categories: those that pursue economic litigation; those engaged in social litigation; and conservative public interest law firms (PILFs). EPSTEIN, *supra*, at 16. We use this framework to compare developments in the first wave of conservative lawyering in the first half of the 1900s, to second-wave developments primarily after the civil rights period.

1. Economic

During the Progressive era, federal and state lawmakers enacted stronger protection for persons in the workplace, including authorizing labor unions and regulating wages, hours, and working conditions in the private sector. *Id.* at 16-30. Some groups consciously developed strategies to combat New Deal economic recovery programs, focusing their efforts on the negative impact such regulation might have on the economic interests of different industries. *Id.* at 18-30. While industry trade associations had existed before this period, organizations such as the American Anti-Boycott Association (AABA), the Executive Committee of the Southern Cotton Manufacturers, and the Edison Electric Institute were formed specifically to engage in litigation to protect private corporate interests. *Id.* at 17-19. As with many contemporary legal organizations, the AABA created its own legal affairs department, recruiting talented lawyers to pursue litigation and a public relations staff to attract more industry members. *Id.* at 19-20. One of its major campaigns involved bringing suits challenging union boycotts as violations of the Sherman Antitrust Act. *Id.* at 20-21. Conservative groups also brought legal challenges to laws prohibiting child labor (including *Hammer v. Dagenhart*, 247 U.S. 251, 271-72 (1918) (invalidating federal law prohibiting child labor), *overruled by United States v. Darby*, 312 U.S. 100, 116 (1941)), and requiring minimum wages. Epstein, *supra*, at 24. Also, these groups consciously selected test cases, not only for the purpose of achieving legal victories with substantial impact, but also to generate positive publicity and enhance their membership rolls. *Id.* at 22. Their success faded as the New Deal Supreme Court began to transform the law under the Commerce Clause and Due Process Clause. *Id.* at 23-24.

2. Social

Other conservative groups employed legal tactics to challenge the expansion of progressive social reforms, such as women's suffrage and federal aid to states to develop programs to reduce infant mortality. *Id.* at 34-37. Unlike the economic conservative groups, these organizations typically opposed government intervention in the private sphere of life on moral, religious, and social grounds, rather than out of concern for economic liberty. *Id.* at 31. While the social issue groups also recruited elite legal talent and were repeat players in the litigation process, they were unable to achieve substantial success during these early years, possibly because their strategies often involved seeking wholesale changes in law, rather than pursuing incremental reform. *Id.* at 37-38. Some groups in both of these first two categories adopted what might have been construed as progressive rhetoric, arguing for the liberty of employers and businesses in the case of the groups opposing economic legislation, and the liberty of the family in the case of opponents of social welfare legislation. *Id.* at 38.

3. PILFs

Finally, in the first half of the twentieth century, conservative activists formed the first conservative PILFs. The most noteworthy of these was the National Lawyers' Committee (NCL) of the American Liberty League (ALL). *Id.* ALL itself grew out of the movement to repeal prohibition, but was officially formed to challenge New Deal legislative reforms. *Id.* at 39. In 1935, NCL was established as an arm of ALL and used legal tactics to advocate for less government regulation, specifically challenging the constitutionality of much New Deal legislation. *Id.* at 38. Whereas ALL engaged in traditional lobbying and public relations campaigns to oppose big government, NCL recruited the best available conservative attorneys and created a library of reports about the constitutional infirmities of many government efforts to deal with economic recovery. *Id.* at 40. Many of the challenges focused on arguments initially accepted by the Supreme Court, such as the claim that these programs exceeded Congress's powers under the Commerce Clause and that state economic regulations violated the Due Process Clause (the theory embraced in *Lochner v. New York*, 198 U.S. 45 (1905)). Epstein, *supra*, at 40.

B. SECOND-WAVE CONSERVATIVE PUBLIC INTEREST LAWYERING

The second wave of conservative legal groups emerged in the latter half of the twentieth century, seeking to emulate—and limit—the success of their liberal counterparts. By many accounts, they surpassed the first-wave conservative groups both in terms of the scope of their institutionalization and their impact on politics.

1. Economic

Conservative economic issue groups in the latter part of the twentieth century focused on opposition to the labor movement and to what they viewed as excessive and costly government regulation of business practices. In 1968, a conservative organization called the National Right to Work Legal Defense Foundation (NRW LDF) was established to attack federal laws creating closed shops in employment settings. *Id.* at 45-46. The groups in this movement argued that the federal recognition of compulsory unions conflicted with the right of people who did not wish to join unions to compete for employment opportunities. *Id.* NRW LDF met with some success, lobbying for state right to work laws and winning some important court cases. *Id.* at 47-48. Initial success led to favorable publicity, as well as an increasing acceptance among the group's leaders that litigation was a useful tool for achieving changes in the law. *Id.* As with many other legal organizations, NRW LDF explicitly modeled itself on the NAACP LDF, recruited top legal talent, and selected test cases to secure broader social goals. *Id.* at 49. In addition to opposing closed shops, its agenda included challenges to compulsory union dues and the use of union fees for political purposes. *Id.* at 49-50. It was successful in many of its efforts, including victories in the U.S. Supreme Court. *See, e.g., Abood v. Detroit Bd. of Educ.*, 431 U.S. 209 (1977); *Seay v. McDonnell Douglas Corp.*, 533 F.2d 1126 (9th Cir. 1976); *Ball v. City of Detroit*, 269 N.W.2d 607 (Mich. Ct. App. 1978).

As the following excerpt describes, another critical development was the collaboration of large business firms to respond to government regulation:

> An important moment in the mobilization of business constituencies behind new public interest law organizations was the publication of the "Powell Memorandum." In 1971, shortly before he was appointed to the United States Supreme Court, Lewis Powell delivered a memo to the U.S. Chamber of Commerce asserting that "[n]o thoughtful person can question that the American economic system is under broad attack." He cited Ralph Nader as "[p]erhaps the single most effective antagonist of American business" and argued that "the time has come—indeed, it is long overdue—for the wisdom, ingenuity and resources of American business to be marshaled against those who would destroy it." Powell asserted that American business had neglected to exercise significant influence in the courts, where "the most active exploiters . . . have been groups ranging in political orientation from 'liberal' to the far left." He urged business to take a more aggressive stance "in all political arenas,"

but he asserted that "[t]he judiciary may be the most important instrument for social, economic and political change."

The Powell memorandum contemplated that the U.S. Chamber of Commerce would become the primary representative of American business in the courts and agencies, and his proposal eventually led to the establishment of the National Chamber Litigation Center [NCLC] in 1977 as a nonprofit, tax-exempt membership organization.

Southworth, *Conservative Lawyers*, *supra*, at 1241-42.

The U.S. Chamber of Commerce had previously stayed away from litigation because of the cost. EPSTEIN, *supra*, at 59. NCLC, in contrast, acted as a law firm representing individual businesses, which funded the litigation rather than using the Chamber's resources. *Id.* at 59-60. As another cost saving measure, NCLC represented these firms mostly through filing amicus curiae briefs rather than bringing direct litigation. *Id.* at 60. As other organizations have done, NCLC established criteria for selecting its cases to most effectively advance its political goals. *Id.* Its criteria for entering a case included the importance of the issue raised to the national business community; whether the broader perspective of business entities was being adequately represented by the parties to the underlying case; whether there was a good likelihood of success; the relationship of the case to NCLC priorities; and the availability of resources. *Id.*

In 1976, lawyers and business leaders formed the Equal Employment Advisory Council, a group concerned about the effects of federal employment discrimination law on businesses. *Id.* at 63-64. Like NCLC, this group emphasized filing amicus briefs rather than direct litigation. *Id.* at 64. Also, fearing adverse publicity and responses by government and civil rights groups, the Council specifically decided to avoid media attention. *Id.* at 65. Instead, it emphasized behind the scenes work, such as publishing materials to help lawyers defend against employment discrimination suits. *Id.* at 66.

As the federal courts in general, and the Supreme Court in particular, have become more receptive to business claims, groups like NCLC have achieved significant success. In 2008, Jeffrey Rosen, writing in the *New York Times Magazine*, reported that NCLC filed amicus briefs in 15 cases before the Supreme Court in the 2007 term and won 13. Jeffrey Rosen, *Supreme Court Inc.*, N.Y. TIMES, Mar. 16, 2008 (Magazine), at 38.

Recall the criteria we outlined in Chapter 1 to help define public interest lawyering. Do you think the work of the NCLC qualifies? Under what criteria?

2. Social

Conservative groups emerged to take on a range of social issues, such as obscenity, crime, and abortion, in the latter part of the twentieth century. A major proponent of the enforcement of obscenity laws against producers and sellers of erotic material was the Citizens for Decency through Law (CDL), which was founded in 1957 and began using litigation in 1963. EPSTEIN, *supra*, at 80. Started as a local group in Cincinnati, Ohio, CDL was launched as a national group by its founder, Charles Keating (later convicted of fraud during the national savings and loan scandal in the late 1980s). *Id.* at 80-82. CDL called for more police enforcement of obscenity laws and saw its role as helping prosecutors obtain convictions in obscenity cases. *Id.* at 83. In conjunction with that effort, CDL identified and developed a pool of experts to provide psychiatric testimony in these cases. *Id.* Their early success was limited in part because their briefs were highly emotional and not sound from a technical legal perspective. *Id.* at 84. The group achieved a higher profile when President Nixon appointed Keating to the President's Commission on Obscenity and Pornography in 1969. *Id.* at 85. Keating found himself in the minority on the Commission, whose final report recommended abolishing obscenity laws as applied to consenting adults. *Id.* at 86. His dissenting report, which Nixon endorsed, gave him a platform to gain national media attention for his cause. *Id.* at 85-86. Through this attention and a direct mail campaign, CDL was able to expand its efforts, professionalize its staff, and hire more experienced attorneys. *Id.* at 86. It used a combination of direct litigation, amicus briefs, and support for local prosecutors to pursue its cause, and began to achieve greater success by the early 1980s. *Id.* at 86-88.

In the law enforcement arena, Americans for Effective Law Enforcement (AELE) was founded in 1966 by Northwestern University law professor Fred Inbau in response to the Warren Court's decisions expanding the constitutional rights of criminal defendants. *Id.* at 89. It was also envisioned as an organization to counter the influence of civil liberties organizations such as the ACLU. *Id.* AELE's Law Enforcement Legal Center, formed in 1973, pursued a litigation strategy emphasizing the filing of amicus briefs in Supreme Court cases. *Id.* at 91. Its role in direct litigation was inherently limited because criminal cases, by definition, are brought by state or local prosecutors. *Id.* AELE's positions were sometimes adopted by the Court or otherwise influenced the shape of constitutional doctrine, achieving notable success, for example, in cases involving the Fourth Amendment as applied to police searches of automobiles. *Id.* at 90-93. It built successful alliances with other organizations, found support through donor funding, and effectively used statistics and law review articles to support its positions. *Id.* at 90-94. AELE was the precursor to more recently formed "law and order" advocacy groups such as the Criminal Justice Legal Foundation, formed in 1982, and the Crime Victims Legal Advocacy Institute, created in 1985. Southworth, *Conservative Lawyers*, *supra*, at 1244.

Formed in 1971, Americans United for Life (AUL) is among several groups that have been influential in the anti-abortion movement. Epstein, *supra*, at 94-95. While AUL worked in opposition to pro-choice groups, lobbying for the retention of abortion prohibitions in the state legislatures, it created a separate legal arm, the AUL Legal Defense Fund (AUL LDF), in the mid-1970s. *Id.* at 95, 98-99. AUL LDF has participated in much of the major abortion litigation in the Supreme Court, focusing on amicus briefs as a vehicle for influencing abortion policy. *Id.* at 101. After the Court decided *Roe v. Wade*, anti-abortion groups lobbied for laws regulating and/or limiting abortion, such as statutes requiring spousal or parental consent for abortions and laws removing public funding for abortion services. *Id.* at 97-98. AUL LDF built up a network of cooperating attorneys to help and routinely filed amicus briefs in favor of these types of state restrictions on abortion when challenged. *Id.* at 99-102. While some observers have argued that AUL LDF, like CDL, achieved limited success in its earlier stages because of the highly charged emotional nature of its briefs, in later years it crafted its briefs with more technical legal rigor and found greater receptiveness to its arguments. *Id.* at 101. It also shifted from a pure amicus strategy to providing direct representation to intervenors in some abortion cases. *Id.* at 102.

AUL LDF is one example of a larger network of conservative organizations that developed based on advocacy surrounding religious faith.

> Religious conservatives produced their own public interest law groups beginning in the 1970s. The Catholic League for Religious and Civil Rights was founded in 1973 to protect the rights of Catholics to participate in public life. Americans United for Life, which began as a nonsectarian educational organization in 1971, was closely allied with the Catholic Church, and in 1976 it established its Legal Defense Foundation to serve as the legal arm of the pro-life movement. The first of the protestant evangelical groups to litigate was the Center for Law and Religious Freedom, established by the Christian Legal Society in 1975 to address First Amendment issues and to promote state accommodation of religious beliefs.
>
> Protestant evangelical groups initially focused primarily on defending private religious schools from government interference. They did not begin to initiate litigation until the mid-1980s, when they mobilized to fight abortion and to promote greater religious expression in the public sphere, particularly in public schools. In 1979, televangelist Jerry Falwell campaigned to persuade fundamentalists to overcome their distaste for politics and to engage with secular legal institutions. In the early 1980s, evangelical leaders began urging lawyers to confront the forces that had removed prayer and Bible reading from schools and that had culminated in the Supreme Court's ruling in *Roe v. Wade.* In 1980, editorials in Christianity Today asserted that evangelicals were "apathetic" in the face of the abortion rulings. "For all practical purposes, the Supreme Court has unwittingly legalized murder," one stated, and "Christians must stand up, speak out, and be counted." In 1981, Francis Schaeffer published A Christian Manifesto, in which he decried the "shift from the Judeo-Christian basis for law" toward a "new sociological law." He asked: "[W]here were the Christian lawyers during the crucial shift from forty years ago to just a few years ago? . . . [S]urely the Christian lawyers should have seen the change taking place and stood on the wall and blown the trumpets loud and clear." In a conference on federalism that launched the Federalist Society for Law & Public Policy Studies in 1982, John T. Noonan, then a Berkeley law professor, noted that the pro-life movement was impaired by "an amateur, predominantly nonlegal leadership" that was "in great need of expert advice," and he urged law students to enlist in the effort to "reverse what, by every standard, is the most serious invasion of state power in our century." The Christian Right began fielding their own legal advocacy organizations to translate dismay about the Supreme Court's rulings on religion and abortion into a new brand of public interest law.
>
> New conservative and libertarian PILFs and legal advocacy groups founded during the 1980s included Christian evangelical groups such as the Rutherford Institute (1982), Home School Legal Defense Association (1983), Concerned Women for America Education and Legal Defense Foundation (1983), National Legal Foundation (1987), and Liberty Counsel (1989).

Southworth, *Conservative Lawyers, supra,* at 1243-44.

In what sense do these groups represent the public interest? Are religious communities underrepresented or otherwise disadvantaged? Which ones? How should we understand the role of religion in the public interest law field? Note that these religious groups seek to challenge governmental restrictions — does that qualify them as public interest organizations?

3. PILFs

As the preceding account by Southworth suggested, the first modern conservative PILFs began to appear in the early 1970s, beginning with the Pacific Legal Foundation, arguably the most successful of these groups to date. EPSTEIN, *supra*, at 121. PLF was founded by members of Ronald Reagan's administration while he was the governor of California. *Id.* at 120-21. The staffers — Ronald Zumbrun, Raymond Momboisse, and Edwin Meese — had witnessed the influence of liberal public interest groups in challenging parts of Reagan's state welfare reform programs. *Id.* In 1973, Zumbrun and Momboisse became the first staff attorneys of PLF, located in Sacramento. *Id.* at 121. PLF's website describes its mission as follows:

> Pacific Legal Foundation is devoted to a vision of individual freedom, responsible government, and color-blind justice. Like America's founders, we believe the blessings of liberty are beyond measure. And like them, we believe each generation must defend those blessings against government encroachment. Every day, PLF attorneys litigate to build a future of economic freedom and equal opportunity.
>
> PLF's litigation focuses on three major projects: to defend the fundamental human right of private property; to promote sensible environmental policies that respect individual freedom and put people first; and to create a nation in which people are judged by the content of their character and not the color of their skin. In addition, PLF's Economic Liberty and Free Enterprise Projects are devoted to protecting the right to earn a living, and protect businesses against unfair burdens.

About PLF: Our Mission, PACIFIC LEGAL FOUNDATION (2012), http://www.pacificlegal .org/page.aspx?pid=262 (last visited July 27, 2012).

PLF began small, but soon added a second office in Washington, D.C. EPSTEIN, *supra*, at 121-22. Initially, it had little funding, but after early success through amicus participation and direct litigation, it drew attention and resources from conservative foundations and individuals. *Id.* at 122. Its docket covers a wide range of conservative issues, including the rights of private property owners against government regulation, especially environmental regulation, opposition to affirmative action, and tort reform. *See PLF Cases*, PACIFIC LEGAL FOUNDATION (2012), http://www.pacificlegal.org/page.aspx?pid=258 (last visited July 27, 2012). Because the group was formed in part to oppose progressive public interest organizations, in its earlier years it steered away from creating its own agenda and bringing test cases (liberal group tactics that PLF had criticized), preferring instead to get involved in systemic litigation initiated by liberal PILFs. *Id.* at 122-23. At the same time, it has successfully emulated many of the strategies that long-standing liberal PILFs have used, such as employing stringent case selection processes, recruiting and training expert attorneys, and engaging in substantial cooperation with other conservative organizations. *Id*. at 123-24. Over time, PLF has become much more comfortable with an active litigation agenda. It maintains a National Litigation Center that manages its cases as well as coordinating the work of its regional offices. *About PLF: PLF National Litigation Center*, PACIFIC LEGAL FOUNDATION (2012), http://www.pacificlegal.org/page.aspx?pid=552 (last visited July 27, 2012). Moreover, it runs an active fellowship program for recent law school graduates, who work closely with an experienced PLF attorney in litigation matters and also are expected to research and write a law review article to both gain expertise and influence judges. *About PLF: College of Public Interest Law*, PACIFIC LEGAL FOUNDATION (2012), http://www.pacificlegal.org/page.aspx?pid=558 (last visited July 27, 2012).

Another influential conservative PILF is the Washington Legal Foundation (WLF), founded by former Nixon staffer Dan Popeo in 1977. EPSTEIN, *supra*, at 130. Like PLF, WLF was formed in response to the success of progressive groups, most notably the Nader organizations and liberal PILFs, which Popeo believed were the cause of unnecessarily increased and arbitrary government regulation. *Id*. WLF's initial mission was to pursue the interests of businesses burdened by excessive government regulation, the rights of crime victims, and the civil liberties of small businesspersons. *Id*. It established its reputation in the conservative community through its participation in high profile litigation, including a case challenging the return of the Panama Canal and a victim's rights suit on behalf of a secret service agent injured during the assassination attempt on President Reagan. *Id*. at 131. WLF has steered away from test case strategies, responding instead to the actions of liberal groups; in addition, it has engaged in the recruitment of expert attorneys and developed ties to law schools in order to enhance its network. *Id*. at 132.

In the mid-1970s, a coalition of conservative PILFs was formed under the umbrella of the National Legal Center for the Public Interest (NLCPI). *Id*. at 125-26. The agenda of these organizations—which include the Southeastern Legal Foundation, Mid-America Legal Foundation, Great Plains Legal Foundation, Mountain States Legal Foundation, and Capital Legal Foundation—was largely oriented toward promoting the interests of the American business community rather than other conservative causes. *Id*. Some critics argued that the NLCPI network was not initially successful because it was viewed as narrowly focused on business interests and because NLCPI ended up competing for funds with its affiliate organizations. *Id*. at 127-29. Some of the affiliate organizations now advocate on behalf of a broader set of conservative causes. *See, e.g.*, *About SLF*, Southeastern Legal Foundation (2011), http://www.southeasternlegal.org/about-slf/ (last visited July 27, 2012) (providing links to the organization's case centers, which include challenges to affirmative action, campaign finance reform, and defending the display of the Ten Commandments, in addition to its general mission of limiting government regulation and promoting individual economic freedom).

Note that these conservative PILFs promote a broad range of conservative causes, but among them are the same types of corporate antiregulatory initiatives championed by first-wave economic groups like the AABA. To what extent does this work advance the public interest? Does it matter how the work is framed—for example, as protecting small businesses from excessive government regulation or advancing corporate interests? Does it matter how the work is funded? For example, would it matter to you if PLF's antiregulatory work was largely bankrolled by corporate donors? What role do you think corporate funding plays in supporting progressive public interest work?

C. THE CONSERVATIVE PUBLIC INTEREST MOVEMENT: CAUSES, COORDINATION, AND CONFLICT

1. The Rise of the Right

Scholars of the conservative public interest law movement have identified a number of related factors that have supported its development. These include high motivation on the part of conservative activists to counteract liberal successes of the civil rights period; a changing political opportunity structure that has been more supportive of conservative legal claims; and enhanced and more focused funding sources.

Beginning in the 1960s, conservative groups perceived themselves as adversely affected by the actions of progressive public interest lawyers and a broader political system that both was shaped by and supported their success. Conservative groups thus began to position themselves as the political counterpart to progressive public interest law and build organizational models that emulated the latter's success—and both promoted and took advantage of the political backlash against their agenda. As Southworth has observed:

> The conservative public interest law movement was a direct response to the creation of public interest law organizations in the late 1960s and 1970s and to the legal and social changes these groups helped produce. A small band of liberal public interest lawyers, dubbed "the new public interest lawyers" in a 1970 comment in the *Yale Law Journal*, created intense interest in an alternative model of legal practice through which lawyers might promote significant social change. The success of these organizations presented an obvious counterstrategy for conservatives: to beat liberals at their own game by creating public interest law groups to speak for competing values and constituencies. They adopted the organizational form and rhetoric of public interest law to serve sometimes conflicting causes of the conservative movement. . . .
>
> Galvanized by the achievements of this new breed of [progressive] lawyers and their organizations, some conservatives responded by attacking the premises of the movement. . . . Conservatives, however, also sought to create their own organizations with similar form and opposing mission. While liberal public interest law groups were thought to resort to the courts to redress their political disadvantage in other arenas, conservative public interest law groups were primarily a response to liberal groups' perceived dominance in the courts and administrative agencies. One libertarian lawyer observed that liberal PILFs were "extremely successful," and "conservatives tried to replicate that." Another said: "[A]ll these liberal litigating organizations are out there bringing citizen suits, . . . and the idea was to take a leaf from their book and start conservative litigating organizations that would bring lawsuits from their side of the spectrum." The organizational counterattack began with business-oriented groups. Christian evangelicals, whose ambivalence about engaging

with secular law delayed their participation in legal rights advocacy, took up the challenge soon thereafter.

Southworth, *Conservative Lawyers, supra*, at 1231-32, 1240-41.

In the early years of conservative legal institution building, conservatives viewed government as relatively inhospitable to their claims. Although Richard Nixon, a Republican, was President, Democrats still controlled Congress by a substantial majority. Moreover, Nixon's appointment of conservative justices Warren Burger and William Rehnquist to the Supreme Court did not alter the Warren Court's progressive bent until years later. *See* THE BURGER COURT: THE COUNTER-REVOLUTION THAT WASN'T (Vincent Blasi ed., 1983). The goal of the conservative movement was to change this institutional equation.

Beginning in the 1980s and growing stronger by the end of the century, conservative lawyering began to more powerfully influence and, in turn, draw support from the transformation in American politics. Just as the establishment of liberal public interest groups during the early and mid-twentieth century was nurtured by sympathetic political elites (recall the federal legal services program) and the federal bench, conservative groups began to thrive at a time when American political institutions, especially at the federal level, were moving significantly to the right. Ronald Reagan's election as U.S. President in 1980 on a conservative platform, and the simultaneous Republican Party ascension to the majority position in the U.S. Senate, began a major shift in partisan politics at the national level. Aron, *supra*, at 14-17. Republicans held the White House and Congress for much of the period between the early 1970s and 2008, and the federal courts have also become increasingly conservative. These changes gave conservative organizations more influence, which they used to reinforce and build the strength of conservatism in politics and the judiciary. *See* Southworth, *Conservative Lawyers, supra*, at 1255; *but see* Mark Tushnet, Op-Ed, *Who's Behind the Integration Decision?: It's the Pacific Legal Foundation, Champion of Right-Wing Causes for 35 Years*, L.A. TIMES, July 7, 2007, at 19 (arguing that conservative groups have not been as successful as progressive organizations because of their lack of follow through, and that they have achieved some successes in the Supreme Court, but have failed to work as successfully in the lower courts to help shape the details of the law after their initial successes). These conditions, the inverse of those during the founding of liberal public interest law, created a favorable opportunity structure for conservative groups to take advantage of:

> Political conservatism has reshaped the field of public interest law. . . . Politically, conservatism has transformed the "social context" of public interest law. From an advocacy perspective, the major change has been the declining role of the federal government as the guarantor of legal rights associated with political liberalism. While deregulation and decentralization have weakened administrative agency oversight, the most striking change has come in the judicial arena, where the struggle over the ideological composition of the federal bench has moved the weight of the judiciary toward a constitutional vision skeptical of economic regulation and minority rights. Republican control of the presidency for seven of the ten terms before the 2008 election of Barak Obama reversed majorities of Democratically appointed judges at both the circuit and district court levels, and solidified the

conservative majority on the U.S. Supreme Court. This has produced profound jurisprudential changes at the federal level, moving the weight of the federal judiciary toward a constitutional vision skeptical of economic regulation and claims of minority rights. The federal court, deemed the final arbiter of liberal claims to social justice during the civil rights period, has thus been transformed into, at best, an unreliable ally and, at worst, a hostile enemy to be avoided. This change has not been uniform and there have been important recent victories for liberal groups in the Supreme Court on noncitizen detention and climate change. However, liberal groups are more circumspect about turning to the federal courts. This reticence was on prominent display in South Dakota in 2006, when women's rights groups refused to bring a legal challenge to a state law enacted by the legislature that prohibited nearly all abortions (and was passed with the aim of provoking a lawsuit enabling the Supreme Court to revisit *Roe v. Wade*) and instead organized to successfully reverse the ban through a statewide ballot initiative.

Scott L. Cummings, *The Future of Public Interest Law*, 33 U. ARK. LITTLE ROCK L. REV. 355, 367-68 (2011).

Conservative legal advocacy has also benefited from focused and sustained funding. For example, pro-business development groups, which are often pitted against environmental, labor, and consumer groups, receive generous funding from corporate members. One of the messages in the Powell memorandum to the U.S. Chamber of Commerce was its call to the national business community to respond to attacks from the "better financed" left by engaging in well-coordinated policy and educational initiatives to be financially supported by American corporations. LEWIS POWELL, JR., CONFIDENTIAL MEMORANDUM, ATTACK OF AMERICAN FREE ENTERPRISE SYSTEM 30 (August 23, 1971) (copy on file with authors) ("The type of program described above (which includes a broadly based combination of education and political action), if undertaken long term and adequately staffed, would require far more generous financial support from American corporations than the Chamber has ever received in the past.").

2. Conservative Networks

Conservative organizations have benefited from deliberate efforts to coordinate distinct factions within their movement. A representative of the conservative think tank, the Heritage Foundation, observed that this organization, "founded in 1972 . . . was to be kind of a clearinghouse for what we might call, for want of a better name, 'conservative' organizations — organizations that were dedicated to individual liberties, limited government, free market economics, a strong national defense." Heinz et al., *Lawyers for Conservative Causes*, *supra*, at 36. As Heinz, Paik, and Southworth describe:

> Last year's annual Heritage meeting convened more than 400 people representing 210 or more organizations from 17 countries. Twice per year, Heritage conducts a "Legal Strategy Forum" with lawyers from about 30 organizations around the country, to "talk about joint efforts and cooperation." A libertarian lawyer interviewed for this project said that these meetings serve "an exceedingly valuable function" in coordinating the conservative movement and

enabling diverse constituencies to operate as "a loose community." Heritage also holds a monthly meeting of legal organizations in the D.C. area to "keep them informed about each others' activities," to educate them about "what's going on on the Hill," and to promote cooperation on amicus briefs and seminars. A lawyer with a long history of work with religious organizations said that these meetings facilitate "philosophical interfacing," allowing him to test his arguments with other smart lawyers "who are not necessarily in our circle." Heritage produces a weekly summary of Supreme Court decisions, delivered by e-mail to organizations around the country, and it sponsors moot court sessions judged by "the best appellate lawyers from the law firms downtown and from some of the public interest groups" to prepare conservative lawyers of all stripes who have arguments before the Supreme Court. One lawyer active in religious liberties issues described the Heritage Foundation (and the Federalist Society) as the "crossroads of the conservative movement."

Id. at 36-37. At the same time, as discussed in the next section, considerable tensions exist within the conservative public interest lawyering community that pose challenges to these networking efforts.

In addition to the coordination of groups such as Heritage, the conservative legal movement has benefited from a deliberate effort to facilitate networking in law school. The Powell memorandum called for "more 'publishing' by independent scholars who do believe in the system" to counteract the work of "liberal and leftist faculty." POWELL, *supra*, at 22. Toward this end, a group of conservative law students formed the Federalist Society for Law and Public Policy Studies in 1981. Southworth, *Conservative Lawyers*, *supra*, at 1244-45. Its stated goals were "to reorder 'priorities within the legal system to place a premium on individual liberty, traditional values and the rule of law.'" *Id.* at 1258 n.196. The Federalist Society was formed in part because of conservative law students' disenchantment with what they perceived as the dominance of liberal viewpoints in legal academia. Jason DeParle, *Nomination for Supreme Court Stirs Debate on Influence of Federalist Society*, N.Y. TIMES, Aug. 1, 2005, at A12; Neil A. Lewis, *A Conservative Legal Group Thrives in Bush's Washington*, N.Y. TIMES, Apr. 18, 2001, at A1; *About Us: Our Purpose*, THE FEDERALIST SOCIETY, http://www.fed-soc.org/aboutus/ (last visited July 17, 2012). By some accounts, it has been successful in transforming the composition of elite law schools in more conservative directions. *See* George W. Hicks, Jr., *The Conservative Influence of the Federalist Society on the Harvard Law School Student Body*, 29 HARV. J.L. & PUB. POL'Y 623, 626-27 (2006).

> The Federalist Society has played an important part in nurturing the political commitments of conservative and libertarian lawyers, helping them network with one another, and facilitating their involvement in legal advocacy for conservative and libertarian causes. It began as a small debating society launched in 1981 by several Yale law students, including Steven Calabresi, with encouragement from Ralph Winter and Robert Bork, who were Yale law professors at the time. The same year, two of Calabresi's friends from Yale College, Lee Liberman and David McIntosh, established a chapter at the University of Chicago Law School, with Antonin Scalia, then a member of the faculty, as their adviser, and professors Richard Epstein, Richard Posner, and Frank Easterbrook providing support. The two chapters convened a

> symposium on federalism in the spring of 1982, with money raised from the Institute for Educational Affairs (on whose board Irving Kristol served), the Olin Foundation, and the Intercollegiate Studies Institute. The national organization grew out of that conference, with the Olin Foundation funding a Federalist Society speakers bureau and helping the organization establish chapters at other law schools. The *Harvard Journal of Law & Public Policy*, launched by Spencer Abraham and Steven J. Eberhard in 1978, became the Federalist Society's official publication.

Southworth, *Conservative Lawyers, supra*, at 1256-57. The Federalist Society has been credited in both academic literature and popular media as an important organizational force in conservative public interest lawyering.

> Although the Federalist Society takes no official public policy positions, admirers and critics alike observe that it has played an important role in staffing the Bush administration and vetting federal judicial nominees. The Society says that it has "created a conservative and libertarian intellectual network that extends to all levels of the legal community."

Anthony Paik, Ann Southworth & John P. Heinz, *Lawyers of the Right: Networks and Organization*, 32 Law & Soc. Inquiry 883, 884-85 (2007).

The success of the Federalist Society in professional networking has subjected it to scrutiny and criticism, particularly from those on the left who believe it has had an undue amount of influence over who is appointed to federal judgeships by Republican presidents. *See, e.g.*, DeParle, *supra*, at A12 (reporting that 15 of 41 federal judges appointed by George W. Bush identified themselves as Federalist Society members). It has also been a source of emulation, with liberal law students launching the American Constitution Society in 1994 to work

> for positive change by shaping debate on vitally important legal and constitutional issues through development and promotion of high-impact ideas to opinion leaders and the media; by building networks of lawyers, law students, judges and policymakers dedicated to those ideas; and by countering the activist conservative legal movement that has sought to erode our enduring constitutional values.

About ACS: Shaping Debate, Building Networks, Making a Difference, American Constitution Society for Law and Policy, http://www.acslaw.org/about (last visited July 20, 2012). Just as the conservative movement proved in building its public interest infrastructure on the successful model of its liberal precursors, imitation is the sincerest form of flattery when it comes to innovative ideas to advance public interest lawyers' competing agendas.

3. Fault Lines in the Conservative Public Interest Law Field

Advocates on the left have attacked the legitimacy of the developing conservative movement. Some have contested the idea that conservative lawyers could be acting in the "public interest," arguing instead that many conservative lawyers are really just shills for the commercial interests of large business entities. *See, e.g.*, Timothy L. Foden, *The Battle for Public Interest Law: Exploring the Orwellian Nature of the Freedom Based Public Interest Movement*,

4 CONN. PUB. INT. L.J. 210, 214, 216 (2005); Houck, *supra*, at 1419. This criticism is rooted in the conception of conservative PILFs as part of the corporate counterstrategy articulated in the Powell memorandum. Southworth, *Conservative Lawyers*, *supra*, at 1241-42. Others have pointed to overt calls from conservatives for business leaders to fund such ventures and the proportion of funding for conservative organizations that comes from business interests. *Id*. at 1226. Even within the circle of advocates who view themselves as conservative public interest lawyers, there has been substantial disagreement about the bona fide nature of conservative beliefs as well as the strategy for constructing a successful movement.

> Within the conservative movement, several influential critics suggested that conservative PILFs established in the 1970s had adopted the form of liberal PILFs without grasping why those groups succeeded. One critic, Michael Horowitz, a lawyer who later served as General Counsel to the Office of Management and Budget in the Reagan Administration, persuaded the Scaife Foundation in the late 1970s to finance a study of conservative public interest groups. His scathing report asserted that "advocates for and members of the traditional public interest law movement have largely isolated their conservative counterparts as hyphenated 'public-interest' pretenders." He predicted that "the conservative public interest movement will make no substantial mark on the American legal profession or American life as long as it is seen as and is in fact the adjunct of a business community possessed of sufficient resources to afford its own legal representation." Horowitz argued that the existing conservative PILFs were parochial, overly dependent upon business patrons, focused excessively on litigation—particularly filing amicus briefs—and, for the most part, staffed by "appallingly mediocre" lawyers. He decried their failure to cultivate relationships with academics and elite law schools. Horowitz urged conservative foundations to withdraw support from most of the existing groups and to invest in organizations that would replicate the strategic choices of liberal public interest law firms and build intellectual and moral content into their programs.
>
> Horowitz argued that challenging the left's definition of public interest practice was critical to the effort: "[W]hat is at stake in public interest law is not so much a battle over cases won and lost as of ideas and ideologies. . . ." He asserted that conservative public interest firms "[have] had essentially no impact on the still-prevailing notions of law students and young attorneys that their career options are largely restricted to serving the public interest (i.e., enhancing governmental power) or 'selling out' (i.e., working for a private law firm and its private sector clients)." He urged conservative foundations to support groups that made plausible claims to speak for unrepresented interests, built relationships with law schools and bar associations, and recruited talented young attorneys. The latter goal, he argued, was particularly important:
>
> > Only when the staffs at conservative public interest law firms are comprised of law review editors, former law clerks and, in no small part, of alumni of national law schools, will the movement be in a position to initiate and participate in a real dialogue and in a truly national competition as to which legal policies and ideologies are truly "in the public interest."

Southworth, *Conservative Lawyers*, *supra*, at 1252-53. One way of reading this passage is to see the conservative public interest lawyering movement as engaged in its own internecine dispute over the bona fide nature of conservative beliefs and their connection to this type of lawyering. Another way might be to see the conservative call to "support groups that made plausible claims to speak for unrepresented interests" as a way to market the policies these groups advocate in a way that packages them in the language of public interest law — though the underlying policy positions would remain unchanged. Which do you find more plausible? Does it matter?

Another tension in conservative public interest lawyering is that one component of conservative ideology is institutional conservatism, which embraces "a narrow role for the judiciary, or at least . . . disfavor[s] judicial innovation." Fallon, *supra*, at 450. One of the principal late-twentieth-century conservative attacks on liberal public interest lawyering centered on the purported illegitimacy of the latter's use of courts to achieve social policy changes, which conservatives argued circumvented the democratic process. Southworth, *Conservative Lawyers*, *supra*, at 1240. This is one reason that some contemporary conservative organizations have eschewed test case litigation of their own. Epstein, *supra*, at 122-23, 132. Rather, they have viewed their mission as counteracting the effect of progressive public interest lawyers and limiting the role of the courts in implementing social change through judicial decisions. Southworth, *Conservative Lawyers*, *supra*, at 1250. This has influenced the way that conservative groups have participated in cases, pushing them toward filing amicus briefs rather than engaging in direct litigation. *Id.*

Finally, tensions exist between business/free enterprise conservatives and social conservatives motivated by religious belief. One study of conservative lawyers

> found considerable antipathy between the core constituencies. An attorney who worked on religious liberty matters described his contempt for law school classmates whose "big ambition was to work for a large, smelly corporate 'big dog' law firm in downtown Chicago and commute from their nice home." A lawyer who had been a partner in a prominent corporate firm before abandoning that position to devote himself full-time to Christian legal work noted that he had become increasingly uncomfortable in a law firm culture that worshiped "two false gods — personal autonomy and wealth." By his own account, his partners were equally uncomfortable with him; he could see that they viewed him as "one of those wild-eyed evangelicals." Eventually his partners confronted him and asked him to stop handling anti-abortion matters *pro bono*. Similarly, a corporate lawyer said that "the religious right . . . makes my skin crawl." Several libertarian lawyers observed that monthly meetings at the Heritage Foundation often generated heated exchanges between socially conservative and libertarian lawyers. We conclude that the lawyers who serve the two core constituencies within the American conservative movement inhabit separate social worlds. For the most part, they identify with the views of their clients. When those views conflict, the lawyers are, perhaps, no more likely to forge consensus than are other interested parties.

Heinz et al., *Lawyers for Conservative Causes*, *supra*, at 40.

Notwithstanding these tensions, the conservative movement has enthusiastically embraced public interest lawyering on its own terms. Going back to the criteria identified in Chapter 1, some conservative lawyers view themselves as engaged in altruistic (as opposed to completely self-interested) advocacy, select the cases in which they get involved based on a specific set of criteria unrelated to the profitability of the work, seek to accomplish goals beyond those of their individual clients, work for nonprofit organizations, and use their professional legal training to change the status quo. What is more, like progressive attorneys, many conservative lawyers see their role as representing un- or underrepresented persons, organizations, and causes. As just one example, Southworth's observations from interviews of conservative lawyers indicate that "[s]ome lawyers for religious and libertarian groups described themselves as champions of vulnerable groups or individuals. Abortion opponents, for example, viewed themselves as protectors of unborn children." Southworth, *Identity and Commitment, supra*, at 92-93. Similarly, advocates representing crime victims, who are dragged into the criminal justice system involuntarily and often do not have financial means for representation, may see their role as taking on the cause of an otherwise unrepresented party. How do you evaluate these claims?

4. Lessons

How has the rise of the conservative public interest movement influenced beliefs about the role of law in social change? It is instructive to compare views on the left and the right. The left, as Chapters 5 and 10 explores in more detail, has been skeptical of the efficacy of law as a social change tool, with scholars arguing that legal decisions cannot change action on the ground, that law deradicalizes and co-opts movements, and that lawyers are prone to dominate clients, particularly poor clients of color. *See* Anthony V. Alfieri, *Reconstructive Poverty Law Practice: Learning Lessons of Client Narrative*, 100 YALE L.J. 2107 (1991); Lucie E. White, *Subordination, Rhetorical Survival Skills, and Sunday Shoes: Notes on the Hearing of Mrs. G.*, 38 BUFF. L. REV. 1 (1990). In contrast, conservatives have invested heavily in building a rights-claiming network and using the opening provided by the changed composition of the federal courts to litigate their issues to the highest levels. In so doing, they have seen some major recent successes in the U.S. Supreme Court. *See, e.g., Citizens United v. Fed. Election Comm'n*, 130 S. Ct. 876 (2010); *Dist. of Columbia v. Heller*, 554 U.S. 570 (2008). By most accounts, the *Citizen United* victory, in particular, has had significant real world impacts on the amount of corporate money in politics. Thus, rather than emphasize collaboration, some conservative groups have prioritized impact litigation integrated into broader political strategies. It may be that the right has similar reservations about law-based social change but has not yet articulated them with the same force as scholars on the left. Or it may be that the right is not as concerned about movement co-optation, which raises the question: Why not? Does the left have a different relationship to principles of democratic accountability and grassroots empowerment that produces a greater anxiety about the law as an elitist tool and a greater affinity for collaborative approaches?

V. POLITICAL ATTACKS ON PUBLIC INTEREST LAWYERS

While we have seen that political fissures may occur within ideological categories, it is when they occur *across* ideological lines (right versus left, or left versus right) that we see those with power attempting to limit the effectiveness of legal strategies pursued by political adversaries. This section examines some instances in which this has occurred in both directions: conservative attempts to restrict progressive public interest lawyering and the opposite.

A. RIGHT VERSUS LEFT

Since the inception of the progressive public interest law movement, there have been political efforts to limit its impact, seen perhaps most notably in the many efforts to decrease funding for and restrict the advocacy of the federal legal services program, discussed in Chapter 2. In the following excerpt, David Luban discusses the legal services funding cuts, in combination with other efforts by conservatives to impose policies to undermine progressive public interest lawyering by restricting funding and the scope of permissible advocacy. Some of the restrictions he discusses — federal limits on legal services lawyers, attacks on Interest on Lawyer Trust Fund Accounts (IOLTA), and judicial constraints on attorneys' fees awards — are discussed in detail in the next chapter.

DAVID LUBAN, *TAKING OUT THE ADVERSARY: THE ASSAULT ON PROGRESSIVE PUBLIC-INTEREST LAWYERS*

91 Cal. L. Rev. 209, 220-24, 226-28, 236-41 (2003)

Silencing doctrines include statutes, rules, and judicial decisions that allow opponents to attack the funding or restrict the activity of their adversaries' advocates.

In recent years, a pattern of silencing doctrines has begun to emerge challenging — to greater or lesser extent — virtually every principal source of support for low-income public-interest lawyering: the [Legal Service Corporation], state IOLTA programs, law school clinics, and fee awards in civil rights cases. Most of these doctrines are the handiwork of judicial and congressional conservatives, and one originates in lawsuits from a probusiness public-interest law firm that has made its mission defunding public-interest lawyers it dislikes. . . .

In 1996, . . . Congress enacted restrictions on legal-services lawyers that went much further [than previous ones]. Not only do they prohibit LSC recipients from taking on certain issues, but they also forbid them from representing entire classes of clients. These include whole classes of aliens, many of whom are legal. The new regulations likewise prohibit the representation of all incarcerated people, including those not convicted of a crime, and those whose cases have nothing to do with why they are in jail, as, for example, in parental-rights lawsuits. The restrictions also prevent LSC attorneys from using specific procedural devices or arguments. They cannot attempt to influence rulemaking or lawmaking, participate in class actions, request attorney's fees under applicable statutes, challenge any welfare reform, or defend anyone charged with a drug offense in a public-housing eviction proceeding. . . .

The congressional restrictions are silencing doctrines, preventing attorneys from advocating for people who have no recourse to non-LSC advocates. Opponents of progressive lawyers quickly took advantage of the regulations. For example, when the restrictions went into effect, New York legal-services lawyer David Udell was helping to monitor an already-settled class action against a federal agency. The LSC threatened that if he continued to participate in the case, it would defund every legal-services lawyer in New York City and fire every employee. The LSC backed down when Udell filed a constitutional challenge to the restrictions, in the form of a motion to withdraw conditional on the restrictions being upheld. In a face-saving explanation, the LSC stated that Udell's participation in an already-settled class action did not violate the new restrictions because his role was nonadversarial. . . . Although this example makes the LSC seem like the heavy, the LSC was only doing what Congress wanted it to do. . . .

[T]hose poor enough to meet legal-aid eligibility criteria are extremely unlikely to have the money to hire a lawyer, and non-LSC-funded public-interest lawyers are rare. Thus, the overwhelming presumption must be that the vast majority of cases that legal-services lawyers turn down [because of Congress's restrictions on their activities] will never be brought by anyone. . . .

IOLTA programs provide the second biggest source of funds for legal-aid lawyers, after the LSC. Lawyers are required to maintain trust accounts for client money that they hold. . . . Lawyers participating in IOLTA programs pool client funds that are too small or held for too short a time to generate collectible interest for the client in an IOLTA account, where the interest goes to the nonprofit foundation funding low-income legal services. . . .

The Washington Legal Foundation ("WLF"), a conservative public-interest law foundation and . . . a stalwart champion of silencing doctrines, challenged IOLTA statutes in Massachusetts, Texas, and Washington. The WLF lost in Massachusetts, but soon won a major victory in its Texas litigation when the United States Supreme Court held in a five-to-four decision in *Phillips v. Washington Legal Foundation* that unrecoverable interest on client funds remains the property of the client. The Court remanded the case to determine whether IOLTA amounts to an unconstitutional taking of that property without just compensation. . . .

[When the *Phillips* case returned to the Supreme Court after remand, the Court held that IOLTA provisions are not unconstitutional because, although the interest belongs to the clients, the collection of that interest by the state imposes no pecuniary loss on the clients, who would otherwise receive nothing anyway. *Brown v. Legal Found. of Wash.*, 538 U.S. 216, 235-37 (2003).—Eds.]

. . . The litigation presents the spectacle of a comfortably funded public-interest law firm — the WLF, which has an annual budget of $4 million, 32% of which comes from corporate contributions — trying to defund other public-interest lawyers because they have different politics. . . .

Today, 182 American law schools offer clinics in more than 130 different subject areas, staffed by more than 1,400 clinical instructors. Counting salaries, fringe benefits, and overhead, law schools annually invest perhaps $280 million in clinical education. In return, clinics provide millions of hours each year of unpaid student legal work. . . .

[V]ery little clinical work is "cause" lawyering, that is, lawyering "directed at altering some aspect of the social, economic, and political status quo." Civil and criminal litigation clinics . . . typically provide one-client-at-a-time, more-or-less routine, direct client representation. . . . While nothing in principle prevents conservatives from starting clinics devoted to issues they favor, for example, crime victims' rights or small business deregulation clinics, it has rarely come to pass, although the WLF started an Economic Freedom Law Clinic at George Mason Law School, which takes a "pro-free enterprise, limited government, and economic freedom perspective." The perception of a leftward tilt makes law school clinics a natural target for adversaries of progressive public-interest law. Although relatively infrequently, law school clinics have indeed been subjected to political attacks and silencing doctrines.

The principal lightning rod has been environmental-law clinics, which sometimes take anti-development stances that put them at odds with business interests. In the 1980s, under pressure from the timber industry, the University of Oregon School of Law's environmental-law clinic came under siege, and eventually had to leave the law school. Environmental-law clinics in the University of West Virginia College of Law and University of Wyoming College of Law have also been attacked by politicians and business interests. Most recently, the University of Pittsburgh School of Law's environmental-law clinic infuriated the state legislature by filing suits delaying highway and logging projects in a national forest. The Pittsburgh Post-Gazette reported that under pressure from the legislature, the University of Pittsburgh law school took back $60,000 of the clinic's $100,000 annual budget, a move denounced by the university faculty's Tenure and Academic Freedom Committee as a violation of academic freedom.

The most notorious effort to silence an environmental-law clinic involves Tulane Law School. . . . After the Tulane environmental clinic successfully stopped a polyvinylchloride factory from locating in a low-income Black residential neighborhood, angry business groups complained to the Louisiana Supreme Court. In response, the court amended its student-practice rule, Rule XX, to make it harder for students to represent environmental groups.

Clinic supporters filed a federal law suit on academic freedom and free speech grounds. . . . The district court sided with the Louisiana Supreme Court and the Fifth Circuit Court of Appeals affirmed. The heart of the Fifth Circuit's argument is that the Louisiana Supreme Court has no obligation to permit unlicensed law students to represent any clients at all. That means its new student-practice rule cannot violate the clinician's rights because they have no such rights. The court adds that it does not matter whether the Louisiana Supreme Court was responding to pressure from groups whose motivation was political and retaliatory. There is no viewpoint discrimination because Rule XX does not prevent anyone from speaking, it merely refuses to promote certain kinds of speech. . . . In effect, the Fifth Circuit told the clinic students that they should be grateful that the Louisiana justices let them into court at all. . . .

[N]o one was complaining about the competence or the ethics of the student lawyers at Tulane or any other Louisiana law school. The complaint was that they represented the wrong causes. The state supreme court had been lobbied by three powerful business associations to clamp down on the law students. The justices were up for re-election. . . .

The attacks on the environmental-law clinics at the University of Pittsburgh and Tulane failed to shut them down. . . . Facing criticism from the Association of American Law Schools and the American Association of University Professors, in March, 2002, the University of Pittsburgh School of Law's dean reversed his decision to assess the clinic its $60,000 overhead costs. And . . . Rule XX has not prevented the [Tulane] clinic from continuing its work. That is not the point, however. If the attacks failed, they were near misses, and eventually some will succeed. Indeed, they may already have succeeded in one of their aims, because clinic directors will undoubtedly hesitate before taking on volatile cases that may provoke dangerous backlash against the clinics or their law schools. Obviously, the degree to which clinicians self-censor cannot be known, but everyone in clinical education with whom I have discussed the subject agrees that self-censorship exists. . . .

In more than half a dozen decisions over the past fifteen years, the U.S. Supreme Court has cut back on statutorily authorized attorneys' fees given to prevailing parties in civil rights and environmental cases. Because they create weapons that adversaries can use to attack the funding of civil rights and environmental lawyers . . . these decisions [also] create silencing doctrines.

Those who disagree with Luban might characterize restrictions on legal services, IOLTA, clinics, and fee statutes differently, emphasizing their importance in reducing frivolous litigation and withdrawing public funding for ideologically charged disputes. Who do you think is right?

B. LEFT VERSUS RIGHT

> Of course it would be just as wrong if the doctrines came from the Left to silence the Right. Someday they may, and then the same criticisms would apply. For the criticism concerns procedural injustice, regardless of its political orientation.

Id. at 220.

While conservative advocates and government officials have sometimes advocated changes in the law seeking to undermine the effectiveness of liberal organizations' social change efforts, the reverse has also sometimes been true. For example, during the late 1930s, progressives attacked the legitimacy of the National Lawyers' Committee of the American Liberty League (NLC), which actively used legal tactics to challenge the constitutionality of much of the New Deal social legislation. EPSTEIN, *supra*, at 38-40. An ethics charge was filed against NLC, arguing that it was engaged in providing free legal advice, a charge for which it was cleared. *Id.* at 41-42. NLC, which prepared reports analyzing the constitutionality of New Deal legislation that formed the basis for litigation, was so successful that its efforts generated a flood of litigation before the National Labor Relations Board. *Id.* at 43. Senator Robert LaFollette, a progressive legislator, held hearings in which evidence was presented to show that NLC was engaged in industrial espionage and other forms of misconduct. *Id.* These claims damaged the group's credibility in the national political arena. *Id.*

Other efforts to limit conservative groups have arisen in the adversarial context of litigation. For example, in 1973, responding to the initial successes of the National Right to Work Legal Defense Foundation (NRW LDF) in challenging closed shops, some unions filed a lawsuit against NRW LDF arguing that it violated a federal law prohibiting employers from financing employees' suits against unions. *Id.* at 53-54. One of the hardest fought battles in this lawsuit was over the unions' claim in discovery that they were entitled to obtain a list of NRW LDF's contributors. *Id.* Because the merits of the suit related to whether it was really employers, rather than NRW LDF, who were financing the challenges to union shops, the discovery request seemed plausibly designed to seek relevant evidence. *Id.* However, disclosure of NRW LDF's membership and donor list could have had a potential chilling effect on its political activity—something that the Supreme Court had disapproved of when the state of Alabama sought to compel the disclosure of NAACP members in the 1950s. *NAACP v. Alabama*, 357 U.S. 449 (1958). Epstein, *supra*, at 54. For this reason, it was viewed by some as a tactical effort by the unions to pressure NRW LDF to stop bringing employee suits. Although NRW LDF was sanctioned for refusing to disclose its list, the circuit court ultimately rejected the unions' claim, holding that the federal law did not apply to the "legitimate litigation program of a bona fide, independent legal aid organization [the NRW LDF], even though the organization receives contributions from interested employers." *United Auto Workers v. National Right to Work Legal Defense and Educ. Found., Inc.*, 590 F.2d 1139, 1150 (D.C. Cir. 1978).

How do you compare the unions' efforts to challenge NRW LDF with the right's effort to, in Luban's terms, "take out the adversary" of progressive public interest lawyers? Do you view them as all part of the same type of partisan struggle in which one side seeks to limit the effectiveness of the other through whatever means are available? Or is there something different about the right restricting the left's ability to advocate for causes?

EXERCISE

Consider the following statement by Nadine Strossen, former President of the ACLU:

> I think public interest work should be understood, broadly and neutrally, as encompassing any case or cause that advances the lawyer's own vision of the common good, *whatever that may be*. Of course, I would be thrilled if all lawyers decided to do volunteer work for the American Civil Liberties Union (ACLU)! But I would also be pleased if each lawyer did any other public service work, as

I have broadly defined it, including work for an organization that opposes the ACLU on particular cases or issues.

Indeed, *in an important sense, I feel more in common with lawyers and organizations whose substantive positions I reject than with lawyers who do not care enough about public issues to take positions at all.* We may disagree about what policies or court rulings will best serve the public interest, but we are all dedicated to expending our professional energies to pursue those policies or rulings.

Nadine Strossen, *Pro Bono Legal Work: For the Good of Not Only the Public, But Also the Lawyer and the Legal Profession*, 91 MICH. L. REV. 2122, 2131 (1993) (emphasis added).

Do you agree with Strossen's view? Why or why not?

WHAT PUBLIC INTEREST LAWYERS DO

The second part of this book examines what public interest lawyers do by looking at the institutional settings in which public interest lawyering occurs, the types of advocacy strategies used to accomplish social change, and the complexities that can arise in the relationship between public interest lawyers, their clients, and their causes.

CHAPTER 4

PRACTICE SITES FOR PUBLIC INTEREST LAWYERING

I. INTRODUCTION

Public interest lawyering may take place in a number of different practice sites: staffed offices of nonprofit groups such as legal aid or the ACLU, small civil rights firms, pro bono programs of large law firms, and government offices like the U.S. Department of Justice (DOJ) or public defender. Each site offers a distinct set of possibilities for, and limitations on, advocacy undertaken by lawyers who work in them. Stuart Scheingold & Austin Sarat, Something to Believe In: Politics, Professionalism, and Cause Lawyering 72 (2004). This chapter explores how the location of public interest lawyering (*where* lawyers work) influences the nature of practice (*how* lawyers work). As the materials suggest, each practice site has tradeoffs. Some may offer more lawyer autonomy, but fewer resources. Others may facilitate lawyering for more radical change, while giving up professional status. These tradeoffs matter both to individual lawyers making choices about where they want to work and to the broader policy debate about how best to allocate scarce public interest law resources — whether society chooses to distribute resources to nonprofit organizations or private firms may influence what types of cases are prioritized in the overall public interest law system. In order to understand the nature and consequences of these choices, this chapter explores the benefits and downsides of a range of sites associated with public interest practice.

As a starting point, we can think of public interest law as comprised of three sectors: a nonprofit sector; a government sector; and a private for-profit sector, encompassing both the pro bono departments of large corporate firms and the access- or policy-oriented activities of small firms or solo practitioners. *See* Figure 1.

Among the many factors that distinguish these practice sites, money is a defining feature. How public interest lawyering is paid for profoundly determines how practice is organized and executed. Richard L. Abel, *State, Market, Philanthropy, and Self-Help as Legal Services Delivery Mechanisms, in* Private Lawyers and the Public Interest: The Evolving Role of Pro Bono in the Legal Profession 295 (Robert Granfield & Lynn Mather eds., 2009); Scott L. Cummings &

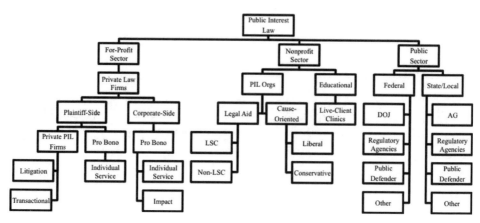

FIGURE 1.

Organizational Chart of the Public Interest Law Industry

Source: Scott L. Cummings, *The Pursuit of Legal Rights — and Beyond*, 59 UCLA L. REV. 506, 526 (2012).

Deborah L. Rhode, *Public Interest Litigation: Insights from Theory and Practice*, 36 FORDHAM URB. L.J. 603, 605 (2009) [hereinafter, Cummings & Rhode, *Public Interest Litigation*]. The funding sources for nonprofit groups are generally different from their governmental and private firm counterparts; in each setting, the funding mechanism influences lawyers' choices to take on certain types of cases and not others. Thus, the old adage: "He who pays the piper calls the tune." Think of that adage as you read the following materials, which investigate different models of funding and how they structure what public interest lawyers do and how they think of their missions across practice sites.

As you do, consider how resources relate to other features of public interest practice settings listed below. How much of the practice lives of public interest lawyers is determined by funding or other structural features of where they work? How much individual control do lawyers have over other important aspects of public interest practice: agenda setting, legal strategy, coalition building, and client relations? Are the factors that influence control internal (specific to the organizational setting in which the lawyers practice) or external (outside of the organization or its lawyers) — or a combination of both? What important choices do lawyers in each practice setting have to make and how do these choices affect outcomes? This chapter engages these questions as it explores the following features of public interest practice across nonprofit organizations, government offices, and private firms:

(1) *Resources.* What resources are available to pursue public interest agendas in each of these sites (financial support, number and quality of legal and nonlegal staff, access to professional development and training for lawyering)? Where do they come from (philanthropic foundations, individual donors, corporations, government, client fees, opposing parties through fee

shifting)? What limits do funders impose? What opportunities do they create?

(2) *Agenda Setting Ability.* To what degree can public interest lawyers in each practice site frame the agenda they wish to pursue? What factors go into the establishment of that agenda? How are the agendas shaped?

(3) *Control Over Legal Strategies.* How much control do lawyers in each of these sites have over the types of advocacy strategies — litigation, lobbying, organizing, education, or other — undertaken in the pursuit of public interest goals?

(4) *Coordination and Coalition Building.* How much freedom and opportunity do lawyers have in each practice site to coordinate their efforts with other organizations?

(5) *The Lawyer-Client Relationship.* How does the nature of practice across these sites affect the lawyer-client relationship? How do the lawyers understand who their clients are? How likely are the lawyers to view themselves as pursuing broader causes versus advancing specific client interests?

II. THE NONPROFIT SECTOR

The practice site that is most commonly associated with public interest lawyering is the nonprofit organization — typically structured (as we saw in Chapter 2) as a charitable, tax-exempt corporation whose resources are devoted exclusively to its public interest mission. The classic studies of public interest practice have all focused on these organizations. *See* Joel F. Handler, Betsy Ginsberg & Arthur Snow, *The Public Interest Law Industry, in* PUBLIC INTEREST LAW: AN ECONOMIC AND INSTITUTIONAL ANALYSIS 42, 76 (Burton A. Weisbrod, Joel F. Handler & Neil K. Komesar eds., 1978) (describing the voluntary, nonprofit public interest law firm as the "core" of the industry). More recent studies have also focused attention on the operation of groups in the nonprofit sector. Laura Beth Nielsen & Catherine R. Albiston, *The Organization of Public Interest Practice: 1975-2004*, 84 N.C. L. REV. 1591, 1601 (2006) (focusing on "organizations in the voluntary sector"); Deborah L. Rhode, *Public Interest Law: The Movement at Midlife*, 60 STAN. L. REV. 2027, 2029 (2008) [hereinafter, Rhode, *Movement at Midlife*] (looking at "the nation's leading public interest legal organizations").

As you will recall from Chapter 2, the nonprofit sector is generally divided between legal aid groups serving the poor and public interest law groups that focus on advancing a cause (like the ACLU or LDF). In addition, the growth of clinical legal education, explored in Chapter 8, has meant that significant public interest law services are rendered by law professors and students working in clinics housed in law schools. Scott L. Cummings, *The Pursuit of Legal Rights — and Beyond*, 59 UCLA L. REV. 506, 531 (2012) (estimating that law school clinical faculty provide public interest law services in amounts equal to that of roughly 290 full-time lawyers each year). Because of their centrality to the public interest law field, this part will focus on the tradeoffs of lawyering in legal aid and public interest law organizations.

A. RESOURCES

Because nonprofit public interest groups do not seek out cases in order to generate fees, they have to raise funds to sustain operations through a combination of sources: membership dues, fundraising from private donors, grants from charitable foundations and government agencies, and attorneys' fees awarded under fee-shifting statutes. Because there are important differences in the funding sources for legal aid and public interest law organizations, this section treats them separately.

1. Legal Aid Organizations

Civil legal aid in the United States is provided through two types of nonprofit groups: those funded (in part) by the federal Legal Services Corporation (LSC), and those funded entirely by other sources. This distinction is important because in exchange for a large amount of federal support, LSC-funded legal aid groups must operate according to specific rules imposed by the federal government (as David Luban's excerpt noted in the last chapter).

Alan Houseman, executive director of the Center for Law and Social Policy (CLASP), reporting in 2009, stated that the "overall funding [for U.S. civil legal aid organizations] is approximately $1.3 billion. The largest element of the civil legal aid system is comprised of the 137 programs that are funded and monitored by LSC." Alan W. Houseman, *Civil Legal Aid in the United States: A Update for 2009* 2, *at* http://www.clasp.org/admin/site/publications/files/CIVIL-LEGAL-AID-IN-THE-UNITED-STATES-2.pdf (last visited July 30, 2012). For LSC-funded groups, the federal government is the largest single funder, although a greater proportion of overall funding comes from non-LSC sources. According to Houseman, "the total funding for LSC funded programs in 2008 is $880,969,889. Of this $354,647,367 came from LSC and $526,322,522 came from non-LSC sources. The largest non-LSC sources were state and local grants of $194,139,032 and IOLTA [Interest on Lawyers Trust Accounts] of $11,797,730." *Id.* at 12. How does this mixture of funding sources affect the operation of legal aid groups?

a. GOVERNMENT

As we discussed in Chapter 2, the creation of a federally supported legal aid system was a transformative event in the history of public interest law. The notion that the federal government would support lawyers as part of an overall War on Poverty changed the provision of civil legal aid from local charity to institutionalized practice. And the ethos of the early legal services program was oriented toward systemic reform to benefit the poor—even though the bulk of program work remained focused on individual case representation. However, over time, federal funding for legal aid has proven double-edged. Although LSC funding remains the biggest single source of support, it has come with tradeoffs.

Focusing on the largest category of legal aid groups—those funded by LSC—spotlights two important resource issues. First, federal funding for LSC groups has declined dramatically over the past 30 years—by roughly

50 percent in real terms. Houseman, *supra*, at 13. This has limited the number of legal aid attorneys per capita. In 1998, David Luban noted that LSC funded "3,590 attorneys at an average salary of just under $40,000, along with 4,637 paralegals," resulting in approximately one LSC attorney for 10,000 poor people. David Luban, *Taking Out the Adversary: The Assault on Progressive Public-Interest Lawyers*, 91 CAL. L. REV. 209, 220-21 (2003). In 2005, LSC reported that there were "3,845 lawyers in LSC-funded programs . . . and an estimated 2,736 in programs that do not receive LSC funding." LEGAL SERVICES CORPORATION, DOCUMENTING THE JUSTICE GAP IN AMERICA 15 (2005). This was equivalent to roughly one legal aid attorney for every 6,861 poor people. *Id.* at 17. These resource constraints limit the extent of services to the poor and place the United States behind many other industrial nations in civil legal aid expenditures. For example, federal allocations for legal assistance are approximately one-sixteenth of Great Britain's budget, one-sixth of New Zealand's, and one-third of that of a few Canadian provinces. Deborah L. Rhode, *Access to Justice: Connecting Principles to Practice*, 17 GEO. J. LEGAL ETHICS 369, 374 (2004) [hereinafter, Rhode, *Access to Justice*]. While recent legislation restored some of the funding that was cut in earlier years, *see* Consolidated Appropriations Act of 2010, Pub. L. No. 111-117, 123 Stat. 3034, few would dispute that there are insufficient funds to address the legal needs of the poor.

The second issue with direct government funding is that the federal government imposes significant restrictions on what lawyers in legal aid groups that receive LSC funding can do, and which clients they can represent. As we saw in Chapter 2, the paltry resources for legal aid "have not prevented decades of political assaults on the program, including the outright lie that poor people have no trouble finding a free lawyer." Luban, *supra*, at 221. "The final blow came with the imposition of congressional restrictions in 1996 banning LSC-funded organizations from redistricting challenges, lobbying, class action lawsuits, representing most aliens, political advocacy, collecting attorney's fees, abortion litigation, prisoner representation, welfare reform activities, and defending public housing tenants evicted for drugs." Scott L. Cummings, *The Politics of Pro Bono*, 52 UCLA L. REV. 1, 22 (2004) [hereinafter, Cummings, *Politics of Pro Bono*]. These restrictions affect agenda setting to the extent that LSC-funded lawyers are prevented from taking certain categories of cases (e.g., redistricting, abortion, and welfare reform) and representing certain clients (e.g., many noncitizens, all incarcerated persons, and public housing residents charged with illegal drug activity in eviction proceedings); they have an impact on strategic considerations to the extent that LSC bans certain types of advocacy (lobbying, political advocacy, and class action lawsuits); they influence coordination with other groups (to the extent that the coordination seeks to advance prohibited advocacy); and they may alter the lawyer-client relationship by requiring reporting to LSC in ways that may affect the type of information that clients reveal to their lawyers (like their immigration status). *See* BRENNAN CENTER FOR JUSTICE, RESTRICTING LEGAL SERVICES: HOW CONGRESS LEFT THE POOR WITH ONLY HALF A LAWYER 6-7 (2000).

> Since [the prohibited activities] . . . are the very strategies most likely to address the causes of poverty and to deter future abuses, legal aid programs

have faced an unpalatable choice. They can do without federal funds and help far fewer individual clients, but in a more effective fashion. Or they can handle greater numbers of cases, but only for politically acceptable claimants, and in ways least likely to promote broader social reforms. . . . Given the difficulties of finding alternative sources of funding, most legal aid programs have opted for the latter course.

Rhode, *Access to Justice, supra*, at 379.

Significantly, LSC bans federally funded programs from using *non-LSC funds* to engage in restricted work. Thus, if a group receives LSC funds, it cannot even use funds raised through other sources (e.g., private donations, IOLTA) to undertake any activities banned by LSC regulations. Omnibus Consol. Rescissions & Approps. Act of 1996, Pub. L. 104-134, §504. Although LSC permits groups to set up separate offices under "program integrity" rules in which they may use non-LSC funds for any purpose, 45 C.F.R. §1610.8, App. 169a, legal services groups have criticized this physical separation requirement as creating waste and duplication (this requirement was challenged — unsuccessfully — in *Dobbins v. Legal Services Corporation*). *See generally* David S. Udell, *The Legal Services Restrictions: Lawyers in Florida, New York, Virginia, and Oregon Describe the Costs*, 17 YALE L. & POL'Y REV. 337 (1998). Despite these restrictions, Houseman notes that "LSC-funded programs can continue to provide representation in over 95% of the cases they were able to undertake prior to the imposition of the 1996 restrictions." Houseman, *supra*, at 9. Yet the debate about the funding restrictions continues to inform discussions over the future of legal aid.

The 1996 restrictions on LSC funding have come under attack, both from policymakers and through litigation. What legal theories are implicated by Congress's decision to selectively fund certain types of cases and not others? In *Legal Services Corporation v. Velazquez*, 531 U.S. 533 (2001), the Supreme Court examined whether Congress's restriction on LSC-funded attorneys' ability to challenge the constitutionality of welfare laws (codified as §504(a)(16) of the Omnibus Consolidated Rescissions and Appropriations Act of 1996) violated the First Amendment. LSC had interpreted the law to permit legal aid attorneys to challenge welfare determinations for individual clients, but not to represent a client for the purpose of changing the welfare laws or challenging their constitutional or statutory validity. The Court declared that the law violated the First Amendment, and also implicated separation of powers concerns because it prevented legal aid lawyers from presenting all valid arguments to the courts. It stated that

> cases would be presented by LSC attorneys who could not advise the courts of serious questions of statutory validity. . . . By seeking to prohibit the analysis of certain legal issues and to truncate presentation to the courts, the enactment under review prohibits speech and expression upon which courts must depend for the proper exercise of the judicial power. Congress cannot wrest the law from the Constitution which is its source.

Id. at 545. In rejecting the LSC's argument that attorneys could simply withdraw from a case to avoid the speech restriction, the Court found that

> [t]he statute is an attempt to draw lines around the LSC program to exclude from litigation those arguments and theories Congress finds unacceptable but

> which by their nature are within the province of the courts to consider. . . . The restriction on speech is even more problematic because in cases where the attorney withdraws from a representation, the client is unlikely to find other counsel.

Id. at 546. Finally, the majority rejected the argument that Congress's discretion whether to fund LSC included the power to withhold funding for specific types of matters. Although Congress "was not required to fund" LSC programs, when it did, it could not constitutionally "confine litigants and their attorneys in this manner." *Id.* at 548.

In dissent, Justice Scalia concluded that the LSC restrictions did not regulate speech at all. He argued that "[r]egulations directly restrict speech; subsidies do not. Subsidies, it is true, may *indirectly* abridge speech, but only if the funding scheme is 'manipulated' to have a 'coercive effect' on those who do not hold the subsidized position. . . ." *Id.* at 552. He found the majority's concern that the restriction would affect the types and nature of claims presented to courts to be wholly unpersuasive. "It may well be that the bar of 504(a)(16) will cause LSC-funded attorneys to decline or to withdraw from cases that involve statutory validity. But that means at most that fewer statutory challenges to welfare laws will be presented to the courts because of the unavailability of free legal services for that purpose. So what?" *Id.* at 556. Moreover, he questioned the relevance of the scarcity of counsel for indigent clients in the welfare system. He observed that "the Court is troubled 'because in cases where the attorney withdraws from a representation, the client is unlikely to find other counsel.' . . . That is surely irrelevant, since it leaves the welfare recipient in no *worse* condition than he would have been in had the LSC program never been enacted." *Id.* at 557.

Justice Scalia's dissent in *Velazquez* is predicated largely on the point that the government is not legally obligated to fund civil legal services for the poor. If Congress decided civil legal services was too expensive and disbanded the entire LSC it would not violate the Constitution. On that view, the government can choose to selectively fund the type of legal work it wishes to prioritize. How would you respond to Justice Scalia's argument?

Under the *Velazquez* majority's reasoning, might other restrictions on LSC funding that limit the scope of representation also violate the First Amendment? Suppose an LSC-funded attorney believes she has a great potential class action case to challenge a particular government application of welfare policy. Current law would forbid her from bringing the case as a class action even if doing so would be the most beneficial option to her clients, because it represented an effective and efficient legal strategy. How is that different from the restriction on challenging the validity of welfare statutes struck down in *Velazquez*? *See Legal Aid Servs. of Or. v. Legal Servs. Corp.*, 608 F.3d 1084 (9th Cir. 2010) (rejecting the claim that restrictions on LSC program lawyers' ability to lobby, solicit clients, and bring class actions violate the First Amendment because the regulations permitted work to be performed by affiliated organizations that comply with federal "program integrity rules"). *But see id.* at 1099 (Pregerson, J., dissenting) (arguing that restrictions distort attorneys' ability to represent clients in the same way as the restrictions struck down in *Velazquez*); *see also*

Andrew Haber, *Rethinking the Legal Services Corporation's Program Integrity Rules*, 17 VA. J. SOC. POL'Y & L. 404 (2010).

b. FOUNDATIONS

In the early 1960s, before the creation of a government-sponsored legal services program, the Ford Foundation was an important early funder for legal services offices. Christine N. Cimini, *Legal Aid/Legal Services, in* 2 POVERTY IN THE UNITED STATES: AN ENCYCLOPEDIA OF HISTORY, POLITICS, AND POLICY 435 (Gwendolyn Mink & Alice O'Connor eds., 2004). Cuts in federal funding have forced federal legal services programs to again look to foundations and elsewhere for funding. However, the diversification of funding sources adds a variety of different constraints. Groups must spend time and money raising funds from private donors and foundations, use targeted funds according to the terms specified in the grants, and adhere to multiple reporting requirements. All of these may require that legal services personnel spend more time on fundraising and grant administration. In addition, as discussed below with reference to other types of nonprofit organizations, foundation funding may also constrain and influence legal aid organizations' ability to pursue particular strategies and agendas.

c. IOLTA

State-based IOLTA programs are another important source of legal aid funding. IOLTA refers to Interest on Lawyers Trust Accounts, the interest earned on funds that lawyers sequester on behalf of clients.[1] All of the states and the District of Columbia have an IOLTA program that uses some of that interest to fund legal services organizations serving poor clients. "In 2009, the U.S. IOLTA programs generated more than $124.7 million nationwide." What Is IOLTA?, iolta.org (last visited Sept. 23, 2011). The impact of IOLTA programs on legal aid work is indisputable. Close to 90 percent of grants awarded by IOLTA programs in 2008 supported legal aid offices and pro bono programs. AMERICAN BAR ASSOCIATION'S COMMISSION ON INTEREST IN LAWYERS' TRUST ACCOUNTS, http://www.americanbar.org/groups/interest_lawyers_trust_accounts/overview .html (last visited July 30, 2012).

While IOLTA has become an important source for funding legal aid and other public interest work, it also has significant practical tradeoffs. First, because IOLTA funding relies on interest rates that are subject to fluctuation, the expected income from IOLTA funds can vary greatly from year to year. The ABA reported that in 2009, following the U.S. recession, IOLTA grants were substantially reduced in many states. *Id.* For programs relying on such funding, this fluctuation can significantly affect programmatic priorities. Some states were better prepared than others to address the economic downturn because they had created reserve funds and found other sources to fund grants to social change groups. *Id.*

---

1. For a short, but detailed, background on the operation of IOLTA programs, see *Brown v. Legal Foundation of Washington*, 538 U.S. 216, 220-23 (2003).

Another potential limitation on IOLTA's future viability is the impact of technological change on the administration of interest-bearing accounts. IOLTA programs are based on the idea that some individual client funds are so small or are deposited for such a brief time that the administrative and transaction costs of putting them in interest bearing accounts would exceed any interest earned; these are the accounts that are aggregated for IOLTA purposes (large funds generally are not since these produce net gains for clients). As computer systems become more sophisticated, however, banks may be able to calculate and distribute interest on small amounts of client funds at a relatively low cost and it may be simpler to determine what interest would inure to the clients' benefits. This could undercut the rationale for IOLTA or expose it to new constitutional challenge. *See* Tarra L. Morris, Comment, *The Dog in the Manger: The First Twenty-Five Years of War on IOLTA*, 49 St. Louis U. L.J. 605, 628 (2005).

Thus far, constitutional challenges to IOLTA programs have been fueled in part by concerns that IOLTA money goes primarily to liberal groups. One conservative advocate claimed that IOLTA programs are a "hidden scheme" by "left-wing lawyers" to "reach into the pockets of small businessmen and the middle class to fund their radical agenda." John C. Scully, *Hidden Scheme to Finance Radical Lawyers Plagues Pacific Northwest*, Wash. Legal Found. Legal Backgrounder, Mar. 31, 1992 (*quoted in* W. Frank Newton & James W. Paulsen, *Constitutional Challenges to IOLTA Revisited*, 101 Dick. L. Rev. 549, 559 n.57 (1997)). These legal challenges are based on several arguments.

First, challengers have argued that IOLTA programs constitute an unconstitutional taking of clients' property in violation of the Takings Clause, which prohibits government action that takes private property for public use without providing just compensation to the property owner. U.S. Const. amend. V. While the Supreme Court initially suggested that there might be a plausible takings argument, *Phillips v. Washington Legal Foundation*, 524 U.S. 156, 172 (2000) (holding that interest on accounts is the clients' property), it later held that IOLTA programs do not constitute an unconstitutional taking because the clients whose funds generated the interest for IOLTA had not suffered any net loss in value. *Brown v. Legal Foundation of Washington*, 538 U.S. 216, 237 (2003). Because the IOLTA program challenged in that case required that lawyers "deposit client funds in non-IOLTA accounts whenever those funds could generate net earnings for the client," funds were placed into IOLTA accounts only when there was no possibility that they could earn interest for a particular client. *Id.* at 239. Though the aggregated funds generated a gain for IOLTA, if disaggregated for each individual client, they would not have earned interest, so the clients did not "lose" anything in the process.

The Court's opinion drew a strong dissent from Justice Scalia, joined by three other Justices, who disagreed that the IOLTA program did not cause a loss to clients whose funds were deposited in IOLTA accounts. "Once interest is earned on petitioners' funds held in IOLTA accounts, that money is petitioners' property. . . . It is at *that* point that the State appropriates the interest . . . —*after* the interest has been generated in the pooled accounts— and it is at *that* point that just compensation for the taking must be assessed." *Id.* at 245. (Scalia, J., dissenting).

Challengers also have argued that the taking of interest to fund particular types of litigation is tantamount to state-compelled speech, in violation of the First Amendment's free speech guarantee. In a separate dissent in *Brown*, Justice Kennedy observed that "[b]y mandating that the interest from these accounts serve causes the justices of the Washington Supreme Court prefer, the State . . . grants to itself a monopoly which might then be used for the forced support of certain viewpoints." *Id.* at 253 (Kennedy, J., dissenting). Kennedy argued that the collection of interest to pay for public interest lawyering that may be ideologically incompatible with the clients' personal views is a form of forced subsidy of another person's speech. The Supreme Court has recognized such claims in the context of the collection of labor union dues, *Abood v. Detroit Bd. of Education*, 431 U.S. 209 (1977), and mandatory bar association dues, *Keller v. State Bar of Cal.*, 496 U.S. 1 (1990).

The court's decision was predicated in part on the conclusion that the interest on client accounts that qualified for IOLTA was not client property. The *Phillips* decision rejected that characterization, 524 U.S. at 172, although *Brown* found that the disaggregated interest had no net value to clients. Because of this ambiguity, some commentators have suggested that the First Amendment issue is unresolved, though others have discounted this line of attack. *See* Morris, *supra*, at 624; *see generally* Terence E. Doherty, *The Constitutionality of IOLTA Accounts*, 19 Whittier L. Rev. 487 (1998); Kevin H. Douglas, Note, *IOLTAs Unmasked: Legal Aid Programs' Funding Results in Taking of Clients' Property*, 50 Vand. L. Rev. 1297 (1997); Hillary A. Webber, Comment, *Equal Justice Under the Law: Why IOLTA Programs Do Not Violate the First Amendment*, 53 Am. U. L. Rev. 491 (2003).

Finally, some have argued that when IOLTA rules are imposed by the state supreme court as a function of their oversight of the organized bar, the IOLTA program may implicate state separation of powers issues. In his dissent in *Brown*, Justice Scalia observed that because the IOLTA scheme was promulgated by the state supreme court, rather than the legislature, it "circumvents politically accountable decisionmaking, and effects a taking of clients' funds through application of a rule purportedly regulating professional ethics, promulgated by the Washington Supreme Court." 538 U.S. at 242 n.2 (Scalia, J., dissenting). Although IOLTA may implicate legitimate state separation of powers issues, should a successful claim be brought, the problem could be cured by a legislative enactment endorsing the state supreme court's rules. Morris, *supra*, at 626.

Given the legal challenges to IOLTA and political opposition to its implementation, as well as potential technological changes that may reduce the costs of calculating interest on these accounts, what do you predict will happen to IOLTA in the future? The elimination of IOLTA would have severe consequences for funding legal services. Houseman's figures show that IOLTA accounted for 17 percent of overall legal aid funding in 2009. Houseman, *supra*, at 12. Do other options exist that might be used to replace this funding source but would not draw the same types of objections?

2. Public Interest Law Organizations

Distinct funding issues face nonprofit, cause-oriented public interest law organizations that pursue reform agendas. This category includes local issue-oriented organizations, as well as the nationally prominent public interest law groups examined in Deborah Rhode's 2008 study, such as the ACLU, Asian Pacific American Legal Center, Disability Right Advocates, Lawyers' Committee for Civil Rights Under Law, Legal Momentum, MALDEF, NAACP LDF, Natural Resources Defense Council (NRDC), Public Citizen, and the Youth Law Center. Rhode, *Movement at Midlife*, *supra*. As Rhode reports, maintaining funding support is fundamental to their successful operation.

> Virtually all organizations faced major challenges raising revenue. Expenses and needs have never stopped escalating, and few had relatively secure sources of income, such as membership dues or interest on endowment or reserves. For most groups, the budget had "to grow just to stay current," and "every January 1 we're back to zero." Even leaders of the wealthiest membership organizations experienced "bone-crushing" pressure to make their budgets. When the "economy goes south" or a particular region experiences a downturn, such as the technology bubble burst in the San Francisco Bay Area, then public interest funding becomes still harder to secure.

Id. at 2056.

Despite these challenges, in terms of overall resources, Laura Beth Nielsen and Catherine Albiston showed that the operating budgets of public interest law organizations (PILOs) had grown between 1975 and 2004: "[I]n 2004, nearly half (42%) of PILOs had annual operating budgets greater than $1.4 million while in 1975 only 25% of PILOs had budgets in this range. The percentage of PILOs operating with budgets of $3.5 million and greater more than doubled in the period." Nielson & Albiston, *supra*, at 1610. What do you think explains this growth? Although there is no systematic data, the 2008 recession has had a negative impact on the financial environment for nonprofit fundraising and likely affected these trends.

With cause-oriented nonprofit groups, funding considerations can be different from legal aid organizations. There is not necessarily a primary funder that tells groups what to do, but rather a mix of multiple funding sources, each of which may have their own priorities and strings attached, and which may pose other limitations on nonprofit groups' operational priorities. Rhode's study concluded that foundations accounted for 37 percent of mean funding for prominent public interest law organizations, while other sources included individual donations (28 percent), corporations (14 percent), attorneys' fees (8 percent), membership dues (4 percent), and sales and events (3 percent). Rhode, *Movement at Midlife*, *supra*, at 2055 tbl. 4. Legal scholars have examined the features and limitations of these various sources, which raise important considerations for public interest groups as they determine their organizational priorities. In this section, we focus on the main funding sources for nonprofit public interest law organizations: foundations, individuals, and corporations. Attorneys' fees, which are also important to nonprofit organizations, are treated later in the discussion of private public interests firms (Section IV.B.1), for which such fees are often the financial lifeblood of practice.

a. FOUNDATIONS

Foundation funding has long played a central role in supporting public interest lawyering. As discussed in Chapter 2, many of the major public interest organizations that emerged in the early twentieth century depended heavily on charitable foundation support. Similarly, during the 1970s, generous funding from foundations, most notably the Ford Foundation, led to the proliferation of public interest law organizations. Roger Alan Stone, *The Mass Plaintiff: Public Interest Law, Direct Mail Fundraising and the Donor/Client*, 25 Colum. J.L. & Soc. Probs. 197, 212 (1992). Today, numerous national and local foundations provide funding for a wide range of social change activity throughout the country. According to Rhode's survey, 98 percent of prominent public interest law organizations received at least some foundation support, which constituted on average a little more than one-third of their budgets. A little over half of the groups received at least 40 percent of their revenues from foundation grants, while a fifth of the groups received at least 60 percent of their support this way. Rhode, *Movement at Midlife, supra*, at 2054.

Nielsen and Albiston, looking at a different universe of public interest organizations (a nationally representative sample that included federally funded legal aid groups), noted a dramatic historical change in the source of funding over the past generation:

> Sources of income also changed for PILOs from 1975 to 2004. In 1975, the single largest income source for PILOs was foundation grants; 42% of all funding for PILOs came from foundation grants in that year. This percentage is not surprising considering that many large granting organizations (including the Ford Foundation) made access to justice and law reform a high priority for funding efforts at that time. The low proportion of PILO income from federal funds in 1975 (8%) may have been due to the fact that the LSC had not yet become a major source of funds.
>
> By the year 2004, sources of income changed dramatically. In 2004, the greatest sources of funding were state and local funds, accounting for 28% of PILO funding. This funding trend is a dramatic reversal from 1975 when state and local funds were at the bottom of the list, accounting for only 1% of PILO funding. In 2004, federal funds and foundation grants were the second greatest sources of income (21% each). This number represents a drop by half in the percentage of foundation grant money supporting PILOs (in 1975, 42% of funding came from foundation grants) and a significant increase in federal funds.

Nielsen & Albiston, *supra*, at 1616. What do you think accounts for these trends and what impact might they have? What differences are there between the results of the Rhode study and the one by Nielsen and Albiston, and how would you explain them?

Foundation money can also support lawyers who wish to work with public interest law groups. Organizations such as Equal Justice Works (http://www.equaljusticeworks.org/ (last visited Aug. 7, 2012)) and the Skadden Fellowship Foundation (http://www.skaddenfellowships.org/ (last visited Aug. 7, 2012)) provide funding for young lawyers to work with established public interest groups and to develop creative projects to advance those groups' missions.

Both have been responsible for providing opportunities for elite law school graduates with demonstrated commitment to enter public interest practice by providing full salary and loan assistance. The impact of these programs has not been studied, but one would expect that they have had a profound influence on the public interest sector, both in terms of staffing needed programs and promoting innovation. Skadden funded over 500 fellows in the program's first 20 years; EJW added approximately another 500 between 1992 and 2008. One question relates to the type of work promoted by the fellowship programs based on their funding sources (large law firms). Skadden has explicit restrictions: it does not fund environmental or immigration projects. EJW does not have stated restrictions, but its movement toward big firm sponsorship after 1998 may lead to limits on the type of projects that it is willing to fund. Fellowships also raise questions of stratification within the public interest bar and career mobility. One would predict fellowship recipients to have more career options and to exercise them to maximize income and prestige. As one rough indicator of the scope of career opportunities for elite public interest lawyers, as of 2008, there were 34 former Skadden Fellows listed in the Association of American Law Schools (AALS) law school faculty directory.

There are other advantages to foundation funding. An organization that has a wide range of programs may be able to target foundations that prioritize a particular project within the organization, but might not support (or may even be opposed to) another one of the organization's missions. For example, a group such as the ACLU, which has a number of diverse specialty areas, may apply for a project-specific grant from a foundation that wants to invest in protection of children's rights, but may not support the ACLU's position on reproductive freedom (or vice-versa). Whereas it might be difficult to raise money from that foundation for the ACLU's general mission, some funders may be willing to support a discrete legal project dedicated to a specific issue.

While foundation funding is quite attractive at many levels, there are important tradeoffs. First, differences in ideological or strategic vision may prompt foundations to limit the type of work that its recipients can carry out. Foundations may have priorities that differ from public interest organizations' preferences. Some foundations may even condition the receipt of funding on the funded organization's willingness to alter its approaches, thus undermining that organization's autonomy. As Rhode's study found, "[m]ost [foundations] were unwilling to fund operating expenses and many were unwilling to support litigation. As one director of a youth law center put it, 'Foundations like children, not lawyers.' Even program officers who were most receptive to legal work sometimes lacked the expertise to know where programs could have the greatest impact." Rhode, *Movement at Midlife, supra*, at 2056. Or consider the following observations:

> When charities do fund antipoverty efforts, their funding strategies are likely to reflect ideas about the pathology of the poor. Traditional efforts to improve the morality of the poor reappear in funding determinations designed to support counseling or mentoring programs. Noncontroversial poverty programs, such as food banks, are more likely to be funded than grassroots

organizations, advocacy initiatives, or public policy efforts. Charities often require donees to avoid activism in general and provide narrow services at the expense of structural reform. Mainstream groups such as the United Way have historically resisted the inclusion of social change groups in their on-the-job giving campaigns. Civil rights organizations that focus on racism and discrimination are forced to modify their strategies in order to obtain foundation support. Although a new generation of philanthropists has emerged with profits earned largely from technology, current patterns differ little from traditional foundations that avoid funding organizations that advocate social change.

Philanthropic organizations not only fail to provide significant material aid to the poor, they also interfere with goals of organizational recipients by requiring modification of programs hoping to qualify for charitable dollars, often at the expense of organizational priorities. Organizations dependent on philanthropy are required to "prospect" for funders at a cost of time, money, and efficiency, while always mindful of donor interest as a primary concern. The unequal power between donor and recipient often forces organizations to adopt donor-determined projects. This results in fragmented organizations in competition with each other, often at the expense of those who rely on their services.

Deborah Weissman, *Law as Largess: Shifting Paradigms of Law for the Poor*, 44 WM. & MARY L. REV. 737, 809-11 (2002); *see also* Cummings & Rhode, *Public Interest Litigation*, *supra*, at 620. What role do you think foundations should play in influencing the work of nonprofit groups? What is the best way to effectively manage the "unequal power" dynamic identified by Weissman?

A related issue is that foundations concerned about their public image may avoid supporting legal work that is perceived as controversial. Concerns about foundations steering away from controversial issues are not new. In the late 1970s, the Ford Foundation decided to terminate funding that it had been providing to some of the nation's most prominent consumer, environmental, and other public interest groups.

> Often litigating against large corporations, Henry Ford II felt that the public interest law groups were "biting the hand that fed them, because they were challenging the corporations funding them." . . . In view of the Ford Foundation's pivotal role in public interest law funding, many commentators believed that its move might bring public interest advocacy to a halt.

Stone, *supra*, at 213. But concerns about the ultimate impact of these cuts may have been overestimated.

> [T]he withdrawal of Ford Foundation funding was the genesis of today's mass plaintiff because the Foundation gave final termination grants for the express purpose of transforming the organizations into self-sufficient membership organizations. Along with this money the Ford Foundation also provided the groups with technical advice on the mechanics of direct mail, membership communications and recruitment crucial to transforming themselves into mass plaintiff organizations.

Id.

Corey Shdaimah offers insights into the impact of funding on the work of legal services lawyers. One lawyer recounted his experience when a community welfare rights organization that had a close working relationship with his legal services office asked him to help disrupt the Olympics as part of a political strategy. His response was directly related to private funding for his office.

> [A]n institutional constraint is we get funding. Our funders do not fund us to disrupt the Olympics. They fund us to help people on welfare who are getting their benefits cut off by the welfare system. . . . And we have much fewer institutional constraints than all those other legal services organizations that have congressional restrictions that are imposed upon them. Which they can't do some of the very things that Lucie White and Gerry López say they *must* do. They can't do organizing, they can't do administrative advocacy, so that's sort of institutional constraints.

COREY S. SHDAIMAH, NEGOTIATING JUSTICE: PROGRESSIVE LAWYERING, LOW-INCOME CLIENTS, AND THE QUEST FOR SOCIAL CHANGE 75 (2009). Not only do such constraints operate to limit lawyers' strategic options, but also they can have an indirect effect on the lawyer's relationship with his client. In the case of the lawyer who gave the previous statement, his denial of representation led his client to question his commitment to their cause. *Id.*

Another issue raised by foundation funding is that sometimes there may be unrealistic expectations for groups to show a positive return on philanthropic investments. Understandably, foundations are themselves accountable to their boards and donors, and must justify their decisions to invest in public interest organizations. As a result, foundations sometimes require their grantees to demonstrate the success of projects that they have funded. Consider these comments from public interest organization officials reported in Rhode's survey.

> Foundations' desires for "newer hotter issues" and "measurable outcomes" also created frustration. Program officers were "always looking for the next new thing. And civil rights seem same old. . . ." To demonstrate quantifiable results, groups sometimes had to shift priorities or, as one leader put it, "stretch the truth." Well versed in the art of foundation spin, that director would "sometimes laugh when I read newsletters of other organizations."
>
> These foundation policies raise broader issues about strategic philanthropy that deserve further research. Leaders who expressed frustration echoed concerns by other experts on the nonprofit sector that some of the progress that reform organizations were seeking could not be readily quantified. Yet funders distributing limited resources have an obvious and justifiable interest in having some way to assess cost-effectiveness. Well designed evaluations can often help both funders and recipients improve their performance. Demands for assessment are among the few structures of formal accountability for public interest law. It would be useful to know more about how the oversight process could be made most productive for all concerned.

Rhode, *Movement at Midlife, supra*, at 2056-57.

Finally, work to secure foundation funding is often time consuming, putting a strain on already under-resourced staff at public interest organizations. ELLEN KARSH & ARLEN SUE FOX, THE ONLY GRANT-WRITING BOOK YOU'LL EVER NEED 58-64 (3d ed. 2009). Organizations must invest their own resources to establish and manage relations with their benefactors — such as writing grants, providing regular reports, and hosting site visits. This adds a layer of responsibility on staff engaged in substantive work. It is not uncommon for a nonprofit lawyer, after spending a day in court or meeting with client groups, to have to spend extra time editing a draft grant proposal, meeting with development staff, or writing a litigation bulletin for a direct mail solicitation campaign.

Given these limitations, should public interest groups continue to rely on foundation support? Do they have any choice? Are there ways to navigate their relationships with foundations that could alleviate some of these concerns?

b. INDIVIDUALS

In addition to foundation grants, individual donations are a cornerstone of financial support for public interest law organizations. In Rhode's study, 85 percent of the groups were funded in part by individual donors, which made up about 28 percent of their revenues on average. Nearly 60 percent of the groups received at least 40 percent of their support from individuals. *Id.* How do nonprofits tap individual donors and what are the tradeoffs of reliance on such funding?

For many years, direct mail solicitations were a relatively efficient vehicle for raising money for public interest lawyering.

> The public interest law movement's growth and need for a new source of funding to replace foundation grants fortunately coincided with the "golden age" of direct mail prospecting, the 1970s and early 1980s. The importance of direct mail prospecting technology in the development of the mass plaintiff organization is incalculable. In 1968, computer technology emerged that allowed organizations to "merge and purge" new lists with old lists. This function permitted non-profits to buy or rent lists from other organizations and combine those lists with existing donor lists without duplicating names. Combined with existing reduced postal rate for non-profit groups, this allowed non-profits to greatly increase the volume of solicitations to potential new donors (direct mail prospecting). In 1969, a non-profit could mail solicitations at a cost of approximately eighty-five dollars per thousand letters and receive a return usually between $125-$175 per thousand. Profitable prospecting for donors led to an explosion in the charity industry in general, and mass plaintiff organizations in particular.
>
> The direct mail funded mass plaintiff organization has become the dominant form of organization in a number of areas of public interest law. The largest litigation organizations in environmental law, the NRDC, the Environmental Defense Fund, the Sierra Club Legal Defense Fund and the National Wildlife Federation, which together receive ninety percent of the funding for environmental public interest litigation, are all mass plaintiff organizations dependent on direct mail. Women's law centers are also organized along mass plaintiff lines. By 1983, sixty-five public interest law groups were using direct mail appeals, several of which have over 100,000 members. . . . Because of the economics of direct mail, the large, mature mass plaintiff organizations can maintain themselves and grow without devoting excessive resources to fundraising.

Stone, *supra*, at 217-18.

In the proper environment, direct mail fundraising can yield substantial benefits for public interest groups. As the excerpt above suggests, the technique has been successful with larger, more well-established groups. In addition, direct mail has been an effective way of fundraising during times of perceived crisis concerning particular issues. *See, e.g., id.* at 215 (citing statistics reflecting that contributions to major public interest law organizations dropped by 32 percent during the term of President Carter, but rose 83 percent during the early period of President Reagan's first term). It is most successful when organizations build up established lists of donors, who are more likely to contribute again once they have given initially. *Id.* at 219.

Direct mail fundraising also has evolved from a money-making tool to become part of larger mobilization strategies. Organizations can use it as part of a comprehensive and sophisticated plan to keep their members informed and invigorated by helping them to feel more invested in a particular issue that they are solicited to support. As part of a larger direct mail campaign, for example, People for the American Way once asked its members to send in local television listings as part of a national effort to address issues related to religious broadcasters. *Id.* at 222. The NRDC incorporates direct mail fundraising into a program of membership communication that includes newsletters and litigation bulletins. *Id.* at 223.

However, direct mail fundraising is not a realistic option for many types of public interest groups. First, the process itself can be costly. Like other fundraising tools, it requires a devotion of financial resources, staff time for monitoring mailing lists, defining fundraising campaigns, and drafting fundraising letters, or coordination with an outside organization that will perform many of these tasks. This has become a bigger problem as postal rates increase and other expenses have risen as well. *Id.* at 220-21. A second issue is that direct mail is likely to yield substantial funds only if the constituency for a particular cause is relatively large. That is, it is a better option for groups with large membership bases. There is also the problem of dilution. A wide variety of organizations use mass funding appeals and it is easy for a public interest organization to get lost in the shuffle. It remains to be seen whether the emergence of email, web sites, and social networking as tools for direct fundraising will affect the ability of organizations with fewer resources to reach a wide constituency.

Like other fundraising tools, direct solicitation of funds can lead to controversies as well. Many public interest organizations have benefitted from their inclusion in the Combined Federal Campaign, which was established in the 1960s to coordinate solicitation of government employees. *Id.* Under this program, the federal government allows charitable organizations to solicit donations from its employees once a year, and facilitates this by distributing materials about various organizations and coordinating donations through payroll deductions or lump sum payments. *Id.* Many private employers participate in similar coordinated giving programs. The Campaign creates a substantial advantage to charitable organizations included because it provides an efficient way of reaching large numbers of potential donors. *Id.* Access to the Campaign is necessary for some groups to succeed and an organization's ideology might affect that access. A controversy arose during the 1980s, when the Reagan Administration banned some public interest organizations from the Campaign. *Id.* at 215-16. This action appeared politically motivated because several progressive public interest organizations were excluded, but the government allowed conservative groups such as the Moral Majority to raise money through the Campaign. *Id.* In *Cornelius v. NAACP Legal Defense and Educational Fund, Inc.*, 473 U.S. 788 (1985), the Supreme Court held that the Campaign was not a public forum under the First Amendment and rejected a challenge to the government's decision to restrict access to it. Congress later amended the law, however, to restore some public interest groups' ability to participate in the Campaign. Stone, *supra*, at 215-16.

c. CORPORATIONS

In addition to individual donations, Rhode found that over half of public interest law organizations receive corporate donations, which constituted an average of 14 percent of overall funding. Rhode, *Movement at Midlife, supra,* at 2055 tbl. 4. Although less than one-sixth of overall funding, corporate donations are nonetheless a substantial, and growing, funding component. *Compare* Handler, Ginsberg & Snow, *supra*, at 54 (showing that corporate donations did not constitute a large enough category to be listed as a funding source for public interest law firms in 1975).

What are the implications of substantial corporate support? Rhode suggests that corporate donors are not generally interested in supporting litigation because they do not see it "as valuable to their bottom line." Rhode, *Movement at Midlife, supra,* at 2057. Consider this observation:

> [Rhode's study] suggests that elite public interest groups may be as dependent — or even more dependent — on private individuals and corporations for financial support (42% of total income) than foundations. What does this mean for organizational governance and programmatic content? One interpretation might be that such private donations reflect significant law firm financial involvement in these organizations. And one would expect such involvement to be accompanied by law firm representation on the groups' boards of directors. How far such financial relationships extend and how much they influence organizational policy are questions that have troubled observers of public interest law since Bell charged the Legal Defense Fund with "serving two masters" in its pursuit of school desegregation. If it is the case that law firms and other private sector actors are exercising more financial control over public interest law organizations, business considerations may compete with ideology in shaping their dockets.

Scott L. Cummings, *The Future of Public Interest Law*, 33 U. Ark. Little Rock L. Rev. 355, 362 (2011).

Do you think that corporate donations are helpful or a threat to public interest law? Why? Might the answer depend on the type of work done by a particular public interest group? How? Should public interest groups accept corporate funding even when no strings are attached?

B. AGENDA SETTING ABILITY

To what extent are public interest lawyers in the nonprofit sector able to set their own agendas? Legal aid lawyers generally set agendas around the needs of individual clients. While they can and do plan affirmatively for how to allocate scarce resources to meet demands across different substantive areas (like housing, employment, family, and consumer law), they are by virtue of their structure and mission focused on promoting individual service. Additionally, for lawyers in LSC-funded groups, the statutory restrictions on the scope of their work and the types of tactics they can pursue also limit their ability to plan an affirmative agenda. Lawyers in cause-oriented public interest law organizations do not face government imposed restrictions but funder priorities are still a key factor influencing agenda setting.

From an agenda-setting perspective, there are some important advantages to the nonprofit structure. Nonprofit groups' reliance on external funding lessens (or even eliminates) organizational reliance on client fees. To the degree that nonprofit lawyers treat fundraising separately from client relations, they may experience greater freedom to determine their overall organizational priorities and select cases to achieve them. Lawyers in these groups may choose which funds to seek as a way of controlling the type of work that they ultimately do. In practice, however, as we have seen, groups sometimes respond to priorities set by the funders, who may restrict the use of grants to certain types of activities. Ultimately, the agendas of nonprofit public interest law organizations are set through negotiation—and sometimes contestation—by various internal and external stakeholders: lawyers, funders, organizational members, community residents, influential political actors, and others.

The iconic historical example of the power and peril of nonprofit agenda setting is the NAACP LDF's development of its assault on public school segregation, culminating in the Supreme Court's decision in *Brown v. Board of Education*. *See generally* Mark V. Tushnet, The NAACP's Legal Strategy Against Segregated Education, 1925-1950 (1987). Derrick Bell's classic critique of LDF charged the group with pursuing integration to the exclusion of educational quality in a manner inconsistent with the views of many African Americans in the affected class. Derrick A. Bell, Jr., *Serving Two Masters: Integration Ideals and Client Interests in School Desegregation Litigation*, 85 Yale L.J. 470 (1976). Part of the reason for this divergence, he argued, rested on the fact that LDF's middle class funders had different priorities than many clients in the class: "The hardline position of established civil rights groups on school desegregation is explained in part by pragmatic considerations. These organizations are supported by middle class blacks and whites who believe fervently in integration. . . . Many of these supporters either reject or fail to understand suggestions that alternatives to integrated schools should be considered, particularly in majority-black districts. They will be understandably reluctant to provide financial support for policies they think unsound, possibly illegal, and certainly disquieting." *Id.* at 489-90.

As the LDF example highlights, a critical component of lawyers' agenda setting power in the nonprofit setting is the ability to identify their own clients for mission-advancing purposes. Whereas in traditional legal practice, clients often seek assistance from attorneys, nonprofit public interest groups sometimes seek clients whose cases will be good for testing or changing the law. Thus, public interest lawyers practicing in this setting can try to identify plaintiffs whose cases present sympathetic facts, who are credible witnesses, and who are supportive of the broader social change effort a nonprofit may be pursuing. Lawyers do not want to expend their limited resources on clients who do not have these types of cases or who may ultimately undermine the relevant cause. Tushnet, *supra*, at 53-54.

Dale Carpenter's account of the legal strategy of LGBT rights lawyers to challenge anti-sodomy laws in *Lawrence v. Texas* reveals the types of important choices lawyers make with respect to client selection in order to advance substantive agendas. Dale Carpenter, Flagrant Conduct: The Story of Lawrence v. Texas (2012). In that case, lawyers from the LGBT rights group Lambda Legal heard of the arrest of two men for allegedly violating Texas's anti-sodomy law: one was white (John Lawrence), the other was black (Tyron Garner); both had criminal records. The Lambda lawyers found out because the police clerk that processed the booking was closeted gay and referred the case. As it turns out, the two men were not involved in a relationship and were not, in fact, engaged in sexual relations at the time of their arrest. However, the Lambda lawyers believed that their case provided the best shot for a frontal Supreme Court challenge to antisodomy laws, which were so underenforced it was difficult to find anyone actually arrested under the law. The lawyers, in collaboration with pro bono counsel, were able to persuade Lawrence and Garner to plead no contest even though they were factually innocent and then to keep quiet about the true nature of their relationship throughout the litigation, which resulted in a monumental Supreme Court victory for the LGBT movement. As this case suggests, one potential advantage of public interest lawyering in nonprofit groups like Lambda is the ability to select and carefully craft the optimal case to advance a cause.

How do contemporary nonprofit groups set and execute priorities? Rhode's study provides some insights into this process. She observed that only about a third of the organizations she studied had either highly or moderately formal processes for setting priorities. Groups with formal processes tended toward annual or biannual retreats that produced planning documents, with periodic staff meetings in between retreats to facilitate additional planning. Those with only moderately formal processes used less frequent staff retreats to carry out planning. Organizations had different assessments of these planning processes, but some valued the opportunity to sit back and take a longer view of strategic priorities. Two-thirds of the surveyed groups used only informal processes for setting priorities, which for the most part worked well, often because the groups were smaller. Rhode, *Movement at Midlife, supra*, at 2050.

In terms of who made the decisions about organizational priorities, the vast majority (95 percent) of the groups relied on their legal staffs. Only about a quarter of the groups sought input from other stakeholders, such as group members, clients, or community organizations. One exception was groups receiving LSC funding, which are required to do client and community outreach. None of the membership groups surveyed reported being significantly influenced by their members' views on priorities. Similarly, the vast majority of groups did not report that their boards of directors had significant input in planning. There were important exceptions, including the ACLU, whose board participates in all controversial litigation decisions. Board involvement can be a mixed blessing. Some board members can add expertise not only in legal matters, but also in financial affairs, media, and public relations. The reality of many nonprofit boards is that their organizations rely on them heavily for fundraising, and this is sometimes an important factor in selecting new board members. *Id.* at 2050-52. On the other hand, board members can be perceived as intruding on staff decision making. As one respondent to Rhode's study put it, "Wealthy and powerful individuals who were used to being in control sometimes have overstepped their role." *Id.* at 2051.

As we have seen, funders can significantly shape institutional priorities. Although the majority of groups in Rhode's study reported that funders had only a limited impact on priorities, nearly 40 percent of the organizations admitted that they had a moderate impact. The influence of funders was seen in both conservative and liberal organizations. While organizations were cognizant of the influence of funders, they could not always resist the pressure. Some groups reported specific instances of pursuing programs their funders wanted, which had important and unsettling effects on staffing decisions and priorities. As Margaret Fung, director of the Asian American Legal Defense and Education Fund conceded, "We try to avoid having our agendas driven by funders but the reality is that they are partially driven." Groups that were well and diversely funded, such as some environmental organizations, had more flexibility. Others, such as LSC-funded offices and groups that relied on only a few sources of financial support, were more susceptible to pressure to modify their strategic plans. *Id.* at 2052-53.

The criteria, aside from funding, for setting organizational priorities varied somewhat among different groups. Of course, most organizations sought to determine how to best achieve their primary substantive goals and have the greatest impact given available resources. But there were varying understandings of measuring impact. Some groups sought to first address the most severe or extreme needs of their constituencies. Others, such as the Environmental Defense Fund, took into account their likelihood of success in pursuing projects. Another important value for some groups was to prioritize work that would not otherwise be performed by any other organization. Still others considered as a priority work that would likely draw additional public and donor support. Even given these specific criteria, it is difficult to assess the degree to which the choices organizations make are the best ones. As Rhode concluded, "It was generally hard to know whether different choices would have been more cost-effective. So informed judgments by experienced staff generally drove the priority-setting process and attracted reasonable consensus in strategic decision making." *Id.* at 2053.

C. CONTROL OVER LEGAL STRATEGIES

As with agenda setting, control over strategy is influenced by a nonprofit's different stakeholders. Funders have an important role setting the basic framework within which strategy is set — limiting the use of resources to certain types of cases and clients. However, within these frameworks, lawyers are relatively free to make strategic decisions about how best to deploy their limited resources in the pursuit of their organizational mission. Because they do not have the same pressure to take on cases to generate fees (although they may sometimes account for the availability of attorneys' fees under fee-shifting statutes), nonprofit lawyers may have relatively more freedom to decide which strategy best advances their cause. For instance, they can make decisions about the degree to which the organization should pursue litigation, and if so, whether that litigation should focus on law reform or on serving a substantial number of individual clients. Similarly, lawyers in nonprofit groups may have greater flexibility to opt for non-litigation strategies, such as community organizing and public education. They can even decide to allocate some resources to more traditional forms of political lobbying. The latter strategy, however, is at least partially limited by federal tax law for organizations formed under 26 U.S.C. §501(c)(3). *See* Chapter 1. But even this can be addressed. If the organization decides that substantial lobbying is a strategy critical to its mission, it can restructure itself to create an independent arm under §501(c)(4), or can use its resources to generate materials that other individuals or groups can draw on to engage in their own lobbying efforts. In Chapter 5, we examine in greater detail the advantages and disadvantages of different strategic approaches.

The empirical evidence lends support to the idea that nonprofit public interest lawyers exercise flexibility in choosing different advocacy approaches. Nielsen and Albiston suggest that public interest organizations have shifted to multiple functions over time. Their study of public interest law organizations between 1975 and 2004 showed that there was a slight increase in the mean amount of time organizations devoted to legal work (63 percent, up from 60 percent), but other trends pointed in the direction of greater strategic diversification. Nielsen & Albiston, *supra*, at 1612. First, 10 percent of the groups studied spent less than one-fifth of their time on legal work in 2004, in contrast to 1975, when there were no groups in that category. *Id.* The percentage of organizations that reported 100 percent of their activities as legal fell from 3 percent to 1 percent during the same period. *Id.* At the same time, PILOs spent more time on research, education, and outreach (19 percent, up from 14 percent in 1975). *Id.* Nielsen and Albiston did not have a definitive explanation for this shift away from legal work and toward research, education, and outreach, but speculated that "[i]t might be . . . a necessity for fundraising. Yet, given that a much larger share of PILO funding came from government sources in 2004, it is more likely that this shift represents a change in how PILOs define their mission. Our research suggests that PILOs have moved beyond litigation as the sole focus of social change." *Id.* What do you think accounts for this move "beyond litigation"? How much control over this shift do you think the lawyers exert—as opposed to other stakeholders, particularly funders?

D. COORDINATION AND COALITION BUILDING

Because of their limited resources and differing areas of expertise, nonprofit public interest organizations can sometimes benefit from interorganizational collaborations. One important example was the collaboration of interest groups representing African Americans, women, and labor in lobbying Congress to enact the Civil Rights Act of 1991, which overturned a number of Supreme Court opinions narrowly interpreting federal employment discrimination law. *See* William N. Eskridge, Jr., *Overriding Supreme Court Statutory Interpretation Decisions*, 101 Yale L.J. 331, 364 (1991).

Overall, it appears that nonprofit groups find significant benefits in collaboration. Rhode reports extensive collaboration between nonprofit public interest groups and (1) nonlegal entities (grassroots, government, and private sector organizations), (2) other public interest groups, and (3) private law firms. Rhode found that over 60 percent of organizations had extensive collaboration and another 25 percent had moderate levels of collaboration with grassroots groups. Collaborations involved public interest lawyers helping to represent or form grassroots groups, working with them to provide services to the community, and teaming up to push for legal and policy reform. In comparison, less than 50 percent of public interest groups worked with government and private sector organizations. Rhode, *Movement at Midlife*, *supra*, at 2064. Establishing coalitions among all of these groups had several significant advantages:

> Expanding the number of organizations cooperating on an issue brought additional resources, perspectives, and legitimacy. As Marcia Greenberger, co-president of the National Women's Law Center noted, "Almost never will a single organization have the capacity to achieve major policy change." For conservative groups, long-term relationships with industry and trade associations have helped to "broaden our influence and share expenses." For technology organizations, relationships with companies that develop and market products have been essential in promoting core values. Youth organizations often have worked closely with government agencies handling foster care, child welfare, and probation, because "they have control over our clients" and cooperative relationships could serve mutual interests.
>
> Many groups have worked hard to expand their political base beyond conventional partners. For example, Lambda Legal has reached out to local black ministers in the push for same-sex marriage. The Mexican American Legal Defense and Education Fund has worked with the business community on immigration issues, which builds its credibility in policy settings. Earth Justice has partnered with ranchers, commercial fishers, Native American tribes, Latino farm workers, health service providers, and the American Lung Association. Such alliances not only have increased policy leverage, they have also challenged the stereotypes that environmental groups "just represent rich backpackers."
>
> Coalition work has served other functions as well. One is to ensure accountability. Gen Fujioka of the Asian Law Caucus emphasized that lawyers in their programs—immigration, employment, and housing—worked extensively with local community groups to "keep us grounded and responsive. They provide a reality check that helps define our policy agenda and identify important cases." Other civil rights groups have similarly found that on issues like environmental justice, "grassroots coalitions are key. The local folks have to live in the community when the national folks go home." Such coalitions also have helped bridge divisions among racial and ethnic groups on divisive issues such as immigration reform. From both a political and public relations standpoint, it has been useful to have both individual clients and activist organizations involved; "the organizations have staying power and the individuals have stories." And for groups that offer direct legal services, partnering with other

community organizations has been essential to ensure effective referral networks and cross-professional assistance.

Id. at 2064-65

Though public interest leaders recognized the value in collaboration, they also recognized some potential costs. First, the coupling of legal organizations with grassroots groups sometimes created unrealistic expectations from the latters' members, who mistakenly believed that the public interest groups would address their individual needs as well as the coalition's. *Id.* at 2066. Indeed, lawyers in such coalitions may need to exercise caution to avoid unintentionally creating an attorney-client relationship. In addition, a small, but notable, percentage of leaders reported issues about allocation of credit for the coalition's successes, as well as disputes about how to resolve strategic or substantive disagreements among the groups. *Id.*

> In some cases, the problem arose because a local group was "less interested in the issue than in creating leadership opportunities and building organizational strength. They will insist on doing the press conference where [our lawyers] have done the work. They need to share." In other contexts, tensions emerged because the public interest organization was the "big boy in the boat." Its greater size and visibility led to disproportionate media coverage, which created resentment and sometimes difficulties in donor relations for the smaller group. Yet for the most part, these issues were not significant obstacles in grassroots collaboration. Although tension over credit was an occasional "annoyance," it seemed never to "undermine an important policy objective. By and large, people are in it for the issues."
>
> The same was true for questions of control. . . . Coalition work often required compromises in pursuit of common ground, and the larger the group, the greater the challenges. Even smaller partnerships could be problematic, particularly if a corporate player was involved and lacked sufficient "buy in" at the leadership level. Environmental groups were especially wary about joining private sector alliances that might do more to "greenwash" businesses than to promote significant reform.
>
> Whether to engage in radical tactics and to accept a partial victory were also occasional sources of disagreement. Grassroots constituencies sometimes saw issues in "black and white" and assumed "the sky would fall" if they settled for only incremental gains. Other tensions, well documented in the literature on cause lawyering, involved lawyers' reluctance to be involved in "raising hell"; by training and temperament, even progressive attorneys have been wary of seeming to undercut a system they are socialized to accept. Additional complications arose when public interest organizations like the ACLU had to consider whether a coalition position was consistent with their own national policies. In other cases, local groups were internally divided or had unrealistic expectations; lawyers were more apt than lay partners to recognize that "just because there's a wrong, [it doesn't mean] there is necessarily a legal solution." Occasionally, the result was that coalition group members had to "agree to disagree." But again, most organizations seemed able to work through their differences when important issues were at stake.

Id. at 2066-67.

Collaborations among different public interest law groups occurred even more frequently, with 55 percent of groups reporting extensive collaboration and around 40 percent more indicating moderate collaboration. Groups reported formal and ongoing relationships through mechanisms such as planning networks, listservs, and regular meetings. Collaboration occurred among conservative groups as well as liberal ones, and in some cities networks were formed from all public interest organizations without regard to their substantive issue focus. *Id.* at 2067-68.

As with other forms of collaboration, these groups work together to pool their energy and resources and avoid duplicating efforts. In addition, the new perspectives sometimes offered by leaders of a different organization can lead to the reassessment of strategic priorities and directions. As Shannon Wilber of Legal Services for Children noted, " '[t]he danger with direct services is that you get so overwhelmed by the need. Collaboration gives opportunities to stand back and be reflective about larger issues. The least effective approach is to work in isolation pulling people out of the river one at a time.' " *Id.* at 2068.

On the downside, public interest groups reported a much higher incidence of conflict over turf and credit for work when collaborating with each other than in their work with other organizations.

> In explaining the frequency of these issues, Gen Fujioka of the Asian Law Caucus noted, "There are always problems of roles, responsibility, and credit, which relate to money and publicity." Often the problems are driven by funders, who want to see concrete payoffs for their investment. In many fields, organizations are competing for a limited pie from the same donors. Funders themselves occasionally recognize this difficulty. As the environmental director of the Nathan Cummings Foundation acknowledged, "We set [groups] up to compete rather than cooperate." Organizations that rely heavily on law firms, corporations, and individual donors also have to worry about publicity and about being seen as the "go to" group on particular issues. Even lawyers willing to take a low profile may have boards of directors that want greater recognition in the press.

Id. at 2068-69.

Somewhat less frequent, but still noticeable, conflicts arose over control of legal decisions and strategies. Leaders sometimes disagreed about substantive decisions, including when and whether to compromise. As discussed in Chapter 2, conflict also occurred around divisions between libertarian and social conservative groups. *Id.* at 2069.

Perhaps compounding issues over turf and control were clashes arising from individual lawyers' personalities.

> "Not everyone plays well with others," was the observation of several leaders; staff who were "very aggressive in positioning themselves" inevitably created tensions. As Public Advocates President Jamienne Studley also pointed out, because "so much of the reward [of public interest work] involves recognition," it is hard for lawyers not to care how credit is allocated. Yet despite "occasional friction," most organizations had developed workable strategies for dealing with these concerns. One was an "informal division of terrain"; groups tried to steer clear of each others' major donors and priority issues. Other approaches included joint development efforts, expansion of fundraising strategies, and explicit sharing of credit in public relations strategies. On the whole, the

> consensus seemed to be that turf-related tensions were "part of the cost of
> doing business," but that "most people . . . are adults about it."

Id.

Finally, there was substantial cooperation between public interest groups
and private law firms providing pro bono legal work. Around 80 percent of
groups reported extensive or moderate collaboration with the private bar.
Those groups that did not work with private firms tended to be smaller and
preferred to maintain control over their cases, or worked in such specialized
fields that expertise from lawyers in private practice was unlikely to be
prevalent. Most large national organizations focusing on impact litigation
drew substantial support from private firms. *Id.* at 2070.

> A few organizations, including the ACLU, the Electronic Frontier Foundation,
> the Lawyers Committee, and the New York Lawyers for the Public Interest,
> served a referral function. They investigated and screened cases to place with
> cooperating attorneys, while keeping some cases to handle on their own or to co-
> counsel with the private bar. Other organizations developed ongoing relation-
> ships with particular firms and relied on their pro bono assistance for litigation
> requiring substantial time and resources. The role of these volunteer lawyers
> varied considerably, depending on their expertise and availability. In some
> instances, they handled 90% of the work; in others, it was closer to 20%.

Id.

Although issues about taking credit for work were less common in pro bono
collaborations than with other alliances, issues did arise in some instances.

> Pro bono attorneys varied in their preferences. Occasionally they might not
> even want to be listed on a brief or would be "willing to give [the public interest
> organization] the limelight;" others had "very aggressive public relations
> departments." When problems arose, the reasons were usually straightforward.
> Public interest organizations "want our lawyers to take the lead. [Firms] want
> their lawyers to lead. Ours have expertise." The more prestigious the opportu-
> nity and the less experienced the pro bono lawyer, the more likely the diffi-
> culty; "individuals and institutions have egos." The press sometimes
> compounded the problem by ignoring one partner in the relationship.

Id. at 2070-71.

Public interest organization leaders attempted to address such conflicts by
clearly communicating their expectations with pro bono lawyers in advance
and by taking a flexible approach to allocating credit, depending on the type of
case the private lawyers were working on and the degree of their experience
and expertise. *Id.* at 2071.

With regard to issues of control, there seemed to be less frequent conflict
between public interest groups and the firms that worked with them. Although
on rare occasions a firm would take an extreme view and want to be in complete
control of decisions about strategy and substance, most groups were clear and
unbending in their desire to be the final decision maker in light of organizational priorities. *Id.*

Another consideration, at least for larger nonprofit groups, is the coordination of a centralized, national organization with local chapters, affiliates, or

other subdivisions that may operate somewhat independently. First, there is the issue of logistical coordination. Given the limited staff and resources of even the largest nonprofits, the national organization may not always be able to coordinate activities of the local sub-groups, particularly if the latter have legal staff and take their own cases. Second, there may be the same types of turf battles that affect coordination with outside groups. Lawyers within an organization, for example, might dispute who is going to be lead counsel at trial or present oral argument in an important appellate case. Third, depending on the amount of autonomy granted to the local groups by the national organization's charter, the local organizations may on occasion take a position adverse to that of the national organization. *See* Nadine Strossen, *In the Defense of Freedom and Equality: The American Civil Liberties Union Past, Present, and Future*, 29 Harv. C.R.-C.L. L. Rev. 143, 154-57 (1994). The adverse position can involve disagreement over strategic options. *See, e.g.*, Tushnet, *supra*, at 82-104. It can even manifest itself in a division over a substantive legal position. These issues can be exacerbated when the network of attorneys working on a matter extends beyond the organization's paid staff to private attorneys cooperating on a pro bono basis with the organization in conducting its legal work. Finally, there can be tensions between the national and local chapters of public interest organizations over fundraising, for which they may actually compete. *Id.* at 98-100 (noting that local campaign to raise money for litigation fund for LDF lawsuit undermined fundraising for local NAACP branches).

E. THE LAWYER-CLIENT RELATIONSHIP

All lawyers owe a duty of loyalty to their clients and must zealously advocate for their clients' best interests. In general, public interest practice can raise challenges for client representation. In the nonprofit context, the lawyers' ability to set agendas and control strategy may, in certain circumstances, make them more directive with their clients about decisions that are typically left to the clients' control. This may occur for multiple reasons. For instance, because of case load pressures or the power differential embedded in the representation of low-income clients, public interest lawyers may assume greater control in case decision making. Tensions may also arise when decisions that advance an organization's cause conflict with the best interests of the client. In turn, client commitment to a case and the broader cause may not always be sustainable. For example, NAACP lawyers had a difficult time keeping clients in some of their cases challenging segregation in higher education in the 1940s.

> [T]he university suits usually had a small number of plaintiffs. As the litigation dragged on, these plaintiffs were vulnerable. Economic pressures or the simple desire to get on with one's life made it hard to sustain the interest of individual plaintiffs, and in some instances lack of local support contributed to even greater disaffection.

Tushnet, *supra*, at 88. The practical and ethical issues related to these aspects of the public interest lawyer-client relationship are explored in more detail in Chapters 6 and 7.

III. THE GOVERNMENT SECTOR

As of 2000, about 8 percent of the nation's lawyers worked for some government entity. CLARA N. CARSON, THE LAWYER STATISTICAL REPORT: THE U.S. LEGAL PROFESSION IN 2000 6 (2004). Paid by taxpayer dollars, lawyers who work for federal, state, and local government departments and agencies might be considered, quite literally, as "public interest" lawyers. Their jobs are to represent the public at large. Yet these lawyers have more specific, identifiable clients, too. They represent government officials and government agencies. Do the interests of the public at large always coincide with the interests of the government?

In this section, we divide government lawyers into two general categories: those lawyers in government agencies and prosecutor offices who act on behalf of the state (by carrying out affirmative civil litigation or criminal prosecution for the government or by defending the government in civil litigation) and public defenders whose work places them in opposition to the state (by defending indigent defendants against government prosecution). In the first part of this section, we examine the ways in which government lawyers can advance the public interest both by affirmative litigation to advance policy reform and by defending the policy status quo from external legal attack. In this context, we explore whether, and in what circumstances, lawyers defending the government may have a broader ethical duty to represent the best interests of the public as well as their specific "clients." In the second part of this section, we look at the tradeoffs for lawyers in public defender offices who defend individual clients from prosecutions carried out by their government counterparts.

A. LAWYERING FOR THE STATE

Michael Pertschuk, chair of the Federal Trade Commission under President Carter, referred to the FTC as the largest liberal public interest law firm in the United States.

DAVID BRODER, CHANGING OF THE GUARD 227 (1980).

Some government lawyers work in positions that permit them to carry out an affirmative policy agenda and thus can sometimes resemble their professional counterparts in nonprofit organizations. The emergence of this role for government lawyers coincided with the rise of the regulatory and administrative state nearly a century ago. In particular, a pro-active social change role was forged by New Deal lawyers, who helped federal and state governments address the social problems associated with the Great Depression. Handler, Ginsberg & Snow, *supra*, at 45.

Perhaps the most widely recognized way for a lawyer to serve the public interest in the past was by working for the federal government. According to Charles Horsky, author of *The Washington Lawyer*, the focus on government service developed in the 1930's. At that time, the various state governments had in large measure been taken over by powerful, moneyed interests. Roosevelt convinced the public that there was a significant opportunity to effect economic, social, and political change through the federal government. Young lawyers flocked to Washington to "save the Union from the states." In the thirties,

Horsky reflects, "to join one of the federal administrative agencies was seen as a way of fighting the enemy; now it is more often perceived as just joining the club."

Note, *The New Public Interest Lawyers*, 79 YALE L.J. 1069, 1069 n.1 (1970); *see also* Handler, Ginsberg & Snow, *supra,* at 54.

Another important aspect of this role for government emerged in the late 1950s and early 1960s, when a significant number of young, talented lawyers joined the DOJ's Civil Rights Division. Handler, Ginsberg & Snow, *supra*. In the following decade, Jimmy Carter made an effort to build ties between the federal government and public interest law bar.

[P]ublic interest law firms' access to the executive branch was greatly expanded by President Jimmy Carter. According to David Broder, Carter was the first President "to recruit large numbers of public interest advocates into the executive branch." Examples of important Carter appointees drawn from the ranks of liberal public interest firms include Assistant Attorney General and Chief of the Civil Rights Division within the Department of Justice, Drew Days III, a former LDF attorney; Joan Claybrook, who headed the National Highway Traffic Safety Administration and formerly worked for Ralph Nader; and Joseph Onek, a former director of the Center for Law and Social Policy (CLSP) who worked on the White House Domestic Policy staff from 1977 to 1979.

Karen O'Connor, *Rebalancing the Scales of Justice: Assessment of Public Interest Law*, 7 HARV. J.L. & PUB. POL'Y 483, 492-93 (1984).

Government activism has not been limited to liberal administrations. President Reagan used his Justice Department to influence public policy and carry out a conservative agenda in important ways. For example, the DOJ under both President Reagan and President George H.W. Bush took the specific position in all abortion litigation that *Roe v. Wade* should be overruled. *See* Brief for the United States as Amicus Curiae in Support of Petitioners, *City of Akron v. Akron Ctr. for Reprod. Health, Inc.*, 462 U.S. 416 (1983) (No. 81-746); Brief for the United States as Amicus Curiae Supporting Respondents at 8, *Planned Parenthood of Se. Pa. v. Casey*, 505 U.S. 833 (1992) (Nos. 91-744 & 91-902). In addition, as discussed further below, the Reagan Administration chose not to actively enforce certain aspects of federal antitrust, environmental, and civil rights laws.

In addition to designing and enforcing law, government lawyers are often in the position of defending challenges to statutes, regulations, policies, and practices that are the current state of the law. In this posture, government lawyers defend the status quo. For example, when Colorado voters enacted Amendment 2, a sweeping anti-gay measure that was eventually struck down in *Romer v. Evans*, 517 U.S. 620 (1996), Colorado's Governor Roy Romer, who had opposed the ballot initiative, nonetheless pronounced that it was his duty, along with the state's attorney general, to defend the measure's constitutionality. Thaddeus Herrick, *Is Trust an Amendment 2 Value? Backers Challenge Governor's Resolve for Pursuing Appeal with Sufficient Vigor*, ROCKY MTN. NEWS, Feb. 8, 1994, at 6A. Because government lawyers in this position act from a responsive posture, they do not generally set their own agendas. Yet, in some contexts, this type of defensive lawyering is key to advancing important public policy initiatives. For instance, the defense of an administration's political agenda may be a crucial part of a larger, systematic law reform effort. Even apart from such coordinated efforts, government lawyers may advance causes through the manner in which they conduct themselves in defensive cases that have larger public significance.

1. Resources

Unlike public interest lawyers in the nonprofit setting, government lawyers do not have to raise money from multiple philanthropic sources and, unlike their private sector counterparts, government lawyers do not have to rely on client fee generation. This allows government lawyers to take on cases based on intrinsic merit and public impact without considering these external constraints; however, the tradeoff is that government lawyers operate in deeply political environments in which the expansion or contraction of resources depends on the degree of political support for the lawyers' work and on overall budgetary conditions. Thus, resources for government lawyering can vary across multiple dimensions, including the type of departmental work, where it is located (federal, state, or local), and the political sympathies of those in charge.

Resources for government lawyering can depend significantly on the level and scope of a government's legal department. Some departments are well funded. At the federal level, the DOJ has numerous lawyers in many different divisions, while other cabinet departments and regulatory agencies have lawyers working to carry out their own agendas. The federal government has substantial resources to devote to legal work, including that which seeks to effectuate social change. *See, e.g.*, Philip Elman & Norman Silber, *The Solicitor General's Office, Justice Frankfurter, and Civil Rights Litigation, 1946-1960: An Oral History*, 100 HARV. L. REV. 817, 833-34 (1987) (noting that DOJ was able to assign five or six lawyers solely to research the legislative history of the Fourteenth Amendment during the briefing for *Brown v. Board of Education*). In addition, government lawyers are able to undertake their social change efforts without the pressure of worrying about the profitability of their legal work. At the state and local level, there is often greater variance in the resources available for carrying out the functions of legal departments. In times of economic crisis and fiscal austerity, resources can dry up, undercutting or even in extreme cases eliminating certain types of enforcement activities. *See, e.g.*, Steven W. Bender, *Oregon Consumer Protection: Outfitting Private Attorneys General for the Lean Years Ahead*, 73 OR. L. REV. 639, 643-44 (1994) (discussing how budget cuts limited the state justice department's ability to enforce consumer protection laws and caused every local district attorney to eliminate its consumer protection unit at the same time that complaints about consumer law violations were increasing).

Even where funding is available to support government lawyers, it is always subject to the constraints of politics. Resources for government lawyering are deeply contingent on the political support of the administration in charge. Political control over government legal departments operates in different ways. Politicians can cut budgets, set different priorities, and change staff. For example, during Ronald Reagan's presidency, the conservative government used its control of the budget to curtail funding for federal enforcement of civil rights protection and antitrust law. U.S. Commission on Civil Rights, Funding Federal Civil Rights Enforcement 71 (1995) (describing 1983 fiscal year budget request for civil rights enforcement as a low point and concluding that "both the President and the Congress have retreated from their obligation to ensure that adequate resources are provided for civil rights enforcement"); William E. Kovacic, *The Modern Evolution of U.S. Competition Policy Enforcement Norms*, 71 Antitrust L.J. 377, 397 n.69 (2003) (noting federal budget for antitrust enforcement cut by roughly half). With regard to environmental regulation, the Reagan Administration cut the budget for the Environmental Protection Agency and also imposed oversight of the EPA by the Office of Management and Budget to assess the cost of environmental regulation on businesses. Robert V. Percival, *Checks Without Balance: Executive Office Oversight of the Environmental Protection Agency*, 54 Law & Contemp. Probs. 127, 174-75, 186-87 (1991); *see also* Stephen Fotis, Comment, *Private Enforcement of the Clean Air Act and the Clean Water Act*, 35 Am. U. L. Rev. 127, 130 n.15 (1985) (noting EPA budget cut by a third).

An administration's power over personnel resources also allows it to influence policy through its appointments to key positions. In some offices, like the DOJ, there are "political" and "career" legal positions; political appointees set and implement policy and are subject to change when new administrations take power. However, there are different norms regarding when political appointees should be removed. Some, like United States Attorneys in charge of prosecuting federal crime, are viewed as more independent and less directly under the influence of executive control. Attempts to influence their judgment through the appointment process can generate controversy. A high profile example was President George W. Bush's removal of several U.S. Attorneys, reportedly in part for their lack of "loyalty" to the President and resistance to administration initiatives. David Johnston & Eric Lipton, *"Loyalty" to Bush and Gonzales Was Factor in Prosecutors' Firings, E-Mail Shows*, N.Y. Times, Mar. 14, 2007, at A18. A career attorney is not typically subject to removal because of political transitions, but may find conditions intolerable when a new administration dramatically changes the mission of an agency for which a career attorney works. For instance, many career attorneys in the DOJ Civil Rights Division left out of frustration with the lack of enforcement under President George W. Bush.

Resource issues for government defense lawyers are not systematically different from those for government lawyers who have a pro-active social agenda. There are taxpayer dollars available to defend government action; the main issue is how political considerations influence their use.

2. Agenda Setting Ability

To a large extent, the agendas of government lawyers originate from the will of elected officials, who may set affirmative and defensive agendas. In some instances, the executive branch may take the lead. One widely examined example is the coordinated effort of the DOJ during Franklin Roosevelt's presidency to work with the President and Congress to establish radically new economic recovery programs and defend them in court. This effort required lawyers to seek changes in federal constitutional doctrine to recognize broader discretion for Congress to enact laws that advanced the growth of interstate commerce. PETER H. IRONS, THE NEW DEAL LAWYERS (1982). Legislatures may also identify a problem and create a special unit or project for the government's attorneys to undertake. For example, Congress enacted the Civil Rights for Institutionalized Persons Act of 1980, which authorized the DOJ to bring civil rights suits against mental health institutions and prisons (though it has been more vigorous about pursuing the former). Charles F. Sabel & William H. Simon, *Destabilization Rights: How Public Law Litigation Succeeds*, 117 HARV. L. REV. 1015, 1029 (2004). Or sometimes the agendas might derive from the work of government commissions or studies that identify a pressing social need. *See, e.g.,* Elman & Silber, *supra*, at 817-18 (describing how the report of President Truman's Committee on Civil Rights spurred the DOJ to become more actively involved in litigation concerning race discrimination).

In general, government lawyers are asked to implement policy dictated from above. Their ability to promote social goals is therefore influenced in large part by how government officials prioritize the allocation of resources for the enforcement, or non-enforcement, of specific laws and policies. For example, an administration may decide to make it a priority to enforce federal fair housing laws on behalf of individuals claiming discrimination. Eugene R. Gaetke & Robert G. Schwemm, *Government Lawyers and Their Private "Clients" Under the Fair Housing Act*, 65 GEO. WASH. L. REV. 329, 336-37 (1997); *but see* Michael Selmi, *Public v. Private Enforcement of Civil Rights: The Case of Housing and Employment*, 45 UCLA L. REV. 1401 (1998) (suggesting that federal government lawyers have lagged behind private lawyers in bringing fair housing and employment discrimination claims). Conversely, an administration may decide to influence a policy area through deliberate non-enforcement. As suggested earlier, during the Reagan Administration, the President and his highest level officials consciously and publicly declared that the federal government would not enforce certain provisions of federal antitrust law, particularly restrictions on mergers and monopolies. Kovacic, *supra*, at 385-86. As another example, the Reagan Administration failed to file any new claims to enforce Section 2 of the federal Voting Rights Act. Anthony Q. Fletcher, Book Review, 32 HARV. J. ON LEGIS. 301 (1995) (reviewing LANI GUINIER, THE TYRANNY OF THE MAJORITY: FUNDAMENTAL FAIRNESS IN REPRESENTATIVE DEMOCRACY (1994)).

In some contexts, government lawyers may have significant autonomy to develop their own agendas. This is particularly true when government lawyers are elected and enter office with a popular mandate. For example, in states where voters elect the state's attorney general, such officials can have a fair amount of control over how they employ their resources to enforce the state's laws and regulations, and engage the state legislature to advance legislative reforms. New York Attorneys General Eliot Spitzer and Andrew Cuomo made names for themselves actively policing illegal Wall Street practices—and did so against the backdrop of relative inaction by federal enforcement agencies. In 2012, California Attorney General Kamila Harris gained national attention by helping to negotiate a $26 billion nationwide settlement with banks to help homeowners facing foreclosure. Nelson D. Schwartz & Shaila Dewan, *$26 Billion Deal Is Said to Be Set for Homeowners*, N.Y. TIMES, Feb. 8, 2012, at A1.

Similarly, the heads of county and city legal departments may, depending on the structure of the local government, have authority to develop priorities for their agendas. Staff attorneys in government offices do not have the same power as their elected bosses, but sometimes are given discretion to craft specific aspects of strategies that advance an elected official's broader agenda.

In addition to pursuing social change through affirmative litigation, governments and their lawyers frequently participate in cases as amicus curiae, submitting briefs to advocate positions on important public law matters. In this context, government lawyers are not actively shaping an agenda, but can use their official positions to try to influence the courts in cases involving other parties. As is true with other public interest organizations, government lawyers' participation as amici in litigation is comparatively less costly than direct litigation, though it also results in less control over the litigation of the case.

Government lawyers are also called to court, along with their clients, to provide a legal defense to all manner of challenges. This position is typically unsuited to agenda setting. But government lawyers may anticipate challenges to newly enacted laws that might draw significant challenges (sometimes from other public interest lawyers). For example, in the wake of the Supreme Court's decision in *District of Columbia v. Heller*, 554 U.S. 570 (2008), state and local governments could expect and plan for an increase in challenges to laws regulating the ownership and use of guns. *See* Robert Barnes, *Cases Piling Up Seeking Supreme Court's Clarification of Second Amendment Rights*, Wash. Post, Aug. 15, 2011, at A15. Similarly, government lawyers anticipated, planned for, and successfully defended the federal health care law recently upheld by the Supreme Court. *National Federation of Independent Business v. Sebelius*, __ U.S. __, 132 S. Ct. 2566 (2012).

One interesting way that government lawyers may attempt to influence agendas is by *declining* to defend laws that they believe are illegal, unjust, or against the popular will. Just as the government lawyers responsible for enforcing a law can choose not to bring enforcement actions, government lawyers opposed to a current law may decide not to defend it against outside legal challenge. This occurred in California, where then-Attorney General Jerry Brown refused to defend Proposition 8—a statewide ballot initiative outlawing same-sex marriage—against a constitutional challenge brought by private lawyers Ted Olson and David Boies. In their absence, Christian Right legal groups were allowed by the court to intervene to defend the law, and were found to have standing to do so. *Perry v. Brown*, 265 P.3d 1002 (Cal. 2011). Another recent example of agenda setting by nonenforcement is the Obama Administration's decision to no longer defend the Defense of Marriage Act in federal litigation. Adam Liptak, *The President's Courthouse*, N.Y. Times, Feb. 27, 2011, at WK5.

3. Control Over Legal Strategies

Once an agenda is established, how much control do government lawyers have in the strategies used in its pursuit? When part of an overall plan, government lawyers may develop highly sophisticated, technical legal strategies to achieve their goals. The following excerpt from Peter Irons's study of the New Deal federal agency lawyers shows the careful planning by lawyers for the National Labor Relations Board in enforcing the law's provisions and establishing a foundation for the defense of its constitutionality—a strategy that culminated in the Supreme Court's decision in *NLRB v. Jones & Laughlin Steel Corp.*, 301 U.S. 1 (1937).

> The NLRB "master plan" recognized that: selection of test cases would be dictated by commerce clause issues. There was little question, the memo's authors felt, that "relations between an employer and those of his employees actually engaged 'in interstate commerce' (e.g., engaged in selling or transporting goods across state lines) ordinarily are subject to regulation." It was likely, however, that most NLRB cases would arise not in classic "interstate commerce" industries but in those based on manufacturing, mining, or processing, which required confrontation with the body of Supreme Court precedent holding that manufacturing and commerce were distinct. . . .
>
> [T]he Board lawyers were thinking in terms of preparing cases to be presented in sequence to the Supreme Court, with the strongest cases first. Consequently, the memo's authors recommended a two-stage strategy: "Once the authority of the Board has been established by the Supreme Court with respect to these industries, the Board should bring cases to test the extent of its authority with respect to other situations." Included in this second round would be those industries in which goods flowed into but not out of the state of manufacture. Additionally, they saw little hope of success "at least for the indefinite future" in such areas as service trades, amusements, and intrastate transportation. Finally, they recommended that industries "with a long record of industrial unrest are preferable to those in which there have been few strikes or other disturbances." Under this criterion, coal, steel, textiles, and the garment industry were the leading candidates. . . .
>
> Dominated by the commerce clause question, litigation strategy planning focused on the nature of the industry; but [the NLRB lawyers] also paid attention to which category of unfair labor practices would present the best test case. . . .
>
> It would be hard to overestimate the importance of this initial plan for an overall litigation strategy. . . . [I]t showed keen insight into the psychological dimension of litigation—which cases would involve the most "flagrant" violators and the most compelling victims; which would most appeal to the sense of fairness of the judges; and which would most easily fit into the certainty of existing law. And, most important, it gave a clear guide to NLRB lawyers in sifting through their massive case loads in search of ideal test cases, charting a clear path from the picket line to the Supreme Court.

Irons, *supra,* at 241-43.

Government lawyers can do much more than engage in litigation. Irons's study describes the New Deal agency lawyers' engagement in not only litigating to defend the Roosevelt Administration's economic recovery programs, but also in drafting legislation, writing regulations, participating in enforcement proceedings, advising policy makers, and negotiating with those who were affected by their agencies' functions. Irons, *supra,* at 10. Federal attorneys sometimes conduct investigations and issue reports concerning civil rights violations relating to state or local government institutions. *See, e.g.,* Monica

Davey, *Federal Report Finds Poor Conditions at Cook County Jail*, N.Y. TIMES, July 18, 2008, at A12 (describing extensive investigation of local jail by DOJ's Civil Rights Division and U.S. Attorney's office concluding that jail had "systematically violated the constitutional rights of inmates"). In the case of conditions affecting institutionalized persons, federal officials can negotiate with local officials to correct problems identified by such investigations and federal attorneys can also bring enforcement actions pursuant to 42 U.S.C. §1997a (providing for courts to grant equitable relief to require compliance with the Constitution). Depending on whether there are statutory or regulatory constraints on the types of activities particular government lawyers can undertake, they may also pursue other strategies, such as public education and lobbying of legislatures and administrative rule makers.

In defending civil litigation, government lawyers can face pressures that complicate their public mission. Daniel Jacobs identifies five institutional factors that influence how government lawyers perceive their role in defending against lawsuits and argues that these factors push them in a defensive posture that inhibits resolution of cases to promote the public interest. Daniel S. Jacobs, *The Role of the Federal Government in Defending Public Interest Litigation*, 44 SANTA CLARA L. REV. 1, 43-48 (2003). First, government law offices have institutional pressure to "win" their cases, and this cultural value is passed onto their lawyers. *Id.* at 44. Second, government agencies do not face the same direct consequences from losing litigation as do private parties. "Because a government agency therefore has less of a monetary incentive to resolve a case than a private-party litigant, the government may well be more inclined to defend a public interest suit even when resolving it would benefit the public at large." *Id.* at 45. Third, there is often a culture within government agencies that favors vindication of their actions, and "key government players in a case may well not interpret their role to include a candid assessment of the merits of the case. . . ." *Id.* Fourth, it may not be clear who the government lawyer represents. "[A] government legal team might adopt the program or individuals directly implicated in a given suit that it defends as essentially its 'client(s).' The legal team might then operate under the assumption that its primary role is to serve the perceived interests of these client(s) above other interests." *Id.* at 46. This can result in the adoption of the agency's bias toward protecting the status quo. *Id.* Finally, institutional factors place the government on the defensive when a lawsuit is filed against it. Cases are typically first assigned to a trial level government attorney who views her job as answering or moving to dismiss, a process Jacobs argues "is not particularly conducive to identification of the potentially meritorious case." *Id.* at 47-48. "As a result of all of these factors, a meritorious public interest lawsuit that in and of itself stimulates reform of a government program, policy, or action is likely to be the exception, not the rule. Rather, the filing of such a lawsuit is more likely to trigger only a defense, and often a spirited one at that, even if ill-deserved." *Id.* at 48.

Jacobs proposes several institutional reforms that would enhance government lawyers' incentives to settle meritorious public interest litigation. Among the things that he suggests are increasing the government's accountability by amending federal attorneys' fees legislation to require federal agencies that are sued to pay fee awards in litigation from their own budgets rather than from a central judgment fund, increasing congressional oversight over agency litigation costs, enforcing Executive branch measures designed to minimize litigation costs and encourage settlements, and engaging in rigorous review (including independent review by DOJ lawyers in addition to the agency's lawyers) of high impact cases at the front end to evaluate the merits of the case and the possibility of early resolution through negotiation. *Id.* at 48-54.

Do you think the pressure on government lawyers to defend their clients is sometimes in conflict with the public interest? Considering the factors Jacobs identifies, are government lawyers less likely to settle meritorious cases than private lawyers? Are the proposals for changing their incentives likely to make a difference?

4. Coordination and Coalition Building

There is historical precedent for the government working closely with non-governmental organizations in developing and carrying out social change agendas. During the civil rights movement, lawyers with the DOJ worked closely with the NAACP LDF in coordinating a legal strategy to challenge racial segregation laws. Elman & Silber, *supra.* One high level DOJ attorney even coordinated a letter writing campaign with private groups to pressure decision makers within the Department to get involved in the major civil rights era case of *Shelley v. Kraemer.*

> I had friends working with the NAACP, the American Civil Liberties Union, the American Jewish Congress, the American Jewish Committee, and other organizations. [We] got them to write letters to the President and Attorney General urging the government to intervene in the Supreme Court. All of these letters eventually came to me. I don't remember how many of them there were, but it was a large, impressive number. . . . These letters all came pouring in, and as each came in I would show it to the Solicitor General, Philip Perlman. I then wrote a formal memorandum recommending that the United States file an amicus brief.

Id. at 818. Other examples of government attorney collaboration with private lawyers and attorneys from nonprofit organizations are described in Chapter 2 and Chapter 3, including the work of Louis Brandeis to defend New Deal era legislation and the work of conservative morality groups supporting prosecuting attorneys enforcing obscenity laws.

A more contemporary example of collaboration occurred in Los Angeles, where a coalition of labor and community organizations formed the Los Angeles Worker Advocates Coalition in 2002. Susan Garea & Sasha Alexandra Stern, *From Legal Advocacy to Organizing: Progressive Lawyering and the Los Angeles Car Wash Campaign, in* WORKING FOR JUSTICE: THE L.A. MODEL OF ORGANIZING AND ADVOCACY 125 (Ruth Milkman et al. eds., 2010). The group launched the Community-Labor-Environmental Action Network (CLEAN) campaign in 2008, seeking to improve conditions in the car wash industry, in which labor exploitation was rampant. Although CLEAN succeeded in advocating for a statewide car wash law mandating fair labor treatment, legal enforcement remained a significant problem. To address it, CLEAN advocates coordinated their efforts with the Los Angeles City Attorney's Office, which agreed to prosecute car wash owners for egregious nonpayment of wages. Sam Quinones, *Carwash Workers Celebrate Union Pact*, L.A. Times, Oct. 26, 2011, at 1. In 2009, the city successfully sued the owners of Vermont Hand Wash in Hollywood, who were sentenced to a year in jail and made to repay workers. CLEAN activists then persuaded the Attorney General to seek $6 million in back wages, fines, and penalties from Bonus Car Wash in Santa Monica. To resolve the suit, the car wash agreed to recognize the union representing its workers and to provide a 2 percent raise, as well as a procedure for worker grievances. *Id.*

Despite the success of some collaborations, tensions may exist when multiple players are involved in advocacy efforts. As when nonprofit groups collaborate, there can be difficult issues concerning control of the cases and strategy decisions. A related concern may arise if there are doubts about who bears the ultimate responsibility and accountability for decisions. Lawyers working in these situations need to be conscious of the potential for serious disagreement about important decisions, and how they will be resolved. For example, drawing again on the civil-rights-era DOJ, when the desegregation battle reached a certain point, NAACP lawyers wanted to take a much more aggressive stance whereas Justice Department lawyers wanted to continue a more gradualist strategy. Elman & Silber, *supra*, at 830. This manifested itself in both the desegregation litigation and in the decision about whether, and when, to challenge the constitutionality of anti-miscegenation laws. *Id.* at 830, 846.

Moreover, for many of the same reasons that nonprofit organizations seek to claim credit for advances, government lawyers may also sometimes seek such credit for their own political and professional benefit. This can manifest itself in uncomfortable ways. For example, in an oral history of DOJ's role in the desegregation cases, Philip Elman, an attorney in the U.S. Solicitor General's office, claimed that the Justice Department was the first entity to initiate a wholesale challenge to the constitutionality of de jure segregation. *Id.* at 821. Elman also questioned the decisions made by the NAACP LDF during this era, describing LDF's strategies as poorly conceived and badly implemented because they "'made the wrong arguments at the wrong time in the wrong case.'" *Id.* at 837. He even disputed the significance of Thurgood Marshall's role in arguing *Brown v. Board of Education* before the Supreme Court, claiming that "nothing that the lawyers said made a difference. Thurgood Marshall could have stood up there and recited 'Mary had a little lamb,' and the result would have been exactly the same." *Id.* at 852.

There are, however, many other instances of generosity and mutual support between government lawyers and their nonprofit counterparts. As the following excerpt from the same DOJ oral history suggests, working for social change can not just foster collaborations but be a transformative experience for government lawyers.

> [W]e filed the brief [in *Shelley v. Kraemer*, the case in which the Supreme Court declared that state courts' enforcement of racially restrictive covenants

violated the Fourteenth Amendment] and [United States Solicitor General Philip] Perlman argued for the United States as amicus curiae. . . . He argued in a courtroom full of blacks, and he was very moved by the whole experience. It was a transforming experience for Perlman, a lawyer from Baltimore, a southern city where racial segregation and discrimination were commonplace. People like Walter White of the NAACP called on him to express their profound gratitude for what the Department of Justice had done. I think it changed Perlman entirely. He couldn't wait to go back to the Supreme Court again and again, arguing for equality, for liberty, for decency. He loved it. And it was a good thing for the United States that he did.

Id. at 820.

While collaboration with nongovernmental lawyers seems less likely as an issue in the context of government defense work, it does on occasion occur. When there are issues of great public import at stake, a range of nongovernmental groups may intervene or participate as amici in defense of government policy, sometimes with the government's consent or invitation. An example can be drawn from the University of Michigan's defense of its affirmative action programs at issue in *Grutter v. Bollinger*, 539 U.S. 306 (2003), and *Gratz v. Bollinger*, 539 U.S. 244 (2003). The government's successful defense of the university's law school admissions program benefited substantially from the close coordination of a record number of amicus briefs from the fields of law, education, business, and the military. *See* Jonathan Alger & Marvin Krislov, *You've Got to Have Friends: Lessons Learned from the Role of Amici in the University of Michigan Cases*, 30 J.C. & U.L. 503, 528 (2004). In an example from the local level, the Los Angeles City Attorney's Office worked closely with outside labor and community groups to craft — and then protect against legal challenge by business groups — an extension of Los Angeles's living wage law that applied to hotels around the Los Angeles International Airport. *See* Steve Hymon, *L.A. Living Wage Law Is Upheld*, L.A. TIMES, Dec. 28, 2007, at B1.

5. The Lawyer-Client Relationship

Complications for government lawyers may sometimes arise when it is unclear whose interests they represent. First, for lawyers working on the staffs of federal agencies, it is not always easy to identify the "client." Is it the agency itself? The heads of the agency? The federal government? One model suggests that agency lawyers should view themselves as if they were private lawyers representing an institutional client, and that their duties of loyalty, confidentiality, and zealous representation are all owed only to the agency. Note, *Rethinking the Professional Responsibilities of Federal Agency Lawyers*, 115 HARV. L. REV. 1170, 1173-76 (2002). A conflicting model, however, argues that although agency lawyers represent agencies, they ought to also have the interests of the public in mind in carrying out their representation. *Id.* at 1176-77. One common critique of the latter approach is that it may not always be clear to the agency what course of action is in the public interest. *Id.* at 1177.

An important example of this confusion about government attorneys' relationship with their clients arises out of the controversy surrounding the role of the U.S. President's Office of Legal Counsel (OLC). The OLC is made up of a group of elite lawyers whose duty is to provide legal advice to the President and other members of the Executive branch. DEBORAH L. RHODE & DAVID LUBAN, LEGAL ETHICS 545 (5th ed. 2009). During the Administration of George W. Bush, OLC head Jay S. Bybee issued the so-called torture memo (authored by OLC attorney John Yoo), which provided a legal analysis concluding that extreme interrogation tactics widely considered to be torture did not violate international or U.S. law. *Id.* at 548-50. While there is a divisive debate about the Bybee-Yoo memo on legal and moral grounds, the controversy also resurrected previously debated questions about the proper role of OLC lawyers. Some maintain that, as government lawyers, OLC staff should provide disinterested legal advice to the President with a view to the broader public good. *See* Cornelia T.L. Pillard, *The Unfulfilled Promise of the Constitution in Executive Hands*, 103 MICH. L. REV. 676, 726-28 (2005). Others defended Yoo's actions as falling within the bounds of ordinary attorney-client counseling and rejected the claims of those who argued that OLC had a public duty to give disinterested advice as "providing a sentimental, distorted and self-serving picture of a complex reality." *See* Eric Posner & Adrian Vermeule, *A "Torture" Memo and Its Tortuous Critics*, WALL ST. J., July 6, 2004, at A22. The fact that the role of lawyers as counselors, rather than advocates in a public proceeding, is hidden from public view makes these issues even more important, as lawyers in such positions may not be accountable for their actions. Which of these roles do you think OLC staff lawyers should properly assume? Why?

Lawyer-client relationship and ethical concerns also can arise in certain hybrid contexts in which government lawyers bring enforcement claims on behalf of private clients, with the dual interest of gaining relief for the client and vindicating the government's interest in compliance with the law. Potential conflicts in such cases raise important questions about who the government attorneys' client is, and to whom these attorneys owe their duty of loyalty. For example, under federal fair housing law, government lawyers from the DOJ and the Department of Housing and Urban Development (HUD) are authorized to file housing discrimination claims on behalf of private persons who have been the victims of discrimination in the sale or rental of housing. Gaetke & Schwemm, *supra*, at 336-37. Where there is a plausible claim of discrimination, HUD lawyers may file claims in administrative proceedings on behalf of individual victims, but where either the complaining party or the respondent elects, the case goes to federal court, where the complainant is represented by DOJ lawyers. Tensions can arise, however, where the interests of the private "client" and the government agency diverge. For example, government lawyers may disagree with the complainant about the wisdom of appealing an adverse ruling, perhaps because the lawyers are not confident about their position. *Id.* at 345-46. Moreover, as repeat players, government lawyers might want to pursue certain courses of action with which the complainant disagrees if the lawyers believe that choice will establish a precedent favorable to the government's interests in future litigation (or, conversely, the government lawyers might want to avoid a course of action that might set a bad precedent). *Id.* at 349-51.

More unusual tensions can arise. In one case, a fair housing complainant being represented by HUD lawyers in an agency proceeding lost before an administrative law judge and wanted to appeal the adverse ruling. *Id.* at 348. The HUD lawyers felt they did not have the authority to appeal beyond the internal procedural setting of their agency, so they withdrew from the case. *Id.* After the complainant retained private counsel to represent her on appeal, DOJ attorneys entered the case to represent the agency in defending the appeal. *Id.* "Thus, within the same FHAA matter, [the complainant] was represented by government lawyers from HUD, abandoned by those same lawyers, and directly opposed in her appeal by other government lawyers from the DOJ." *Id.* at 348. Does this situation put government lawyers at odds with their private clients' interests? With their loyalty to the agency that employs them?

As in the context of affirmative governmental lawyering (and as suggested in the article by Daniel Jacobs above), government defense raises issues about the nature of the client and the duties owed — particularly whether the government lawyer has a higher public duty than conventional lawyers. These issues are explored in detail as part of our public interest legal ethics analysis in Chapter 7.

B. LAWYERING AGAINST THE STATE

What are the responsibilities of public defenders, who are also government lawyers, yet at the same time adversaries of the state? And how do their practice sites influence their public interest roles?[2]

1. Resources

Although indigent criminal defense, at least for felony offenses, is constitutionally guaranteed, *Gideon v. Wainwright*, 372 U.S. 335, 342-43 (1963), one of the biggest challenges to the public defender system has always been insufficient resources. Kim Taylor-Thomson articulates the problem:

> Spurred in part by rising crime rates that ignited the fears of the electorate, legislators had license to impose stiffer controls in the fight against crime. The Reagan and Bush administrations waged war against crime and legislated policies defenders often described as Zero Tolerance for criminal defendants and their lawyers. Moreover, this anticrime tide swept resources away from criminal defense and into law enforcement coffers. Not only did prosecutors reap the benefits of this attitudinal shift, but they gained new and improved weapons in their fight against crime: mandatory minimum penalties, sentencing guidelines at both the state and federal levels, and preventive detention schemes that increased prosecutorial discretion in charging and sentencing.
>
> Public defender budgets, in contrast, suffered crippling blows from the government's fiscal axe. Because public defender offices represent a constituency composed of the unpopular, often dangerous members of our society who could neither vote nor wield power in traditional political ways, funding authorities drastically cut public defender budgets without fear of electoral

---

2. This section discusses only the practice of government-funded public defenders. Different institutional pressures may affect the large number of private attorneys who are appointed to represent indigents in a pro bono capacity or defenders working in community-based practices.

repercussions. At the same time, because of an escalation in arrests and subsequent prosecutions, cases began to flood the criminal justice system. As costs billed by members of the appointed defense bar began to skyrocket, state and local governments and courts turned increasingly toward public defender offices, expecting defenders to handle additional cases within a newly circumscribed and inadequate budget. Denied sufficient funding to hire additional lawyers, and often subjected to hiring freezes that meant that lawyers who left the office could not be replaced, public defender offices simply operated on overload.

Kim Taylor-Thompson, *Individual Actor v. Institutional Player: Alternating Visions of the Public Defender*, 84 GEO. L.J. 2419, 2430-31 (1996) [hereinafter, Taylor-Thompson, *Alternating Visions*]. Resource constraints limit indigent criminal defense across the board, affecting public defender salaries, budgets for expert witnesses, investigative services, support staff, and training. *See* AMERICAN BAR ASSOCIATION STANDING COMMITTEE ON LEGAL AID & INDIGENT DEFENDANTS, *GIDEON'S BROKEN PROMISE: AMERICA'S CONTINUING QUEST FOR EQUAL JUSTICE* 7-26 (2004). Fiscal constraints have been exacerbated by the recent financial crisis. *See* Heather Baxter, Gideon*'s Ghost: Providing the Sixth Amendment Right to Counsel in Times of Budgetary Crisis*, 2010 MICH. ST. L. REV. 341 (2010).

The funding problem arises acutely in the context of capital defense. For many years, those who have studied capital litigation in the state criminal justice system have called for greater resources for capital defense work. *See, e.g.,* ABA TASK FORCE ON DEATH PENALTY HABEAS CORPUS, TOWARD A MORE JUST AND EFFECTIVE SYSTEM OF REVIEW IN STATE DEATH PENALTY CASES, A REPORT CONTAINING THE AMERICAN BAR ASSOCIATION'S RECOMMENDATIONS CONCERNING DEATH PENALTY HABEAS CORPUS AND RELATED MATERIALS FROM THE AMERICAN BAR ASSOCIATION CRIMINAL JUSTICE SECTION'S PROJECT ON DEATH PENALTY HABEAS CORPUS 16 (1990). Observers have suggested that more resources would reduce the number of errors made in capital trials and provide more opportunities for capital defendants to have legitimate claims heard. At the same time, opponents of more funding for capital defense have complained that more resources are likely only to facilitate long delays in the administration of the death penalty. *See* Roscoe C. Howard, Jr., *The Defunding of the Post Conviction Defense Organizations as a Denial of the Right to Counsel*, 98 W. VA. L. REV. 863, 912-14 (1996). At one point, the federal judiciary sought to alleviate the problem by invoking its powers under the Criminal Justice Act, 18 U.S.C. §3006(A)(g)(2)(B), to establish 20 post-conviction defender organizations to provide representation to capital defendants in both state post-conviction proceedings and federal habeas litigation. These organizations, known as Resource Centers, ably handled much capital defense representation in post-conviction proceedings and had a substantial level of expertise and experience on their staffs. Randall Coyne & Lyn Entzeroth, *Report Regarding Implementation of the American Bar Association's Recommendations and Resolutions Concerning the Death Penalty and Calling for a Moratorium on Executions*, 4 GEO. J. ON FIGHTING POVERTY 3, 21-22 (1996). The centers were widely lauded by federal and state judges and by the organized bar as an effective way of providing competent representation. *Id.* In 1996, however, Congress defunded all of the Resource Centers, in part as a response to pressure from those who viewed the centers as obstructionist. Howard, *supra*, at 914-15.

2. Agenda Setting Ability

Like many legal aid lawyers, public defenders are often focused on individual client representation and therefore might not naturally be considered to have much room for agenda setting or long-range strategic planning about criminal justice issues. In fact, however, public defender offices have often paid close attention to larger issues affecting indigent criminal defendants. Charles J. Olgetree & Randy Hertz, *The Ethical Dilemmas of Public Defenders in Impact Litigation,* 14 N.Y.U. REV. L. & SOC. CHANGE 23 (1986). As Taylor-Thompson observes, "As the Warren Court era ended, the climate in which defender offices operated abruptly changed, forcing defenders to take greater notice of larger issues rather than concentrating on the representation of individual clients. . . . Having lost many procedural and substantive tactical options made available through the Warren Court decisions, public defenders needed to explore and experiment with new styles of defense." Taylor-Thompson, *Alternating Visions, supra,* at 2429-30.

In this context, many defenders have embraced a more proactive role. Kim Taylor-Thompson, *Tuning Up Gideon's Trumpet,* 71 FORDHAM L. REV. 1461, 1486-87 (2003). For example, some offices have pursued affirmative legislative agendas, become engaged in community activism to address local criminal justice issues, and taken on national leadership roles to address criminal justice policy at a broader level. *Id.* In an example outside of the public defender setting that nonetheless highlights the possibility of impact-oriented defense work, Ingrid Eagly describes her law school clinic's representation of *loncheros,* local ethnic food truck vendors, after the City of Los Angeles began strictly enforcing an ordinance restricting how long they could park in one space. Ingrid V. Eagly, *Criminal Clinics in the Pursuit of Immigrant Rights: Lessons from the* Loncheros, 2 U.C. IRVINE L. REV. 91 (2012). Although the clinic students defended a *lonchero* in an individual enforcement action by the City, they also took on a broader role, coordinating closely with local community organizers to challenge the ordinance and to address concerns about its impact on immigrant workers in particular. *Id.* at 109. Eagly also catalogues historical examples — from the work of Charles Hamilton Houston to Fred Gray (Rosa Parks's counsel) to William Kunstler — to illustrate that cause lawyering and individual criminal defense work can be a collaborative enterprise that achieves both social change and client representation goals. *Id.* at 110-12; *see also* Margareth Etienne, *The Ethics of Cause Lawyering: An Empirical Examination of Criminal Defense Lawyers as Cause Lawyers,* 95 J. CRIM. L. & CRIMINOLOGY 1195 (2005).

3. Control Over Legal Strategies

During the Progressive era, public defenders were envisioned as having a limited role in advocating for their clients. Their duty was to protect the innocent and enter pleas for the guilty, not to zealously advocate for their client's defense in all circumstances. Barbara Allen Babcock, *Inventing the Public Defender,* 43 AM. CRIM. L. REV. 1267, 1274-75 (2006). The modern public defender's role is more widely conceived of as checking the substantial power of the state and facilitating the adversarial model of justice. This has given public defenders more autonomy over their choice of legal strategies, at least within the framework of criminal defense litigation. At the same time, limited resources make it challenging to provide an adequate defense to each client and often constrain the type of legal strategies that defenders may employ.

Moreover, public defenders may grow frustrated at the inability of individual representation to affect the larger socioeconomic forces — poverty, the lack of good jobs, inadequate housing, poor schools, racism, and other types of inequality — that influence their clients' lives. For this reason, some defender organizations have developed community-based models that seek to represent fewer clients in a more "holistic" manner — addressing not just their criminal case, but also the underlying causes and consequences of criminality. Such community defender groups typically operate as nonprofits outside of the government, taking on fewer cases and employing a much broader range of strategies to affect community conditions and assist clients in dealing with addiction, mental health issues, and the impacts of involvement in the criminal justice system on eligibility for government programs, housing, and jobs.

4. Coordination and Coalition Building

Although primarily focused on protecting the rights of clients in individual cases, public defenders also make efforts to coordinate with other public defender offices, as well as community groups and other advocacy organizations. For example, as Taylor-Thompson observes, in the post-Warren Court era,

> defenders began collaborating on issues common to the clients they represented. Cooperative action had already begun to occur in the form of civil class actions brought by the offices on behalf of indigent prisoners challenging, for example, the conditions of confinement in state prisons and jails. Designed to force states to comply with minimum constitutional guarantees within their prison facilities, these suits often persuaded federal courts to impose numerical caps on the prison population. And in the face of these new population limits, defenders leveraged local judges to consider alternatives to incarceration when sentencing clients.
>
> More significantly, the manner in which defenders litigated certain issues arising in their criminal cases assumed a decidedly institutional character. Some offices consciously looked for broader issues of concern shared by many clients in the criminal justice system, and joined forces with other offices, pooling resources and developing common strategies to tackle them. For example, during my tenure as Director of the Public Defender Service for the District of Columbia, we coordinated efforts with public defenders in Cook County, Illinois to prevent evidence derived from deoxyribonucleic acid (DNA) testing from being admitted in our respective jurisdictions. We shared the costs of ordering transcripts of earlier DNA proceedings and we worked together to identify experts who could provide testimony to challenge the accuracy of this new technology as a means of identification. Within each office, defenders formulated arguments to be raised in every case in which the government sought to introduce DNA test results against an accused. In being forced to pursue more institutional strategies, public defender offices were not only developing new options to advance clients' positions, but also were re-creating themselves in the process.

Taylor-Thompson, *Alternating Visions, supra,* at 2431-32.

In comparison, Eagly's case study of her law school clinic's work for the *loncheros* provides an example of close collaboration between a criminal defense project and local community groups. Student lawyers met with members of a local association to consider alternative approaches to reform, including a legislative campaign to amend the parking ordinance, a public education campaign, an affirmative test case to challenge the ordinance, and defense of an individual member who had been subjected to multiple enforcement actions. Eagly, *supra*, at 104-05. Ultimately, through a collaborative decision-making process, the group decided that it did not want to detract from its organizing efforts to pursue time-consuming litigation, and opted to pursue the individual defense in conjunction with those efforts. *Id.* at 105. The example illustrates the range of possibilities of public defender-community cooperation to pursue law reform.

5. The Lawyer-Client Relationship

The context of public defender practice influences the lawyer-client relationship in a number of different ways. Resource limitations put pressure on defenders to deal with high volumes of clients in a routinized manner, challenging their ability to provide a zealous individual defense to all clients. As with lawyers in other public interest practices, tensions may exist between public defenders' primary duty to their individual clients and the broader criminal justice causes they may wish to pursue. This can be of particular concern given the vulnerability of indigent criminal defendants.

In addition, public defenders — as repeat players in the criminal justice system who face the same prosecutors and judges in case after case — may have incentives to make decisions in individual cases that preserve the lawyers' own reputations or maximize the benefits to future defendants who will have to confront the same system. Taylor-Thompson suggests how the repeat player problem has influenced the approach of some defender offices:

> Recognizing that the office viewed as an institution was a repeat player in the criminal justice system, [one] approach sought to maximize efforts in individual cases by insisting that a given client's position reflect the institution's view of a given question. To develop a more coherent institutional stance, the office required individual defenders to reconcile divergent positions on matters affecting the class of clients the office represented, so that defenders could assert office-wide policies when defending individual clients. While the individualized model encouraged autonomy and idiosyncratic approaches, the institutional vision attempted to orchestrate positions according to overriding priorities. . . .
>
> These alternating impulses — individualized and institutional — arose in my own practice as a public defender. From 1981 to 1991, I observed decisionmaking in defender offices from a variety of vantage points. As a staff lawyer in the District of Columbia's Public Defender Service, and later as director, I necessarily prioritized cases and issues. While I may have attempted, and at times publicly claimed, to give one hundred percent of the effort possible to every case, the reality of juggling thirty-five or more active cases simply did not permit such an allotment of time or effort. Although I may not have fully recognized it at the time, individualized concerns dictated my actions in the representation of clients. Without regard for consistency among cases or similarity of issues, my colleagues and I formulated strategies and developed arguments tailored to

the individualized objectives of clients, only rarely examining or acknowledging the motivations or justifications for the decisions we made.

This approach has its dangers. On one occasion, for example, I represented a young man in a felony case who had entered a plea of guilty. During the course of my argument at sentencing, it became clear that the judge was hesitant to place my client on probation. I needed to think fast. I began arguing that this client was quite different from other young men who had appeared before the judge. I searched for ways to make my client appear unique that would resonate with this judge. Only later as I reflected on my success in getting this client placed on probation did I recognize a problem: I could only make this argument effectively before this judge once. In my efforts to distinguish this client from all other clients, I was potentially harming other clients I was representing or would represent before that same judge. Had I anticipated the judge's reluctance, I could perhaps have developed a different strategy that would not have put my other clients at risk. At the time, however, getting this client released was foremost on my mind.

Taylor-Thompson, *Alternating Visions, supra*, at 2432-33. Do you think Taylor-Thompson should be thinking of future clients when arguing for a current one? What approach would you have taken to the problem she identifies? Do you think it is possible, or desirable, to be zealous for each and every defendant a lawyer represents in the defender context? Do you think it is justifiable for public defenders to think and act strategically in order to reform laws that affect the broad category of criminal defendants?

IV. THE ROLE OF PRIVATE LAWYERS

Prominent corporate law attorney Arthur Garfield Hays once referred to his volunteer work with the ACLU as the "'salt' that livened up the otherwise mundane practice of law. . . . [He said that] [t]he ACLU 'brought me into contact with a variety of circles, usually the poor, defenseless, and unpopular, always the dissenters and persecuted. It has shielded me from the corroding influence of the particular groups who would normally be my associates.'"

Samuel Walker, In Defense of American Liberties: A History of the ACLU 67 (1990).

[F]rom an historical perspective, the assumption that "public interest" law involves lawyering in arrangements funded through means other than client-paid fees is a strong but virtually unexamined precept in many "public interest" circles. There is, however, no principled basis for this requirement, which tends to exclude from recognition the many lawyers throughout our history who, while organized in "private" law practice arrangements, have worked on the same kinds of legal issues as "public interest" lawyers. The very use of language to divide up the world of law practice into "public" and "private" spheres renders invisible the contributions of such lawyers.

Susan D. Carle, *Re-Valuing Lawyering for Middle-Income Clients,* 70 Fordham L. Rev. 719, 729-30 (2001).

As of 2000, less than 2 percent of lawyers in the United States worked for legal aid, public defender offices, or other nonprofit organizations; about

8 percent worked for the government. CARSON, *supra*, at 6. The overwhelming majority of lawyers, roughly three-fourths, work in private practice.

Generally, public interest lawyering in the private sector maps onto the two "hemispheres" of legal practice found by John Heinz and Edward Laumann in their classic study of Chicago lawyers. JOHN P. HEINZ & EDWARD O. LAUMANN, CHICAGO LAWYERS: THE SOCIAL STRUCTURE OF THE BAR 171 (rev. ed. 1994). One hemisphere consists of large corporate law firms that do defense work for corporate clients. These firms contribute to public interest lawyering primarily through pro bono service. The other hemisphere consists of smaller law firms, often from the plaintiffs' bar. Some of these firms do pro bono work as well, while a subset also adopt "public interest" missions of their own—representing clients in fee-generating cases that advance political causes like antidiscrimination, labor rights, environmentalism, and consumer rights. We will treat these small firms separately from their large firm counterparts.

A. LARGE FIRMS

Whereas, for the most part, nonprofit public interest groups and government lawyers with public missions are largely phenomena of the twentieth century and later, members of the private bar have contributed to public interest work as far back as the nation's founding period (see Chapter 2). The systems through which such work takes place, however, have evolved substantially since those early days. The emergence of pro bono as an organized practice in the public interest arena is of relatively recent vintage.

> Although American lawyers had always provided some services for free, they were never generous in their gratuity, which often simply involved helping out friends, relatives, and groups such as the local church, Little League, or opera. In fact, the very concept of "pro bono"—understood as a professional duty, discharged outside the normal course of billable practice, to provide free services to persons of limited means or to clients seeking to advance the public interest—did not exist until quite recently. Service to the individual poor client had historically been treated as charity to be dispensed by organizations like legal aid, while the free representation of public interest groups was sporadic and controversial. Indeed, it was not until the 1980s that the profession's ethical rules even referred to the term "pro bono" in discussing a lawyer's public service responsibility. . . . [But] within the last twenty-five years [pro bono work] has become centralized and streamlined, distributed through an elaborate organizational structure embedded in and cutting across professional associations, law firms, state-sponsored legal services programs, and nonprofit public interest groups. This network of organizations, in turn, has developed a system of values and practices that have become deeply ingrained as part of the culture of legal professionalism, defining how lawyers understand their role in making legal services available to poor and underrepresented groups.

Cummings, *Politics of Pro Bono, supra*, at 4, 6.

Today, private attorneys may undertake pro bono work in a wide variety of circumstances. Sometimes cases arise out of opportunity or circumstance. Other times, cases are brought in cooperation with an established nonprofit public interest organization. One of the most important roles that private law firm lawyers have played in the past several decades has been as "cooperating attorneys" with large scale organizations such as the NAACP and ACLU. Constrained by limited financial resources to pay full-time in-house legal staff, organizations such as these have relied on the development and recruitment of large networks of cooperating attorneys to help them carry out their agendas. *See, e.g.*, Robert L. Rabin, *Lawyers for Social Change: Perspectives on Public Interest Law*, 28 STAN. L. REV. 207, 217-18, 223-24 (1976); *see also* NAN ARON, LIBERTY AND JUSTICE FOR ALL: PUBLIC INTEREST LAW IN THE 1980s AND BEYOND 33-34 (1989) (describing proliferation of cooperating attorneys and concluding that outside private volunteer attorneys perform about 28 percent of the legal work for nonprofit organizations).[3]

A number of factors have contributed to the private bar's expanded role in carrying out pro bono work in the late twentieth and early twenty-first century, contributing to what has been called the "institutionalization" of pro bono. Cummings, *Politics of Pro Bono, supra*, at 6. One factor was the decreasing state financial support for legal services work, and the increasing restrictions on the type of cases that lawyers receiving legal services funding could undertake; against this backdrop, the need for private lawyers to fill in the gap left by declining state funds led to increased investments in pro bono service. *Id.* at 19-25. Another reason for the rise of pro bono has been the expansion of nonprofit public interest organizations that have consciously developed close relationships with private law firms. *Id.* at 25-33. Particularly for nonprofits focused on larger, law reform cases, reliance on pro bono contributions from the private sector has become crucial to advancing their missions. *Id.* at 26.

One of the most significant factors in the institutionalization of pro bono practice has been the evolution and economic success of the large corporate law firm.

> Pro bono's institutionalization has depended critically on the rise of the big corporate law firm. Although small-scale practitioners have been important actors in the pro bono system, it has been big firms that have provided the resources and prestige to promote pro bono as a central professional goal. At one level, the big firm's organizational structure provides very practical advantages over smaller practice sites in delivering pro bono services. Since the pro bono model seeks to deploy large numbers of lawyers to provide free services, it relies heavily on the big firm as a mass supplier of pro bono personnel. In addition, because big firms are highly leveraged, they can generally absorb the costs associated with pro bono more readily than their smaller counterparts, which cannot afford to forgo significant amounts of billable work. Finally, big firms have the administrative capacity to coordinate large-scale pro bono efforts that small firms cannot match.

---

3. Some critics have argued that the expansion of nonprofit organizations calling themselves "public interest law firms" has undermined the private bar's sense of obligation to do more pro bono work as part of their professional identity. *See* Kenney Hegland, *Beyond Enthusiasm and Commitment*, 13 ARIZ. L. REV. 805, 805-06 (1971).

Yet the relationship between pro bono and big firms has not been one-sided, with pro bono programs merely the lucky recipients of big-firm largesse. Pro bono has also provided critical organizational benefits to big firms themselves. Law firms, like other organizational structures, adapt to the demands of their environments in order to gain economic resources. A key resource for big firms is talented lawyers. As part of the intense market competition to attract elite law school graduates, many of whom care deeply about pro bono opportunities, big firms have therefore designed pro bono programs to complement broader recruitment and retention plans.

Big firms are also highly attuned to professional status. Indeed, lawyers' standing as self-regulating professionals relies heavily on the legitimacy of their enterprise in the public eye. The ideology of professionalism has provided this legitimacy, as lawyers' claims of expertise, ethical responsibility, and altruism have been invoked to justify professional efforts to assert market control. Particularly for big firms, whose bottom-line focus has long elicited public cries of commercialism, the ability to define organizational activity in terms of professional ideology becomes an important goal. In this way, big-firm pro bono serves not merely as a vehicle to advance the public good, but also as a source of professional legitimation.

Id. at 33-34.[4]

A related development supporting large firm pro bono programs was the increasing importance of ranking systems and the publicity large law firms garnered through reporting their pro bono commitments in publications such as THE AMERICAN LAWYER. *Id.* at 40.

The American Lawyer's 1994 decision to begin publicly ranking firms based on the depth and breadth of their pro bono performance dramatically altered firm behavior. The emergence of law firm and law school pro bono efforts over the previous decade had led graduates to expect pro bono opportunities. *The American Lawyer's* pro bono rankings offered a readily accessible and ostensibly objective method of evaluating those opportunities in particular firms. . . . The stakes escalated in 2003 when *The American Lawyer* began publishing its "A-List" of the top twenty firms based on a combined score, which incorporated a firm's overall pro bono performance as an important factor (in addition to economic performance, associate satisfaction, and diversity measures). *The American Lawyer's* pro bono rankings are based on two quantitative measures: the average number of pro bono hours per attorney and the percentage of firm attorneys who contribute at least twenty hours of pro bono work. . . . Part of the impetus for the ranking structure was to create a counterweight to the revenue-based rankings developed a decade earlier, now known as the Am Law 200. The addition of pro bono information in the online version of the NALP Directory in 2006 and the incorporation of pro bono information in the Vault.com database on law firms reflected similar concerns, and added further pressure on firms to demonstrate their pro bono commitment.

---

4. Even some large corporations, such as Coca-Cola and McDonald's, have pro bono committees and encourage their in-house lawyers to participate in pro bono work. Cummings, *Politics of Pro Bono, supra,* at 65. There is even an organizational web site supporting pro bono work by in-house counsel. *See* www.corporateprobono.org (last visited Aug. 7, 2012).

As in other contexts, the movement to rank pro bono contributions produced a "Heisenberg effect": the rankings changed the phenomenon they claimed to measure. By creating a highly visible and easily interpreted metric of law firm evaluation, this ranking structure established pro bono as an even more prominent factor in firm reputation and influenced the recruitment of associates. Moreover, by measuring only the quantity and extent of participation, rankings encouraged firms to focus on these goals, rather than on harder to assess outcome measures such as the quality or social impact of their work.

Scott L. Cummings & Deborah L. Rhode, *Managing Pro Bono: Doing Well by Doing Better*, 78 Fordham L. Rev. 2357, 2371-72 (2010) [hereinafter, Cummings & Rhode, *Managing Pro Bono*].

1. Resources

A key advantage of private law firm participation in public interest legal work is that they can mobilize significant personnel and monetary resources. In addition to having lawyers to work on cases, large corporate law firms in particular have substantial financial resources to cover litigation and other legal costs, libraries, electronic legal research databases, paralegals and other support staff, state of the art computers, software, copiers, and other technological assets. *See generally* Cummings, *Politics of Pro Bono, supra*. At the same time, firm training does not focus on public interest issue areas and thus pro bono attorneys often must rely on the support of full-time public interest lawyers who can offer their expertise and experience. *Id.* at 71. Firms sometimes receive a benefit back from pro bono work because of the training and experience their young lawyers gain working on public interest cases. *Id.* at 111.

Law firm resources, however, are not unlimited and there are significant financial pressures on pro bono even in the best of economic times — and certainly in the worst. Law firm economic performance tends to be positively correlated with pro bono activity. Those firms that are "doing well" are typically the best at "doing good." *See* Steven A. Boutcher, *The Institutionalization of Pro Bono in Large Law Firms: Trends and Variation Across the AmLaw 200*, in Private Lawyers and the Public Interest, *supra*, at 135. This is because in good times firms have a fair amount of "organizational slack" from which to draw upon for free pro bono services. *See* Rebecca L. Sandefur, *Lawyers' Pro Bono Service and American-Style Civil Legal Assistance*, 41 Law & Soc'y Rev. 79, 93-94 (2007); *see also* Rebecca L. Sandefur, *Lawyers' Pro Bono Service and Market-Reliant Legal Aid*, in Private Lawyers and the Public Interest, *supra*, at 95. However, even in good times, this slack only funds pro bono up to a limit. Pushing against the professional duty to do pro bono is the economic imperative to pursue profit. And when there is an economic downturn, pro bono service is often a liability, since firms retrench and allocate less toward pro bono activity. This occurred after the Great Recession. *See* Chris Johnson, *Pro Bono Report 2011: Choppy Waters*, The American Lawyer, July 1, 2011 ("Average pro bono hours for lawyers at Am Law 200 firms plummeted 8 percent in 2010 to their lowest level in three years, reversing a decade of steady growth."). Thus, one of the downsides of relying on private firm largesse to fund public interest work is that in a moment of economic crisis—when we would expect the legal needs of the poor and other vulnerable groups to peak—financial support for pro bono may decline.

2. Agenda Setting Ability

Law firms set their pro bono agendas through collaboration among the stakeholders involved in the pro bono system: partners and associates inside the firms, and nonprofit public interest groups and their constituencies on the outside. In this process, the types of cases firms take on reflect a match between internal lawyer preferences and external client need. Sometimes agendas are defined through a centralized planning process and others are based on the interests of influential partners who value a specific cause. Law firm pro bono dockets may reflect individual lawyer choices or a comprehensive decision to support a particular project. Some law firms may simply encourage their lawyers to take on any cases that they find social usefully. Other firms may consciously develop expertise in a particular public interest area and channel volunteer resources into specific types of cases. Cummings & Rhode, *Managing Pro Bono, supra,* at 2429. Through the creation of "signature programs," the firm may set its agenda and establish a foundation for large investments in specific areas. *Id.* To the extent that law firms get their pro bono cases through referral organizations, those organizations play an agenda setting role by selecting the cases referred. Such organizations "set service priorities, make triage decisions, engage in client education and outreach, and conduct initial client screening." Cummings, *Politics of Pro Bono, supra,* at 42. Furthermore, because they are typically granted a great deal of discretion to shape the firm's policies on intake and outreach, pro bono coordinators frequently play a critical role in what types of public interest work a firm pursues. *Id.* at 60.

However, there are important tradeoffs. For instance, while firms are free to develop specialty programs, they may pick clients and causes that minimize conflicts with their paying clients and avoid public controversy. Pro bono cases may present actual conflicts of interest with firms' paying clients, thus precluding firms from taking those cases. *Id.* at 116. In other circumstances, a firm may choose not to take a pro bono case if it will require the firm to advocate a position that is contrary to the business interests of its paying clients (a so-called positional conflict). *Id.* While firms are not strictly barred from taking such cases, these types of routine business considerations are nonetheless an important constraint on firms' freedom to pursue public interest agendas. *Id.* at 116-17. For instance, there is evidence that large law firms are not inclined to take on cases involving consumer, environmental, or employment law claims that are likely to involve suits against major corporations. *Id.* at 119-20; Cummings & Rhode, *Managing Pro Bono, supra,* at 2393. In one prominent example, a large New York law firm withdrew from helping the city with a lawsuit against the gun industry after one of the gun company's lawyers contacted one of the firm's large corporate clients, which pressured the firm to back out because the suit could have negative implications for that client's interests in potential future cases. Cummings, *Politics of Pro Bono, supra,* at 147.

Overall, pro bono programs walk a line between responding to community needs and promoting the economic objectives of their law firms. Consider the following findings from a 2010 study of pro bono counsel on the role of firm lawyer preferences in shaping pro bono dockets at large firms.

> Lawyer preferences . . . influence pro bono programs through case selection. . . . [O]ur survey data suggest that key considerations in selecting matters are whether a case is likely to appeal to firm associates and provide good training. The pro bono counsel whom we interviewed confirmed that "trying to find the perfect case" was a major part of their role. They made efforts to learn "what people are interested in and match that with what is happening on the ground." This motivation drove many of the efforts to poll lawyers and summer associates about their preferences. . . . The job was easiest when lawyers expressed clear substantive preferences, such as "I'm really interested in animal rights." Somewhat greater challenges involved corporate lawyers who wanted matters squarely within their expertise. "I get questions like 'I'm a communications regulation lawyer. What could I do at the FCC?'" Even for summer associates, case selection was often "driven by what they want and not necessarily by what is easiest to get their hands on."
>
> Although most pro bono counsel seemed to accept the necessity of matching cases to lawyer interests, a few expressed frustration. Some found it difficult to focus attorneys on "responding to community needs" rather than just their own preferences. As one noted, "There are areas where I know that there is a huge legal need . . . but I can't get lawyers to sign on. Homeless issues — it is difficult to sell those matters. . . . People are scared of working with homeless, mentally ill clients." For some of these counsel, their role involved efforts to reshape, not simply respond to, lawyer interests: "Pro bono counsel should remain public interest lawyers — focused on social justice, not just financial resources or the quality of life of their firm. They have to be more mission based than firm-goal based." From this perspective, privileging lawyer preferences in developing case dockets gets the priorities backward. The "relationship between the public interest and private bar can't be 'We are so grateful.' It should be collaborative, the leader should be the public interest [groups] . . . and we firms [should be] honored to play on their team."

Cummings & Rhode, *Managing Pro Bono*, *supra*, at 2421-22.

3. Control Over Legal Strategies

Within the broader pro bono system, there is space for lawyers to engage in activities across a range of legal strategies.

> Because of its fluid structure, the pro bono system offers significant opportunities for lawyers to deploy different types of advocacy strategies. Although formal rules and practices have developed, there is considerable latitude within the system for practitioners to bring a range of legal cases using a variety of lawyering techniques. The clearest illustration of this is by way of comparison with the federal legal services program, which now operates under a web of restrictions. While LSC-funded organizations cannot bring class actions, engage in abortion or prisoner litigation, or represent most undocumented immigrants, big firms can — and do — through pro bono. While legal services has drawn political fire as a government-sponsored organization that turns

around and sues the government, big firms are generally free to aggressively pursue cases against government agencies.

The flexibility of the pro bono system also makes room for programs to develop creative problem-solving approaches to issues facing low-income and underserved client communities, taking advantage of the absence of institutional traditions shaped by a particular law reform or individual service imperative to craft programmatic approaches that depart from conventional models. San Francisco's VLSP [Volunteer Legal Services Program], for instance, promotes a "holistic" approach that emphasizes client problem-solving over discrete case representation. Instead of simply responding to identified legal concerns, VLSP works to gain a more complete picture of the multiple legal and nonlegal issues that confront clients. On the basis of a careful screening process, VLSP staff attorneys attempt to devise comprehensive solutions to the problems clients face — linking them with legal resources, while also helping them apply for government benefits, secure an affordable place to stay, and obtain necessary health services. Another example of this problem-solving approach is Public Counsel's Homeless Court Project, which operates in connection with the Los Angeles Superior Court, City Attorney, and Public Defender to resolve minor quality of life and traffic offenses for homeless clients who connect with residential and rehabilitative service programs. By emphasizing informal dispute resolution and prioritizing social service provision, these programs underscore the range of nontraditional advocacy strategies that pro bono programs deploy.

Cummings, *Politics of Pro Bono, supra*, at 103-04.

Although there is strategic flexibility in the pro bono system, law firm lawyers representing pro bono clients tend to deploy relatively conventional legal tools. This likely reflects the fact that they are often relied upon by their nonprofit partners to provide the legal resources nonprofit groups often lack. Typically, law firms are called on for their comparative advantage, which is litigation support in large, resource-intensive cases. Yet firms engage in a range of other types of pro bono activities. For example, firms that specialize in governmental relations work also sometimes do so for pro bono clients. *See* Jeffrey H. Birnbaum, *Sometimes Lobbyists' Advice Really Is Priceless*, WASH. POST, Dec. 27, 2004, at E01. Some firms provide pro bono representation on the transactional side of public interest practice, often helping groups engaged in community economic development initiatives. This type of pro bono activity — as the D.C. Bar's mission statement below reflects — is targeted to transactional business lawyers, who often feel left out by the pro bono system's main emphasis on litigation:

> The D.C. Bar Pro Bono Program established the Community Economic Development (CED) Pro Bono Project in 1998 to provide a vehicle for corporate, transactional, and business lawyers seeking nonlitigation pro bono assignments. The project is designed to deliver critically needed legal services to organizations operating in and serving low-income and distressed communities in the District of Columbia. . . .

Community Economic Development Project, D.C. BAR (2012), http://www.dcbar.org/ for_lawyers/pro_bono/about_the_program/serving_the_community/ced.cfm (last visited July 31, 2012); *see also Business Law Pro Bono Project*, AMERICAN BAR ASSOCIATION (2012), http://www.americanbar.org/groups/probono_public_

service/projects_awards/business_law_pro_bono_project.html (last visited July 31, 2012). In addition to allowing transactional lawyers the opportunity to engage in meaningful volunteer work, community development-oriented pro bono service also has the virtue, from the firms' point of view, of being less likely to generate actual or positional conflicts, since the firm is not engaged in litigation against members of its client base.

As between pro bono lawyers and the nonprofit lawyers with whom they collaborate, who gets to control strategic decision making? The answer depends on the particular context, but sometimes tension may arise. This can occur, for example, when a pro bono lawyer thinks a case should be settled, but the nonprofit lawyers she is working with believe the case should proceed, either because it has important precedential value or to generate public attention for a broader social issue. Of course, the opposite may be true as well. The pro bono lawyer may wish to continue pursuing a case when the nonprofit lawyer thinks doing so risks creating a bad precedent. As Rhode reports:

> Issues of control sometimes arose but rarely posed serious difficulties. No public interest leaders experienced extensive difficulties over decision making in pro bono collaborations; eight percent (n=49) reported moderate problems, and 14% reported limited problems. Occasionally, firms "want[ed] to go to the wall," or took the view that "if it's our money, we should have control over spending it." Allowing private counsel to exercise such authority was generally unacceptable to public interest organizations, which had long-term policy objectives to consider. Most attempted to make it clear at the outset that they would retain control over strategic decisions.

Rhode, *Movement at Midlife*, *supra*, at 2071. Who do you think should have the ultimate strategic decision-making authority on pro bono cases? Does it depend on how the representation is structured — i.e., on whether the case is formally co-counseled by the firm and nonprofit group?

4. Coordination and Coalition Building

As the discussion of strategic decision making suggests, pro bono service delivery hinges on coordination between law firm lawyers and external legal groups and clients. The emergence of institutional structures to support and facilitate pro bono work has played a role in the expansion of this practice. Among these structures are referral organizations, often connected with local bar associations, whose primary mission is to direct cases to private law firms. There are also traditional legal services and public interest groups that have developed structures to facilitate the strategic use of pro bono resources to advance their cause. Cummings, *Politics of Pro Bono*, *supra*, at 42-49. Coordination is also facilitated by the increasing involvement of the organized bar and the establishment by many private firms of pro bono committees and pro bono coordinators to facilitate the firms' efforts. *Id*. at 49-52, 57-62.

A number of models exist for promoting firm-nonprofit collaboration around the signature pro bono projects referred to earlier:

> Law firms have experimented with different approaches to achieving greater scale. One is the adoption of large "signature" pro bono projects that focus firm

resources on a particular issue, client group, or geographic area. Signature projects are designed to coordinate firm resources around a well-defined goal, create synergies between different practice groups, and build institutional knowledge and resources. By marshaling the firm's resources in this way, firms seek to "maximize[ ] efficiency, allowing the firm and its attorneys to make a larger impact." Signature projects also have the benefit of serving as useful marketing vehicles. Latham & Watkins is a prominent example in this regard, recently initiating a well-publicized firm-wide project to represent unaccompanied refugee children detained by the government. Similarly, San Francisco-based Heller Ehrman White & McAuliffe has focused on assisting individuals with HIV/AIDS.

From the perspective of pro bono organizations, signature projects have the benefit of providing stable institutional commitments by firms that can be counted on and therefore easily planned around. Thus, a pro bono organization can move large numbers of clients to a firm in connection with a signature project, reducing the costs associated with coordinating among multiple firms. There is also a reduction in uncertainty to the extent that organizations can more confidently take on cases knowing that pro bono resources will be available.

Signature project relationships are structured in different ways. A firm can agree to take cases from multiple pro bono organizations that relate to a specific issue, along the lines of the Latham & Watkins model. Another arrangement involves a firm agreeing to partner with a single pro bono organization, taking on a large number of cases from that referral source. This is the model adopted by New York's Stroock & Stroock & Lavan, which has developed a partnership with the New York Lawyers for the Public Interest's Disability Law Center. A final model has a law firm "adopting" a community-based organization working in a particular low-income neighborhood, handling all types of legal issues that arise in the course of the organization's work.

Cummings, *Politics of Pro Bono, supra,* at 72-74. The 2010 Cummings and Rhode study of pro bono at large law firms found that "[n]early sixty percent of the firms in our survey (n=33) reported [a signature] project. Of these, eleven projects focused on some aspect of immigration, particularly matters involving asylum, refugees, juveniles, and domestic violence. Eight focused on children's rights or family law (including domestic violence). Another four concentrated on economic development, particularly microenterprise; three on criminal defense/death penalty work; and two each on veterans' issues, human rights, education, and Holocaust survivors. Other firms reported having projects on HIV/AIDs, employee rights, the environment, and civil rights." Cummings & Rhode, *Managing Pro Bono, supra,* at 2385.

In the wake of the economic downturn, law firms developed different types of partnerships with nonprofit groups, turning to "temporary public interest placements as a way station for incoming or currently underemployed associates. By the summer of 2009, over 50 Am Law 200 firms were offering subsidies of between $50,000 and $80,000 for associates to spend a year working for nonprofits or government agencies." *Id.* at 2409.

> The primary impetus for the placements was economic. Each deferred associate is estimated to save the firm between $60,000 and $100,000 because the salaries and support for these junior lawyers would exceed the profit they generate

at current billing rates. In addition, deferral gives firms a way to quickly restock their associate ranks with minimal transaction costs once the worst of the recession passes. Training was another important reason for the placements. As surveyed counsel noted, providing pro bono opportunities enables lawyers to "continue to build their skill sets" while also meeting urgent legal needs of vulnerable groups.

Id. at 2410. Do you think that such placements are a good deal for nonprofit partner organizations? What are the potential downsides? How easy would it be for nonprofit groups to say no to the firms' offer to place deferred associates?

As the deferral example suggests, law firms have developed a range of pro bono collaborations with government agencies. In the early 2000s, "Debevoise & Plimpton ha[d] instituted a five-month externship program with the Queens County District Attorney's office; [and] Cleary, Gottlieb, Steen & Hamilton ha[d] . . . a three-month program at the city Corporation Counsel." Cummings, *Politics of Pro Bono, supra,* at 78. In the wake of the recession, one large firm reported plans "to launch a misdemeanor criminal program in connection with the local public defender's office. The impetus was to support criminal defense work while providing courtroom experiences for its attorneys that did not take 'a lot of time.'" Cummings & Rhode, *Managing Pro Bono, supra,* at 2427. As both of these examples illustrate, large firm-government collaboration around pro bono serves the twin goals of supporting under-resourced government programs, while training law firm lawyers in skills that are relevant to commercial practice.

5. The Lawyer-Client Relationship

In theory, the quality of private firm representation is supposed to be the same for paying and nonpaying clients. However, the structure of private law firm practice, which is organized around commercial goals, creates pressures on pro bono service that can affect the nature of the lawyer-client relationship. How law firm lawyers perceive certain types of cases can affect whether they make it into the pro bono system in the first instance and, even when they do, how and where clients are served.

> Clients who might be perceived as difficult or not mainstream are discouraged, while "deserving" clients are promoted. Clients at San Francisco's VLSP, for instance, include children with disabilities and special needs, battered women, people with cancer, low-income people with credit problems, abused immigrant children, disabled and elderly immigrants, people who are HIV positive or have AIDS, women on welfare seeking to reenter the workforce, and nonprofit organizations. Clients who are less sympathetic are kept at a greater distance. Homeless clients, for instance, are generally served outside the offices of law firm volunteers at legal clinics or public agencies.

Cummings, *Politics of Pro Bono, supra,* at 141. Similarly, firms may be discouraged from collaborating with organizations that are perceived as more radical or controversial by either the clients or the firm's own lawyers. *See, e.g., id.* at 122-23 (reporting incident where a law firm ordered one of its lawyers to stop representing the activist group, Queer Nation, because of criticism from other lawyers in the firm).

In addition, economic pressures on law firm lawyers mean that sometimes, despite their best intentions, pro bono clients receive less attention. At the extreme end, this can result in bad consequences for clients. In one widely reported incident, a court found that an associate from Skadden Arps Slate Meagher & Flom made "careless and inaccurate" statements to her pro bono divorce client, "including informing her that Skadden could withdraw from the case if [the client] raised the issue of her relocation or pursued an equitable distribution claim." Noeleen G. Walder, *Failure to Supervise Pro Bono Attorney Dooms Divorce Pact*, N.Y.L.J., June 18, 2009. As a result, the court set aside a settlement stipulation because the lawyer "made serious errors and was inadequately supervised." *Id.* In another case that reached the United States Supreme Court, two pro bono attorneys from Sullivan & Cromwell represented a death row defendant, Cory Maples, in seeking post-conviction relief in the Alabama state courts. When those attorneys left the firm, they failed to tell their client or the court. When the Alabama trial court denied Maples's petition, the notice was sent to the pro bono attorneys at Sullivan & Cromwell. Because they were no longer at the firm, the notice was returned to the state court clerk unopened. As a result, Maples never learned of the trial court's ruling and therefore missed the deadline to file an appeal in state court. Because of this state default, Maples then had his federal habeas petition denied by the federal district court. He appealed and the Supreme Court reversed, holding that the pro bono attorneys' abandonment of Maples constituted sufficient "cause" justifying his procedural default. *Maples v. Thomas*, 132 S. Ct. 912 (2012).

Although such extreme cases are atypical, quality concerns are not. As Rhode reports:

> The most common difficulty in pro bono collaboration . . . involved not credit or control, but quality. About three fifths of organizations experienced some quality concerns; fourteen percent . . . reported extensive problems, 33% reported moderate problems, and 8% reported limited problems. For some organizations, the highly specialized nature of their work made it inefficient to rely on inexperienced counsel, and few pro bono attorneys had the relevant skill sets. In death penalty work, for example, "getting people to the point of real competence takes years, not weeks." Immigration, voting rights, and technology cases also presented challenges for non-specialists, and lack of language skills amplified problems in assisting non-English-speaking clients. Some organizations were willing to provide volunteers with the necessary background in substantive law, but could not afford to "train a junior associate in how to take a deposition."

Rhode, *Movement at Midlife, supra*, at 2071-72. Partner supervision of pro bono cases poses particular challenges.

> Despite efforts to guarantee partner supervision, many [pro bono] counsel nonetheless conceded that "monitoring cases is a large challenge." At times, it is simply difficult to get overcommitted partners to pay attention to unpaid matters under their supervision. As one counsel put it, "I strongly believe that most partners are not focused on pro bono, so someone else has to catch trips and falls." For this counsel, the lack of partner oversight caused "a great deal of

headaches. Getting more partner involvement is critical." Supervision breaks down not simply because partners are "too busy," but also because associates may be too "intimidated" to ask for help. Partner expertise can also be a problem. Although one counsel noted that "[e]very matter has a supervising partner," she acknowledged that "in some areas the associate knows more than the partner."

Cummings & Rhode, *Managing Pro Bono, supra*, at 2395.

B. SMALL FIRMS

Small firms and solo practitioners also play important roles in public interest service delivery. Such practitioners provide significant pro bono services, although unlike at large firms, small and solo practitioners tend to either write off or write down fees after services are delivered in order to accommodate clients' inability to pay. Leslie C. Levin, *Pro Bono Publico in a Parallel Universe: The Meaning of Pro Bono in Solo and Small Law Firms*, 37 HOFSTRA L. REV. 699, 701 (2009); *see also* LYNN MATHER ET AL., DIVORCE LAWYERS AT WORK: VARIETIES OF PROFESSIONALISM IN PRACTICE (2001); CARROLL SERON, THE BUSINESS OF PRACTICING LAW: THE WORK LIVES OF SOLO AND SMALL-FIRM ATTORNEYS (1996); Philip R. Lochner, Jr., *The No Fee and Low Fee Legal Practice of Private Attorneys*, 9 LAW & SOC'Y REV. 431 (1975). Some argue that this type of "low bono" work is a crucial and overlooked part of the American system of legal services delivery that should be enhanced as a tool to promote access to justice among the "near poor." Luz E. Herrera, *Rethinking Private Attorney Involvement Through a "Low Bono" Lens*, 43 LOY. L.A. L. REV. 1 (2009).

In addition, there are small firms that specialize in work they define to be in the "public interest." Unlike other private firms, lawyers in these "private public interest law firms" are politically motivated by particular causes and financially motivated by receiving attorneys' fees. Such firms "have been held out as an alternative site for 'doing well' and 'doing good,' allowing lawyers to take on large-scale social change litigation that nonprofit groups cannot because of resource limits — and big-firm pro bono programs will not because of business conflicts — while also addressing other deficits associated with NGO [nongovernmental organization] practice, such as low salaries, lack of training, and high turnover." Cummings, *The Future of Public Interest Law*, *supra*, at 364-65.

Private public interest law firms are, quite literally, in the business of pursuing justice. What defines them? The following description of this practice setting comes from a guide prepared by the law schools at Harvard and Columbia:

> Like traditional not-for-profit public interest organizations, public interest law firms usually have a particular social, political, or economic vision that includes helping underrepresented groups and/or promoting change. Public interest firms, like traditional not-for-profits, bring cases that will advance their vision. A public interest law firm may, for example, represent employees charging their employers with unlawful discrimination, or consumers charging a financial institution with deceptive practices.

But unlike traditional not-for-profits, public interest firms operate as for-profit businesses. Public interest firms rely on the fees generated by their cases, rather than foundation grants or tax dollars, to pay the rent and their lawyers' salaries. Thus, a public interest firm looks not only at the merits but also at the potential profitability of a case in deciding whether to take it on. Firms have different means for ensuring their financial solvency. Some firms split their practice so that profit-driven client work can subsidize the public interest docket. At most such firms, associates will usually be required to work on both kinds of matters. Other firms choose only to represent clients that further their public interest agenda, but more strictly scrutinize the financial implications of each case.

What distinguishes a public interest firm from other private law firms? One public interest firm lawyer describes the difference this way: "Subject matter of the cases is the key to defining a firm as a private public interest law firm. The lawyers at my firm have 'religion'; they really care about what they do. They are committed to their beliefs." A second important distinction, offers another attorney, is the kind of clients public interest firms represent: "I represent people who are disenfranchised and powerless. We do a lot of similar things that government attorneys and public interest groups do, but we are able to make some money while accomplishing something good at the same time."

Private Public Interest and Plaintiff's Firm Guide, THE PRESIDENT AND FELLOWS OF HARVARD COLLEGE, 4 (2010), http://www.law.harvard.edu/current/careers/opia/toolkit/guides/documents/privatepiguide2010.pdf (last visited July 31, 2012) [hereinafter, Harvard Guide].[5]

These firms, distinguished by a commitment to fuse profit and principle, have existed since at least the early part of the twentieth century, with some playing important roles in the civil rights movement. Scott L. Cummings & Ann Southworth, *Between Profit and Principle: The Private Public Interest Firm, in* PRIVATE LAWYERS AND THE PUBLIC INTEREST, *supra*, at 183, 184. A recent study suggests that they have grown substantially over the past 40 years. Scott L. Cummings, *Privatizing Public Interest Law*, 25 GEO. J. LEGAL ETHICS 1, 12-13 (2012). While it is difficult to make precise comparisons, research from the 1970s reported estimates ranging from 44 to 66 firms that devoted a significant portion of their practices to public interest work. *Id.* They were generally small and low paying. *Id.* at 13. "The firms relied on varying economic arrangements to promote

---

5. An important, but somewhat disputed, type of practice organization that could arguably be included in this category is the plaintiffs' personal injury firm. As the report suggests:

> Firms that represent plaintiffs in relatively routine personal injury cases — for example, car accidents, workplace injuries, and medical malpractice — are not generally considered public interest law firms. Less clear is how to characterize a firm that handles personal injury cases that raise a broader social issue such as an allegedly defective automobile or other consumer product. Such firms may consider themselves to be a breed of public interest firm. Similarly, a firm that handles the occasional personal injury case as a means of generating income to subsidize its public interest docket may consider itself a public interest firm. Adding to the complexity of characterizing plaintiff-side personal injury firms is the criticism some such firms have drawn for seeking huge damage awards in which they would reap large contingency fees.

Harvard Guide, *supra*, at 6.

stability, such as establishing ongoing cooperative relationships with nonprofit PIL [public interest law] groups, taking advantage of federal programs subsidizing the cost of public participation in regulatory agencies, participating in prepaid legal services plans, and relying on non–PIL cases to supplement their income." *Id.* The most common areas of public interest practice for these early hybrid firms were consumer protection, environmental law, employment discrimination, housing, criminal law, and civil rights work; most of the firms' paying work came from personal injury cases, with labor and general commercial law work also important for fee generation. *Id.* Most of these early firms were located in the Northeast. *Id.* In contrast, there are now approximately 670 such organizations. "Of these, most (66%) are located outside of the Northeast. California alone is home to 222 firms, which is more than in New York, Massachusetts, and Washington, D.C., collectively (187). The mean size for all firms was approximately seven lawyers, with a median of three." *Id.* at 13-14.

Why do lawyers start these firms and how do they operate? In 1980, three lawyers working in the environmental unit of the California Attorney General's office formed Shute, Mihaly & Weinberger, a small San Francisco law firm devoted to an environmental law practice. Bob Egelko, *Mark Weinberger— Lawyer for Environment*, S.F. CHRON., July 22, 2005, at B7. It set out with a philosophy of representing only preservationists, not developers, a challenging agenda for a for-profit firm. *Id.* The firm's client base includes a mix of local government agencies and community environmental groups. *About Us*, SHUTE, MIHALY & WEINBERGER, LLP, http://www.smwlaw.com/ (last visited Aug. 12, 2012). The firm counsels its governmental clients on matters regarding environmental regulation and land use. *CEQA/NEPA*, SHUTE, MIHALY & WEINBERGER, LLP, http://www.smwlaw.com/practice-areas/ceqa-nepa (last visited Aug. 12, 2012). It engages in both litigation and contract drafting work on behalf of these entities. *Id.*

In the next passage, the founders of one well-known private public interest firm, Bernabei & Katz (now Katz, Marshall & Banks, LLP, and Bernabei & Wachtel), discuss the features of their firm and their reasons for starting it:

> Bernabei & Katz is a four-lawyer, private, public interest law firm based in Washington, D.C. The firm specializes in litigating civil rights and civil liberties cases, employment and AIDS discrimination cases, whistleblower cases, and prisoner rights cases. . . . [W]e view ourselves as public interest lawyers whose primary obligation—and indeed professional duty—is to provide high quality legal representation to public interest clients. These clients have a vital interest in shaking up the system. To that end, our representation necessarily involves aggressively challenging the existing power structures and institutions to try to force them to operate in a non-discriminatory and equitable manner. . . .
>
> Private public interest law firms, like ours, are distinguished from nonprivate public interest law firms such as the NAACP Legal Defense Fund and the American Civil Liberties Union, for example, in that they are not dependent upon grants from foundations or governmental assistance and are not membership organizations. Nor are they considered "charitable

organizations" exempt from federal income tax under section 501(c)(3) of the Internal Revenue Code. They operate in the traditional attorney-client mode by accepting fees for legal representation, and thereby make their public interest practices self-sustaining. Similarly, our firm has survived with minimal foundation funding: (1) by charging clients at hourly rates substantially less than market rates, depending upon their incomes and other factors affecting their abilities to pay; (2) by receiving the award of statutory attorneys' fees in cases in which the plaintiff prevails or reaches a successful settlement; and (3) by maintaining our salaries at levels commensurate with those of our non-profit, public interest counter-parts.

We have chosen to operate in this organizational structure because it provides maximum discretion to select cases, guided by our own views of social justice, and ensures that, once having made that selection, we remain true to the interests of that particular client. Moreover, we believe that the private public interest law firm structure is best suited to achieve independence from the requirements of funders and Boards of Directors, to permit maximum flexibility in the types of strategies that can be pursued on behalf of our clients, and to ensure long term viability.

Obviously, our litigation practice is not programmatic in nature — that is, we do not map out an agenda for law reform in a specific area and select only those cases which advance that agenda. Nor does it have a singular ideological commitment. Rather, our practice reflects, to a considerable degree, our decision as to which cases best serve the public interest, often defined by the exigencies and needs of our client base and the community in which we practice.

Debra S. Katz & Lynne Bernabei, *Practicing Public Interest Law in a Private Public Interest Law Firm: The Ideal Setting to Challenge the Power*, 96 W. Va. L. Rev. 293, 294-97 (1993). As this discussion highlights, private public interest law firms have distinct funding mechanisms that create different tradeoffs when it comes to agenda setting, legal strategy, collaboration, and lawyer-client relationships.

1. Resources

Unlike any of the other practice sites discussed, private public interest law firms rely heavily — and often exclusively — on fees. The development of private public interest law firms initially benefitted from the opportunity presented by fee-shifting statutes under both federal and state law, which allowed such firms to build practices in areas such as employment discrimination and police abuse. Cummings, *Privatizing Public Interest Law*, *supra*, at 11-12. At the same time, these firms have grown in response to limits on nonprofit public interest groups.

While the availability of fees has made private PIL firms economically feasible, a variety of constraints associated with NGO practice have encouraged lawyers to move into the private sector. Lawyers' complaints about the NGO sector focus on lower pay, the scarcity of jobs, limited training opportunities, and insufficient resources for large-scale litigation. These general limitations have been compounded by specific funding and substantive restrictions imposed on the federal legal services program over the last twenty-five years. Accordingly, the NGO sector has become a less congenial arena for litigators: Groups have found it difficult to raise foundation funds to sustain ongoing litigation operations, while restrictions on federal legal services programs have eliminated the

> ability to pursue class actions, attorneys' fees, and cases involving most undocumented immigrants. Against this backdrop, private PIL firms have offered lawyers the chance to pursue public goals, while enjoying some of the advantages associated with private practice, such as greater freedom to shift agendas and more autonomy from funding sources.

Id. at 12. As this passage suggests, the private public interest law firm's reliance on fees has allowed many to flourish — freed from the mandates of foundation or government funding — but it also imposes constraints on client selection and other aspects of firm governance.

A key resource issue is the degree to which private public interest firms supplement cause-oriented cases with "straight" cases taken on purely to generate a fee. Firms have different approaches to this issue.

> The literature reveals that private public interest firms adopt a variety of economic models. Some claim to pursue *only* work that the principals believe in — and sacrifice income to do so. [The Los Angeles-area firm] Traber & Voorhees, for instance, reports that it has never taken a case outside its core practice of civil rights, housing, and human rights law. Similarly, Bernabei & Katz . . . declined to supplement its caseload with cases taken purely for financial reasons (though they did receive a small amount of foundation funding) and paid its attorneys on a nonprofit scale. The community-based El Centro practice, studied by Trubek & Kransberger, also combined foundation grants with client fees, which were limited based on ability to pay. Many firms, however, supplement their mission-driven work with other matters that are consistent with their commitments but not especially dear to them. Other firms take cases that do not further their political ideals at all, in order to subsidize the work they deem to be in the public interest. [The Los Angeles-area firm] Hadsell & Stormer, for instance, represented wealthy executives in employment contract disputes in what one lawyer called its "white male cases." Scheingold and Bloom's research similarly found that attorneys in small firms, whose financial status tended to be "precarious," subsidized "transgressive" work with "paying non-political clients."

Cummings & Southworth, *supra*, at 196. Other models exist as well. Some firms charge fees on a sliding scale based on ability to pay while others supplement fee-generating work with outside donations. Louise Trubek & M. Elizabeth Kransberger, *Critical Lawyers: Social Justice and the Structure of Private Practice, in* Cause Lawyering: Political Commitments and Professional Responsibilities 201 (Austin Sarat & Stuart Scheingold eds., 1998). Note that some law firms that work on affordable housing and other community development matters may be able to get fees out of the public financing available for such transactional deals. Other firms with institutional clients, like unions, may also rely on regular fee payments.

While private public interest law firms provide many benefits, such as higher salaries, there are tradeoffs. These firms are unlikely to have as many resources as their large corporate firm counterparts because of their organizational structure and reliance on fee-shifting statutes. There may be occasions in which this affects their practice, such as when they need to retain costly expert witnesses. In addition, reliance on fees exposes private public interest firm lawyers to a number of challenges based on political and judicial efforts to limit fee-shifting statutes, which we turn to now. Keep in mind that these challenges also affect nonprofit groups that litigate cases for which fees are recoverable.

a. FUNCTION OF FEE-SHIFTING STATUTES

In the twentieth century, with the emergence of statutory civil rights laws, Congress adopted fee-shifting measures to promote access to counsel and encourage enforcement.[6] In *Newman v. Piggie Park Enterprises, Inc.*, 390 U.S. 400 (1968) (*per curiam*), the Supreme Court held that fees under Title II of the 1964 Civil Rights Act ordinarily ought to be awarded to assist in the private enforcement of civil rights laws. *Id.* at 401-02. It acknowledged that Congress's purpose was to facilitate such enforcement because when "a plaintiff obtains relief, he 'does so not for himself alone but also as a "private attorney general," vindicating a policy that Congress considered of the highest priority.'" *Id.* at 402 (footnote omitted). In the wake of the Court's decision in *Newman*, some lower courts began to award attorneys' fees in cases involving other civil rights statutes that did not have fee-shifting provisions, claiming authority to award fees under their equitable power. *Evans v. Jeff D.*, 475 U.S. 717, 747-48 (1986) (Brennan, J., dissenting). However, in *Alyeska Pipeline Service Co. v. Wilderness Society*, 421 U.S. 240, 241, 247 (1975), the Court rejected the idea that federal courts had power to award fees in the absence of a federal statute or certain narrow equitable exceptions.

Congress responded to *Alyeska Pipeline* by enacting the Civil Rights Attorney Fee Awards Act of 1976, 42 U.S.C. §1988. Section 1988(b) provides that in any action to enforce a wide range of federal civil rights provisions "the court, in its discretion, may allow the prevailing party, other than the United States, a reasonable attorney's fee as part of the costs." *Id.* Thus, courts may at their discretion require civil rights defendants to pay the reasonable attorneys' fees of the prevailing plaintiff, which is a statutory reversal of the "American rule," at least in these specified cases. Fee-shifting statutes are also available in numerous other contexts, including suits under environmental law statutes, *see, e.g.*, 42 U.S.C. §6972(e) (2006), 33 U.S.C. §1365(d) (2006), the 1964 Civil Rights Act, 42 U.S.C. §2000e-5(k) (2006), and the Fair Labor Standards Act (FLSA), 29 U.S.C. §216(b) (2006), just to name a few. Fees are available on a more limited basis against the federal government under the Equal Access to Justice Act (EAJA). 28 U.S.C. §2412 (2006 & Supp. IV 2010).[7]

Prior to the enactment of §1988, attorneys in civil rights damages claims could afford to take cases only on a contingency fee basis. Even the prospect of

---

6. Congress enacted its first fee-shifting provision during the Reconstruction era as a means of securing enforcement of voting rights. *See* Marjorie A. Silver, *Evening the Odds: The Case for Attorneys' Fee Awards for Administrative Resolution of Title VI and Title VII Disputes*, 67 N.C. L. Rev. 379, 384 n.36 (1989). As with many of the most ambitious civil rights reforms of that era, that provision was not ultimately effective because the underlying causes of action were repealed. *Id.* Attorneys' fees provisions also appeared during the New Deal as part of the federal securities laws. *Id.* at 384 n.35.

7. The Supreme Court has ruled that a court may, in rare cases, award attorneys' fees to a defendant, but only where the plaintiff's claim was "frivolous, unreasonable, or groundless" or "the plaintiff continued to litigate after it clearly became so." *Christiansburg Garment Co. v. Equal Employment Opportunity Comm'n*, 434 U.S. 412, 422 (1978); *see also Fox v. Vice*, ___ U.S. ___, 131 S. Ct. 2205, 2214 (2011).

a contingency fee was unlikely to draw the interest of an attorney to a meritorious civil rights case where the monetary damages were likely to be minimal. Moreover, no market incentives existed to encourage a lawyer to take a civil rights claims for injunctive relief, as there was no damages recovery from which to draw a fee. It was against this backdrop that §1988 and other fee-shifting provisions were enacted.

> Congress enacted fee-shifting statutes to encourage private enforcement of civil rights laws by making it easier for victims of civil rights violations to find lawyers willing to represent them. Congress intended these statutes "to ensure that there would be lawyers available to plaintiffs who could not otherwise afford counsel." Congress saw the need for fee-shifting statutes based in part on evidence that the vast majority of civil rights victims could not afford representation, and that private attorneys were refusing to take civil rights cases because of the limited potential for compensation. Congress explicitly noted that civil rights enforcement "depend[s] heavily upon private enforcement," and that "fee awards" are essential "if private citizens are to have a meaningful opportunity to vindicate the important Congressional policies which these laws contain." . . .
>
> Fee-shifting statutes support an extensive system of rights enforcement by encouraging private litigants to bring enforcement actions that benefit not only the litigant but also the broader public interest. These litigants are sometimes referred to as "private attorney[s] general." More than 150 important statutory policies, including civil rights and environmental protections, provide statutory fees to encourage private litigants to mobilize a private right of action. . . . This private enforcement system decentralizes enforcement decisions, allows disenfranchised interests access to policymaking, and helps insulate enforcement from capture by established interests. It is also less expensive for taxpayers because it does not place the cost of enforcement solely upon government actors. . . .
>
> Fee-shifting statutes also address structural disincentives inherent in decentralized enforcement that might otherwise discourage public interest litigation. First, they help mitigate power disparities between individual claimants and more sophisticated and resourceful institutional defendants. Reflecting this function, fee-shifting provisions historically emerged in the context of individual claims against government or corporate defendants who were better able to absorb litigation costs, and thus resist or deter claims against them. Second, fee-shifting statutes solve the public good problem that arises when no one individual has sufficient incentive to enforce rights that nevertheless would significantly benefit society as a whole. For example, voting rights claims, school desegregation cases, or environmental enforcement actions can involve complex issues, require time-consuming and costly litigation, and require class actions against government entities or corporations. Absent fee-shifting provisions, there are few resources for private attorneys or public interest organizations to take on these expensive cases, even though these claims may be essential to enforcing important public policies. By overcoming these structural challenges, fee-shifting provisions help preserve a decentralized enforcement scheme without undermining incentives to enforce statutes that benefit the public interest.

Catherine R. Albiston & Laura Beth Nielsen, *The Procedural Attack on Civil Rights: The Empirical Reality of* Buckhannon *for the Private Attorney General,* 54 UCLA L. Rev. 1087, 1088-89, 1095-96 (2007).

b. LIMITS ON ATTORNEYS' FEES

While attorneys' fees are an important source of public interest funding, they are also limited in significant ways that affect how public interest firms operate. Some limits stem from the practical realities of the system of administering attorneys' fees. Others come from Supreme Court interpretations of the attorneys' fees statutes.

One practical limitation on attorneys' fees funding is that it is only available in the context of specific types of litigation (other types of public interest advocacy do not generate attorneys' fees). Organizations that choose to focus on lobbying, public education, and/or community organizing cannot pursue this funding option. This may help explain why half of the public interest groups in Rhode's study received no attorneys' fees and that overall such fees amounted to only 8 percent of organizational funding on average. Rhode, *Movement at Midlife, supra,* at 2055 tbl. 4.

Another practical limitation is that court-awarded attorneys' fees are somewhat unpredictable. Fee awards are sporadic and lawyers who rely on them may have to address more regular funding needs to get through long droughts without any fee awards. Fee awards may not arrive until many years after the underlying legal victory has been achieved. This is even more problematic if the firm sponsoring the case has expended substantial costs up front and experiences long delays before being reimbursed. *Id.* at 2056.

As a result, one could imagine a public interest lawyer stating the following view:

> Our practice is heavily focused on statutory civil rights claims, and we are fortunate to have won some major court cases and received substantial fee awards. But relying on attorneys' fees is like riding a roller coaster. I have been working here for 25 years, and we go back and forth between periods when we have plenty of money and times when we are worried about making next month's payroll. We always manage to get by, but the uncertainty adds an enormous amount of stress to my role as managing attorney. We finally came up with a partial solution when we instituted a policy requiring us to set aside a reserve fund from every fee award we received. After we pay off the expenses from a case, we take 10% of the remainder of the fee award and put it in an account that cannot be touched except in the case of extraordinary and unforeseen financial emergencies. That helps, but I still feel like we're living from award to award, just as many of our clients sometimes have to live paycheck to paycheck.

A related problem is that if the fee issue is not settled at the time the underlying legal claim is resolved, there can be protracted litigation over the plaintiffs' legal entitlement to fees and the proper amount that should be awarded. Such litigation can itself be costly and time consuming and draw lawyers' energy away from the substantive work. If the plaintiffs prevail in the fee litigation, they are entitled to petition the court for an award for the attorneys' fees relating to the fee litigation as well. *See, e.g., Commissioner, INS v. Jean,* 496 U.S. 154, 160-61 (1990); *Hernandez v. George,* 793 F.2d 264, 269 (10th Cir. 1988); *Hernandez v. Kalinowski,* 146 F.3d 196, 199-201 (3d Cir. 1998). But, again, it may be a long time before those fees are awarded.

Another problem can arise from distorted public understandings of fee awards. News of large fees in public interest cases can make it appear that lawyers or organizations are getting rich because the figures awarded for complex litigation can be in the hundreds of thousands of dollars or even over a million dollars. This can look unusual to the public, particularly in cases in which the monetary award to the clients is relatively modest or where the only relief is injunctive and declaratory. In these contexts, it is not always clear that fee awards include long awaited reimbursements of expenses firms have advanced toward the case over years of litigation or, in the case of recovery by nonprofit groups, that the fees typically go to the organizations, not the individual lawyers who work for them. As a result, politicians have long attacked fee awards as a windfall for greedy plaintiffs' attorneys. *See, e.g.*, David Margolick, *Pro Bono Lawsuits at Park Avenue Prices*, N.Y. TIMES, Dec. 18, 1983, §4, at 8.

These concerns have been codified in the context of prisoner litigation. In 1996, Congress enacted the Prison Litigation Reform Act (PLRA), a law designed to address the perceived problem of frivolous prisoner litigation and to constrain what were argued to be overzealous federal judges in their administration of remedies in prisoner cases. *See* Margo Schlanger, *Inmate Litigation*, 116 HARV. L. REV. 1555, 1565-66 (2003). In addition to making it more difficult even for prisoners with meritorious cases to proceed, the PLRA also limited access to counsel by placing limitations on attorneys' fees. The PLRA imposes additional restrictions on fee awards in prisoner litigation that are not required in other civil rights suits. To recover fees, the prisoner must show that the fee "was directly and reasonably incurred in proving an actual violation of the plaintiff's rights protected by a statute pursuant to which a fee may be awarded under section 1988." 42 U.S.C. §1997(e)(d)(1)(A). The PLRA limits the amount of recovery as well. Attorneys' fee awards must be shown to either be "proportionately related to the court ordered relief" or "directly and reasonably incurred in enforcing the relief ordered for the violation." 42 U.S.C. §1997(e)(d)(1)(B). Where a prisoner recovers damages, a portion of the judgment that would otherwise go the prisoner, not to exceed 25 percent, is taken out and awarded as part of the attorneys' fee award. 42 U.S.C. §1997(e)(d)(2). That section also indicates that "[i]f the award of attorney's fees is not greater than 150 percent of the judgment, the excess shall be paid by the defendant." In other words, the defendant cannot be forced to pay fees that amount to more than 150 percent of the monetary judgment. Finally, the hourly rate that can be awarded is capped. Under typical §1988 fee claims, attorneys are permitted to claim an hourly rate that comports with the prevailing market rate for lawyers of similar experience in the area where the claim was brought. *Blum v. Stenson*, 465 U.S. 886, 895-96 (1984). Under the PLRA, attorneys can recover no more than "150 percent of the hourly rate established" under federal law for payment of court-appointed counsel. 42 U.S.C. §1997(e)(d)(3). That rate is sometimes adjusted, but as of 2003 it was a maximum of $169.50 per hour. Schlanger, *supra*, at 1631.

In addition to these practical and statutory limits on fee awards as a funding source for public interest lawyers, some of the rationales for fee-shifting statutes have been undercut by important developments in case law interpreting §1988 and parallel federal attorneys' fees provisions.

i. FEES ON NOMINAL DAMAGES AWARDS

In *Farrar v. Hobby*, 506 U.S. 103 (1992), the Supreme Court considered an attorneys' fees claim for more than $300,000 by a civil rights plaintiff who won his case, but was awarded only a $1 nominal damages award. The Court held that the plaintiff was the "prevailing party," because he won "actual relief on the merits of his claim [that] materially alter[ed] the legal relationship between the parties by modifying the defendant's behavior in a way that directly benefit[ed] the plaintiff." *Id.* at 111-12. But in evaluating the reasonableness of the fee award, the Court held that "[w]hen a plaintiff recovers only nominal damages because of his failure to prove an essential element of his claim for monetary relief, . . . the only reasonable fee is usually no fee at all." *Id.* at 115.

As we have discussed, fee-shifting statutes such as §1988 were designed, in part, to create incentives to take cases with modest damage claims because contingency fee arrangements would not produce a sufficient recovery to induce attorneys to take such cases, thus limiting access to the justice system. Given what you have read about Congress's goals in enacting fee-shifting statutes, does the result in *Farrar* make sense? Does this case create an incentive for a plaintiff to be relatively conservative in the amount of damages she requests in her pleadings? How far would the reasoning in *Farrar* extend? Consider a case where the jury awarded $50 as compensatory damages for a due process violation. Or $200. Would *Farrar* allow a court to award a substantial amount for attorneys' fees for such results? Would it matter if the right vindicated through the litigation was a very important one?

ii. FEE WAIVERS AS A CONDITION OF SETTLEMENT

Ironically, some Supreme Court decisions have also facilitated the ability of *defendants* to use fee awards strategically in the course of ongoing litigation. Because fee awards in complex public interest litigation can be substantial, defendants' potential exposure to such awards can be a major factor in how they conduct themselves in the litigation, including whether they are willing to settle a case and how much they are willing to pay to do so. In *Evans v. Jeff D.*, 475 U.S. 717 (1986), the plaintiffs were a class of children who were, or in the future would be, placed in the care of the State of Idaho for treatment for emotional and mental disabilities. They filed suit against state officials complaining that serious deficiencies in educational programs and health care services violated the U.S. Constitution, the state constitution, and several federal and state statutes. The federal trial court appointed a legal aid attorney to represent the plaintiff class. After a couple of years of litigation on one of the plaintiffs' major claims, the parties were preparing for trial. The defendants then presented the plaintiffs with a settlement proposal offering them the injunctive relief sought in their complaint, but conditioning the offer on the plaintiffs' agreement to waive their entitlement to statutory attorneys' fees. The plaintiffs' lawyer accepted the offer because he determined that he had an ethical obligation to accept the proposal in the interests of his clients. After entering the agreement, however, he petitioned the court to refuse approval of the fee waiver on the ground that the defendants had exploited his ethical duty to his clients to extract that waiver.

The Supreme Court held that no legal or ethical provision precluded operation of the fee waiver. In fact, the Court observed that there was technically no ethical conflict in this case, because the duty of the plaintiff's counsel was unambiguous. *Id.* at 727-28. Although this put him in a difficult position, he was not required "to choose between conflicting duties under the prevailing norms of professional conduct. Plainly, Johnson [the plaintiffs' attorney] had no *ethical* obligation to seek a statutory fee award. His ethical duty was to serve his clients loyally and competently. Since the proposal to settle the merits was more favorable than the probable outcome of the trial, Johnson's decision to recommend acceptance was consistent with the highest standards of our profession." *Id.* The Court found no statutory barrier to approving settlements that included a fee waiver.

> The text of the Fees Act provides no support for the proposition that Congress intended to ban all fee waivers offered in connection with substantial relief on the merits. On the contrary, the language of the Act, as well as its legislative history, indicates that Congress bestowed on the "prevailing *party*" (generally plaintiffs) a statutory eligibility for a discretionary award of attorney's fees in specified civil rights actions. It did not prevent the party from waiving this eligibility anymore than it legislated against assignment of this right to an attorney, such as effectively occurred here. . . . In fact, we believe that a general proscription against negotiated waiver of attorney's fees in exchange for a settlement on the merits would itself impede vindication of civil rights, at least in some cases, by reducing the attractiveness of settlement. . . . Most defendants are unlikely to settle unless the cost of the predicted judgment, discounted by its probability, plus the transaction costs of further litigation, are greater than the cost of the settlement package. If fee waivers cannot be negotiated, the settlement package must either contain an attorney's fee component of potentially large and typically uncertain magnitude, or else the parties must agree to have the fee fixed by the court. Although either of these alternatives may well be acceptable in many cases, there surely is a significant number in which neither alternative will be as satisfactory as a decision to try the entire case.

Id. at 730-34.

Justice Brennan dissented. He argued that permitting fee waivers such as the one exercised here was inconsistent with the broader purpose of the attorneys' fee act. "It seems obvious," he wrote, "that allowing defendants in civil rights cases to condition settlement of the merits on a waiver of statutory attorney's fees will diminish lawyers' expectations of receiving fees and decrease the willingness of lawyers to accept civil rights cases." *Id.* at 754.

> Because making it more difficult for civil rights plaintiffs to obtain legal assistance is precisely the opposite of what Congress sought to achieve by enacting the Fees Act, fee waivers should be prohibited. We have on numerous prior occasions held that "a statutory right conferred on a private party, but affecting the public interest, may not be waived or released if such waiver or release contravenes the statutory policy."

Id. at 759.

Justice Brennan called on Congress to amend the fee statute to preclude conditional fee waivers and on state and local bar associations to declare it unethical for defense counsel to seek fee waivers in such cases. *Id.* at 765. Indeed, as he pointed out, a couple of local bar associations had already adopted such rules. *Id.* But his hopes for federal statutory reform and/or widespread professional disapproval of the defense counsel practice of seeking fee waivers remain unmet nearly 25 years after the *Jeff D.* case. At the same time, the extent to which the dire predictions of widespread seeking of fee waivers were accurate is unclear. There has been limited empirical study of whether and how *Jeff D.* has affected negotiated settlements in injunctive relief cases that have fee-shifting statutes for those who prevail on the substantive claim. One scholar who interviewed civil rights plaintiffs' attorneys found that while some respondents suggested that *Jeff D.* has affected settlement negotiations, the majority indicated that requests for fee waivers were not a major problem. *See* Julie Davies, *Federal Civil Rights Practice in the 1990's: The Dichotomy Between Reality and Theory*, 48 HASTINGS L.J. 197, 215 (1997). Another scholar, based on his own personal experience and common knowledge, concluded that *Jeff D.* has "destroyed" §1983 as a remedy for plaintiffs seeking injunctive relief or modest damages claims. Paul D. Reingold, *Requiem for Section 1983*, 3 DUKE J. CONST. L. & PUB. POL'Y 1, 4, 38 (2008).

One cure suggested by Justice Brennan was that civil rights attorneys might be able to secure agreements from their clients not to waive attorneys' fees claims. 475 U.S. at 766. If the dilemma presented by fee waiver requests has not had a substantial impact, one explanation might be that public interest attorneys have indeed adjusted their retainer agreements to ensure that their clients will not agree to waive fees before the merits of the case have been settled. Davies's anecdotal study suggested that:

> After *Jeff D.*, attorneys very quickly developed fee agreements with clients which offer some protection from waivers in the form of financial disincentives. In addition to providing for attorney payment on a contingent fee basis, some agreements provide that if fees are waived in a settlement, the client must pay at the lodestar rate for all the hours the attorney expended, or at 75% of lodestar. Attorneys also discourage fee waivers by exercising caution in client selection and by educating clients about the importance of fees in a civil rights practice to prepare clients in the event of a settlement offer contingent on a waiver.

Davies, *supra*, at 215. Several other scholars and lawyers have focused on this as a response to the Court's decision. *See* Steven M. Goldstein, *Settlement Offers Contingent upon Waiver of Attorney Fees: A Continuing Dilemma After* Evans v. Jeff D., 20 CLEARINGHOUSE REV. 692 (1986); Jeff Scott Olson, *A New Model Retainer Agreement for Civil Rights Cases: Nailing Things Down on Settled Ground, in* CIVIL RIGHTS LITIGATION AND ATTORNEY FEES ANNUAL HANDBOOK 391-415 (Steven Saltzman & Barbara M. Wolvovitz eds., 1991); Stephen Yelnosky & Charles Silver, *A Model Retainer Agreement for Legal Services Programs: Mandatory Attorney's Fees Provisions*, 28 CLEARINGHOUSE REV. 114 (1994). For a critical examination of whether these retainer agreements are consistent with professional ethics rules and whether they would address the fee waiver problem, see Reingold, *supra*, at 21-28. Do you think a public interest lawyer should present the fee waiver option to her clients at the outset of representation? Are there any concerns with that type of negotiation between lawyer and client? If so, how might they be addressed?

iii. NARROWING THE DEFINITION OF PREVAILING PARTY

A critical aspect of evaluating entitlement to attorneys' fees under federal fee-shifting statutes is determining when a plaintiff is a "prevailing party." The Court has been quite clear in stating that attorneys' fees should not be awarded to a party who is able to resolve a dispute before litigation has even commenced. *North Carolina Dep't of Transportation v. Crest St. Community Council, Inc.*, 479 U.S. 6 (1986). This is true even though the pre-filing resolution of the dispute may consume vast amounts of attorney resources. More recently, the Court addressed whether attorneys' fees should be awarded to a plaintiff who resolves the dispute *after* the lawsuit has been filed, but not through a formal judgment or settlement agreement. Some lower court decisions had previously suggested that plaintiffs in such circumstances might recover attorneys' fees under a "catalyst" theory if they could demonstrate that their lawsuit prompted the defendant to change its behavior in ways that were consistent with what the plaintiffs sought in the case.

In *Buckhannon Bd. & Care Home, Inc. v. W. Va. Dep't of Health & Human Resources*, 532 U.S. 598 (2001), the Court rejected the catalyst theory. In that case, a class of residential care facilities and their residents sued the state to enjoin enforcement of a state fire code provision that had resulted in the closing of facilities because some of the homes' residents were incapable of "self-preservation" as defined under West Virginia law. The plaintiffs claimed that the state's self-preservation requirement violated federal fair housing and disability discrimination laws. While the case was pending, the state agreed not to enforce its order closing the residential care facilities, and the next year the state legislature repealed the self-preservation requirement that was at the heart of the lawsuit. The district court then granted the state's motion to dismiss the case as moot. The plaintiffs' lawyers filed a petition for attorneys' fees, arguing that they were the prevailing party and that their lawsuit had been the catalyst for the change in state law.

In rejecting the fee claim, the Court concluded that "a 'prevailing party' is one who has been awarded some relief by the court. . . ." *Id.* at 603. Thus, where the plaintiff secures a judgment on the merits or a settlement agreement enforceable by consent decree it can be said to have prevailed. *Id.* at 604. Both of those outcomes result in a "court-ordered 'chang[e] [in] the legal relationship between [the plaintiff] and the defendant.'" *Id.* Conversely, in this case, "[a] defendant's voluntary change in conduct, although perhaps accomplishing what the plaintiff sought to achieve by the lawsuit, lacks the necessary judicial *imprimatur* on the change. Our precedents thus counsel against holding that the term 'prevailing party' authorizes an award of attorney's fees *without* a corresponding alteration in the legal relationship of the parties." *Id.* at 605. The Court also rejected the plaintiffs' claims that the legislative history of the attorneys' fees act supported a broader understanding of "prevailing party." *Id.* at 607-08.[8]

---

8. The Court's decision suggests that the legislative history is ambiguous. But the Senate Committee report regarding the relevant fee statute stated that "prevailing party" may include parties who vindicate their rights through a consent judgment "or without formally obtaining relief." *See generally* Albiston & Nielsen, *supra*, at 1088-89.

Finally, the Court rejected the plaintiffs' contentions that in the absence of a catalyst theory, defendants could unilaterally moot cases prior to judgment specifically to avoid liability for attorneys' fees and that plaintiffs would be dissuaded from taking the risk of pursuing meritorious, but expensive, cases. First, it argued that there was no empirical evidence to suggest these developments would materialize. *Id.* at 608. The Court observed that the opposite incentives were just as likely, with defendants *unwilling* to change their conduct because of their potential exposure to large fee awards. *Id.* Furthermore, it argued, even if the plaintiffs' theory was correct, it would only create such incentives in injunctive cases, since damages claims would not become moot even after a change in the defendants' conduct. *Id.* at 608-09. And even in injunctive cases, the defendants' change in behavior might not moot the case if it were viewed as a voluntary cessation of unlawful conduct that qualified as an exception to the mootness doctrine. *Id.* at 609.[9] The Court also expressed concern that the question of whether the plaintiffs' lawsuit was the catalyst for the defendants' change in conduct would be highly contested, thus enhancing the chance of protracted fee litigation after the central components of the case were resolved. *Id.* at 609-10.

Four Justices dissented. In an opinion by Justice Ginsburg, the dissenters viewed the catalyst theory as consistent with Congress's purpose in adopting fee-shifting provisions to create incentives for lawyers to represent plaintiffs in civil rights cases. *Id.* at 635. "Under a fair reading of the . . . provisions in point, I would hold that a party 'prevails' in 'a true and proper sense,' when she achieves, by instituting litigation, the practical relief sought in her complaint." *Id.* at 634. "The plaintiffs' objective was to stop enforcement of a rule requiring Buckhannon to evict residents like centenarian Dorsey Pierce as the price of remaining in business. If Buckhannon achieved that objective on account of the strength of its case—if it succeeded in keeping its doors open while housing and caring for Ms. Pierce and others similarly situated—then Buckhannon is properly judged a party who prevailed." *Id.* Finally, the dissenters disputed the majority's suggestion about the incentives likely to be created by acceptance of a catalyst theory. They argued that if the catalyst theory were in effect, that "may lead defendants promptly to comply with the law's requirements: the longer the litigation, the larger the fees. Indeed, one who knows noncompliance will be expensive might be encouraged to conform his conduct to the legal requirements before litigation is threatened." *Id.* at 639.

The majority and dissent disagree about the incentives for both plaintiff and defense attorneys under the rule in the *Buckhannon* case. Is the majority correct that without a catalyst theory there is a substantial incentive for defendants to settle cases in ways that are favorable to plaintiffs? Will the

---

9. In some contexts, it may be possible for plaintiffs to argue that their legal claims are not moot despite the defendants' apparent capitulation. An important exception to mootness applies when the defendant voluntarily ceases engaging in the conduct the plaintiff has challenged as unlawful. *See Friends of the Earth, Inc. v. Laidlaw Environmental Services, Inc.*, 528 U.S. 167 (2000). But "courts evaluate voluntary cessation of allegedly illegal conduct by government officials with more deference and solicitude than similar actions by private actors." Albiston & Nielsen, *supra*, at 1112.

possibility of non-recovery discourage plaintiffs' attorneys from taking on complex cases in the first instance? Are there ways in which the results in *Jeff D.* and *Buckhannon*, when combined, disadvantage plaintiffs in settlement negotiations?

As was the case after the Court decided *Jeff D.*, many scholars and other observers predicted that the *Buckhannon* decision would have adverse effects on the ability to find legal counsel to invest their resources and time into public interest cases. Albiston and Nielsen conducted an empirical survey of civil rights organizations to determine whether *Buckhannon* affected the way they carried out their work. After analyzing their survey results, they reached the following conclusions:

> First, organizations that engage in litigation directed at systemic social change are more likely than others to report that they were negatively affected by the *Buckhannon* decision. Organizations that engage in impact litigation, litigate against government actors, bring class actions, and work in the environmental, civil rights, or poverty areas were the most likely to report negative effects from this decision. Second, qualitative data from our survey indicate that *Buckhannon* affects far more than fee recovery. These data indicate that *Buckhannon* both discourages settlement and discourages lawyers from representing plaintiffs in enforcement actions. . . .

Albiston & Nielsen, *supra*, at 1120-21. Their study went further, and looked at three case studies that demonstrated the types of circumstances in which *Buckhannon* is most likely to affect lawyers' ability to bring cases. They examined an injunctive case seeking to challenge a state welfare policy, a claim against the Immigration and Naturalization Service for disclosure of documents under the federal Freedom of Information Act, and a claim for equitable relief requiring a school district to implement an individualized education program under federal law. *Id.* at 1104-10.

In assessing these three case studies, Albiston & Nielsen observed that *Buckhannon* was most likely to influence the lawyering in cases with three common features:

> First, these actions sought to enforce important constitutional or statutory rights, and therefore advance the public policy interests behind the private attorney general doctrine. Second, these were claims against government defendants seeking a change in policy or a judicial mandate to government actors to comply with the law; if there were no private enforcement in claims such as these, it would be hard to imagine government actors stepping into the breach. Third, the plaintiffs in these cases were limited to injunctive relief or other equitable relief, and thus could not rely on a claim for monetary relief to avoid mootness. Together, these cases present a set of structural conditions not uncommon in public interest cases that render claims vulnerable to fee loss as a result of defendants' strategic behavior.

Id. at 1104.

Furthermore, other issues in the wake of *Buckhannon* may make it even more difficult for plaintiffs to avoid strategic capitulation. As Albiston & Nielson also point out:

> [A] circuit split has developed on whether a preliminary injunction is sufficient to support a fee award should the defendant subsequently change its position

in accordance with this injunctive relief. This question is important because preliminary relief may be the primary form of success in complex actions seeking significant institutional reform, and it is an important signal about the likely outcome of the litigation. If an injunction is not sufficient to support a fee award, a plaintiff who obtains preliminary injunctive relief is especially vulnerable to strategic capitulation because the court's order may simply prompt wise defendants to alter their conduct voluntarily to avoid a fee award. There is also a circuit split on the question of whether *Buckhannon* extends beyond strategic capitulation to include settlement agreements, even though *Buckhannon* did not involve a settlement. Courts generally agree, however, that settlements that allow the court to retain jurisdiction provide sufficient judicial imprimatur to support a fee award under *Buckhannon*. As a result, plaintiffs must be very careful to structure settlement agreements in a way that preserves their right to recover fees, assuming defendants will agree to such a settlement after *Buckhannon*.

Id. at 1113-14.

As this suggests, limits on fees may be a challenge for the future of private public interest firms that rely on fee-shifting statutes for financial support. These limits also affect nonprofit groups that either collect fees directly or through collaborations with private law firms that donate such fees to nonprofit partners when they are awarded in pro bono cases.

2. Agenda Setting Ability

Because of the importance of fee recovery, agenda setting within private public interest law firms must take into account the firms' overall profitability in addition to their social mission. Not having to rely on external funding frees private public interest firm lawyers from having to shape their dockets around foundation or government mandates. This type of autonomy is one appeal of the private firm context.

The existing research suggests that one attraction of private public interest law firms is that they allow lawyers to structure practices to match their political commitments. Lawyers profiled in the literature emphasize the strong advantage of flexibility in case selection. . . . When [Los Angeles-based] Hadsell & Stormer formed its partnership in 1992, the lawyers asserted that "we wanted to be as unfettered as possible and we knew that the closer you get to a grant-funded organization the more restrictions there's going to be. And we really, literally, wanted to be able to take any case we wanted." [R]esearch on conservative and libertarian lawyers similarly found lawyers who gravitated toward small firms where they could build practices consistent with their political and/or religious values.

Cummings & Southworth, *supra*, at 195.

However, reliance on client fees also means that lawyers may have to define their agenda in terms that are broad enough to encompass a range of fee-generating cases that generally align with the lawyers' sense of justice. Thus, some firms that set themselves up as for-profit organizations avoid adopting a specific mission, preferring instead to take cases based on the partners' sense of what serves the public interest. Katz & Bernabei, *supra*, at

296-97. Others adopt a broad mission. Los Angeles-area firm Hadsell & Stormer, for instance, asserts that its goal is "fighting injustice, no matter what form it takes." Cummings, *Privatizing Public Interest Law, supra*, at 34-35. The breadth of this mission permits firm lawyers to allocate resources as they see fit to meet the twin goals of impact and profitability. "Because it is not tied to a specific movement goal, the firm can evaluate how it wants to allocate its litigation resources in light of the shifting terrain of progressive politics in Los Angeles and beyond. Of course, part of this analysis involves finding the types of cases that generate fees; but the firm members are also concerned with evaluating political impact. . . . The breadth of the firm's articulated mission also creates space for individual lawyers to define the firm's goals as compatible with their own political commitments and to advocate that the firm take on cases that advance the causes they believe in." *Id.* at 35. This type of flexibility can also serve other goals, such as helping the sustainability of social change efforts because lawyers can adapt to different clients and causes, potentially minimizing burn out. Overall, private public interest firms must balance political goals in agenda setting with managing a stream of fee-generating cases sufficient to pay the bills over time.

3. Control Over Legal Strategy

Private public interest law firm lawyers may also experience flexibility in choices of legal strategy. Many studies of these firms "highlight the attraction of private public interest firms for lawyers seeking to experiment with unconventional client relationships and advocacy tactics." Cummings & Southworth, *supra*, at 195. Firms may have the flexibility to engage in community organizing, at least as a complement to more traditional legal strategies, such as litigation. However, the fee structure may limit how much control lawyers have over strategic decisions. Because the lawyers in private public interest firms depend on fees, they have a strong economic incentive to take on traditional cases that generate them. Thus, most such firms are organized as litigation boutiques that rely on attorneys' fee awards or contingency fees.

4. Coordination and Coalition Building

Private public interest law firms have different approaches to coordination and coalition building. In order to advance the causes they believe in, private public interest firm lawyers sometimes co-counsel with nonprofit groups on cases of mutual political concern. Thus, it is not uncommon to see private public interest firms on the pleadings in cases with firms like the ACLU and other nonprofit groups.

There have been high profile examples of collaborations between private law firms, government lawyers, and nonprofit organizations. As described in Chapter 2, the battle against large tobacco companies involved the unusual, but effective, alliance between the plaintiffs' personal injury bar and state attorneys general. John J. Zefutie, Jr., Comment, *From Butts to Big Macs— Can the Big Tobacco Litigation and Nation-Wide Settlement with States' Attorneys General Serve as a Model for Attacking the Fast Food Industry?*, 34 Seton Hall L. Rev. 1383, 1392-93 (2004).

Another noteworthy collaboration was in the employment discrimination suit against Wal-Mart, *Dukes v. Wal-Mart Stores, Inc.* The massive sex discrimination class action against the retailer involving a class of 1.6 million women was coordinated by a team of nonprofit groups—the Impact Fund, Equal Rights Advocates, and the Public Justice Center—and private plaintiffs' firms—Cohen, Milstein, Hausfeld & Toll of Washington, D.C.; Davis, Cowell & Bowe of San Francisco; and Tinkler & Firth and Merit Bennett P.C. from Santa Fe. Nathan Koppel, *Firms, Nonprofits Team in "Wal-Mart": Is Pairing of Plaintiffs' Lawyers Merely to Hide a Motive for Profit?*, 26 Nat'l L.J. 7 (2004). The coalition of nonprofits and firms helped to close the resource gap between the plaintiffs and Wal-Mart, which was represented by a large national corporate law firm. By associating with nonprofit groups, the plaintiffs' firms identified with the public interest bar and thus distinguished themselves from ambulance chasing stereotypes. *Id.* It also allowed the team to have geographic breadth and depth of expertise.

> [Team coordinator and Impact Fund director Brad] Seligman assembled the plaintiffs' team. He enlisted 45-lawyer Cohen Milstein to provide much of the infrastructure. Its paralegals have loaded nearly 2 million documents into a database. The firm's Joseph Sellers, a well-known civil rights lawyer, has assisted Seligman with courtroom duties. San Francisco's Equal Rights Advocates was retained because of its contacts with women's rights groups. It has spent a lot of time talking to news media.
>
> The Public Justice Center in Baltimore was added partly because of contacts with low-wage workers who might become class members. The Davis Cowell firm is focused on investigating discrimination at the Sam's Club retail outlets owned by Wal-Mart. Tinkler and Bennett, the originators of the suit, continue handling depositions and other duties.

Id. There are other prominent examples of this type of inter-organizational coordination in large-scale public interest litigation. San Francisco's Lieff Cabraser Heimann & Bernstein developed a coalition with the NAACP and the Mexican American Legal Defense Fund to sue Abercrombie & Fitch Co. for race discrimination. *Id.* Successful collaborations, however, do not ensure successful results. Despite the effective coordination of lawyers across the for-profit and nonprofit sectors, the Supreme Court recently rejected certification of the plaintiff class in the Wal-Mart litigation. *Wal-Mart Stores, Inc. v. Dukes, ___ U.S. ___*, 131 S. Ct. 2541 (2011).

Los Angeles's Hadsell & Stormer also has a reputation for co-counseling with nonprofit partners because it allows the firm to advance its mission while giving nonprofit partners much needed resources and expertise. Cummings, *Privatizing Public Interest Law, supra*, at 78-80. The ACLU of Southern California's Director of Litigation emphasized the benefits of these collaborations: "[Y]ou don't have to be concerned in terms of the themes that will be developed in the case and the integrity of the case with respect to civil liberties objectives. . . . When they sign on to do a case . . . they are aggressive and committed and you never have to look back." *Id.* at 79-80. Nonprofits also indicated that they are inclined to work with Hadsell & Stormer because its "associate dependent" structure makes it set up to litigate. *Id.* at 79-80. As one legal aid lawyer put it: "[T]hey do all that discovery grunt work and legal research — and we do all the people work." *Id.*

While co-counseling is well within the operating norm for private public interest firms, coalition building with other types of organizations is more of a challenge. Consider again the case of Hadsell & Stormer:

> [T]ight accountability to a broader political constituency is generally traded off for greater lawyer autonomy in case selection and organizational practice. The result is that — without institutional clients like unions — H&S lawyers are given greater freedom to chart their own conception of the public good and determine how to fit their litigation work into that vision. In Stormer's terms, "I get to do what I want to do. That's why I signed up to do this. . . . I think I'm a reasonably political person . . . but the bottom line for me is I like doing it." "I get to make my own way. I get to eat what I kill. . . . I get to make my own decisions."
>
> This autonomy opens up possibilities for radical work since it places the firm outside the strictures of governmental oversight or foundation mandates. But by individualizing determinations of what constitutes appropriate political investments, it also relieves lawyers of having to answer to a broader political constituency. As a consequence, there may be an incentive to identify cases that make the firm money with cases that advance the public good. Case decisions may also be made on the basis of partial information about community need or to advance pet political projects.
>
> [Hadsell & Stormer] attempts to counteract the tendency toward becoming too self-referential by encouraging all of its lawyers to engage with community groups and other PIL organizations, by doing outreach and serving on boards of directors. The partners nevertheless recognize the challenge of this type of external engagement "when all we're really doing is working every day and then [we] go home and collapse." The partners themselves try to set an example: [Named partner Barbara] Hadsell, for her part, is on the board of the Impact Fund and has served on the local [National Lawyers Guild] board for thirty years. The firm also attempts to mitigate accountability concerns by hiring a diverse range of attorneys who bring different political commitments and community ties. But these efforts are inevitably partial and can lead to case decisions that are politically idiosyncratic.

Id. at 39-40. As this example suggests, close engagement with outside groups in sustained coalitions may be traded off for some private public interest law firms attempting to leverage their resources to compete against more well-resourced adversaries.

5. The Lawyer-Client Relationship

In terms of client relations, we might expect private public interest firm lawyers in general to be more traditional in their approach to client decision making. Because their firms are the most financially dependent on client satisfaction with legal outcomes, their lawyers are likely to be most deferential to client decision making. Although there are no systemic data, some qualitative studies support this view. For instance, at Hadsell & Stormer, lawyers explicitly adopt a client-centered approach.

> On the question of balancing client interests and political commitments, however, the lawyers at H&S tend to locate themselves on the client-centered

side of the lawyering spectrum. They achieve close identification between lawyer and client goals through the case selection process — screening in cases that fit within the firm's ideological parameters. Once clients have retained the firm, the lawyers emphasize the paramount nature of client interests in guiding litigation decisions, referring to their professional duty to the clients as the touchstone. . . .

H&S sometimes co-counsels cases with the ACLU in which the goal is to litigate to judgment in order to create precedent that shapes prospective government or corporate conduct. In these situations, firm lawyers attempt to memorialize an understanding with the client at the outset of the representation that makes clear that the objective of the suit is to achieve a specific outcome, rather than gain the client compensation. Where a conflict still arises, the lawyers defer to client wishes: "Basically we have an ethical obligation to our clients that takes precedence over the political goals that we would like to accomplish." Hadsell emphasized the importance of building trust with the client and resolving conflicts with an eye to client interests:

> Hopefully they're trusting you in the end . . . and if they're asking you should I go forward or not, you can't really say, "Well there is a fifty percent chance you're going to lose or who knows how it's going to grind out, but do it for the cause." It's difficult to do that.

Id. at 43. Other firms report adopting more radical approaches to client relations, attempting to promote client empowerment through enlisting them more broadly in firm operations. *See* Trubek & Kransberger, *supra*, at 211-15. In each case, the picture is distinct from the domineering lawyer wresting control from clients common in the literature on nonprofit attorneys.

———————————

What practice site do you think offers the best platform to pursue public interest work? Why? What are the limitations of public interest lawyering in those sites, and how can they be addressed?

5
PUBLIC INTEREST
ADVOCACY STRATEGIES

I. INTRODUCTION

Public interest lawyers deploy a range of advocacy strategies and techniques to advance causes. Some require the use of technical legal skill, while others draw on lawyers' problem-solving backgrounds, but enlist skills less closely linked to their formal law school training. Public interest lawyering is most frequently associated with traditional litigation, which continues to play a pivotal role in practice. Yet public interest lawyers commonly employ other approaches, both legal and nonlegal. This chapter examines different modes of advocacy undertaken by public interest lawyers and considers the conditions under which they can be most effective, as well as the ways in which they sometimes complement each other.

We begin with a scenario depicting a challenging, contemporary social problem—homelessness—as a way of providing a background against which to discuss different advocacy strategies. Throughout the chapter, we will return to this scenario to explore the ways in which different approaches to advocacy may be useful, as well as to understand their limitations.

Because of the historical centrality and continued importance of litigation, we include an extensive discussion of litigation strategies. In it, we consider the structure of public interest litigation, compare litigation models, outline the advantages and disadvantages of pursuing change through the courts, and evaluate when litigation is most effective for achieving public interest objectives.

We then examine four non-litigation modes of advocacy. The first is *transactional lawyering*, which involves advising organizational clients, like nonprofit groups, on traditional corporate issues (corporate organization and governance, tax, real estate, and contract law) but toward a distinctively egalitarian goal: promoting economic development within low-income communities. Here, we see lawyers primarily engaged in the planning and execution of projects designed to provide affordable housing and living wage jobs to low-income people who experience significant barriers to economic opportunity. In general, transactional public interest lawyers emphasize community control and seek to play a facilitative rather than a directive role in promoting collective action and community empowerment—although some lawyers become centrally involved in community struggle. As this suggests, transactional lawyering is related to the second mode of advocacy: *community organizing*. Public interest lawyers since the civil rights period have played important roles organizing constituencies and mobilizing them for political action. In the contemporary political context, organizing has become more salient for some lawyers on the political left, for whom judicial conservatism and mainstream political marginalization have raised the importance of fostering grassroots democratic action. The third mode of non-litigation work we explore—*policy advocacy*—has a lengthy pedigree. Public interest lawyers have long taken an active role in lobbying legislators, administrative agencies, and other policy makers, often using their background legal knowledge, research, and drafting skills to influence policy making. When policy advocacy works, it allows lawyers to use their legal skills of argumentative persuasion and precise drafting to craft laws that directly respond to the needs of the constituencies they represent. The challenge, of course, is amassing enough political power to pass good laws—and it is the absence of such power that may lead lawyers back to pursuing countermajoritarian strategies, like litigation. Public interest lawyers, irrespective of ideology, emphasize the ultimate importance of winning in the court of public opinion as well as in front of judges. Indeed, the struggle for public acceptance may be more important than judicial decisions in effectuating and sustaining long-term social change. Thus, the final mode of advocacy involves *public education and media strategies* designed to sway the opinions and beliefs of the general public.

While we break advocacy strategies down by category in this discussion, that is not to suggest that some forms are better than others, or that there is an optimal public interest lawyering approach. Rather, advocacy strategies should be thought of as a set of tools that lawyers can use and adapt, depending on the clients involved, the goal to be attained, the resources available, the potential for countermovements, and the social, economic, and political conditions that underlie the issues being addressed. In the end, public interest lawyers often view their roles as multifaceted and integrated, rejecting the idea that these strategies can be separated out into discrete lawyer and nonlawyer categories. In Chapter 10, we return to this discussion and consider how public interest lawyers "put it all together," linking these different modes of advocacy into a holistic and multidimensional approach to social change.

PROBLEM

The Center for Homeless Advocacy (CHA) is a nonprofit public interest law organization whose mission is "to improve the well being of homeless adults and families." The CHA currently has five staff attorneys, a paralegal, a fundraising director, and a half-time staff person with some media relations expertise. The attorneys are mainly experienced in litigation and policy analysis. CHA has hired you to work on a special project. It has received a foundation grant that will support you and two of the other current attorneys, and provide $250,000 per year for other activities, for the next five years. The grant may be renewed at reduced levels if CHA shows the funder "adequate evidence of progress."

CHA is located in an urban area with a population of 3.2 million people. The homeless population is estimated to be somewhere around 12,000 people, but is expected to grow because of a significant economic downturn. There are several public and private shelters that provide temporary housing for transient persons, but the total capacity in the community is 2,400 beds per night. In addition, there are concerns about the safety of persons who receive housing at these shelters because several incidents of violence among homeless persons at such shelters have occurred in recent months. Most experts believe that homelessness is caused by a combination of structural changes in the economy, a serious shortage in affordable housing, reduction in government welfare programs, increases in the rate of incarceration (former prisoners are a substantial portion of the homeless), and an increase in mental illness coupled with a reduction in public mental health services. There is no federal constitutional right to receive shelter, welfare, or other social services, though in some states courts have recognized a state constitutional or statutory right to emergency shelter.

The surrounding legal community has five large private law firms (more than 200 lawyers per firm) and two law schools (one private and one public). The city also is the State's capital. The city's policy-making authority resides in a seven-person, elected city council. There is also a strong multi-faith religious coalition in the community that is active in coordinating volunteer help to provide social services. The city council recently adopted the following ordinances in response to the efforts of Citizens for Peace and Safety, a local community group that has complained about the increasing presence of homeless people on the streets.

City Ordinance 100.561
It shall be unlawful for any person to use a public street, highway, alley, lane, parkway, or sidewalk for lying or sleeping except in the case of an imminent physical emergency or the administration of medical assistance.
City Ordinance 100.564
It shall be unlawful and a class C offense for anyone to beg or solicit alms in the streets or public places of the city or exhibit oneself for the purpose of begging or obtaining alms.

What goals would you set for your special project? How would you define them and what input from community stakeholders would you use? What strategy or combination of strategies would you deploy to advance the goals? What would you seek to do about the ordinances and what strategies would you employ? What role would litigation play? How, if at all, would you incorporate transactional lawyering, community organizing, policy advocacy, and community education?

As you study the materials in this chapter, consider how each strategy or combination of strategies might be used effectively to address the CHA's objective "to improve the well being of homeless adults and families."

II. PUBLIC INTEREST LITIGATION

Litigation is an indisputably central tool in the struggle for social justice. As we learned in Chapter 2, litigation has been used to challenge government action from the earliest days of the republic, although the litigation-centered vision of public interest law did not emerge as a defined legal movement until the 1950s. JOEL F. HANDLER, SOCIAL MOVEMENTS AND THE LEGAL SYSTEM: A THEORY OF LAW REFORM AND SOCIAL CHANGE 1 (1978). The NAACP employed litigation early in its history, and support for this strategy grew quickly after the group's early race litigation yielded initial successes, leading to increased support for the organization. MARK V. TUSHNET, THE NAACP'S LEGAL STRATEGY AGAINST SEGREGATED EDUCATION, 1925-1950 1 (1987). As early as 1926, the NAACP's annual report called courtroom victories "definite" and "clear-cut" and observed that they could be "built upon." *Id.* In many ways, the public perception of the NAACP's success in *Brown* and other noteworthy victories in the Supreme Court has perpetuated the idea that litigation is a foundational tool of social change. Some of the major accounts of the *Brown* litigation in the academic literature, most notably Richard Kluger's SIMPLE JUSTICE (1977), have reinforced this perception.

In addition to its high public profile, litigation is often viewed as the quintessential lawyering activity. It is common to think of going to court to vindicate someone's rights as the lawyer's basic stock-in-trade. For lawyers interested in public interest work, litigation's power and prominence make it an appealing social change tool. We could imagine a hypothetical public interest lawyer framing her commitment to litigation in the following terms:

> To me, public interest law is about litigation. I mean, let's face it: the most significant inroads in changing society have come from path breaking Supreme Court cases, such as *Brown*. The federal courts, even in today's climate, are the only institutions with the independence from everyday politics to be able to enforce the rule of law. Plus, I didn't go to lobbying school; I didn't go to public speaking or public education school; I didn't go to community organizing school. I went to LAW school!

The materials in this section explore the rewards—and risks—of public interest litigation. We begin by highlighting some structural aspects of public interest litigation and comparing different litigation models: impact litigation vs. individual client representation and direct litigation vs. amicus participation. We then discuss some critiques of the traditional model of public interest litigation and the conditions and factors that enhance or limit its usefulness.

A. LITIGATION AND SOCIAL CHANGE: STRUCTURAL CONSIDERATIONS

Litigation occurs in two contexts: civil and criminal. In the civil context, public interest litigation tends to be *affirmative*, with lawyers representing an individual or a group of plaintiffs in lawsuits seeking to enforce or extend their rights against individual, governmental, or corporate defendants.[1] In the criminal context, the posture of the litigation depends on one's frame of reference. If the focus is on representing the criminally accused, then litigation tends to be *defensive*, with public defenders representing individual defendants against the state. If, in contrast, the focus is on criminal prosecution, then cases are brought affirmatively by prosecutors based on the facts of the alleged crime. In both the civil and criminal contexts, cases may be *individually ori-ented*—with the objective being simply to resolve a dispute between two dis-crete parties—or they may be *reform oriented*—with the goal of systemic change that affects a broader class of people.

1. Civil

As with all civil litigation, public interest lawyers must consider basic struc-tural features of the litigation system and fundamental tactical choices: the identity of the parties, the substance of the legal claim and type of remedy sought, and the forum for adjudicating the claim. But certain issues arise in public interest litigation more commonly than in private lawsuits.

a. WHO?

In the public interest context, civil claims are usually brought on behalf of individuals or groups against defendants—often the government or a commercial entity—in order to vindicate rights. The playing field tends to be unequal. As Marc Galanter famously noted, there are two general categories of litigants: "one-shotters" who "only have occasional recourse to courts" and "repeat players" who "are engaged in many similar litigations over time." Marc Galanter, *Why the "Haves" Come Out Ahead: Speculations on the Limits of Legal Change*, 9 LAW & SOC'Y REV. 95, 97 (1975). A repeat player is an entity "which has had and anticipates repeated litigation, which has low stakes in the outcome of any one case, and which has the resources to pursue its long-run interests." *Id.* at 98. As such, a repeat player enjoys a number of advantages, including "advance intelligence" about how the system operates, easy access to expertise, and the ability and incentive to "play for rules"—seeking to carefully select cases in order to achieve favorable legal rulings that will have precedential value in future cases. *Id.* at 98-101. By contrast, one-shotters, who would include low-income individuals and members of other marginalized groups, lack these advantages and, as a result, face systematic barriers in the litigation process. Public interest organizations are meant to correct for some of this inequality by providing expert lawyers, with long-term experience and a com-mitment to "play for rules," to make up for some of the informational and resource disadvantages that typical public interest plaintiffs confront. Never-theless, public interest lawyers can rarely ever match the resources of their adversaries, which makes it crucial that they skillfully litigate the cases that they do accept.

---

1. Recall from the discussion in Chapter 4 also that government lawyers may play a defensive role in protecting enacted legislation from legal challenge.

b. WHAT?

A critical aspect of public interest litigation is what remedies are available and the likelihood of attaining them, as well as whether they will be sustainable over the long term. Court-awarded damages can serve both a compensatory and deterrent function. In many types of public interest cases, however, damages may not yield the desired result. Some conduct may violate the law but not produce a tangible harm. Some types of damages are difficult to quantify and demonstrate to a court or jury. *See Memphis Comm. Sch. Dist. v. Stachura*, 477 U.S. 299, 308 (1986) (precluding award of damages for violation of constitutional rights in the absence of other tangible harm). Other types of law violations, such as relatively minor forms of harassment by law enforcement officers, may simply not be worth a lot in money damages. In these types of cases, plaintiffs may not regard the available damages as being worth the trouble and expense of litigation. And as a practical matter, it may be difficult to secure legal counsel to represent a plaintiff. Even if such cases could be brought successfully, they might serve the compensatory goal, but not the deterrent one. It may simply be worth it to defendants to pay a small amount of damages to be able to continue behaving in ways that are desirable to them. Class action litigation may allow public interest lawyers to aggregate small claims and circumvent these barriers, but the Supreme Court has narrowed the scope of class action law in recent years. *See Wal-Mart Stores, Inc. v. Dukes*, ___ U.S. ___, 131 S. Ct. 2541 (2011) (holding that the claims of a class of 1.5 million female employees or former employees did not satisfy Rule 23's requirement that the class members' claims involve common questions of law and fact because the substantive claim in the case was premised on Wal-Mart's allocation of discretion to local supervisors, whose actions did not necessarily constitute a common discriminatory policy). Courts may award punitive damages, which punish the defendant for egregiously wrongful behavior, thus enhancing the deterrent impact of the lawsuit. But the Court has imposed a high mental state threshold for establishing entitlement to punitive damages in constitutional rights cases, *Smith v. Wade*, 461 U.S. 30, 56 (1983), and has recognized constitutional limits on the amount that courts can properly award in punitive damage claims, *see, e.g., BMW of North America, Inc. v. Gore*, 517 U.S. 559 (1996).

Equitable remedies are also an important element of public interest litigation. Prohibitory injunctions are court orders that stop a party from engaging in a particular form of behavior. In contrast, mandatory injunctions are court orders requiring a party to affirmatively act in a specific fashion. Equitable relief can be a powerful remedy that can affect a wide range of persons — all children in a school district, all inmates in a state prison, all female employees — or it can be relatively narrow. Equitable relief can also be extraordinarily expensive to comply with and may require regular monitoring on the part of the parties and the court. It is also considered to be an extraordinary form of relief and is therefore subject to numerous legal limitations. Moreover, in the types of cases typically brought in public interest litigation, a number of procedural and justiciability rules may make it more difficult to obtain equitable relief, at least in the federal courts. A routine consideration in any federal injunctive action, for example, is whether the plaintiff has standing to assert a particular legal claim. The Supreme Court has narrowed standing law in ways that make it difficult to address some types of law reform issues in an injunctive action. *See, e.g., City of Los Angeles v. Lyons*, 461 U.S. 95, 105 (1983) (rejecting injunctive claim of plaintiff who allegedly had been subjected to chokehold pursuant to city police department policy because he could not show that he was likely to be subject to such conduct again in the future). So-called *Lyons* problems routinely face litigators who seek prospective injunctive relief for their clients in social change cases. *See* Myriam E. Gilles, *Reinventing Structural Reform Litigation: Deputizing Private Citizens in the Enforcement of Civil Rights*, 100 Colum. L. Rev. 1384 (2000).

c. WHERE?

Public interest litigation, precisely because it can be controversial and high profile, may be affected by the forum in which it is brought. Thus, in litigation where there are numerous possible places to file a case, some of which might be more favorable to the interests of one's clients, lawyers consider the forum in evaluating the chance of success. This assessment can be particularly important in public interest litigation, which may raise politically sensitive, controversial issues. Public interest lawyers must be cognizant of whether the forum for litigating a case is likely to be receptive or hostile to their clients' claims and whether the judges have expertise in the area and are likely to be able to act independently of political pressure. Another practical factor is the size of the court docket. How quickly can the client's case be moved along through the ordinary adjudication process? Yet another factor is whether evidentiary and procedural rules are more favorable in one jurisdiction than another. For example, one might consider what discovery rules exist in each forum and how that might affect the case. *See, e.g.,* Sameer M. Ashar, *Public Interest Lawyers and Resistance Movements*, 95 Cal. L. Rev. 1879, 1908 (2007) (explaining how movement lawyers representing undocumented workers chose to bring wage enforcement claims in federal court because "discovery guidelines were more stringent, federal judges had lower caseloads since they try to move cases off their dockets as quickly as possible, and federal magistrate judges usually took charge of discovery and issued schedules and orders quite expediently"). Another factor may be as practical as the forum's physical location. How far away is the court from the clients? Is it located in a community that might be particularly hostile to the claims in the case, particularly if the lawyer is pursuing a jury trial and the juror pool will be drawn from that community?

2. Criminal

The work done every day in the courts by public defenders and attorneys appointed to represent indigent defendants is an important form of public interest litigation focused on individual client representation. Because of the nature of the criminal process, this type of litigation is generally reactive — defending the rights of the accused — making it less subject to the type of carefully orchestrated social change strategizing that characterizes affirmative public interest litigation in the civil context.

Despite the individual orientation of day-to-day practice, criminal defense lawyers do nonetheless sometimes pursue broader systemic reform through different avenues, as Kim Taylor-Thompson's discussion in Chapter 4 of the "institutional" vision of some public defender's offices highlighted. For instance, defense lawyers often seek to create new legal rights for criminal defendants through the development of constitutional precedents in the context of motions to suppress evidence at trial, appellate litigation, and, where still permissible by law, collateral attacks on convictions through habeas corpus. Sometimes criminal defense lawyers may identify an important legal issue ex ante and wait for a case with the right facts to present it most forcefully to an appellate court.

Criminal litigators also engage in organized efforts to persuade courts to adopt precedents promoting the rights of those accused of crimes by filing amicus briefs in cases where new precedents may be established. At times, an outside group may enter a case as amicus curiae to try to shape the law, independent of the representation of the defendant. In some of the major constitutional criminal procedure reform cases from the Warren Court era, *Mapp v. Ohio*, 367 U.S. 643 (1961), and *Miranda v. Arizona*, 384 U.S. 436 (1966), the ACLU played this role by providing arguments to the Supreme Court in amicus briefs that the defendants' own attorneys did not assert. *See* Samuel Walker, In Defense of American Liberties: A History of the ACLU 249-51 (1990). In many criminal cases, amicus efforts take place through national coordinating organizations, such as the National Association of Criminal Defense Lawyers (NACDL).

Another exception to the reactive nature of criminal litigation is the law reform work of a specialized core of criminal defense lawyers seeking to abolish the death penalty, and to ensure full and fair procedural protections for capital defendants in jurisdictions where it is administered. Some of these advocacy groups also engage in pro-active efforts to persuade policy makers to repeal or modify laws affecting capital defendants through the political process.

Criminal litigators pursue law reform in other creative ways as well. As Ingrid Eagly suggests in an analysis of her clinic's work with a group of immigrant lunch truck vendors in Los Angeles (discussed in the last chapter), criminal defense lawyers sometimes work directly with community-based organizations seeking to promote legal change that benefits their members. Ingrid V. Eagly, *Criminal Clinics in the Pursuit of Immigrant Rights: Lessons from the* Loncheros, 2 U.C. Irvine L. Rev. 91 (2012). In Eagly's account, her clinic defended an individual lunch truck owner who had been fined for violating a city parking ordinance as part of a coordinated campaign by a community group to repeal the law; the individual representation of the owner, who was hand-picked by the community group to test the law's validity, resulted in a court decision declaring it unconstitutional — thus realizing the group's law reform objective. *Id.*

B. LITIGATION MODELS

Before turning to a discussion of the advantages and disadvantages of public interest litigation as a social change strategy, we describe some features of different litigation models. One important distinction is between *impact litigation*, which seeks to change legal rules and ultimately institutional behavior, and *individual client service*, which seeks to achieve a positive resolution to an individual client's dispute. Both are generally viewed as important and, at some level, complementary tools. Any disagreement about these models tends to be over the degree to which public interest lawyers should invest resources in one approach over the other. Another distinction relates to the *form* of public interest lawyers' participation in litigation. When should public interest lawyers pursue the direct representation of clients in lawsuits of their own selection and when should they submit amicus curiae briefs in cases brought by others?

1. Impact Litigation and Individual Service

Public interest lawsuits designed to advance social change are characterized as "impact" or "law reform" litigation when they are part of a conscious, strategic effort to change the law and address a social issue that affects a wide range of people. The predominant version involves lawyers seeking change through large test cases (sometimes brought as class actions) to establish new rights or legal principles. An example of this type of broader social change effort is a litigation campaign to challenge a law as an infringement of the constitutional rights of a large group of persons. The NAACP's campaign to end racial segregation and invalidate Jim Crow is the most prominent historical example. The anti-abortion movement's broad strategy to overrule *Roe v. Wade* is another. Sometimes a litigation campaign is designed to ensure the enforcement of existing laws and rights rather than to create new legal rules. After the adoption of numerous federal laws protecting the environment, for example, the environmental movement focused for many years on litigating cases asking courts to require federal officials to enforce those laws. Conversely, public interest lawyers can also mount a systematic campaign to defend the validity of a law or set of laws that are designed to further social reform. Yet another version of the impact lawsuit involves lawyers coordinating litigation with an organizing campaign in order to advance the campaign's objective.

In contrast to impact litigation, the client service model favors an approach that seeks to extend services to a wide range of individual clients in order to vindicate their individual interests. This type of public interest litigation involves bilateral disputes between parties. For example, an arrestee may file a claim against a law enforcement officer who allegedly used an unreasonable amount of physical force on him under the circumstances resulting in physical injuries and medical expenses. A landlord may serve a tenant with an eviction notice for failure to pay rent, but the tenant asserts a counterclaim that she has withheld rent because of the landlord's severe neglect in maintaining the rental property in a habitable condition. A local government agency may terminate public aid payments to a single parent, claiming that the parent no longer meets legal eligibility requirements for such aid. Sometimes a client seeks the intervention of the state to protect her from another, as in the case of a person who requests a state court civil protection order to restrain an abusive intimate partner. These types of cases focus on vindicating client interests and thus have a critical impact on the lives and welfare of the individual claimants; nonetheless, some may raise generalizable issues and set important legal precedents.

One question for individual public interest lawyers, their organizations, and the overall legal services system is how to best allocate limited resources to individual and impact approaches. The answer to this question depends on a number of factors. What do the clients want in a particular case? Under what conditions might an impact approach be most effective in addressing the underlying social problems and improving people's lives? Sometimes, lawyers are confronted with a choice about which approach to follow. The following excerpt considers the tradeoffs:

> A law reform orientation might lead a lawyer to assist a client wanting changes in nursing home conditions, by helping the client organize a group of similarly minded nursing home residents, by obtaining media coverage for them to air their grievances and demands, by aiding the group in drafting petitions and testimony before legislative committees, and most importantly . . . by initiating a class action law suit against the owners of the nursing home. In this way, the initial unequal power relationship that existed between the poor person and the nursing home owners might be overcome with the additional possibility of far-reaching changes for nursing home residents other than the individual who came to the Legal Services office. By contrast, the equal access model would normally favor only the individual negotiations or suit brought in behalf of this one poor resident against the nursing home owners, a suit which would be vigorously pursued, but which would not be supplemented by any non-court representation and would probably not seek classwide relief.
>
> Equal access proponents agree that poor people do not normally confront the non-poor on equal footing in the legal process. However, they believe that if all poor clients had competent and zealous legal counsel, the judicial proceedings would produce results that were much fairer. Courts are presumed to be relatively independent of other political, social or economic influences. Additionally, the factual record at trial is thought to be sufficiently closed to these legally extraneous matters so that an impartial decisionmaker can regard the two parties fairly. But such fair decisionmaking requires that each party have an articulate defender, marshalling relevant facts to support his or her client's position, as well as challenging and exposing weaknesses in the opponent's case. According to these proponents, if such defenders' skills are roughly equal, a fair verdict can then be rendered regardless of who the parties are. Since each side is represented by savvy, articulate, and respectable lawyers (who in these respects resemble the judge), outside bias will not be likely to enter into the judge's decisionmaking.
>
> The equal access proponents thus put exclusive emphasis on providing high quality legal counsel for those who seek and yet who cannot afford such counsel. These proponents argue forcefully that the law reform proponents contribute to the plight of individual poor persons by disregarding the particular problems and desires of those who seek their help, instead lumping the poor together into one homogenous group for class representation.

According to equal access proponents, only by viewing the poor as discrete individuals can the poverty lawyer represent the poor in the same way his or her counterparts represent the non-poor clients and thus ensure that the legal rights of the poor are as secure as those of all other citizens.

The proponents of the two models claim that their differences come out most clearly in the type of case selection procedures sanctioned by their respective views. Put simply, law reform proponents sanction case selection procedures which would consistently choose the suit or legal action which has the greatest impact on the greatest number of poor persons' interests; whereas equal access proponents sanction case selection procedures which give equal weight to the unique interests of individual poor persons who seek legal help. Assuming that funds for Legal Services programs for the poor are scarce, how will these models help lawyers decide which poor persons' cases to handle? It appears that group-oriented, utilitarian schemes are favored by law reform models, and random schemes, which put equal weight on each poor person's case, are favored by equal access models.

Marie A. Failinger & Larry May, *Litigating Against Poverty: Legal Services and Group Representation*, 45 Oʜɪᴏ Sᴛ. L.J. 1, 15-16 (1984) (citations omitted). For one of the principal critiques of the law reform model, see Marshall Breger, *Legal Aid for the Poor: A Conceptual Analysis,* 60 N.C. L. Rᴇᴠ. 282, 286-97 (1982) (arguing that the interests of the poor can only be advanced by individual client representation that does not account for the larger interests of the class or classes to which the client may belong).

While the debate between client service and impact litigation is an intense one, it also may create somewhat of a false choice. Even given limited resources for public interest lawyering, individual case representation and impact litigation can co-exist, and often may complement each other. In fact, some have argued that doing individual case work can provide lawyers with a view of problems at a broader level, thus generating potential opportunities to bring larger impact cases to address the needs of the larger population. Gary Blasi, *Framing Access to Justice: Beyond Perceived Justice for Individuals*, 42 Lᴏʏ. L.A. L. Rᴇᴠ. 913 (2009). Leading public interest lawyer and Harvard Law School Professor Gary Bellow famously argued that individual client representation could be used to generate institutional reform. Writing about legal aid lawyers, he called for a "focused case" strategy that involved the representation of large numbers of individual clients against target institutions in ways that would pressure them to reform practices that violated program client rights. Gary Bellow, *Turning Solutions into Problems: The Legal Aid Experience*, 34 NLADA Bʀɪᴇꜰᴄᴀsᴇ 106, 122 (1977).

What is more, the distinctions between the models are not as rigid as some may characterize them. As Failinger and May observe:

> Most equal access proponents prefer [case] selection procedures which are not totally random, some allowing emergency cases to override all others. But as with any other exceptions, what counts as an emergency is often hard to determine without weighing the interests in the so-called emergency case against those who would have to be turned away, and thus the equal weight principle is not consistently adhered to. A second preference is for non-random procedures which put case selection into the hands of client boards. But such

procedures also fail to give equal weight to each poor client's desires and needs, for such boards will consistently look to many of their own subjective factors. The ideal of giving equal weight to each poor person's problem is at least partially abandoned by these more realistic legal services allocation considerations. By contrast, law reform proponents often stress that programs should consider exceptions to the rule of greatest group impact, such as emergencies, hardship cases, or problems of serious concern to the clients. Like equal access proponents, their proposed allocation schemes are by no means "pure."

Failinger & May, *supra*, at 16-17 (citations omitted).

What do you think is the better approach to public interest litigation — impact or individual service suits? Under what conditions does one approach seem preferable to the other? How different are they in practice? How might they best be used together?

2. Direct Litigation and Amicus Participation

Direct sponsorship of public interest litigation — i.e., when a public interest law organization selects, files, and litigates a case on its own — has a number of important benefits. First, lawyers can be pro-active, selecting and shaping a legal claim on behalf of a particular client and cause precisely because the case represents an opportunity for changing or enforcing the law. Many of the advantages discussed above, such as careful selection of good clients with helpful facts, timing, choice of forum, and other strategic litigation decisions are available when the lawyers engage in direct representation of clients. *See* Lee Epstein, Conservatives in Court 10-11 (1985).

Lawyers pursuing direct cases also have substantial control over the conduct of the litigation, the structure of the legal claims, the strategic choices made as the case evolves, and (perhaps most important) whether the case is brought at all. Public interest lawyers sometimes make a conscious choice *not* to bring a case if the circumstances are unfavorable or the case presents a great risk of establishing a legal precedent that will be antithetical to the lawyers' social change mission. (This, of course, does not prevent other lawyers from doing so.) In pursuing direct representation, public interest organizations frequently advance litigation expenses for clients, often because the clients do not have the resources to pay for a lawyer, much less expenses associated with typical litigation claims. Whether lawyers are representing individual clients with unmet legal needs or carrying out large, law reform class actions, standard litigation costs associated with court filings, discovery, copying and printing, staff time, trial transcripts, and other items can pose a substantial barrier to the pursuit of litigation.

Public interest lawyers can also play a more limited role in cases brought by other parties as amicus curiae, or friends of the court. Joseph D. Kearney & Thomas W. Merrill, *The Influence of Amicus Curiae Briefs on the Supreme Court*, 148 U. Pa. L. Rev. 743, 744 (2000); Michael K. Lowman, Comment, *The Litigating Amicus Curiae: When Does the Party Begin After the Friends Leave?*, 41 Am. U. L. Rev. 1243 (1992). The rise of amicus briefs in Supreme Court litigation corresponds roughly to the period in which public interest litigation emerged as a distinct realm of legal practice. At the beginning of the twentieth century, lawyers filed amicus briefs in only about 10 percent of Supreme Court cases, but by the end of the century they submitted amicus briefs in 85 percent of cases before the Court. Kearney & Merrill, *supra*, at 744.

By many accounts, the initial conception of the amicus curiae was as a neutral "friend" offering to assist the Court in its deliberations on difficult cases. Samuel Krislov, *The Amicus Curiae Brief: From Friendship to Advocacy*, 72 YALE L.J. 694, 695 (1963). Many amici now come in on behalf of one or more parties to the case, offering a slightly different perspective and perhaps providing information on how the case might affect other constituencies that are not directly involved. Well-done amicus briefs can present legal theories and arguments or authorities that were not cited by the parties. Kearney & Merrill, *supra*, at 745. They can also supply technical, statistical, or other types of information that may be useful to a court's decision making. *Id.* On the other hand, critics of partisan amici warn that they may unfairly influence judicial decisions, and are problematic because they may be a backdoor method allowing parties to circumvent page limitations for briefs, *Voices for Choices v. Ill. Bell Tel. Co.*, 339 F.3d 542, 544 (7th Cir. 2003), or introduce information or evidence into the case without being bound by the formal rules of evidence, other procedural limitations, or standards of scientific and social science validity. *See, e.g.*, Michael Rustad & Thomas Koenig, *The Supreme Court and Junk Social Science: Selective Distortion in Amicus Briefs*, 72 N.C. L. REV. 91 (1993). These differing perceptions about the appropriate role for amici are reflected in the views of the Justices themselves. *Compare Justice Breyer Calls for Experts to Aid Courts in Complex Cases*, N.Y. TIMES, Feb. 17, 1998, at A17 (quoting Justice Breyer expressing the value of amicus briefs in educating judges on technical matters) *with Jaffee v. Redmond*, 518 U.S. 1, 36 (1996) (Scalia, J., dissenting) (expressing dismay at the proliferation of partisan amici and arguing that "[t]here is no self-interested organization out there devoted to pursuit of the truth in the federal courts").

For public interest lawyers, the most fundamental question is whether amicus briefs influence courts' decisions and are therefore effective tools for change. The efficacy of amicus briefs is highly contested in the available research. A number of studies have concluded that amicus briefs have some impact on the outcomes of U.S. Supreme Court and state supreme court cases. *See, e.g.*, Paul M. Collins Jr., *Friends of the Court: Examining the Influence of Amicus Curiae Participation in U.S. Supreme Court Litigation*, 38 LAW & SOC'Y REV. 807 (2004); Kearney & Merrill, *supra*; Donald R. Songer & Ashlyn Kuersten, *The Success of Amici in State Supreme Courts*, 48 POL. RES. Q. 31 (1995). Some of these studies conclude, however, that success is dependent on the identity of the parties. Collins, *supra* (concluding that amicus success is dependent on the level of useful information provided in the briefs); Kearney & Merrill, *supra* (concluding that the U.S. Solicitor General, and to a lesser degree the ACLU, the AFL-CIO, and the States, are more successful as amicus than other parties). Others are more skeptical about the role of amicus briefs in litigation. *See, e.g.*, Nathan Hakman, *Lobbying the Supreme Court — An Appraisal of "Political Science Folklore,"* 35 FORDHAM L. REV. 15 (1966); Songer & Sheehan, *supra; but see* Karen O'Connor & Lee Epstein, *Amicus Curiae Participation in U.S.*

Supreme Court Litigation: An Appraisal of Hakman's "Folklore," 16 Law & Soc'y Rev. 311 (1981-82).

One might reasonably ask why lawyers and organizations have filed amicus briefs in increasing numbers if their effectiveness is in doubt. First, lawyers will turn to this strategy as long as they *believe* that it works, and there is sufficient evidence that amicus briefs have the potential to wield influence that this is a reasonable perception. Second, whether or not the amicus brief is successful, public interest groups may benefit from the profile that amicus participation gives them. They may highlight their role as an amicus to gain publicity for the organization's mission, which can serve as a useful organizing tool for their community, further the organizations' credibility with the courts, facilitate fundraising efforts, and draw other potential clients to their organization's attention. Third, for historically underrepresented groups, amicus briefs can play an important role in facilitating a participatory voice in the legal process. *See generally* Ruben J. Garcia, *A Democratic Theory of Amicus Advocacy*, 35 Fla. St. U. L. Rev. 315, 320 (2008) (arguing for a view of amicus participation that values it as serving a significant role in a participatory democracy).

Amicus participation also offers a number of tactical tradeoffs. When lawyers participate on behalf of amici, they are, by definition, not in control of the course of the case, or whether it was filed in the first instance. Their role is, initially, a passive one. However, in some situations amicus briefs may be the only way for a group to provide input to litigation when legal barriers would otherwise preclude them from participating. For example, when public interest groups want to take the government's side in an existing case, they cannot play a direct role, but they can weigh in through an amicus role. Epstein, *supra*, at 149. Also, parties who might otherwise not have justiciable claims in the underlying legal case may still participate as amici. In addition, amicus participation can be a cost effective way in which groups can influence ongoing litigation. *Id.* (describing how some groups have viewed amicus briefs as a low cost way to have a role in shaping or changing precedent). The relatively low cost of amicus participation can especially facilitate the ability of nascent organizations to get involved in social causes until they can build up a membership and fundraising support base. *Id.* at 135 (describing how the Pacific Legal Foundation started out filing amicus briefs until it established a stronger reputation and then moved toward more direct sponsorship of litigation).

As with individual and impact litigation, direct sponsorship and amicus participation are also importantly complementary tactical options. Many organizations consider the factors discussed above in balancing how many and which types of cases to pursue in direct litigation, and which ones are better suited for amicus briefing.

C. APPRAISAL

The lure of litigation is strong, fed by popular cultural accounts of epic courtroom battles and the simple binary elegance of their outcomes — wins and losses—which can be tallied as a way of defining success and failure. Should litigation's appeal pull lawyers in to do battle on behalf of less powerful groups, leveraging the moral and legal force of the courts to advance their causes? Or is litigation a trap—enticing lawyers to devote resources to a strategy unlikely to produce meaningful long-term change? In this section, we explore some of advantages and challenges of relying on traditional litigation as a tool for social change. These arguments are not exhaustive, but rather are meant to introduce the basic framework of the debate.

1. Advantages

a. ACCESS AND EFFICIENCY

One benefit of public interest litigation—upon which the classic representation rationale for public interest law is based—is that it provides an alternative route for advancing the interests of groups that historically have been excluded from equal participation in the political process. American courts play a central role in protecting the rights of minority groups, political dissidents, and others who might not command sufficient attention from elected officials because of their marginalized status. The inaccessibility of politics may be the product of institutionalized discrimination and, in some cases, actual formal exclusion from voting, holding office, and other access to the political system. Or the inattention of political actors to the needs of certain constituencies may reflect the reality that they are a numerical minority and therefore do not represent the majority will (or have interests that conflict with groups that do represent a majority of voters).

Courts, in contrast to elected officials, are theoretically open to any person with a cause of action (assuming, of course, that the aggrieved party can secure legal representation or present the case on his or her own). Federal courts and many (though not all) state courts are also insulated from the partisan political process and therefore may be freer to enforce the rule of law to protect minorities even when that decision may be politically unpopular. These arguments are familiar in the context of constitutional judicial review in the federal court system. *See, e.g., United States v. Carolene Products Co.*, 304 U.S. 144, 152 n.4 (1944).

Another element of access is that law reform litigation can be an efficient mechanism for accomplishing significant change for large numbers of individuals. *See* HANDLER, *supra*, at 31; Robert L. Rabin, *Lawyers for Social Change: Perspectives on Public Interest Law*, 28 STAN. L. REV. 207, 223 (1976). Although litigation can be complex and expensive, it has the advantage of focusing all of the issues related to a particular legal claim in one forum. Impact litigation in particular can yield widespread changes that affect the rights of substantial numbers of people in one case. This can occur both in class action litigation and in individual cases that are brought to establish a legal principle. For example, the litigation resulting in the invalidation of the death penalty as applied to juveniles, *Roper v. Simmons*, 543 U.S. 551 (2005), established a broad constitutional principle that ensured no such laws could be enforced. Rather than continuing to have defense lawyers challenge these sentences on an individual basis, the precedent effectively ended capital punishment for minors. Similarly, a litigation challenge to the anti-solicitation ordinance in the homelessness fact pattern above might yield a ruling declaring the ordinance to be in violation of federal or state law. This could be a more efficient outcome than recruiting attorneys to represent individual homeless people who are charged with violating the law. Indeed, in an ethics opinion issued in 1974, the American Bar Association embraced this approach, concluding that public interest lawyers, unlike other members of the bar, must use their professional skills to maximize benefit to the community or group that makes up its client base. ABA Formal Opinion 334 at 6 (1974) ("[T]o achieve the goal of maximizing legal services, services to individuals may be limited in order to use the program's resources to accomplish law reform in connection with [a rsqb; particular legal subject matter."). In assessing the value of impact litigation, however, it is important to keep in mind that efficiency works both ways. Impact litigation can be efficient for defendants, too. Instead of facing an army of lawyers representing many individual clients, the defense can focus its resources on the large impact case. And, of course, a defense victory in such a case can foreclose individual litigants from later bringing similar claims.

b. DIRECT EFFECTS

Public interest litigation can be an effective form of social change because of the direct impact on changing and enforcing the law. Appellate cases can establish important and controlling precedents. Lower courts can issue injunctions that stop defendants from engaging in conduct harmful to plaintiffs, or ordering defendants to take action that they are under a legal duty to carry out. Courts can award compensatory, and sometimes punitive, damages as remedies for past harms. Such outcomes provide specific, tangible benefits to current and future parties. Litigation not only can produce new legal precedent, but also promote institutional reform and behavioral change in response to changes in the law.

Impact litigation may also be an effective tool of social change because courts, and especially federal courts, may be particularly well suited to managing complex social change cases and implementing remedies. A litigation victory has only symbolic value if it is not enforced. Courts have the ability to ensure compliance and maintain oversight of a defendant's conduct through the power of contempt sanctions. In some types of public interest litigation, courts may engage in ongoing monitoring of compliance with its orders, either directly or through a special master. Lawyers can also use the threat of the courts' enforcement power as a tool for securing negotiated compliance or other forms of relief outside of the formal judicial process. In this way, the enforcement power behind a court order has value as currency in a broader social change plan.

An important aspect of assessing litigation as a social reform tactic is identifying the conditions that enhance the possibility of success, such as legal capacity, the receptivity of the judiciary to the right asserted, the mechanism of legal enforcement, and the extent of rights saturation in group members.

Legal capacity hinges on the existence and strength of legal organizations advancing an issue and the degree to which they have relevant technical expertise, both substantive and procedural. The receptivity of the judiciary depends on the doctrinal availability and precedential strength of the legal right asserted and the ideological proclivities of the judges with final decisionmaking power. The type of enforcement mechanism is a function of the nature of the remedy and its mode of implementation. Enforcement may be one-shot or require a long-term commitment of resources; it may involve injunctive or monetary relief; and it may require bureaucratic action or occur through voluntary conduct (and, in that sense, be self-enforcing). Finally, the depth of legal consciousness may be understood in terms of rights saturation: Do members of groups affected by legal action understand the nature of the rights conferred and feel empowered to assert them? . . .

[S]ocial change litigation is most likely to succeed when . . . reformers have the resources to pursue litigation effectively, there is a supportive political and legal culture, the right asserted is a negative one designed to protect voluntary activity (and therefore no bureaucratic enforcement is required), there is strong political organization and monitoring resources, and the legal and political strategies are coordinated toward the same goal. We presume in this context that, although political decisionmakers may be generally supportive of the reformers' goals, litigation provides the more expeditious and effective route to achieve them. Conversely, social change litigation is most likely to fail when there [is] . . . weak [legal] capacity, hostile decisionmakers, bureaucratic enforcement, and strong opposition.

Scott L. Cummings, *Litigation at Work: Defending Day Labor*, 58 UCLA L. Rev. 1617, 1624-25 (2011) [hereinafter, Cummings, *Defending Day Labor*]. How do you suppose lawyers in the field would access information about these factors? Where would it come from? How reliable would it be? How much certainty would lawyers need about the likely outcome to justify proceeding with a social change lawsuit?

As the foregoing excerpt suggests, the ability of courts to monitor and enforce their orders is a key factor in determining the effectiveness of litigation as a social change tool. There is a rich debate about the desirability and efficacy of placing courts in the position of monitoring the implementation of institutional reforms over time — a debate shaped by the emergence of large-scale "public law litigation" in the second half of the twentieth century. Until then, litigation was largely seen as a binary dispute resolution mechanism through which private parties could clarify their rights and obligations. Abram Chayes, *The Supreme Court 1981 Term — Foreword: Public Law Litigation and the Burger Court*, 96 HARV. L. REV. 4, 4-5 (1982) [hereinafter, Chayes, *Burger Court*]. As described by Abram Chayes, this traditional model was also marked by courts' retrospective focus, which sought to provide a remedy for past conduct, and by the limited role of the judge, who would act as a neutral arbiter of claims only for the duration of the resolution of the discrete dispute. *Id.* In contrast, the concept of "public law litigation" developed as a mechanism for advancing broader social reform. Unlike private litigation, public law cases were shaped by the parties and courts, were designed to affect parties beyond the actual litigants, embraced forward-looking relief, involved remedies that were negotiated and often required monitoring by the court after the initial phase of the litigation was completed, and addressed broad public policy issues rather than individual grievances. Abram Chayes, *The Role of the Judge in Public Law Litigation*, 89 Harv. L. Rev. 1281, 1302 (1976) [hereinafter, Chayes, *Public Law Litigation*]. Chayes's seminal analysis centers on large institutional reform cases commonly brought in the late twentieth century, such as attacks on public school segregation, prison and police practices reform suits, reapportionment cases, and environmental enforcement litigation. As we have already seen, there are varying accounts of the degree to which these types of cases were ultimately successful. But they represented a new model for the role of courts, especially federal courts, and of lawyers representing clients in these cases. Chayes argued that courts are particularly well suited to addressing broad public issues in this type of litigation.

> First, and perhaps most important, is that the process is presided over by a judge. His professional tradition insulates him from narrow political pressures, but, given the operation of the federal appointive power and the demands of contemporary law practice, he is likely to have some experience of the political process and acquaintance with a fairly broad range of public policy problems. Moreover, he is governed by a professional ideal of reflective and dispassionate analysis of the problem before him and is likely to have had some experience in putting this ideal into practice.
>
> Second, the public law model permits ad hoc applications of broad national policy in situations of limited scope. The solutions can be tailored to the needs of the particular situation and flexibly administered or modified as experience develops with the regime established in the particular case.
>
> Third, the procedure permits a relatively high degree of participation by representatives of those who will be directly affected by the decision, without establishing a liberum veto.
>
> Fourth, the court, although traditionally thought less competent than legislatures or administrative agencies in gathering and assessing information, may have unsuspected advantages in this regard. Even the diffused adversarial structure of public law litigation furnishes strong incentives for the parties to produce information. If the party structure is sufficiently representative of the interests at stake, a considerable range of relevant information will be forthcoming. And, because of the limited scope of the proceeding, the information required can be effectively focused and specified. Information produced will not only be subject to adversary review, but as we have seen, the judge can engage his own experts to assist in evaluating the evidence. Moreover, the information that is produced will not be filtered through the rigid structures and preconceptions of bureaucracies.
>
> Fifth, the judicial process is an effective mechanism for registering and responding to grievances generated by the operation of public programs in a regulatory state. Unlike an administrative bureaucracy or a legislature, the judiciary must respond to the complaints of the aggrieved. It is also rather well situated to perform the task of balancing the importance of competing policy interests in a specific situation. The legislature, perhaps, could balance, but it cannot address specific situations. The bureaucracy deals with specific situations, but only from a position of commitment to particular policy interests.

> Sixth, the judiciary has the advantage of being non-bureaucratic. It is effective in tapping energies and resources outside itself and outside the government in the exploration of the situation and the assessment of remedies. It does not work through a rigid, multilayered hierarchy of numerous officials, but through a smallish, representative task force, assembled ad hoc, and easily dismantled when the problem is finally resolved.

Chayes, *Public Law Litigation, supra*, at 1307-09.

As Chayes observes, the social reform elements of these cases were bound up in the nature of the disputes, which were about public policy issues, the nature of the remedies, which often required ongoing and extensive supervision by the courts, and by the wide participation of institutions and other parties. The evolution of this type of litigation coincided with, or was precipitated by, changes in legal and procedural rules, such as the relaxation of the standing doctrine, the availability of the class action procedure, and the recognition of the courts' broader discretion to shape and enforce equitable remedies. Chayes, *Burger Court, supra*. These changes each brought a form of backlash by those who were critical of the expanded role of courts in social reform and branded the courts, among other things, as "activist." *Id.* at 4. As the Supreme Court became increasingly skeptical about such institutional reform litigation, it began to cut back on some of the same doctrines whose expansion led to increased public law litigation in the first instance. Those reversals, however, have not eliminated the courts as a forum for social change, and some have argued that the trends toward public law litigation are highly resistant to change. *Id.* at 56.

Charles Sabel and William Simon have observed that public law litigation has moved from a court-centered "command and control" model of remedial implementation to what they call an experimentalist approach, which "combines more flexible and provisional norms with procedures for ongoing stakeholder participation and measured accountability." Charles F. Sabel & William H. Simon, *Destabilization Rights: How Public Law Litigation Succeeds*, 117 Harv. L. Rev. 1015, 1019 (2004); *see also* Susan P. Sturm, *The Legacy and Future of Corrections Litigation*, 142 U. Pa. L. Rev. 639, 706-35 (1993). Under this model, public law litigation pursues what the authors call "destabilization rights."

> A public law destabilization right is a right to disentrench or unsettle a public institution when, first, it is failing to satisfy minimum standards of adequate performance and, second, it is substantially immune from conventional political mechanisms of correction. In the typical pattern of the new public law suit, a finding or concession of liability triggers a process of supervised negotiation and deliberation among the parties and other stakeholders. The characteristic result of this process is a regime of rolling or provisional rules that are periodically revised in light of transparent evaluations of their implementation.

Id. at 1062. On this view, public law litigation is more deliberative and transparent, and provides the parties with more control over a negotiated solution to problems with the public institution involved, whether it is a prison, police force, school system, or mental hospital. It also reflects the reality that social change is an ongoing and dynamic process. "Destabilization induces the institution to reform itself in a process in which it must respond to previously excluded stakeholders." *Id.* at 1056.

Another feature of impact litigation that enhances its ability to produce a direct impact on the law is that it is strategic: it can take place as part of a planned campaign. Organizers of litigation campaigns can carefully contemplate and control many of the important variables. They may carefully select which cases to bring. Assuming there is a substantial group of potential plaintiffs who have standing to sue in a particular litigation campaign, lawyers may select sympathetic clients to best represent the cause because of their potential appeal to a jury and to the public, and whose facts most potently illustrate the legal harm and the need for a remedy. In the NAACP's campaign to desegregate higher education institutions, Charles Hamilton Houston was quite selective about choosing plaintiffs to challenge state school segregation, picking only black plaintiffs who clearly had credentials sufficient to be admitted to the white universities. TUSHNET, NAACP, *supra*, at 36-37. An advocate affiliated with recent litigation efforts to challenge state law bans on gay marriage remarked that she looked for plaintiffs who were likely to stay together as couples despite the stress of being involved in high profile litigation, appeared to be typical gay couples who were adversely affected by the laws, rather than political activists, and would be relatively at ease in front of the press or testifying in a courtroom. Margaret Talbot, *A Risky Proposal*, THE NEW YORKER, Jan. 18, 2010, at 45. Lawyers may also design suits to maximize the chance of creating important precedents — by, as mentioned above, choosing the forum in which to bring the case and determining the timing of the litigation in relation to other political or societal events (e.g., an upcoming election). Some of these choices may in retrospect turn out to be less than optimal, but control over the features of public interest litigation can make it an appealing social change vehicle.

c. INDIRECT EFFECTS

Litigation may also serve purposes apart from achieving a direct outcome in a case. This can occur in at least three distinct ways. First, litigation may be used as a preliminary approach to enable other tactics to succeed. HANDLER, *supra*, at 210-12. An example of this comes from the civil rights movement, when litigation was used to block or limit criminal prosecutions of protestors and to represent them when arrested. The principal goal was to accomplish change through sit-ins, but litigation was used to ensure those tactics would be possible. *Id.* A second way that litigation can be used indirectly is to enhance the leverage of social reform groups, with the goal of enhancing other non-litigation tactics. Litigation, or the threat thereof, can sometimes increase a group's bargaining power in ways that allow it to negotiate stronger rules or craft better legislation on behalf of its constituents. *Id.* at 212-13. Again, the goal is not to win the litigation, but to move officials to implement reforms in other arenas. Finally, successful or not, litigation may help call public attention to social problems. *Id.* at 214-22. In this way, litigation serves an educative function for legislators and other policy makers, political constituencies within and outside of a social movement, community organizers and activists, the media, and the general public. Litigation can help inform public debate and build community support for a cause by focusing attention on the issue it addresses. This public attention can promote fundraising to support the current litigation as well as build a funding base for future litigation campaigns. Public attention can have adverse consequences as well, perhaps leading to alienation and entrenchment by defendants, possibly souring the atmosphere for negotiation and settlement.

Lawyers may pursue litigation for its public impact even at the risk of losing on the merits. *See, e.g.,* Catherine Albiston, *The Rule of Law and the Litigation Process: The Paradox of Losing by Winning,* 33 Law & Soc'y Rev. 869 (1999); Jules Lobel, *Courts as Forums for Protest,* 52 UCLA L. Rev. 477 (2004); Doug NeJaime, *Winning Through Losing,* 96 Iowa L. Rev. 941 (2001). Jules Lobel has argued that there is a long tradition in American justice of lawyers using courts as a forum for social protest even if they lose the case.

> The lawyers' and plaintiffs' interest in the lawsuit is not solely winning or losing in court, but in getting their message out to the broader public or a particular group. The lawsuit serves as a means for the plaintiffs and their counsel to transform the court into a forum to broadcast their point of view. While the plaintiffs do have a legal claim that they believe is valid and want the court to decide, they also seek to use the litigation as a vehicle for their protest, and as a catalyst for aiding or developing a broader social movement.
>
> The efficacy of lawsuits in generating publicity has been well documented. Social scientists have observed "that litigation is one of the most effective ways to win publicity for a cause." Public interest litigators and organizations have come to view litigation as a vehicle for attracting the media. Reflecting this recognition, it is now a common practice to announce a pending or filed public interest lawsuit at a press conference. Often, litigation attracts the media's attention in a way that nothing else does. Professor Joel Handler concludes that in general "a 20-page complaint and a temporary injunction are worth more than a 300 page report in the media." . . .
>
> The educational value of litigation is often substantial even where the case does not result in a legal victory. Professor Michael McCann demonstrates that pay equity advocates used lawsuits as "a crucial organizing tool," and that for many of the activists "[w]hether you win or lose [in court], awareness rises through this type of action." For Professor McCann, while the pay equity litigation resulted in only modest policy reforms, "perhaps the single most important achievement of the movement has been the transformations in many working women's understandings, commitments, and affiliations."

Lobel, *supra,* at 487-88.[2]

Can you think of some indirect effects that might arise from litigation to challenge either of the ordinances in the homelessness problem above? Would those effects encourage or discourage you from choosing a litigation approach? What do they suggest about the opportunities for integrating a litigation strategy with other advocacy methods?

---

2. Litigation for the purpose of calling attention to a social cause, as opposed to the primary goal of winning the underlying legal claim, raises ethical issues for lawyers engaged in social change work. We take this subject up in Chapter 7.

2. Challenges

a. ACCOUNTABILITY

While the power of litigation to bypass the political process is often charac-terized as an asset, critics of litigation as a means of social change suggest that this circumvention is actually a fundamental flaw. Interestingly, this criticism of litigation has come from both conservatives and progressives in the academic and practice world. These attacks are not simply academic exercises — they have influenced contemporary approaches to public interest lawyering in important ways.

i. CLIENT DISEMPOWERMENT

An important counterpoint to the argument that law reform litigation enhances access for disempowered constituencies is that the litigation process can also result in a dynamic that privileges the lawyers' power and diminishes the clients' autonomy and capacity to be responsible for their own destinies.

There are potential costs borne by plaintiffs that must be considered in evaluating the value of litigation as a social change strategy. These are not just the typical resource costs required to pay for litigation (which we consider below) because those out-of-pocket costs are ordinarily paid for by the organization sponsoring the litigation. But other important costs may affect the decision whether to litigate. Litigation can be a burdensome and time-consuming activity for the parties. Plaintiffs may, in some cases, want to sim-ply live their lives without the external burden of participating in a case, par-ticularly a case that may draw unwanted attention to them.

In controversial cases, litigation often places the plaintiffs in a position to be harassed or targeted for retaliation, ostracized from the community, or to suffer other negative professional and personal consequences. These problems can be magnified where the defendants use their own tactics to create divisions in the local community. For example, in the NAACP Legal Defense Fund's litigation campaign to achieve salary equity between white and black public schoolteachers in the 1940s, some local officials threatened to respond to charges of discrimination not by increasing the salaries of African-American teachers, but by *decreasing* white teachers' salaries, thus breeding dissension and political opposition to the equity effort. TUSHNET, NAACP, *supra*, at 93. This created tensions within the black teachers' own professional communities. Another example can be drawn from one of the largest impediments to LDF's attack on segregation in elementary and secondary schools — the concern about the backlash against black teachers should such a strategy be chosen. The desegregation of the public schools would inevitably result in the loss of teaching positions in desegregated school districts and many black teachers feared they would lose their jobs if LDF's campaign succeeded. *Id.* at 113.

Perhaps more troubling is the danger in large impact cases that lawyers may impose their own views of the underlying cause on their clients, pursuing broader social goals at the expense of their clients' interests. The concept of lawyer domination arises from concerns about the nature of the lawyer-client relationship in social reform litigation, in which lawyers may have a tendency, conscious or unconscious, to wield their professional expertise over their clients and control the course of the litigation in a top-down manner that devalues client autonomy. The concerns are particularly acute in impact lawsuits in which lawyers are managing complex litigation and clients are diffuse and/or lack sophistication, making them more inclined to defer to the lawyers. The lawyers, in turn, may view their clients in a manner that perpetuates stereotypes about low-income people as "subordinate, dependent, and helpless." Ascanio Piomelli, *Appreciating Collaborative Lawyering,* 6 Clinical L. Rev. 427, 438-39 (2000); *see also* Lucie E. White, Goldberg v. Kelly *on the Paradox of Lawyering for the Poor,* 56 Brook. L. Rev. 861 (1990). To ensure that litigation is effective and does not result in a reduction in client autonomy, public interest litigators must pay close attention to structuring the attorney-client relationship in a manner that is sensitive to these concerns. We explore these issues more extensively in Chapter 6.

ii. DEMOCRATIC LEGITIMACY

The movement toward litigation as a social reform strategy in the latter part of the twentieth century spawned a great deal of criticism, particularly from conservatives. Critics argued that public interest litigation was an illegitimate tool for changing law precisely because it bypassed the democratic process. David Luban has styled this argument the "objection from democracy." Luban, *supra,* at 303. As Luban states it, the contention is that "[i]t is wrong for groups that are unable to get what they want through ordinary democratic means (pressure-group politics, the legislative process, electing an executive who does things their way) to frustrate the democratic will by obtaining in court what they cannot obtain in the political rough-and-tumble." *Id.* Critics also maintained that the courts should not be laboratories for social engineering because they were not institutionally competent to engage in policy making and were not accountable to the public for their decisions. *See* Ann Southworth, *Conservative Lawyers and the Contest over the Meaning of "Public Interest Law,"* 52 UCLA L. Rev. 1223, 1240 (2005) (providing general account of this critique). This perspective is mirrored in the criticisms of judicial review by federal courts in enforcing the Constitution against the decisions of democratically elected officials who theoretically reflect the public will—the so-called countermajoritarian difficulty. Alexander M. Bickel, The Least Dangerous Branch: The Supreme Court at the Bar of Politics 16 (1962). Some conservatives, particularly those who highly valued judicial restraint, took the view that courts should have a very limited role in a democratic society—in the political rhetoric of the day, they argued that judges should interpret law, not make it. Of course, some conservatives have benefited from impact litigation, particularly cases brought to protect constituencies in the political minority, such as gun owners and certain religious groups.

The conservative critique relies on relative faith in the political process and also assumes that the majority should usually prevail in a constitutional democracy. The American constitutional system, however, has many devices that reflect a collective desire to protect minorities from the majority will in specific circumstances. Substantive rights of free speech, freedom of religion, equal protection, and others are clearly countermajoritarian in their thrust. *See, e.g., United States v. Carolene Products Co.*, 304 U.S. 144, 152 n.4 (1944). The conservative critique could accept these specific exceptions from the majority rule principle while still arguing for a much more limited role for courts in social change.

In recent years, progressive critics have also argued that litigation is not an optimal strategy for the development of constitutional rights, asserting that litigation has undermined the role of popular participation, through organizing and protest, in the development of constitutional principles, which might yield a more sustainable and legitimate rights regime. *See* LARRY KRAMER, THE PEOPLE THEMSELVES: POPULAR CONSTITUTIONALISM AND JUDICIAL REVIEW (2004) (arguing that constitutional judicial review has undermined the capacity for citizen deliberation about the interpretation of the Constitution); MARK TUSHNET, TAKING THE CONSTITUTION AWAY FROM THE COURTS (1999) (maintaining that Congress is the appropriate forum for deliberations about the meaning of the Constitution with the participation of interest groups, which can organize to protect their interests); *but see* Emily Zackin, *Popular Constitutionalism's Hard When You're Not Very Popular: Why The ACLU Turned to Courts*, 42 LAW & SOC'Y REV. 367 (2008) (reporting on a study of the ACLU's history in which the organization moved away from a popular constitutionalism approach to protecting rights precisely because such methods failed when pursuing the rights of politically unpopular minority groups).

b. EFFECTIVENESS

i. CRITIQUE OF RIGHTS

The widely cited "myth of rights" critique suggests that relying on public interest litigation to achieve social change misunderstands the role that rights play in a democracy and risks undercutting more effective political mobilization. This argument was articulated by political scientist Stuart Scheingold in his now classic book evaluating the success of litigation and rights-based strategies for social change.

> Legal frames of reference tunnel the vision of both activists and analysts leading to an oversimplified approach to a complex social process — an approach that grossly exaggerates the role that lawyers and litigation can play in a strategy for change. . . . Instead of thinking of judicially asserted rights as accomplished social facts or as moral imperatives, they must be thought of, on the one hand, as authoritatively articulated goals of public policy and, on the other, as political resources of unknown value in the hands of those who want to alter the course of public policy. The direct linking of rights, remedies, and change that characterizes the *myth of rights* must, in sum, be exchanged for a more complex framework, the *politics of rights*, which takes into account the contingent character of rights in the American system.

Stuart A. Scheingold, The Politics of Rights: Lawyers, Public Policy, and Political Change 5-7 (2d ed. 2004).

On this view, litigation-centric social change strategies reinforce and perpetuate the myth of rights at the expense of a more realistic view of the role of judicially enforced legal rights in the larger landscape of social movements. One way it does this is by draining resources from potentially more effective methods of social activism, Michael W. McCann, Taking Reform Seriously: Perspectives on Public Interest Liberalism 200 (1986) ("[L]egal tactics . . . absorb scarce resources that could be used for popular mobilization . . . [and] make it difficult to develop broadly based, multi-issue grass-roots associations of sustained allegiance."); Gerald N. Rosenberg, The Hollow Hope: Can Courts Bring About Social Change? 339 (1991) (asserting that litigation "siphons off crucial resources and talent, and runs the risk of weakening political efforts").

ii. CONTINGENCY OF COURT IDEOLOGY

Another important limit on litigation as a tool of social change is the degree to which its success is dependent upon a favorable audience in the courts. A critical condition necessary for the emergence of litigation as a social change strategy was the increasing receptivity of the courts to such cases and the willingness of the judges to be more activist in their opinions. Handler, *supra*, at 1-2. One explanation for the reported decrease in the amount of law reform litigation by progressive groups in recent years is that the increasing conservatism among the Supreme Court Justices and the judges on the lower federal courts have made litigation a less attractive option. Tushnet, NAACP, *supra*, at 159 ("[B]y the end of the twentieth century most of the planned litigation campaigns had petered out. Liberal-oriented groups continued to litigate, but on a far more catch-as-catch-can basis, looking for targets of opportunity in an increasingly conservative judicial climate."). Of course, ideological contingency can work both ways. In the same period in which liberal groups have shied away from courts, conservative public interest lawyers have seen new opportunities for success, finding a receptive audience to claims for the rights of gun owners, *Dist. of Columbia v. Heller*, 554 U.S. 570 (2008), minority religious groups seeking to use public spaces, *Rosenberger v. Rector & Visitors of the Univ. of Va.*, 515 U.S. 819 (1995), and limits on campaign finance reform, *Citizens United v. Fed. Election Comm'n*, __ U.S. __, 130 S. Ct. 876 (2010).

If the success of public interest litigation is contingent upon the vagaries of the ideological composition of judges, the courts are potentially unstable and unreliable institutions for sustainable reform. Successes during one generation can be vanquished by the next. The inability to foresee what future courts will look like also makes it difficult to design a long-term litigation strategy, and could deter donors and other supporters of litigation from making substantial investments. Moreover, in historical periods (or in specific jurisdictions) in which the political branches of the government are more progressive than the courts, impact litigation may not be a particularly valuable tool.

iii. ENFORCEMENT AND MONITORING

Suppose in the homelessness problem set out at the beginning of this chapter, lawyers for CHA brought a class action claim against the city arguing that the health and safety conditions at the city's homeless shelters were inadequate under state law and seeking an injunction requiring prompt improvement of those conditions. After filing the suit, a consent decree is negotiated and entered with the court. Under the consent decree, the city agrees to a staged plan to implement improved conditions over the course of one year and to report its progress to the court on a monthly basis. As the year progresses, the city fails to implement the decree and provides the court with reports indicating that fiscal constraints and bureaucratic complexities have caused substantial delays in compliance with the decree. How should CHA's lawyers proceed?

As this scenario suggests, a significant challenge to the effectiveness of litigation is the degree to which the remedies achieved must be enforced and monitored by the attorneys after the initial litigation success. A critical variable in determining success is the degree to which a courtroom victory is dependent upon implementation by bureaucrats who have discretion to ignore or under-enforce the court's order. HANDLER, *supra*, at 192-94. Law reform efforts are more likely to be successful where the principal benefit derives from the actual change in legal rules from the court's decision without the need for bureaucratic enforcement (e.g., striking down a law prohibiting a public protest) or where the court issues an injunction that blocks specific conduct (e.g., preventing the siting of a hazardous waste facility in an already over-burdened low-income community). *Id.* at 194-96.

While discrete, identifiable litigation victories can sometimes be declared — such as a court order halting enforcement of an ordinance that discriminates against persons based on their political beliefs or an injunction requiring a state prison to provide basic medically necessary health care for its inmates — a variety of factors may impede actual compliance with the court's orders. The defendants may resist compliance or drag their feet after the court order if the court's decision is likely to be unpopular with the defendants' constituents. Government officials responsible for implementing the court's order may first have to secure funding to finance the necessary changes, as in the case of the prison medical care injunction. Thus, courts are not the only relevant institutions when it comes to carrying out changes that are required by their own orders.

> That courts can sometimes be induced to propound rule-changes that legislatures would not make points to the limitations as well as the possibilities of court-produced change. With their relative insulation from retaliation by antagonistic interests, courts may more easily propound new rules which depart from prevailing power relations. But such rules require greater inputs of other resources to secure effective implementation. And courts have less capacity than other rule-makers to create institutional facilities and re-allocate resources to secure implementation of new rules. Litigation then is unlikely to shape decisively the distribution of power in society.

Galanter, *Why the "Haves" Come Out Ahead, supra* at 149-50.

Moreover, court-ordered implementation of legal and social change may be complex if it involves major alterations to large institutional practices. After the Supreme Court declared racially segregated public schools to violate the Equal Protection Clause in *Brown v. Board of Education*, public interest lawyers spent a generation litigating desegregation remedies. *See* Paul Brest, Sanford Levinson, J.M. Balkin & Akhil Reed Amar, Processes of Constitutional Decisionmaking: Cases and Materials 768-94 (4th ed. 2000). And even when remedies are clear, plaintiffs' counsel may have to spend years, perhaps an entire career, monitoring compliance with the ongoing order. For example, ACLU lawyers found that after Supreme Court decisions banning school prayer and reading the Bible in public schools, many local school districts around the country simply failed to comply. Walker, *supra*, at 226. Ensuring universal compliance would be a nearly impossible task given the sheer number of school districts in the United States. It would be impracticable for an organization to find an attorney to bring an enforcement action, or even send a letter threatening enforcement, in each district. It is because of this problem that ACLU founder Roger Baldwin once said, "no victory ever stays won." *Id.* at 227.

The enforcement of a legal principle often requires filing additional lawsuits in related cases citing the precedent won as authority for compliance — e.g., using the order in *Brown* as authority to end desegregation in other public school districts. But this is not always an easy task. In his account of the NAACP's litigation campaigns, Tushnet observes:

> It is even more difficult to use the appellate decisions as precedents to affect the behavior of those who were not a party to the initial lawsuit. The same contingencies that attended the initial litigation recur: plaintiffs are hard to find and, once found, can disrupt the negotiations that are an essential part of the use of precedents by accepting settlement offers for less than they could win by litigating, or by rejecting offers for more than they could win. In addition, nonparties can read precedents too, and can adapt what they do as to escape the direct force of the appellate decision. Contingencies and especially adaptation can in turn force those directing the litigation campaign to spend as much energy on the follow-up cases as they had on the initial ones.

Tushnet, NAACP, *supra*, at 82.

Another limitation on enforcement is the degree to which the remedial stage of litigation can be expensive and time consuming for the lawyers monitoring the court order or consent decree. "Advocates who embrace the test case model frequently fail to understand at the outset that the remedial stage will consume the bulk of their time and resources." Sturm, *supra*, at 715. As Sturm argues:

> Th[e] failure to appreciate the significance of remedy is important for a number of reasons. Effective lawyering at the remedy stage requires different skills and processes than those needed to participate effectively in formal adjudication. Much of the remedial process takes place outside the courtroom and the adversary model of dispute resolution. Because cooperation by crucial insiders is critical to implementation, effective remedial advocacy requires creative uses of negotiation, mediation, and experts. The test case model simply ignores the

political and institutional dimension of implementation, and relies on legalistic approaches to compliance that do not take into account the complexities
of organizational change. The model also blinds advocates to the importance
of building coalitions with insiders . . . and linking litigation to other methods
of advocacy, such as public education as well as administrative advocacy and
legislative advocacy.

Id. at 714.

iv. COSTS

An important consideration in pursuing a litigation strategy is the cost —
both in terms of actual outlays (human resources and other expenses) and
forgone opportunities. Depending on the type of case, litigation can be a significant resource drain. One critical factor in public interest cases is deciding
who is going to pay for the out-of-pocket costs up front.[3] A separate question is
whether the benefits achievable are worth those costs. Are there internal organizational or resource reasons for adopting a litigation strategy? Organizers of
litigation must assess the most cost effective way to pursue the litigation, particularly for a broad, nationwide social change campaign. Another cost is simply time. Litigation cannot only drain financial and human resources, but also
can take many years to reach any sort of definitive outcome.

Litigation can also impose opportunity costs by creating a structure that
diminishes the incentives and opportunities for other types of important social
reform work. Thus, some observers have raised concerns about what Orly Lobel
calls "legal cooptation" — the tendency of legal strategies to dissipate activism
and limit a movement's transformative potential. Orly Lobel, *The Paradox of
Extralegal Activism: Critical Legal Consciousness and Transformative Politics*, 120
Harv. L. Rev. 937, 939 (2007) [hereinafter, Lobel, *Extralegal Activism*].

v. RISK OF BACKLASH AND ACCOMMODATION

Another potential risk of public interest litigation (related to the problem
of democratic legitimacy) is that its very success could polarize public opinion
and provoke a countermobilization by adversaries — triggering a so-called
backlash. *See* Michael J. Klarman, *How* Brown *Changed Race Relations: The Backlash Thesis*, 81 J. Am. Hist. 81 (1994); Gerald N. Rosenberg, *Courting Disaster:
Looking for Change in All the Wrong Places*, 54 Drake L. Rev. 795, 813 (2006).
Those who raise concerns about backlash suggest that only strategies that
cause cultural change can accomplish enduring social reform. *See* Thomas B.
Stoddard, *Bleeding Heart: Reflections on Using the Law to Make Social Change*, 72
N.Y.U. L. Rev. 967, 985 (1997) ("I prefer legislative lawmaking because I view it
as the avenue of change most likely to advance 'culture-shifting' as well as

---

3. In some types of cases, fees and costs may be recoverable by the plaintiff should she prevail
in the litigation. *See generally* Chapter 4. The defendants in such cases may ultimately have to
reimburse the plaintiffs for their costs and also pay the plaintiffs' attorneys' fees. But even in
that setting, someone has to pay for costs during the litigation, and the reimbursement, if any,
could be years down the road.

'rule-shifting' — the method of lawmaking most likely to lead to absorption into the society of new ideas and relationships."); *see also* Katz & Bernabei, *supra*, at 302-03 ("The legal decisions and laws that fared the best in the otherwise conservative era of the 1980s were those supported by strong, vocal, and national constituencies, such as the reproductive rights movement."). To the extent, therefore, that litigation victories are viewed as illegitimate — as the product of unelected judges thwarting the will of the people or imposing their own views too far outside the mainstream of popular opinion — they can potentially trigger a negative public reaction. This reaction can fuel (and be fostered by) opponents who work to limit or reverse the victory achieved through courts. The classic examples of backlash are the "massive resistance" to *Brown* and the growth of the religious right's power after *Roe v. Wade*. Scholars debate how much the *court decision* itself triggered backlash (as opposed to the general success of the outsider movement), with the dominant view that there is something about judges trumping popular will that inflames passions and contributes to countermobilization.

Responding to the backlash concern, some scholars and advocates have critiqued litigation from the perspective of the alternative dispute resolution movement, arguing that a broader, inclusive, and collaborative process involving all stakeholders is a superior method of reaching common ground and solving conflict in a more sustainable way than a court order. This process can bypass litigation completely or be a mechanism for more productively resolving disputes that originate in the litigation system. It may require a separate set of procedural structures to permit the collaborative process to work, which allows all stakeholders to become part of the discussion, as distinguished from the typical binary relationship between plaintiffs and defendants.

> Conventional public interest advocacy often assumes that there are good guys and bad guys. For justice to prevail, a third party, the courts, must hear the facts and rule the bad guys out of order establishing good legal precedent in the process. Problems arise when there are many actors and good guys and bad guys meld together, when there are not enough resources to share between the bad guys and the good guys, or when the processes are simply gridlocked with competing sides or overworked with too-big-to-handle-dockets. When the losers in the electoral process[,] or the defeated in the litigation process, seek to upset their losses with constant battles, new elections, appeals, and attempts to dethrone or reverse "settled" outcomes, the paradigm again fails. Occasionally, the interested parties are so turned off by the complexities, expense, and wastefulness of these traditional processes they simply refuse to participate. Because of these concerns, and others, creative lawyers, attempting to find social justice for the many, rather than for the few, use the structured processes of mediation and consensus building to arrive at negotiated solutions to very complex legal and social problems.

Carrie Menkel-Meadow, *When Litigation Is Not the Only Way: Consensus Building and Mediation as Public Interest Lawyering*, 10 Wash. U. J.L. & Pol'y 37, 53-54 (2002); *see also* Jeffrey R. Seul, *Settling Significant Cases*, 79 Wash. L. Rev. 881 (2004) (arguing for wider acceptance of settlement in resolving socially significant litigation). If mediation and consensus building are more likely to build sustainable solutions, why do you think public interest lawyers continue to turn to courts? Are there risks of alternative dispute resolution (ADR) processes for less powerful social groups? What are they and how do you think they would affect outcomes? What role do you think ADR should play as a public interest law strategy?

Going back to our problem, can you anticipate ways in which a successful lawsuit against the city arguing that the health and safety conditions at the city's homeless shelters are inadequate under state law might generate backlash? Which stakeholders might organize opposition? As a lawyer for CHA, how might you anticipate such a reaction, and what steps could you plan to reduce opposition? Would those steps relate to litigation, or might they incorporate other advocacy strategies?

The backlash concern is that public interest litigation may be too successful in producing change and thus galvanize opponents to use their power to limit its reach through the political process. On the other side, there is a risk that litigation will be too weak an instrument for reform, resulting in outcomes that accommodate the status quo rather than challenge it. This might occur because defendants alter their activities to blunt the legal claim. For instance, a defendant may make it more difficult for the plaintiff to succeed by modifying its policies or behavior in ways that make the claims less clear cut. Defendants can engage in conduct that may make the plaintiff's claim moot or try to "pick off" individual claimants by offering them personally desirable settlements. These types of maneuvers make it difficult for plaintiffs to develop a legal theory or approach to a case because they are litigating against a "moving target."

Accommodation may also result from negotiated settlements, which result in a tangible outcome ostensibly benefiting the plaintiff, but undercutting the effort to effect social change. In an essay challenging the ADR movement, Owen Fiss argued that settlements in many social change contexts are likely to be undesirable because of the substantial power imbalance between the parties typically engaged in such litigation.

> The disparities in resources between the parties can influence the settlement in three ways. First, the poorer party may be less able to amass and analyze the information needed to predict the outcome of the litigation, and thus be disadvantaged in the bargaining process. Second, he may need the damages he seeks immediately and thus be induced to settle as a way of accelerating payment, even though he realizes he would get less now than he might if he awaited judgment. All plaintiffs want their damages immediately, but an indigent plaintiff may be exploited by a rich defendant because his need is so great that the defendant can force him to accept a sum that is less than the ordinary present value of the judgment. Third, the poorer party might be forced to settle because he does not have the resources to finance the litigation, to cover either his own projected expenses, such as his lawyer's time, or the expenses his opponent can impose through the manipulation of procedural mechanisms such as discovery. It might seem that settlement benefits the plaintiff by allowing him to avoid the costs of litigation, but this is not so. The defendant can anticipate the plaintiff's costs if the case were to be tried

fully and decrease his offer by that amount. The indigent plaintiff is a victim of the costs of litigation even if he settles.

Owen M. Fiss, *Against Settlement*, 93 YALE L.J. 1073, 1076 (1984).

The same power imbalances discussed by Fiss may encourage defendants to engage in "strategic settlements." As many scholars have observed, litigation outcomes are often distorted by the different incentive structures for resolving litigation through adjudication versus settlement. In his landmark work on the subject, Marc Galanter concluded that litigation, and particularly public interest litigation, frequently involves "repeat players," parties who are likely to be in court on the same issue against multiple opponents. Galanter, *supra*, at 97. Classical economic theory suggests that a party will settle a specific case for an amount that is less than the total of the anticipated cost of litigation plus the cost of a realistic award of damages (or other relief). Galanter illustrated how repeat players may have other reasons to settle that are not based on the anticipated outcome of a specific case. When allowing the case to go to judgment may result in a precedent that might adversely affect the repeat player defendant's position in its litigation with other parties, that defendant may engage in a strategic settlement — even paying more than the case's individual value — to avoid that precedent from being established. *Id.* at 100-03. Thus, the repeat player may behave differently than a one-time litigant, who may settle for terms that are favorable to her but ultimately less favorable for the broader class of similarly situated people.

The legal system has created some adaptations to procedural law that can counteract the defendants' strategic advantage in settling cases to avoid creation of an adverse new rule. As we have seen, one such device is the class action, pooling the collective interests of similarly situated parties and making the defendant's settlement strategy less appealing. Frank B. Cross, *In Praise of Irrational Plaintiffs*, 86 CORNELL L. REV. 1, 8 (2000). However, in addition to the legal and practical barriers to bringing such actions, the defendant still has a strategic advantage if it settles the case with the class but fails to change its behavior or the relevant legal rule, thereby putting future potential plaintiffs, who might have benefitted more from the precedent, at risk. *Id.* at 8-9. Another possibility that might counteract strategic settlement is that plaintiffs may not always behave rationally in settling their own cases. "[P]laintiffs may litigate for reasons other than purely financial ones and may not be willing to settle for even a lucrative offer from the defendant that exceeds their likely award at trial. If so, defendants who make large settlement offers to sympathetic plaintiffs may not succeed in avoiding a precedent because these plaintiffs may refuse even highly lucrative offers." *Id.* at 16.

Consider these issues in the following problem. As the lawyer for the plaintiffs, what steps could you take to make these outcomes less likely? Should you even take such steps?

Suppose the CHA brings litigation on behalf of five homeless clients challenging the constitutionality of the city ordinance prohibiting lying or sleeping in public.

Scenario 1: In initial negotiations, after the city's policy was the target of some negative editorials in the local newspapers, the city's lawyers indicate that the mayor has instructed the police department not to enforce the ordinance. The case is settled under these terms. The following week, one of your clients calls you from the city jail, where she has been arrested and charged under the public sleeping ordinance. You return to court, seeking an order of contempt, but the judge accepts the city's argument that there has been inadequate time to re-train its police officers, and orders you to return for a status hearing in two months. The next week, another client calls you to inform you that he has been arrested for sleeping in public, but not under the public sleeping ordinance. Rather, the police charged him with violating two different ordinances, one that prohibits "obstructing the public way" and another that prohibits "disturbing the public peace."

Scenario 2: In initial settlement negotiations, the city's attorneys suggest a settlement under which the city places each of the plaintiffs in a city-run residence for persons in transition for the next six months in exchange for dismissing the lawsuit. Unlike the city's other homeless shelters, there are better conditions and fewer safety concerns at the transitional residence. When you communicate this offer to your clients, they ask you to settle the case. The settlement leaves the ordinance in place and does not increase the shelter capacity or services for local homeless citizens.

III. PUBLIC INTEREST ADVOCACY OUTSIDE LITIGATION

The "essentialist" public interest lawyer tends to think of litigation and adjudication as the normative ways of accomplishing public good, perhaps because the model set by *Brown v. Board of Education* appeared so successful. At least some sophisticated lawyers, who care about public interest and seek social justice, recognize that litigation, although it has its uses, may not be optimal for all forms of legal change. Many public interest groups use, and have recently intensified their use of, legislative and lobbying efforts. Many groups in the civil rights, civil liberties and environmental movements use, or had to defend against, the referendum process. In the administrative context, some public interest groups participate in negotiated rule-making, one of the hybrid forms of dispute resolution. . . . Poverty lawyers and community development activists always explore other models of social and legal change, from organizing, to street or court theater, to community education, to collaborative joint venture strategies. More recently, even the most avid of traditional poverty law advocates recognize the importance of "facilitating coalitions" and encouraging "collaborative relationships across professions."

Menkel-Meadow, *supra*, at 44-45.

Though conventional accounts of the early years of public interest lawyering heavily emphasize litigation, the literature demonstrates that organizations and advocates never limited their work to the courts. HANDLER, *supra*, at

3. Advocacy was important in all institutions, public and private, that made decisions affecting client interests, as well as in the media. *Id.* Law reform activity of all types also served important consciousness-raising and legitimizing functions in earlier eras. *Id.* Even the NAACP LDF and the ACLU, two of the nonprofit organizations most closely associated with law reform litigation, had many internal debates about balancing litigation with other advocacy strategies. TUSHNET, NAACP, *supra*, at 8-9, 11-13; WALKER, *supra*, at 53. Thinking about the nature of public interest lawyering and its relationship to a wide range of advocacy models continued to evolve in the post-civil rights era. Several prominent legal scholars began to reexamine public interest advocacy in ways that envisioned litigation not as a central tool for social reform, but as one element among multiple strategies that could mobilize and empower communities to accomplish change. These scholars suggest that the ultimate goal is mobilization and organizing to accomplish changes in the dominant configurations of power. Viewed this way, litigation is one of several different political instruments that can play a role in accomplishing social reform. *See* SCHEINGOLD, *supra*, at 95-96; Scott L. Cummings & Ingrid V. Eagly, *A Critical Reflection on Law and Organizing*, 48 UCLA L. REV. 443, 447-48 (2001).

The remainder of this chapter explores some of the non-litigation options that lawyers and others have developed to pursue social change. It examines the features, advantages, and limitations of these strategies, as well as how they relate to each other and to litigation approaches. In the next chapter, we examine the implications of some of these models for the relationship between public interest lawyers and their clients.

A. TRANSACTIONAL LAWYERING

1. Features

Outside the domain of litigation, many public interest lawyers engage in transactional law, particularly in the field of community economic development (CED). In this work, lawyers often play the role of facilitators — advising, counseling, negotiating, and drafting documents to promote development in low-income communities. *See* Brian Glick & Matthew J. Rossman, *Neighborhood Legal Services as House Counsel to Community-Based Efforts to Achieve Economic Justice: The East Brooklyn Experience*, 23 N.Y.U. REV. L. & SOC. CHANGE 105 (1997); Daniel S. Shah, *Lawyering for Empowerment: Community Development and Social Change*, 6 CLINICAL L. REV. 217 (1999); Ann Southworth, *Representing Agents of Community Development: A Comment on Recent Trends*, 8 J. SMALL & EMERGING BUS. L. 261 (2004); Ann Southworth, *Business Planning for the Destitute? Lawyers as Facilitators in Civil Rights and Poverty Practice*, 1996 WIS. L. REV. 1127-29. Though a variety of factors define CED work, its basic features include: "(1) efforts to develop housing, jobs, or business opportunities for low income people, (2) in which a leading role is played by nonprofit, nongovernmental organizations and (3) that are accountable to residentially defined communities." William Simon, *The Community Economic Development Movement*, 2002 WIS. L. REV. 377, 378-79.

With respect to legal tactics, CED differs sharply from its litigation counterpart. In the litigation context, lawyers file claims of legal rights in an adversarial process to either change state practice vis-à-vis marginalized groups or invoke the power of the state to reform private conduct. The CED lawyer's role, in contrast, requires the type of nonadversarial transactional skills that are the stock-in-trade of the corporate bar: structuring business entities, arranging access to capital, counseling compliance with tax and corporate regulations, negotiating partnerships and other legal agreements, and navigating the process of real estate development.

Scott L. Cummings, *Mobilization Lawyering: Community Economic Development in the Figueroa Corridor, in* CAUSE LAWYERS AND SOCIAL MOVEMENTS (Austin Sarat & Stuart A. Scheingold eds., 2006) [hereinafter, Cummings, *Mobilization Lawyering*]. CED lawyers commonly provide transactional support to nonprofit organizations developing affordable housing, supporting needed community services, and creating commercial enterprises, including large-scale retail or industrial developments, small businesses, and worker cooperatives. *See* Carmen Huertas-Noble, *Promoting Worker-Owned Cooperatives as a CED Empowerment Strategy: A Case Study of Colors and Lawyering in Support of Participatory Decision-Making and Meaningful Social Change*, 17 CLINICAL L. REV. 255 (2010); Susan R. Jones, *Promoting Social and Economic Justice Through Interdisciplinary Work in Transactional Law*, 14 WASH U. J.L. & POL'Y 249 (2004). CED lawyers have also been involved in negotiating agreements with private developers that require those developers to provide specific types of benefits to local residents — housing, local hiring, living wage jobs, green space — in exchange for community support and public subsidies. Cummings, *Mobilization Lawyering, supra,* at 313.

Echoes of the CED movement can be heard in the early discourse between Booker T. Washington and W.E.B. DuBois about the optimal approach to advancing economic opportunity in African-American communities. Scott L. Cummings, *Community Economic Development as Progressive Politics: Towards a Grassroots Movement for Economic Justice*, 54 STAN. L. REV. 399, 410-13 (2001) [hereinafter, Cummings, *Community Economic Development*]. Washington believed that prioritizing economic development and self-sufficiency was the principal way to address racial equality, and advocated job training and facilitating entrepreneurial business development in the black community. *Id.* at 410-11. While DuBois believed in greater reliance on direct advocacy for civil rights, he did not reject the idea that economic development would yield important gains for blacks. *Id.* Throughout the civil rights movement, a rights-focused social change campaign took precedence, but concerns about economic opportunity were never far in the background. By the mid-1960s, leaders became more focused on the failure of African Americans to make substantial economic gains, and growing concern about poverty in America supported the expansion of social welfare programs.

In the 1980s, the election of Ronald Reagan and the emergence of a conservative political climate focused policy attention on free market reforms, which included efforts to promote market-based approaches to addressing poverty, in contrast to what were viewed by critics as dependency-inducing government welfare programs. *Id.* at 422-23. It was in this context that a market-based approach to CED began to develop:

> The current CED paradigm . . . rests on the premise that the market does not function properly in low-income communities and that creative efforts to build market capacity are necessary to stimulate flagging local economies. The main programmatic goal, advanced primarily by [nonprofit community development corporations, or] CDCs, has been to restructure market incentives to leverage private investment for the development of community-based businesses, affordable housing, and financial institutions.
>
> A central component of market-based CED strategies has been the promotion of local business development as a vehicle for creating jobs for low-income workers. Toward this end, community organizations have acted as financing intermediaries for neighborhood businesses, provided technical assistance to community entrepreneurs, and developed local real estate projects such as shopping centers, supermarkets, and industrial business parks. A significant portion of the funding for these efforts has come through federal, state, and local economic development agencies, supplemented by foundation grants, private investments, and commercial loans. Community groups have also made efforts to stimulate economic growth through microenterprise and nonprofit business ventures. Thus, many organizations have provided technical assistance and microloans to very small businesses owned by low-income community residents. In addition, some nonprofit groups have sought to employ low-income people directly by starting their own business ventures, often termed social enterprises. CED lawyers have played a variety of roles in these business development projects, establishing appropriate legal structures, reviewing contracts and financial instruments, evaluating the tax consequences of development projects, and handling real estate matters.
>
> Affordable housing development constitutes another important programmatic element of the market-based CED model. The Low-Income Housing Tax Credit (LIHTC) has, perhaps more than any other program, exemplified the market-based approach to CED. The LIHTC, enacted as part of the Tax Reform Act of 1986, was created as a financial incentive to boost private sector investment in affordable housing. Its enactment underscored the move away from the concept of housing as a public good and toward increased reliance on the private market to supply housing to the poor. By establishing a process for syndicating tax credits to private investors, the LIHTC has provided a substantial subsidy to affordable housing development since its introduction. Under the tax credit program, the construction or rehabilitation of eligible residential rental properties may qualify for the LIHTC if a minimum number of rent-restricted units for low-income tenants is set aside. Although estimates of the production effect of the LIHTC vary, it is clear that the credit has spurred the construction of a significant number of low-income units; the cost-effectiveness of the program, however, remains the subject of debate. Given the technical complexity of LIHTC deals, CED lawyers have been critical to their implementation, assisting developers to apply for tax credits, form limited partnerships, draft tax opinions, and review financing and real estate documents.
>
> Consistent with the goal of market expansion, CED has also focused on increasing access to financial institutions in low-income communities to augment the flow of capital resources to areas that have suffered disinvestment. One of the main efforts in this regard has been to develop banking alternatives

in economically distressed neighborhoods. Most prominently, the Community Development Financial Institutions Act (CDFI Act) of 1994 created a fund to invest in community development financial institutions (CDFIs), which are community-based organizations dedicated to investing, lending, and providing basic banking services in support of community development efforts. The CDFI Act is structured to increase direct federal investment and technical assistance to CDFIs, and to create incentives for private banks to invest in CDFIs. The CDFI program has stimulated the establishment of community development banks, credit unions, community development loan funds, venture capital funds, and micro-enterprise loan funds that serve low-income communities. These CDFIs target investments to support job creation projects, affordable housing, and community infrastructure development. They offer financial products such as checking and savings accounts, mortgages, small business loans, individual development accounts, and equity investments, while often providing other community services, such as job training courses and homeownership programs. By providing access to capital markets, CDFIs have complemented efforts to increase business development and expand affordable housing in low-income communities.

Cummings, *Community Economic Development, supra*, at 438-41.

Although the market-based CED model was successful on some measures in reversing the trend of disinvestment in poor, urban communities, it was limited by its focus on leveraging private market resources through existing governmental programs rather than advocating to redefine legal relations in order to address the underlying structural causes of poverty and inequality. In response, a newer "politically engaged" CED model that some have termed "accountable development" emerged. The accountable development model links transactional CED work with grassroots community organizing and political advocacy. It seeks to build upon the benefits of market-based approaches while also mobilizing to address structural political and market relations, and promote redistributive policy making. This model has three defining features.

First, the politically engaged model applies legal advocacy to support community organizing around economic justice issues. Its goal is to deploy transactional lawyering in a way that builds organized low-income constituencies that can challenge the distribution of political power. The integration of CED and community organizing represents a rapprochement between two types of grassroots practice that have largely diverged since the increasing professionalization of CED work in the late 1970s. This has occurred as organizing—with its emphasis on using public confrontation and direct action to influence political institutions—has re-emerged during the 1990s as a viable social change practice with a newly energized leadership and an active grassroots presence. The increasing visibility of organizing has shifted the terrain of social change work, highlighting the need for an advocacy strategy that challenges the distribution of political power in addition to promoting bricks and mortar construction in low-income areas. . . .

The second key attribute of this new model is that it seeks to situate CED advocacy within the context of a broader progressive movement on behalf of marginalized communities. This has been most evident in the increasing formation of strategic alliances between CED practitioners and other grassroots actors—such as community organizers, labor representatives, and clergy—

who have the mass-based constituencies necessary to leverage structural change. These grassroots formations, particularly the community-labor coalitions, have become increasingly powerful, advocating for living wage and resident hiring provisions, promoting publicly funded job creation, negotiating worker factory buy-outs, providing strike support, and blocking industrial plant closings. By tapping into these emerging economic justice networks, CED lawyers have developed a more comprehensive approach to redressing poverty that coordinates the multi-faceted efforts on behalf of low-wage workers and welfare recipients. Moreover, CED lawyers have recognized that collaboration with organized labor, faith-based entities, and poor people's organizations — which have large, relatively cohesive memberships and, in the case of unions, financial power — is critical to achieving the political clout necessary to push through economic justice measures.

Finally, unlike the conventional market-based model, the new approach to CED is spatially decentered, actively cultivating cross-racial coalitions that cut across traditional community boundaries. Instead of targeting economic resources in specific neighborhoods, CED practitioners are forging linkages with community groups in different localities in order to create regional, national, and transnational structures to combat the economic deterioration of marginalized populations. This effort to extend the geographic scope of CED promotes multiracial coalition building and establishes the structural links necessary to build a broad-based progressive movement. In this way, CED advocates are transforming the meaning of community to encompass racially and geographically dispersed groups that share common grievances arising from their economically marginalized status.

Id. at 459-64; *see also* Cummings, *Mobilization Lawyering, supra*, at 313.

One of the principal elements of the accountable development approach has been an emphasis on local community participation in the approval and implementation of private development projects. The first wave of CED operated in economically distressed neighborhoods and sought to attract private capital through a variety of economic and social incentives in order to build housing and viable businesses. However, when some of these neighborhoods became more attractive to private investments during the real estate boom of the 2000s, they confronted a distinct problem: the rapid influx of private capital began to impose significant costs on existing residents in the form of gentrification and displacement. Scott L. Cummings & Ben Beach, *Community Benefits Agreements, in* COMMUNITY ECONOMIC DEVELOPMENT: A TEXT FOR ENGAGED LEARNING 322 (Susan D. Bennett et al. eds., 2012). "In the face of this reinvestment boom, poor communities had to confront a new dilemma: how to either slow down private investment or condition it on the provision of community benefits such as affordable housing and living wage jobs for existing residents." *Id.*

> One of the [accountable development] movement's central goals was to change city redevelopment practices by increasing community participation in the planning process and forcing local developers and governmental officials to commit to redevelopment projects responsive to the needs of low-income residents, who contributed their tax dollars to subsidize development but were often rewarded by being displaced. . . .
>
> [Community Benefits Agreements, or] CBAs were conceived as a tool to shape major development projects through direct agreements with developers.

Because the goal of conditioning private investment on the provision of community benefits involved the exercise of local political power, a central issue was who had the power to shape local decision making in the interests of low-income residents. In most campaigns resulting in a CBA, the answer has been the "community-labor coalition." . . .

A primary goal of community development corporations (CDCs) created to advance CED was to mesh government incentives with community initiatives in order to lure reluctant private investment dollars back into the central city. Toward this end, CED projects attempted to attract outside capital by creating public-private partnerships facilitated by federal laws such as the Low-Income Housing Tax Credit program to leverage private investment from public subsidies. Criticizing this approach for its incrementalism and absence of a broader redistributive vision, some community groups began pursuing accountable development as an alternative (though not incompatible) path that sought to build community-based political power as a means to demand more resources than contemplated by existing development policy and practice. In particular, this approach sought to ensure that private developers who received public subsidies to revitalize low-income communities created projects that actually benefited community members — instead of simply driving them out. To advance this goal, local groups turned to community organizing, labor organizing, and social movement models to "redefine redevelopment" and promote "economic justice." In addition to CDCs, important actors included Alinsky-style organizing groups, national organizing networks such as ACORN, church-based organizations, and other neighborhood-based economic justice groups such as Strategic Actions for a Just Economy (SAJE), which was a lead organization in the first CBA negotiated in Los Angeles. Environmental groups also entered CBA coalitions in an effort to mitigate specific environmental harms associated with development projects.

However, despite the range of these groups, they often lacked the financial resources to influence political and development decisions. That is where organized labor came in. Labor leaders have promoted community-labor alliances as a national strategy through organizations such as Good Jobs First, which was created to build networks of local activists to support labor rights. In addition, unions in major metropolitan areas have sponsored the formation of local labor rights organizations, which have mediated between organized labor and other community- and faith-based groups. The Los Angeles Alliance for a New Economy (LAANE), formed in 1993 by the Hotel Employees and Restaurant Employees union, has become nationally known for its innovative labor campaigns, which include securing passage of the Los Angeles Living Wage Ordinance in 1997, and more recent efforts to promote accountability in publicly subsidized redevelopment. Similar groups in cities around the country have joined with LAANE to form the Partnership for Working Families to advocate for greater social and economic returns on public investments.

Organized labor has promoted CBAs for a set of interlocking reasons. First, CBAs provide concrete benefits — such as living wage jobs, affordable housing, and environmental safety — to union and nonunion workers alike, which is a goal that organized labor has supported on its own terms. Second, CBAs may advance specific union organizing campaigns by including provisions requiring living wage, card-check neutrality, and responsible contracting that can complement organizing strategies. Third, organized labor has viewed CBAs as part of a broader, long-standing strategy to broaden its constituency.

Community-labor coalitions have become an umbrella for a range of urban constituencies frustrated by economic development and willing to forge strategic alliances in order to advance a local political agenda with redistributive aims. The coalitions that have led and supported recent CBA campaigns suggest that this formula has the potential to attract a diverse group of stakeholders. For example, the "One Hill" coalition that in 2008 obtained a CBA for the proposed new sports arena to house the Pittsburgh Penguins professional hockey team consisted of more than 90 local stakeholders, including small businesses, clubs and associations, political organizations, advocacy groups, and service providers. The 2008 CBA for the Dearborn Street project in Seattle included the Washington Vietnamese Chamber of Commerce, UFCW Local 21, LIUNA NW Regional Organizing Coalition, and the Jackson Place Community Council. . . .

CBA campaigns offer coalition members an opportunity to accomplish several types of goals. Most tangibly, CBA campaigns can shape major development projects in a way that delivers real and meaningful benefits to low-income communities. The immediate substantive goals of CBA campaigns, dictated by community needs, have included living wage and unionized jobs; job training and targeted hiring programs for local residents; affordable housing; community services, parks, and environmental benefits; contractor compliance with labor standards; and community oversight of project implementation. A single CBA campaign may seek to obtain most of these kinds of benefits in connection with a single project. For example, the 2008 CBA for a major mixed-use project in San Francisco's Bayview Hunters-Point ultimately provided many of these benefits, including living wage standards, card-check neutrality, first-source hiring, substantial funding for job training and affordable housing, the replacement of existing public housing units, and the creation of an implementation committee. Of course, for these goals to be meaningful, they must be enforceable by community groups. The most effective CBAs are therefore explicitly drafted to permit the direct enforcement of community benefits provisions by coalition members against the developer (and sometimes the city).

CBA campaigns may have less immediate, but no less important, goals as well. Most significantly, CBA campaigns may offer a vehicle for enhancing the power of workers and communities in local economic development relative to developers and local officials. Similarly, CBA campaigns may contribute to efforts to change local government behavior by normalizing higher development standards in the local market. Finally, CBA campaigns may lay the groundwork for further community and worker organizing, by strengthening the political capacity of community-labor coalitions and creating legal leverage for future organizing.

Id. What kind of lawyering do you think accountable development involves? How is it different, if at all, from the type of transactional lawyering associated with traditional CED?

2. Appraisal

a. BENEFITS

The CED movement has been associated with a model of public interest lawyering that deemphasizes litigation and other traditional tactics in favor of an approach that builds new institutions, while also cultivating a lawyer-client relationship in which the community, represented by a locally accountable organization, is empowered to advance its interests. These benefits can be described in several categories.

i. LOCAL CONTROL

CED, as a set of policies and practices, emphasizes the importance of local control. Lawyers who work with CED organizations, therefore, may advance that goal. CED provides communities with access to government and market structures that might not be achievable through litigation and other types of advocacy. It also emphasizes direct decision making by local residents, bounded in a discrete neighborhood, who identify and solve community problems. In this way, local control is viewed as facilitating a more effective and accountable approach to social change and redressing local poverty.

> Different justifications have been offered in support of localized CED efforts. Some have argued that the local focus is a strategic necessity — an effort to maximize the impact of advocacy undertaken with limited financial resources. Others have suggested that there is a stronger imperative for localism, one rooted in a model of "bottom-up" social change that relies on the active participation of community residents to produce meaningful, long-term results. In either case, there has been a powerful tendency to treat the local neighborhood as a discrete economic unit in need of rebuilding. Commentators have generally presumed the fixity of local neighborhood boundaries, suggesting that the primary objective of CED should be the creation of new investment, jobs, and development projects within defined geographic spheres. CED has therefore evolved as a "place-based" strategy that attempts to enlist the support of community residents to effect changes in their immediate surroundings.
>
> Analyses of CED have concentrated on demonstrating how community-based groups have worked to facilitate the expansion of economic activities within specific low-income neighborhoods. CED has thus been promoted as a method of counteracting the deterioration of communities through the development of community-oriented enterprises that increase local economic viability and neighborhood autonomy. In particular, CDCs have been presented as catalysts for local economic growth, working to correct market failures by channeling resources into areas with high concentrations of poverty. In the legal services context, CED has been offered as a way of supporting local development through the representation of CDCs on real estate, tax, corporate, and regulatory matters. By focusing on neighborhood-level interventions, market-based CED has demonstrated its strategic commitment to local action and underscored the primacy of local communities as sites for social change.

Cummings, *Community Economic Development, supra*, at 442-43.

ii. COMMUNITY EMPOWERMENT

Another advantage of CED is that it attempts to give power to the community and its leaders, rather than the lawyers who work with them. This addresses one of the principal critiques of public interest litigation and places control of the movement to alleviate poverty directly in the hands of affected community members. Indeed, "one of the most frequently cited justifications for CED as a social change strategy is its capacity to 'empower poor people to work for their own economic and social betterment.'" *Id.* at 443-44. This feature is also closely related to the emphasis on local control.

> CED scholars have suggested that if neighborhood residents are incorporated as active participants in the reconstruction of their local economies, they will be empowered through the process. In particular, CED proponents have argued that communities build power by exerting ongoing influence over local decision-making structures in a way that ensures that development efforts are responsive to community needs. CED work has therefore been focused on establishing mechanisms for ensuring that ultimate control of neighborhood-based initiatives resides in low-income community members. Generally, the establishment of CDCs accountable to residents has been viewed as the main vehicle for achieving community empowerment. Community business ownership and community involvement in redevelopment efforts have also been cited as effective mechanisms for promoting empowerment.
>
> What emerges from the CED literature is a picture of empowerment as a complex process that occurs on a variety of different planes—political, social, and psychological. Empowerment is described as both the expression of individual capacity and group political strength. Often, empowerment occurs on the individual and the group level simultaneously, in a mutually reinforcing cycle. Some have described empowerment in process-oriented terms, suggesting that CED efforts facilitate self-help strategies that teach community members how to handle their own problems more effectively. Others have characterized empowerment as tethered to the results of community action, claiming that empowerment occurs when community members see their projects come to fruition. What these descriptions have in common is an understanding of empowerment as a measurable good: Empowerment is viewed as a discernable transformation—a quantum of influence that can be cultivated by active participation in local community life.

Id. at 444-45.

As the community grows more empowered, the risks of a power imbalance between lawyer and client, to which lawyer domination is often attributed, can be reduced. This may occur organically given the fact that the nature of CED projects and the ability to monitor their development is typically less reliant on professional knowledge or training in the way that litigation may be.

> In the legal scholarship, CED lawyers have been portrayed as particularly effective in fostering community empowerment. For instance, it has been argued that CED lawyers can empower their clients both by demystifying the law and by ensuring that the development process is successfully implemented. Some feminists have claimed that bottom-up CED strategies, such as microenterprise development, can lead to women's empowerment by creating "new patterns of social interaction" that promote feelings of enhanced social and political capacity. It has also been suggested that lawyers can augment community power by helping clients to structure organizations that integrate mechanisms of local control, such as CDFIs. Others have argued that CED

lawyers may promote empowerment by collaborating with client groups to address the problems of poverty "in creative, power-sensitive, and politically engaged ways."

Scholars have also claimed that the nature of the lawyer-client relationship in the CED context promotes empowerment by minimizing the potential for lawyer domination. Since the representation of organizational clients requires that lawyers plan and structure future client projects as well as properly maintain existing programs, CED lawyers tend to adhere to client objectives and defer to client expertise. As a result, client autonomy is respected in the CED context to a greater extent than in other advocacy settings, thereby enhancing the potential for client-empowering experiences to occur.

Id. at 445-46. Nonetheless, "[t]here remains considerable variation in the degree of lawyer-client collaboration, ranging from more passive facilitation of client projects . . . to greater lawyer participation in defining and executing community goals. . . . The degree of lawyer participation in client decision making is a function of the governance style of the client organizations, the personal commitments of the lawyers . . . , and the influence of the lawyers' practice settings." Cummings, *Mobilization Lawyering, supra*, at 309.

b. CHALLENGES

While CED has contributed to successful development projects in local communities and promoted community empowerment, there are (as with all advocacy strategies) important tradeoffs.

i. DISADVANTAGES OF LOCAL CONTROL

One tradeoff occurs in relation to local control, which is double-edged. First, some have argued that local control is problematic because it cannot address the structural determinants of poverty. By emphasizing development projects at the local level, CED may take both attention and resources away from larger reform efforts to eradicate poverty. Cummings, *Community Economic Development, supra*, at 455. Because of their geographically limited focus, local development projects cannot fundamentally redistribute political and economic power, address impediments to economic equality in a liberal capitalist system, or reach across geographic boundaries to address the increasing interconnectedness of urban economies. *Id.*

There also may be reasons to question how powerfully local economic development contributes to the broader enlargement of economic opportunity for the poor. *See id.* Some observers have concluded that CED initiatives have not been sufficient to reverse the decline of urban neighborhoods. For instance, one study found that only 20 to 30 percent of CDC-sponsored housing and business development programs have had a substantial impact on their neighborhoods. *Id.* at 447-48. Even successful development projects have not necessarily led to economic opportunity for local residents, who may still earn below poverty level wages from jobs created by revitalization efforts. *Id.* at 449. Efforts to create more low-income housing in urban neighborhoods do not always increase the overall supply of affordable units and may in some cases lead to gentrification and displacement. *Id.* at 448, 450.

Another potential drawback to the local control focus of CED projects is that this emphasis may create impediments to cross-community and cross-racial coalitions to address poverty. Some scholars argue that "[r]ather than concentrating exclusively on neighborhood development as a poverty reduction strategy, practitioners must begin to look beyond community boundaries to a more comprehensive antipoverty approach that acknowledges the significance of regional and transnational networks in the process of economic reform." *Id.* at 456. Similarly, because many high-poverty neighborhoods are disproportionately composed of people of color, the local focus may create a kind of tunnel vision that precludes reaching out to foster inter-community collaboration among the urban poor. "By accepting existing neighborhood configurations, the market approach tends to reinforce racialized community borders and maintain existing patterns of racial segregation. This place-based focus impedes efforts to forge a cross-racial coalition to advance a political agenda sensitive to the needs of low-income workers." *Id.* at 458.

A final challenge of localism is how to extend the benefits of CED to other communities. Some observers of CBAs wonder whether the negotiation of different development standards in individual communities will result in inconsistency that works against a comprehensive approach to urban poverty. Cummings & Beach, *supra*. Some networks exist to foster the diffusion of best practices, and many developers now view CBAs as a routine part of their business planning. However, there are limits to how far CBAs might be able to reach. Significantly, some of the factors that promote CBAs—such as a strong local labor movement—may not exist everywhere, making it more difficult to imagine that CBAs can be effectively used by all communities facing gentrification and displacement pressures.

ii. DEPOLITICIZATION OF ANTIPOVERTY ADVOCACY

Some types of CED work have also tended to steer clear of advocacy oriented toward economic reform in favor of facilitating deals within the context of existing government and private sector programs. "The market-based model has conceptualized poverty alleviation as primarily a matter of structuring the appropriate economic incentives to spur capital inflow and business expansion in distressed neighborhoods. Within this framework, the notion of building political power among the poor to challenge institutional arrangements is viewed as inimical to the goal of packaging low-income communities as attractive business environments." Cummings, *Community Economic Development*, *supra*, at 451. Such an approach ignores the critical ways in which government decisions and regulations regarding zoning, residential segregation, red-lining by mortgage lenders, and the location of public housing have shaped urban communities and are responsible for many of the problems of entrenched poverty. *Id.* In this sense, CED may be more oriented toward playing within the existing rules of the game than challenging the rules through political action. Observers suggest that deemphasizing political mobilization has compromised the ability of CED projects to make greater progress in addressing urban poverty. Moreover, the emphasis on market-based strategies may also undermine the fight for economic opportunity by diverting resources away from grassroots political work and providing an excuse for government agencies to withdraw aid and economic support programs from struggling communities. *Id.* at 453.

Overall, CED's approach to politics emphasizes collaboration over confrontation, distinguishing it from other types of legal and political action.

> CED's emphasis on collaboration as a form of legal action reflects its distinct orientation toward the fairness of the legal system. . . . CED does not seek to reform public law rules through judicial decree or legislative change. Therefore, in contrast to more traditional rights-oriented cause lawyering, which was designed to achieve universal public benefits, the goal of CED is the more modest production of partial private benefits. . . .
>
> The focus on cultivating and maintaining relationships with external state and market elites thus influences the *nature* of mobilization within CED, privileging collaboration over systemic disruption. In this sense, CED stands in contrast to social movements, which have historically been defined by direct challenges to "existing institutional authority—whether it is located in the political, corporate, religious, or educational realm". . . . Moreover, unlike social movements that rely on "disruptive 'symbolic' tactics such as protests, marches, strikes, and the like that halt or upset ongoing social practices" . . . , CED adheres closely to institutional channels of collective action. There are instances of disruptive activity within CED. . . . However, disruptive activity is de-emphasized among CDCs. . . .

Cummings, *Mobilization Lawyering, supra,* at 309-10, 312.

iii. EFFECTIVENESS

As has already been suggested, there are questions about how to define and measure CED's effectiveness. The factors contributing to community revitalization are multifaceted and it is often hard to disentangle the effects of local efforts versus broader economic trends. There are always questions of opportunity costs—that is, whether investments in CED might produce greater housing or job gains elsewhere. And there is no agreement on how to understand or measure the impact or value of community empowerment.

Even in projects that can potentially be measured, it is not always easy to judge their success. Take the community benefits agreements (CBAs) mentioned above—private contracts negotiated between community groups and developers directing "benefits" (housing, jobs, training) to local residents in exchange for community support (and often public subsidies). One challenge is that the community benefits negotiated in CBAs do not become operational until the economic development has been completed. Because development projects can take years to finish, it can be difficult to determine tangible results. Moreover, the time frame for these projects can also affect the ability of groups to maintain ongoing energy to organize their communities. Consider the following description of the preliminary results of a major CBA in Los Angeles:

> The slow progress on the L.A. Live development—the country's first [CBA] in 2001—highlights the challenges facing CBA implementation and suggests potential differences between the affordable housing and jobs-related

components of the agreements. After the CBA was signed, contributions from developers (including those that subsequently purchased discrete parcels from the original developer) helped to fund over 200 affordable housing units in close proximity to the project. In terms of jobs, phase one of the development was not completed until 2007 with the opening of the 7100-seat Nokia Theatre, which hosts events such as the American Music Awards and the Emmys. According to the developer, all of the jobs in the Nokia Theatre meet the living wage requirements of the CBA and half of the jobs are held by local residents in compliance with the local hiring requirement. There is no information available, however, on CBA compliance for the recently completed phase two of the project, which includes restaurants and entertainment venues (such as The GRAMMY Museum, ESPN Zone, The Farm of Beverly Hills, Lawry's, and Starbucks) that are in industry sectors generally associated with lower wage rates. The third (and final) phase of development—which includes hotels and residences—is not yet complete. A 2006 Status Update from the coalition stated that a job training program was established in August 2003 and that the developer had provided $62,000 (out of a promised total of $100,000) in seed funding to support the program.

Cummings & Beach, *supra*.

In addition to timing issues, some elements of CBAs may be easier to enforce than others. Because the housing agreements require developers to "either build a specified portion of units or pay into an affordable housing fund, they may be easier to enforce because the developers' obligations are clear and discrete (and may be as simple as cutting a check). In contrast, jobs provisions may be more difficult to enforce over time, since they continue on throughout the duration of the project, raising challenges to ongoing monitoring." *Id.* Having some form of stable, ongoing monitoring organization may be critical to sustaining the success of CBAs.

As this discussion suggests, monitoring and enforcement are significant issues in CED work—just as they are in the context of litigation. How should public interest lawyers approach monitoring and enforcement in the CED context? How are the monitoring and enforcement challenges different in the transactional and litigation spheres of public interest law?

iv. ACCOUNTABILITY

As with litigation, CED lawyering raises complex issues of accountability. Who speaks for the community and how representative are these members of the community's diverse interests? How accountable are CED lawyers to the communities on whose behalf they claim to serve? Even within the local paradigm of CED practice, accountability issues do not disappear—they just change. This issue will be treated more fully in Chapter 7. For now, consider the complexity of representing coalitions of community groups in the context of negotiating CBAs:

> . . . CBAs raise another set of questions that revolve around the issue of the accountability of CBA coalitions to the communities that they attempt to benefit. The legitimacy of CBAs rests on their ability to represent diverse community interests. Thus, the composition of the coalition is key and the strongest CBAs are negotiated by groups that have the broadest and deepest

community connections. One issue relates to the differential power of organized labor versus other community groups. While union leverage brings developers to the table, union partners are typically supportive of development projects that will create jobs for their members and thus may be more likely than their community partners to want to negotiate a deal.

Another key issue is the representativeness of the CBA coalition and its ties to a broad range of community interests. Coalitions that do not represent a broad enough range of community concerns risk undermining the legitimacy of a resulting CBA. The Brooklyn-based Atlantic Yards CBA—negotiated around a mixed-used development that included a basketball arena designed to be the future home of the New Jersey Nets — was finalized by a coalition that included only eight community groups (including ACORN), and has been subject to criticism from a range of community organizations and outside commentators for its lack of representation. In extreme cases, developers may seek to influence the composition of coalitions, cutting side deals with groups they perceive as willing to support their project in order to create the veneer of community approval.

Another axis of accountability is between the lawyer for a CBA coalition and the client. Researchers have raised concerns about lawyers dominating poor clients. These concerns are, to some degree, mitigated in the CBA context, where the coalitions are frequently comprised of relatively powerful organizations governed by politically savvy and influential leaders. Because the coalitions approach the lawyers as empowered political actors, the lawyering itself may be focused on achieving a political result defined by the coalition rather than on promoting goals envisioned by the lawyers.

Nonetheless, lawyering for CBA coalitions presents unique challenges. Group representation generally raises difficult questions about who speaks for the group, but in the CBA context, this is exacerbated because the client itself is an amalgam of several groups that operate with a range of organizational formality and at times very different resources. Often, the lack of a formal governance structure within the coalition complicates the lines of client communication and has led some commentators to argue for creating separate organizational entities to facilitate CBA negotiations. However, to the degree that a coalition has a strong internal system for making decisions and a clear understanding of members' respective bottom lines, the lack of formal organization may be less important because the groups can arrive at a unified position that can be easily conveyed to the lawyer. Further, a CBA lawyer may minimize the potential for conflicts among coalition members by obtaining conflict waivers in advance or agreeing to only provide representation as to matters about which coalition members are in agreement.

Id.

v. PUBLIC VERSUS PRIVATE

The fact that CED generally results in the formation of private entities (housing developers, businesses) or privately negotiated agreements (CBAs) raises questions about its ultimate scope. It does not, as has been suggested, typically result in redistributive policy reform generally applied across neighborhoods or cities (though lawyers do, as discussed below, sometimes engage in policy advocacy to promote new and expanded CED initiatives). There are other limits to the focus on private transactions that characterizes CED practice.

Consider again CBAs, which are the result of negotiations between community groups and developers. Although groups are able to use legal and political leverage to extract real benefits for their communities, often developers will have greater bargaining power, leading to contractual provisions that are not strictly enforceable, such as soft targets for meeting CBA goals like living wage standards. And for developers, there are advantages for containing CBA negotiations to specific private development sites rather than permitting the principles of accountable development to be embedded in citywide policy. "An inequality of power between developers and community groups may also explain why the development standards created in CBAs have generally not been translated into city-wide public policy." *Id.*

> The private nature of CBAs raises other important issues. First, there are concerns that CBAs may benefit some groups at the expense of others. For instance, critics have suggested that coalition members may use the process of CBA negotiation to extract "sweetheart deals" for their organizations, such as funding that goes to support specific organizational projects. Although this is an important concern, it is worth noting that most CBAs do not provide direct funding to signatory groups, which often explicitly disclaim such funding in order to avoid conflicts of interest and ensure political legitimacy.
>
> More broadly, critics of CBAs have expressed concern that they may result in misallocated development resources and skewed public policymaking. CBAs, these critics contend, at best bypass and at worst distort established democratic processes to determine how best to allocate public dollars to low-income communities. Supporters of CBAs respond that the established democratic channels for decisions regarding development have historically benefited powerful developers to the detriment and exclusion of communities and thus CBAs offer a necessary corrective—both in terms of creating meaningful channels for community input and establishing community-oriented rules governing major developments. Moreover, CBAs do not change the existing formal development regulatory structure, but rather are private agreements negotiated in the shadow of that structure; as such, they resemble a range of other familiar contracts (such as collective bargaining or settlement agreements) that interact with—but do not supplant—extant policy.
>
> Finally, the private nature of CBAs raises concerns about who ultimately bears their costs. As developers come to understand CBAs as a "cost of doing business," they can mitigate the direct impact on their bottom line by requesting more public subsidy, passing through the price of CBAs to the taxpaying public. Depending on how much power developers have to pass on the costs, they could shift some, if not all, of the cost of CBA compliance to the public, while still reaping the legitimacy benefits that the CBA affords. Public money would thus be allocated through private bargaining. The political desirability of this allocation would depend on whether CBA negotiations in fact expand development resources or, if not, how we judge what cities are forced to ultimately give up in order to redirect public money to CBA projects.

Id.

What do you think about these criticisms? Are they fair? How do they compare to criticisms of litigation strategies? What do they say about the lawyer's role?

Returning to the homelessness scenario set out at the beginning of the chapter, can you think of some ideas for CED projects that might benefit the homeless? One idea that might come to mind is a project to develop low-income housing that would help address, in part, the lack of available housing units. Another project might involve a small business that engaged homeless persons as both employees and in the business's operation and design. In order to advance such a project, who would the stakeholders be in the local government and the private sector? How might you bring them to the bargaining table? What role would the lawyers play in such an endeavor? How might you address some of the challenges discussed in the preceding section of this chapter? For a general discussion of some ongoing CED projects involving the homeless, see Susan R. Jones, *Tackling Homelessness Through Economic Self-Sufficiency*, 19 St. Louis U. Pub. L. Rev. 385 (2000).

B. COMMUNITY ORGANIZING

The political organization of intermediate-sized groups is perhaps the highest service anyone can perform in the service of democracy.

Luban, *supra*, at 387.

Give a [person] a fish, and he [or she] will eat for a day. Teach a [person] to fish and he [or she] will eat for a lifetime.

The Yale Book of Quotations 527 (Fred R. Shapiro ed., 2006).

The latter, commonly invoked, sentiment emphasizes the value of allowing individuals to take control of their destinies, rather than helping them in a discrete, episodic, but ultimately unsustainable, manner. It could just as well be a comment on public interest lawyering. In response, as the discussion of CED underscores, some lawyers have sought to develop strategies that mobilize communities to use their collective power to fight for social change on their own terms. An important tool in this effort is community organizing, which public interest lawyers have sought to support — both on its own terms and in connection with traditional strategies like litigation — in order to advance different types of causes.

1. Features

While the label "community organizing" has been attached to a variety of activities designed to accomplish social change, its definition is fluid. There is no uniform understanding of what community organizing is, or how lawyers operate within such activities. "Organizing is often used as shorthand for a range of community-based practices, such as organization building, mobilization, education, consciousness raising, and legislative advocacy." Cummings & Eagly, *supra*, at 481. In this section, we examine some of the activities that have been grouped under this category and then explore the degree to which lawyers can play a role in such work.

Lawyers have long sought to use legal and organizing strategies in synergistic ways. Even in its relatively early stages, the NAACP's legal strategy to end racial segregation paid attention to the connection between its litigation campaign and mobilization of the black community. TUSHNET, *supra*, at 29. A pivotal figure in the history of organizing is Saul Alinsky, who organized groups of poor people in the 1930s. SAUL ALINSKY, REVEILLE FOR RADICALS (1946); SAUL ALINSKY, RULES FOR RADICALS (1971). "The central tenets of 'Alinskyism' included building local power through the strategic mobilization of poor people, developing indigenous leadership to articulate specific community interests, and ensuring that organizing efforts evolved organically out of the needs of local communities." Cummings & Eagly, *supra*, at 462. While Alinsky's early efforts focused on organizing people who shared common interests within their geographical area, others built on this model and began forming community organizations that were organized around specific issues rather than geographical communities. *Id.* For example, Fred Ross, an ally of Alinsky's, worked with César Chávez to help organize migrant farm workers to challenge their working conditions. *Id.* Community organizing became an important tool in the civil rights movement, and national attention to campaigns such as the Montgomery bus boycott fueled support for the effectiveness of collective action. *Id.* at 462-63.

> Over the past several decades, community organizing has emerged as a self-conscious social justice movement with the primary goal of "community building." The movement has focused on fostering grassroots participation in local decision making, coordinating the strategic deployment of community resources to achieve community-defined goals, and building community-based democratic organizations led by local leaders who advocate for social and economic change. In practice, community organizations have worked at the local level to create more equitable social and economic policies, redistribute resources to low-income communities, and empower marginalized constituencies by giving voice to their concerns. As a result of the community organizing movement, there are now more than six thousand community organizations in the United States. Movement historians have pointed to its many accomplishments, including the development of skilled community-based leaders and national community organizing networks, the refinement of replicable community organizing models, and numerous successful campaigns that have effectively shifted the balance of power toward disadvantaged communities.

Id. at 460-61.

Lawyers may play a variety of roles in supporting community organizing. Some are straightforwardly technical: helping organizations with their specific legal problems, such as incorporating a nonprofit or dealing with run-of-the-mill organizational legal issues such as leases and contracts. LUBAN, *supra*, at 389-90. Yet sometimes lawyers may make deeper contributions.

Jennifer Gordon is one of those lawyers. Gordon has been a creative and introspective thinker about community organizing approaches to social change, and comes from a position that is skeptical of traditional litigation models. Her scholarly accounts of her experiences have been influential in both academic and practice circles. *See* JENNIFER GORDON, SUBURBAN SWEATSHOPS: THE FIGHT FOR IMMIGRANT RIGHTS (2005) [hereinafter, GORDON, SUBURBAN SWEATSHOPS]; Jennifer Gordon, *We Make the Road by Walking: Immigrant Workers, The*

Workplace Project, and the Struggle for Social Change, 30 Harv. C.R.-C.L. L. Rev. 407 (1995).

For several years, Gordon was Executive Director of the Workplace Project, which sought to advance the rights of immigrant workers on Long Island, New York. The Workplace Project is a workers center, an organization designed to address the legal, political, economic, and social issues confronting low-wage, predominantly immigrant, workers. In her path-breaking work, Gordon found that many traditional avenues of workplace redress were not available for immigrant workers. First, it was difficult to organize immigrant workers into unions in low-wage sectors because of a variety of factors: the decentralized nature of industries in which subcontracting was pervasive; xenophobia within some elements of the organized labor movement; the difficulty of motivating workers from a highly transient population to invest time and energy in union organizing; and the perception from some immigrants that unions in their home countries were ineffective or subject to retaliation. Gordon, Suburban Sweatshops, *supra,* at 27-39. Second, many immigrant workers in Gordon's community were undocumented, and therefore vulnerable to exploitive employers who could threaten to expose workers who tried to enforce their rights to immigration authorities. *Id.* at 46-50. Third, although there are legal protections in place to protect undocumented workers (e.g., the right to payment of wages for labor performed), there are insufficient resources available to government agencies responsible for enforcing the rights of such workers and weak incentives for private attorneys to take on such cases. *Id.* at 24-26.

Overall, Gordon viewed conventional legal strategies as offering little promise for immigrant workers.

> Even if legal representation had been more widely available, individual legal victories in the sweatshop world are both hard to enforce and fleeting in their impact. Once caught, many employers continue to pay sub-minimum wages to other workers not involved in the lawsuit. Another approach might be to seek a more effective body of law through impact litigation. But in a setting where every law on the books is flouted, the incentive to add one more rule to the list of those already ignored is minimal. Lobbying for changes in the law faces the same problem. Both litigation and stronger legislation can be important tools arsenal of the fight against sweatshops, but without effective government enforcement or organizations of workers that have the power to see that legal rulings and new laws are enforced, they are unlikely to have much of an impact.

Id. at 27.

The Workplace Project sought to organize the community through a worker-led membership center to combat low wages, workplace injuries, and pervasive abuses of immigrant workers through "self-organization, supported by community education, leadership training and legal services." *Id.* at 68. Gordon summarizes some of the group's successful efforts as follows:

> Against the odds, the group had carried out a series of innovative organizing experiments in the underworld of immigrant work. Each was at least a limited success, and some succeeded far beyond the organization's dreams. In its first five years, the Workplace Project and its immigrant leaders raised wages on

Long Island day labor streetcorners by over 30 percent—at least most of the time, in most places. They created a domestic worker bill of rights and a model contract for domestic employers, and forced placement agencies to promise to adhere to them—a promise that they sometimes kept. They founded a very small but successful worker-owned landscaping cooperative, and were planning for what would become a much larger housecleaning cooperative. The Workplace Project's legal clinic and its "Justice Committee" pickets of recalcitrant employers collected hundreds of thousands of dollars in unpaid wages for workers who had earned them. And despite the fact that almost no Workplace Project members could speak fluent English or vote, with training by the Workplace Project staff they changed New York state law, creating and winning passage of a bill that made failure to pay the minimum wage a felony, and raised by 800 percent the civil penalty against employers who did not pay workers in full, from a quarter of the total owed to double the total owed. At any one time, too, a handful of smaller organizing projects were in progress—a shop steward election campaign in a unionized factory to win representation for Latino workers within an existing all-white union structure, an effort to beat back anti-immigrant sentiment in a neighborhood where day laborers waited for work in the morning.

Id. at 68-69.

Law and organizing initiatives, such as workers centers, incorporate lawyers in specific ways designed to maximize the organizing power of the community. Lawyers can be used to attract new members to a community organization. One key to a successful organizing campaign is building up a critical mass of members to undertake the campaign's essential work. Toward this end, worker center lawyers may operate legal clinics to address the discrete enforcement of rights for members of the campaign's constituent group. In the Workplace Project, for example, the clinic took cases for individual clients to enforce wage claims or other legal rights. While the clinic followed a traditional method of rights enforcement, it was not the focus of the center. In fact, the clinic was viewed as a means of drawing new members into the group's organizing efforts. *Id.* at 121-22.

> Through the new clinic, workers who came in with a labor issue met first with an organizer, who listened to their problem, introduced them to the Project as a membership organization, and described its collective goals. They were then joined by a lawyer or law student volunteer, who worked with the organizer and workers to develop a strategy to resolve the problem. These strategies incorporated self-help, mutual support, and organizing as well as more traditional legal advocacy. In exchange for the support they received, workers were asked to take the Workers Course [a nine-week course about labor law, immigration and labor history, and organizing techniques]. This structure was designed to address individual problems effectively, and simultaneously to invite workers to look critically at the broader causes of those problems and to consider collective action as a response.

Id. at 122. Workers could not join the organization or receive assistance from the legal clinic unless they agreed to complete the Workers Course.

Additionally, within organizing groups, lawyers can be used to engage community members in a discussion to help assess the disjunction between formal legal rights and the experiences of those whose rights are supposed to be protected. "The gap between the legal ideal and practical reality can then be used to chart a course for political action and community mobilization." Cummings & Eagly, *supra*, at 468.

Lawyers can also pursue conventional legal tactics to facilitate an organizing campaign, rather than merely to achieve a litigation victory as an end in itself. Under this model, litigation is used to complement a broader organizing strategy. "[T]he law serves as a strategic mechanism to support or advance organizing campaigns in practical ways — for example, by filing a lawsuit to call attention to a broader structural issue or to put pressure on an employer or industry to undertake systemic reforms." *Id.; see also* Lucie E. White, *To Learn and Teach: Lessons from Driefontein on Lawyering and Power*, 1988 Wis. L. Rev. 699, 758-59 (1988) ("[T]he measure of the case's success is not who wins. Rather, success is measured by such factors as whether the case widens the public imagination about right and wrong, mobilizes political action behind new social arrangements, or pressures those in power to make concessions. To accomplish these goals, the lawyer must design the case with the audience — the subordinated group and the wider public — in mind.").

Another, more expansive and imaginative, role that lawyers might play is one of facilitating critical discourse and consciousness-raising about the problems of the communities they are working to help empower. Lawyers can play a role in generating discourse in the community to help its members understand that the source of their problems may actually be the political or legal system rather than a product of their own misfortune. These are "people who feel cheated but have no clear sense of who is responsible, people who describe their suffering to outsiders as their lot in life, or people who distrust the 'system' and the remedial processes that it offers. Such people will not give the right answers when the well-meaning lawyer innocently asks, 'What's wrong?'" White, *supra*, at 760. Consider the following elaboration of White's conception of what she calls a "third-dimensional" practice of law.

> In contrast to the norm of "professional distance," the outsider [lawyer] strives to open the norms of her profession to critique by the group. She takes the lead in questioning her own expertise and the values on which it is based and invites other group members to deepen the critique. Rather than manipulating the group to preserve her own authority, she tries to engage the group to displace her as authority, and to relocate the very concept, transformed, in their own process of conversation. This does not mean that she withholds her own judgments. Rather, she tries to speak honestly, as a person with a different experience, and to demand that her views be taken seriously in the group's practice of understanding.
>
> Challenging subordination on the level of consciousness entails educational work in the broadest sense, working with people to engender changes in how all participants view themselves and the world. . . .
>
> In addition to pedagogy, lawyering in the third dimension also includes strategic work. The lawyer must help the client-group devise concrete actions that challenge the patterns of domination that they identify. This strategizing is also a learning process. Through it, the group learns to interpret their relationship with those in power as an ongoing drama rather than as a static

condition. They learn to interpret the particular configurations that the oppressor's power takes on over time and to respond to those changing patterns with pragmatism and creativity. They learn how to design context-specific acts of public resistance, which work, not by overpowering the oppressor, but by revealing the wrongness and vulnerability of its positions to itself and to a wider public.

Thus, third-dimensional lawyering involves helping a group learn how to interpret moments of domination as opportunities for resistance. The lawyer cannot simply dictate to the group what actions they must take. Neither the lawyer nor any single individual is positioned to know what actions the group should take at a particular moment. Sound decisions will come only as those who know the landscape and will suffer the risks deliberate together. The role of the lawyer is to help the group learn a *method* of deliberation that will lead to effective and responsible strategic action.

This image of lawyering bears little resemblance to traditional professional practice. The lawyer who would challenge domination within the client's consciousness is not a psychoanalyst in disguise. He does not interpret the group's experience from without, according to a fixed theory of self or society. . . .

Why should this "third-dimensional" work be thought of as lawyering at all? It certainly can be done without an attorney's license and, indeed, without any legal training at all. Nevertheless, fluency in the law—that is, a deep practical understanding of law as a discourse for articulating norms of justice and an array of rituals for resolving social conflict—will greatly improve a person's flexibility and effectiveness at "third-dimensional" work. An understanding of law as discourse on norms will help him work with the clients to deepen their own consciousness of their injuries and their needs. Knowledge of the law's procedural rituals will give the group access to a central arena for public resistance and challenge. It is also possible, however, that professional identification as a lawyer can narrow one's strategic imagination. Perhaps the best arrangement is for lawyer-outsiders to work side by side with outsiders trained in other fields.

Id. at 763-65. For further exploration of lawyers' possible roles in community organizing efforts, see Luban, *supra*, at 389-90. For more elaboration of the workers center model of organizing, see Saru Jayaraman & Immanuel Ness, *Models of Worker Organizing, in* The New Urban Immigrant Workforce (2005).

As Gordon and White both suggest, lawyers can collaborate with organizers to develop creative tactics to address injustice, particularly when conventional avenues of legal redress have been blocked. Lawyer-activist Julie Su's advocacy on behalf of enslaved Thai garment workers on the outskirts of Los Angeles is a seminal example of this type of innovative work. In 1995, after a group of Thai garment workers was discovered to have been held as captives and forced to work in virtual slave labor conditions in El Monte, California, the Immigration and Naturalization Service (INS)—rather than freeing them—locked the workers in a detention facility because they were undocumented. Community advocates from Su's organization (the Asian Pacific American Legal Center, or "APALC") and allied groups tried to persuade the INS that detaining workers who reported unlawful practices would discourage such violations from being reported in the future, but to no avail. In her description of her work with the Thai community, Su describes the advocacy response:

> We quickly learned that the INS is not convinced by sound policy arguments. So we resorted to aggression and street tactics. We set up a makeshift office in the basement waiting room of INS detention. We used their pay phones, banged on windows, and closed down the INS at one or two in the morning, refusing to accept "paperwork" and bureaucracy as an excuse for the continued detention of the Thai workers. By the end of the nine long days and nights before the workers' release, both pay phones were broken, as we had slammed them back onto the receivers in frustration each time we received an unsatisfactory and unjust response. . . . I am convinced that we succeeded in getting the workers released in just over a week in part because we did not know the rules, because we would not accept procedures that made no sense either in our hearts or to our minds. It was an important lesson that our formal education might, at times, actually make us less effective advocates for the causes we believe in and for the people we care about.

Julie A. Su, *Making the Invisible Visible: The Garment Industry's Dirty Laundry*, 1 J. Gender Race & Just. 405, 408 (1998).

In the aftermath of the workers' release, a coalition of community groups and nonprofit organizations, as well as the government, were involved in other tactical responses. Scott L. Cummings, *Hemmed In: Legal Mobilization in the Los Angeles Anti-Sweatshop Movement*, 30 Berkeley J. Emp. & Lab. L. 1 (2009). A federal criminal prosecution for kidnapping and other offenses was brought against the operators of the El Monte shop. *Id.* at 21-22. The workers' immigration status was resolved first by securing them temporary S visas, which allowed them to remain in the country if they testified against the shop operators, and later, when advocates negotiated permanent resident status for them. *Id.* at 22. The back wages owed to the workers were collected through a combination of approaches. First, a state labor agency seized assets of the sweatshop operator and fined manufacturers who benefited from their work to secure some of the wages. *Id.* at 22-23. Second, a group of lawyers from large and small nonprofit groups and private public interest law firms formed a legal team to bring a complex lawsuit against the shop operators as well as the manufacturers who contracted with them for their goods. *Id.* at 23-28. Ultimately, a large settlement was negotiated against the backdrop of substantial media coverage that created a great deal of community sympathy for the workers. *Id.* Building from this success, APALC implemented a law and organizing strategy that combined strategic litigation against garment manufacturers and retailers with coordinated media campaigns and public protests in front of retail shops (such as Forever 21). This innovative law and organizing approach resulted in a number of significant legal victories for garment workers, mobilized support for the passage of a statewide law assigning liability to garment manufacturers for the workplace violations of their contract shops, and led to public awareness of the continuing crisis of garment sweatshops. To implement this strategy, APALC helped create and collaborated with the Garment Worker Center as the organizing base of the antisweatshop movement, as well as Sweatshop Watch, the movement's policy advocacy arm. This integrated approach permitted the advocates to educate and empower individual workers, mobilize in the streets to put pressure on recalcitrant employers, and use the voices of affected workers to persuade policy makers to extend greater workplace protections.

2. Appraisal

a. ADVANTAGES

i. EFFECTIVENESS AND DEMOCRATIC LEGITIMACY

As the example of APALC's antisweatshop advocacy and the law and organizing approach of the Workplace Project show, organizing marginalized communities can mobilize their power to strengthen court cases (by pressuring employers to settle favorably) and advance policy making through the legislative process. In both instances, organizing is used as a confrontational tactic to leverage reform. Such efforts are important when entrenched power interests are not responsive to other overtures.

There are also examples of more collaborative organizing approaches. There exist many successful examples of community-based organizations (CBOs) that have established relationships with government agencies to develop a problem-solving approach to addressing social issues that may enhance both the effectiveness and the political legitimacy of community organizing work. These CBOs take a pragmatic approach by working in tandem with government agencies to promote change. CBOs may act as experts and information gatherers and help government decision makers understand the structural changes necessary to engage in meaningful reform. CBOs may even take on responsibilities that are traditionally performed by government agencies, and share a stake in the outcomes resulting from their actions.

One example of this comes from Julissa Reynoso's account of the relationship between a CBO that advocated for improved conditions in low-income housing in the Bronx, New York, and a local housing agency. In it, she describes how the agency began to relinquish its direct control over a substantial amount of housing and allowed the CBO to not only help monitor the housing conditions, but also in some cases to actually play a part in managing distressed properties and administering housing programs. Julissa Reynoso, *Putting Out Fires Before They Start: Community Organizing and Collaborative Governance in the Bronx, U.S.A.*, 24 Law & Ineq. 213, 223-25 (2006). The CBO also collaborated with the agency by reporting problems and protecting against abandonment. This type of collaboration places CBOs in a new position vis-à-vis the government actors whose performance they are monitoring. They are at once critics and partners. As Reynoso describes:

> [G]rassroots organizations, which historically have been instrumental in demanding reform and public accountability through adversarial means, can collaborate, in such evolving relationships, with government institutions in new ways, while maintaining their own independent and critical practices — developing new forms of accountability. Such collaboration and attempts at coordination involve both formal arrangements with local government but

also informal negotiations and pressure tactics. CBOs have community insight into public problems to which government does not have access. As street-level monitors then, community organizations assist in preserving the adequacy of public goods and services by tracking early warning indicators and by tackling problems at the source rather than leaving them to be corrected at the "the end of the pipe," when often government has lacked the capacity to solve and contain the problem. Indeed, as strategic allies, organizations like Northwest Bronx are increasingly co-participants with government in identifying and solving public problems. Northwest Bronx has gone beyond developing countervailing power. The organization arguably has taken on certain roles of those in "official" power.

Id. at 262; *see also* Julissa Reynoso, *The Impact of Identity Politics and Public Sector Reform on Organizing and the Practice of Democracy*, 37 COLUM. HUM. RTS. L. REV. 149 (2005); *but see* Douglas Nejaime, *When New Governance Fails*, 70 OHIO ST. L.J. 323 (2009).

ii. COMMUNITY EMPOWERMENT

Community organizing work reformulates lawyers' power relationships with their clients. To the extent that community members are directing their own destinies, rather than having lawyers "take care of" them, they are empowered to carry out actions to help themselves. The empowerment of individuals and community groups is not only desirable on its own terms, but also may lead to greater sustainability and longevity for a social change effort. Rather than relying on a small corps of lawyers to carry out their social change mission, change can be driven by members of the community itself, who may be greater in number and also are the ones who have the most at stake.

b. CHALLENGES

i. SCOPE AND RESOURCES

In advancing direct mobilization at the local level, community organizing also faces constraints. Some are related to the mode and geographic scope of local organizing work and thus echo the issues identified in the previous discussion of CED. For instance, although organizing may be coordinated with broad-based policy or legal reform efforts (as the Thai worker story highlights), it sometimes can be localized and its proponents skeptical about the benefits of formal legal change. Commentators have thus wondered whether organizing is able to build into a broader movement with the power to transform legal relations and institutional practice on a wide scale or address the structural causes of poverty and inequality. Cummings & Eagly, *supra*, at 484-87 (summarizing criticisms).

Moreover, there may be practical limitations to organizing certain constituencies.

Clients escaping abusive relationships can be so busy participating in various legal and social service activities—such as petitioning for divorce, requesting restraining orders, testifying in criminal proceedings, attending counseling, and applying for public benefits — that they find little time to become meaningfully involved in organizing. Lawyers must also consider whether the safety of these women would be jeopardized by requiring them to engage in organizing efforts, because domestic violence survivors must take great care in leaving the home, making phone calls, and going to community meetings. Once women have escaped their abusive situation, some may be interested in participating in organizing activities, but ongoing issues of safety and a need to hide their identity might impede organizing efforts. Indeed, many domestic violence shelters impose strict limitations on residents' movement in order to protect them from abusers. Thus, as this example suggests, practitioners must be sensitive to how the circumstances of particular client groups impose obstacles to effective organizing. In particular, as lawyers continue to experiment with organizing-centered approaches, they must do so with a keen awareness of the context-specific nature of their advocacy.

Id. at 499-500.

Financing organizing can also be a challenge. Foundation support is available and important to many groups, but may be limited. To the extent that community groups are membership organizations, dues may be hard to collect or sporadically paid, particularly if the members are from low-income communities. GORDON, SUBURBAN SWEATSHOPS, *supra*, at 68-72.

Community organizing also requires a great investment of time by organizers and community members. Particularly when community members are economically marginalized and politically subordinated, it may be difficult to sustain the level of commitment and energy necessary to carry out ongoing, long-term goals. Cummings & Eagly, *supra*, at 498-99. Jennifer Gordon, for example, recounts the impressive efforts made by members — many working more than one job and dealing with child care, transportation, and other issues — just to make it to the Workplace Project, attend courses and engage in organizing. GORDON, SUBURBAN SWEATSHOPS, *supra*, at 113-14.

ii. PROFESSIONAL ROLE

Law and organizing are not always synergistic — there can also be tensions. The literature on lawyers and organizing emphasizes the importance of lawyers playing a subordinate role to the community groups they are trying to assist. *See, e.g.*, LUBAN, *supra*, at 389-90. But some commentators have cautioned that an emphasis on organizing might too readily discard the value that traditional strategies might provide. Cummings & Eagly, *supra*, at 490-91. The promotion of organizing work could also shift legal resources away from addressing traditional legal needs through the representation of underserved clients. *Id.* at 491-92. This tradeoff — which is similar to that discussed in the impact versus individual service lawsuit context, and applies with equal force to any redirection of lawyer resources away from traditional representation — may be an optimal approach to addressing community problems. Yet it is one that public interest lawyers must consider in deciding how to distribute their scarce legal resources.

One issue raised when lawyers attempt to directly engage in organizing is whether they have adequate training or the right skill set. *Id.* at 500-01. Finding the time and energy necessary to coordinate organizing on top of a law practice may be difficult, and diminish a lawyer's ability to do either activity in an optimal fashion. *Id.* at 500. One way to address these issues is for lawyers to work collaboratively with experienced organizers to accomplish community-defined goals. By playing a supporting role, lawyers can complement the organizers' work to maximize their social change impact. Even in these collaborative contexts, however, lawyers may have to compete with nonlawyer organizers for the time and attention of their common client groups and for organizational resources.

What is the appropriate role for lawyers in organizing contexts? Some have argued that lawyers' knowledge of the legal system and its relationship to power allows them to meaningfully participate in organizing efforts. Others have suggested, however, that "one could just as easily claim, based on the general distrust of lawyers at the grassroots level, that lawyers are singularly ill-equipped to organize. . . . [A] lawyer's penchant for narrow, legalistic thinking and tendency to dominate community settings can undermine his effectiveness as an organizer." *Id.* at 494. Even in the best situations, combining law and organizing does not eliminate concerns about lawyers controlling community members with whom they are working. Notwithstanding the subordinated role lawyers might try to play in organizing campaigns, their elite status and training may still lead community members to defer to their decisions about organizing strategies or options. *Id.* at 496.

Moreover, some community members may simply not care to be organized, but rather may just want a lawyer to provide them basic legal services. Promoting organizing activities to such members or making legal services contingent on their participation in organizing may undercut their sense of autonomy and agency, rather than foster their empowerment.

> The imposition of an organizing model on clients who are seeking legal services raises questions about lawyer domination and paternalism. Are these clients really interested in being organized, or are they agreeing to do so only because they have no other means of obtaining needed legal services? [Lucie] White has cited several examples from practice of participants who agree to receive unwanted services because of lack of resources to seek out alternatives. For instance, students have attended literacy classes using popular education despite the fact that they viewed these classes as "an intrusion — an unwanted attempt to indoctrinate them with out-dated Marxist propaganda." Similarly, homeless shelter residents required to attend an empowerment support group "resented having to pay for their shelter with what they viewed as an intrusion into their personal lives."
>
> Even when clients have voluntarily agreed to engage in organizing activities, it is not clear that the outcome will be free of lawyer domination. Lawyers practicing in organizing contexts may be reluctant to cede control in group settings and restrain their more adept verbal skills in order to advance client empowerment. Even skillful facilitators may subtly impose their own ideas and political agendas on the marginalized communities they are working to organize.

Id. at 496-97.

Finally, there may be ethical issues raised when lawyers attempt to combine law and organizing activities. Attorneys who do organizing work may find it unclear when they have formed an attorney-client relationship with some community members. Coordinating an organizing campaign with a legal case can also raise potential conflicts and problems of client confidentiality. *Id.* at 502-15.

Does engaging in or supporting organizing seem like a good use of lawyers' time and energy? What are the biggest rewards? What are the most significant potential problems?

Using the scenario outlined at the beginning of the chapter, consider a community organizing project to address the concerns of the homeless community. What might be the goals of such a project? How would the organizing work, and who would it target? What are some of the possible limitations or challenges you would face? How might you link an organizing campaign to other advocacy strategies you might choose to pursue?

C. POLICY ADVOCACY

Advocacy in the legislative and administrative arenas is another important facet of public interest lawyering work. Social change is pursued in the halls of all branches of government, and advocacy of policy change can be an effective way to achieve social reform. This type of advocacy has a long pedigree: in the 1980s, about three-fourths of public interest law centers surveyed were at least supplementing litigation with other forms of advocacy, including legislative activity. NAN ARON, LIBERTY AND JUSTICE FOR ALL: PUBLIC INTEREST LAW IN THE 1980S AND BEYOND 32 (1989). What does policy advocacy involve and what are the advantages and disadvantages of this approach?

1. Features

In advancing policy change, lawyers may perform a wide range of tasks: they may draft statutory language for new bills or amendments to existing laws; draft memoranda laying out constitutional, statutory, and policy arguments opposing legislation that may harm the interests of their constitute groups (or supporting good legislation); and conduct background research, legal and otherwise, to provide policy analysis to support their positions or counter the arguments of proponents of legislation they oppose.

Not only must successful advocates have a firm grasp of the underlying policy issues, budgetary implications, and implementation details, but also they need to understand and be able to comply with the many, sometimes byzantine, procedural rules that pervade most legislative settings. And just as litigators are more effective if they have credibility with the courts in which they practice, legislative advocates must establish credibility with legislators and their staffs (by, for example, having a strong reputation for providing accurate and reliable factual information to support the policy choices they advocate). Professional legal skills can be valuable in this realm.

> Lawyers are among the most important lobbyists, for reasons that are not hard to fathom: lawyers, unlike other lobbyists, understand the legal consequences

of legislation. When they talk to legislative staff, they can make concrete suggestions about how to redraft language, burying prizes for their clients in the legalese. If a staff member solicits the lobbyist's opinion of an on-the-spot suggestion for a change, only the lawyer-lobbyist can respond with an on-the-spot analysis. The lawyer may in addition be familiar with a client's pending legal problems and can see how legislation will affect them. And, rightly or wrongly, the lawyer-lobbyist is perceived by some to be more independent (and hence more trustworthy) than the full-time paid professional lobbyist. Legislators need the help that lobbyists offer. . . . Obviously the lawyer-lobbyist is in a favorable position to draft a bill and notice traps; and without the lobbyist's services the legislature must "do all the leg work," which of course lessens the likelihood that a bill will be introduced.

Luban, *supra*, at 377-78.

Policy work is not limited to traditional advocacy in the formal legislative process. Lawyers can also play an important role in influencing federal and state administrative agencies' promulgation of regulations. Through the rule-making process, agencies are generally required to publish proposed rules and provide a period for public comment before they become effective. This process is a formalized way of permitting input into, and ultimately influencing, agency decisions. As with other types of policy making, the more effective advocates in the administrative rule-making process are those with resources to participate, who are highly organized, and who can be mobilized to respond to proposed rules with thoughtful commentary and information that might influence the agencies' final decisions.

It oversimplifies the public interest lawyer's role in the policy-making arena to describe it as simply lobbying for legislation. Effective policy advocacy incorporates a range of tactics, including public education and relations, media coverage, public pressure, policy analysis, and direct contact with lawmakers and other government decision makers. In this context, lawyers must anticipate and negotiate the political process in ways that comprehend the interests of diverse constituencies. Neta Ziv describes these issues in relation to the legislative campaign on behalf of the Americans With Disabilities Act in Congress:

[W]ithin the legislature cause lawyering underscores the indeterminate and relational aspects of political interests and of political choices. Within a legislative campaign, these shift constantly and are modified through the formation of contingent political, personal, and ad hoc alliances between the clients, their legal representatives, and those holding official elected positions in Congress, together with their political, legal, and administrative staff. . . . If lawyers wish to enlist the support of members of Congress to a certain cause they must bear in mind the political considerations of those politicians. These oftentimes include the political worthiness of a specific legislative initiative for a particular member as well as the barriers the member is likely to encounter during the course of transforming a social interest into law. Lawyering for a cause under these circumstances frequently entails considering and suggesting possible financial resources to cover the costs of a new law or accepting trade-offs due to financial constraints. As long as lawyers and members of Congress carry a mutual interest to pass a law, lawyers cannot discount these aspects of legislative reform. This is not to say that lawyers are to provide solutions to questions of financing, but that in the course of negotiation they are expected to incorporate such political or economic considerations into their professional decision-making responsibilities. These have to be reconciled with their duties to continue and act "with zeal" (to use the term of conventional lawyering) on behalf of their client group and constituency.

Neta Ziv, *Cause Lawyers, Clients, and the State: Congress as a Forum for Cause Lawyering During the Enactment of the Americans With Disabilities Act, in* Cause Lawyering and the State in a Global Era 211, 213-14 (Austin Sarat & Stuart Scheingold eds., 2001); *see also* Barbara Hinkson Craig, Courting Change: The Story of the Public Citizen Litigation Group 8 (2004) (describing Ralph Nader's approach to legislative and policy advocacy). As Ziv observes, legislative advocacy "entails being partly a community organizer, a legal analyst, a drafter, a lobbyist, and a statesperson and bears the potential to build better alliances between lay people, experts, and officials inside and outside formal state institutions." Ziv, *supra*, at 237.

2. Appraisal

a. ADVANTAGES

i. *DYNAMIC DECISION MAKING*

Advocacy that results in the enactment of a new law, regulation, or government policy constitutes direct structural legal change. Conversely, preventing the enactment of a bill that has adverse impacts on a particular constituency is a direct method for protecting that group. Of course, direct legal change does not always lead to social change. The legislative process is full of compromise among different constituencies, including lawyers and interest groups, legislators and their staffs, and members of affected communities. Its effectiveness is highly contingent on a number of variables. But its capacity to produce change is also quite high. As Ziv describes the dynamics of the campaign for the ADA:

> One can remain skeptical about the potential of legislation to bring about actual progress in the lives of persons with disabilities. However, access to political institutions remains an essential course to obtain many desired policy changes. Private and corporate interests aided by their "power lawyers" have long been utilizing these channels to gain prevalence over powerless groups in influential juncture points. Lawyers who represent politically disempowered groups are therefore utilizing similar strategies to rectify injustice on behalf of previously underrepresented people. In this respect, the ADA cause lawyers merged between the dynamics of social movements and the politics of the state. The path they paved through their professional activity—together with others—opened an opportunity for constant flow, input, and feedback of information, knowledge, and understanding between the disability community and Congress.

Ziv, *supra*, at 215-26.

ii. DEMOCRATIC LEGITIMACY

As described above, a principal critique of pursuing social change through litigation is that it circumvents the ordinary political process. Critics who level these claims argue that courts are not the appropriate institutions to implement social change. To the extent that advocates do, in fact, participate directly in the democratic process, those critiques are less powerful. Even more, successful legislative activity may, because of its perceived legitimacy, receive less resistance from opponents than litigation victories (or at least less resistance about the process, if not the substance). One problem with this argument is that the types of claims that may be litigated are typically the same types of claims that are unlikely to succeed in the political process because they are brought on behalf of politically powerless or unpopular groups.

Whatever the structural disadvantages of less powerful groups, effective policy advocacy on their behalf may nonetheless address some of the imbalances in the democratic system. That is, if lawyers and other activists can devise effective advocacy strategies that leverage the bargaining chips they have and build coalitions with strong partners, they may be able to defeat political adversaries — at least some times. Thoughtful and well-executed policy campaigns can provide an effective, organized response to more powerful and better financed groups, which routinely hire lobbying firms to advocate for their interests. As Luban has observed:

> We must not forget, however, that lawyers are advocates. And when they are acting as lobbyists, they are advocates without opponents. . . . This is the fundamental reason that lobbying by public interest lawyers is so important. Taking the pressure-group theory at face value, we can see that if no lawyers were around to lobby for outsider groups, pressure-group politics would not be merely in danger of undemocratic legislative failures — it would become one long, uninterrupted embodiment of undemocratic legislative failure.

Id. at 378-79. Is this true? Might some observers view organized advocacy on behalf of relatively powerless groups as a form of special interest politics?

Another element that must be considered in terms of democratic legitimacy in a legislative campaign is that there may be internal tensions within the group seeking reform. Unlike in a traditional attorney-client relationship, it is not always clear who the client or clients are when a lawyer engages in lobbying activity on behalf of a coalition. Indeed, "in situations in which lawyers represent the general interest of a diffuse group, the notion of lawyer-client relationship is essentially undermined." Ziv, *supra*, at 224. How should a lawyer leading a legislative campaign mediate the diverse interests of the constituency she represents? In the ADA campaign, "[t]he lawyers interviewed did not feel uncomfortable with the notion that they were representing the interest of a diffused and unidentifiable group of people, a constituency practically impossible to communicate with. The professional experience they all had acquired through past representation of this group made them feel that they were connected to their constituency, aware of the issues the law needed to address and the best solutions." *Id.* at 223. Do you think that attitude is appropriate? Given that there are some 29 million disabled persons in the United States, what would be the alternative?

iii. CONDITIONS FOR LEGISLATIVE ADVOCACY

Policy advocacy can be effective under appropriate circumstances, and it is important for lawyers to understand what conditions enhance or diminish the opportunities for progress. Consider the following:

> The degree of political mobilization is . . . measured across four variables: political capacity, the degree of support from political elites, the availability of resources to monitor legal compliance, and the strength of countermovement opposition. Political capacity depends on the existence and effectiveness of promovement political organizations, which wield power by mobilizing financial resources, staff expertise, and relationships with other political actors. Strong support from political elites increases the potential that promovement policies will be enacted or upheld in the legislature. Weak support means that elites are motivated (and have the power) to block promovement legislation or to reverse court victories. Strong political mobilization also includes the availability of resources to monitor legal enforcement over time. The final variable is the degree to which countermovement opposition might either be able to block legislative advances or mobilize a backlash that reverses court victories. . . .

Cummings, *Defending Day Labor, supra,* at 1624.

The issue, of course, is how less powerful groups can find the leverage and allies necessary to succeed in the political arena. Consider the following example from the Workplace Project. In it, Jennifer Gordon describes an improbable legislative victory: the 1997 passage of New York's Unpaid Wages Prohibition Act, which significantly increased the civil and criminal penalties imposed on employers who fail to pay workers. The bill was advanced by a coalition led by immigrant workers, the Workplace Project, and a number of other workers centers, business, labor, religious, and community groups. How did they do it?

> The first theory, that Republican senators supported this legislation because they saw Latino immigrants as a group soon to have economic and voting power, is rational given the demographics of Long Island and the state. It becomes more complicated, however, given the demographics of our membership and the other beneficiaries of the legislation. . . .
>
> On Long Island, the percentage of Latino residents has surged over the past decade and a half, increasing by 80 percent between 1980 and 1990, even according to census data that most advocates believe represents a drastic undercount. In New York state generally, the Latino population grew by 50 percent over the same period. While many of these residents are not yet voters, immigrants are becoming citizens at rates unheard of in previous years. Although Latinos still do not control large amounts of money in the state, their importance as consumers and increasingly as a voting bloc is undeniable, even outside the traditional stronghold of New York City. And the local Republican Party has responded in kind. . . .
>
> Given that we were running a legislative campaign with almost no voters, we realized that we needed a wide range of allies to show support for the Act.

Although the endorsement of labor, religious, and community groups was crucial for the success of the campaign, in the end our most important allies would be the ones no one expected we could get: business groups.

The first question that Long Island senators asked us in our early lobbying forays was: "what is the industry associations' point of view on this?" It quickly became clear that we would have a difficult time finding the sponsors that we wanted unless we could show business backing for the proposal.

The process for gaining the support of the Long Island Association (LIA), Long Island's most respected business group, was simple. We sent them a letter setting forth the unfair competition arguments and others that our members had developed. . . . I met with Mitchell Pally, the LIA's vice president for legislative and economic affairs, and we discussed the proposal briefly. He then presented it to their committees and board, won approval, and wrote a letter of support.

In a recent interview, Pally told me that the main factor behind the LIA's support was the "equity issue." Eighty to eighty-five percent of the Association's membership is made up of small businesspeople, largely in the retail and service industries. (Significantly, few of their members are in the landscaping and restaurant industries, which do a considerable amount of underground hiring of immigrant workers.) According to Pally, "a lot of small businesses on Long Island are impacted when other employers do not pay legal wages, so this is a matter of fairness that affects our members." Pally also feels that the timing for the legislation was right: "The economy is good, so people feel better about making sure everyone gets a piece of the pie. It would have been more difficult for us to support this in hard times," given the perception that the legislation put money into the pockets of immigrants. . . .

Strong media support was crucial to our effort to make the bill unopposable. Through media coverage, we built a climate of outrage about the treatment to which immigrant workers were subjected, made our issue into a hot topic, put pressure on legislators, and gained supporters for our cause.

Our media message related to the campaign was threefold and specifically targeted at the Long Island delegation of the New York State Senate. First, given the invisibility of immigrants on the Island, we had to show that sweatshops were a common local phenomenon, though not in the traditional form. Unless the public knew about the scores of busboys and dishwashers earning less than $2.50 an hour for eighty-hour weeks, the gardeners and landscape workers who often went without pay for weeks on end, and the domestic workers who labored from 6:00 a.m. to 11:00 p.m. for wages of less than two dollars an hour, they would have no reason to support this legislation. This was a real challenge: in 1996, although many on Long Island were aware of some immigrants in their midst, few were cognizant of the sweatshop-like working conditions that prevailed in many service industries.

Second, we wanted to make clear that part of the fault for these circumstances lay in weak state laws and inadequate New York State Department of Labor enforcement practices. Third, we wanted the press to communicate our "universal appeal" points: that the bill was supported by business organizations and that it would bring revenue to the state in a number of ways.

We were largely successful both in shaping the message about the problem and the legislation that appeared in the press and in timing press coverage to crucial points in the campaign. . . .

Some of these stories had effects on the campaign that went deeper than simply spreading the word. For example, when *Newsday* did a Sunday full-cover story on restaurant workers on Long Island being paid less than half the minimum wage (an article on which we worked with them for months), featuring the legislation as an important part of the solution to the problem, it put senators who would have liked to ignore the bill in an awkward position. For example, during the months leading up to the publication of that story, we had been in frequent contact with Senator Spano's office about our request that he sponsor the legislation. As Ken Crowe, *Newsday*'s labor reporter, put the finishing touches on the story, the Senator's aide called to tell us that he had decided not to become a sponsor. Crowe called him and told him the substance of the story he would be publishing, informed him that the Unpaid Wages Prohibition Act would be featured in the article, and asked if the Senator could confirm and explain his refusal to sponsor the legislation. Senator Spano's assistant called back within half an hour to state that the Senator would be co-sponsoring the bill. . . .

Finally, it is worth considering that some part of what moved the senators had nothing to do with money or votes but instead with empathy for the workers before them, a sense of identification with the immigrant stories that they presented, and thus a moral discomfort with the suffering they described.

During the lobbying visits, immigrant workers spoke directly to the senators or their staff about the abuse that they and their families faced. These were not sob stories or tales from a token "client" brought along to speak on an advocacy visit. Instead, immigrants ran the entire meeting, mixing their personal experiences with statistics from the Workplace Project database, appealing to the senators' own interests, answering their questions and responding to their concerns. The fact that the bill's provisions were developed by immigrant workers to remedy the problems that they faced, rather than being designed by advocates on behalf of the workers, gave the workers a passion for the bill that would have been impossible to achieve otherwise. For these reasons, our meetings had an immediacy and a strength that is all too often lacking in traditional lobbying visits on behalf of poor people. As Senator Skelos said, "I think they did a great job. In government, we're used to seeing professional lobbyists constantly, whether it's for a small group, a large group, whatever. But when you see a real human face on it, I believe it has a real emotional impact on the process, and certainly they had that emotional impact."

The opportunity to speak directly with an organized and prepared group of immigrants may have moved senators from possible sympathy — a common but ineffectual reaction to sad stories — to empathy, the ability to see the victims of the abuse as in some way the same as themselves. Almost all of the Long Island and other sponsoring senators were second or third generation immigrants. They had justified their support of Proposition 187-like legislation with descriptions of illegal aliens who had come to this country to take from the system, an image safely distant from stories about their own family's immigration experience, which inevitably featured hard work and sacrifice. But it was hard for the senators to separate *these* immigrants, sitting before them with dignity and talking about their struggle to be paid for their labor, from their own family's experiences of building a life in the United States.

JENNIFER GORDON, THE CAMPAIGN FOR THE UNPAID WAGES PROHIBITION ACT: LATINO IMMIGRANTS CHANGE NEW YORK WAGE LAW (Carnegie Endowment for International Peace, Global Policy Program, Working Paper No. 4, 1999).

What does this example teach you about effective legislative work? Are there general lessons to be learned or was the victory contingent on the specific circumstances?

b. CHALLENGES

i. EFFECTIVENESS

Just as there have been concerns with exaggerating the effectiveness of public interest litigation, it is easy to overstate the degree to which policy advocacy changes society. First, the enactment of a new law may be merely symbolic if the government does not then create mechanisms for its enforcement. Second, formal legal changes, whether achieved through litigation or legislation, do not always yield changes in culture. Legal scholar and social change advocate Thomas Stoddard observed that changes in legal rules will only have an impact on the culture where four conditions exist — the change "is very broad or profound," there is "[p]ublic awareness of that change," "[a] general sense of the legitimacy (or validity) of the change" exists, and there are mechanisms for "[o]verall, continuous enforcement of the change." Stoddard, *supra*, at 978. Unless advocates for policy changes are sensitive to the conditions surrounding the issues they pursue, they risk limited success.

Third, legislative campaigns for social change also can be less than optimal because there is more pressure to develop and agree to compromise positions to ensure the necessary number of votes. Because of the nature of interest group pluralism in the legislative process, there may be a great need to accommodate a wider range of interests than is necessary (or even permissible) in the litigation process. *See* Theodore J. Lowi, The End of Liberalism: The Second Republic of the United States (1979). The need to compromise also presents itself in public interest litigation, particularly in the context of settlement negotiations, but there are fewer constituencies that need to be satisfied in litigation than in the open-ended political process. As Ziv notes, "In this setting, the 'best' law is the consequence of the consideration and accommodation of competing interests, procured through negotiation and compromise. Legislation is not about adjudication of rights but primarily aims to alter policy, and the 'truth' thus assumes a different meaning." Ziv, *supra*, at 218.

Fourth, like litigation, legislative work can produce backlash from opposing groups. For example, as we discuss at greater length in Chapter 10, an early legislative success in conjunction with the marriage equality movement came in 1999 when California enacted a law extending hospital visitation rights to those who signed up for a domestic partnership registry and health benefits for the domestic partners of government employees. But the response to even that modest movement of the law was a successful statewide initiative campaign that resulted in the enactment of Proposition 22, which prevented California from recognizing same-sex couples as married. Scott L. Cumming & Douglas NeJaime, *Lawyering for Marriage Equality*, 57 UCLA L. Rev. 1235, 1256-62 (2010).

Finally, legislative and policy work may be difficult to finance, thus undercutting its potential efficacy. As we have seen, some forms of legislative advocacy are not viable options for all public interest lawyers. Federal tax code restrictions preclude 501(c)(3) corporations from engaging in substantial lob-bying efforts, though they can set up parallel 501(c)(4) organizations to do so. Donors to the latter, however, may not deduct their contributions from their taxes. Second, there are restrictions on lobbying activity by federally funded legal services offices. In general, lobbying at the federal level is heavily regu-lated without regard to whether the lobbyists are advocating the interests of wealthy and powerful interests or the interests of the powerless. Also, there are no attorneys' fees-shifting provisions or comparable provisions to help finance legislative advocacy, even when successful.

Returning to our problem, as a lawyer for CHA, how would you design a legislative campaign to promote the well-being of the homeless community in your city? How would you identify the priorities of that community? Would you focus on state or local legislation, or on administrative advocacy? What other groups would you reach out to in developing a coalition? What groups are likely to oppose your campaign? How would you incorporate and coordi-nate other social change strategies?

D. PUBLIC EDUCATION AND MEDIA STRATEGIES

1. Features

Lawyers can effectively incorporate media and public education strate-gies as part of a coordinated public relations effort that advances a social movement or cause. Like legislative advocacy, public education and media relations work are not new to social change advocates, but have been incor-porated into their strategies for decades. Nearly two-thirds of the public interest law centers surveyed in the 1980s engaged in community education or public education work. ARON, *supra*, at 32. Sometimes these strategies can be carried out to enhance the effectiveness of other approaches, such as lit-igation or lobbying campaigns. Thus, public interest lawyers frequently use newsworthy events in litigation, such as the filing of a new suit, to attract media and public attention to the problem they are addressing. This has the dual function of educating the general public, gaining public sympathy for their case and cause, and generating pressure on the defendant to resolve the case. As an example, some lawyers who brought a sexual harassment claim on behalf of a female student against a local school district described their strat-egy as follows.

> After researching the legal claims of the young woman, we sent a demand letter to the school superintendent setting forth not only her legal claims entitling her to damages, but explaining that the larger underlying problem was that the school was not ensuring a non-discriminatory educational environment as required under federal law. We then assisted the students in calling a press conference to expose the pervasiveness of the problem of sexual harassment at the high school and to explain the changes that the students had asked the administration to make, as well as the need for the larger community to recognize the seriousness of the problem of sexual harassment at area schools. Speaking at the press conference were law professors, who applauded the students' efforts, and affirmed that it was they, rather than the school

administration, who were in the forefront of progressive legal thinking about the problem of sexual harassment and how to eliminate it. The story was covered in the local and national press.

Katz & Bernabei, *supra*, at 307. The publicity helped the students generate widespread attention, which facilitated efforts to organize and put pressure on school officials. *Id.* It also yielded changes in the environment at the school, leading to a decline in sexual harassment. *Id.* Coupled with a complaint filed with the U.S. Department of Education, this strategy led to the adoption of all of the changes to school policies that the plaintiffs had sought. *Id.; see also* Deborah J. Cantrell, *Sensational Reports: The Ethical Duty of Cause Lawyers to Be Competent in Public Advocacy*, 30 Hamline L. Rev. 567 (2007) (providing case studies about the effective use of media by both progressive and conservative social change groups).

Similarly, press conferences and press releases may serve to promote the advocates' agenda in a legislative campaign as well. In this case, however, the public pressure associated with media strategies can be brought to bear on elected officials whose votes are necessary for success. In large campaigns, advocates can dispatch workers and media strategists to the districts of legislatures who are vulnerable in upcoming reelection campaigns to publicize their votes (or failures to vote) on important legislative measures.

Lawyers can also coordinate media campaigns solely for the sake of educating the public and/or policy makers about various issues. The types of meticulously researched policy reports prepared by Nader's organizations, think tanks, and other groups following this model can be enormously influential in public policy debates. These do not necessarily have to be linked to a pending piece of legislation or an ongoing court case, but can serve the function of putting the issue on the map for many public officials and calling the public's attention to a social problem in need of attention.

While media strategies have long been part of public interest law efforts, media work is not always something that lawyers are comfortable with, either because they may not feel that they have the skill set necessary to competently address such efforts or because of concerns about professionalism or other ethical considerations. Lawyers may feel that their time is better spent doing the tasks that are unique to the legal profession and leaving media relations functions to persons trained to engage the public. But as Deborah Cantrell argues:

> [C]ause lawyers are often the public voice for the cause by virtue of the places in which they perform their advocacy work. When a cause lawyer walks out of the courtroom after winning a case or legal argument, and the media is waiting, it is the cause lawyer who must be prepared and competent to answer the media's questions. When a cause lawyer goes to a community center to teach a "know your rights" class, it is the cause lawyer who is the public face of the advocacy effort. In many situations, the cause lawyer cannot duck the responsibility of being part of the public voice on behalf of the cause. Thus, while cause lawyers need not be the only advocates skilled in public advocacy, they at least must be part of the group of advocates with such skills.

Cantrell, *supra*, at 576.

With regard to the ethical considerations, it is worth noting that media work was at one time considered to be unseemly or unprofessional by some bar leaders. *Id.* at 568. The emergence of public interest lawyering and the substantial changes in the profession have broadened the conception of lawyering in important ways. As Professor Cantrell argues, one could even make the case that becoming facile with media strategies is one component of a public interest lawyer's professional competency.

Finally, some public education campaigns can be designed to inform people of existing rights that are under-enforced because there isn't sufficiently wide awareness of their existence. The ACLU publishes a series of paperback books to inform the lay public about their rights in a wide range of specific contexts. So-called know your rights campaigns can be effective not only in deterring legal harms from occurring in the first instance, but also in gauging the extent to which rights are being violated. That is, they can serve an information gathering function for public interest advocates. Some ACLU offices publish and distribute wallet sized cards describing in detail the rights that protect certain constituencies and making it easy for those persons to reference them. The cards also contain a phone number for the local ACLU affiliate office so that people can report incidents quickly and easily to ACLU attorneys. To expand the reach of public education campaigns, public interest lawyers can work cooperatively with print and television journalists, documentary makers, bloggers, and others with access to a public audience, by feeding them information that is newsworthy and trying to facilitate sympathetic coverage to gain wider (and free) exposure for the issue at stake.

Community-based education efforts can also help to diffuse local knowledge of rights and promote the empowerment of marginalized groups. *See* Stacy Brustin, *Expanding Our Vision of Legal Services Representation — The Hermanas Unidas Project*, 1 AM. U. J. GENDER & L. 39 (1993). In Ingrid Eagly's description of her work at the Legal Assistance Corporation of Chicago, she described using media campaigns to publicize workplace laws, disseminating bilingual educational materials, providing trainings for social service providers, and workshops and workers' rights courses for community members. Her assessment was that such community education strategies were able to reach populations "that would not otherwise find out about Legal Services," provide support "for clients to learn about issues relevant to their cases and to meet others who are facing similar circumstances," respond to "problems that cannot be redressed by the legal system," and foster problem-solving and leadership skills in community members, while raising their consciousness about workplace issues. Ingrid V. Eagly, *Community Education: Creating a New Vision of Legal Services Practice*, 4 CLINICAL L. REV. 433, 472-79 (1998). Yet implementing community education programs was not without its challenges:

> One issue that I confronted while conducting community education work was questioning whether I had the ability or background to play the role of an educator. My experience made me think more generally about the power dynamic between poverty lawyers and their poor clients in the context of educational work. Can poverty lawyers, as outsiders to the communities that they serve — better educated, more highly paid, and often racially and ethnically different from their clients — effectively facilitate the educational

process? Will middle-class poverty lawyers necessarily end up dominating discussions they attempt to facilitate, resulting in the same dependence on lawyers as litigation produces?

As a young, white, middle-class, female attorney working with low-income, Latina, immigrant women, I was, in most respects, different from the groups that I served. My outsider status created tensions and gaps in understanding and reinforced hierarchies already prevalent in our society. The communities that I worked with received me with a critical skepticism, and at times openly acknowledged and discussed my status within society. As a group facilitator, I struggled to remain attuned to these tensions and, to the extent possible, to re-distribute power within the group. When such hierarchies were manifested in workshops, I would attempt to defuse them with techniques discussed in this Article, such as allowing the group to select discussion topics and returning questions that were addressed to me as the "expert" to the group as a whole. Although at times I departed from the rebellious ideal and instead imposed my own structure and ideas on the discussion, I struggled to continually re-evaluate my work with the goal of collaborative lawyering in mind.

Id. at 480-81.

2. Appraisal

a. ADVANTAGES

Whether established as part of a multi-pronged social movement campaign or a stand-alone effort, public education and media strategies can yield a number of important advantages as an approach to social change.

i. *DIRECT EFFECTS*

In any social movement, gaining sympathy and support from the general public, as opposed to the directly affected constituencies, is an important building block of enduring change. This can take the form of simple education about scientific data, statistical information, or other relevant factual information that can transform the social landscape against which the campaign takes place. Public acceptance and sympathy can be as critical as formal legal change, particularly when there is widespread misunderstanding about a particular issue. For example, in early litigation on behalf of persons with HIV or AIDS who were discriminated against in employment and educational settings, lawyers and others associated with protecting civil rights had to devote substantial energy to educating the public (and the courts) that HIV was not transmissible through casual contact or exposure. Caroline Palmer & Lynn Mickelson, *Many Rivers to Cross: Evolving and Emerging Legal Issues in the Third Decade of the HIV/AIDS Epidemic*, 28 WM. MITCHELL L. REV. 455, 457-58 (2001). Thus, lawyers enlisted the support of public health officials and doctors to help inform the broader public about the relevant facts.

Similarly, another advantage of public education and media strategies is that they may help ensure the sustainability of any legal reform by helping to promote cultural change. Public education can help to mitigate backlash against formal legal victories. *See* Stoddard, *supra*, at 978. Furthermore, an informed public that is sympathetic to a particular cause helps create pressure on elected officials who may be in a position to make decisions that can effectuate formal change. It is far easier for a legislator to do the "right" thing if she knows that her constituents will not vote against her for doing so when the next election comes.

Education strategies can also be used synergistically with other approaches to move policy reform forward. For instance, public media campaigns can be effective in drawing attention to social problems that may have no plausible litigation solutions. In this vein, a public education and media campaign was effectively used to support a successful state legislative effort to ban racial profiling in Missouri. Leland Ware, *Prohibiting Racial Profiling: The ACLU's Orchestration of the Missouri Legislation*, 22 ST. LOUIS U. PUB. L. REV. 59, 60-64 (2003). The campaign was developed in part as a reaction to the courts' resistance to traditional constitutional discrimination claims under the Equal Protection Clause and Fourth Amendment. *Id.* at 65-70.

ii. INDIRECT EFFECTS

As this suggests, it is important not to view public education and media campaigns in isolation, but to consider how they can relate to and complement other approaches. Public education can generate important internal support for social movements themselves. Successful publicity about a cause or group can help attract new members for organizations, thus reinforcing the ranks of supporters. Furthermore, positive media relations and public education can generate increased fundraising opportunities, which can in turn sustain a public interest group's ability to carry out future campaigns. And public education can be a critical component of community organizing, legislative advocacy, and litigation.

b. CHALLENGES

Strategies focused on public education and media relations also have important limitations that social change advocates must consider.

i. INABILITY TO DIRECTLY CHANGE LAW

If a campaign's primary goal is to implement direct changes in law or policy, public education strategies are an indirect, rather than direct, approach to such change. While informing the public about relevant issues is an important foundation for other types of advocacy, it does not, of course, change the law itself. Thus, advocates sometimes may question whether implementing a public education strategy is a circuitous route to social change—although any effort that seeks to empower communities to mobilize legally or politically requires a commitment to equipping them with critical knowledge.

Finally, even a well-planned public education and media strategy may be difficult to control. Whereas lawyers have some control over the structure of a litigation or legislative campaign, they may have less control where third parties, such as journalists or filmmakers, are creating the message that the public actually hears. While advocates can produce their own educational materials and deliver them directly to the relevant audience, in other cases the message will be filtered through surrogates who may not convey the precise facts or ideas that the advocates might desire. Moreover, like other social change strategies, public education campaigns can motivate countermovements to engage in their own efforts designed to influence the public in the opposite direction.

Suppose you are designing a public education and media campaign to complement CHA's efforts to improve the welfare of the homeless community. What would be the goal of your campaign? How, if at all, would it relate to your other advocacy strategies? What is your target audience? For a discussion of how advocacy can shape public attitudes about homelessness, see Gary Blasi, *Advocacy and Attribution: Shaping and Responding to Perceptions of the Causes of Homelessness*, 19 St. Louis U. Pub. L. Rev. 207 (2000).

EXERCISE

Returning to the scenario from the beginning of the chapter, what, if any, litigation options would you consider as part of the strategy to address the homelessness problem? What are the potential remedies that could be sought? Would they immediately advance the cause? Would they address the cause in the long run?

1. What are some alternative strategies besides litigation?
2. Develop a media strategy.
3. Develop a policy strategy.
4. Could community organizing be an effective social change strategy? Why or why not?
5. How would you recommend combining and sequencing strategies?

Present your findings to the CHA board and executive director.

6

THE PUBLIC INTEREST LAWYER-CLIENT RELATIONSHIP

[N]o social role encourages such ambitious moral aspirations as the lawyer's, and no social role so consistently disappoints the aspirations it encourages.
WILLIAM SIMON, THE PRACTICE OF JUSTICE: A THEORY OF LAWYERS' ETHICS 1 (1998).

I. INTRODUCTION

This chapter explores the dynamics of the lawyer-client relationship in the public interest law context. There are several important issues to consider. One is the recurrent question of lawyer accountability and client autonomy. As we have seen, a central issue within public interest lawyering concerns whose interests the lawyer is, or should be, advancing. There may be broad and narrow understandings of what actions are in the client's best interests. On one view, the lawyer's goal should be to carry out only actions that protect the client's legal rights or interests, without regard to other considerations. Another view is that the lawyer should be attentive not only to advancing the client's primary legal interests, but also to broader concerns about the client's well-being—a more holistic approach to representation. Under yet another view, the public interest lawyer's objective should be to advance the underlying cause, however that may be defined. How much input clients and communities have into the process of agenda setting and tactical execution is a key concern. Thus, the cause-oriented vision could be entirely compatible with strong accountability to clients; or it might risk undermining the client's autonomy in choosing the best course of action for herself in ways that raise ethical concerns (discussed in Chapter 7).

As this suggests, how we understand the lawyer-client relationship depends in part on how we define "success" in the public interest context. Success may be assessed along several different metrics, not all of which are consistent with one another. One measure could be the degree to which public interest lawyering achieves a formal rule change or the implementation of a new policy. Under this metric, a lawyer might approach her relationship with her clients in ways that advance that goal. At the same time, doing so may not serve other interests that a public interest lawyer may value, such as client autonomy and empowerment. If a lawyer's goal is not simply to achieve a short-term objective, such as a court order, but to empower her clients to independently address long-term structural problems in their community, the lawyer might approach the relationship with her clients in different ways.

A final consideration is how context influences lawyer-client relations. Who the clients are and what they aspire to, and where the lawyers work and what they value are factors that may influence the scope and content of representation. You will note that, unlike the other chapters in this book, our discussion in this chapter is centered on public interest lawyers working for nonprofit organizations. This is because research on the public interest lawyer-client relationship has tended to emphasize nonprofit lawyers. However, even though the examples and analysis tend to be drawn from nonprofit settings, they have applications for lawyering in other practice sites. As you review the material, ask yourself how the analysis would apply to a private firm lawyer representing a pro bono client. What about a lawyer in a private public interest law firm? A government lawyer representing an agency?

Our focus in this chapter is on comparing different models of lawyering in the public interest context. For organizational purposes, this chapter divides the discussion of the public interest lawyer-client relationship into four distinct categories: conventional lawyering, cause lawyering, client-centered lawyering, and community lawyering. Though we distinguish them conceptually, there are many connections. Our goal is to reflect upon the normative aspirations and practical challenges associated with each—and evaluate which models seem most appealing as approaches to public interest practice.

II. CONVENTIONAL LAWYERING

A. CONCEPT

Understanding the particular features, goals, and challenges of the lawyer-client relationship in the public interest context requires that we compare it to the standard conception of conventional lawyering. In the standard account, lawyers are viewed as detached professionals—neutral partisans who are not identified with the morality, causes, and beliefs of their clients. Rule 1.2(b) of the Model Rules of Professional Conduct codifies this position: "A lawyer's representation of a client . . . does not constitute an endorsement of the client's political, economic, social, or moral views or activities."[1] This model of

---

1. Neutrality does not attach until the moment of representation. A lawyer can typically refuse to represent a client if he disagrees with that client's moral position, in which case he owes no duty at all. We examine the ethical implications of client selection in Chapter 7.

the "hired gun" is often associated with lawyers in private practice, to whom clients pay a fee to advance a position with which the lawyer need not agree, but only must think is legally defensible. The lawyer's advocacy for that position is a function of the agency relationship established by the market transaction. The lawyer may share a client's values, objectives, or agendas (and many often do), but this is incidental to, rather than constitutive of, the lawyer-client relationship. Robert W. Gordon, *The Independence of Lawyers*, 68 B.U. L. Rev. 1, 56 (1988). It is precisely the zealous pursuit of client objectives irrespective of the lawyer's assessment of their ultimate moral worth that defines the "ideology of advocacy." William H. Simon, *The Ideology of Advocacy: Procedural Justice and Professional Ethics*, 1978 Wis. L. Rev. 29, 36-37.

> Conventional lawyers are not . . . supposed to have any qualms about switching sides or representing clients whose values and behavior are reprehensible to them. The prevailing codes of professional ethics expressly allow lawyers to represent clients without endorsing their views or goals. The rules allow the sale of legal expertise without requiring a lawyer to take into account any of the moral or political implications of their representation. Indeed, to do so is a point of professional pride and a demonstration of professional responsibility.

Stuart A. Scheingold & Austin Sarat, Something to Believe In: Politics, Professionalism, and Cause Lawyering 7-8 (2004) [hereinafter, Scheingold & Sarat]; *see also* Austin Sarat & Stuart Scheingold, *Cause Lawyering and the Reproduction of Professional Authority: An Introduction, in* Cause Lawyering: Political Commitments and Professional Responsibilities 3-4 (Austin Sarat & Stuart Scheingold eds., 1998) [hereinafter, Sarat & Scheingold].

B. BENEFITS

Defenders of the standard conception of neutral partisanship justify it in terms of the benefits it confers on both individual clients and the broader adversarial system.

1. Effective Advocacy

An important potential benefit of neutral partisanship is simple effectiveness. Lawyers who assume a morally detached role may more capably represent their clients by advising them in an objective, dispassionate manner that enables the lawyers to identify and pursue the clients' best interests. On this view, lawyers who are detached from their clients are more likely to give sound, objective advice.

2. Client Autonomy

Proponents of neutral partisanship also suggest that it promotes client independence and protects against attorneys who might wield their professional expertise to influence client views. In an influential article, Stephen Pepper defended the lawyer's "amoral ethical role" as a means of according clients "first-class citizenship" premised on the core value of client autonomy. Pepper contended that the ethical rules stood for the notion that "the role of the professional is to serve the client ahead of himself or herself" as a way of protecting client autonomy from the moral whims of lawyers.

> Our first premise is that law is intended to be a public good which increases autonomy. The second premise is that increasing individual autonomy is morally good. The third step is that in a highly legalized society such as ours, autonomy is often dependent upon access to the law. Put simply, first-class citizenship is dependent on access to the law. And while access to law — to the creation and use of a corporation, to knowledge of how much overtime one has to pay or is entitled to receive — is formally available to all, in reality it is available only through a lawyer. Our law is usually not simple, usually not self-executing. For most people most of the time, meaningful access to the law requires the assistance of a lawyer. Thus the resulting conclusion: First-class citizenship is frequently dependent upon the assistance of a lawyer. If the conduct which the lawyer facilitates is above the floor of the intolerable — is not unlawful — then this line of thought suggests that what the lawyer does is a social good. The lawyer is the means to first-class citizenship, to meaningful autonomy, for the client.

Stephen Pepper, *The Lawyer's Amoral Ethical Role: A Defense, a Problem, and Some Possibilities*, 1986 AM. B. FOUND. RES. J. 613, 617-18.

3. Access and Legitimacy

Institutional justifications for neutral partisanship focus on its value in fostering access to justice and supporting the legitimacy of the adversarial system. The access rationale suggests that not attributing the client's views or objectives to the lawyer facilitates the representation of unpopular clients. In Deborah Rhode's terms,

> if . . . advocates were held morally accountable for their clients' conduct, less legal representation would be available for those most vulnerable to popular prejudice and governmental repression. Our history provides ample illustrations of the social and economic penalties directed at attorneys with unpopular clients. It was difficult enough to find lawyers for accused communists in the McCarthy era and for political activists in the early southern civil rights campaign. Those difficulties would have been far greater without the principle that legal representation is not an endorsement of client conduct.

DEBORAH L. RHODE, IN THE INTERESTS OF JUSTICE: REFORMING THE LEGAL PROFESSION 54 (2000). This view is particularly powerful with respect to criminal defendants whose alleged actions invite moral reproach that would make it difficult to secure adequate representation by lawyers worried about public disapproval.

The access justification for conventional lawyering may advance the public interest by increasing the likelihood of representation of underrepresented client groups. In Norman Spaulding's view, "thin professional identity," in which lawyers serve clients irrespective of their own personal approval of the client's objectives, serves the principle of open access to law by orienting lawyers toward the achievement of the client's lawful objectives. "[I]t strikes me as the highest order manifestation of service through thin identity — being willing to serve where the most dire need exists quite irrespective of whether one identifies with the personal attributes or positions of the clients one serves and quite irrespective of the prospects for material reward or social approval." Norman W. Spaulding, *Reinterpreting Professional Identity*, 74 U. Colo. L. Rev. 1, 101 (2003). As one example, if a lawyer in a large private firm represents an unpopular client in a pro bono matter, the standard conception suggests that her paying clients should not associate her with the views of the pro bono client and understand that she is simply discharging her professional role. If the reverse were true, it could discourage that lawyer from representing the pro bono client for fear of losing business.

This principle of access is related to the systemic legitimacy of the adversary system, which depends on the public's belief that individuals can participate fully in the legal process. Because this participation requires access to lawyers, a system in which lawyers were viewed as either denying representation because of disagreement with client objectives or disciplining client choice during representation would erode the belief in full participation necessary to sustain the system. Daniel Markovits, A Modern Legal Ethics: Adversary Advocacy in a Democratic Age (2008).

C. CHALLENGES

The justifications for neutral partisanship can be thought of as resting on an implicit conception of what it means for lawyers to serve the "public interest," whether that is promoting individual choice or systemic legitimacy. Critics of the neutral role for lawyers also invoke the public interest for the opposite point: to show how amorality can produce systemic distortions. In particular, they emphasize the risks of neutral partisanship in a system in which the ideology of advocacy (particularly on behalf of powerful clients) can too easily shade into adversarial abuse and access to lawyers is not evenly distributed across socioeconomic categories.

Critics point out that client autonomy is not the only systemic value lawyers should promote and, even if it is a paramount one, should be judged according to what it produces. Drawing upon David Luban's work, Deborah Rhode puts it this way:

> It is, for example, morally desirable for clients to make their own decisions about whether to attempt to defeat a needy opponent's valid claim through a legal technicality; it is not morally desirable for them actually to make the effort. Autonomy does not have intrinsic value; its importance derives from the values it fosters, such as personal creativity, initiative, and responsibility. If a particular client objective does not, in fact, promote those values, or does so only at much greater cost to third parties, then neither that objective, nor an advocate's assistance, is ethically justifiable.

Rhode, *supra*, at 57.

From a systemic perspective, others criticize neutral partisanship on the grounds that it actually ends up reinforcing inequality in the marketplace for legal services, not (as proponents suggests) promoting greater access. In a system in which access to lawyers depends largely on the ability to pay, the systemic consequence of facilitating client autonomy through lawyers is that the autonomy of particular clients (those with resources) will be given more scope than others (those without). As a result, having lawyers neutrally facilitate client ends will end up according more legal resources to advancing the objectives of wealthy, powerful clients against parties who lack the resources to pursue justice in a truly adversarial manner.

Furthermore, an emphasis on neutrality can have legitimacy costs. The model of the "hired gun" is associated with what much of the lay public views as the worst of the legal profession. The American public generally holds lawyers as a group in low repute, suspecting that they are more concerned with collecting fees than serving the public good. *See* Leo J. Shapiro & Associates, Public Perceptions of Lawyers: Consumer Research Findings 19 (Am. Bar Ass'n 2002). The lack of attachment to client goals can reinforce the view that lawyers are simply empty vessels who would just as soon represent the other side of a dispute in an equally zealous manner for the right price. Such moral flexibility can lead some lawyers to push the bounds of ethical propriety in the zealous pursuit of victory. It also places lawyers in the position of disclaiming responsibility for client actions that justifiably receive public condemnation. Is a lawyer who chooses to represent a tobacco company that knowingly covered up false information about the health effects of cigarettes and marketed tobacco products to minors truly not responsible for the company's actions? This type of question leads some critics to wonder whether neutral partisanship is simply self-serving, allowing lawyers to justify getting paid for work that facilitates morally reprehensible actions.

How public interest lawyers relate to their clients spans the range from a model that is close to conventional lawyering to one that is dramatically different from it. Their relationships are driven by a number of contextual factors: the type of case, the fee arrangement, the lawyer's personal values and commitments, whether the case is about law reform or individual service, and the nature of the clients themselves. Some of these contextual factors were explored in Chapter 4's examination of public interest practice sites and how they shape lawyer-client relationships. The remainder of this chapter focuses on frameworks for understanding these relationships in the public interest context. Rather than focus on what causes variation in practice, it explores different conceptual models of how public interest lawyers do — and should — approach client relations. As we will see, all of these models respond to, and offer criticisms of, conventional lawyering, even while sometimes building upon it.

In general, all public interest lawyers care about something beyond mere client service and thus can be viewed as embracing a cause that distinguishes them from the amoral technician assumed in the conventional lawyering model. Chapter 1 introduced the concept of "cause lawyering" and its definitional challenges. Here, we approach cause lawyering from a different perspective by asking how a lawyer's commitment to a cause influences her relations with clients. Are cause lawyers more effective advocates for justice, more attuned to client needs, more capable of promoting access to justice? What are the tradeoffs? The idea of cause lawyering raises the question of just what the lawyer's cause is. For some lawyers, the cause may be a particular type of social transformation — changing law and practice, for instance, to promote greater racial justice, gender equality, environmental protection, or immigrant rights. In this context, lawyers may act with or through clients to achieve particular types of legal and behavioral change. For other public interest lawyers, the clients themselves may be the "cause" in the sense that the goal is to foster a certain sense of client agency or power. Our discussion of cause lawyering thus leads us to explore two alternative lawyering concepts that focus more directly on client empowerment. The first, "client-centered lawyering," argues for an approach that places the lawyer in the role of helping clients solve problems based on a deep understanding of the client's point of view. The second, which we call "community lawyering," encompasses a range of lawyering styles that are connected by an emphasis on the goal of ultimately building power within client communities.

Each model asserts a vision of public interest lawyering that is distinct from neutral partisanship, though each may share some affinities with it. As you review these models, consider how they relate to conventional lawyering — and each other. How do the models relate to the goals of promoting client autonomy? Which seem most likely to produce significant social transformation? Which seem most likely to enhance access to justice and reinforce systemic legitimacy? Which, in your view, offer the most appealing ways of being a lawyer? How different are they in practice?

III. CAUSE LAWYERING

A. CONCEPT AND VARIATIONS

Public interest lawyers who advocate for a cause, in contrast to their conventional counterparts, are driven by moral commitment. This is not to say that public interest lawyers always are on the "right" side of an issue, but rather that they take ownership of the position they advocate — expressing moral and political dedication to their clients and/or the causes they represent. Austin Sarat and Stuart Scheingold suggest that it is precisely the commitment to cause that distinguishes such lawyers from the mainstream of the legal profession. Sarat & Scheingold, *supra*, at 3.

> [Conventional] lawyering . . . is neither a domain for moral or political advocacy nor a place to express the lawyer's beliefs about the way society should be organized, disputes resolved, and values expressed. . . . For cause lawyers, such objectives move from the margins to the center of their professional lives. Lawyering is for them attractive precisely because it is a deeply moral or political activity, a kind of work that encourages pursuit of their vision of the right, the good, or the just. Cause lawyers have *something to believe in* and bring their beliefs to bear on their work lives. In this sense, they are neither alienated from their work nor anxious about the separation of role from person.

SCHEINGOLD & SARAT, *supra*, at 2. Within this framework, the notion of cause lawyering "conveys a determination to take sides in political and moral struggle." *Id.* at 5.

How a public interest lawyer defines her cause affects how she approaches her clients. In the following excerpt, Thomas Hilbink examines three lawyer-client models that he associates with different visions of cause lawyering: proceduralist lawyering, which is "marked by a belief in the separation of law and politics, and a belief that the legal system is essentially fair and just"; elite/vanguard lawyering, which "trades on the faith that law has the capacity to render substantive justice and that legal institutions do so"; and grassroots lawyering, in which lawyers are "skeptical of law's utility as a tool of social change" and "work with grassroots movements, often as supporting players." Thomas M. Hilbink, *You Know the Type . . . : Categories of Cause Lawyering*, 29 LAW & SOC. INQUIRY 657, 665, 673, 681 (2004).

> [T]he proceduralist type incorporates a traditional/mainstream conception of the lawyer-client relationship. Clients, from the perspective of this type, are seen as atomized individuals, their cases discrete from any larger cause or group (aside from the proceduralist cause itself). Legal Services director Clinton Bamberger outlined just such a vision for . . . lawyering: "Once a client is accepted . . . , the lawyer's obligation is clear — regardless of any group interests which the client may represent or oppose — the lawyer must represent the interest of the client with absolute dedication."
>
> Thus, proceduralist lawyering doesn't deviate from established professional norms. . . .
>
> Another aspect of the lawyer's role central to proceduralist lawyering is the idea that lawyers are nonpartisan and don't adopt their clients' causes as their own. Proceduralist lawyering embraces the notion of neutrality. . . . In describing its early involvement in the civil rights-era South, the [Lawyers' Committee for Civil Rights Under Law] made clear that its representatives went to Mississippi not as "activists" or "civil rights lawyers." Their goal was not to "target" southern white racism, but rather to simply serve as lawyers for a client . . . who approached them and requested assistance. It was only later that they became enmeshed with the substantive goals of the civil rights movement. . . .
>
> With [an elite/vanguard] conception of the cause comes a distinct formulation of the lawyer's role, the client's place, and the relationship between the two. . . . They file briefs in courts, they are open about their intentions, and they make "principled constitutional arguments." Indeed, the profession shows great respect for and professional acceptance of such approaches. Yet to the extent that the traditional or mainstream conception of the lawyer-client relationship exists, such lawyering deviates quite seriously from that norm. Lawyers choose the clients, lawyers determine the strategy and goals, and sometimes they stage the events necessary to create a valuable set of facts.
>
> Another way in which elite/vanguard lawyering deviates from the expressed norm of the profession is the lawyer's overt commitment to the substantive cause. Elite/vanguard lawyering transgresses the traditional professional ideology that presumes neutral partisanship. Whereas Proceduralist lawyering entails a professional (and procedural) basis for the commitment, elite/vanguard lawyering entails an investment in the substantive goals of the cause for which lawyers advocate. Clarence Darrow and the ACLU were deeply invested

in defeating Tennessee's antievolution law in the Scopes trial. Thurgood Marshall and Charles Houston were similarly devoted to the cause of racial equality in their litigation. . . .

In cause lawyering aimed at vindicating or advancing a broad principle, the individual client fades into the background. With the individual case a vehicle for the advancement of general principles, the client is seen as of secondary importance. . . .

What is the [grassroots] lawyer's role in a professional sense in a situation where, as one lawyer said, the "legal stuff is secondary. . . . It's probably not even secondary. It's relatively unimportant"? The question that arises again is "who's in charge"? . . . Sometimes [grassroots lawyers] are leaders, while other times they are not. But, unlike elite-vanguard lawyers, grassroots lawyers work closely and in solidarity with social movements. In determining strategy, grassroots lawyering typically involves working with (or as part of) social movements — planning litigation or legal action not in isolation from the movement but as part of an integrated approach in solidarity with movement actors.

The grassroots lawyer-client relationship generally avoids the rigidity of traditional lawyer-client interactions. Often this grassroots approach involves a collaboration between partners rather than an "expert-client" relationship. . . . Lawyers strive, in the course of representation, to connect with the person they represent. . . . As such, lawyers and clients ideally develop solidaristic bonds that facilitate and enhance communication and cooperation. . . .

Some grassroots lawyers see it as part of their political and cause lawyering identity to *violate* the rules of the profession. For one, they reject neutrality in favor of solidarity with clients. Their work entwines them in their clients' agendas "in order to make a political statement."

Hilbink, *supra*, at 672-89. If, as Hilbink suggests, some versions of cause lawyering incorporate traditional conceptions of the lawyer's role, how useful is it as a concept for understanding public interest lawyer-client relations? Is the important distinguishing feature of cause lawyering commitment to a cause or is the key issue what that cause is? Are proceduralist lawyers any different from big law firm lawyers who neutrally represent corporate clients? Are grassroots lawyers "hired guns" for social movements?

B. BENEFITS

The tradeoffs of cause lawyering from the standpoint of lawyer-client relations can be measured according to the same criteria with which we evaluated conventional lawyering: individual impacts (effective advocacy and client autonomy) and systemic impacts (access to the legal system and systemic legitimacy). In terms of individual criteria, do you think that close identification with client objectives — what Spaulding calls "thick identification" — would make a lawyer more or less effective as a client advocate? Proponents of cause lawyering suggest that lawyers who are morally committed can be more effective — both as advocates for clients and broader causes — precisely because they are passionate, not dispassionate. Close identification with client objectives is motivating in a way that propels the lawyer to do her best for the client. A commitment to cause can likewise be energizing and provide the lawyer with a vision beyond a particular case, which may inspire thinking strategically about broader social reform. In this sense, cause lawyers may be more likely to develop a long-term relationship with clients and organizations to advance the causes and beliefs they share, as opposed to hopping from case to case in a technical, professional role. *See* SARAT & SCHEINGOLD, *supra*, at 9 ("Indeed, cause lawyers often argue that the more closely they identify with their clients' values, the better advocates they will be. Shared values, according to this perspective, are conducive to a deeper understanding that will enable them to engage in context-sensitive advocacy."); *see also* Susan Sterett, *Caring About Individual Cases: Immigration Lawyering in Britain, in* SARAT & SCHEINGOLD, *supra.*

The relationship between cause lawyers and client autonomy is contingent on the type of approach lawyers take. For Hilbink's grassroots lawyers, who view their cause as empowering clients and communities, representation is organized around identifying and advancing client goals, and thus is deeply autonomy-enhancing. Similarly for proceduralist lawyers, who view their cause as facilitating access to the legal system, the approach to client relations mirrors their conventional lawyering counterparts in ways that produce the same autonomy benefits.

For similar reasons, we would expect cause lawyering to promote access to justice by directing lawyer resources toward underrepresented groups. It is not necessarily the case that cause lawyering is always aligned with enhanced access; again, it depends on what "cause" the lawyers adopt. For those who care primarily about procedural justice — that everyone who needs a lawyer should have one — access *is* the cause. And other types of cause lawyering can also be access-enhancing, such as the civil liberties work of groups like the ACLU, which support freedom of speech for unpopular views, or public defenders who care deeply about the rights of indigent clients to the best defense, or issue-oriented groups that advocate for clients and constituencies that would not otherwise have equal representation.

There are systemic benefits of cause lawyering as well. As Scheingold and Sarat argue, the organized bar has, to a degree, embraced cause lawyering in a "fragile alliance" that allows the bar to assert its commitment to the professional value of public service and distance itself from the charge of commercialism. Yet in so doing, cause lawyering also destabilizes the ideology of advocacy in ways that threaten mainstream professionalism:

> On the one hand, cause lawyering is rooted in traditions of civic responsibility that long have been intrinsic to the ethical ideals of lawyering in the United States. Cause lawyers serve the interests of the profession by reconnecting law and morality and by making tangible the idea that lawyering is a "public profession" — one whose contribution to society goes beyond the acquisition, aggregation, and deployment of technical skills. Yet cause lawyering exposes the limitations of the dominant conception of professionalism. It stretches the meaning of civic professionalism well beyond the Tocquevillian vision of social responsibility and engagement while at the same time directly assailing the profession's core standard of ethical behavior, which weds lawyering to political and moral neutrality and to technical competence.

SCHEINGOLD & SARAT, *supra*, at 23. Do you agree that cause lawyers enhance the reputation of the profession by expressing its highest commitment to service? What are the systemic costs? Are they worth it?

C. CHALLENGES

As Hilbink's discussion of cause lawyering highlights, commitment to cause can have different impacts on client relations—depending on what the cause is and how it influences the lawyer's understanding of the client's role. Tensions may arise either when lawyers identify primarily with the client or primarily with the cause. How those tensions are managed and whether they are justified by the pursuit of the ultimate outcome are crucial questions.

1. Connection to Clients: Problems of Attachment

What are the advocacy tradeoffs of strong identification with one's clients? While one benefit of cause lawyering may be high motivation to "win," close identification also may carry risks. Can a strong affinity between attorney and client lead to confusion about the boundaries of the lawyer's proper role in representing clients? In the following segment, Nancy Polikoff provides an introspective reflection on her practice, much of which involved representing activists who had engaged in civil disobedience to protest discriminatory treatment of gays and lesbians in the wake of the 1987 National March on Washington for Lesbian and Gay Rights. Note how she identifies the difficulty of balancing her professional role as a lawyer representing gay and lesbian activists with her place as someone who is personally affected by the struggle for gay and lesbian rights.

Polikoff examines these tensions from different perspectives. In the first part of her article, excerpted below, she explores the conflicts that arise because of her need to maintain legitimacy and credibility as an attorney with other actors in the legal system, which sometimes requires her to distance herself from her clients. That distance, in turn, may reduce her effectiveness as a lawyer if it causes the activists she represents to be less trustful of her precisely because of her close association with the legal system.

NANCY D. POLIKOFF, *AM I MY CLIENT?: THE ROLE CONFUSION OF A LAWYER ACTIVIST*

31 Harv. C.R.-C.L. L. Rev. 443, 449-54 (1996)

[I]A. "They" Are the Clients; "I" Am the Lawyer

Civil disobedience activists misbehave: they break the law, breach decorum, and disregard order. Lawyers behave: they uphold the law, maintain decorum, and cooperate in preserving order. I cannot be in both groups at the same time.

In 1991, I represented approximately sixty demonstrators who had been arrested for blocking a Washington D.C. street in a protest against government AIDS policy. . . . [O]ne . . . demonstrator . . . chose to go to court in order to plead guilty, make a statement, and request that he be permitted to pay the equivalent of his fine to an AIDS service organization. . . . Most of his fellow demonstrators were in the courtroom to support him.

As we were waiting, one of the demonstrators seated behind me leaned over and asked, "Can we applaud and cheer when he comes in the courtroom?" The first thought that came to my mind was, "Of course you can't do that in a courtroom." The second thought was, "That's the wrong answer, Nancy. You are the lawyer; they are the clients. Just tell them the consequences of their actions so that they can make a decision that best meets their goals." My third thought was, "Get me away from these people." I was in a courtroom where I often appear, and a part of me could not bear to be associated with a major breach of courtroom decorum. If they were going to cheer and clap, I wanted to say, "It's not me; it's them," even though I was there as their lawyer precisely because they are me and because we represent each other.

I would have been less troubled by this scenario had I felt less connected to and less associated with my clients. As I think back on other activist groups I have represented, I realize that I would not have felt uncomfortable sitting near them during their disruptive courtroom behavior as a statement of professional connection. I would have expected the judge to see me as their lawyer, nothing more and nothing less. Had a judge suggested that it was my job to enforce rules of courtroom decorum, I would have resisted while still feeling that I was separate from my clients.

With lesbian and gay clients, however, I feel vulnerable. I do not know what the judges think about me when I represent such activists. Some certainly know I am a lesbian, as I have never been secretive about my sexuality. In these situations, however, my need to preserve the judge's ongoing respect for my professional judgment compels me to distance myself from my clients. Otherwise, I assume the judge will see me in the way that I see myself: as connected to my clients and in some way represented by them. If, however, the judge does not know that I am a lesbian and therefore sees me as being merely their lawyer, then I stand before the court absolved of my clients' misbehavior but also as a fraud — labeled as separate when in fact I am not.

To distance myself is to betray both myself and my relationship with my clients. To allow myself to be distanced by the system also feels dishonest. Nonetheless, I am not prepared to throw my lot in with those who disregard the rules of courtroom behavior by which I must live if I am to have any credibility or respect within the judicial system.

That day in 1991, I acted as a lawyer should. I explained the possible consequences of disruptive behavior to my clients without making their decision for them. They chose to remain quiet, so I had no further discomfort. Yet, I felt in that moment the inevitability of role confusion. . . .

[S]eparation . . . occurs between my clients and me as a result of the lawyer-client relationship both during civil disobedience actions and afterwards in court. . . . As the lawyer, I am speaking for others, not myself. It is "they," not "we," who are planning for a certain number of people to be arrested, who will stage the action at a particular location, and who plan whether to stay in jail. This rational, professional "I'm doing my job" conversation covers up the rage and pain that motivate me, as well as my clients, to work against injustice. . . .

[I]B. "You" Are the Lawyer; "I" Am the Activist

Many of my gay and lesbian activist clients who come from around the country to demonstrate in Washington, D.C. have no way of knowing whether I will understand their goals and sympathize with their tactics. If they are experienced in civil disobedience, they have had their share of bad lawyers, and if not, they have heard horror stories. They know that lawyers often go to great lengths to protect their insider status. Although I approach my relationship with each client with the assumption that we share a common cause, they make no such assumption about me. Some may even see me as part of a hostile system. Because feeling connected is so important to me, I work hard to demonstrate my commitment to my clients' goals and values.

Inevitably, some client choices make my lawyering tasks more difficult. For example, some clients refuse to give their name or give a false name to the police. When a client takes such a position, not only with official court personnel but with me, she is identifying me with the system rather than with the protest action. I try to resist this misidentification by being patient and empathetic. To do otherwise is to accept my client's judgment of me as alien and hostile. The client's judgment, however, is not entirely off the mark as she gazes at me from her side of the cell bars, a visible reminder of the insider/outsider distinction between us. . . .

I am able to narrow the gap between my clients and me by doing something not normally considered lawyering work: carrying messages back and forth between those arrested and their supporters. Since only a lawyer has access to those behind bars, only a lawyer can connect the arrested activists to those doing support work on the outside. Lawyers with a more narrow view of their role may minimize the importance to their clients of this work and may even resist it. Yet in my experience it is one of the few ways in which my clients and I can clearly see ourselves as part of a common struggle. . . .

Polikoff's reflective narrative reveals a role dilemma that many public interest lawyers face on a routine basis. On one hand, to best serve their clients, lawyers must establish and maintain professional credibility with other actors in the legal system. This can be difficult when the lawyer has a strong political and emotional connection to the groups she represents. Lawyers who share such connections must contemplate how they will react to situations that compel them to choose between those roles. On the other hand, lawyers also need to have credibility with their clients, and deeply activist clients engaged in protest and forms of civil disobedience may mistrust lawyers precisely because of the way in which they comport themselves in professional settings in what may appear to be a foreign and detached manner. Are there ways in which a lawyer can address these concerns in advance of client representation? If so, how? Consider the fact that lawyers do not always have the opportunity to consult with clients (or even meet with them) before assuming their professional roles.

2. Cause versus Client: Problems of Autonomy

What happens when cause lawyers — such as those in Hilbink's "elite/vanguard" model — view their cause primarily or even exclusively in terms of changing law and social practice? What are the potential costs to client relations?

One casualty of this type of cause lawyering may be client autonomy. Particularly to the extent that cause lawyers are directing reform litigation, their clients' views can sometimes be devalued or even ignored. When that occurs, the cause lawyering model may be less respectful of clients than conventional lawyering, which more clearly places the lawyer in the role of a technician advancing goals that the client determines are important. In Martha Davis's account of welfare rights litigation in the 1960s and 1970s, she describes the preparation of the seminal case of *Goldberg v. Kelly*, which established a welfare recipient's due process right to a hearing before the termination of welfare benefits. One of the legal services lawyers on the case was David Diamond, from Mobilization for Youth Legal Unit in New York.

> Preferring a behind-the-scenes role rather than direct contact with clients, the soft-spoken Diamond supervised the preparation of the brief, affidavits, and other papers to be filed with the complaint. Brief writing was what Diamond . . . liked best about his job. "I wanted [plaintiff] John Kelly to get some money," he later recalled, "but John Kelly was not a real person to me. He was an occasion."

MARTHA DAVIS, BRUTAL NEED: LAWYERS AND THE WELFARE RIGHTS MOVEMENT, 1960-1973, 90 (1993). What are the risks of treating plaintiffs as "occasions"? What are the tradeoffs of this approach? *Goldberg* is understood as one of the monumental victories of public interest law of the twentieth century. However, critics also note that it was succeeded by a backlash against welfare that has dramatically curtailed its scope.

Do you think similar autonomy problems are confronted by lawyers on the left and right? Do conservative lawyers treat them in the same way? Ann Southworth's study of conservative lawyering revealed some lawyers who articulated views similar to their liberal law reform counterparts — emphasizing the importance of changing the law and expressing little concern about client autonomy. ANN SOUTHWORTH, LAWYERS OF THE RIGHT: PROFESSIONALIZING THE CONSERVATIVE COALITION 73 (2008) (citing a conservative cause lawyer who reported that "when asked to represent someone who is 'really not interested in pursuing the law,' she and her colleagues 'suggest they go somewhere else, because we really want to move the law forward' ").

As the welfare rights litigation example above highlights, cause lawyers may be morally aligned with the underlying cause, but not necessarily personally invested in the individual client. Distancing themselves from their clients may allow lawyers to take on an unpopular cause, while divorcing themselves from accountability for their clients' underlying conduct (as, say, in the case of a lawyer representing a criminal defendant in a capital case). But can that personal detachment also adversely affect the manner in which the lawyer carries out her professional duties? This issue is illustrated in the following excerpt. Burt Neuborne, former national legal director of the ACLU, discusses his relationship with his clients in a somewhat tongue-in-cheek response to George H.W. Bush's criticisms of the ACLU during the 1988 presidential campaign. Bush had attacked his opponent, Michael Dukakis, for admitting that he was a card-carrying member of the ACLU and for vetoing a state law requiring schoolchildren to recite the Pledge of Allegiance while he was the Governor of Massachusetts. ROBERT GOLDSTEIN, BURNING THE FLAG: THE GREAT 1989-90 AMERICAN FLAG DESECRATION CONTROVERSY 74 (1996). Bush successfully made doubts about Dukakis's patriotism a centerpiece of his campaign, which had previously trailed Dukakis in public opinion polls, and also attacked the ACLU and Dukakis for being "liberal."

BURT NEUBORNE, *CONFESSIONS OF AN ACLU LAWYER*

Wall Street Journal, October 20, 1988

Please allow me to express my gratitude to the tribunal for permitting me to expose my errors of libertarian deviationism.

As the tribunal well knows, I served for more than 20 years as a lawyer for the American Civil Liberties Union, most recently as its National Legal Director from 1982 to 1986. I stand accused by Leader Bush of excessive zeal in the defense of individual liberty. It is true that I defended the rights of accused criminals. I defended the rights of political extremists. I defended the rights of bigots and atheists. I defended books that I would never read and speakers whom I loathed; religions that I did not understand and unsavory individuals whom I understood all too well.

When I look back over the hundreds of ACLU cases that I handled, I can recall only a handful of clients I would have had to dinner and relatively few that I would have welcomed as a close friend. In many of those cases, I was protecting people whose ideas or actions were as far from my relentlessly middle-class life style as one can imagine.

Why then, as Leader Bush so artfully puts it, did I devote so much of my career to the defense of a "criminals lobby"? What is the hidden "liberal political agenda" that explains why I fought so fiercely and so long against so many policies favored by the people?

I beg the tribunal to understand that my zeal did not flow from sympathy with the goals or behavior of most of my clients. While I was privileged to represent an occasional saint, many of my clients were thoroughly unpleasant, hopelessly foolish or painfully incompetent. Sometimes all three. I fought their battles as an ACLU lawyer in the hopelessly naive belief that the continued existence of individual freedom for average people depends on protecting the rights of everyone, even the most despised among us. I believed that individual freedom is not a natural phenomenon. I believed that left to itself, the government would inexorably expand its power to control people's lives and that only an organized defense of individual freedom could hope to preserve a tolerable degree of liberty.

I viewed the ACLU as the institution with the responsibility for defending every inch of personal liberty guaranteed in the Bill of Rights. I feared that unless an organized (if you can call the ACLU organized) group spoke up for the rights of individuals—even unpleasant individuals—our personal liberties would erode to the point where the government would always defeat the individual. I did not expect to win all my cases. I did not even want to win all my cases. But I feared that unless the argument in favor of the individual and against the government was raised vigorously every time the government sought to restrict individual freedom, the government would win by default.

I've already told the tribunal that I would not want to live in a world where the ACLU won all its cases. But I would not want to live in a world where there was no ACLU to bring the cases. By stubbornly defending every inch of personal freedom as vigorously as we knew how, we believed that the final equilibrium would come to rest at a point somewhere in the middle; a point where the interests of the individual and the group would be harmonized.

Until very recently, I believed that the system was working. We had achieved a degree of personal liberty in this country that is the envy of the entire world. Our geopolitical rivals like Russia and China looked enviously at the way our respect for the dignity of the individual made us a vibrant and innovative society. All over the globe, people turned to us as the symbol of freedom.

But freedom isn't an accident. It is the result of painstaking work to maintain the structure of liberty against inevitable erosion at the hands of the government. I thought that my work for the ACLU was an integral part of maintaining freedom for everyone. I now confess my error and embrace Leader Bush's perception that the ACLU is a politically suspect liberal conspiracy.

In mitigation, I ask the tribunal to note that I did not understand that defending Nazis or Ku Klux Klan members was part of a liberal conspiracy. Neither did I realize that defending the free-speech rights of tobacco companies was high on the liberal agenda. I doubt it occurred to any ACLU lawyer that the defense of Rupert Murdoch or Oliver North or Meier Kahane was part of the liberal ideology. I confess that I was misled by the words of former Leader Goldwater when he said that "moderation in the defense of liberty is no virtue."

I now realize that the ACLU interferes with the will of the people as expressed in the views of our current Leaders. I realize that my concern with the individual interferes with the desires of the group. I thought I was a civil libertarian. I now learn that I was really a liberal. I accept Leader Bush's criticism and ask only that I be permitted to merge my individual concerns into the greater needs of the group. I await Vice Leader Quayle's guidance.

Neuborne's opinion piece is an excellent articulation of a cliché often attributed to the ACLU's institutional view of its role vis-à-vis clients. Former ACLU director Melvin Wulf is quoted as once having said, "Our real client is the Bill of Rights." *See* Note, *The New Public Interest Lawyers*, 79 YALE L.J. 1069, 1092 (1970). But, of course, from a technical professional standpoint, that is not true. ACLU lawyers do represent live human beings and organizations even if their ultimate goal is the systemic protection of individual liberty.

What do you think of Neuborne's statement that he would seldom want to have any sort of social relationship with many of his hundreds of clients? Should that matter to a lawyer? What about his statement that his zeal for civil liberties did not come from sympathy with most of his clients' goals and behaviors? Finally, how do you feel about Neuborne's statement that he did not even want to win all of his cases? What do you suppose he means by that? How do you think these statements reflect on Neuborne's idea of the lawyer-client relationship in the setting of public interest lawyering? Do you think his attitudes, if understood by his clients, would affect that relationship? If so, how? How do you think his clients would view his statement that many of them are "thoroughly unpleasant, hopelessly foolish or painfully incompetent"?

Does the relationship of public interest lawyers who do not have a strong affinity with their clients start to more closely resemble the relationship of private lawyers to their clients? Or are they different because, unlike private lawyers, these lawyers identify with a broader social cause, even if not with the clients?

3. Cause versus Client: Problems of Accountability

A related concern is the degree to which cause lawyers represent the constituencies they purport to serve. This tension can arise in individual representation cases, but is heightened when the public interest lawyer represents a larger, diverse group in class action or other complex litigation. An important example of this phenomenon comes from Derrick Bell's classic work examining the tension between NAACP lawyers and their clients in the legal battle to desegregate public schools. Derrick A. Bell, Jr., *Serving Two Masters: Integration Ideals and Client Interests in School Desegregation Litigation*, 85 YALE L.J. 470 (1976). Bell explored the desegregation litigation led by the NAACP and LDF in several major metropolitan areas in the post-*Brown* era. As he observed, after years of litigation, the accomplishment of desegregation was slowed by disputes over remedies (such as busing), which were met with substantial resistance from many whites and some courts, and contributed to the relocation of white families to surrounding suburban neighborhoods. Bell claimed that, despite increasing evidence that busing did not necessarily improve educational quality for black schoolchildren, "civil rights lawyers continue to argue that black children are entitled to integrated schools without regard to the educational effect of such assignments." *Id.* at 480. A significant number of families in the black community expressed concern that improving the quality of public education received by their children was a more important goal than desegregation per se. But LDF's middle class black and white leaders and lawyers were singularly focused on desegregation as the ultimate goal of the litigation. *Id.* at 489-90. In this context, it was unclear which "clients" the NAACP and LDF were actually representing, or whether the lawyers leading the desegregation litigation were following the direction of the nonprofit organizations for which they worked at the expense of the concrete interests of the clients whom they, at least nominally, represented. Do you think Bell was right to suggest that LDF lawyers were primarily responsive to their middle class black and white patrons rather than the community at large? What would it have meant to represent "the black community's interest" in the desegregation context? How would the lawyers have accurately determined what that interest was? What if, as Bell suggests, the community had multiple and conflicting interests? What faction should the LDF lawyers have represented? What recourse would clients have had if they believed the lawyers were not advancing their interests in educational quality? We discuss the ethical implications of this conflict in Chapter 7.

IV. CLIENT-CENTERED LAWYERING

A. CONCEPT

During the 1970s, as the first wave of public interest lawyering was taking shape, a new body of scholarship began to promote the concept of "client-centered" lawyering. Client-centered lawyering emerged from the clinical legal education movement, and is often associated with two textbooks. *See* Gary Bellow & Bea Moulton, The Lawyering Process: Materials for Clinical Instruction in Advocacy (1978); David A. Binder, Paul Bergman & Susan C. Price, Lawyers as Counselors: A Client-Centered Approach (1991). The model responded to concerns about attorney control and the corresponding lack of client autonomy associated with the cause lawyering model. It also distinguished itself from conventional lawyering, as the following excerpt shows.

> Under the traditional conception, lawyers view client problems primarily in terms of existing doctrinal categories such as contracts, torts, or securities. Information is important principally to the extent the data affects the doctrinal pigeonhole into which the lawyer places the problem. Moreover, in the traditional view, lawyers primarily seek the best "legal" solutions to problems without fully exploring how those solutions meet clients' nonlegal as well as legal concerns.
>
> Next, compare client-centered and traditional conceptions of clients. A client-centered conception assumes that most clients are capable of thinking through the complexities of their problems. In particular, it posits that clients are usually more expert than lawyers when it comes to the economic, social and psychological dimensions of problems. The client-centered conception also assumes that, because any solution to a problem involves a balancing of legal and nonlegal concerns, clients are usually better able than lawyers to choose satisfactory solutions. Moreover, the approach recognizes that clients' emotions are an inevitable and natural part of problems and must be factored into the counseling process. Finally, the approach begins with the assumption that most clients seek to attain legally legitimate ends through lawful means.
>
> Clients are less well regarded in the traditional conception. Lawyers adhering to the traditional view have often muttered, "The practice of law would be wonderful if it weren't for the clients." Such lawyers tend to regard themselves as experts who can and should determine, in a detached and rational manner, and with minimal client input, what solution is best. Three common

attributes that lawyers who hold a traditional view tend to ascribe to clients are: (1) Clients lack sophistication; (2) Clients are too emotionally wrapped up in their problems; and (3) Clients do not adequately consider the potential long-term effects (risks) of decisions.

[D]espite these differing conceptions, client-centered and traditional conceptions of lawyering have much in common. Both, for example, recognize the critical importance of legal analysis and have as their ultimate goal maximum client satisfaction. Moreover, most lawyers do not follow one conception to the complete exclusion of the other. However, the client-centered conception "fills in" the traditional approach by stressing that problems have nonlegal as well as legal aspects, and by emphasizing the importance of clients' expertise, thoughts and feelings in resolving problems. In a client-centered world, your role involves having clients actively participate in identifying their problems, formulating potential solutions, and making decisions. Thus, client-centered lawyering emanates from a belief in the autonomy, intelligence, dignity and basic morality of the individual client.

BINDER, BERGMAN & PRICE, *Lawyers as Counselers: A Client-Centered Approach, supra,* at 17-18. The authors identified six attributes of client-centered lawyering. The lawyer helps identify problems from a client's perspective; actively involves a client in the process of exploring potential solutions; encourages a client to make those decisions that are likely to have a substantial legal or nonlegal impact; provides advice based on a client's values; acknowledges a client's feelings and recognizes their importance; and repeatedly conveys a desire to help. *Id.* at 19-22. An extensive exploration of the client-centered model of lawyering also appears throughout Gary Bellow and Bea Moulton's influential textbook on clinical legal education. *See* BELLOW & MOULTON, *supra.* For other important scholarly treatments of the client-centered model, see Gary Bellow, *Turning Solutions into Problems: The Legal Aid Experience,* 34 NLADA BRIEFCASE 106 (1977) [hereinafter, Bellow, *Turning Solutions*]; Stephen Ellmann, *Client-Centeredness Multiplied: Individual Autonomy and Collective Mobilization in Public Interest Lawyers' Representation of Groups,* 78 VA. L. REV. 1103, 1128 (1992); Stephen Ellmann, *Lawyers and Clients,* 34 UCLA L. REV. 717, 739 (1987); Stephen Wexler, *Practicing Law for Poor People,* 79 YALE L.J. 1049 (1970). An important new work argues for the concept of "engaged client-centered lawyering" in which it is not presumed that clients always "know" what they want and that lawyers are sometimes needed to engage clients in moral and political dialogue so that decisions can reflect the client's underlying values. *See* STEPHEN ELLMANN, ROBERT D. DINERSTEIN, ISABELLE R. GUNNING, KATHERINE R. KRUSE & ANN C. SHALLECK, LAWYERS AND CLIENTS: CRITICAL ISSUES IN INTERVIEWING AND COUNSELING (2010); *see also* Katherine R. Kruse, *Engaged Client-Centered Representation and the Moral Foundations of the Lawyer-Client Relationship,* 39 HOFSTRA L. REV. 477 (2011); Katherine R. Kruse, *Fortress in the Sand: The Plural Values of Client-Centered Representation,* 12 CLINICAL L. REV. 369 (2006).

Clinical legal education, as we explore in Chapter 8, developed in tandem with the public interest law movement and was viewed by many as a crucial supplement to it—teaching students effective lawyering that also served clients in need. Accordingly, client-centered lawyering partly grew out of the experiences of lawyers who identified the disparities in the relative power of attorney and client in the context of public interest practice. As Robert Dinerstein noted, "Modern clinical legal education developed in the crucible of political activism of the 1960s and early 1970s. Many of the proponents of the client-centered approach were former legal services or public interest lawyers who entered academia as clinical law teachers. The experience of these lawyer-teachers with poor clients had a profound effect on their assessments of problems in the lawyer-client relationship and their proposed solutions." Robert R. Dinerstein, *Client-Centered Lawyering: Reappraisal and Refinement*, 30 ARIZ. L. REV. 501, 518-19 (1990). Gary Bellow described some of these problems as follows:

> The definition of the client's problems and the "best" available solutions are not mutually explored and elaborated; they are imposed by the lawyer's view of the situation and what is possible within it. In most discussions between lawyer and client, the lawyer does almost all of the talking, gives little opportunity for the client to express feelings or concerns, and consistently controls the length, topics and character of the conversation. Insofar as the client must elaborate the facts, they are obtained by a series of pointed, standard questions rather than any process that resembles a dialogue. Clients take this as "all they can expect" and are rarely aware that a different relationship with a lawyer is possible.

Bellow, *Turning Solutions, supra,* at 108. As Bellow expresses, client-centered lawyering was in one sense a critique of top-down cause lawyering in which lawyers as experts controlled cases with little or no input from those clients they represented. Do you think that client-centered lawyering plays a special role in the public interest law setting? How is it different from conventional lawyering?

B. BENEFITS

As is clear from the Binder, Bergman and Price excerpt above, client-centered lawyering above all seeks to enhance client autonomy. *See* Dinerstein, *supra,* at 512-13. It presupposes that clients have a better and more detailed understanding about the problems they are confronting and the potential solutions for addressing them than do their lawyers. It shifts the lawyer's focus from emphasizing detached professional advice to learning from the clients about the nature and source of their problems, and counseling them based on a fuller, contextualized understanding of their lives. It also advances the value of client autonomy by encouraging lawyers to view clients not in a paternalistic manner, but rather as partners in the effort to solve problems.

Moreover, client-centered lawyering expands the notion of problem solving for clients beyond the formal legal realm to address the complexity of issues affecting their lives, thus focusing lawyers on a more holistic approach to counseling. In this way, the client-centered lawyering model also questions the conventional notion that a dispassionate approach to lawyering would best serve the clients' interests.

The emotional detachment . . . generally considered among lawyers as essential to giving careful legal advice, also permits legal services lawyers a good deal of distance from the exploitation and poverty with which their clients must deal. It is a short step from such detachment to the impersonal routines which [legal services] offices have adopted. Similarly, the "professional focus" on the client's "legal" problems justifies not making inquiries beyond what the client explicitly complains about. Professional neutrality, an essential ingredient of keeping personal biases out of lawyer-client relationships, provides an acceptable rationale for narrowly defining what the lawyer can do, and discourages the lawyer from dealing with the underlying causes of the client's situation or his or her reaction to them.

Bellow, *Turning Solutions*, *supra*, at 118-19.

The client focus of this approach also reduces the risk that lawyers will prioritize the interest of the cause at the expense of the clients' wishes and interests. Thus, for example, a client-centered approach offers a different path for the lawyers in the desegregation litigation discussed in Derrick Bell's work. Operating under a client-centered view, NAACP and LDF lawyers might have made more of an effort to understand the specific goals and interests of their clients and worked closely with them to address the educational quality issues they faced on a daily basis. They also might have embraced a broader vision about the school desegregation issue that focused on community-based solutions or on addressing some of the impediments to desegregation remedies, such as white flight and residential segregation.

Whether that approach would have yielded different outcomes in courts or changed the course of history in any meaningful way — preventing massive resistance, white flight, and Southern backlash — is a deeply contested question. It is a question that underscores the systemic tradeoffs of a client-centered approach. By emphasizing client service, do client-centered lawyers forgo the strategic planning and complex advocacy necessary to change law and social practice? How do you think Gary Bellow, one of the founders of the legal services movement and a fierce advocate for the poor, would view the relationship between client-centeredness and systemic reform? In one sense, the individual focus of client-centered lawyering reminds us of the access orientation of both conventional lawyering and some visions of cause lawyering. It also fits comfortably with conventional notions of the lawyer's role as client advocate. Do you think client-centeredness is compatible with other views of lawyering we have discussed so far? Why or why not?

C. CHALLENGES

1. The Limits of Client-Centeredness

Are there any tradeoffs with actively engaging the client in problem solving and trying to resolve the case from the client's point of view, taking account of both the legal and nonlegal implications? Might client-centered lawyering promote client autonomy and empowerment at the expense of the underlying cause or movement goal? One possible risk of client-centeredness is that lawyers might encounter a tension between promoting client interests and advancing a broader cause — as, for instance, when the client desires a negotiated outcome that does not create strong precedent for the movement. How serious do you think this risk is? How would a client-centered lawyer deal with the tensions that might arise in a law reform campaign?

What happens when a client-centered lawyer is deeply connected, on a personal level, with the cause and clients who are part of a movement? How does that affect the quality of the representation provided? In the following excerpt, Nancy Polikoff reflects on a set of tensions arising from her representation of LGBT activists with whom she felt a strong affinity. Her belief in maintaining a client-centered approach to lawyering produced a conflict with her own strong sense of connection to the gay and lesbian rights movement.

Nancy D. Polikoff, *Am I My Client?: The Role Confusion of a Lawyer Activist*

31 Harv. C.R.-C.L. L. Rev. 443, 458-68 (1996)

... I am a strong proponent of client-centered counseling. This model of lawyering rests upon the conviction that clients bear the consequences of their decisions and are in the best position to understand the full nonlegal as well as legal significance of their choices. Accordingly, lawyers counsel clients best by helping them to explore all of the possible consequences of their actions so that the clients can make decisions that best suit their needs.

My sense that my clients represent me as much as I represent them, however, complicates the implementation of client-centered counseling. When I feel that I, as a member of the group that my clients represent, also bear the consequences of their choices, it is difficult maintaining my role as a counselor. My feelings of connection to my clients imply that we have a common cause, and unless I am careful, may deny my clients the client-centered assistance that they should receive. ...

In speaking around the country about representing activists, I have found a good deal of resistance to the client-centered counseling model. Some lawyers, especially young ones, went to law school to become part of a movement, and they do not want any distance between themselves and their clients; they want to be full participants in their clients' political decision making. Other lawyers hold a belief with which I entirely disagree: that by virtue of being a lawyer they have specialized knowledge that allows them to exert control over the political decision-making process.

I do believe that lawyers can be political activists and can make decisions about civil disobedience actions, but I do not believe that they should do so as lawyers. Rather, I support the position articulated by Martha Minow that "if the lawyer wants to make or help make the choice to violate the law for political reasons, then the lawyer should join the client as a comrade rather than serve in the role of legal advisor" [citing Martha Minow, *Breaking the Law: Lawyers and Clients in Struggles for Social Change*, 52 U. Pitt. L. Rev. 723, 747 (1991)]. When acting as a lawyer, one should participate in the decision-making process as a client-centered counselor rather than as a decision maker. ...

B. Client Resistance to the Client-Centered Model

Clients who feel connected to me and who appreciate that connection may be inclined to defer to me more often than they might defer to another, less connected, lawyer. This observation is especially true of my activist clients who know me well. Even so, clients will bear consequences that I will not, so I must resist their requests to make decisions that I do not feel are mine to make. . . .

The more my clients feel connected to me, the more likely it is that they will ask such questions and defer to my authority without consciously recognizing it as such. Some of my closest friends, for example, were among the first group of demonstrators arrested and processed at the 1987 Supreme Court civil disobedience action. . . . In the District of Columbia, plea bargaining does not include a determination of the sentence. Thus, only after the first person pled guilty before the judicial officer would any of us know what sentence would be imposed. . . .

[T]he protestor whose case would be called first . . . was "Jenifer," a friend of mine. . . . [S]he asked directly what I thought she should do. Then she asked what I would do if I were she. Resolutely, I maintained my role as client-centered counselor. I explained consequences and helped her articulate her goals. I engaged in active listening and reflected back what I heard.

My responses were somewhat frustrating to Jenifer. We had common personal and political bonds, but our relationship in this situation was really no different from that of any client trying to get her lawyer to make a decision and any lawyer resisting with the knowledge that it is the client, not the lawyer, who must live with the consequences of that decision. Jenifer had been arrested in other demonstrations and was not customarily deferential to lawyers. It was because she trusted me both personally and politically that she looked to me to make her decision for her. . . . As long as she turned to me as her lawyer, I felt a strong obligation to respond as her lawyer. In that situation — she was behind bars, I was free to leave — we were not just two friends, one helping the other make a decision.

C. Lawyer Resistance to the Client-Centered Model

A different set of conflicts occurs when a lawyer and her client have different values. These differences may result from the lawyer's self-interest in maintaining professional legitimacy, or they may result from political differences, thus making a lawyer uncomfortable with, or even unwilling to accept, client choices. . . . [I]t is possible for the activist lawyer to confront an action that surpasses her limits. Here I refer to an action that contradicts the lawyer's own political beliefs or judgment to the extent that she no longer wishes to be connected to it. A lawyer who begins representation from a stance of political distance is less likely to be troubled by client decisions. On the other hand, a lawyer with a political connection to her work may face the choice of either assuming the distanced stance of the "hired gun" or withdrawing from representation.

A dramatic example of this type of conflict confronted attorney Urvashi Vaid, who was then the executive director of the National Gay and Lesbian Task Force (NGLTF). In February 1992, Vaid agreed to provide legal assistance for a civil disobedience action by an affiliate group of ACT UP/New York. The action took place in Washington, D.C. at a meeting between officials of the Centers for Disease Control (CDC) and representatives, invited by the CDC, of AIDS and public health organizations. The purpose of the meeting was to discuss a new CDC definition of AIDS. The invited representatives were all part of national organizations that regularly lobbied and worked within the federal bureaucracy. The ACT UP activists entered the meeting, demanding that it be cancelled and that the AIDS and public health advocates leave because the meeting did not include representation of the full spectrum of people with AIDS. The group believed that a lobbyist walkout could encourage the CDC to hold public hearings at which people with AIDS would express their views about changing the definition. When the demand to terminate the meeting was not met, the ACT UP members handcuffed themselves to the representatives from the AIDS organizations.

Vaid, who has a history of both participating in direct action and working within the system, had ties both to the activists whom she had agreed to represent and to the advocates who were the target of the action. From the moment her representation began, her role was a blurry one, both to her and to her clients. Vaid reported that she took the case because she knew and respected the ACT UP activists. In other words, she acted from a perspective of connection and identification with her clients. At the same time, ACT UP selected Vaid because her position of prominence and respect within mainstream groups and direct action lesbian and gay political groups lent credibility to the action. The clients, therefore, also had a vision of their lawyer as connected to and identified with the mainstream in a way that they believed would benefit them politically and legally.

Although the invited advocates supported the ACT UP demands and had agreed in advance to ask the CDC to hold a series of meetings to obtain broader community input, they refused to act under threat. During the action, those who were handcuffed complained of discomfort and distress. After ninety minutes, Vaid spoke with her clients and told them that she disagreed with their tactics. When they would not end their action, she resigned as their legal counselor and left the scene. ACT UP members felt betrayed and abandoned by Vaid. ACT UP member Juan Mendez stated:

> We're not upset that she disagreed with our tactics, even though she knew about them before it happened. What we don't appreciate is that . . . she publicly tried to assume the role of facilitator and blurred the lines of her role; then she tried to use her clout to make us leave. She tried to make herself look good in front of her peers at the table.

Thus, Vaid's clients criticized her for abandoning the role of a neutral and dispassionate lawyer, although they selected her precisely because she would be seen as connected to the action and thereby lend credibility to it.

Vaid admitted that she had knowledge of the handcuffing plan when she undertook her role. She stated, however, that the impact of it did not occur to her until she saw it develop and saw the discomfort of those handcuffed:

> I just feel like I got caught up in something that I didn't actively think through. I sincerely apologize to the activists who felt let down, but I just could not go

through with being a neutral legal observer. . . . I couldn't agree with the tack and the way it unfolded.

Vaid reported that another factor involved in her decision to withdraw her legal support from this action was that the meeting was in the private offices of the American Public Health Association (APHA), and she knew that the APHA staff would not call the police. Thus, she was aware that the activists would not be arrested and that they would not need representation against the state. She asserted that had she believed otherwise, she would have felt obligated to remain. Without the threat of state intervention, Vaid saw her ties to those who were handcuffed, people with whom she worked regularly and with whom she had ongoing relationships, jeopardized by her continued association with her clients, and she therefore chose to withdraw.

Vaid's experience demonstrates what ultimately may be the most difficult conflict for a lawyer representing activists in her own movement. If the lawyer does the work to feel connected and to be an integral part of the action, she is bound to be tormented if she disagrees with a tactic or decision made during the action. It is possible to avoid this conflict by avoiding representation in the first place; I make this choice if I know in advance that the scenario is one with which I have fundamental disagreement — but not every action is neatly choreographed, and not every demonstrator adheres to a predetermined set of rules. . . .

Polikoff's exploration of the role duality of public interest lawyers is entirely in the context of representing activist clients engaged in civil disobedience. Do her observations have relevance to other forms of public interest lawyering, such as impact litigation, community organizing, or public policy work? At the conclusion of her article, she states that

> [c]lient-centered counseling and participation in political decision making cannot occur simultaneously. The dynamics that I have described — lawyers who impose their values on clients or activists who defer to the judgment of a lawyer — are dangers that can be avoided only when a lawyer adheres to the client-centered counseling model.

Id. at 470-71. Do you agree?

2. Whose Autonomy?

Another question raised by the client-centered approach concerns the degree to which certain types of clients may experience client-centeredness as empowering and under what conditions. As Dinerstein noted above, client-centered lawyering was developed in the context of concerns about the autonomy of poor clients within public interest practice. But in seeking to promote the autonomy of poor clients, does the client-centered model make certain assumptions about who those clients are and how they make decisions that may, in some situations, actually work against the autonomy-enhancement goal?

Coming from this point of view, Alex Hurder suggests that client-centered assumptions about how clients arrive at important decisions may reinforce inequality:

> The client-centered process of legal interviewing and counseling not only does not provide space for lawyer-client negotiation to occur, but it fosters an inequality in the lawyer-client relationship that hinders negotiation. The source of inequality is the lawyer's greater access to relevant information. Binder, Bergman and Price stress equally the need for the client to disclose all relevant information and for the lawyer to conceal information that would reveal the lawyer's preferences.
>
> The lawyer's access to client-held information is considered so fundamental to the client-centered approach that questioning techniques intended to manipulate the client into making a full disclosure are regarded as central to the legal interviewing and counseling process. Clients who resist client-centered questioning techniques and continue to withhold information are considered "atypical" and "difficult." The lawyer's need for full knowledge, not only of the facts of the client's case, but also of the client's values and beliefs, outweighs any interests that may cause a client to resist disclosure of information.
>
> Binder, Bergman and Price assume that the most significant barriers to a client's full disclosure of information, values and beliefs to a lawyer are psychological factors. Because the most significant barriers to full communication are deemed to be psychological, techniques taken from psychology and therapeutic counseling are relied upon to question clients effectively. The school of psychotherapy pioneered by the psychologist Carl R. Rogers is the primary source of the psychological techniques used in client-centered counseling.
>
> Binder, Bergman and Price particularly stress the importance of the practice of "empathic understanding." Empathic understanding is the technique of communicating empathy and nonjudgmental acceptance of a client's choices. To communicate empathy and nonjudgmental acceptance, it is necessary for lawyers to project an appearance of neutrality about the alternatives available to a client. Binder, Bergman and Price stress that the appearance of neutrality is necessary to enable clients to participate actively in the resolution of their problems, as well as to encourage clients to reveal information they might withhold if they knew the interests and preferences of the lawyer.
>
> Maintaining the appearance of neutrality inevitably requires pretense. The lawyer is seldom disinterested. In a study of lawyers representing clients in personal injury cases in New York City, Douglas E. Rosenthal identified the lawyer's financial interest in a quick settlement of the case as the most likely source of conflict with the client's interest. Other sources of conflict may lie in the lawyer's personal interests or in the policies of the law firm or institution employing the lawyer. The lawyer's interests might be financial, ideological, institutional, or personal. Because lawyering ordinarily involves not just communication with the client about potential solutions to a problem, but collaboration with the client on activities to solve the problem, every decision about a case has a potential impact on the lawyer.
>
> In Carl Rogers' concept of client-centered therapy, the ability of the therapist to remain nonjudgmental is at the core of the therapeutic approach. In order to remain nonjudgmental the therapist must be a person with no significant emotional investment in the decisions made by the client. Rogers advised spouses not to counsel spouses and advised friends not to counsel

friends because of their emotional stake in the other person's decisions. Like a spouse or a friend, a lawyer cannot be emotionally neutral about decisions made by a client. The lawyer's role as a partner in a joint endeavor makes it inevitable that the lawyer will have interests in the goals of the endeavor as well as in how the goals are carried out.

The practice of disguising the lawyer's true interests while manipulating the client to make full disclosure creates an unequal relationship between the lawyer and client. The client becomes dependent on the lawyer in a way that is characteristic of professional-client relationships in medicine and psychiatry, but is not appropriate for the lawyer-client relationship. In medicine and psychological counseling a relationship of dependency with the professional might be necessary to accomplish the purpose of the service. In law it is not.

The purposes of the human services delivered by physicians and psychologists are fundamentally different than the purposes of a lawyer's services. . . .

By entering the professional-client relationship, the client implicitly accepts the broad goals inherent in the definitions of health or normal social functioning developed by the respective human service discipline.

In contrast, entering a lawyer-client relationship does not manifest acceptance of any implied goal or objective. It does not imply a desire for help in changing how the client functions as an individual. The purpose of a lawyer's services is to work in union with a client to solve a problem external to the client, whether the solution requires resolving a dispute, drafting a document, or planning a transaction. The goals of the lawyer-client relationship must be developed and agreed upon in the course of the relationship between the lawyer and client. By focusing on the lawyer's role as a helper, rather than on the lawyer's dual role as a negotiator and a collaborator, the client-centered approach to lawyering does not equip a lawyer to deal with the complexity of the lawyer-client relationship. It does not recognize the client's role as an equal participant in the creation of the relationship and in the implementation of joint decisions.

Alex J. Hurder, *Negotiating the Lawyer-Client Relationship: A Search for Equality and Collaboration*, 44 Buff. L. Rev. 71, 84-88 (1996). For an empirical study of negotiated lawyer-client relationships, see William L.F. Felstiner & Austin Sarat, *Enactments of Power: Negotiating Reality and Responsibility in Lawyer-Client Interactions*, 77 Cornell L. Rev. 1447 (1992).

In a different analysis of lawyer-client inequality, Michelle Jacobs argues that "lawyers, including clinicians using client-centered counseling, and students have continued the traditional silencing of clients. Lawyers limit the client's legal options both by devaluing racial components of a client's legal claim and through cultural ignorance." Michelle S. Jacobs, *People from the Footnotes: The Missing Element in Client-Centered Counseling*, 27 Golden Gate U. L. Rev. 345, 391 (1997). She notes, in particular, that unconscious racism can shape lawyer-client relations in ways that may cause client-centered lawyers to misinterpret client actions and undermine client power.

> The concept of self-fulfilling prophecy can certainly provide illumination in the area of client-centered counseling. The lawyer or student unaware of her own behavior perceives the client to be exhibiting negative behavior. One of the insidious dangers of the self-fulfilling prophecy is that since individuals are

seldom able to monitor their own behavior, they are more likely to attribute negative behavior from the client, not to their own original nonverbal behavior, but instead to some disposition inherent in the client. Presently, except in one isolated area, skills training material devotes no attention to negative nonverbal behaviors that students and white lawyers in general, might be exhibiting toward their clients. Nor, do we have any idea how clients may decode and reciprocate such behavior. . . .

The issue of expectancies on the part of the provider of counseling is quite complicated. Expectancy refers to a belief, hypothesis, theory, assumption or accessible construct that is brought from a previous experience and is used either consciously or unconsciously as a basis for interpreting or generating behavior in the present context. . . .

One of the frequent complaints heard from the students is that the clients seem apathetic. The students feel that they care more about the client's well-being than does the client himself. Yet, the student/lawyer and the physician share the traits of high levels of education and higher socio-economic status. These factors may be producing, in the legal services client, the same level of intimidation that the lower socio-economic patient feels when visiting a doctor. In fact, it is generally accepted, in client-centered counseling material, that clients may be intimidated by the difference in status between the client and the lawyer. . . .

[I]f we can glean anything from the works in other disciplines, it is that such studies could provide lawyers and students interested in client-centered counseling with a wealth of information about how negative nonverbal behavior exhibited by the lawyer and student/lawyer expectancies can influence the nature and quality of the interaction with the client and hamper our ability to give effective representation. . . .

As clinicians teaching client-centered counseling, we must be willing to adjust our approach to counseling methodology to ensure full representation of our clients. Adherence to the client-centered counseling models in their present race neutral constitution have not and can not cure the problem of client-manipulation. Nor, can they provide a solid blueprint for client empowerment, because the clients and their world views are not truly valued within the models. In fact, as previously noted, in many cases, the use of client-centered counseling resulted in further silencing of our clients.

Id. at 380-84, 401. What do you think of Jacobs's claims? Are they a product of the client-centered model or something else?

Muneer Ahmad raises similar questions about lawyering for clients with limited English proficiency (LEP):

The interpreter does not fit comfortably within the structure of even a client-centered lawyer-client relationship. Like the traditional model, the client-centered relationship is still linear, albeit more level. The lawyer's appreciation of her own subject position and that of the client are enhanced, but the fundamental structure of one lawyer, one client remains the same. The strength of the dyadic model as a cultural feature of lawyering encourages lawyers to imagine the role of the interpreter as merely a conduit of information—a piece of technology, such as a telephone—that transmits data from one point to another, achieving "perfect identity" between one language and the other. But the culturally informed, deeply textured nature of language, combined with the interpersonal consequences of the interpreter's presence, belie such a mechanical understanding of how interpreters operate, and expose the fiction of verbatim interpretation. Because interpreters do not merely transmit information, but mediate it as well, the personhood of the interpreter — her own subject position and associated biases and interests — cannot be removed from the process.

Because the interpreter brings her own subjectivity to the enterprise, the singular relationship between lawyer and client is transformed into three distinct relationships: lawyer and interpreter, interpreter and client, and lawyer and client. We might envision these relationships in a triangular formation — a lawyer-interpreter-client triad — that both multiplies and refracts the client-centered concern for power as between lawyer and client. It multiplies this concern in that we must now attend to power not only between lawyer and client, but also between lawyer and interpreter and between client and interpreter. It refracts the concern because nearly all communication between the lawyer and client is necessarily mediated by the interpreter. In this regard, client-centeredness is a useful point of departure for an analysis of the complex nature of the relationships between and among lawyer, client, and interpreter.

For example, the principles of client-centeredness prove useful in selecting an appropriate interpreter. Just as client-centeredness encourages attention to gender as one potential dimension of power disparity in the lawyer-client relationship, a similar attentiveness to the gender dynamic as between client and interpreter may also be appropriate. In our clinic, many female clients who have been victims of sexual violence express a strong preference for a female interpreter, and that preference is generally honored. This is not merely a matter of subjective client preference, but a recognition of how gender subordination has figured into the client's life and may continue to animate and inhibit the lawyer-client relationship.

While such attention to power disparities is highly productive, the conventional tools of client-centeredness do not address the full complexity of lawyering across language difference. In particular, they are inadequate to the task of managing the role complications that result when an interpreter is involved. Unlike in the traditional lawyer-client relationship, in which the regulatory structure of the ethical rules renders lawyer and client roles relatively well-defined and static, the role of the interpreter is often diffuse and dynamic. Interposed between the client and the lawyer, interpreters often assume characteristics of each. Thus, the interpreter may end up answering the lawyer's question, thereby displacing the client and compromising her autonomy, or asking the client questions of his own, thereby displacing the lawyer and diminishing her control. Even if the interpreter's conduct does not fully displace the lawyer or the client, it may situate the interpreter closer to one or the other, either in function or in perception. Moreover, the interpreter's position with respect to the lawyer and the client may vary across time and according to context. Such role confusion is unsurprising in light of the lack of clear guidance on the use of interpreters in the lawyering context, and is especially likely to occur with untrained interpreters.

Just as client-centeredness seeks to mitigate the effects of power disparities between lawyers and clients, as applied to the multiple relationships of LEP representation, it counsels corrections for interpreter distortions as well. Angela McCaffrey has detailed a series of corrective measures that lawyers can take, including how to identify an appropriate interpreter, prepare the interpreter for a client interview, and frame appropriate questions for the client. However, approaches such as these leave unanswered the fundamental question of what role the interpreter should play. Specifically, the question of how a lawyer may construct a perceptual frame that is shared by the client when their relationship is mediated through the subjective experience of another remains unresolved.

Any interpreter role other than a technological one is bound to agitate many lawyers, precisely because the dyadic one-lawyer, one-client norm is so strongly established within the profession. By the traditional account, the lawyer-client relationship does not accommodate the personhood of the interpreter, thus fueling the lawyerly impulse to confine and control the interpreter. The inevitable expression of the interpreter's personhood is likely to be viewed as an unwelcome intrusion, and the lawyer may feel like she is engaged in a power struggle with an unruly subordinate. While the lawyer's desire for control is, in the abstract, understandable, it is unrealistic in light of the linguistic demands of interpretation. Rather than attempt to repudiate the presence of the interpreter, it would be more productive to the ultimate goals of representation — including the client-centered goal of enhancing client autonomy — to embrace the complexity that the involvement of interpreters necessarily brings.

Muneer I. Ahmad, *Interpreting Communities: Lawyering Across Language Difference*, 54 UCLA L. Rev. 999, 1051-53 (2007). How should a client-centered lawyer respond to the challenge of interpretation Ahmad raises? Do any of the other lawyering frameworks we have encountered do a better job dealing with the problem?

3. Systemic Issues

What are the systemic consequences of client-centeredness? Consider William Simon's critique of the Psychological Vision of lawyering (or lawyer "psychologists"), which he associates with clinical education (among other legal movements) and identifies with a client-centered emphasis on serving the "whole client" and advancing the client's psychological needs (autonomy, empowerment, etc.):

> Clinical courses inspired by the Psychological Vision focus on "conflict" and "struggle," but the conflict and struggle do not occur in society. The psychologists are concerned with conflict and struggle not among individuals, but within them. The student learns to "struggle with his feelings" and to deal with "conflicting feelings." He learns to interpret encounters between people in terms of the feelings which they arouse in each other. He studies not social relations, but "interpersonal relations."
>
> The social world, the world in which people act, appears only dimly and randomly. It has neither history nor structure. It is of interest principally insofar as it is reflected through or impinges upon feelings. For the lawyer, the facts which define the social world are a function of the feelings perceived in the community-of-two. . . . In a chapter entitled "Constructing the Case," Gary Bellow and Bea Moulton assert that "to a large extent good facts . . . are often made, not found." They emphasize the extent to which people can be " 'persuade[d]' . . . to recount facts in a way consistent with the outcome [lawyers] desire." They repeatedly urge that lawyering be conceived in terms of metaphors, such as writing fiction, acting in a play, or playing a game, which imply the unreality of the context in which the lawyer acts. . . .

[T]he knowledge of the client's social context . . . is not only irrelevant, but positively destructive of the kind of psychological understanding the lawyer really needs. In order to empathize sufficiently with the client, the lawyer may have to discard relatively impersonal economic and social categories and concepts. There is a moral as well as an epistemological dimension to this point. To some of the psychologists, there is something inhuman about the abstract, the remote, and the relatively impersonal. "Intellectualizing," thinking about the world abstractly, is often taken as a moral failing. Thinking about people abstractly degrades them by stripping them of what makes them human, that is, their feelings. Shaffer writes that a "lawyer may react negatively to his client if he looks at his client in social or economic terms; viewed in this way, the client may be a conventional middle class prig." But by "tun[ing] in to" the client's feelings, the lawyer understands the client as an individual, and this understanding makes possible a more "positive" attitude toward the client, which makes the relation more satisfying to both. Besides being degrading to others, intellectualizing can be a sign, of cowardice or maladjustment on the part of the lawyer. The lawyer concerned with the abstract, the remote, and the impersonal appears unable or afraid to deal with her own and her client's feelings. She may use concepts to block out an emotional reality which frightens and daunts her.

The psychologists' case against the normative and intellectual orientation of the sociological approach is most vigorously advanced by William Pincus, president of the Council on Legal Education for Professional Responsibility. Pincus's ideas appear to have been strongly influenced by his revulsion at the "destructive university protest movement" of the late 1960s. . . . He argues that the proclivity of traditional legal education to "Think Big!" exacerbates "the natural affinity and the need for the young for arrogance." The student who deals with experience "distilled into abstractions" comes to see "[i]ndividuals and their petty lives . . . reduced in size and consequence." Concern with public policy breeds insensitivity to the concerns of individuals. Pincus argues that the policy orientation reflects an "immoral, antidemocratic, and, thank goodness, nonsensical" assumption that law students will inevitably occupy positions of public prominence. In his view, law schools should produce "lawyers," not "policy-makers." To this end, students should be taught that the profession exists "to serve people" rather than to exercise public power. The principal thrust of the proposed clinical curriculum is thus sensitivity to the personal needs of individual clients. . . .

Yet, as mentioned earlier, it is a striking fact that the majority of the theorists and teachers of legal psychologism seem to be politically to the left of center. Indeed, many and perhaps most of them are veterans of the movements which during the Warren Court era challenged the professional vision of lawyering as apolitical: the public interest and legal services movements. The connection between the clinical versions of psychologism and the legal services movement is particularly striking. A large number of the teachers in the clinical programs came to law teaching from legal services practice. Moreover, many of these programs have provided for students to work for academic credit in legal services offices under the supervision of legal services practitioners. To some extent the explanation of this phenomenon seems to lie in the decline of the public interest and legal services movements. The period of dramatic growth in the clinical movement of the late 1960s and early 1970s coincided with a period of rightward drift in American politics and of growing frustration and demoralization among liberal activist lawyers. For the activists, the disappointments of practice must have come not from the discovery that law-yering was political, but from the discovery of the tension and difficulty of politics. In this climate, the clinical movement became one of the most attrac-tive escape routes from public interest and legal services practice. A majority of the rapidly growing number of clinical teaching jobs went to lawyers leaving this kind of practice. The Psychological Vision thus appears a product not so much of the legal services and public interest practice, as of the abandonment of this kind of practice.

William H. Simon, *Homo Psychologicus: Notes on a New Legal Formalism*, 32 STAN. L. REV. 487, 508, 510-11, 555-56 (1980). Do you agree with Simon? Does client-centeredness represent a retreat from politics? Is it possible to teach students to be client-centered in the poverty law context but expect them not to be client-centered when they take jobs with law firms representing powerful corporate clients? Is it desirable? Is this even a problem that proponents of client-centeredness should care about?

V. COMMUNITY LAWYERING

A. CONCEPT AND VARIATIONS

The client-centered lawyering model is the foundation for understanding lawyer-client relations within clinical legal education. And because of the strong connection between clinical education and public interest lawyering, the model has deeply influenced the practice of public interest lawyers. *See generally* Margaret Martin Barry, Jon C. Dubin & Peter A. Joy, *Clinical Edu-cation for This Millennium: The Third Wave*, 7 CLINICAL L. REV. 1, 13-14 (2000); *see also* Chapter 8. As the last section noted, the client-centered model fits com-fortably with both conventional lawyering and conceptions of cause lawyering that emphasize the autonomy-enhancing representation of individual poor clients. But what happens when the goal of lawyering is not just enhancing autonomy to realize individual goals but building power to change society? And what if that goal extends beyond the individual client to an entire community—understood either in terms of place or identity? What does this type of community lawyering look like? What should it look like? This section explores the elements of community lawyering, points of intersection and tension with other lawyering concepts we have encountered so far, and the benefits and challenges of this approach.

We begin by noting the intellectual and practical origins of community lawyering and highlighting its conceptual breadth. Although community law-yering resonates with and builds upon examples explored throughout this book—from grassroots versions of civil rights lawyering to community eco-nomic development—it grew out of clinical education and can be understood in relation to discussions about practice generated in that space. The notion of community lawyering has affinities with both cause and client-centered law-yering, but asserts both a unique conception of cause—one rooted in building community power—and how it should be achieved through client relations.

See Anthony V. Alfieri, *Fidelity to Community: A Defense of Community Lawyering*, 90 Tex. L. Rev. 635 (2012); Karen Tokarz, Nancy L. Cook, Susan Brooks & Brenda Bratton Blom, *Conversations on "Community Lawyering": The Newest (Oldest) Wave in Clinical Legal Education*, 28 J.L. & Pol'y 359 (2008). At bottom, community lawyering accepts the core principles of client-centeredness: enlisting the client in active problem solving, empowering the client to make decisions, and taking account of legal and nonlegal impacts of problems. These principles are extended from the individual client to community level. "[C]ommunity lawyering involves formal or informal collaborations with client communities and community groups to identify and address client community issues. It assumes a community perspective in the consideration of legal problems." Tokarz et al., *supra*, at 363. This collaborative approach is directed toward the goals of "empowering communities, promoting economic and social justice, and fostering systemic change." *Id.* at 364.

Yet, as these descriptions suggest, community lawyering also rests on critiques of both the client-centered and cause lawyering models. It rejects the client-centered focus on individual dispute resolution, instead seeking broad social change. Yet it also rejects the top-down approach of (some versions of) cause lawyering in favor of a model that is deeply embedded in and sensitive to a community's definition of problems and solutions. In this regard, community lawyering moves beyond the critique of impact litigation leveled by Bell and others to highlight the potential for lawyer domination of poor clients in everyday poverty law settings, in which lawyers either misunderstand client concerns through the prism of class and race, or are too busy or jaded to give them full attention. This is also a theme in client-centered lawyering, from which the community lawyering literature springs, but for community lawyering advocates, the specter of client domination takes on a more central theoretical role.

> [The early clinical scholarship on lawyering] largely assumed that lawyering entails three main activities: (1) litigating claims before adjudicatory bodies, (2) negotiating claims or agreements, usually with or against other attorneys, and (3) counseling clients with respect to decisions that arise in the course of litigation, negotiation, or transactional planning. Despite their characterization of lawyering as fundamentally a process of helping clients solve problems, Binder, Bergman, and Price consistently assumed that lawyers only work on "cases." Neither their work nor the other lawyering literature has fully addressed the significance of the difference between formulating the lawyer's concern narrowly as a "case" or more broadly as a "problem." . . .
>
> In the late 1980's and early 1990's, a new stream of scholarship, specifically focused on the representation of lower-income clients, gained prominence in the literature on lawyering. This literature has been produced primarily by clinical law teachers, reflecting on lawyering experiences. Most of these reflections focus on the authors' own lawyering before joining clinical academia, rather than their clinics' representation of clients. . . .
>
> These scholars share a sense that prevailing lawyering practices disserve lower-income clients. Their individual visions arise largely from a critique of the power attorneys exercise, often unthinkingly, over their lower-income clients. They note that lawyers' practices are unwittingly grounded in, and perpetuate, pejorative conceptions of lower-income people as subordinate,

dependent, and helpless. They focus on how lawyers often see these clients as victims in need of rescue, rather than potential partners in solving their own problems. These scholars often depict attorneys' failures to appreciate clients' goals of preserving dignity and maintaining some control over the manner in which they are depicted in the course of advocacy. The authors value and extol clients' active participation in individual and collective efforts to make themselves heard and to act against their own oppression.

Ascanio Piomelli, *Appreciating Collaborative Lawyering*, 6 CLINICAL L. REV. 427, 438-39 (2000).

From this perspective, proponents of community lawyering challenge public interest lawyers to be more contemplative about their practice and the way they interact with clients so as to avoid—deliberately or inadvertently—substituting their own views. This is important not just to arrive at the appropriate outcome of cases, but also to build client community capacity, ultimately equipping community members with the skills and agency to change the broader power structures that frame their lives. As we saw in the last chapter, a key goal (in Lucie White's terms) is to use lawyering to change the consciousness of subordinated groups—the "third dimension" of power—so that they can fight for change on their own terms.

> On the first dimension [of power] is advocacy which seeks to make the positive law more responsive to the social welfare needs of socially disempowered groups. This dimension encompasses three familiar forms of public interest lawyering: litigation to expand welfare entitlements or improve welfare administration; lobbying to increase resources or improve programs; and monitoring the work of administrative agencies to enhance procedural fairness. On the second dimension is advocacy which seeks to transform values in dominant cultures so as to encourage greater sensitivity to the injustices poor people face, greater respect for their life projects, and a clearer will to mobilize public resources on their behalf. On this dimension, the trial or legislative session becomes an educational or theatrical event that is designed to move its audiences to empathize with poor people and form political coalitions with them.
>
> On the third dimension is advocacy that is focused on poor people's own political consciousness. Its goal is not to change either social policy or elite attitudes toward the poor. Rather, "third dimensional" advocacy seeks to enable poor people to see themselves and their social situation in ways that enhance their world-changing powers. At the same time, lawyering on the third dimension seeks to change the attitudes and self-concepts of lawyers themselves. This work seeks to transform our own political identities, relationships, and commitments, enabling us to work more effectively with historically subordinated groups to achieve social justice.
>
> On the third dimension, lawyering is no longer a unidirectional "professional service." Rather, it is a collaborative communicative practice. This practice demands strategic innovation and critical reflection—about the forces that condition poor people's subordination, as well as the ways they might resist and even redirect those forces to achieve justice. Through such action and reflection, poor people and their lawyer-allies voice aspirations, identify concrete action strategies, and discover grounds for political unity.

Lucie E. White, *Community Lawyering in the Field? On Mapping the Paths from Rhetoric to Practice*, 1 CLINICAL L. REV. 157, 157-58 (1994); *see also* Lucie E. White, *To Learn and Teach: Lessons from Driefontein on Lawyering and Power*, 1988 WIS. L. REV. 699 (hereinafter, White, *Driefontein*). White's description highlights another aspect of community lawyering, which is a shift in perspective in the types of skills that lawyers can effectively use to advance community goals. Rather than focusing on traditional legal work, community lawyering proponents suggested that advocacy to empower communities required a broader range of problem-solving skills to promote organizing and other types of political mobilization.

As the discussion so far suggests, the concept of community lawyering is capacious, providing space for different ideas about what type of work lawyers should do to promote community goals (and what those goals should be). Thus, community lawyering includes "a range of different practice areas, including workers' rights, immigration, children's rights, public benefits, environmental rights, community economic development, and intellectual property," and a variety of "types of work, ranging from litigation to administrative practice, mediation and dispute resolution to community education and legislative advocacy to transactional work and community economic development." Tokarz et al., *supra*, at 362-63; *see also* Susan D. Bennett, *On Long-Haul Lawyering*, 25 FORDHAM URB. L.J. 771 (1998). In part because of contestation over its basic terms, commentators have given a variety of different names to what we are calling "community lawyering" here—most notably Gerald López's "rebellious lawyering," Lucie White's "collaborative" and "third dimensional" lawyering, and Anthony Alfieri's "reconstructive poverty lawyering." GERALD P. LÓPEZ, REBELLIOUS LAWYERING: ONE CHICANO'S VISION OF PROGRESSIVE LAW PRACTICE (1992) [hereinafter, LÓPEZ, REBELLIOUS LAWYERING]; Anthony V. Alfieri, *The Antinomies of Poverty Law and a Theory of Dialogic Empowerment*, 16 N.Y.U. REV. L. & SOC. CHANGE 659 (1988); Anthony V. Alfieri, *Reconstructive Poverty Law Practice: Learning Lessons of Client Narrative*, 100 YALE L.J. 2107 (1991); Lucie E. White, *Mobilization on the Margins of the Lawsuit: Making Space for Clients to Speak*, 16 N.Y.U. REV. L. & SOC. CHANGE 535 (1987-88); White, *Driefontein, supra*; Lucie E. White, *Subordination, Rhetorical Survival Skills, and Sunday Shoes: Notes on the Hearing of Mrs. G.*, 38 BUFF. L. REV. 1 (1990). Although these ideas share basic premises, they are not the same and you should consider differences in the materials that follow. We use "community lawyering" as an admittedly imperfect shorthand to emphasize the embeddedness of the lawyer in community concerns and her efforts to collaborate with clients to challenge pervasive social and economic marginalization. How do different versions of community lawyering understand the lawyer's cause? How do they propose that lawyers approach client relations? What are the tensions you observe?

To illustrate different aspects of the community lawyering model, we draw on foundational early works in the field. Gerald López's path-breaking book, REBELLIOUS LAWYERING, has been widely influential both among academics and public interest practitioners. In the excerpt below, López writes about a fictional law student named Catharine, who is exploring the world of public interest lawyering and trying to figure out how to be both effective and true to her understanding of the lawyer's role. The following segments describe Catharine's experiences discussing lawyering with three different types of public interest lawyers. This first excerpt describes Teresa, an attorney with Advocates for Justice, a nonprofit organization that emphasizes impact litigation advocating for a variety of different progressive social causes. This section describes the way that Teresa relates to and interacts with the clients in her cases.

> Catharine discovered, to her surprise . . . that Advocates for Justice often seeks out litigants to fit cases it has designed in advance, cases that strategically introduce sensitive social issues into the courts. In this search, Teresa seems to assume both that client groups perceive that they suffer injuries which can be redressed and that they are willing to share these perceptions with a lawyer. In turn, she takes it upon herself to coach the client groups to frame their interests in a frame the law can process. Reluctantly, she must sometimes turn away otherwise worthy plaintiffs in the interest of finding the right test case. Catharine was most taken aback when she learned that Teresa must occasionally look for facts that aren't typical of the group she hopes to represent in order to present a more appealing case.
>
> Teresa, says Catharine, is most comfortable taking cases on behalf of Latino clients; she claims she "always knows what they want." Still, Teresa never does any "direct service" kind of work anymore. And she repeatedly insists that, while the organizations and community groups that work with Latinos probably do good things, they're not all that useful to her legal work. Once or twice they have helped find a client for Teresa to use in a test case and, on occasion, have joined in on a press conference. But that's the only sort of interaction that goes on between them. Catharine couldn't understand why Advocates for Justice disregards groups that seemed to her fundamentally important to a lawyer's work. . . .
>
> Teresa accepts educating test-case clients about their upcoming role in the litigation process as part of her responsibility as a lawyer. Once she has recruited appropriate and willing litigants she makes certain that each wants to be a test case. Though she believes their individual lives will be affected by the result, she does not delude them. She makes plain the broad social rather than individual orientation of test cases. She explains that the cases are highly technical actions and that clients don't have to worry about investing much of their time and energy. That's the attorney's job, and that's the way it should be. She believes that most of her clients would rather defer to her expertise anyway. "After all," she told Catharine, "why shouldn't the poor have the same opportunity as the rich to have a lawyer who takes care of their legal problems for them?" Besides, involving members of the client group may cause delay and make things "too messy."
>
> From the beginning of a relationship with a client, Teresa's practices bring to life and reinforce her general sense of how things should operate. She poses specific questions aimed at filling in factual detail and tells clients that she'll get in touch if more information is necessary. Catharine has realized that Teresa never gives much thought to preparing clients for the experience of media-covered litigation—the contrast between the excitement and the

attention of the initial filing, on the one hand, and the uncertainty and invisibility of the long period, usually years, during which the case works its way through the court system, on the other. Because of time pressure, the special expertise necessary, and the broad social purposes of the case, Teresa hardly ever asks clients to help gather information, read materials, or study the law; to take part in planning, preparing, or attending meetings about the drafting of the complaint; to help frame and critique the stories she will be telling on the clients' behalf; or to think about including their friends and supporters as part of anything other than the media show that the lawyer scripts, produces, and directs.

In fact, as far as Catharine can tell, after the filing of the complaint and often throughout the entire trial and appeals process, the client nearly vanishes. Teresa busily researches, prepares, and deposes witnesses; requests and responds to interrogatories; and researches and writes detailed memoranda of points and authority. The client is to stay busy with his own life (Teresa says clients already feel overwhelmed anyway), fully appreciate that the lawyer works better with fewer interruptions, stand ready if Teresa needs him to testify at trial, and find ways to deal with any uncertainties or doubts. If he loses, the client hasn't been prepared at all for what to do. If he wins, the client is usually happy but often remains mystified about how it happened and what the lawyer did.

Id. at 14-16.

In contrast with Teresa, Abe works in a small, union-side labor law firm.

. . . Abe and his colleagues do nearly all the legal work that unions generate: They provide legal advice; negotiate collective bargaining agreements; represent the union in arbitration and proceedings before the National Labor Relations Board (usually against the employer, but sometimes against workers who sue the union for breach of the duty of fair representation); manage the pension fund; and litigate as it becomes necessary and if it doesn't swallow up too much of the firm's limited resources. The firm once did a fair amount of wrongful termination work for non-union workers but over the years decreased this part of the practice because it wasn't very profitable.

Everyone has his place in the labor movement, says Abe, and his is to lend his professional legal expertise. Typically, Catharine has found, Abe gets a call from the president of the union, who explains the union's problem, the union's objective, and the kind of work he'd like the firm to do. The two spend some time together working through some strategic options, and then Abe (actually, one of his associates) researches and writes the memo, brief, or proposal for negotiation. Then before a negotiation or board proceeding, Abe sits down with the union leaders to discuss the law, to fine-tune strategy, or to prepare witnesses. Occasionally Abe presses leadership on views and positions, but the structure of the relationship more routinely leaves those matters to "union discretion." When all is said and done, Abe finds himself regularly doing almost exactly what union leadership wants. . . . That doesn't seem to bother Abe much, though. His general philosophy is that unions *should* run the labor movement. That's their expertise and they are his clients. . . .

Catharine . . . attended a reproductive rights workshop in a unionized factory held at the request of several of the women of color who made up a large percentage of the employees. Halfway through the workshop, a white male union representative burst in and told the young woman who was making the presentation to leave, insisting that the union "had its own education program, thank you, and these women didn't need outsiders stirring things up." When Catharine told Abe what had happened, he shook his head and said that unfortunately things like that did sometimes occur. He used to try to tackle those attitudes head-on, he said, but they now seemed so entrenched that he had just given up. . . .

Catharine found that Abe has never contemplated working with the union to survey the needs and concerns of workers about day-to-day work life, to set up worker support groups, or to discuss strategies for structural change of the workplace. . . . As he sees it, the union leadership doesn't pay his law firm to participate in this kind of legally tangential work. . . .

Abe, like Teresa, seems to dismiss, or maybe never even notices, opportunities for collaboration with others. For example, he doesn't seem to think it necessary to work together with others in the community who are interested in labor issues. . . . Not only do other groups focus too much on non-legal problems, he says, but collaborating with these groups would not be the most efficient and profitable use of his firm's limited time and resources. Anyway, he doesn't want to alienate his clients. Union leadership is often hostile to groups that focus undue attention on the status of women, Latinos, African Americans, Asian Americans, Native Americans, gays and lesbians.

Once again (and in this instance all the more ironically), Catharine found herself with a lawyer who gives no thought to his own law firm as a workplace, particularly to the well-defined status and wage positions of distinct groups within the firm (namely, partners, associates, fellows, secretaries, and other support staff); to the work demands placed on each group; or to the amount of sick leave, vacation, and flex time, The firm's fellowship program, about which Abe was once justifiably proud, now seems simply a cheaper and more convenient way of getting associate work without paying associate rates and without having to promise permanent employment. . . .

Id. at 17-20.

Jonathan is a legal aid lawyer who represents clients in housing cases.

Jonathan is 29, thoroughly committed to helping poor people, and zealous in his dislike of those strongly implicated in their oppression — welfare bureaucrats, landlords, and the like. He feels overwhelmed by the number of people who come into his office with housing problems. Most of them face evictions that cannot be legally prevented. . . . [B]ecause of the sheer numbers involved, he told Catharine he has to accept clients by the "triage" method, selecting the healthiest cases for representation but commiserating with those who have no defense.

Jonathan sees part of his mission as educating the community about housing law: He does this in several ways. With those he cannot help, Catharine has often seen him spend time explaining in plain, lay language what has happened to them, how they can try to forestall eviction for a few days, and how to avoid having this happen to them again. With cases that he does accept for representation, he always takes time with the client (usually right before settlement) to make sure that the client understands her or his legal rights, the legal issues in the case, and what to do if faced again with an eviction (usually to get to a lawyer as quickly as possible). . . . But because of time pressure and, frankly, his own low opinion about the good sense or intelligence of some of his clients, he hardly ever asks them to help him gather information, to identify and choose among strategies, to read the materials he prepares for them, to look at the law, to help fill out any of the forms, to take part in (much less lead) meetings and negotiations. . . .

Jonathan's strategy with most of the cases he accepts is to exploit every procedural tactic he can think of, and time and time again he wins on a "technicality": an error in the three-day notice or a problem with the service of the complaint. He is well aware, however, that the landlord can ultimately outlast him and find some legal reason to evict the tenant, especially if the tenant is having a hard time paying rent. So, most of the cases end in settlements, whereby the landlord agrees to allow the tenant to stay in the apartment or to reduce the rent if the apartment is a mess. . . . Most clients, he says, are happy with a negotiated settlement and feel that they finally beat their landlords out of something. But to Catharine they often seemed mystified about what their lawyer actually did for them. She wondered if they weren't returning to apartments that looked very much like they did before they started complaining, and how on earth that must feel.

Jonathan's general philosophy is that it is his job to help as many people as he can avoid the hardship and suffering of being evicted, harassed by their landlords, or forced to live in substandard housing. For many reasons he tends to work alone, even apart from the attorneys in his own office. . . . He has only minimal contacts with other social service groups in the community or with other people in the community who are interested in housing issues. In fact, Catharine discovered that he wasn't even aware of some of the groups she consistently made contact with on the advice of her clients.

The chief reason that Jonathan gives for his isolation is that he is overworked and that there isn't much going on in the community anyway. In fact, the more hours he puts in just doing straight casework, the more helpful (and beleaguered) he feels. When Catharine told him about a tenants' union that a former client wanted to start in his building, Jonathan told her that while he once believed in developing tenants' groups . . . he no longer thinks that mobilizing others is an efficient way for him to spend his time. Moreover, he gets a lot of personal satisfaction out of helping people out of jams. As his understanding of the difficulty of "solving" poor peoples' problems has developed, he has become resigned that nothing much can be done except to make their lives a little bit more bearable, to win them money when it can be done, and to make landlords think twice before they (openly) "mess with" his clients and former clients. . . .

Catherine noticed that, once Jonathan had agreed to take a case, he almost always worked on it independently from the client. The more she saw, the more she realized that the only real contact he has with the client comes when he calls to get some more information for the petition/complaint and when he comes out to take pictures of the apartment for the hearing. . . . He does not involve the client in any substantive way in preparing the case, nor does he do much to find out if other tenants in the building face the same problems. At the hearing, Jonathan gives and opening and a closing statement and does all of the talking to the examiner. The client sits quietly until the lawyer examines her or him, producing information and documents on cue. Although Jonathan knows (and sometimes even comments to Catharine) that he tends to treat his clients like 8 year olds, and that he would not act this way if he were representing a business-person, he justifies his actions by thinking how much more time it would take if he had to involve the client in all the decisions, in all the basic work that goes into preparing for a hearing.

Id. at 20-23.

What different approaches to the lawyer-client relationship are illuminated by each of these profiles? In what ways do Teresa, Abe, and Jonathan work with their clients in similar ways? In what ways are they different? López uses these narratives to illustrate an approach to lawyering that he concludes is common in the public interest community, particularly among those lawyers representing subordinated persons. He labels this type of approach "regnant lawyering," and defines it by the following characteristics:

- Lawyers "formally represent" others.
- Lawyers choose between "service" work (resolving individual problems) and "impact work" (advancing systemic reforms), largely dichotomous categories.
- Lawyers set up their offices to facilitate formal representation in service or impact work. Lawyers litigate more than they do anything else.
- Lawyers understand "community education" as a label for diffuse, marginal, and uncritical work (variations on the canned "after dinner talk about law"), and "organizing" as a catchword for sporadic, supplemental mobilization (variations on sit-ins, sit-downs, and protests).
- Lawyers consider themselves the preeminent problem-solvers in most situations they find themselves trying to alter.
- Lawyers connect only loosely to other institutions or groups in their communities, and almost always these connections focus on lawyers' use of institutions or groups for some aspect of a case in which they serve as formal representatives.
- Lawyers have only a modest grasp on how large structures — regional, national and international, political, economic, and cultural — shape and respond to challenges to the status quo.
- Lawyers suspect that subordination of all sorts cyclically recreates itself in certain subcultures, thereby preventing people from helping themselves and taking advantage of many social services and educational opportunities.
- Lawyers believe that subordination can be successfully fought if professionals, particularly lawyers, assume leadership in pro-active campaigns that sometimes "involve" the subordinated.
- Lawyers do not know and try little to learn whether and how formal changes in law penetrate the lives of subordinated people.
- Lawyers understand their profession as an honorable calling and see themselves as aesthetic if not political heroes, working largely alone to make statements through *their* (more than their clients') cases about society's injustices.

Id. at 24. Compare this list of characteristics to the features of client-centered lawyering articulated by Binder, Bergman, and Price, *supra*. Is regnant lawyering consistent with or in tension with client-centered lawyering goals? Or are López's descriptions simply a critique of poorly executed client-centered lawyering?

López suggests that the regnant model of lawyering constrains public interest practice in ways that limit the effectiveness of practitioners' efforts to address client problems.

The regnant idea does not acknowledge the connection between different forms of practical know-how inevitably at work in each and every person's effort to get by day to day. And it does not facilitate, much less coordinate, responses to problems that originate outside its understanding of the social world. When all is said and done, the regnant idea of the lawyer for the subordinated helps undermine the very possibility for re-imagined social arrangements that lies at the heart of any serious effort to take on the status quo. In so doing, it wastes the very excellence it sometimes displays and reduces itself to another kind of bondage to formula.

Id. at 29.

López goes on to suggest that this regnant model of lawyering has become deeply embedded in the legal and social culture of those involved in public interest lawyering on behalf of subordinated groups, such that it often goes unnoticed even by those deeply affected by its practice: lawyers, clients and community groups, and professionals and lay people in the community who routinely interact with these clients (e.g., social workers, government administrators, community organizers). These constituencies work under this model because it is what they have come to expect. Lawyers learn it from their formal professional training in law school and their experience working with other attorneys. Clients learn it from watching the way that lawyers treat them and expect them to conduct themselves. López's work has attempted to raise the consciousness of lawyers and law students to help them imagine different ways to organize their practices, relate to their clients and others they routinely work with, and address the broader, structural problems that burden the lives of those who live in subordinated communities.

In trying to help law students and lawyers envision what a rebellious practice would look like, López included in his work the profiles of Sophie and Amos, two lawyers who represent a very different approach to practice than Teresa, Abe, and Jonathan. Here is Sophie's story:

> Sophie works out of the neighborhood center of a legal aid organization, under the auspices of its Immigration Project. Though other attorneys are involved with the project, she is the only one housed in her particular office. She is in her mid-30s, one of ten red-headed Irish Catholic kids in her family. . . . Originally from the Midwest, she now says that she and her family are in California for good. She certainly fits in out here. She speaks great Spanish (a few years ago, she told Catharine, she and her husband spent some time in Mexico assisting start-up worker cooperatives and just traveling around), and she's just about the most down-to-earth person Catharine has ever met. A real "granola head," you might say.
>
> Sophie lives in the neighborhood where she works, and to Catharine that appears to make all the difference in the world. The community is a small one of predominately low-income people, largely of color, part of the metropolitan mosaic that is Oakland. Getting stuck in the role of permanent outsider is a real possibility here—this community has had more than its share of so-called friends flitting in and out trying to make changes. Yet Sophie lives just a few blocks from where she works. She walks to her office each morning and gets her lunch from *La Frontera* (the local taco truck) nearly every day. She has been an active and interested resident throughout the three years she has lived and worked in the community. She and her husband are members of the local

Tenants' Council, and they regularly attend as well as help organize and support community events. Their son is in the first grade at the local elementary school, and they participate in the school's Parent Support Network.

Living in her neighborhood is not all cheery or romantic, though. Like everyone else, Sophie has to watch out for her safety. She has to put up with a local library that is small and understaffed. She has no neighborhood park to take her son to on the weekends, no nearby recreation center where he can play with other kids. She has to travel a long way to get to the bank, or even to a sizable grocery store. With everyone else, she has to fight for more resources in local schools. She has to challenge Pacific Gas & Electric rate hikes seemingly every quarter. And she constantly has to battle with the local rent board to get the rent-control ordinance enforced.

Sophie always has things going on all burners. Even so, she is remarkably good at following through on the commitments she makes. Take her work with a group of immigrant families in her community. The group started out with some parents who individually sought Sophie's advice. They each had taken advantage of the 1986 Immigration Reform and Control Act (IRCA) to become legal residents of this country. But their children remained ineligible to apply for legal status because they arrived after 1982 and therefore hadn't been in the United States for the duration of time required by IRCA. Organizational efforts by both Sophie and these parents have slowly disclosed a number of families with children in the same precarious position. An immigration paralegal from another organization put the group in touch with a Bay Area alliance that's part of a broader-based national coalition trying to mobilize and lobby around this issue. Meanwhile, the group members meet regularly on their own, too, not only to plan strategies but also to help each other cope with the ever-present fear that their children will be discovered and subjected to deportation.

. . . Sophie does indeed appreciate litigation as a strategy and sometimes helps people in her community pursue individual claims—through federal and state court, administrative hearings, and small claims court proceedings. Even when she's helping out with this litigation, and certainly in the rest of her work, she systematically tries to encourage local people to share experiences and to develop the know-how that will enable them to better anticipate and address their needs over time. She seems to look for opportunities in what others experience only as routines.

During the opening months of the legalization program, for example, Sophie spent a great deal of time helping a paralegal from her office develop a group workshop model for processing claims and then train lay volunteers to staff the workshops. At the beginning, Sophie told Catharine, she was challenged and criticized by other lawyers in her office for spending so much time on these "high-octane ideas" that don't get much work done. As it turned out, the Immigration Project was able to assist far more applicants than it could have if each claim had required individual appointments, so the other lawyers begrudgingly acknowledged the value of her efforts. Sometimes they even praised her. At the same time, as Sophie had hoped, participants were not only more involved with their cases than they probably would have been otherwise, but they also developed bonds with one another that have endured long past the filing of their claims.

But, for Sophie, establishing opportunities for people to help themselves and others isn't limited to imaginative case processing. She keeps a constant watch, often spending a lot of time outside of her office, for news of efforts that she can learn from and contribute to. When she heard about a group of recently documented women who wanted to start a housekeeping cooperative, for example, she let them know through a mutual friend that she'd be interested in working with them—offering them what she knew from her own earlier experiences in Mexico and getting a chance to learn from this kind of entrepreneurial effort here in the United States. Such overtures don't often pan out, as Sophie herself told Catherine, but this time those women really hit it off. Together they got the cooperative started, assembled a modest handbook about cooperatives as an organizational arrangement, and put on a series of workshops sharing their own experiences with other housekeepers in the Bay Area. . . .

Before Sophie started working, "staff meetings" entailed a kind of ad hoc case review for lawyers. At Sophie's insistence, these meetings now include all members of the staff and sometimes a broader agenda. For the first time, discussions have touched on intake procedures, file maintenance, and scheduling—what used to be thought of as the concerns of only the secretaries and the receptionist. And when it is Sophie's turn to run the rotating "Free Time" portion of the staff meetings (which she also implemented), she and Irma make the most of the opportunity, introducing recent immigration and labor market studies, and offering practical examples of how to incorporate self-help and community education into legal work. . . .

Id. at 30-33.

Amos's story is much different from the rest. While he is trained as a lawyer and spent time as a public defender and legal aid attorney, he works for a new nonprofit organization that seeks to respond to the lack of governmental and private resources and services for children and families in a poor community. The organization was initiated with this fairly broad goal, and hired Amos to undertake a systematic assessment of the community's needs before developing a strategy. Amos's efforts start with the development of an open-ended needs assessment survey that he uses to find out what's going on in community members' lives. Unlike many lawyers, his work emphasizes going out into the community and building relationships with the people who live and work there, sorting through the bureaucracy to help coordinate the limited services available, and thinking creatively about how to attract more resources into the community. *Id.* at 34-37.

Sophie and Amos represent lawyers who structure their practice under López's rebellious lawyering model. He describes this practice as follows:

In this idea—what I call the rebellious idea of lawyering against subordination—lawyers must know how to work with (not just on behalf of) women, low income people, people of color, gays and lesbians, the disabled and the elderly. They must know how to collaborate with other professional and lay allies rather than ignoring the help that these other problem-solvers may provide in a given situation. They must understand how to educate those with whom they work, particularly about law and professional lawyering and at the same time they must open themselves up to being educated by all those with whom they come in contact particularly about the traditions and experiences of life on the bottom and at the margins.

To move in these directions, those who would "lawyer rebelliously" must, like Sophie and Amos, ground their work in the lives and in the communities of the subordinated themselves, whether they work for local outfits, regional offices, or national policymaking agencies. They must, like Sophie and Amos, continually evaluate the likely interaction between legal and "non-legal" approaches to problems. They must, like Sophie and Amos, know how to work with others in brainstorming, designing, and executing strategies aimed at responding immediately to particular problems and, more generally, at fighting social and political subordination. They must understand how to be part of coalitions, as well as how to build them, and not just for purposes of filing or "proving up" a lawsuit (as Teresa, Abe or Jonathan might do). They must appreciate how all that they do with others requires attention not only to international, national, and regional matters but also to their interplay with seemingly more mundane local affairs. At bottom, the rebellious idea of law-yering demands that lawyers (and those with whom they work) nurture sensibilities and skills compatible with a collective fight for social change.

Id. at 37-38.

———————————

Compare López's account of rebellious lawyering with the following exchange between Anthony Alfieri and Lucie White. Do they describe the same problems as López? Are their approaches to solving problems consistent? What is their disagreement?

> I met Mrs. Celeste in the neighborhood legal aid office where I used to work. She told me this story over the five years I helped represent her in a food stamp case. In the years since, I often have revisited the story to gather lessons of lawyering for my teaching and to settle doubts which arose later when those lessons were tested by clients, colleagues, students, and my own research. What I have discovered is that the story Mrs. Celeste told is not the story I originally heard nor the one I told in advocacy.
>
> Mrs. Celeste, a divorced Hispanic foster parent, was a long time food stamp recipient dependent on public assistance for survival. As a consequence of a state food stamp reduction and economic need, she was forced to reallocate her public assistance income to pay rent and purchase food and clothing. The reallocation caused her twice to forego payment of gas and electricity until the local utility discontinued her service, at which time she sought emergency assistance. In short, Mrs. Celeste's story is about state-sanctioned impoverishment. . . .
>
> This Essay is a study of interpretive practices in the context of the lawyer-client relation in an impoverished urban community. Within that social text, lawyer and client wage an interpretive struggle. The struggle is violent. Voices are silenced and stories are forgotten. The voices silenced are the voices of clients. The stories forgotten are the stories of client self-empowerment.
>
> Story forms the core of the lawyer-client relation in the practice of poverty law. Located within this core are competing lawyer and client narratives containing opposing meanings and images of the client's world. Sometimes lawyer narratives speak of the client in terms of independence and power. More often, the narratives describe the client in the language of dependency and powerlessness.
>
> The dominance of the narrative meanings and images of client dependency in lawyer storytelling brings rational order to poverty law practice. The order is expressed in well-defined lawyer-client roles, tactics, and strategies. Such order is crucial given the extraordinary number of clients served by the practice.

What is communicated, both publicly and privately, is a vision of the world constructed by lawyer-spoken narratives. Omitted from this vision is an alternative set of meanings and images articulated by client narratives. In this respect, the order of poverty law practice depends on interpretive omission.

My thesis is that situated outside lawyer-told client story is an alternative client story composed of multiple narratives, each speaking in a different voice of the client. The different voices of client narratives imbue client story with normative meanings associated with values such as selfhood, family, community, love, and work. In this view, client story presents a rich text of interwoven voices and narratives. In poverty law advocacy, the integrity of client story stems from the revelation and integration of client voices and narratives in lawyer storytelling. When the client's voices are silenced and her narratives are displaced by the lawyer's narratives, client integrity is tarnished and client story is lost. . . .

The story of [my client] Mrs. Celeste and the voices of her narratives furnish a social text for studying the poverty lawyer's interpretive practices. The lessons of this text are singular to Mrs. Celeste and should not be extrapolated to construct an essentialist vision of the voices and narratives of impoverished clients. The starting point is Mrs. Celeste's initial interview with me at a legal aid office on the morning of welfare intake. Upset by the interrogation of the intake interview, Mrs. Celeste told her story hesitantly, often speeding up, halting suddenly, alternating subjects, then doubling back. This oblique style of telling intertwined the constitutive narratives of her story. . . .

Subordination [occurs through] interpretive violence. . . . [I]t holds firm to the image of client dependence and inferiority. By means of subordination, the lawyer objectifies that image, transmuting the client into an object, a thing to be handled, manipulated, and remolded. This practice silences client narratives of struggle by superimposing lawyer narratives. Manifested by hierarchy, subordination imposes subject-object relations between lawyer and client. Hierarchy institutionalizes the transformation of the private subject seeking help into the public object: "client." . . .

[An] alternative vision affirms the client's ability to muster and assert power both in the lawyer-client relation and in associated legal settings, such as welfare offices, administrative hearings, and courts. Because each client is different, the assertion of power is distinctive in each case. For Mrs. Celeste, the twice-asserted demand for an emergency assistance grant is one form of power. Her insistence on the court-ordered increase of her granddaughter's child support payments is a second form. Her request for an administrative hearing to halt the reduction of her family's food stamps is a third form, and her sharing information with other foster parents about her effort to challenge the reduction in a lawsuit is a fourth.

Specific to each form is a substantive assertion of power tailored expressly to the context in which Mrs. Celeste found herself. When the context switched (for example, from welfare office to foster parent meeting), the substance of her assertion changed. Mrs. Celeste's ability to adjust her assertion to combat the fluctuating aggressions of impoverishment in public and private life is a mark of an empowering subject. That mark is available to the poverty lawyer in client voices and narratives. But as Mrs. Celeste's demands for emergency assistance grants demonstrate, the incidents of power recounted by the client may seem mundane and even redundant to the lawyer.

The client's daily struggle to assert power enables her to resist depictions of dependence and inferiority. In the case of Mrs. Celeste, her struggle materialized in commonplace acts of dignity, caring, community, and rights. Unnoticed in the routine spaces of her public and private life, these acts symbolized alternative forms of knowledge, practices of discourse, and models of individual and collective social action. The experience of daily struggle is the bond connecting client knowledge, discourse, and action.

Alfieri, *Reconstructive Poverty Law Practice, supra,* at 2110, 2118-19, 2122, 2128, 2133-34.

Several theorists, all of them thoughtful critics of Foucault, warn of the risks inherent in theorizing about "interpretive" violence. This is a danger that Professor Alfieri does not fully escape. In order to define a concept of "interpretive violence," he must create a dichotomy between his "metaphor" of "interpretive violence" and a "real" violence — the actual conduct of violent acts — to which his metaphor is opposed. After constructing this dichotomy, Alfieri's story emphasizes the metaphor, and thereby devalues the opposite pole. Thus, the essay unwittingly works to de-emphasize the "actual conduct of violent acts" in poor communities. It turns our attention away from cops kicking poor people — with boots and with racist slurs — and of landlords locking them out. By repressing these images, Professor Alfieri's story has to ironic effect of doing precisely what it seeks to avoid. His story of lawyers' interpretive "violence" shifts our attention away from these other kinds of violence. His admonition that we listen for stories of dignity and power from our clients, as well-founded as this advice may be, renders us less attentive when a client attempts to name for us the violence that threatens her life.

Professor Alfieri should not be faulted for the "violence" done by his essay; that risk is entailed by any monologic, abstract approach to theoretical work. He cannot avoid the risk by rejecting discourse-awareness and shifting his focus from "interpretive" violence to the "actual" violence in the "real" world. As his philosophical mentors show us, he will find no firm footing in the quicksand of "the real world." The challenge, rather, is to critique the "violence" we inflict through language without thereby creating a dichotomy, a hierarchy, that privileges this "interpretive" violence and thereby represses the violence of blood.

This path — this edge — will reveal itself only through a less impatient practice of theory: the situated piece-work of reflecting together as we get on with our work. Only such contextualized reflection can plot the paradox of interpretive/corporal violence, tracing how the subordinating power of "real" violence comes from its social meaning, and how disempowering traditions of law practice arise from, and enhance, the violence imposed by guns and knives. The task is to tell stories that reveal how "literal violence" cannot be experienced separately from the power/knowledge regimes in which it is embedded, and how "interpretive violence" cannot be disentangled from the threat, and the execution, of corporal violation.

Lucie E. White, *Paradox, Piece-Work, and Patience,* 43 HASTINGS L.J. 853, 858-59 (1992).

B. BENEFITS

The attraction of community lawyering is its promise to unite client/community autonomy with systemic reform so that community members become the authors of their own stories and the agents of their own change. Thus, a key benefit is the emphasis on client/community decision making and empowerment. One aspect of this approach is that it links the empowerment of individuals in case-by-case representation to the empowerment of broader subordinated communities. As lawyers help to disrupt the domination of clients within the lawyer-client relationship, that empowerment can spread outward in virtuous circles to endow clients with greater agency to challenge bigger social problems. *See* Lucie E. White, *Seeking ". . . the Faces of Otherness . . .": A Response to Professors Sarat, Felstiner, and Cahn*, 77 Cornell L. Rev. 1499, 1504 (1992).

It is, in the end, the goal of systemic change defined and driven by communities that is viewed as the core benefit of community lawyering:

> Our society has been working to isolate the poor for a long time. The choice to concentrate poverty was reflected in the public housing models of the mid 20th century—the high-rise structures that were justified as a way to concentrate the delivery of services to the poor but, in fact, allowed the concentration of poverty, so that the poor no longer lived scattered out into neighborhoods around our cities and towns. This concentration also bore the consequence of creating centers of deep urban poverty.
>
> Through housing patterns, traffic patterns, and increasingly, over the last twenty years, incarceration, we have chosen, as a public policy matter, to respond to poverty by concentrating it and placing it so that those of us who do not suffer the burdens of poverty do not have to see it. Law has been an essential element in creating and maintaining policy choices relating to poverty and law must be an essential element in remedying the situation. Community lawyering clinics help better prepare new law graduates to develop their social justice consciousness and take on the challenges of addressing poverty in our society in systematic ways.

Tokarz et al., *supra*, at 398.

C. CHALLENGES

The strengths of community lawyering—its emphasis on multidisciplinary problem solving, community empowerment, and systemic reform—also pose important challenges, which this section explores.

1. Effectiveness and Professional Identity: Legal versus Nonlegal Tools

Are there tensions between lawyers' engagement in community lawyering and the retention of their professional identity and roles as attorneys? Referring back to López's account of rebellious lawyering above, to what extent does Sophie's and Amos's work, however valuable, require skills or abilities that are taught (or able to be taught) through our existing legal education system? López anticipates the legal profession's possible doubts about this question in his own narrative. After listening to Catharine's admiring description of Sophie's practice, Catharine's father "seems unimpressed. 'What are you, kidding?' [he] has asked skeptically. 'Three years of law school for that?' " *Id.* at 30. What do you think about this reaction? Is it fair? How would you respond?

Some have suggested that the community lawyering literature seems apologetic about the role of lawyers, even though it is very much written by, about, and for lawyers. *See* Paul R. Tremblay, *Rebellious Lawyering, Regnant Lawyering, and Street-Level Bureaucracy*, 43 Hastings L.J. 947, 949 (1992). From this perspective, while community lawyering's critique of conventional law-yering raises valid questions about the legitimacy of traditional legal work as a tool of social change, it also could be read as arguing against traditional strat-egies that may, when conducted thoughtfully as part of a larger campaign, still prove effective.

While such an interpretation is plausible, proponents of community law-yering have generally underscored the compatibility of traditional tactics with community-centered values. *See, e.g.*, Nancy Cook, *Looking for Justice on a Two-Way Street*, 20 Wash. U. J.L. & Pol'y 169 (2006). For them, the key point is that tactical decisions should be driven by those affected — not that conventional tools shouldn't be used at all. Along these lines, scholars have described how collaboration may effectively operate within the context of traditional strate-gies, like litigation. For instance, Binny Miller embraces the notion of incor-porating client narrative more extensively into the problem-solving process and advocates a broader conception of how client narrative can be valuable in helping construct case theory in litigation. Binny Miller, *Give Them Back Their Lives: Recognizing Client Narrative in Case Theory*, 93 Mich. L. Rev. 485 (1994). While the construction of case theory might in traditional circles be viewed as strategic and thus within the lawyer's realm, she argues for a collaborative role that involves the client in the development of that strategy.

> Case theory discussions are likely to reveal new factual dimensions because clients tell lawyers what they think is important and case theory reveals which facts matter. Once the lawyer broadens the frame of what is relevant, then the lawyer, assisted by the client, will see new facts and emphasize those facts consistent with case theory. In this dialogue, the client is truly a teacher and a contributor, not simply a recipient of the lawyer's noblesse oblige, as in the prototypical client-centered discussion about nonlegal consequences. The client engages deeply in the process of developing case theory because of what he knows and what the lawyer does not. The client might educate us in ways we cannot even imagine. Once we cede control over case theory to our clients, we must remember that as lawyers we may not be in the best position to under-stand their choices. We want desperately to ascribe a "why" to their words, yet our understanding is limited by our own frame of reference. We perceive legal strategy as the reason for their actions and only reluctantly consider other possible strategic goals. We forget that the legal consequences of their actions may be entirely accidental. They may have intended something completely different.

Id. at 566-67.

Miller's account further underscores the challenge of understanding the appropriate role of "expertise" within the community lawyering model. In general, community lawyering emphasizes the co-eminence of client and community expertise in constructing problems and solutions. How does that model become operationalized in practice? How does lawyer expertise relate to that of the clients or community? For certain types of client problems, reliance on lawyer expertise may substantially advance the clients' short-term needs and desires. *See* Tremblay, *supra*, at 955-56. And the traditional lawyer-client role may be integrated into a broader social movement in sophisticated ways that both take advantage of the professional skills that attorneys can offer and respect clients' autonomy.

The question of expertise, in the end, is part of a broader set of questions about appropriate professional role. Community lawyering proponents suggest that there is value added in having lawyers participate in organizing campaigns and other types of community-based, collaborative work. Among other things, they are trained to understand the technical nature of the legal system and its sometimes byzantine processes, their association with community groups may offer some immediate legitimacy and credibility to outsiders that these groups otherwise might take some time to develop, and the availability of their counsel and representation might be used instrumentally to attract people to a broader social change campaign. JENNIFER GORDON, SUBURBAN SWEATSHOPS: THE FIGHT FOR IMMIGRANT RIGHTS (2005); LÓPEZ, REBELLIOUS LAWYERING, *supra*, at 32; Cummings & Eagly, *supra*, at 494, n.214; White, *Driefontein, supra,* at 765. At the same time, these very professional attributes may endanger the autonomy of the community that the lawyer serves or result in role confusion. Cummings & Eagly, *supra*, at 494. The lawyer might think to herself, "Am I here *because* I'm a lawyer, or *in spite of* the fact that I'm a lawyer?"

> While the positional ambivalence of lawyer-organizers may foster a self-critical awareness that enhances their ability to work in grassroots settings, it can just as easily produce a sense of role confusion that is demoralizing and causes them to doubt their own efficacy. This ambivalence can also have negative consequences for clients by encouraging lawyers to engage in organizing activities without a clear sense of purpose. In addition, the lack of role definition can actually inhibit effective collaboration with community organizers, who might think it presumptuous for lawyers to believe that they can, with minimal training, implement sophisticated organizing projects.

Cummings & Eagly, *supra*, at 496. Do you think that the risk of this type of role confusion is real? How would you address the possibility for misunderstanding between lawyers and organizers?

2. Power

a. HOW MUCH DO LAWYERS DOMINATE?

One scholarly reaction to the community lawyering emphasis on the potential for lawyer domination has been to explore the extent to which it occurs in order to better understand how to manage it. There has been a great deal of empirical literature exploring the exercise of power within lawyer-client relations. Here, we highlight two different scholarly investigations, both of which suggest that while lawyer domination of clients in public interest lawyering does occur, lawyers are often keenly sensitive to it and make efforts to avoid it.

Ann Southworth conducted an empirical study that involved interviews of Chicago lawyers engaged in poverty law or civil rights practice. Ann Southworth, *Lawyer-Client Decisionmaking in Civil Rights and Poverty Practice: An Empirical Study of Lawyers' Norms*, 9 Geo. J. Legal Ethics 1101 (1996). The lawyers in her study worked in a variety of practice settings, including legal services offices, law school clinics, legal advocacy groups, small plaintiffs' civil rights firms, grassroots organizations, and private law firms (in which she focused on business lawyers offering advice on community economic development projects).

Based on this data, Southworth made several observations. First, the level of lawyer control over client decisions in her sample varied by practice setting. Generally, lawyers who were less dependent on their clients for their salaries, such as lawyers working in legal services offices, law school clinics, and advocacy groups, tended to play a larger role in decision making than those in other practice settings. *Id.* at 1124. These lawyers were also likely to feel the pressure of substantial resource constraints, which affected their ability and willingness to devote a lot of time to client counseling. *Id.* at 1125; *see also* Tremblay, *supra*, at 950 (arguing that the limitations of poverty lawyering may be caused not by lawyers' attitudes, but by structural, institutional, political, economic, and professional defects). In contrast, attorneys in civil rights firms (who usually work on a contingency fee basis or in anticipation of statutory fee-shifting) were relatively more deferential to their clients' views. Southworth, *supra*, at 1125-26.

However, deference to clients did not vary only by practice site; it also depended to some degree on the substantive area of practice and the type of client involved. Thus, lawyers working for grassroots organizations and in private firms counseling community development groups showed greater deference to client decision making even though their salaries were not dependent on case outcomes. *Id.* at 1127-28. Southworth observed that lawyers for grassroots organizations were often involved in ongoing projects and had long-term relationships with their client groups and that they may have been ideologically committed to client-centered practices. *Id.* Many of the business lawyers were working on a pro bono basis, but she speculated that they may have been more deferential because they were used to deferring to the decisions of their paying clients. *Id.* at 1128. Conversely, lawyers who represented poor, unemployed clients were more likely to make decisions for them than attorneys who represented well-educated, sophisticated clients who had financial resources. *Id.* at 1128-29. Lawyers who worked for individual clients on a one-time basis and in litigation matters were more likely to direct their clients' decisions than lawyers who represented "repeat players" in ongoing, long-term projects that were not litigation oriented. *Id.* at 1129-30. Finally, the study data indicated that lawyers' deference to client autonomy might vary with the degree to which the lawyers had "transformative" political visions, though it depended on what those visions entailed.

> [M]any lawyers in legal services, law school clinics, and legal advocacy organizations indicated that they believed that current economic and political institutional arrangements were basically unfair. They may have believed that clients would benefit if lawyers were able to modify at least some of the

harshest inequities. The political and social views of lawyers in grass-roots organizations were similar to those of lawyers in legal services, law school clinics, and advocacy organizations, except that these lawyers were strongly committed to client autonomy.

Id. at 1131. The business lawyers who represented community groups and tended to be more politically conservative were less likely to be motivated by a social change agenda and also more likely to defer to their clients' wishes. *Id.*

In addition to these observations, Southworth noted that the interviews revealed that the actual conduct of attorneys did not always reflect purely paternalistic or purely client-centered practices, but rather a combination of the two. *Id.* at 1106. Thus, some lawyers committed to client-centeredness believed that their clients expected them to lead, while others emphasized "their obligations to advise and recommend." *Id.* How do Southworth's findings square with López's account of "regnant" lawyering excerpted above? Are Southworth's legal services lawyers regnant? If not, how does that affect López's critique and normative account of the rebellious lawyering alternative?

Corey Shdaimah conducted a more recent study of lawyers' practices and client relationships. COREY S. SHDAIMAH, NEGOTIATING JUSTICE: PROGRESSIVE LAWYERING, LOW-INCOME CLIENTS, AND THE QUEST FOR SOCIAL CHANGE (2009). For this study, Shdaimah interviewed lawyers who worked for a large legal services office in a major urban area in the northeastern United States and some of their clients. *Id.* at 29-34. Many lawyers in her study recognized the value of promoting client autonomy, but struggled with incorporating the idea into their practices. As with some of the lawyers in Southworth's study, resource constraints were a significant impediment to the type of client-centered practice advocated in the lawyering scholarship. One lawyer reported difficulty in counseling his client about a proposed settlement, saying to himself: "I got a hundred other clients, this is a really good solution, I think I've solved your problem. I really need you to say yes now because I need to move on to something else." *Id.* at 74. Even lawyers who value and believe in client autonomy must find ways to manage their day-to-day professional lives.

Some of the lawyers interviewed for Shdaimah's study also reflected on the complexity of promoting autonomy when their clients expressed no interest in engaging in the problem-solving process. How can lawyers counsel clients who resist taking control of their problems (whether out of false consciousness, lack of time, energy, and resources, or for other reasons) without undermining the very type of autonomy they are trying to honor? In one scenario, Pete, a lawyer representing a poor client engaged in a dispute with a government agency, advised his client to call a case worker's supervisor and resolve the problem directly, and to call him back if that approach failed. *Id.* at 73. The client resisted, asking Pete to make the call himself because he was the lawyer. Pete refused and offered the following rejoinder to the client: "I'm not going to enable you not to have the experience of being able to solve your own problem and learning from it." *Id.* As Shdaimah observed, "[T]here is a tension between . . . [respect for] autonomy and notions of what is the proper role of the lawyer. According to Pete, lawyers should provide advice and opinions to their clients, but they should not make decisions for them. Lawyers should act where clients need them, but where clients can act on their own they should be encouraged, perhaps even forced, to do so." *Id.*

A lawyer's commitment to address a range of issues that affect her clients' lives could also sometimes be in tension with client autonomy. In one narrative, a lawyer named Liz struggled with the fact that her client wanted only to resolve a discrete and easy tax problem, even though Liz had identified another problem that she viewed as both more important and capable of legal resolution. *Id.* at 76. She expressed her frustration that the client was not interested in pursuing the issue but acknowledged that it was his decision. *Id.* Liz recognized that her natural instinct to care for her clients was sometimes in conflict with her need to respect their autonomy. *Id.* at 77. Another lawyer was more blunt, suggesting that scholars who promoted the client autonomy ideal "may be out of touch with what she knows of her clients' lives and desires." *Id.*

Shdaimah also spent time interviewing clients about their needs and perceptions. There were several noteworthy findings. For instance, some of the clients did not experience their reliance on lawyers for advice as either interfering with their independent decision making or as manipulation. *Id.* at 78. Rather, they saw their lawyers as a resource or tool to help them work through the legal system. *Id.* In addition, some clients believed that seeking expert assistance was itself an act of independence, one component of pulling together their resources to address their problems and increasing their options. *Id.* at 78-79. As Shdaimah observed, "[T]he marshalling of resources, including professional advice, is an exercise of agency and self-determination that further enables clients to retain or regain control of their lives in difficult circumstances." *Id.* at 97.

Some of the clients expressed a desire to understand what their lawyers described to them about their legal issues, but "many did not seem to know or care about the legal arguments or even necessarily what stage their case had reached. Understandably, most clients were more interested in the bottom line or the outcome of their case: Will I get my children back? Will I be reinstated for public housing? Will my disability make me eligible for Social Security benefits?" *Id.* at 82. But even when the clients were principally concerned about results, they described their lawyers' efforts to communicate with them as being clear and understandable. *Id.*

The study also focused on understanding the lawyer-client relationship within the context of clients' lives. While in an ideal world, lawyers would have endless time to meet with each client and provide a completely client-centered experience, and clients would be able to participate fully in their cases, the reality was that clients, like lawyers, had resource constraints. "If a client can shift the burden of one problem to the lawyer, this frees her up to cope with other problems. Although this is a logical allocation of resources in the context of the clients' circumstances, it fits uncomfortably with ideal notions of their autonomy in relations with lawyers." *Id.* at 86. Similarly, as Martha Minow has argued:

> Most poor people have to negotiate for themselves daily, maneuvering through social and economic frameworks where they are systematically disadvantaged. Sometimes, the best way to honor the dignity of disempowered

persons is not to expect them to advocate for themselves, but instead to ensure their representation by the toughest, most high-powered lawyer available — just as a wealthy corporate client can expect.

Martha Minow, *Lawyering for Human Dignity*, 11 Am. U. J. Gender Soc. Pol'y & L. 143, 155 (2002).

Moreover, in Shdaimah's study, it was challenging for attorneys to honor client autonomy when they believed in good faith and based on their professional expertise that clients' decisions were not in their best interests. While most lawyers in the study deferred to their clients' decisions in such cases, some felt it necessary to strenuously advise the clients that they disagreed with their decisions and that the clients would be harmed if they made those decisions. Shdaimah, *supra*, at 90. Is this type of advice itself an infringement on the client's independence? Also, if lawyers are truly dominant in these relationships, why would clients adhere to the decisions that their lawyers advise them against?

None of this is to suggest that lawyer domination of their clients does not occur. Indeed, one attorney in Shdaimah's study clearly prioritized good outcomes over client autonomy, to the extent that he claimed that he typically wouldn't let a client ask him to withdraw from a case. *Id.* at 92. However, the accounts provided in the Southworth and Shdaimah studies paint a complex picture of lawyer-client relationships in public interest practice. Do they affect your view of the justifications for community lawyering? Do they influence how you think it should be practiced?

b. WHO DECIDES?

The focus on community as the agent and locus of change raises two important questions for community lawyers. Who is the client or community group that the lawyer represents? And what is the lawyer's role in shaping the community's agenda and response?

i. DEFINING THE "CLIENT"

Consider the following analysis of the challenges facing clinics that teach community lawyering practice:

Community collaborations inevitably lead those involved to raise questions about what assumptions might be embedded in their notions of community. Clarifying who is the client and getting a clear view of the client's wishes is a first level concern for those working in community settings. What is this community that is receiving the benefits of community building? Who are the spokespersons, the decision-makers, the stakeholders? Who are insiders, outsiders? In community economic development clinics, clients range from large community development corporations with fairly complete strategic plans for their neighborhoods, to small, single focused, non-profits or community-based businesses with little or no plan in hand. The questions that must be answered in all of these cases include, who is "the" client?

With much potentially at stake in terms of setting goals and priorities, and in terms of power and resource allocation, community lawyering clinic faculty and clinic students must also wrestle with the meaning of community. They must struggle with questions of roles, process, and infrastructure that flow from the central task of defining community. It can be fairly said that an essential aspect of community lawyering is defining community and locating the boundaries within and between communities. The scale and complexity of the work, and the capacity of the lawyers and clinics to handle the work must also be identified.

Ethical dilemmas sometimes arise with respect to identifying the client community. Sometimes we approach a community or an issue believing that there is a shared view among the community members as we have identified them, only to learn that there may be factions within the community that may have conflicting interests, or at least interests that are in some tension with each other. Sometimes, the composition of the community changes. In such situations, the clinical law teacher may have to make difficult decisions about how to navigate these very risky waters. The clinic instructor may be challenged to come up with a way to frame the issues and the representation such that she and her clinic students can realistically continue doing community lawyering. In the worst case scenario, the clinic may have to withdraw the clinic from the representation if genuine conflicts of interest arise that cannot be resolved.

As a way of addressing the definitional issues, in the University of Maryland community development and community justice clinics, the semester begins with a tour of "the other Baltimore." Clinic students and faculty spend a day on a bus, touring the city's most disinvested neighborhoods, along with a tour guide who talks about the history of these communities, community development efforts, and current statistics on challenges and opportunities. This exercise is designed to introduce students to the complex web of social and economic forces in their clients' lives. The tour also includes some of the "power neighborhoods" and gentrified neighborhoods to help students identify the differences that come with the investment of resources, both private and public. The clinic faculty underscore the importance of understanding the neighborhoods by hanging large maps of neighborhoods in the hallways of the clinical offices, with designated client neighborhoods and functioning community associations identified. For most clinic students, this clinic is the first time they have been exposed to the full scope of the city—from the docks to the entertainment district, from the open air drug markets to the mansions of our oldest and most wealthy communities.

An introductory exercise used by the Rogers Williams Community Justice & Legal Assistance Clinic and the Washington University Civil Rights & Community Justice Clinic requires students in the first two weeks of the semester to conduct in depth "on the street" investigations of their client communities, their partnership sites, and related community organizations, and to develop an initial definition of the "community" with whom they will be working. In addition to meeting with and interviewing selected individuals, students are encouraged to do research online, at the library, and in local publications. Students also are encouraged to visit schools, shelters, community centers, shopping areas, and neighborhoods. Students are pushed to explore various questions about their client communities: where do their clients live, work, eat, shop, and go to school? What community groups are active with the community? In the process of their investigations, students are urged to inquire about community organizations: what is the nature of the organization? what kind of work do they engage in? How do they define the community they work in or with? What is their philosophy about community empowerment, community building, community engagement, or similar things? What, if any, role do they see for lawyers in this work?

Through these pedagogies, clinic faculty hope that clinic students will see themselves and their clients in a different context and begin to understand better the interconnections among themselves and their clients.

Tokarz et al., *supra*, at 386-89; *see also* Stephen Ellmann, *Client-Centeredness Multiplied: Individual Autonomy and Collective Mobilization in Public Interest Lawyers' Representation of Groups*, 78 Va. L. Rev. 1103 (1992). Do the efforts described help you to clarify who a community lawyer's client or constituency is? Does it matter? Why or why not?

ii. LAWYERS' ROLE IN CONSTRUCTING THE "PROBLEM"

If client empowerment is one of the goals, how is it achieved? What role does it give lawyers, themselves part of the community, in helping set agendas and executive strategies?

Consider this view of the lawyer's role in community-based group representation:

> There surely is a need for client autonomy. Community lawyers should foster and maintain it. There is also a need, however, for professional intervention by the community lawyer, particularly where the lawyer is an ongoing collaborator rather than merely a technical adjunct in the group's activities. In this participatory role, the lawyer has information and, perhaps, a perspective that would benefit the client. Therefore, if the lawyer is to participate in client activities, then he or she has a right, if not a duty, to express his or her views about client goals and strategies.
>
> Consider [this scenario]. Tenants of a building seek the help of an attorney in what is most likely a legally hopeless situation. Certainly no standard legal remedy will meet the needs of the tenants. They may win a legal battle with the owner but the victory is unlikely to bring improvements in the conditions of the building. The lawyer knows this, although the client may not.
>
> What, then, is the lawyer's role here? To what extent is presenting the option of tenant ownership, or at least of tenant appropriation of the building, an improper attempt to influence the tenants to accept the lawyer's position? The line between presenting options and advocating for a particular outcome is minutely thin. But failing to present this option will, as a practical matter, leave the tenants without a remedy. Yet by introducing this highly unusual concept, the attorney appears to endorse it. As such, the attorney pushes the tenants toward a conclusion they did not seek.
>
> An activist lawyer must present options such as these. If one or more of them is adopted by the client, the activist lawyer takes on the tasks necessary to assist the group in achieving its aims. These may include activities such as assisting in organizing the residents, locating and packaging financing, and helping to obtain services for the buildings and for the residents. All of these tasks are outside the purview of the traditional lawyer.

Michael Diamond, *Community Lawyering: Revisiting the Old Neighborhood*, 32 Colum. Hum. Rts. L. Rev. 67, 121-23 (2000). Do you agree with Diamond that the lawyer has an obligation to express substantive views? Or should the lawyer's role be confined to establishing a fair decision-making process? We will return to these questions in Chapter 7 when we discuss the potential for conflicting views among members of a community organization. For now, it is worth noting that the goal of empowerment is complicated by the fact that client groups are composed of diverse individuals who may disagree on the best course of actionand whose opinions may be different than those held by some members of the broader community. Whether a lawyer assumes an interventionist role, as described by Diamond, or passively facilitates decisions arrived at by the client group may affect precisely who among various members of the community is ultimately empowered.

c. CAN LAWYERS AVOID INFLUENCE?

As Michael Diamond suggests in his description of community lawyering above, some scholars sympathetic to the community lawyering project have questioned its concern with lawyer power. In the following excerpt, William Simon agrees with the central theme of the literature that lawyers ought to be sensitive to and aware of their power relative to their clients and that lawyer paternalism toward clients is problematic. Simon, however, is skeptical that lawyers can in practice ever completely empower their clients because lawyers influence their clients' decisions in important, and perhaps valuable, ways. He argues that

> any plausible conception of good practice will often require lawyers to make judgments about clients' best interests and to influence clients to adopt those judgments. The argument, however, does not amount to an embrace of paternalism. The issue of paternalism remains moot until we can clearly distinguish a judgment that a client choice is autonomous from a judgment that a choice is in the client's best interests, and my argument is that in practice we often cannot make such distinctions.

William H. Simon, *Lawyer Advice and Client Autonomy: Mrs. Jones's Case*, 50 Md. L. Rev. 213, 213 (1991). He continues, suggesting that "[e]ven where they think of themselves as merely providing information for clients to integrate into their own decisions, lawyers influence clients by myriad judgments, conscious or not, about what information to present, how to order it, what to emphasize, and what style and phrasing to adopt." *Id.* at 217. In the following excerpt, Simon provides a more extensive account of this view.

WILLIAM H. SIMON, THE DARK SECRET OF PROGRESSIVE LAWYERING: A COMMENT ON POVERTY LAW SCHOLARSHIP IN THE POST-MODERN, POST-REAGAN ERA

48 U. Miami L. Rev. 1099, 1099–1100, 1102–1111 (1994)

In the late 1980s and early 1990s, a large body of literature on poverty practice emerged. This literature focused intensely on the problem of lawyer domination, which it portrayed not . . . as a necessary evil, nor . . . as a remediable failing, but as an overwhelming menace stalking the most sophisticated and well-meaning efforts to respect autonomy. In this literature, client empowerment means liberation from lawyers as much as obtaining leverage on the outside world. The scale of practice portrayed is typically small — often one on one—and the benefits are often as much psychological as they are material. . . . At each stage in this remarkable evolution, the concern with lawyer oppression of clients has increased, while the scale of material and organizational ambitions has declined. . . . I admire this literature and am pleased to have had my own work associated with it. However, I have reservations about it that I want to explore here. . . .

The Dark Secret of Progressive Lawyering is that effective lawyers cannot avoid making judgments in terms of their own values and influencing their clients to adopt those judgments. This is so for the following reasons:

First, lawyers choose their clients. Even if they delegate the choice to other people, organizations, or the market, the decisions to delegate involve choices that influence the outcomes.

Second, the advice lawyers give clients and the representational tactics they choose on behalf of clients are inevitably influenced by the lawyers' own values. This advice and these tactics in turn influence clients' perceptions of their interests. There is no value-free mode of communication in which clients could be presented with unfiltered information needed for decision. Advice has to be limited and structured in ways that will reflect the advisor's values. Similarly, tactical choices that the lawyer makes may affect not only opposing parties but also the client's sense of his own interests.

Third, collective practice involves commitments to multiple clients with potentially differing interests. To engage in this kind of practice, lawyers have to make choices that influence the balance of power among these interests. If conflicts materialize, lawyers will have to take sides. (Even if they react by withdrawing or deferring to the instructions of someone else, those decisions will affect the balance of power.) If conflicts do not materialize, lawyers will make decisions (or will choose others to make decisions) that affect the contours of organizational power.

Lawyers have to make all these choices and decisions in terms of their own values. Even a decision to defer to someone else is a decision that, if not arbitrary, must be based on some judgment about why the other is entitled to deference in this matter. What potentially redeems this situation from constituting oppression is that the lawyers' values may include notions such as democracy, autonomy, and equality that mandate respect and empowerment for the client. People, however, tend to differ over what such values mean in any given context. Except in the highly unlikely circumstances in which all clients fully understand and share the lawyer's values at the outset of the relationship, the lawyer's efforts to respect and empower the clients are likely to involve power over the clients, that is, the imposition of lawyer values.

I call this situation a "Dark Secret" because the established bar has been at pains to deny it for the past hundred years. Mainstream lawyers have long aspired to see their work as apolitical—as not involving choices for which they have substantive responsibility or which might legitimate public concern or regulation. Thus, the bar has insisted that effective lawyers merely carry out the will of their clients. They have tended to ignore the fact that lawyers choose their clients (aside from ineffectual laments that the resulting distribution of legal services is so skewed). They have mistakenly portrayed the practice of counseling as the neutral presentation of information for autonomous client decision. . . .

Because it does not adequately acknowledge the Dark Secret, the new scholarship suffers from at least three major problems:

First, the client "empowerment" recommended by the new scholarship seems quite similar to the client autonomy exalted in the traditional doctrine. In this respect, the new scholarship seems much less radical in principle than in rhetoric. If "empowerment" means simply respecting the client's own sense of her goals, then this is exactly what mainstream doctrines prescribe. If it means enhancing the client's potential for self-help, it is, if not required by mainstream doctrine, certainly not discouraged by it.

[T]he new poverty law scholars recognize myriad ways in which well-intentioned lawyers can misunderstand and dominate their clients. This recognition, however, involves them in a difficulty. The scholars are committed both to a post-modernist belief that identities and relations are constantly constructed in the process of interaction . . . and a pre-modernist belief in the ingrained virtue and insight of poor people. . . . These conflicting commitments make it difficult to explain the lawyer's intervention.

The pre-modernist commitment leads to the prescription that the lawyer leave the client alone (not dominate her). But this raises the question of what the lawyer can usefully contribute. The post-modernist premise suggests that only a fairly minor intervention could avoid changing the client. Indeed, one tendency of the scholars is to describe lawyering in terms that connote a fairly minor intervention — for example, as a form of "translation" of obscurantist professional rhetoric into lay terms that enables clients to act on the basis of their pre-existing insight. But this approach seems to trivialize poverty and subordination. One would almost think that a good dictionary would be enough to overcome them. . . . Thus, on the premises of this literature, it is hard to imagine a role for the lawyer that would make a difference without oppressing the client.

The second major problem is that the normative premises of the new literature are not plausible. The problem is not so much with the idea of client empowerment as with the idea of lawyer self-effacement. . . .

Radical lawyers . . . cannot think that their work is valuable and fulfilling just because they help enforce their clients' legal rights. The fact that their clients are poor is critical to their sense of professional worth and satisfaction. But the new scholarship seems hostile to allowing the expression of any personal commitments of the lawyer beyond the general commitment to the poor. Once the client is identified as poor, her values are supposed to determine the relation. . . . Yet this position seems to condemn the radical lawyer to an experience that, in almost any other context, she would call alienation, since the values of even poor clients will sometimes be different from those of the lawyer. The left has always considered the ability to express one's values in one's work as a defining quality of a just, humane society. Presumably this is part of what lawyers are trying to help poor clients achieve. Why should they be denied this benefit themselves?

To say that lawyers have a legitimate interest in expressing their values in their work is not to say they should be able to control their clients. It is to say that not all lawyer power and influence should be seen as illegitimate domination. I don't have any formulas about the legitimate range of lawyer influence. . . . But I think consideration of this issue has been inhibited by a reluctance exemplified in this literature to acknowledge any legitimate lawyer interest in participating in formulating the goals of the relation. . . .

The third problem with the new literature is that it has difficulty squarely addressing some of the critical aspects of collective practice. . . . The reason mainstream doctrine deems lawyering ill adapted to situations of conflicting interests is that such situations might require lawyers to make value judgments about the relative validity of competing client claims. Since the choice among client interests would involve resort to some value other than those asserted by clients, such a choice would require the lawyer to look to some commitment of her own or of some authoritative source other than the clients. And this would have to be seen as oppressive power.

So the reason why collective action seems less problematical to the new scholars cannot be their greater willingness for lawyers to resolve client conflicts of interest. It must be that they are less prone to see the interests of poor people as in conflict. And this, in turn, seems related to their commitment to viewing poor clients as attractive people. But this is naive. The client premise is valuable or at least harmless as long as it is treated as a presumption designed to inhibit the lawyer's instinct toward arrogance or paternalism, but it is untenable as a categorical dogma. Poor people are capable of the same kinds of selfishness, false consciousness, and incompetence as non-poor people. Such qualities are destructive of efforts at collective action, and a lawyer who blinds herself to them is incompetent to assist collective action. Moreover, even smart, virtuous, capable people are prone to have different views of what their own and their groups' interests are. . . .

Organization on the basis of consensus is difficult generally, and especially difficult for the poor. Thus, to maintain an existing group it may be necessary to rely either on coercion (for example, binding a minority to majority rule) or selective incentives (rewarding members on an individual basis for contributions to the group). The same principles apply to organizing unaffiliated people; only here the coercive power or selective incentives would have to come from some source outside the unorganized community, perhaps from "outside agitators" or social reformers.

Now if this argument is correct, it means real trouble for any attempt to integrate collective practice into the perspective of the new poverty law scholarship. For the application of coercion and selective incentives can only look like illegitimate power in this perspective. . . . I want to illustrate the difficulty that collective practice poses for the new scholarship by mentioning two traditional approaches to organizing disadvantaged people.

The first might be called cathartic. The organizer structures a situation to induce a sense of common interest, hope, and potency among the people she is trying to organize. In one variation, the organizer encourages people to engage some project of mutual assistance that they considered beyond their abilities. For example, in John Steinbeck's *In Dubious Battle*—a romantic portrayal of Communist Party style organizing—the organizer, by pretending to have medical expertise, gets a group of farmworkers to collaborate in delivering a baby. . . . In another variation, the organizer "rubs raw," as Saul Alinsky put it, a sense of grievance among individuals; she brings them together so they can discover that they share this sense; she then arranges a confrontation between the aggrieved and some powerful adversary in which the adversary feels compelled to yield something to them. The organizer chooses an issue big enough for people to care about, but small enough so that success in the confrontation is likely. In an Alinsky classic, the grievance involves trash that the City has allowed to accumulate on an abandoned lot, and a confrontation at City Hall forces municipal officials to promise to clean it up. . . .

The other approach to organizing involves the conditional provision of benefits. The organizer recruits members by touting the material advantages of membership—for example, the prospect of job security, or wage increases, or strike or sickness benefits that a union might negotiate for its members. Organizational discipline is maintained in part by conditioning continued membership on compliance with the organization's rules and by providing for the forfeit of benefits when a member is expelled. Or the organization may sanction noncompliance through fines or other such penalties. For example, unions believe that it is very important to be able to penalize members who resign and cross picket lines during a strike.

Sometimes lawyers assist in the conditional benefit strategy by helping to design and enforce the rules of the organization. Sometimes they become the conditional benefit themselves; organizers use a promise of legal services as an inducement to join. Thus, a union might recruit by promising its members legal help with unlawful discharge or workers' compensation claims; a welfare rights movement might recruit by promising members legal help with public assistance claims. . . .

The striking fact about both these organizing approaches is that they are equally inimical to the mainstream conception of advocacy and that of the new poverty law scholarship. The cathartic approach is unacceptably manipulative. It violates the principle that the client is supposed to be taken as she is, not transformed in accordance with the lawyer's vision of how she ought to be. . . . [T]he new poverty law scholarship, with its sensitivity to the pervasiveness and subtlety of power and the ways in which oppression can take the form of consent by the oppressed, should have no trouble recognizing this type of practice as an exercise of power by the organizer, and it seems committed to condemning it categorically.

Mainstream doctrine is uncomfortable with the conditional benefit strategy because it puts the lawyer in a position where, if conflict emerges between the organization and its members, he will feel pressure to betray one to the other. Mainstream doctrine prefers to resolve such conflicts by having the lawyer assume responsibility to only the organization (reified as a unity and usually identified with its senior officials) or to the individual member. The established doctrine of the bar views it as unacceptable for a lawyer asserting an individual claim on behalf of a member to defer to the organization in conducting his litigation strategy, and it is uncomfortable with the idea that a lawyer might condition individual representation on the individual's loyalty to the organization. . . . The new poverty law scholarship has yet to focus on the strategic issues of collective advocacy, but I don't see how its doctrines can be any more hospitable. The idea that the individual could be legitimately constrained by the group, though essential to effective collective action, doesn't sit easily with the tendency to see all constraint as power and all power as oppressive. Moreover, the lawyer's choices between individual and group or among different group constituents will have to be made on the basis of commitments or principles independent of the individuals and constituents themselves, and I don't see how this can be portrayed as anything but cultural imperialism in the framework of the new poverty law scholarship. . . .

[W]hile there have been important changes in the organization of protest groups in recent years, the corresponding changes in the organization of the dominant, establishment groups seem less dramatic. The dominant groups in the society still make extensive use of collective coercion, material incentives, and the assertion of encompassing ideological identities, and the efficacy of their efforts does not seem to be declining. It seems mere wishful thinking for the left to suppose that it can avoid the traditional moral and practical difficulties of organization. . . .

What do you think of Simon's argument? Is he right that lawyers inevitably influence clients? If so, what consequences should flow from that? How would a community lawyering proponent respond to his critique?

3. Access: Should Lawyers Empower or Represent?

We know that the aim of community lawyering is some type of systemic change. What are the systemic tradeoffs of its approach in terms of access to justice and broader reform? Consider the following reflections on this question:

> [E]xaggerating the ineffectiveness of traditional legal interventions minimizes the significant institutional restructuring that legal advocacy has achieved. Indeed, creative litigation and court-ordered remedies have changed many aspects of the social, political, and economic landscape. An analysis that obscures this fact truncates progressive legal practice by closing off potential avenues for redress.
>
> In addition, the suggestion by proponents of law and organizing that lawyers should act as organizers, facilitators, and educators would require that less time be spent providing conventional representation to low-income clients, who are already drastically underserved. . . . Given the scarcity of resources in legal aid programs, a shift toward an organizing-centered approach would result in a reduction of basic services to these clients.
>
> In the end, this type of resource reallocation may be beneficial—it may, as law and organizing advocates argue, ultimately allow poverty lawyers to effect greater institutional reform. However, it would be short-sighted to undertake such a shift without a careful evaluation of how law and organizing relates to existing legal services priorities. This evaluation should be grounded in an empirical analysis of the relative effectiveness of conventional legal practice and law and organizing activities. Thus, to advance the dialogue on social change lawyering, scholars and practitioners must move beyond discussions of law and organizing that merely magnify the deficiencies of traditional legal tactics and instead begin to articulate a new type of interdisciplinary collaboration.

Scott L. Cummings & Ingrid V. Eagly, *A Critical Reflection on Law and Organizing*, 48 UCLA L. Rev. 443, 491-93 (2001); *see also* Orly Lobel, *The Paradox of Extralegal Activism: Critical Legal Consciousness and Transformative Politics*, 120 Harv. L. Rev. 937 (2007) (suggesting both that the effectiveness of traditional legal reform has been understated and that the same problems that plague traditional legal reform confront other contemporary approaches to social change).

In a similar vein, Paul Tremblay has suggested that in carrying out collaborative, community mobilization strategies, community lawyers may risk sacrificing short-term benefits to clients for the possibility of long-term and lasting structural changes. *Id.* at 955-56. While acknowledging the substantial value of long-term structural change, he notes that this may not always be what clients desire. "[W]e cannot expect clients, if offered a free and informed choice, willingly to sacrifice their present benefits for future benefits unless the promised benefits are substantially assured and will accrue to those clients themselves." *Id.* at 967. Thus, he suggests, there may be important and often unrecognized tensions between the notion of client-centeredness and empowerment and the collectivist impulses of rebellious lawyering. *Id.* at 950. Without important structural changes in the way poverty law is practiced, he argues, "we may have to conclude that increased client-centeredness will lead to more, rather than less, conventional lawyering." *Id.* at 951. Do you agree?

PART III

CONTEMPORARY CHALLENGES FOR PUBLIC INTEREST LAWYERING

7
LEGAL ETHICS IN THE PUBLIC INTEREST

I. INTRODUCTION

Commentators have long focused on lawyers' professional obligation to do justice. *See* DAVID LUBAN, LAWYERS AND JUSTICE: AN ETHICAL STUDY (1988); DEBORAH L. RHODE, IN THE INTERESTS OF JUSTICE: REFORMING THE LEGAL PROFESSION (2003); WILLIAM H. SIMON, THE PRACTICE OF JUSTICE: A THEORY OF LAWYERS' ETHICS (2000). Whether and how they do so is a source of endless controversy that has spurred countless proposals for reform. Within this debate, public interest lawyers play a crucial, albeit contested, role: connecting practice to the profession's highest ideals of public service, while simultaneously pushing the limits of conventional advocacy and revealing the inadequacy of the profession's overall commitment to justice. STUART SCHEINGOLD & AUSTIN SARAT, SOMETHING TO BELIEVE IN: POLITICS, PROFESSIONALISM, AND CAUSE LAWYERING (2004); *see also* LAWYERS' ETHICS AND THE PURSUIT OF SOCIAL JUSTICE: A CRITICAL READER (Susan D. Carle ed., 2005). This chapter explores the relationship between public interest lawyering and the profession's ethical rules and norms.

A lawyer's conduct is governed by an intersecting web of legal regulations. The most familiar are ethical codes, adopted by state courts and administered by state bar associations. These codes set the ground rules of ethical practice—dealing with such issues as competence, confidentiality, and conflicts of interest—and are enforced through state bar disciplinary committees. Each state has its own code, though most are based on the American Bar Association's Model Rules of Professional Conduct, which was adopted by the ABA in 1983. Although ethical codes are what we generally think of as the main source of professional regulation, they are only one part of a broader "law of lawyering," which includes a range of other federal and state laws, many of which are specific to distinct fields of practice. DEBORAH L. RHODE & GEOFFREY C. HAZARD, JR., PROFESSIONAL RESPONSIBILITY AND REGULATION 8 (2d ed. 2007). All lawyers, for instance, face potential malpractice liability (arising from state tort law) for violation of their duty of care, while lawyers practicing in specialized fields like securities law may have to adhere to rules laid down by the federal agencies in which they appear. This chapter will address the "law of public interest lawyering" generally, although it will focus much of its discussion on the particular challenges public interest lawyers face in navigating ethical codes.

Our analysis of the law of public interest lawyering is organized around the twin dilemmas of *access* and *accountability*. The notion of *access* relates to the unequal distribution of legal resources in society and the legal profession's responsibility for redressing it. One commonly espoused professional goal is greater "access to justice," measured in terms of more lawyers for poor and underrepresented groups. DEBORAH L. RHODE, ACCESS TO JUSTICE 5-7 (2004). Ethics codes deal with this issue through aspirational pro bono standards that urge lawyers to "provide legal services to those unable to pay." MODEL RULES OF PROF'L CONDUCT R. 6.1. The movement to promote access to justice raises questions about what has caused the current state of inequality, and what role lawyers in general—and public interest lawyers in particular—may play in expanding legal resources to fill the so-called justice gap.

The idea of *accountability* focuses our attention on how public interest lawyers negotiate relationships with multiple stakeholders—individual clients and broader communities—in the pursuit of their respective causes. In ethical terms, the concern (discussed throughout the book) is that a conflict of interest might arise between the lawyer's duty to clients and her commitment to advancing a political mission, or among multiple client interests. The classic critique of public interest lawyers, discussed in Chapters 5 and 6, is that they are only weakly accountable to the clients and communities they purport to help, often driven by their own political agenda. Whether or not this is an accurate characterization—either of contemporary public interest lawyers or their earlier counterparts—is a complex and contested issue. It does, however, underscore the challenge of navigating accountability problems in the day-to-day context of public interest practice. In this chapter, we examine key pressure points for accountability—both in litigation and non-litigation practice—around client selection, lawyer-client decision making, and case resolution. In doing so, we set out the framework of legal ethics that guide public interest lawyering and examine how lawyers confront ethical challenges in practice.

II. THE REGULATION OF PUBLIC INTEREST LAWYERING

A. THE ROLE OF PROFESSIONAL REGULATION

In 1981, Richard Abel provocatively asked: Why does the ABA promulgate ethical rules? Richard L. Abel, *Why Does the ABA Promulgate Ethical Rules?*, 59 TEX. L. REV. 639 (1981). He argued that the rules did not resolve the ethical dilemmas of legal practice, which were caused by the fact that clients could buy their lawyers' allegiance, and thus operated to legitimate a profoundly unequal system of justice. Abel's criticism was leveled against the entire system of professional regulation. But it is a useful starting point for considering the role that professional regulation plays in governing the work of public interest lawyers. Do ethical rules promote or limit public interest lawyering and its central objectives?

The Model Rules of Professional Conduct begin by asserting that a lawyer is at once "a representative of clients . . . and a public citizen having special responsibility for the quality of justice." MODEL RULES OF PROF'L CONDUCT PREAMBLE [1]. These two roles—zealous client advocate and protector of the public good—are meant to coexist, even to reinforce one another. Thus, a lawyer is obligated to "zealously . . . protect and pursue a client's legitimate interests, within the bounds of the law," but is also called to "ensure equal access to our system of justice" and "help the bar regulate itself in the public interest." *Id.* at [6] & [9].

Yet, despite the Model Rules' aspirations, conventional legal ethics have long been viewed with suspicion by lawyers working for the vulnerable and oppressed. In practice, the public interest goals of the ethical rules often give way to the focus on zealous individual representation. And although some have argued that the zealous representation of individual clients, in itself, serves the public good (as we saw in the last chapter), others have noted that in a society in which not everyone has access to lawyers, zealous advocacy may advantage the haves at the expense of the have-nots. *Compare* Stephen Pepper, *The Lawyer's Amoral Ethical Role: A Defense, a Problem, and Some Possibilities*, 1986 AM. B. FOUND. RES. J. 613, *with* David Luban, *The Lysistratian Prerogative: A Response to Stephen Pepper*, 1986 AM. B. FOUND. RES. J. 637.

In addition, the basic premises of the ethical rules—client autonomy and lawyer neutrality—may operate in tension with robust legal reform efforts, which seek to transform social relations and not simply effectuate client desires. You will remember, for example, that Austin Sarat and Stuart Scheingold's concept of "cause lawyering" is specifically defined in opposition to the standard ethical ideal of lawyer neutrality: cause lawyers pursue ends that transcend mere client service. Austin Sarat & Stuart Scheingold, *Cause Lawyering and the Reproduction of Professional Hierarchy: An Introduction, in* CAUSE LAWYERING: POLITICAL COMMITMENTS AND PROFESSIONAL RESPONSIBILITIES 3, 3-4 (Austin Sarat & Stuart Scheingold eds., 1998).

Moreover, as some scholars have noted, lawyer regulation may be deployed not merely to promote the public good and protect client interests, but also to thwart legal practice that challenges established configurations of power. Susan Carle summarizes the NAACP LDF's fight against legal ethics charges in its pursuit of desegregation:

> The legal attacks against the NAACP acquired new venom after the United States Supreme Court decided *Brown v Board of Education* in 1954. The state of Texas sued the NAACP after local counsel sent out letters urging students to apply to segregated colleges and go to segregated parks in order to create the facts to file test cases. In 1956, Texas succeeded in enjoining the NAACP Legal Defense and Education Fund from soliciting litigation anywhere in the state.
>
> During the same period, five other southern states—Georgia, Mississippi, South Carolina, Tennessee, and Virginia—adopted stricter anti-barratry statutes aimed at curtailing the NAACP's activities within their borders. These initiatives were part of a broad campaign to cripple the NAACP's post-*Brown* desegregation efforts. Other legislative avenues included laws requiring

political organizations to register and disclose their membership lists to the state, use of reporting and disclosure requirements under corporate and tax laws, and outright prohibitions against advocating school integration.

Susan Carle, *From Buchanan to Button: Legal Ethics and the NAACP (Part II)*, 8 U. Chi. Law School Roundtable 281, 299 (2001).

Jerold Auerbach tells a similar story about lawyers for the National Lawyers Guild during the McCarthy era:

> The National Lawyers Guild was a primary target for the government and for the American Bar Association. . . . The Smith Act trial of Communist Party leaders, with the hysteria it both expressed and generated, was the turning point. . . . With guilt by associat[ion] endemic in postwar public life, vilification of the guild inevitably followed. The House Un-American Activities Committee issued a report denouncing it as "the foremost legal bulwark of the Communist Party, its front organizations, and controlled unions." . . .
>
> The [ABA] explored proscriptive and punitive measures of professional discipline, imploring other professional groups to follow its lead. First it recommended that lawyers take a loyalty oath and file an affidavit declaring whether they had ever belonged to, or supported, an organization that advocated the forcible overthrow of the government. It urged that lawyers who had once belonged to the Communist Party should be investigated to determine their fitness to remain in practice. . . . The House of Delegates recommended to all bar associations that disciplinary action leading to expulsion commence against lawyers who were party members or who advocated Marxism-Leninism.

Jerold Auerbach, Unequal Justice: Lawyers and Social Change in Modern America 234, 238 (1976).

From a more contemporary perspective, David Luban argues that intersecting regulatory changes have interacted to undermine the effectiveness of public interest lawyers by "taking out the adversary." As we discussed in Chapter 3, he suggests in particular that attacks on the Legal Services Corporation (LSC), state IOLTA programs, law school clinics, and civil rights attorneys' fees have limited the ability of "progressive public interest lawyers" to robustly represent their constituencies. David Luban, *Taking Out the Adversary: The Assault on Progressive Public Interest Lawyers*, 91 Cal. L. Rev. 209 (2003).

On occasion, and in a range of contexts, academics and practitioners have made the argument that the nature of public interest practice sometimes requires the relaxation or modification of some of the concrete ethical restrictions that apply to traditional lawyers. *See generally* Shauna I. Marshall, *Mission Impossible?: Ethical Community Lawyering*, 7 Clinical L. Rev. 147 (2000); Christine Zuni Cruz, *[On the] Road Back In: Community Lawyering in Indigenous Communities*, 24 Am. Indian L. Rev. 229 (2000). Why should this be? One argument relates to scarcity in the public interest law context. Under this view, it may not be appropriate to hold public interest lawyers to the same ethical standards to avoid conflicts or to prohibit nonlawyer practice when such restrictions further limit the ability of low- and moderate-income people to access lawyers. Or is it realistic to impose adherence to certain ethical rules on lawyers in under-resourced contexts where they do not have the ability to collect and monitor information in the way large firms do? This is not to suggest that ethical rules should be stricken in the public interest context, but perhaps they should be relaxed. One example of this relaxation that is already on the books is Model Rule 6.5, which lowers the burden of conflict rules in the context of pro bono representation provided through a nonprofit organization or court-based program. Specifically, it states that if a lawyer associated with one of these programs "provides short-term legal services to a client without expectation by either the lawyer or the client that the lawyer will provide continuing representation in the matter," the lawyer is subject to conflict-of-interest rules "only if the lawyers knows that the representation of the client involves a conflict of interest." MODEL RULES OF PROF'L CONDUCT R. 6.5(a). Do you think pro bono lawyers should have lower standards when it comes to checking conflicts? In general, do you agree that client or lawyer resources should factor into deciding which ethical rules public interest lawyers should have to follow?

Might public interest lawyering deserve different ethical rules because the moral hazards of public interest work are different than those in other contexts? For instance, it might be that we are worried less in the public interest context about lawyers ignoring the interests of third parties or the general public in ways that argue in favor of modifying some ethical mandates; or, conversely, it may be necessary to strengthen certain types of restrictions for lawyers who are not tightly accountable to the power of a high-paying client.

B. COMPETING REGULATORY REGIMES

Public interest lawyers are governed by a variety of sometimes overlapping rules that extend beyond ethical codes and depend both on what lawyers do and where they work. For example, lawyers who practice in front of federal immigration judges and the Board of Immigration Appeals are bound by a distinct set of professional rules that set specific grounds for disbarment or suspension. 8 C.F.R. Part 1003. Lawyers who work in tax-exempt charitable organizations are limited in the amount of political advocacy they can undertake.

While these multiple regulations give lawyers guidance, they may also present dilemmas when they are perceived to conflict. As we have seen, one of the most comprehensive regulatory schemes applies to lawyers who work in LSC-funded legal services organizations, who face advocacy restrictions that govern what types of cases they can file and who they can represent. Those restrictions constitute a set of regulations that interact with, and sometimes may conflict with, ethical rules embodied in state codes of professional responsibility. For example, in recent years a dispute arose between LSC and the California Rural Legal Assistance Corporation (CRLA), a legal aid office receiving LSC funding, when LSC's inspector general subpoenaed information about CRLA's clients and their cases. The inspector general, Kirt West, asserted that the information was sought as part of an audit to ensure that CRLA was using LSC funds for the purposes designated by Congress. Margaret Graham Tebo, *A Privilege to Serve: Battle over Legal Aid Funds Spills over to Attorney Client Privilege*, A.B.A. J. (Feb. 21, 2007). Specifically, West claimed that his office had received reports that CRLA lawyers were soliciting clients, had taken a fee-generating case, sought attorneys' fees in a case they had won, and engaged in political activity. *Id.* While CRLA is subject to LSC oversight, its executive director, Jose Padilla, resisted the subpoena on the ground that it would reveal information that was protected by the attorney-client privilege as well as by state privacy laws. *Id.* Moreover, Padilla argued that the information might subject clients who had asserted labor rights to retaliation by their employers and domestic violence victims to retribution by their abusers. *Id.* He also asserted that LSC's oversight actions were spurred by local ranchers who opposed CRLA's work for labor rights. *Id.* West conceded that LSC was trying to get more information to determine "whether CRLA 'disproportionately focuses its resources on farm worker and Latino work, and, if so, whether such practice is inappropriate for an LSC grantee.'" *Id.* In response, Padilla suggested that because local ranchers often hired both legal and undocumented Latino workers, the inspection was generated by LSC's suspicion that CRLA was representing undocumented laborers. *Id.* He argued that CRLA is careful to ensure that its labor case plaintiffs are documented workers and raised concerns about LSC's actions interfering with his organization's establishment of priorities for its legal work as well as the potential civil rights implications of LSC's focus on persons of a specific ethnicity. *Id.* Who do you think is right here? Should a funder be allowed to require a grantee to take action that might raise ethics concerns? Is there a way for CRLA to resolve this dispute consistently with its dual obligations to federal regulators and the state bar?

As we discussed in Chapter 4, after the 1996 LSC regulations were promulgated, some legal services organizations asserted legal challenges to block them, asserting among other things that they impaired the ability of lawyers to effectively represent their clients. Courts have rejected most challenges to the regulations, though the Supreme Court did strike down one section that prevented a legal services lawyer from seeking to "amend or otherwise challenge" welfare law in the context of representing a client seeking specific relief. *Legal Services Corporation v. Velazquez*, 531 U.S. 533 (2001). However, many other restrictions on legal services lawyer conduct still stand, including those that prevent lawyers from engaging in class actions or collecting attorneys' fees. Do you think that such restrictions are fair responses to limit legal services lawyering to individual case representation? Or do they hinder the effective representation of the poor? Can a legal services lawyer follow ethical guidelines requiring competence and zealousness in such a context?

III. THE ACCESS PROBLEM: PROFESSIONAL CAUSES AND RESPONSES

A. DOCUMENTING THE PROBLEM

It is widely understood that low- (and even moderate-) income people often lack effective *access* to the legal system because they find themselves priced out of the market for lawyers. It is frequently too expensive to pay a lawyer for services by the hour, and only certain types of cases qualify under fee-shifting statutes or make economic sense for lawyers to take on a contingency basis. As a result, many poor people are unable to afford a lawyer and thus forgo legal assistance for problems that require a legal solution. Legal needs surveys consistently show that poor people experience between one and three legal needs a year, and that "only a small fraction" are addressed with the help of a lawyer, resulting in a "justice gap." Legal Services Corporation, Documenting the Justice Gap in America: The Current Unmet Civil Legal Needs of Low-Income Americans 17 (2009); *see also* Gillian K. Hadfield, *Higher Demand, Lower Supply? A Comparative Assessment of the Legal Landscape for Ordinary Americans*, 37 Fordham Urban L.J. 129 (2010); Rebecca L. Sandefur, *Access to Justice: Classical Approaches and New Directions, in* Access to Justice, 12 Soc. Crime, Law & Deviance ix (2009).

As we saw in Chapter 4, there are far too few legal aid lawyers to respond to the legal needs of the poor. The most recent report by the American Bar Association and Legal Services Corporation concludes as follows:

> Nationally, there are *well over ten times more* private attorneys providing personal legal services to people in the general population than there are legal aid attorneys serving the poor. While there is only one legal aid lawyer (including all sources of funding) per 6,415 low-income people in the country, this report estimates that there is one lawyer providing personal legal services (that is, services aimed at meeting the legal needs of private individuals and families) for every 429 people in the general population.

Legal Services Corporation, Documenting the Justice Gap, *supra*, at 19.

B. CAUSES: THE PROFESSIONAL MONOPOLY

In a free market system, it is puzzling why there should be such a market imbalance. One would assume — in a world of no market barriers — that there would be lawyers (or even nonlawyers) who would emerge to provide low-cost services to the poor. Why doesn't that occur?

Many commentators point to the *structure of professional self-regulation*, in which the organized bar has the ultimate authority to determine who can be a lawyer and who can provide legal services — thus wielding an effective monopoly over the legal field. The bar uses this monopoly power to limit the supply of lawyers through entry barriers (such as mandatory legal education and bar examinations), while limiting competition by defining who can — and cannot — provide legal services. Richard L. Abel, American Lawyers 27 (1989). The ultimate impact of these limitations is to reduce the supply of legal services and drive up prices, leaving low-income people unable to afford representation. As Deborah Rhode concludes, "Bar efforts to restrain lawyers' competitive practices have inflated the costs and reduced the accessibility of legal assistance. Although the courts have increasingly curtailed these efforts through constitutional rulings, the bar's regulatory structure has remained overly responsive to professional interests at the expense of the public." Rhode, Access to Justice, *supra*, at 69.

One way the bar reduces competition is by generally prohibiting nonlawyers from providing legal services. *See* Deborah L. Rhode, *Policing the Professional Monopoly*, 34 STAN. L. REV. 1 (1981). ABA Model Rule 5.5 restricts the practice of law to lawyers admitted to a given jurisdiction. The justification for such restrictions is consumer protection. Comment [2] to Rule 5.5 notes that "limiting the practice of law to members of the bar protects the public against rendition of legal services by unqualified persons." Historically, the ABA has promoted an expansive definition of legal practice that involves "the application of legal principles and judgment with regard to the circumstances or objectives of a person that require the knowledge and skill of a person trained in the law." TASK FORCE ON THE MODEL DEFINITION OF THE PRACTICE OF LAW, PROPOSED MODEL DEFINITION OF THE PRACTICE OF LAW, §(b)(1) (Sept. 18, 2002). Although never adopted, this broad notion of practice is reflected in many state ethics codes. Nonlawyers who cross the line and engage in the "practice of law" may be enjoined and, if they persist in the face of an injunction, prosecuted for criminal contempt.

As a practical matter, state enforcement of unauthorized practice restrictions has declined, and several jurisdictions have experimented with permitting nonlawyers to undertake out-of-court activities that pose little risk to consumers, such as document preparation. *See* RESTATEMENT, THE LAW GOVERNING LAWYERS §4 cmt. c (2000). In California, for example, nonlawyer "legal document assistants" may be licensed to provide "[s]elf-help services" that include "completing legal documents in a ministerial manner," "[p]roviding general published factual information that has been written or approved by an attorney," and "[f]iling and serving legal forms." CAL. BUS. & PROF. CODE §6400(d)(1)-(4).

Yet, although nonlawyer services can help low-income people navigate routine legal matters, the potential for abuse remains, as this report from Los Angeles indicates:

> An immigration scam exploiting the use of the Spanish word notario has bilked thousands of Latino immigrants seeking to legalize their United States residency status and prompted Los Angeles officials to launch a crackdown.
>
> In some Latin American countries, a notario is a lawyer. In others, the title denotes someone who holds public office. In the United States, however, a notary is simply someone legally empowered to witness and certify documents and take affidavits and depositions.
>
> Unscrupulous operators are using confusion over the meaning of the word to dupe unsuspecting immigrants into thinking they are attorneys who can help people get U.S. work permits and legalize their residency status, officials said.
>
> They charge their clients exorbitant fees, file frivolous paperwork and keep them waiting—and paying—often for years, according to authorities.
>
> In many cases, immigrants unknowingly sign applications for asylum, which lawyers say can greatly improve the possibility of being awarded a work permit while the petitioner's case is pending adjudication. But when the client is called up for an asylum interview, their case is usually revealed as being invalid. Successful political asylum applications for Mexican nationals are rare, lawyers said. Still, the fraud thrives.

Such scams have been going on for decades, but local officials said they've noticed a [sic] uptick in complaints in recent months. The rip-off can spell disaster for immigrants desperate for a shot at permanent residency in the United States.

Ann M. Simmons, *Immigrants Exploited by "Notarios,"* L.A. Times, Aug. 10, 2004. It is important to note, however, that lawyers may also take advantage of vulnerable clients. *See* Richard L. Abel, Lawyers in the Dock 105-87 (2008) (describing sustained client neglect leading to the disbarment of an immigration lawyer). Do you think the risks of unauthorized practice justify the limits on entry to the profession? How would you calculate the costs and benefits of unauthorized practice restrictions from the perspective of promoting access to justice? Do you think that liberalizing practice rules to permit more nonlawyers to perform legal services would help or hurt low-income clients? How might the system regulate abuses of such practice?

C. TOWARD GREATER ACCESS TO JUSTICE

What should be done in the face of the justice gap? The answer depends on what effective "access to justice" ultimately means—a subject on which there is a great deal of disagreement. Is it procedural (*access*) or substantive (*justice*)? Does it involve providing lawyers to redress individual client grievances or using them to solve collective social problems? Beyond the definitional question, how should access to justice be achieved—through volunteerism, state subsidies, or some other mechanism?

1. What Does Access to Justice Mean?

The easiest way to understand access to justice is in terms of providing a lawyer to individuals with ripe legal disputes. But is this sufficient? Consider the range of the following perspectives.

A common tendency in bar discussions of access to justice is to conflate procedural and substantive justice, and to treat the provision of services as an end in itself. According to the Massachusetts Access to Justice Commission, "[i]n most instances, if competent legal assistance were available, justice would be within reach, even for those of modest means." Yet the more sophisticated the discussion, the harder it is to maintain that assumption. Even the Massachusetts Commission somewhat inconsistently acknowledged that "[n]ot all barriers [to justice] are in the judicial system"; some are part of a larger problem of economic disadvantage. Many factors affect the justness of the legal process apart from the adequacy of legal assistance: the substance of legal rights and remedies; the structure of legal processes; the attitudes of judges and court personnel; and the resources, expertise, and incentives of the parties. On almost all of those dimensions, as law professor Marc Galanter famously put it, the "'haves' come out ahead."

There are, of course, obvious reasons why bar commissions and commentators want to avoid the divisive task of defining justice in substantive rather than procedural terms. But overlooking the difference can lead to reform priorities with unwelcome effects. For example, research on housing courts has found that providing legal assistance for formerly unrepresented tenants does not always improve outcomes. In one early case study in the South Bronx, legal aid lawyers' procedural victories provoked strong backlash. Judges unable to clear their dockets and landlords unhappy about deadbeat tenants united behind reforms that eliminated certain defenses and ultimately undermined defendants' bargaining position. In other contexts, changes in the substantive law, inadequate lawyer expertise, or provision of information about the unavailability of defenses has led to poorer outcomes for tenants despite the availability of legal assistance.

That is not, however, an argument against providing such assistance. Most studies show that increasing legal representation dramatically improves tenants' ability to win at trial or to negotiate favorable settlements. The result is to reduce the incidence of homelessness and all its accompanying social, economic, and health costs. Indeed, several studies have found that every dollar spent on preventing eviction through legal assistance ends up saving taxpayers substantial amounts in shelter costs and related social services. Appointing lawyers for parents in child abuse and neglect proceedings also saves money by enabling families to comply with court orders and to devise plans that keep their children out of foster care systems. The lesson of this and other research reviewed below is that if our goal is improving not just the legal process but also the life circumstances of disadvantaged groups, then the value of legal services should be assessed in context, and lawyers should focus on long-term impact as well as short-term results.

Deborah L. Rhode, *Whatever Happened to Access to Justice?*, 42 Loy. L.A. L. Rev. 869, 872-74 (2009). Do you agree that increasing access to lawyers tends to improve legal outcomes for clients? In an important recent study, James Greiner and Cassandra Wolos Pattanayak cast doubt on the idea that access to lawyers increases the probability of claimants' success in their legal case. Their study tracked persons seeking assistance from the Harvard Legal Aid Bureau (HLAB) in their appeals of initial rulings regarding eligibility for unemployment insurance. In contrast to prior studies of actual representation, the authors, in connection with HLAB, created a randomized experiment in which a group of claimants was made offers of representation while a control group was not. The case outcomes of members of each group were then evaluated. Surprisingly, the authors found that "an offer of HLAB representation had no statistically significant effect on the probability that a claimant would prevail, but . . . the offer did delay the adjudicatory process." D. James Greiner & Cassandra Wolos Pattanayak, *Randomized Evaluation in Legal Assistance: What Difference Does Representation (Offer and Actual Use) Make?*, 121 Yale L.J. 2118, 2124 (2012). Greiner and Pattanayak's study provoked the following response by the Executive Director of Greater Boston Legal Services:

> I am concerned . . . that the results reported in the study with respect to *offers* of representation by HLAB are misleading at best and of little utility at worst. This is because nearly half of the control group were represented by counsel and, more significantly, probably that many and perhaps more in the control group got an offer of free representation from my program or another providing free legal services in unemployment cases. To make an analogy to the medical world, suppose there was a Pfizer drug trial where 50% of Pfizer's control group were offered the exact same medication from Merck. Wouldn't that cast serious doubt on the outcome of the study? There is no mention of

this 49% in either the abstract or introduction which unfortunately are all many readers will read.

Bob Sable, What Different Representation — A Response, Symposium (What Difference Representation, at http://www.concurringopinions.com/archives/category/representation-symposium (last visited Aug. 7, 2012). What do you make of this exchange? For some additional data on the impact of counsel, see Russell Engler, *Connecting Self-Representation to Civil Gideon: What Existing Data Reveal About When Counsel Is Most Need*, 37 FORDHAM URB. L.J. 37 (2010).

Gary Blasi, a long-time poverty lawyer and law professor, views the problem of access to justice not simply in terms of access to lawyers.

GARY BLASI, *FRAMING ACCESS TO JUSTICE: BEYOND PERCEIVED JUSTICE FOR INDIVIDUALS*

42 Loy. L.A. L. Rev. 913, 920-25 (2009)

As a beginning legal services lawyer in 1978, I knew that many of my clients reported having problems of the kinds that caused David Quail to withhold his rent: lack of heat and hot water, cockroach and rat infestations, broken windows and doors, cracked walls, and peeling paint. One of those clients was Celia Carbajal, an immigrant mother and garment worker from El Salvador who lived in a sixty-unit building on Main Street, a mile south of downtown Los Angeles and only one block from my office. In order to try to pressure the landlord, she gave the manager a list of serious problems in her apartment and in the building, along with a note that she would not pay rent until they were repaired. Shortly thereafter, she appeared on my intake day with an eviction notice. I had represented scores of tenants before, particularly in eviction cases, and I knew what to do. I had visited their homes, taken pictures, and helped them collect "Roach Motels" (many evidencing signs of "No Vacancy") along with the proceeds of mouse and rat traps (these were useful for settlement purposes but not popular with court clerks who might be called to mark them as trial exhibits). At the time, I thought that each of my clients received excellent representation (as a matter of fact and not just ego) and real access to justice, even when we lost at trial. Although I worked with some tenant organizations, I generally framed my job as helping one family at a time, the family having effectively been selected for my help by a landlord through the service of an eviction notice.

I also knew Ms. Carbajal's landlord, Dr. Milton Avol. I had represented another one of his tenants when he tried to evict her with no notice at all. Dr. Avol was a Beverly Hills neurosurgeon with a lucrative side business as a slumlord, owning several large apartment buildings in the poorest neighborhoods of Los Angeles. I had not visited Ms. Carbajal's building, however, until I accompanied her to see her apartment and take photographs. Perhaps partly because I knew her landlord, I grew increasingly angry with what I saw: children playing in darkened hallways (light bulbs cost money), stairwells with broken railings, inoperable fire escapes and fire hoses, heaters that had not worked in years, leaky plumbing, fresh evidence of vermin, and other violations of basic housing and health codes. And the rent for Ms. Carbajal's unit was not cheap; on a per-square-foot basis, it was more expensive than my own house.

I went back to the office determined to do more than just defend Ms. Carbajal's eviction. After meeting with the senior lawyers in the office, my colleague Barbara Blanco and I decided we would sue Dr. Avol on behalf of all the building's tenants who would agree to representation, seeking both injunctive relief and damages under every legal theory possible. Doing this for Ms. Carbajal alone would not have made sense because of our limited resources and because the other tenants in the building shared virtually all of Ms. Carbajal's problems. The common areas were obviously, well, common. The lack of heat resulted from a single decrepit furnace boiler in the basement. The cockroaches lived in every interstice of the building; cleared from one room, they would quickly return. Ms. Carbajal's problem required a collective solution, so we enlisted the help of a tenant organization, Inquilinos Unidos, to help us work with the tenants.

At the hearing on the preliminary injunction, Dr. Avol's lawyer offered to settle the case. Under the terms of the stipulated judgment, an injunction would issue requiring Dr. Avol to fix a detailed list of problems that we would specify, and Dr. Avol would pay our clients a few thousand dollars in general damages. The repairs were made, and heaters were installed. A stipulated judgment for a few thousand dollars in damages was entered. Although we had to have the sheriff threaten to tow away the Oldsmobile belonging to Dr. Avol's wife in order to collect the money judgment, Dr. Avol began to make repairs. Our clients were satisfied, as were we, that some justice had been done.

Unfortunately, the story of the Main Street building does not end there. Although repairs were made as the result of our settlement, Dr. Avol maintained the same business model of "milking" the building, and the slum conditions returned within a few years. Once again, legal services lawyers (joined this time by a private litigation firm) sued Dr. Avol on behalf of the tenants, almost all of whom were new since the first case. And once again, the tenants secured an injunction requiring repairs. This time, however, they collected much more money in damages from Dr. Avol (or rather his insurers), and the plaintiffs' lawyers got more than one million dollars in attorneys' fees. The story after that gets more complicated, but in essence, the same building was the subject of yet another round of complicated litigation, resulting in the appointment of a receiver and the eventual removal of Dr. Avol as the owner. About twenty years elapsed between the first case and the last.

Now the building, which lies on the border of a gentrifying downtown Los Angeles, has been rehabilitated once again by another owner, and the units are being marketed as "affordable luxury in the heart of downtown Los Angeles." Rents have risen beyond the reach of garment workers like Ms. Carbajal. Ms. Carbajal and her neighbors, both in the building and in the neighborhood, might have benefited from organizing and legal assistance well beyond what they received. For example, the use of government funds that are ostensibly intended to benefit low-income people has enabled much of the gentrification of the area. Litigation, organizing, and other modes of advocacy might have reduced or ameliorated the gentrification pressure that led to their eventual displacement from the neighborhood. Advocacy also might have focused on pressuring the responsible government agencies to take a more active and effective role. Put another way, although expanding the framing of Ms. Carbajal's problem as one that she shared with the other tenants was a positive step, the framing never really went beyond the actual building in which she lived. Doing so, however, might have ultimately been more effective, a more efficient use of resources, and a greater contribution to equality of access to adjudicative systems.

This leads us to the questions at hand. First, under a definition of "access to justice" to which we should reasonably aspire, would Ms. Carbajal and her neighbors be entitled to the kind of collective, affirmative representation that we—legal aid lawyers and tenant organizers—provided? Under most current conceptions, the answer is no. To begin with, the tenants did not have a legal problem that might be addressed by litigation until lawyers combined their circumstances with untested legal theories and produced a complaint. . . . [E]ven the most forward-leaning current discourse regarding a right to counsel in civil matters frames the issue in terms of individuals or families rather than buildings, neighborhoods, or classes of similarly situated people. And, of course, when Ms. Carbajal came to our office, she had the same framing: she had a legal notice and, therefore, a legal problem, but it was relevant only to her and her family. It was only through discussion, meetings, organizing, and considerable effort by our office and our organizer partners that the tenants and lawyers came to frame Ms. Carbajal's problem as a common or group legal problem that was capable of an affirmative, collaborative, and collective solution.

Furthermore, under a reasonable construction of access to justice, would Ms. Carbajal and other poor tenants in her neighborhood have access to assistance in responding to the failures of the housing code enforcement system or the misuse of redevelopment funds? As I note below, one will find few arguments to that effect in the current discourse about access to justice. I will argue for such access, however, at least as a matter of first principles. In a world of finite resources, there will always be tradeoffs between the time spent assisting individuals like Mr. Quail or Ms. Carbajal with their individually framed problems and time spent dealing with problems common to the tenants in a building or the residents in a neighborhood. Those tradeoffs deserve careful considerations that do not prejudge an outcome. But, by framing access to justice in individual terms and with regard to problems already defined as "legal," we do not merely prejudge the outcome; we preempt the discussion.

Here, I argue that we should begin with a wider framing of access to justice—for at least some populations and some kinds of problems—that would encompass a right to assistance to (1) claims making, which would include assistance not only with problems that have ripened into clear legal controversies but also with those that might do so with the benefit of legal assistance; (2) organizing and coordination, which would include legal or organizing assistance to overcome collective action problems and to assert group claims, where doing so is either necessary or demonstrably more efficient or effective; and (3) monitoring and enforcement, which would include legal and investigative assistance to monitor and enforce compliance with equitable relief obtained through litigation or organizational or institutional change obtained by other means.

———————

Do you agree with Blasi that access to justice should be framed in terms of a right to assistance in "organizing and coordination" to "overcome collective action problems and to assert group claims"? If so, how would you decide which group claims merited representation? If not, how would you propose to deal with the problem of the landlord in this case, Dr. Arvol, continuously "milking" the building?

2. How Should Greater Access Be Achieved?

Even if one were to assume that the justice gap could be filled by simply increasing the number of lawyers serving the poor, how would that increase be achieved? There are two basic approaches. On one side there is an *internal professional* approach centered on lawyers' obligation to serve the public good through pro bono activity. The discussion around pro bono generally concerns whether it should be mandatory, how much service should be required, what counts as pro bono, and other technical details. On the other side is an approach *outside the domain of professionalism* that looks to alternative structures for distributing legal services, such as government-funded legal aid; this discussion focuses on the inadequacy of the current legal aid regime and how to fix it. Here, we present the tradeoffs of these approaches and some alternatives.

a. THE INTERNAL PROFESSIONAL APPROACH: PRO BONO SERVICE

Ethics codes generally respond to the justice gap by promoting volunteer pro bono service as a professional obligation. ABA Model Rule 6.1 provides that every lawyer "should aspire to render at least (50) hours of pro bono publico legal services per year," and that a "substantial majority" should assist "persons of limited means" or organizations that help them. Additional assistance should go to activities that improve the law, legal profession or legal system, or that support "civil rights, civil liberties or public rights, or charitable, religious, civic, community, governmental and educational organizations" if payment of fees would "significantly deplete the organization's economic resources or would be otherwise inappropriate."

By all accounts, pro bono service has become a major resource for poor and underserved clients, with large law firm pro bono programs leading the way. Steven Boutcher reports that the total pro bono hours for firms in the Am Law 200 in 2005 was just over 3.75 million. Steven A. Boutcher, *The Institutionalization of Pro Bono in Large Law Firms: Trends and Variation Across the AmLaw 200, in* PRIVATE LAWYERS AND THE PUBLIC INTEREST: THE EVOLVING ROLE OF PRO BONO IN THE LEGAL PROFESSION 135, 144 (Robert Granfield & Lynn Mather eds., 2009). AFTER THE JD, a longitudinal study of newly certified lawyers by the American Bar Foundation and NALP Foundation for Law Career Research and Education, reported that about half of total pro bono hours by private practice lawyers came from lawyers in firms with more than 250 attorneys. Ronit Dinovitzer et al., Am. Bar. Found. & NALP Found. for Law Career Research & Educ., After the JD: First Results of a National Study of Legal Careers 37 tbl.4.3 (2004); *see also* Rebecca L. Sandefur, *Lawyers' Pro Bono Service and Market-Reliant Legal Aid, in* Private Lawyers and the Public Interest, *supra,* at 95, 101. Solo and small-firm lawyers also provide significant no-fee or reduced-fee ("low bono") services, although — instead of taking on volunteer cases *ex ante* — they tend to write down fees after cases are accepted and it becomes clear that clients cannot afford to pay. *See* Leslie C. Levin, *Pro Bono Publico in a Parallel Universe: The Meaning of Pro Bono in Solo and Small Law Firms,* 37 Hofstra L. Rev. 699, 701 (2009); *see also* Lynn Mather et al., Divorce Lawyers at Work: Varieties of Professionalism in Practice (2001); Carroll Seron, The Business of Practicing Law: The Work Lives of Solo and Small-Firm Attorneys (1996); Philip R. Lochner, Jr., *The No Fee and Low Fee Legal Practice of Private Attorneys,* 9 Law & Soc'y Rev. 431 (1975).

As we saw in Chapter 4, the ascendance of pro bono has marked a transformation in the provision of legal services in the United States. "Whereas pro bono had traditionally been provided informally — frequently by solo and small firm practitioners who conferred free services as a matter of individual largesse — by the end of the 1990s pro bono was regimented and organized, distributed through a network of structures designed to facilitate the mass provision of free services by law firm volunteers acting out of professional duty." Scott L. Cummings, *The Politics of Pro Bono,* 52 UCLA L. Rev. 1, 4 (2004); *see also* Deborah L. Rhode, Pro Bono in Principle and Practice: Public Service and the Professions (2004); Robert Granfield & Lynn Mather, *Pro Bono, the Public Good, and the Legal Profession, in* Private Lawyers and the Public Interest: The Evolving Role of Pro Bono in the Legal Profession 1 (Robert Granfield & Lynn Mather eds., 2009); Rebecca L. Sandefur, *Lawyers' Pro Bono Service and American-Style Civil Legal Assistance,* 41 Law & Soc'y Rev. 79 (2007). Such services have augmented legal aid to the poor, as well as supported cause-oriented, nonprofit legal groups taking on large-scale cases. This transformation has resulted from a number of interlocking trends, including pressure from the organized bar to increase volunteer service in the face of declining funding for federal legal aid. In 1980, there were about 90 programs dedicated to pro bono referrals. Today there are approximately 900 such programs, whose combined pro bono activity accounts for between one-quarter and one-third of overall U.S. legal aid services. Sandefur, *Lawyers' Pro Bono Service, supra,* at 102. As we discussed in Chapter 4, in addition to these bar efforts, there have been important market-based pressures promoting pro bono's development, particularly large law firm rankings by publications such as *The American Lawyer. See* Scott L. Cummings & Deborah L. Rhode, *Managing Pro Bono: Doing Well by Doing Better,* 78 Fordham L. Rev. 2357, 2370-72 (2010).

The rise of pro bono has not been a panacea and comes with its own trade-offs. Despite the important efforts by private lawyers, pro bono service still is not able to close the justice gap. Moreover, its growth raises other concerns. For one, there are questions about "what counts" as pro bono — and whether the ABA's emphasis on private volunteerism by large-firm lawyers undervalues the service provided to low-income communities by solo and small-firm practitioners on a daily basis. *See, e.g.,* Luz E. Herrera, *Rethinking Private Attorney*

Involvement Through a "Low Bono" Lens, 43 Loy. L.A. L. Rev. 1 (2009). Even within large firms, there are still significant barriers to pro bono service. In her survey of pro bono activity, Rhode reported that only "a quarter of surveyed lawyers' workplaces (25%) fully counted pro bono work toward billable hours." Rhode, Pro Bono in Principle and Practice, *supra*, at 138. The pressure to prioritize billable hours, combined with the lack of strong supervision by partners, may contribute to less than exemplary pro bono representation. Furthermore, the number of hours suggested is relatively small, though if every lawyer in the country fulfilled this quota, there would certainly be a lot more legal services being offered than under the status quo.

Moreover, there are deeper tradeoffs involved in erecting a system of legal services to the poor and underserved upon a foundation of private sector largesse. Consider the following view:

> [P]rivate lawyers do a tremendous service representing individual poor clients in routine matters and lending their institutional resources to support the reform agendas of public interest groups. Their volunteer work ranges from the mundane to the transformative and includes matters of intense personal interest and immense social import. But the central dilemma of pro bono remains: A system that depends on private lawyers is ultimately beholden to their interests. This means not just that private lawyers will avoid categories of cases that threaten client interests, but also that they will take on pro bono cases for institutional reasons that are disconnected from the interests of the poor and underserved — and often contrary to them. This is most apparent in the use of pro bono for law firm associate training: Associates who gain skills in the volunteer context spend most of their time using them to vigorously advocate against the interests served through pro bono representation. In so doing, they become zealous partisans for corporate clients — defending them from tort claims, consumer suits, employment and labor grievances, and environmental challenges. The time they spend engaged in pro bono work provides a respite from this world, but does not change it.
>
> There are other drawbacks to the pro bono system. Pro bono lawyers do not invest heavily in gaining substantive expertise, getting to know the broader public interest field, or understanding the long-range goals of client groups. Particularly in contrast to the way big-firm lawyers seek to understand and vigorously advance the goals of their client community, the partiality and narrowness of pro bono representation is striking. And the disparity of the resources devoted to billable versus pro bono work — which, even at the most generous firm, rarely constitutes more than 5 percent of total hours — underscores the vast inequality in legal services that persists. Indeed, there are no parallel resources available to press the interests of marginalized social groups. Legal services is too restricted and nonprofit groups are too financially constrained. This is not accidental. Opponents of the reformist agenda of legal services have championed pro bono as an acceptable alternative, knowing that it does not pose the threat to business interests that an unrestricted legal services would. Marginalized groups, then, are left to depend heavily on volunteer efforts to respond to their needs — a fact that distinguishes them from all of their adversaries, who spend lavishly to purchase the best legal counsel money can buy.

Cummings, *The Politics of Pro Bono, supra*, at 147-48.

Would it be appropriate for the legal profession to mandate that all licensed attorneys perform a specific number of pro bono hours per year? Can you imagine any problems with such a system? How do you think members of the legal profession who oppose such a mandate might respond? Do you think there would be an impact on clients? Note that the Legal Services Corporation has been one of the staunchest critics of mandatory pro bono. Why do you think that is? For further discussion of mandatory pro bono for practicing attorneys, see Donald Patrick Harris, *Let's Make Lawyers Happy: Advocating Mandatory Pro Bono*, 19 N. Ill. U. L. Rev. 387 (1999); Esther F. Lardent, *Mandatory Pro Bono in Civil Case: The Wrong Answer to the Right Question*, 49 Md. L. Rev. 78 (1990); Michael Millemann, *Mandatory Pro Bono in Civil Cases: A Partial Answer to the Right Question*, 49 Md. L. Rev. 18 (1990).

b. REFORM PROPOSALS OUTSIDE THE PROFESSION

If pro bono isn't a complete solution, what else could be done to promote greater access to justice? We do not lack in reform proposals, although we frequently lack political will. There are, for instance, recurrent calls to lift the restrictions on LSC-funded groups and restore funding to sustainable levels. In 2009, Senator Tom Harkin of Iowa introduced the Civil Access to Justice Act, which (in addition to increasing funding to 1980 levels) would have repealed many of the restrictions put in place in 1996, including the prohibition against using non-LSC funds for otherwise restricted activities. However, in the hyperpartisanship of Washington, the bill never gained sufficient support. To make up for lost funding, Blasi has proposed a tax on law firms to support legal services to the poor. Gary Blasi, *How Much Access? How Much Justice?*, 73 Fordham L. Rev. 865 (2004). Do you think that would be a good idea? What might be some of the tradeoffs?

Another proposal goes in the opposite direction and advocates moving away from the goal of full-scale legal representation for the poor (i.e., a lawyer for every individual who needs one). Instead, proponents of "unbundling" legal services suggest that legal problems can be broken down into smaller parts (writing a demand letter, filing a grievance, attending a mediation session) and that clients and nonlawyers can be trained to undertake some of these tasks without the need for lawyers. Resources like telephone hotlines and pro se assistance centers in courts can provide individuals with basic information allowing them to fill out standardized forms or take some steps toward advocating for themselves to solve problems. Not only can this conserve scarce legal assistance resources, it can also promote client empowerment. Critics suggest that unbundling, while useful in very basic situations, risks leaving poor people with a second-class version of legal assistance that could harm their basic interests. Note that new online providers like *legalzoom.com* offer access to basic information and a variety of legal documents and forms at low or no cost. Is this the future of legal services for the poor? Is this a positive development?

Even were more resources for legal services available, some critics question whether mere redistribution would ultimately produce more equal justice. True equalization, such critics suggest, would require not simply giving more lawyers to the disempowered, but *withdrawing* lawyers from the already empowered. *See* Richard L. Abel, *Socializing the Legal Profession: Can Redistributing Lawyers' Services Achieve Social Justice?*, 1 Law & Pol'y Q. 5 (1979). Critics of the professional monopoly have also called for deprofessionalizing legal services as a way to expand access. But these proposals have gotten little political traction.

The so-called Civil Gideon movement has been one bright spot on the access to justice horizon. As Clare Pastore notes,

> The American Bar Association ("ABA") unanimously passed a historic resolution in 2006 endorsing the provision of "counsel as a matter of right at public expense to low income persons in . . . adversarial proceedings where basic human needs are at stake, such as those involving shelter, sustenance, safety, health or child custody. . . ." Numerous state and local bar associations have endorsed the ABA resolution. . . . Encouraging legislative developments have occurred as well. . . . [S]even states have recently enacted laws expanding the right to counsel in certain civil cases. A bill is currently pending before the New York City Council to provide counsel as of right to low-income seniors facing eviction or foreclosure, and a separate effort is underway in the New York State Assembly to provide counsel more broadly to homeowners facing mortgage foreclosures. In October 2009, California enacted the Sargent Shriver Civil Counsel Act, establishing a six-year pilot program (to begin in 2011), funded at approximately $11 million per year, to test the effects and feasibility of expanding access to counsel in cases involving housing, domestic violence and other harassment, conservatorships and guardianships, elder abuse, and child custody. Likewise, there have been some successes in the courts. Several state courts have held that when a state statute requires appointment of counsel for parents in state-initiated proceedings to terminate parental rights, equal protection requires such appointments in privately-initiated termination cases.

Clare Pastore, *A Civil Right to Counsel: Closer to Reality?*, 42 Loy. L.A. L. Rev. 1065, 1067-68 (2009); *see also* Laura K. Abel, *Keeping Families Together, Saving Money, and Other Motivations Behind New Civil Right to Counsel Laws*, 42 Loy. L.A. L. Rev. 1087 (2009). Yet not all observers are so sanguine. Benjamin Barton argues that

> the corrosive effects of *Gideon* would likely be greatly amplified in the civil setting. First, note that the problems of crippling caseloads and woeful funding occur in the context of serious crimes. In fact, many of the most powerful examples of *Gideon*'s failures come in death penalty cases. If reviewing courts and legislatures cannot see the worth in adequately funding capital defense, what hope is there for adequate funding for defense of a termination of parental rights proceeding, let alone a landlord-tenant action?

Benjamin H. Barton, *Against Civil Gideon (and for Pro Se Court Reform)*, 62 Fla. L. Rev. 1227, 1262-63 (2010). Is Barton right? Is some funding better than none at all?

EXERCISE

Imagine that you are on the ABA's Access to Justice Task Force and have been charged with developing a new rule to bridge the "justice gap." Which approach would you choose? How would you go about marshalling political support? How would you evaluate your chances for success?

IV. THE ACCOUNTABILITY PROBLEM: WHO IS THE "PUBLIC" IN PUBLIC INTEREST LAWYERING?

A. THE FUNDAMENTAL DILEMMA: ACCOUNTABILITY TO WHOM?

While the access to justice dilemma concerns the structure of the profession and appropriate policy responses, the issue of lawyer *accountability* in the public interest context goes more directly to the representational choices that lawyers make in day-to-day practice. Such choices have been the focus of critical commentary since the early days of the public interest law movement, with concerns expressed by those generally sympathetic to its aims. *See* William H. Simon, *Solving Problems vs. Claiming Rights: The Pragmatist Challenge to Legal Liberalism*, 46 Wm. & Mary L. Rev. 127 (2004). The central target of critical scholarship has generally been the lawyer working in a nonprofit group — and thus financially independent from clients — who undertakes impact litigation asserting rights that affect a larger community. But all forms of public interest lawyering in which lawyers represent clients in cases with broader community or policy impact raise accountability concerns. Generally, such concerns relate to the appropriate allocation of control among the actors with a stake in such cases: lawyers, clients, and the affected community. The question is who gets to decide key aspects of the case — particularly, its goals and the terms upon which it is resolved? In this section, we look at how public interest lawyers confront and manage these accountability issues in both the litigation and non-litigation contexts. The key ethical issues involve how lawyers select a public interest case in the first instance (implicating rules regarding client solicitation), and how lawyers manage potential disagreements among stakeholders as the case unfolds and is resolved (implicating issues of decision-making authority and conflicts of interest).

As we investigate these issues, keep in mind the basic accountability critique of public interest lawyers that we have encountered in our discussions of public interest strategies and the lawyer-client relationship. One version of this critique holds that the public interest lawyer, by effectively manufacturing cases to advance substantive legal rights identified as important by the *lawyer himself*, uses the legal system to engage in policy making without having to answer to the very group he purports to help. Under this view, the lawyer may lack accountability either to clients or the broader community. Another version of this critique focuses on the potential conflicts among groups and the lawyer's role in facilitating some views over others. Here, the argument is not that the public interest lawyer is a rogue rights claimer, but rather that she effectively chooses sides in a contested policy debate — perhaps helping minority factions to pursue a policy agenda that is at odds with the will of the majority of the affected community. In both types of situations, the question is whether there is an actual or potential conflict of interest that might affect the lawyer's ability to effectively represent clients. Outside of the test case litigation context, similar issues arise regarding whether and how public interest lawyers relate to the multiple stakeholders involved in community change.

More generally, as you read the following material, ask how much of a real-world concern lawyer accountability is in the public interest context. If it is a problem, what can be done about it? Also, keep in mind that social change efforts that occur outside of the legal arena may also raise accountability problems. For instance, when an organization purports to represent the interests of a broad social movement (think of the Southern Christian Leadership Conference or Student Nonviolent Coordinating Committee during the civil rights movement), there are inevitable questions about how carefully that group represents the interests of the movement writ large. Would it change your analysis of public interest lawyer accountability to compare it to the conflicts that occur between leaders and their constituents more generally?

B. THE LITIGATION PARADIGM: ACCOUNTABILITY IN THE LIFE CYCLE OF THE CASE

One way to understand accountability in the context of public interest litigation is by looking at the "pressure points" of lawyer accountability as they arise in the life cycle of the case. Here, we focus on accountability issues that emerge at three key moments during the basic chronology of a legal matter: (1) *at the beginning of representation*, when lawyers exercise discretion in soliciting and selecting clients; (2) *during the course of representation*, when issues arise regarding the appropriate allocation of decision making between lawyer and client, and the potential for conflicts emerges; and (3) *at the resolution of representation*, when key issues involve settlement and the incentive effects of attorneys' fees.

1. Initiating Representation: Choosing Clients

a. REJECTION

For impact-oriented legal groups like the ACLU or NAACP LDF, client selection is closely linked to the group's substantive aims: clients are chosen if their cases present issues that promote the group's policy agenda. For legal aid lawyers, client selection is part of organizational "triage": without sufficient resources to represent everyone who walks in the door, a legal aid group must set criteria for deciding who gets what type of services—and who does not.

As a doctrinal matter, it is at the selection stage that lawyer autonomy is at its apex. Generally speaking, a lawyer may decline to represent almost any prospective client. Even when a lawyer is appointed by the court to represent an indigent client, she may generally decline the appointment for good cause, which includes financial hardship. MODEL RULES OF PROF'L CONDUCT R. 6.2.

Nonetheless, just because a public interest lawyer can decline to represent someone begs the question of whether she should. Particularly in the context of legal aid scarcity, triage standards implicate ethical choices about who deserves representation. In an influential article, Paul Tremblay argued that triage criteria are ultimately a function of the underlying practice vision of a legal services office; thus, an access to justice mission—maximizing services to deserving clients—would yield a different set of criteria than one based on community empowerment. Paul R. Tremblay, *Acting "A Very Moral Type of God": Triage Among Poor Clients*, 67 FORDHAM L. REV. 2475 (1999). Tremblay ultimately asserts that a legal services office, adopting a "trustee model," should strive to have a "balanced portfolio" of cases, some of which meet the individual representation goals of access and others that perform more of a mobilizing role. Within this framework, a number of "weighted triage" criteria would guide the "microallocation" of resources to potential clients, which he describes in relation to a fictional office called the Essex Legal Services Institute (ELSI):

ELSI should choose its clients with the following principles in mind:

- The principle of legal success: ELSI should favor those prospective clients for whom the staff's talent, resources, and time will make a difference in the outcome desired by the individual. This principle would rule out, or suggest lower preference for, those individuals with very weak cases or very strong cases. It is a justifiable operating maxim, as the limited resources of ELSI should be directed to areas where the resources can make a palpable difference. It may be imperfect in execution, particularly since screening takes place without an enormous level of case detail, but when it is available it ought to count in a significant way.

- The principle of conservation: For reasons similar to those just discussed, ELSI ought to offer priority to those applicants whose cases require proportionally smaller amounts of the program's resources to accomplish the benefits that ELSI wishes to achieve. A goal of ELSI's triage must be the efficient use of its limited assets, and this maxim privileges efficiency. If ELSI's staff can prevent the homelessness of four families with the same resource allocation as it would take to prevent the homelessness of one family, then, everything else being equal, the office ought to turn down the latter client family and accept the first four, subject to the preceding principle of legal success. Or, to use a different example, a family whose homelessness can be avoided with some quick but significant legal input would be preferred to another family, everything else being equal, whose eviction can be avoided only through months of active litigation.

- The principle of collective benefit: ELSI ought to prefer cases that are likely to affect the lives of a larger group of poor people over cases that promise benefit only to the actual represented client. The norm of efficiency again justifies this principle, which seeks to use the limited goods of the program in a more widely effective way. This maxim is nearly self-evident, but it may often conflict with the principle of legal success, as more deeply transformative legal work will tend to be more speculative. That conflict serves as the basis of later discussion, for it represents one of the central tensions in legal services case selection: that between quicker, surer work and longer-term, more speculative projects.

This principle also implies a necessary corollary. Not only ought ELSI prefer cases which maximize benefits over its constituent base, but it also ought to reject cases which undercut community interests. This maxim not only influences which prospective clients ELSI ought to accept, but it also may limit the advocacy permitted by ELSI staff on behalf of any already-accepted client. In this respect ELSI's broader mandate favoring collective interests serves as a kind of "positional conflict" of interest operating as a constraint on its advocacy strategies.

• The principle of attending to the most serious legal matters: Some legal matters are apparently more "serious" than others. The term "serious" is not self-defining, but it is fair to understand it as reflecting the level of pain, discomfort, or harm associated with the legal matter if left unresolved. This axiom holds that ELSI ought to seek to reduce pain and harm at the greatest rate possible consistent with its other commitments. Among those legal matters satisfying the "legal success" maxim above (in that their likelihood of resolution may increase substantially with the aid of the ELSI staff), some will create more discomfort for its victims than others, and ELSI ought to prefer the former to the latter. Marshall Breger's recognition of a priority for "emergency" cases exemplifies this principle.

This maxim will obviously play an important role in any legal services case selection, and may be applied presumptively, if imperfectly, to "types" of legal matters. For example, by and large the specter of eviction and resulting homelessness is more serious than the specter of a bad credit rating, even though the latter problem can present great difficulties for a consumer. Therefore, eviction cases can be preferred to credit rating matters. Within categories, though, there may exist wide ranges of potential harm. One family facing homelessness may have a place to which to move or resources to find suitable replacement housing, while another family facing eviction will have to live in a car. If an applicant screener knows of these differences, then he is entitled to prefer the latter applicant to the former.

• The principle favoring long-term benefit over short-term relief: The goal of efficiency of resource use suggests this next maxim. Given two otherwise equally worthy cases, ELSI ought to prefer a case that will effect a longer-lasting change over one offering short-term relief. If nothing else, this principle tends to reduce the universe of legal matters to be faced in the future and may be deemed a subset of the "seriousness" criterion above. Consider an eviction matter in which the tenant has been brought to court for non-payment of rent and her monthly disability benefit is less than the contract rent for the apartment where she lives. Even if the applicable law permits some defense to the landlord's claim now, the likelihood is substantial that this tenant will be the subject of another similar action in a month or two. The long-term benefit maxim would suggest that this case should have a lower priority than an eviction case in which ELSI could assist a tenant to remain in her apartment for an indefinite period of time.

Id. at 2489-93. Do you agree with these criteria? Could you come up with different ones? Do you agree that whatever criteria are chosen should reflect the underlying mission of the organization?

b. SOLICITATION

While public interest lawyers must inevitably reject cases they do not want or cannot handle, they may also — particularly in the context of impact lawsuits — seek out plaintiffs with compelling claims for representation. Under the dominant ethical view, public interest lawyers in these contexts may generally take some affirmative steps to solicit clients for representation. The contemporary professional rules generally distinguish between solicitation for "pecuniary" and "nonpecuniary" purposes, with tighter restrictions on the former. MODEL RULES OF PROF'L CONDUCT R. 7.3. What this means in practice is that public interest lawyers who are not significantly motivated by collecting legal fees may directly contact prospective clients for participation in a cause-advancing lawsuit. *Id.* Indeed, as the excerpts below discuss, lawyers have a constitutionally protected right to solicit clients for cause-advancing cases, subject to limits on abusive practices that involve "coercion, duress or harassment."

However, as we mentioned earlier, there was a time when it was not clear that the solicitation of clients for test case purposes was constitutionally protected activity. As a result, opponents of public interest lawyering sought to use traditional bans on lawyers' "stirring up litigation" and other solicitation activity to curtail public interest litigation. These attempts were justified on the grounds that they reduced frivolous suits by unaccountable lawyers who were pressuring clients into filing cases. In the classic example, some Southern states attempted to undermine LDF's school desegregation litigation campaign by enforcing prohibitions against client "solicitation" in order to prevent its lawyers from recruiting plaintiffs. This issue ultimately reached the U.S. Supreme Court in the following case.

NATIONAL ASSOCIATION FOR THE ADVANCEMENT OF COLORED PEOPLE V. BUTTON

371 U.S. 415 (1963)

Mr. Justice BRENNAN delivered the opinion of the Court.

. . . [T]he dispute centers about the constitutionality under the Fourteenth Amendment of [Virginia Acts of Assembly] Chapter 33, as construed and applied by the Virginia Supreme Court of Appeals to include NAACP's activities within the statute's ban against "the improper solicitation of any legal or professional business." . . .

. . . In litigation involving public school segregation . . . [t]ypically, a local NAACP branch will invite a member of the legal staff to explain to a meeting of parents and children the legal steps necessary to achieve desegregation. The staff member will bring printed forms to the meeting authorizing him, and other NAACP or Defense Fund attorneys of his designation, to represent the signers in legal proceedings to achieve desegregation. On occasion, blank forms have been signed by litigants, upon the understanding that a member or members of the legal staff, with or without assistance from other NAACP lawyers, or from the Defense Fund, would handle the case. It is usual, after obtaining authorizations, for the staff lawyer to bring into the case the other staff members in the area where suit is to be brought, and sometimes to bring in lawyers from the national organization or the Defense Fund. In effect, then, the prospective litigant retains not so much a particular attorney as the "firm" of NAACP and Defense Fund lawyers, which has a corporate reputation for expertness in presenting and arguing the difficult questions of law that frequently arise in civil rights litigation. . . .

Statutory regulation of unethical and nonprofessional conduct by attorneys has been in force in Virginia since 1849. These provisions outlaw, inter alia, solicitation of legal business in the form of "running" or "capping." Prior to 1956, however, no attempt was made to proscribe under such regulations the activities of the NAACP, which had been carried on openly for many years in substantially the manner described. In 1956, however, the legislature amended . . . the provisions of the Virginia Code forbidding solicitation of legal business by a "runner" or "capper" to include, in the definition of "runner" or "capper," an agent for an individual or organization which retains a lawyer in connection with an action to which it is not a party and in which it has no pecuniary right or liability. Virginia Supreme Court of Appeals held that the chapter's purpose "was to strengthen the existing statutes to further control the evils of solicitation of legal business. . . ." The court held that the activities of NAACP, the Virginia Conference, the Defense Fund, and the lawyers furnished by them, fell within, and could constitutionally be proscribed by, the chapter's expanded definition of improper solicitation of legal business, and also violated Canons 35 and 47 of the American Bar Association's Canons of Professional Ethics, which the court had adopted in 1938. Specifically the court held that, under the expanded definition, such activities on the part of NAACP, the Virginia Conference, and the Defense Fund constituted "fomenting and soliciting legal business in which they are not parties and have no pecuniary right or liability, and which they channel to the enrichment of certain lawyers employed by them, at no cost to the litigants and over which the litigants have no control." . . .

We reverse the judgment of the Virginia Supreme Court of Appeals. We hold that the activities of the NAACP, its affiliates and legal staff shown on this record are modes of expression and association protected by the First and Fourteenth Amendments which Virginia may not prohibit, under its power to regulate the legal profession, as improper solicitation of legal business violative of Chapter 33 and the Canons of Professional Ethics.

A.

We meet at the outset the contention that "solicitation" is wholly outside the area of freedoms protected by the First Amendment. . . . In the context of NAACP objectives, litigation is not a technique of resolving private differences; it is a means for achieving the lawful objectives of equality of treatment by all government, federal, state and local, for the members of the Negro community in this country. It is thus a form of political expression. Groups which find themselves unable to achieve their objectives through the ballot frequently turn to the courts. Just as it was true of the opponents of New Deal legislation during the 1930's, for example, no less is it true of the Negro minority today. And under the conditions of modern government, litigation may well be the sole practicable avenue open to a minority to petition for redress of grievances. . . .

The NAACP is not a conventional political party; but the litigation it assists, while serving to vindicate the legal rights of members of the American Negro community, at the same time and perhaps more importantly, makes possible the distinctive contribution of a minority group to the ideas and beliefs of our society. For such a group, association for litigation may be the most effective form of political association.

B.

... We conclude that under Chapter 33, as authoritatively construed by the Supreme Court of Appeals, a person who advises another that his legal rights have been infringed and refers him to a particular attorney or group of attorneys (for example, to the Virginia Conference's legal staff) for assistance has committed a crime, as has the attorney who knowingly renders assistance under such circumstances. There thus inheres in the statute the gravest danger of smothering all discussion looking to the eventual institution of litigation on behalf of the rights of members of an unpopular minority. Lawyers on the legal staff or even mere NAACP members or sympathizers would understandably hesitate, at an NAACP meeting or on any other occasion, to do what the decree purports to allow, namely, acquaint "persons with what they believe to be their legal rights and * * * (advise) them to assert their rights by commencing or further prosecuting a suit * * *." We cannot close our eyes to the fact that the militant Negro civil rights movement has engendered the intense resentment and opposition of the politically dominant white community of Virginia; litigation assisted by the NAACP has been bitterly fought. In such circumstances, a statute broadly curtailing group activity leading to litigation may easily become a weapon of oppression, however evenhanded its terms appear. Its mere existence could well freeze out of existence all such activity on behalf of the civil rights of Negro citizens.

... We hold that Chapter 33 as construed violates the Fourteenth Amendment by unduly inhibiting protected freedoms of expression and association.

C.

The second contention is that Virginia has a subordinating interest in the regulation of the legal profession, embodied in Chapter 33, which justifies limiting petitioner's First Amendment rights. ...

However valid may be Virginia's interest in regulating the traditionally illegal practices of barratry, maintenance and champerty, that interest does not justify the prohibition of the NAACP activities disclosed by this record. Malicious intent was of the essence of the common-law offenses of fomenting or stirring up litigation. ...

Resort to the courts to seek vindication of constitutional rights is a different matter from the oppressive, malicious, or avaricious use of the legal process for purely private gain. Lawsuits attacking racial discrimination, at least in Virginia, are neither very profitable nor very popular. They are not an object of general competition among Virginia lawyers; the problem is rather one of an apparent dearth of lawyers who are willing to undertake such litigation. There has been neither claim nor proof that any assisted Negro litigants have desired, but have been prevented from retaining, the services of other counsel. We realize that an NAACP lawyer must derive personal satisfaction from participation in litigation on behalf of Negro rights, else he would hardly be inclined to participate at the risk of financial sacrifice. But this would not seem to be the kind of interest or motive which induces criminal conduct. ...

Mr. Justice HARLAN, whom Mr. Justice CLARK and Mr. Justice STEWART join, dissenting. . . .

[I]t is claimed that the interests of petitioner and its members are sufficiently identical to eliminate any "serious danger" of "professionally reprehensible conflicts of interest." . . .

The NAACP may be no more than the sum of the efforts and views infused in it by its members; but the totality of the separate interests of the members and others whose causes the petitioner champions, even in the field of race relations, may far exceed in scope and variety that body's views of policy, as embodied in litigating strategy and tactics. Thus it may be in the interest of the Association in every case to make a frontal attack on segregation, to press for an immediate breaking down of racial barriers, and to sacrifice minor points that may win a given case for the major points that may win other cases too. But in a particular litigation, it is not impossible that after authorizing action in his behalf, a Negro parent, concerned that a continued frontal attack could result in schools closed for years, might prefer to wait with his fellows a longer time for good-faith efforts by the local school board than is permitted by the centrally determined policy of the NAACP. Or he might see a greater prospect of success through discussions with local school authorities than through the litigation deemed necessary by the Association. The parent, of course, is free to withdraw his authorization, but is his lawyer, retained and paid by petitioner and subject to its directions on matters of policy, able to advise the parent with that undivided allegiance that is the hallmark of the attorney-client relation? I am afraid not.

[T]he interests of the NAACP go well beyond the providing of competent counsel for the prosecution or defense of individual claims; they embrace broadly fixed substantive policies that may well often deviate from the immediate, or even long-range, desires of those who choose to accept its offers of legal representations. This serves to underscore the close interdependence between the State's condemnation of solicitation and its prohibition of the unauthorized practice of law by a lay organization. . . .

The *Button* majority was clearly concerned that the Virginia legislature was using the ethical codes to undermine the political goals of the NAACP   that the solicitation rules were part of a broader offensive against desegregation. This is clear from Court's frank admission: "We cannot close our eyes to the fact that the militant Negro civil rights movement has engendered the intense resentment and opposition of the politically dominant white community of Virginia." In this battle, the Court seemed willing to presume an identity of interests between the NAACP lawyers and the community of African-American families it was seeking to represent. It was, perhaps, easier to make such an assumption given the broader civil rights movement for inclusion and equality, and the significant nonlegal infrastructure that existed to promote those aims. In addition, there was no evidence that the NAACP was benefiting financially through the collection of legal fees.

But what about situations in which the lawyers are clearly in the driver's seat — identifying a contested practice and crafting a case to challenge it? Does the lawyers' right to political expression outweigh the risks to client autonomy that might occur? What if a lawyer seeks to advance a cause *and* collect fees in so doing?

IN RE PRIMUS

436 U.S. 412 (1978)

Mr. Justice POWELL delivered the opinion of the Court.

We consider on this appeal whether a State may punish a member of its Bar who, seeking to further political and ideological goals through associational activity, including litigation, advises a lay person of her legal rights and discloses in a subsequent letter that free legal assistance is available from a nonprofit organization with which the lawyer and her associates are affiliated. Appellant, a member of the Bar of South Carolina, received a public reprimand for writing such a letter. The appeal is opposed by the State Attorney General, on behalf of the Board of Commissioners on Grievances and Discipline of the Supreme Court of South Carolina. . . .

I

Appellant, Edna Smith Primus, is a lawyer practicing in Columbia, S. C. During the period in question, she was associated with the "Carolina Community Law Firm," and was an officer of and cooperating lawyer with the Columbia branch of the American Civil Liberties Union (ACLU). She received no compensation for her work on behalf of the ACLU, but was paid a retainer as a legal consultant for the South Carolina Council on Human Relations (Council), a nonprofit organization with offices in Columbia. . . .

During the summer of 1973, local and national newspapers reported that pregnant mothers on public assistance in Aiken County, S. C., were being sterilized or threatened with sterilization as a condition of the continued receipt of medical assistance under the Medicaid program. Concerned by this development, Gary Allen, an Aiken businessman and officer of a local organization serving indigents, called the Council requesting that one of its representatives come to Aiken to address some of the women who had been sterilized. At the Council's behest, appellant, who had not known Allen previously, called him and arranged a meeting in his office in July 1973. Among those attending was Mary Etta Williams, who had been sterilized by Dr. Clovis H. Pierce after the birth of her third child. Williams and her grandmother attended the meeting because Allen, an old family friend, had invited them and because Williams wanted "[t]o see what it was all about. . . ." At the meeting, appellant advised those present, including Williams and the other women who had been sterilized by Dr. Pierce, of their legal rights and suggested the possibility of a lawsuit.

Early in August 1973 the ACLU informed appellant that it was willing to provide representation for Aiken mothers who had been sterilized. Appellant testified that after being advised by Allen that Williams wished to institute suit against Dr. Pierce, she decided to inform Williams of the ACLU's offer of free legal representation. Shortly after receiving appellant's letter, dated August 30, 1973 — the centerpiece of this litigation — Williams visited Dr. Pierce to discuss the progress of her third child who was ill. At the doctor's office, she encountered his lawyer and at the latter's request signed a release of liability in the doctor's favor. Williams showed appellant's letter to the doctor and his lawyer, and they retained a copy. She then called appellant from the doctor's office and announced her intention not to sue. There was no further communication between appellant and Williams.

On October 9, 1974, the Secretary of the Board of Commissioners on Grievances and Discipline of the Supreme Court of South Carolina (Board) filed a formal complaint with the Board, charging that appellant had engaged in "solicitation in violation of the Canons of Ethics" by sending the August 30, 1973, letter to Williams. . . . The [state bar] panel filed a report recommending that appellant be found guilty of soliciting a client on behalf of the ACLU, in violation of Disciplinary Rules . . . of the Supreme Court of South Carolina, and that a private reprimand be issued. . . . On March 17, 1977, the Supreme Court of South Carolina entered an order which adopted verbatim the findings and conclusions of the panel report and increased the sanction, *sua sponte,* to a public reprimand.

We now reverse.

***

IV

. . . The Supreme Court of South Carolina found appellant to have engaged in unethical conduct because she "'solicit[ed] a client for a non-profit organization, which, as its primary purpose, renders legal services, where respondent's associate is a staff counsel for the non-profit organization.'" It rejected appellant's First Amendment defenses by distinguishing *Button.* . . . Whereas the NAACP in that case was primarily a "'political'" organization that used "'litigation as an adjunct to the overriding political aims of the organization,'" the ACLU "'has as one of its primary purposes the rendition of legal services.'". . . The court also intimated that the ACLU's policy of requesting an award of counsel fees indicated that the organization might "'benefit financially in the event of successful prosecution of the suit for money damages.'" . . .

[T]he record does not support the state court's effort to draw a meaningful distinction between the ACLU and the NAACP. From all that appears, the ACLU and its local chapters, much like the NAACP and its local affiliates in *Button,* "[engage] in extensive educational and lobbying activities" and "also [devote] much of [their] funds and energies to an extensive program of assisting certain kinds of litigation on behalf of [their] declared purposes." The court below acknowledged that "'the ACLU has only entered cases in which substantial civil liberties questions are involved. . . .'" . . . For the ACLU, as for the NAACP, "litigation is not a technique of resolving private differences"; it is "a form of political expression" and "political association."

We find equally unpersuasive any suggestion that the level of constitutional scrutiny in this case should be lowered because of a possible benefit to the ACLU. The discipline administered to appellant was premised solely on the possibility of financial benefit to the organization, rather than any possibility of pecuniary gain to herself, her associates, or the lawyers representing the plaintiffs in the *Walker v. Pierce* litigation. It is conceded that appellant received no compensation for any of the activities in question. It is also undisputed that neither the ACLU nor any lawyer associated with it would have shared in any monetary recovery by the plaintiffs in *Walker v. Pierce*. . . .

Contrary to appellee's suggestion, the ACLU's policy of requesting an award of counsel fees does not take this case outside the protection of *Button*. Although the Court in *Button* did not consider whether the NAACP seeks counsel fees, such requests are often made both by that organization, . . . and by the NAACP Legal Defense Fund, Inc. In any event, in a case of this kind there are differences between counsel fees awarded by a court and traditional fee-paying arrangements which militate against a presumption that ACLU sponsorship of litigation is motivated by considerations of pecuniary gain rather than by its widely recognized goal of vindicating civil liberties. Counsel fees are awarded in the discretion of the court; awards are not drawn from the plaintiff's recovery, and are usually premised on a successful outcome; and the amounts awarded often may not correspond to fees generally obtainable in private litigation. Moreover, under prevailing law during the events in question, an award of counsel fees in federal litigation was available only in limited circumstances. And even if there had been an award during the period in question, it would have gone to the central fund of the ACLU. Although such benefit to the organization may increase with the maintenance of successful litigation, the same situation obtains with voluntary contributions and foundation support, which also may rise with ACLU victories in important areas of the law. That possibility, standing alone, offers no basis for equating the work of lawyers associated with the ACLU or the NAACP with that of a group that exists for the primary purpose of financial gain through the recovery of counsel fees.

Appellant's letter of August 30, 1973, to Mrs. Williams thus comes within the generous zone of First Amendment protection reserved for associational freedoms. The ACLU engages in litigation as a vehicle for effective political expression and association, as well as a means of communicating useful information to the public. . . .

V
***

Appellee contends that the disciplinary action taken in this case is part of a regulatory program aimed at the prevention of undue influence, overreaching, misrepresentation, invasion of privacy, conflict of interest, lay interference, and other evils that are thought to inhere generally in solicitation by lawyers of prospective clients, and to be present on the record before us. . . .
***

The record does not support appellee's contention that undue influence, overreaching, misrepresentation, or invasion of privacy actually occurred in this case. Appellant's letter of August 30, 1973, followed up the earlier meeting—one concededly protected by the First and Fourteenth Amendments—by notifying Williams that the ACLU would be interested in supporting possible litigation. The letter imparted additional information material to making an informed decision about whether to authorize litigation, and permitted Williams an opportunity, which she exercised, for arriving at a deliberate decision. The letter was not facially misleading; indeed, it offered "to explain what is involved so you can understand what is going on." The transmittal of this letter—as contrasted with in-person solicitation—involved no appreciable invasion of privacy; nor did it afford any significant opportunity for overreaching or coercion. Moreover, the fact that there was a written communication lessens substantially the difficulty of policing solicitation practices that do offend valid rules of professional conduct. See *Ohralik*, 436 U.S., at 466-467. The manner of solicitation in this case certainly was no more likely to cause harmful consequences than the activity considered in *Button*.

Nor does the record permit a finding of a serious likelihood of conflict of interest or injurious lay interference with the attorney-client relationship. Admittedly, there is some potential for such conflict or interference whenever a lay organization supports any litigation. That potential was present in *Button*, in the NAACP's solicitation of nonmembers and its disavowal of any relief short of full integration. But the Court found that potential insufficient in the absence of proof of a "serious danger" of conflict of interest, of organizational interference with the actual conduct of the litigation. As in *Button*, "[n]othing that this record shows as to the nature and purpose of [ACLU] activities permits an inference of any injurious intervention in or control of litigation which would constitutionally authorize the application," of the Disciplinary Rules to appellant's activity. . . .

We conclude that South Carolina's application of its DR2-103(D)(5)(a) and (c) and 2-104(A)(5) to appellant's solicitation by letter on behalf of the ACLU violates the First and Fourteenth Amendments.

Mr. Justice REHNQUIST, dissenting. . . .

I believe that constitutional inquiry must focus on the character of the conduct which the State seeks to regulate, and not on the motives of the individual lawyers or the nature of the particular litigation involved. . . .

Here, South Carolina has not attempted to punish the ACLU or any laymen associated with it. Gary Allen, who was the instigator of the effort to sue Dr. Pierce, remains as free as before to solicit potential plaintiffs for future litigation. Likewise, Primus remains as free as before to address gatherings of the sort described in *Button* to advise potential plaintiffs of their legal rights. Primus' first contact with Williams took place at such a gathering, and South Carolina evidently in response to *Button*, has not attempted to discipline her for her part in that meeting. It has disciplined her for initiating further contact on an individual basis with Williams, who had not expressed any desire to become involved in the collective activity being organized by the ACLU. While *Button* appears to permit such individual solicitation for political purposes by lay members of the organization, it nowhere explicitly permits such activity on the part of lawyers.

As the Court understands the Disciplinary Rule enforced by South Carolina, "a lawyer employed by the ACLU or a similar organization may never give unsolicited advice to a lay person that he or she retain the organization's free services." That prohibition seems to me entirely reasonable. . . . I cannot agree that a State must prove such harmful consequences in each case simply because an organization such as the ACLU or the NAACP is involved.

I cannot share the Court's confidence that the danger of such consequences is minimized simply because a lawyer proceeds from political conviction rather than for pecuniary gain. A State may reasonably fear that a lawyer's desire to resolve "substantial civil liberties questions," may occasionally take precedence over his duty to advance the interests of his client. It is even more reasonable to fear that a lawyer in such circumstances will be inclined to pursue both culpable and blameless defendants to the last ditch in order to achieve his ideological goals. Although individual litigants, including the ACLU, may be free to use the courts for such purposes, South Carolina is likewise free to restrict the activities of the members of its Bar who attempt to persuade them to do so. . . .

As Justice Rehnquist's dissent emphasizes, a key element of the case was the apparent lack of a pecuniary motive by Primus, which the majority found reduced the risk of possible overreaching. What if Primus had sought to bring the identical suit, which the court concedes was politically driven, as ACLU counsel under a policy of awarding legal fees to cooperating attorneys? What if she had brought the suit on her own (i.e., not as an ACLU cooperating attorney) and sought statutory attorneys' fees? What if Primus had brought the suit on her own on a contingency fee basis? Or what if she was a partner in a personal injury firm seeking clients for a class action (on contingency) against doctors who performed sterilizations? Should the fee arrangement affect the level of constitutional protection that a lawyer receives? Recall our discussion in Chapter 4, in which we highlighted the public interest legal work that is done by lawyers in private law firms. Would any of this be protected under *Primus*? Should it be?

c. CONFLICTS

In addition to selecting clients in accordance with solicitation rules, public interest lawyers must also consider how client selection may be affected by conflicts of interests. There are a number of proscriptions. A lawyer may not, without client consent, accept the representation of a client if it would be "directly adverse" to another current client, MODEL RULES OF PROF'L CONDUCT R. 1.7(a)(1), or if it would be directly adverse to a former client in a matter that is the same or substantially related. MODEL RULES OF PROF'L CONDUCT R. 1.9(a). These rules apply to both an individual lawyer and to an entire legal organization by imputation. MODEL RULES OF PROF'L CONDUCT R. 1.10.

The Model Rules also state that it is a conflict for a lawyer to represent a client if there is "a significant risk that the representation . . . will be materially limited by the lawyer's responsibilities to another client, a former client or a third person or by a personal interest of the lawyer." MODEL RULES OF PROF'L CONDUCT R. 1.7(a)(1). We will discuss below how a lawyer working alongside organizers in a multifaceted law and organizing campaign may avoid such a conflict. However, for now we note that this rule might apply if a lawyer's strong "personal interest" in a particular outcome limited his ability to effectively represent a client. Generally, such a conflict can be waived by informed client consent, but a public interest lawyer should understand at the outset that, as an ethical matter, a strong commitment to a particular outcome may fall within a conflicts analysis.

Even if no conflict exists, there is the broader ethical question of whether a lawyer should take on a case in the first instance to advance a policy position about which there are strongly held and divergent opinions in the affected community. Discussing conflicting opinions within the LGBT community regarding the desirability of pursuing different types of policy claims, William Rubenstein poses the issue this way:

> Given the conflicting opinions on these subjects among the litigators, they face a dilemma: How are they to decide which depictions of gay identity to present in the cases that they litigate?
>
> Several possibilities are evident. One approach would be to yield decision-making to the individual clients, allowing those persons to determine how to present homosexuality to the courts in their own cases. By contrast, the professional litigators have largely approached the issue as appropriate for debate, consultation, and consensus among themselves; for example, the Lesbian/Gay Litigators Roundtable regularly discussed the issue throughout the late 1980s and early 1990s, reaching a formal consensus . . . in 1994. A third approach, espoused by many attorneys not involved in the professional meetings, has been to view the decision as one requiring the application of their own technical "expertise."

William B. Rubenstein, *Divided We Litigate: Addressing Disputes Among Group Members and Lawyers in Civil Rights Campaigns*, 106 YALE L.J. 1623, 1643 (1997). Rubenstein voices skepticism about the model of allowing individual clients to decide whether to pursue policy-oriented cases, and concludes by proposing "procedural and ethical innovations that would make the resolution of group member disputes more democratic and would value expertise more in the resolution of lawyer disagreements." *Id.* at 1680-81. Do you agree that the decision to file policy reform cases should effectively be put to a constituency vote? How would this work? How could you stop lawyers and clients from violating the democratic decision-making process and filing a suit contrary to the community's majority wishes? Is it even desirable to try?

2. Accountability During the Conduct of Litigation

Once a lawyer accepts a client (or group of clients) for representation, of course, she assumes a professional obligation to zealously represent the client's interests within the bounds of the law. This obligation gives rise to two areas of ethical inquiry that we cover in this section. The first involves the allocation of decision-making authority in both individual and class representation. Who gets to decide which questions and how? The second again involves the possibility of conflicted interests and how they should be managed. We will treat these issues first in the context of civil litigation and then highlight some special problems in the criminal context.

a. CONTROL AND CONFLICTS

In general, the professional regulation of lawyer-client decision making adopts an "ends-means" dichotomy, in which "a lawyer shall abide by a client's decisions concerning the objectives of representation" but "may take such action on behalf of the client as is impliedly authorized to carry out the representation." MODEL RULES OF PROF'L CONDUCT R. 1.2(a). In addition, the same conflict of interest rules discussed above would apply through the representation. We next consider these issues of control and conflict from the point of view of individual and class representation.

i. INDIVIDUAL REPRESENTATION

Although clients have the ultimate authority to define the goals of representation, as many commentators have noted, the line between "ends" and "means" is not so neat, and lawyers may use their position of relative power to advance agendas that may diverge from the clients', thus undercutting client autonomy.

In the context of individual representation, the problem arises when the client is relatively weak, which permits the lawyer to make crucial case decisions, often persuading the client to go along. As we saw in the last chapter, the lawyer may also reinforce client domination by offering a story of client victimization and passivity as a strategy to win the case. *See* Anthony V. Alfieri, *Reconstructive Poverty Law Practice: Learning Lessons of Client Narrative*, 100 YALE L.J. 2108 (1992). However, as Corey Shdaimah found, poverty lawyers often take steps to promote client autonomy—even if it may conflict with the lawyer's best judgment. Consider the reflections of Martin, a legal aid lawyer Shdaimah interviewed:

> [I]f the client has clearly said that's what they want to do, then that's what's done. I mean, you have to respect the client's wishes. . . . If I feel extremely strongly that the client is making a decision that's going to have significant harm to them, I tell the client, "This is your decision to make; it's not the one that I would make." I would explain why I would make a different decision. I would tell, make it clear to the client that regardless of the client's decision that I will respect that wish, and I would probably put it in writing, that I'm advising you to do this; however, if you choose to do something else that's what I'm going to do.

COREY S. SHDAIMAH, NEGOTIATING JUSTICE: PROGRESSIVE LAWYERING, LOW-INCOME CLIENTS, AND THE QUEST FOR SOCIAL CHANGE 90 (2009). What would you do if your client wanted to pursue a course of action you thought was likely to fail?

Oftentimes, the control problem flows from the lawyer's perception that "she knows best" based on her legal experience what a client should do. But, as Lucie White recounts in her powerful story of representing a welfare client, Mrs. G., even lawyers who are well meaning and have the best intentions may misunderstand clients' true wishes and thus guide them in ways that are inconsistent with the clients' own desires. Lucie E. White, *Subordination, Rhetorical Survival Skills and Sunday Shoes: Notes on the Hearing of Mrs. G*, 38 Buff. L. Rev. 1 (1990). In Mrs. G.'s case, the lawyer wanted the client not to reveal that she had used her welfare payment to purchase new Sunday shoes for her children—which was an impermissible use of the grant. However, when the client told her story on her own terms, the hearing officer dismissed the complaint against her and the lawyer realized that the shared cultural norms around churchgoing ultimately trumped technical law. In a historical example from the abolition era, Paul Finkelman reinforces the same theme: that clients often times have a clearer understanding of their options, and the consequences that may flow from exercising them, than their lawyers.

> Burns [the escaped slave] declined Dana's offer [of legal services]. Burns certainly had no reason to trust this unknown white man who suddenly appeared at his side. Moreover, Burns seems to have had a better understanding of the realities of his situation than Dana did. Burns told Dana, "It is of no use, they have got me." Dana, with a rather naive faith in the legal system, persisted, "I told him there might be some flaw in the papers, or some mistake, [and] that he might get off." But, legal technicalities meant nothing to a man who had grown up as a slave. Burns predicted—correctly as it turned out—that any attempt to interfere in this rendition would only make things worse when he was finally sent back. Burns did not want to anger his master by making his rendition any more expensive and time-consuming than necessary. He told Dana, "I shall fare worse if I resist." . . . Dana, a lawyer with no previous relationship to Burns, ignored his refusal of aid and argued directly to the Commissioner for a delay. The Commissioner, who would ultimately send Burns back to slavery, decided that Burns really did want a delay though Burns himself refused to speak to the issue. Despite the Commissioner's intention to conduct a summary hearing, Dana maneuvered him into turning the proceeding into something close to a full blown trial. . . . As events unfolded, Burns might have been better off if the antislavery lawyers and Commissioner Loring had acceded to his initial request. When Burns was finally returned to the South, Suttle [his master] punished him harshly, keeping him in chains for many months. The experience left Burns weak, ill, and permanently lame. It probably shortened his life.

Paul Finkelman, *Legal Ethics and Fugitive Slaves: The Anthony Burns Case, Judge Loring, and Abolitionist Attorneys*, 17 Cardozo L. Rev. 1793, 1804-07 (1996).

ii. CLASS REPRESENTATION

Contemporary analyses of public interest lawyer accountability have generally attended to problems peculiar to the classic civil rights impact litigation model, in which strong lawyers (who work full time in nonprofit groups to control case selection and execution) represent a class of weak clients (who are diffuse and disorganized) in the pursuit of policy change through courts. Although this model of lawyering represents only one slice of contemporary reform efforts, it continues to remain an important vehicle of advocacy and to dominate ethical analyses of public interest practice. The issue is how lawyers comply with their duties to represent their clients in the context of multiparty representation in which group interests are diverse and potentially in conflict.

It is here that lawyers may exercise their power in ways that they view as cause-advancing but others may view as infringing on client autonomy or not acting in the community's best interests. As you recall, the conventional view of legal representation deems lawyers as neutral agents of client wishes. David Luban suggests that this view is inadequate in the reform context, in which public interest lawyers may legitimately influence clients in order to advance the cause. Luban argues that the pursuit of a cause renders inadequate "an ordinary lawyer-client relationship based on agency conceptions of fiduciary responsibility" and instead calls for "a relationship of comradeship, of primary commitment to the cause." LUBAN, LAWYERS AND JUSTICE, supra, at 338.

Yet commentators have expressed concerns about the risks of lawyer power in these situations. One risk is that public interest lawyers — in the pursuit of what they believe to be the community's best interests — may in fact end up advancing one set of community interests over another. Recall Derrick Bell's article questioning whether LDF's commitment to desegregation — supported by its middle-class white and black constituents — ignored the needs of black communities by privileging litigation to achieve integration over political strategies to promote educational quality.

> . . . The NAACP and the LDF, responsible for virtually all school desegregation suits, usually seek to establish a racial population at each school that (within a range of 10 to 15 percent) reflects the percentage of whites and blacks in the district. But in a growing number of the largest urban districts, the school system is predominantly black. The resistance of most white parents to sending their children to a predominantly black school and the accessibility of a suburban residence or a private school to all but the poorest renders implementation of such plans extremely difficult. Although many whites undoubtedly perceive a majority black school as ipso facto a poor school, the schools can be improved and white attitudes changed. All too little attention has been given to making black schools educationally effective. Furthermore, the disinclination of white parents to send their children to black schools has not been lessened by charges made over a long period of time by civil rights groups that black schools are educationally bankrupt and unconstitutional per se. NAACP policies nevertheless call for maximizing racial balance within the district as an immediate goal while supporting litigation that will eventually require the consolidation of predominantly white surrounding districts.
>
> * * *
>
> The hard-line position of established civil rights groups on school desegregation is explained in part by pragmatic considerations. These organizations are supported by middle class blacks and whites who believe fervently in integration. At their socioeconomic level, integration has worked well, and they are certain that once whites and blacks at lower economic levels are successfully mixed in the schools, integration also will work well at those levels. Many of these supporters either reject or fail to understand suggestions that alternatives to integrated schools should be considered, particularly in majority-black districts. They will be understandably reluctant to provide financial support for policies which they think unsound, possibly illegal, and certainly disquieting. . . .

Jack Greenberg, LDF Director-Counsel, acknowledges that fundraising concerns may play a small role in the selection of cases. Even though civil rights lawyers often obtain the clients, Greenberg reports, "there may be financial contributors to reckon with who may ask that certain cases be brought and others not." He hastens to add that within broad limits lawyers "seem to be free to pursue their own ideas of right, . . . affected little or not at all by contributors." The reassurance is double-edged. The lawyers' freedom to pursue their own ideas of right may pose no problems as long as both clients and contributors share a common social outlook. But when the views of some or all of the clients change, a delayed recognition and response by the lawyers is predictable.

School expert Ron Edmonds contends that civil rights attorneys often do not represent their clients' best interests in desegregation litigation because "they answer to a miniscule constituency while serving a massive clientele." Edmonds distinguishes the clients of civil rights attorneys (the persons on whose behalf suit is filed) from their "constituents" (those to whom the attorney must answer for his actions). He suggests that in class action school desegregation cases the mass of lower class black parents and children are merely clients. To define constituents, Edmonds asks, "[To] what class of Americans does the civil rights attorney feel he must answer for his professional conduct?" The answer can be determined by identifying those with whom the civil rights attorney confers as he defines the goals of the litigation. He concludes that those who currently have access to the civil rights attorney are whites and middle class blacks who advocate integration and categorically oppose majority black schools.

Edmonds suggests that, more than other professionals, the civil rights attorney labors in a closed setting isolated from most of his clients. No matter how numerous, the attorney's clients cannot become constituents unless they have access to him before or during the legal process. The result is the pursuit of metropolitan desegregation without sufficient regard for the probable instructional consequences for black children. In sum, he charges, "A class action suit serving only those who pay the attorney fee has the effect of permitting the fee paying minority to impose its will on the majority of the class on whose behalf suit is presumably brought." . . .

The position of the established civil rights groups obviates any need to determine whether a continued policy of maximum racial balance conforms with the wishes of even a minority of the class. This position represents an extraordinary view of the lawyer's role. Not only does it assume a perpetual retainer authorizing a lifelong effort to obtain racially balanced schools. It also fails to reflect any significant change in representational policy from a decade ago, when virtually all blacks assumed that integration was the best means of achieving a quality education for black children, to the present time, when many black parents are disenchanted with the educational results of integration. . . .

Derrick A. Bell, Jr., *Serving Two Masters: Integration Ideals and Client Interests in School Desegregation Litigation*, 85 Yale L.J. 470 (1976). Did the LDF lawyers violate any ethical duties in pursuing an integration agenda? How might they have handled this differently?

For other excellent discussions of the tensions in class actions, see Shauna I. Marshall, *Class Actions as Instruments of Change: Reflections on* Davis v. City and County of San Francisco, 29 U.S.F. L. Rev. 911 (1995); Deborah L. Rhode, *Class Conflicts in Class Actions*, 34 Stan. L. Rev. 1183 (1982).

Note that the issue of class conflicts can come up in different ways. In *Fiandaca v. Cunningham*, 827 F.2d 825 (1st Cir. 1987), the First Circuit heard an appeal of a motion to disqualify a legal aid group, New Hampshire Legal Assistance (NHLA), from proceeding as plaintiffs' class counsel in a case challenging the state's failure to establish a facility to house female inmates with the same services and programs provided to male inmates in state prison. When the state offered to settle by creating such a facility on the grounds of New Hampshire's sole mental health institution, the Laconia State School and Training Center, NHLA declined the offer after consulting with its clients. The state then moved to disqualify NHLA, arguing that it faced a conflict of interest because in a separate lawsuit NHLA also represented a class of mentally retarded persons housed at Laconia, who did not want the new facility built on the center's grounds. The First Circuit agreed and held that NHLA should have been disqualified because the settlement offer placed it "in the untenable position of being simultaneously obligated to represent vigorously the interests of two conflicting clients." *Id.* at 829. NHLA had argued that the state made the settlement offer precisely to manufacture the disqualifying conflict in order to get it out of the case — an argument the court rejected. But it is notable, as Rhode and Luban observe in their treatment of the case, that none of the plaintiffs from either class were complaining. Deborah L. Rhode & David Luban, Legal Ethics 663 (5th ed. 2009). Is it fair for a defendant to be able to disqualify plaintiffs' counsel for a conflict that does not involve the defendant directly (i.e., NHLA did not represent the state of New Hampshire)?

b. PUBLIC REPRESENTATION

There is a general consensus that government prosecutors, because they wield the power of the state, have ethical duties that set them apart from other public or private lawyers. *See generally* Model Rules of Prof'l Conduct R. 3.8. Specifically, a prosecutor's ethical duty points toward fulfilling her role in a manner consistent with the broader public interest. Should, and do, the same responsibilities extend to government lawyers in civil litigation? The following excerpts ask this question, first in a general sense, and then in the context of federal government lawyers defending the government in certain types of litigation.

Bruce A. Green, *Must Government Lawyers "Seek Justice" in Civil Litigation?*

9 Widener J. Pub. L. 235, 235-37, 240-42, 249-50, 252 (2000)

Lawyers for private parties are generally expected to serve as zealous advocates. Although there is disagreement about the lengths to which lawyers as advocates may go, should go and should be permitted to go, they are generally expected to pursue their private clients' objectives, even if the truth is derailed or the outcome is unjust. . . . In comparison, the professional responsibility of government lawyers, at least in criminal litigation, is to "seek justice."

Criminal prosecutors have been characterized as "minister[s] of justice." Although the precise implications of their quasi-judicial role are contested, it has been understood since the nineteenth century that criminal prosecutors must seek just outcomes. Most importantly, they must avoid "the conviction of the innocent" and they must promote the fairness of the judicial process. . . . The assignment of a quasi-judicial role to prosecutors reflects a recognition that the adversary process is an imperfect means of achieving the truth and a belief that, if prosecutors temper their advocacy, unfair and erroneous convictions are less likely to occur. . . .

Unlike in the criminal context, in the civil context it is generally not accepted that government lawyers must "seek justice." To be sure, some government law offices publicly acknowledge this obligation. The United States Department of Justice is one such example. The facade of its building in Washington, D.C. bears a quotation from former Solicitor General Frederick W. Lehmann: "The United States wins its case whenever justice is done one of its citizens in the courts." Yet, individual lawyers who represent the federal, state or local government in civil litigation may have a different understanding. They may perceive the civil government litigator solely as a zealous advocate, not as a minister of justice.

How the government's civil litigators envision their role will influence a range of decisions, which individually or collectively can have considerable importance for the administration of civil justice in cases involving the public interest. . . . Must government lawyers refrain in civil litigation, as in criminal prosecutions, from bringing "bad" or undeserving cases, or, like private lawyers, are they subject only to restrictions against taking frivolous positions?

Similarly, how government lawyers envision their role will influence their procedural decisions. For the benefit of private litigants, lawyers generally may exploit legal and factual errors made by the court or the opposing party. . . . Must the government's civil litigators, like its criminal prosecutors, correct or "confess error," or, like private lawyers in civil litigation, may they freely encourage and exploit it? . . .

As a practical matter . . . the question whether government lawyers must seek justice in civil litigation is a question about the role of all government lawyers. That is because a large amount of authority is delegated to subordinate lawyers in the typical government law office. . . .

When the government . . . is a civil plaintiff in an ordinary business dispute (e.g., a breach of contract case) or is a civil defendant, the government is arguably no different from a private litigant. Therefore, one may assume that the government lawyer's role becomes more akin to the role of a private lawyer.

Charles Gardner, a former State Deputy Attorney General in Nevada, offered a personal experience which tests this intuition:

> [W]hile representing the state prison in an institutional reform suit, [I discovered] that the prison was in violation of state fire codes worse than even the complaint suggested. For a decade the state fire marshal and prison officials had agreed to cover it up, while the problems grew worse every time the prison was inspected. It was all very well documented, down to the minutes of the truly conspiratorial meetings. Nothing worked, not the sprinklers, not the fire truck, not the alarms — even the fire exit signs were upside down. It was

simply agreed that the fire marshal would look the other way for its sister state agency.

As Gardner described it, there was disagreement in his office about what position to take. Many deputy state attorneys in Gardner's office thought they had an obligation to defend the state officers. One can understand why this might be so. The lawyers might have considered the state officers to be their clients and therefore felt duty-bound to take direction from those officers or to serve their objectives. Alternatively, the lawyers might have perceived that in order to achieve a just result, the prisoners' claim had to be tested in an adversarial proceeding at which it was zealously opposed; that is to say, for every action against the government, "justice" required an equal and opposite reaction by the government's lawyers. Gardner's position, in contrast, "was that state officers had violated the law and i[t] was our duty to prosecute them." He described, "I wrote it all up in a memo to the state attorney general, who, it turned out, was quite upset that I had violated the tradition of plausible deniability that the subordinate is supposed to offer to the elected official."

District Judge Jack B. Weinstein offered another example, drawing on his prior experience as county attorney. Judge Weinstein raised the question whether county lawyers could properly seek "to forestall reapportionment" as required after the Supreme Court recognized the principle of one-man-one vote. He noted that many counties took positions in litigation that were contrary to the Court's reading of the Constitution, but in his view, government lawyers must take a firm position in favor of conforming government practices to the law. . . .

[In the context of asserting procedural objections,] . . . the following scenario was recently discussed by lawyers in the New York State Attorney General's Office:

> Counsel for a losing party in an administrative proceeding against the State advises the assistant attorney general that she intends to bring [a judicial] proceeding challenging the agency's decision. She indicates that she plans to commence the proceeding by a particular date that the assistant attorney general knows would be outside the time required by the four month statute. The assistant attorney general recognizes that the opposing party's attorney is generally unfamiliar with the technical requirements of [the applicable law]. She also believes that the proceeding, if timely, would have a good chance of success on the merits. May she advise opposing counsel of the timing requirements? Must she refrain from doing so?

The question here, it should be stressed, is not whether the government lawyer should seek to dismiss an appeal for failure to meet the timing requirements after the fact. Rather, the question is whether the government lawyer may alert opposing counsel to the requirement before the fact so that the opposing counsel will be more likely to comply with the technical requirement. Alternatively, does the government lawyer have an obligation, as a zealous advocate for the government agency, to seek to gain a strategic advantage by refraining from notifying the other lawyer of the law's technical requirements and, indeed, insofar as possible, by discouraging the other lawyer from discovering that she is operating under an erroneous understanding of the law? . . .

While acknowledging that there is no definitive expression of the government lawyer's obligations in civil litigation, Green goes on to identify several potential sources that might support such a lawyer's decision to comply with a different set of norms than those that apply to private lawyers. First, in any given jurisdiction, there may be extrinsic sources of ethical obligations, such as professional ethics codes, judicial decisions, or standards set internally by a particular government law department. *Id.* at 256-63. Second, Green suggests that government lawyers may be held to different obligations because of their unique constitutional and statutory roles. *Id.* at 265-79. Although government lawyers technically represent specific government agencies and officials, under one view their real client is the sovereign itself. Thus, the government lawyers' distinct professional obligations derive in part from the fact that their client owes a special duty to the public good.

c. LITIGATING IN THE CONTEXT OF BROADER ADVOCACY

i. *COORDINATING LAW AND ORGANIZING*

Efforts to combine litigation with organizing and other forms of advocacy have created additional questions about the ethical conduct of lawyers. *See* Sameer M. Ashar, *Public Interest Lawyers and Resistance Movements*, 95 CAL. L. REV. 1879, 1910 (2007). How do lawyers manage their obligations to clients when they are involved in broader efforts that invite them to coordinate with other political stakeholders? Are there any restrictions on how they may use litigation to advance campaign goals? The following excerpt discusses some of the ethical issues confronted by lawyers engaged in law and organizing.

2. Confidentiality

Confidentiality is a central tenet of the legal profession. A lawyer is required to maintain the confidentiality of all attorney-client communications and may not reveal any information related to the representation of a client to third parties. The duty of confidentiality applies to all information obtained during the course of representation, regardless of the source. Confidentiality rules can apply even in situations in which the lawyer receives confidential information, but does not take on representation or perform legal services for the prospective client.

Perhaps the most perplexing confidentiality issues emerge when lawyers and organizers collaborate on a common project. A good illustration of how such ethical tensions could arise is found in the Workplace Project, which uses a multidisciplinary staff to provide legal services. When an individual comes to the Workplace Project for assistance, he first meets with an organizer and describes his workplace problem, which may or may not be amenable to a legal solution. The organizer describes the way that the Workplace Project operates, including its organizing mission. Next, the client meets with a non-lawyer counselor who also listens to the client's problem. In deciding how to respond to the client's concerns, the counselor might consult with a lawyer on staff. If the client is found to have a complex problem, the client will meet with a team of advisors, including the attorney, organizer, and counselor. Through the course of these strategy sessions, the team decides whether legal action is necessary. If the client's case is accepted for legal representation, the team continues to work together on the matter.

While the interdisciplinary team approach to working with the client is appealing for a variety of reasons, this form of advocacy raises serious questions regarding the protection of client confidentiality. In order to include non-lawyer organizers within the scope of confidentiality protections, strict procedures—similar to those in place at a law firm—must be established before collaboration begins. Protocols regarding how confidential information must be handled should be reduced to writing so that all parties involved, including clients, organizers, and lawyers, understand the rules that apply to the collaboration. A lawyer who fails to create such procedures exposes herself to possible discipline. Furthermore, lawyers working together with organizers on legal matters must provide training for the nonlawyer organizers regarding confidentiality rules and explain that their work on legal matters must comply with the lawyer's ethical responsibilities. At all times, the attorney must carefully supervise and remain responsible for the organizer's work product and conduct.

Lawyers collaborating with organizers in this manner might ask the client to sign a waiver of confidentiality. However, consent to disclosure of confidential information is extremely problematic because such consent may only be sought if it is in the best interests of the client, there is full disclosure, and the client's consent is knowing and voluntary. Not only will it be difficult to explain to a client the many possible scenarios that could arise as a result of such a waiver, but it is also questionable whether such a waiver is voluntary when made in a situation in which organizing is a required condition to receiving legal services.

One solution to the client confidentiality dilemma is to entirely separate the legal work from that of the organizing work and not involve any organizers in the lawyering process. Under such a model, clients must be informed of the potential consequences of sharing their confidential information with individuals outside the attorney-client relationship, such as organizers. In addition, steps should be taken to ensure that other aspects of the representation, such as the physical setup of client meetings and the location of client's files, are conducive to maintaining the client's privacy.

3. Conflict of Interest and Scope of Representation
The ethical rules of conflict of interest and scope of representation provide important guidance for law and organizing practitioners in determining the proper path to follow when working with community members and organizations. It has long been held that the lawyer has a duty of loyalty to her clients. Accordingly, the lawyer may not allow her personal interests, the interests of other clients, or the interests of third parties to interfere with her representation of the client. If interests of a third party potentially conflict, the lawyer may accept representation only if the lawyer reasonably believes that the client's interests will not be negatively affected and if the client consents after full disclosure. Even if a third party is paying for the client's legal services, the third party may not interfere with the attorney-client relationship.

Under the scope of representation rules, the attorney must allow the client to articulate his objectives and to make any key decisions regarding his substantive legal rights. In contrast, the attorney has the responsibility of making final decisions regarding questions of legal strategy. However, the attorney must consult with the client regarding the means by which client objectives will be pursued. In general, "the lawyer should assume responsibility for technical and legal tactical issues, but should defer to the client regarding such questions as the expense to be incurred and concern for third persons who might be adversely affected."

Tension between the interests of the client and the interests of the organizers is one of the principal ways in which ethical dilemmas arise. Consider, for example, a situation in which lawyers and organizers are working together on a matter and a decision must be made regarding whether to file an action on behalf of a client in state or federal court. Each option offers advantages and disadvantages, but after learning that the potential for recovering damages is greater in federal court, the client expresses his desire to pursue the federal remedy. The attorney also feels that, as a matter of strategy, federal court is preferable because the federal law on the matter is more favorable to the client and the judges in federal court have a history of finding in favor of clients in similar situations. However, the organizers do not agree. The federal court is a good distance away from the community in which the events occurred, and the organizers believe that this will prevent mass mobilization around the suit. The organizers are adamant that the suit be filed in the local state court so that it can be used as the centerpiece of an organizing campaign.

The attorney in the hypothetical is in a difficult situation. If she decides to file in state court, despite the fact that both she and the client believe that federal court is the preferable forum, she risks violating her ethical duties as an attorney. Although the state filing might be best from the organizing standpoint, the attorney must properly give the authority to make decisions regarding the goals and objectives of the case to the client, not to the organizers. Furthermore, she must not allow a third party to influence the course of the litigation and must insist on pursuing the client's goals zealously, within the bounds of the law, applying her best tactical judgment as an attorney.

It has been suggested that conflict of interest problems could be avoided by carefully crafted client retainers. For example, the attorney could draft a "limited retainer" explaining to the client that the attorney will only continue to represent him so long as the client's interests do not diverge from broader public interest or community organizing goals. Alternatively, the client could be asked to sign a "prospective waiver" in which the client would waive any conflicts of interest that might evolve in the future between the lawyer-organizer and the client. Yet, whether such contracts would be found valid by a court of law remains unclear. The simplest strategy for averting conflicts is for the lawyer to avoid simultaneously serving as an organizer and a legal representative.

Scott L. Cummings & Ingrid V. Eagly, *A Critical Reflection on Law and Organizing,* 48 UCLA L. Rev. 443, 506-13 (2001).

In addition to tensions in organizing practices, lawyers' roles in public media communication have also raised issues about the limits on lawyers' conduct. Deborah Cantrell suggests that ethical rules not only permit cause lawyers to engage in public advocacy but may even require them to do so in order to fulfill their professional duty of competence, which is defined in reference to what similarly situated lawyers would do to effectively advance the cause. Deborah J. Cantrell, *Sensational Reports: The Ethical Duty of Cause Lawyers to Be Competent in Public Advocacy,* 30 Hamline L. Rev. 567, 572 (2007).

Ethical issues also come up in the context of other types of lawyer-nonlawyer collaborations. Sometimes these are ad hoc or situational. Think back to Muneer Ahmad's discussion of using translators to facilitate the representation of Limited English Proficient (LEP) clients in the last chapter. Does it break the bond of lawyer-client confidentiality when an LEP client uses a friend or family member as a translator? Other types of collaborative enterprises are more systematic and raise different ethical issues. For instance, "multidisciplinary practice" (MDP) involves lawyers "working closely with other professions, law advocates and community agencies to meet a variety of needs and overcome barriers." Louise G. Trubek & Jennifer J. Farnham, *Social Justice Collaboratives: Multidisciplinary Practices for People,* 7 Clinical L. Rev. 227, 229 (2000). Some MDPs adopt a social justice orientation to promote holistic service provision and effective collaboration around broader social change goals and involve collaborations between lawyers and social workers, psychiatrists, business consultants, and other types of professionals. *Id.* In such situations, the ABA Model Rules express concern for a lawyer's "professional independence." Model Rule 5.4 prohibits a lawyer from forming a "partnership with a nonlawyer if any of the activities of the partnership consist of the practice of law," and prohibits a lawyer from permitting "a person who recommends, employs, or pays the lawyer to render legal services for another to direct or regulate the lawyer's professional judgment in rendering such legal services." Model Rules of Prof'l Conduct R. 5.4(b) & (c). Do MDPs risk violating these rules? If so, do you think that the rules should be amended to permit greater flexibility for MDP activity? Note that Rule 5.4(d) prohibits lawyers from practicing "in the form of a professional corporation or association" if "a nonlawyer is a corporate director or officer thereof." Many nonprofit public interest groups have nonlawyer board members from the corporate world who help raise funds. Could this pose an ethical problem for a nonprofit public interest lawyer? How could such practices be structured to avoid nonlawyers from exercising control over the lawyer's professional judgment? Is this another situation where the rules as written may not be well suited to public interest practice?

ii. *LITIGATING CASES FOR PURPOSES OTHER THAN COURTROOM VICTORY*

While public interest lawyers generally litigate to enforce law, sometimes they do so to gain other political advantages. Michael McCann has argued that litigation can play multiple roles in social movements: "litigation can work initially to expose systemic vulnerabilities and to render legal claims sensible or salient to aggrieved citizens. As marginalized groups act on these opportunities, they often gain sophistication and confidence in their capacity to mobilize legal conventions to name wrongs, to direct blame, to frame demands, and to advance their cause." Michael McCann, *Law and Social Movements: Contemporary Perspectives,* 2 Ann. Rev. L. Soc. Sci. 17, 26 (2006). In addition, "litigation offers formidable tactical leverage for social policy advocates" by imposing "substantial costs" that may pressure decision makers to negotiate settlements. *Id.* at 29; *see also* JOEL F. HANDLER, SOCIAL MOVEMENTS AND THE LEGAL SYSTEM: A THEORY OF LAW REFORM AND SOCIAL CHANGE 209-22 (1978) (discussing the "indirect effects" of law-reform activity).

Even unsuccessful litigation may have positive long-term effects on social movements. Doug NeJaime argues that losing may ultimately advance movements by helping

> a specific organization stake out an identity in a competitive social movement by committing itself to an important issue area susceptible to judicial rejection; and . . . contribut[ing] to mobilization and fundraising by inspiring outrage and signaling the need for continued activism in light of courts' failure to act. . . . [In addition, loss] may prompt advocates to shift more attention and resources to other law-making institutions, but it may do so in a way that allows advocates to carve out a specific need for action by other state actors; and . . . [a]dvocates may use loss to appeal to the public by encouraging citizens to rein in an "activist," countermajoritarian judiciary.

Douglas NeJaime, *Winning Through Losing*, 96 IOWA L. REV. 941, 969 (2011).

Although public interest lawyers do not typically bring cases intending to lose, they may bring cases when they know that the odds of victory in court are slim in order to gain some of these other positive benefits. In an influential article, Peter Gabel and Paul Harris argued for a "power-oriented approach to law practice" designed to expand "political consciousness through using the legal system to increase people's sense of personal and political power." Peter Gabel & Paul Harris, *Building Power and Breaking Images: Critical Legal Theory and the Practice of Law*, 11 N.Y.U. REV. L. & SOC. CHANGE 369, 375-76 (1982-83). In one example, lawyers for "Los Siete," a "brown power" organizing group in San Francisco's Mission District, took a radical approach to representing group members arrested for obstructing the sidewalk while selling their newspaper, *Basta Ya*. Instead of advising their clients to plea bargain, as "apolitical professionals" would have done, the lawyers took the cases to trial, where their radical approach "was to stress the political realities involved; to admit and defend the true nature of *Basta Ya*, and to expose the police department's racism and its attempts to harass and intimidate members of Los Siete." *Id.* at 392. "The trial ended successfully for the defendants despite the judge's persistent attempts to ridicule the attorneys and to prohibit their making any mention of the first amendment." *Id.*

What is your reaction to the lawyers' "radical" approach to this case? Would it change your analysis if their clients had lost at trial? Under what circumstances do you think this type of approach would be most effective? Most risky?

One constraint on a lawyer's ability to use litigation for broader political purposes is Rule 11 of the Federal Rules of Civil Procedure, which provides that a lawyer may be sanctioned for violating its terms:

> (b) Representations to the Court
>   By presenting to the court a pleading, written motion, or other paper — whether by signing, filing, submitting, or later advocating it — an attorney or unrepresented party certifies that to the best of the person's knowledge,

information, and belief, formed after an inquiry reasonable under the circumstances:

> (1) it is not being presented for any improper purpose, such as to harass, cause unnecessary delay, or needlessly increase the cost of litigation;
>
> (2) the claims, defenses, and other legal contentions are warranted by existing law or by a nonfrivolous argument for extending, modifying, or reversing existing law or for establishing new law;
>
> (3) the factual contentions have evidentiary support or, if specifically so identified, will likely have evidentiary support after a reasonable opportunity for further investigation or discovery; and
>
> (4) the denials of factual contentions are warranted on the evidence or, if specifically so identified, are reasonably based on belief or a lack of information.

For a general discussion of the application of Rule 11 to litigation that is brought without a specific intent to win, see Jules Lobel, *Courts as Forums for Protest*, 52 UCLA L. Rev. 477 (2004) (arguing that Rule 11 should not be imposed where lawyers use courts as a forum for protest). The federal circuit courts have split on the issue of whether a lawyer who files a case or motion for the purpose of gaining publicity for a cause or client has an "improper purpose" and may be sanctioned under Rule 11, even when the claim is otherwise nonfrivolous. *Id.* at 515-20 (collecting cases). Or consider a lawyer's decision to push for a possible negative court decision to influence the political process. In *The Nine* (2007), Jeffrey Toobin provides an account of the ACLU's legal strategy in the lower courts in *Planned Parenthood v. Casey*. According to Toobin, the ACLU expressly expedited its pursuit of certiorari from the Supreme Court after losing the case in the Third Circuit, bypassing an opportunity to have the case heard, and possibly reversed, by the Third Circuit sitting en banc. *Id.* at 40-43. The lawyers purportedly sought to get the case in front of the U.S. Supreme Court and have it decided, perhaps in a way that would have overruled *Roe v. Wade* (the opposite of what they desired), so that the decision might have an influence on the 1992 presidential election. *Id.*

Do you think that litigation filed to advance a cause but not necessarily to win on the legal merits always complies with Rule 11? Only in certain circumstances? Never?

d. SPECIAL PROBLEMS IN THE CRIMINAL CONTEXT

Thus far, we have been focusing on the ethical choices of public interest lawyers in civil practice. In addition, the special ethical problems faced by public defenders and government prosecutors in the criminal context deserve attention. There are systemic justifications for the roles of both public defenders and government prosecutors that are thought of as imposing special duties. For defense lawyers in general and public defenders in particular, the fact that their clients face the full force of government prosecution threatening a deprivation of their liberty is said to justify an enhanced version of zealous advocacy. Under this rationale, defense lawyers exist in part to ensure that the government always meets its burden of proof and thus may zealously advocate for a client they suspect to be guilty. For prosecutors, because they wield enormous power, they are also required to do so in ways that do not simply achieve convictions, but rather promote justice.

i. DEFENSE

The criminal defense context raises a host of ethical issues that could, by themselves, occupy an entire discussion on their own terms. *See* Martin Guggenheim, *Divided Loyalties: Musings on Some Ethical Dilemmas for the Institutional Criminal Defense Attorney*, 14 N.Y.U. REV. L. & SOC. CHANGE 13 (1986). In this section, we highlight two issues that are relevant to our discussion of the connection between lawyering and the public interest. The first, as suggested above, is the systemic question of role justification for public defenders. Should we expect them to be zealous in defending clients in ways that we would not in other contexts because of what is at stake? What does it mean to do justice in the context of criminal defense?

In a classic exchange on the topic, William Simon argues that criminal defense is not ethically exceptional in that criminal defense lawyers, like any other lawyer, must exercise ethical discretion in pursuing justice in each case and, accordingly, cannot rely on any systemic rationale to justify "aggressive defense" all the time. William H. Simon, *The Ethics of Criminal Defense*, 91 MICH. L. REV. 1703 (1993). Luban disagrees:

> Consider . . . the typical, overburdened defender of the indigent. For such a lawyer, Simon's implicit question — "Is it ethically proper to engage in aggressive defense in every case?" — is wholly beside the point. Her caseload and resources make it impossible for this lawyer to offer aggressive defense in every case; it may be impossible for her to offer capable defense in every case. At the same time, however, her clients are most likely to be threatened with the evils of overpunishment, racism, and assembly line justice that Simon and I agree would make aggressive defense permissible. Thus, her dilemma of aggressive defense is a problem of desperate triage; her moral question is not "May I engage in aggressive defense?" but "Given that many of my clients deserve aggressive defense, how do I choose whom to provide with aggressive defense?" My own view is that she should utilize her scarce resources on behalf of those clients who are in greater jeopardy and who are less dangerous, rather than the other way around; probably Simon would agree. However, for reasons I explained earlier, I think that a blanket permission or even encouragement for indigent defenders to engage in aggressive advocacy is better than an injunction to assess each candidate for aggressive defense on its merits, because the latter rule would lead to too many wrong decisions to curtail zeal.

David Luban, *Are Criminal Defenders Different?*, 91 MICH. L. REV. 1729, 1765 (1993). Who do you think is right? Should public defenders "aggressively defend" every case they can given the disparity in resources and other disadvantages attendant to criminal defense practice? Or does that let public defenders off too easily, sanctioning "dirty tricks" and other advocacy designed to get a client off without regard to the underlying merits?

A second issue in the defender context relates back to the issue of client autonomy with which we began. As Luban notes in the above article, nearly all criminal cases end in plea bargains, which give both prosecutors and defense lawyers enormous discretion to shape the terms of defendants' ultimate case disposition. Although the Model Rules make it clear that a defendant has the absolute power to decide the terms of any plea, in reality he may rely heavily on his lawyer for guidance. Simon's experience representing "Mrs. Jones" illustrates the authority lawyers may have in this regard:

> The only criminal case I ever handled involved defending a woman who worked as a housekeeper for the senior partner in the firm where I worked. The client, Mrs. Jones, was charged with leaving the scene of a minor traffic accident without stopping to identify herself.
>
> According to her, she *had* stopped to identify herself; it was the other driver—the complainant—who had both caused the accident by hitting her car in the rear and who had left the scene without stopping. The other driver then called the police and reported Mrs. Jones as leaving the scene.
>
> Mrs. Jones was black; the other driver was white. The police, without investigation, had taken the other driver's word for what had happened, and when Mrs. Jones came down to the station at their insistence, they reprimanded her like a child, addressing her—a sixty-five-year old woman—by her first name while referring to the much-younger complainant as "Mrs. Strelski."
>
> Mrs. Jones lived near Boston in a lower middle class black neighborhood with a history going back to the Civil War. She was a homeowner, a churchgoer, and a well known and respected member of the community. This was her first brush with the police in her sixty-five years. Nervous and upset as her experience had made her, she was obviously a charming person. As far as I was concerned, her credibility was off the charts.
>
> Moreover, I had a photograph of her car showing a dent and a paint chip of the color of the other driver's car in the rear—just where she said the other driver had struck her. When we got to the courthouse, we located the other car in the parking lot, found the dent and a paint chip of the color of my client's car in the front, and I took a Polaroid picture of that.
>
> The case seemed strong, and the misdemeanor procedure gave us two bites at the apple. First, there would be a bench trial. If we lost that, we were entitled to claim a trial de novo before a jury.
>
> Thus, things looked fairly good. Mrs. Jones's main problem was that her lawyer—me—was incompetent. I had never tried a case and had never done any criminal work. But I tried to remedy that by getting a friend with a lot of experience in traffic cases to co-counsel with me. The first thing my friend did was to dismiss, with a roll of his eyes, my plan to expose the police's racism through devastating cross-examination. The judge and the police were repeat players in this process who shared many common interests, he told me. We could never get a dismissal on a challenge to prosecutorial discretion, and if an acquittal would imply a finding of racism against the police, it would be all that harder for the judge to give one. The second thing my friend did was to start negotiation with the prosecutor, which he told me was the way nearly all such cases were resolved. He told the prosecutor some of the strengths of our case and showed him my photographs, but he didn't say a word about racism.
>
> The prosecutor made the following offer. We would enter a plea of, in effect, nolo contendere. Under the applicable procedure, this, if accepted by the judge, would guarantee a disposition of, in effect, six months probation. Mrs. Jones would have a criminal record, but because it would be a first offense, she could apply to have it sealed after a year.

We considered the advantages: It would spare her the anxiety of a trial and of having to testify. In the unlikely but possible event that we lost this trial, the plea bargain would have spared her six further months of anxious waiting, and the anxiety of a second trial. In the even more unlikely but still possible event that we lost both trials, it would have spared her certain loss of her driver's license, a probably modest fine, and a highly unlikely but theoretically possible jail term of up to six months.

What was the downside? I couldn't say for sure that the criminal record Mrs. Jones would have for at least a year wouldn't adversely affect her in some concrete way, but I doubted it. (She was living primarily on Social Security and worked only part-time as a housekeeper.) What bothered me was that the plea bargain would deprive her of any sense of vindication. Mrs. Jones struck me as a person who prized her dignity, deeply resented her recent abuse, and would attach importance to vindication.

Mrs. Jones had brought her minister to the courthouse to support her and serve as a character witness. Leaving my friend with the prosecutor, I went over to her and the minister to discuss the plea bargain. I spoke to them for about ten minutes. For about half this time, we argued about whether I would tell her what I thought she should do. She and her minister wanted me to. "You're the expert. That's what we come to lawyers for," they said. I insisted that, because the decision was hers, I couldn't tell her what to do. I then spelled out the pros and cons, much as I've mentioned them here. However, I mentioned the cons last, and the last thing I said was, "If you took their offer, there probably wouldn't be any bad practical consequences, but it wouldn't be total justice." Up to that point, Mrs. Jones and her minister seemed anxiously ambivalent, but that last phrase seemed to have a dramatic effect on them. In unison, they said, "We want justice."

I went back to my friend and said, "No deal. She wants justice." My friend in disbelief and then said, "What? Let me talk to her." He then proceeded to give her his advice. He didn't tell her what he thought she should do, and he went over the same considerations I did. The main differences in his presentation were that he discussed the disadvantages of trial last, while I had gone over them first; he described the remote possibility of jail in slightly more detail than I had, and he didn't conclude by saying, "It wouldn't be total justice." At the end of his presentation, Mrs. Jones and her minister decided to accept the plea bargain, and as I said nothing further, that's what they did.

William H. Simon, *Lawyer and Advice and Client Autonomy: Mrs. Jones's Case*, 50 MD. L. REV. 213, 214-16 (1991). Did Simon's friend do the right thing?

ii. Prosecution

Government prosecutors at the federal, state, and local level face a different set of ethical dilemmas. Their role, as commonly understood, is to seek justice, not just convictions. *See* STANDARDS RELATING TO THE ADMIN. OF CRIM. JUST. §3-1.2(c) (stating that prosecutors must "seek justice [and] not merely convict"); MODEL RULES OF PROF'L CONDUCT R. 3.8 ("A prosecutor has the responsibility of a minister of justice and not simply that of an advocate."). Yet prosecutors do face real institutional pressures to convict. How do they balance doing justice and winning? Consider the following skeptical view by Abbe Smith:

ABBE SMITH, *CAN YOU BE A GOOD PERSON AND A GOOD PROSECUTOR?*

14 GEO. J. LEGAL ETHICS 355, 376-91 (2001)

Ethical standards, rules, and codes all proclaim that the central duty of prosecutors is to "seek justice [and] not merely . . . convict." This overarching and "rigorous" duty, which has been recognized for well over a century, requires that prosecutors "do the right thing," not merely the easy or popular thing. It is a righteous exaltation, a call to rise above the Machiavellian, win-at-all-costs nature of ordinary law practice. While these same standards, rules, and codes also acknowledge the multiple roles of prosecutors as "administrators of justice," "advocates," and "officers of the court," the duty to seek justice is the chief and abiding ethic, marking prosecution as a grand and noble vocation, unlike any other.

But, what does it mean to be both an advocate and an administrator of justice? How does one balance these competing and sometimes inconsistent obligations? And how much do prosecutors actually care about—or even think about—their competing duties, especially when they are immersed in a case? The reality is most don't.

And what does it mean to "seek justice"? The concept could not be more ambiguous and subject to multiple interpretations.

Moreover, what prosecutor doesn't think that he or she is "seeking justice," doing "right," or doing "good"? Perhaps this sense of righteousness is a good thing; it might reflect awareness on the part of an individual prosecutor that he or she is *obliged* to be righteous, no matter the competing impulses. But too often righteousness becomes *self*-righteousness. Too often prosecutors believe that because it is their *job* to do justice, they have extraordinary in-born wisdom and insight. Too often prosecutors believe that they *and only they* know what justice is.

There is an inherent vanity and grandiosity to this aspect of the prosecution role. Many prosecutors genuinely believe they are motivated only by conscience and principle. But many prosecutors come to believe they are the only forces of good in the system.

The reality is that justice is an elusive and difficult concept. Most defenders recognize this on a daily basis. Wise prosecutors do, too. Justice, like many an abstract notion, is in the eye of the beholder. It can mean one thing in one case and something totally different in another. Ethical standards are turned on their heads, however, when prosecutors claim with confidence to have a special understanding of the meaning of justice.

The Tendency Toward Narrowness and Cynicism

Prosecutors have a tendency to see things as black and white, right or wrong, guilty or not guilty. There is little interest in the various shades of grey that color most people's lives. Both as interpreters and enforcers of the law, prosecutors have a preference for the literal over the figurative, for *what* happened over *why* it happened, for the trees over the forest.

To prosecutors, the record is everything: police reports, criminal records, chemical analysis, physical evidence, documentary evidence. This is the stuff you can put your hands on; it speaks for itself. The fact that the record may not tell the whole story, or that there is another story altogether, is a complicating detail to be dealt with at trial or sentencing.

Most prosecutors believe that if someone breaks the law, he or she ought to be prosecuted. Individual accountability is everything. Individual circumstances, the forces that cause an event to happen, and the broad context of the matter only clutters things up. If the law is sometimes harsh, this is the responsibility of those who make the law, not those who enforce it.

This tendency to see things in black and white may be related to prosecutors not having clients. Prosecutors represent the government, not a flesh-and-blood client. They represent an abstract entity, not someone with frailties, weaknesses, vulnerabilities. Although some prosecutors claim to be "representing victims"—and some prosecutors may develop close bonds with some victims—the relationship between prosecutors and alleged victims is a complicated one, not fairly analogized to the lawyer-client relationship. The reality is that alleged victims are prosecution *witnesses*, not clients.

Defenders, on the other hand, undertake the representation of *people* in all their ugliness and splendor. We represent clients who have made mistakes, who have problems, and who may have done some terrible things—but who didn't arrive at that point from nowhere. In order to effectively represent a client, a lawyer must understand the client in all his or her complexity and make an effort to walk in the client's shoes. The best lawyers are those who are able to "submerge" themselves in the client—at least for a time.

The ability to submerge oneself in another is related to the capacity for empathy. In the context of criminal law practice, empathizing with the client—connecting with and embracing the client no matter what he or she is alleged to have done, and no matter whether he or she is guilty or innocent—can be difficult. It requires both generosity and the suspension of *judgment*. It also requires acknowledging the random nature of good and bad fortune in life.

But prosecutors are in the business of *judging*, of upholding standards, of exacting penance. To prosecutors, luck is irrelevant. People make choices. The humility and liberation that defenders experience when they connect with a client may be antithetical to what prosecutors need to do. Compassion, while laudable, may not be something prosecutors can afford on a regular basis.

Perhaps to compensate for the lack of knowledge that comes from working closely with clients, prosecutors often act as if they have heard it all before no matter how inexperienced they may be. Too often, a prosecutor's immediate reaction to an alternative version of the facts—an exonerating or mitigating circumstance, or simply a different perspective—is to reject it. What defender hasn't begged, pleaded, explained, or cajoled, only to be told, "I don't buy it, counselor."?

For many prosecutors, cynicism takes over in both style and substance. In order not to be played for a fool, taken for a ride, considered a *sucker*—a nightmarish reputation for a prosecutor—prosecutors often become suspicious, untrusting, disbelieving. Notwithstanding the legal presumption of innocence, the cultural and institutional presumption in most prosecutor offices is that *everybody is guilty*.

At its best, there is a clarity and consistency in a narrow, letter-of-the-law approach and perspective of prosecutors; if the focus is on the act and not the actor there is less opportunity for prejudice or unfairness. At its worst, however, there is a kind of moral fascism.

The Paradox of Discretion

Many commentators have noted the discretionary power of prosecutors. Prosecutors have the power to direct investigations, define the crime to be charged, affect punishment both in plea offers and sentencing arguments, and decide whether or not to prosecute at all. Indeed, this power is an enormous draw for many would-be prosecutors. The well-intentioned believe they will have the power to do good, to make a difference, or, at the very least, to moderate the excesses of the system.

The truth is most prosecutors have very little discretion. For newer prosecutors and those at the lower levels in an office, there is often little autonomy and independence. This is not necessarily different for more experienced prosecutors. As often as not, there is someone higher up in the office hierarchy who must be consulted before a prosecutor can act.

There are some cases in which prosecutors, no matter how experienced, often have no discretion at all. Cases alleging assault on a police officer are a prime example. High profile cases are another. However, sometimes prosecutors abdicate—or at best share—their discretionary authority even in ordinary cases.

Although prosecutors have discretion to go forward with a prosecution and may decline to prosecute for any number of reasons, there is generally not a lot of soul searching about the decision to prosecute. Too often, prosecutors decide *not to decide* and cede responsibility to the fact-finder. This is an especially troubling occurrence.

When prosecutors *do* have power, they too often abuse it. They throw their weight around to show defense lawyers who is the boss. They throw their weight around to show defendants that they are prosecutor, judge, and jury rolled into one. They throw their weight around because they *can*.

Winning

In view of the institutional culture of prosecutor's offices and the culture of the adversary system generally, it is perhaps inevitable that the overriding interest of prosecutors would be winning. This is so notwithstanding the prosecutor's ethical obligation to embrace justice over winning, or the ambiguity of what it means to "win."

There is a courthouse saying—known by anyone who has ever practiced criminal law—that expresses the ethos of winning over everything else in a grisly, sardonic way: "Any prosecutor can convict the guilty. It takes real talent to convict the innocent." This would be just another cheap (but clever) shot about prosecutors if there weren't so many cases in which prosecutors *have proudly convicted the innocent* and refused to back down even upon compelling proof that the conviction was wrongful.

It is not just the big, high profile cases — too frequently capital cases — that create pressure on prosecutors to win. The same pressure is present in ordinary, run-of-the-mill cases. The pressure is both external, the result of the inherently political nature of prosecution, and internal, the result of policies relating to salary and promotion.

The desire to win inevitably wins out over matters of procedural fairness, such as disclosure. It is remarkable from the standpoint of both fairness and *efficiency* how reluctant most prosecutors are to provide meaningful discovery in advance of trial, and how little the situation has changed in the past forty years. The concealment of exculpatory evidence by prosecutors remains a serious problem.

The desire to win takes over and corrupts the plea negotiation process as well. There is no other explanation for the frequent, troubling occurrence of prosecutors making generous plea offers when a case is weak. The practice is troubling because it puts pressure on innocent people to plead guilty and avoid the cost and uncertainty of a trial. No doubt, prosecutors come to believe that the defendants to whom they make such offers are guilty of *something*, and the deal simply reflects problems of proof, not truth.

A prosecutor's desire to win also prevails over reservations about the harshness of sentencing guidelines, mandatory minimums, recidivist statutes, and longer prison terms generally. Whether prosecutors simply become numbed by the *numbers*, no matter how high they are, or actually believe in the sentences they urge, they often seem untroubled by unfairness.

Are Smith's arguments fair? How do you suppose prosecutors would respond? Who is right?

3. Case Resolution

As the preceding discussion suggests, the plea bargaining phase of criminal cases poses ethical challenges for both prosecution and defense attorneys. Back on the civil side, the endgame phase of litigation can present another set of accountability issues, particularly when a lawyer views the case as a vehicle for affecting policy, while the client may simply want to resolve the matter or gain a monetary settlement. How fees are allocated (or not) in settlement may also present a potential conflict between lawyer and client interests in the public interest context. The following discussion considers these issues.

a. LITIGATING TO JUDGMENT

A public interest lawyer may ultimately care about getting law on the books — winning a favorable judicial ruling that will have widespread impact. This desire, however, may run up against the reality that clients in a particular matter may prefer to settle rather than risk a negative outcome in court. The classic formulation of this problem is posed by David Luban:

> Mrs. P belongs to a tenant's organization and agrees to be the plaintiff in a suit against D Real Estate ("unhealthiest tenements in town"). P is represented pro

bono by L, a committed tenants' rights lawyer who hopes that P v. D will set an important precedent. D does not want the precedent, and it tries to "buy out" P with a cash settlement shortly before the trial. (By that time L has invested hundreds of hours of work in the case.) If it is clearly in P's personal interests to accept the offer, should L counsel her to do so? If she wants to accept it, should L nevertheless try to pressure her into going to trial? Who is L representing — P or "the cause"?

DAVID LUBAN, LAWYERS AND JUSTICE, *supra*, at 320.

Model Rule 1.2 requires deference to the client's wishes should she desire to settle. But the issue is whether her lawyer, who has many tools of persuasion that can be deployed, may convince the client otherwise for the good of the cause. This act of persuasion may be doubly disempowering for clients: not only do they not get what they want out of the lawsuit, but their experience with their lawyers reproduces their sense of marginalization. On the other hand, perhaps the favorable resolution of the case on the merits would have far-reaching benefits beyond the individual client.

A lawyer confronted with this type of a situation is technically required to ultimately defer to the client's decision. However, a lawyer may plan for this type of potential conflict by seeking clients at the outset who share the lawyer's social change goals and requesting a waiver in the retainer agreement stating that the client will not accept a settlement that does not advance the cause. The Model Rules in some situations permit clients to waive their rights to future conflicts, so long as the client is fully informed and understands the reasonably foreseeable adverse consequences of the waiver. MODEL RULES OF PROF'L CONDUCT R. 1.7 cmt. 22. Do you think that a public interest client could understand what she was giving up by consenting to waive her right to settle a case that her lawyer wanted to litigate to judgment for the cause? Should such waivers be permitted?

b. NEGOTIATING SETTLEMENT

In seeking to settle a case, a defendant may wish to do more than avoid bad precedent — it may also desire to hide the terms of the settlement so that they are not available to other potential litigants seeking similar redress. A public interest lawyer would tend toward promoting transparency in settlement in order to publicize victory, promote similar cases, and deter future wrongdoing. But clients may have a different calculus, which pushes them in favor of a confidential settlement even though it may have negative effects for the "cause."

Consider the following hypothetical scenario, faced by a plaintiff's lawyer, in a major products liability case for injuries caused to her client because of the design of Firestone tires on the Ford Explorer:

In a lawsuit, the plaintiff asks for some documents. The plaintiff says that they are clearly relevant and they are; they are essential to the case, which they are; but the defendant says, "Oh, these are trade secrets" or "they are commercial information and you can't have them. They are confidential and are of great value to our competitors." But the law recognizes that in general there are privileges that preclude public disclosure of that kind of information. . . .

So the plaintiff's lawyer agrees and takes everything under the protective order. Sure enough the documents turn out to be dynamite. The depositions turn out to be even better because the lawyer has the documents and the witnesses who wrote the documents, and he gets everything he wants. All of which, of course, is under seal. The defendant at this point decides, "I think I had better settle this lawsuit; things are not looking very good." He offers the plaintiff a very large amount of money. Indeed, there is actually a case involving Firestone where the lawyer told me that they offered much more than the case was worth. But there was, you see, this one condition, which is that the plaintiff's lawyers would have to give back all of the documents, and they could not reveal any of what they learned to anybody else.

The first question is, is this a legitimate position for the defendant's lawyers to take? I think we would all say that, under our current system, the defendant's lawyer can properly do that. Is it unethical for the plaintiff's lawyers to accept that kind of offer? It is clearly an offer in the best interest of their client, and if your job is to represent your client, and do the best you can for them, how can you not accept that offer when doing so truly is in the best interest of the client?

Suppose the plaintiff's lawyer were to say, "Well, I don't want to accept this secrecy. I don't believe in that secrecy stuff. Safety is too important, and so I am not going to accept the secrecy." Then the defendant might reply, "That's all right, you can have non-secrecy, but we are going to cut two-thirds off the price that we are willing to pay to your client." In the real world, of course, the defendant would never have to say that because the plaintiff understands that secrecy is part of the bargain.

"Well, at least," the plaintiff's lawyer asks, "What about other cases that I have or other cases that other lawyers have?" The defendant says, "Well, if the lawyer asks for the documents, I will be glad to give them to them, if they know what to ask for, of course." The defendant's lawyer doesn't quite say that because it is not necessary. The plaintiff's lawyer says, "What about other victims?" The defendant assures the plaintiff's lawyer that this is an isolated case. "We are just keeping these secrets because we don't want all of this bad publicity to get out and there is nothing really wrong with the product. Besides, we have taken the product off the market or made some changes so it won't happen again."

Bringing it up to the present time, of course, the last statement about the Firestone tires is clearly no longer true. It is not an isolated problem. There are tens, scores, hundreds of victims; who knows how many people have been injured by them. What about the protective order that was in existence? Should the plaintiff's lawyer continue to agree to these protective orders knowing that there are other victims out there? Is there somebody else that needs to know this information? What about the officials at the National Highway Traffic Safety Administration? It has subpoena power, unlike some agencies like the Food and Drug Administration. NHTSA's problem is that they do not know what to ask for. They have a limited budget and too many other fish to fry. They are in a very difficult situation.

Lives are clearly at stake and yet under our system of ethical rules, the plaintiff's lawyer continues not to have any choice but to take the money for his or her client and keep the secrets. The rules are pretty clear on that. The client is the boss, and the lawyer must do what the client wants. Of course, the client could say, "Secrecy be damned. We are not going to take this secrecy order." But there are very few clients who are willing to say that.

The defendants do have a point about trade secret materials, bad publicity, and other things. The question again is, is their point controlling? Should the answer to the question be that zealous representation is enough when once again we have a substantial interest of third parties who have no say in this litigation? Are they going to be harmed by this zealous representation?

Alan B. Morrison, *Must the Interests of the Client Always Come First?*, 53 ME. L. REV. 471, 476-78 (2001).

David Luban argues that "secret settlements" may undermine the public interest in cases where there are significant social issues (e.g., health and safety) that affect large numbers of unrepresented people—who may continue to suffer because they lack access to information contained in the settlements. He argues, instead, for greater "sunshine" in the settlement process.

> The biggest worry about sunshine regimes is that secret settlements may be the only way that a weak plaintiff who has suffered serious harm can obtain compensation. If judges make secrecy agreements unenforceable, a weak plaintiff may not receive a serious settlement offer and the case goes to trial. Since plaintiffs can demand a generous settlement in return for secrecy, and trials are expensive, banning secret settlements may cost plaintiffs money.
>
> Defendants, however, will still have all the standard incentives for settlement. They may decide that a settlement with no guarantee of confidentiality is a better bet for keeping information out of the headlines than is a public trial. In any event, the argument behind sunshine regimes is that they recognize situations in which the public interest in matters relating to health, safety, and the operations of government outweighs the plaintiff's interest in gaining a favorable settlement. If, on the other hand, judges retain discretion to seal records at will, . . . their understandable desire not to undercut plaintiffs' best chance at quick compensation will almost surely combine with their desire to clear their dockets and lead them to accede to secret settlements. Judges are unlikely to exercise their discretion to scuttle a settlement in the name of the publicity principle.

David Luban, *Settlements and the Erosion of the Public Realm*, 3 GEO. L.J. 2619, 2657-58 (1995).

Are secrecy agreements as a condition of favorable settlement more likely to arise in public interest litigation than in private litigation contexts? Why? To what extent is a public interest lawyer's ethical duty to zealously advocate for her client put in tension with the broader mission of social change by such offers? Can you think of ways to satisfy both the ethical duty and the social concerns in an individual case? What about systemic reforms or regulations as a manner of addressing secret settlements?

c. FEES

The ability to receive attorneys' fees is crucial for many public interest lawyers—both in the NGO and private sector. Such fees, which are available under some federal civil rights and state "private attorney general" statutes, generally allow lawyers in successful cases to recover fees against their adversaries and thus recoup their significant investments of time. Particularly for lawyers in private public interest firms, who typically rely heavily on fees to sustain their practices, attorneys' fee recovery is an essential part of a viable practice. However, as suggested in Chapter 4, the reliance on fees also creates some ethical dilemmas, as lawyers are faced with potentially losing fees based on "sacrifice offers," in which plaintiffs are given a favorable settlement in exchange for their lawyers waiving fees, *Evans v. Jeff D.*, 475 U.S. 717 (1986), or strategic voluntary compliance by defendants that obviates a lawsuit's claims and thus negates the opportunity for "prevailing party" fees under civil rights laws. *Buckhannon Bd. & Care Home, Inc. v. W. Va. Dep't of Health & Human Resources*, 532 U.S. 598 (2001). Both of these situations put pressure on lawyers, who are placed in the difficult position of losing all of their investment in a case in order to do what is best for their clients. To address this ethical dilemma in advance, some firms have restructured their fee arrangements. Consider how Hadsell & Stormer (H&S), a Los Angeles-area civil rights firm, deals with these issues:

> When damages are at issue, H&S avoids the impact of these cases by structuring its retainer with clients to both prohibit the acceptance of any sacrifice offer, and to provide for a contingency fee in the absence of a statutory fee award. . . . Where fees are recoverable, H&S hedges its downside risk by providing that it is entitled to the statutory fee award or the contingency amount, whatever is higher. Conflicts still arise during settlement when the firm has made a major investment of resources and the settlement amount on the table would result in a contingency fee that would not cover the firm's cost investment. These situations are complex since the firm's economic incentive would be to push for a larger settlement, while the one on the table may be sufficient for the client. In this context, the firm and client may attempt to negotiate a resolution that reduces the firm's loss — for instance, by paying the firm a fixed amount — although the firm must take the loss if the client so insists.
>
> At the other end of the spectrum are cases in which damages are not the goal; instead, the plaintiffs are seeking some type of injunctive relief typically to end a targeted governmental practice. In this type of public law reform case, the issue of fees becomes more complicated. On the one hand, these types of cases are much more susceptible to the *Buckhannon* problem, since the absence of settlement damages from which to take a contingency fee makes them high-risk from the firm's point of view. Thus, voluntary compliance by the defendant negates the opportunity to get fees. In response to this problem, a firm may choose to avoid injunctive relief cases or to try to bring them under state law (when possible) in order to take advantage of the California private attorney general statute, with its broader fee provisions. For its part, H&S has generally opted for the first route — it does not to take many injunctive relief cases. . . .

Scott L. Cummings, *Privatizing the Public Interest*, 25 Geo. J. Legal Ethics 1, 87-88 (2012). Do you think what Hadsell & Stormer does is a good resolution to the fee dilemma?

C. ACCOUNTABILITY IN NON-LITIGATION CONTEXTS

Litigation, of course, is only one legal approach to social change. Lawyers may also assist clients outside the litigation context to build power and solve problems. In these situations, the lawyer's role may involve counseling, fact gathering, negotiation, and transactional work. Accountability concerns persist in these non-litigation contexts, though the tradeoffs may be different. This section considers some ethical issues raised by non-litigation approaches to public interest lawyering.

1. Government Lawyering

Although, as we have seen, many government lawyers—whether in defenders' or prosecutors' offices—engage in litigation, some play a different role: advising government officials on the legality of certain proposed policies. As discussed in Chapter 4, in these contexts, a key question involves how the government lawyer should define the client. Is it the official seeking the legal opinion? A particular agency, like the EPA or State Department? An entire branch of government? The public? How one answers these questions may influence the type of advice given. *See* Jeffrey Rosenthal, *Who Is the Client of the Government Lawyer?, in* ETHICAL STANDARDS IN THE PUBLIC SECTOR: A GUIDE FOR GOVERNMENT LAWYERS, CLIENTS, AND PUBLIC OFFICIALS 13 (Patricia E. Salkin ed., 1999).

2. Community Lawyering

As discussed in Chapter 5, many public interest lawyers do not litigate at all, but engage in the type of non-adversarial transactional practice that is the stock-in-trade of the corporate bar: structuring business entities, arranging access to capital, counseling compliance with tax and corporate regulations, negotiating partnerships and other legal agreements, and navigating the process of real estate development. *See* Ann Southworth, *Business Planning for the Destitute? Lawyers as Facilitators in Civil Rights and Poverty Practice,* 1996 WIS. L. REV. 1121; Brian Glick & Matthew J. Rossman, *Neighborhood Legal Services as House Counsel to Community-Based Efforts to Achieve Economic Justice: The East Brooklyn Experience,* 23 N.Y.U. REV. L. & SOC. CHANGE 105 (1997); Daniel Shah, *Lawyering for Empowerment: Community Development and Social Change,* 6 CLINICAL L. REV. 217 (1999). This type of practice is often associated with the community economic development movement. Scott L. Cummings, *Community Economic Development as Progressive Politics,* 54 STAN. L. REV. (2001); *see also* WILLIAM H. SIMON, THE COMMUNITY ECONOMIC DEVELOPMENT MOVEMENT: LAW, BUSINESS, AND THE NEW SOCIAL POLICY (2001).

It is tempting to view the representation of community groups as solving many of the accountability problems inherent in public interest litigation: lawyers for community groups deal with coherent organizational structures that are rooted in communities and representative of their interests. These groups have their own agendas and look to lawyers for assistance in effectuating pre-defined goals. The groups have leaders that are, at least in principle, accountable to their broader constituency and are thus less likely to be deferential to lawyer power. As an ethical matter, lawyers are bound to represent the "organization" rather than individuals within it and are ultimately charged with taking their instructions from a group's "duly authorized constituents," typically the board of directors. Model Rules of Prof'l Conduct R. 1.13.

Yet, as many scholars and practitioners have noted, accountability concerns do not disappear in the context of organizational representation, they just change their form. As Stephen Ellmann argues, they are "multiplied" in ways that complicate public interest lawyers' attempts to balance the twin goals of client autonomy and collective mobilization. Stephen Ellmann, *Client-Centered Multiplied: Individual Autonomy and Collective Mobilization in Public Interest Lawyers' Representation of Groups*, 78 Va. L. Rev. 1103 (1992).

> The bond between lawyer and client fuels, and is fueled by, the heart of client-centered counseling — the careful, even elaborate, process in which lawyer and client work together to identify the relevant considerations on which the decision should be based. . . . Group discussions may produce more complete assessments than any one individual and his lawyer could, because the members' diverse perspectives will illuminate each others' judgments. But these discussions will not be likely to elicit so many of the particulars of the several members' perceptions and situations as might be brought out during a meeting between a single client and his lawyer. Nor will the lawyer, on whom both individual and group clients must rely for information about consequences beyond their expertise, be able to speak to each uncertainty of each of the group's members. There simply are too many perceptions, with too many nuances, for such exhaustiveness to be achieved. The effort to achieve this, in addition, might actually be counterproductive, for the multiplication of details could serve more to confuse than to clarify the fundamental issues at stake.
>
> Moreover, this is not simply a problem of sheer numbers. For a consideration to achieve notice by the group, it does not need majority concurrence, but it does need to attract attention in the inevitable interpersonal patterns of recognition and approval that develop within any group. These patterns need not be pernicious; on the contrary, it seems entirely proper for groups to accord respect to those of their members who earn it. At the same time, however, such patterns frequently do not foster free and equal participation by all members. Some people will speak and not be heard; others will not talk; others will orate at length.
>
> None of this means that identifying relevant considerations should be abandoned in group representation; this step is generally important to the decisions of groups of people just as it is to the judgments of individuals, and lawyers for groups should encourage their clients to undertake it. But the lawyer's focus must shift in two respects. First, the goal of discussion must now become the eliciting of the major concerns in the group's thinking, rather than the detailed variations. Much as a teacher hearing two students make related points will assist the rest of the class by linking the two together into an overarching point, so the lawyer for a group must digest, translate, and summarize somewhat disparate comments into more coherent themes.
>
> Second, the lawyer must work to ensure that the considerations brought out are those of all of the group's members, rather than only those of a dominant few. In this effort, however, the lawyer must be careful to work within the context of the group, so as to avoid transforming her group client into a series of individual clients. Of course, there are straightforward steps the lawyer can

take to encourage some people to participate more actively. The lawyer can, for example, *say* at the start of the meeting that it is important for all members to speak their minds and hear each other's views; she can make sure that those who have raised their hands get a chance to speak, ask people who have not raised their hands whether they have something to say, and discourage talkative members from chiming in repeatedly before others have spoken at all. She can arrange the chairs for the meeting in a circle rather than in rows to facilitate freer discussion. The lawyer may also find it helpful to talk with individual members outside the group meetings, in order to get a better sense of their concerns and be able to ensure that these members' views get aired. Perhaps the lawyer will also want to express her endorsement of the significance of points raised by less influential group members, so as to add the weight of her influence to that of the speakers.

These steps may seem innocuous enough. In fact, however, the more the lawyer utilizes them the more she will be taking over leadership of the particular meeting and perhaps of the group itself. The lawyer becomes increasingly responsible for deciding who speaks in the meeting; she also becomes increasingly involved in taking the pulse of the members outside the meeting. These are leadership functions, and the lawyer who takes them on fills a role that group members otherwise might have played. They may also have controversial implications, for the patterns of speech and silence within a group are not accidents but rather the product of the interactions group members have had with each other. The lawyer who helps a silenced member to speak empowers him, but she may be undercutting someone else. The very steps that help the group to make decisions, and to realize its autonomy, thus become sources of threat to its self-governance and its internal norms, both of which are also aspects of the group's autonomy. . . .

In the most intractable of these situations, the conflict between what will empower the group and what will empower particular members within the group may be inescapable. This conflict is an issue of ethics as well as of technique. I have defended the principle of group representation on the ground that, in addition to giving expression to the potential values of group connection, such representation also increases individuals' power over their lives and vindicates the exercises of individual autonomy entailed in group membership. Here, however, supporting the group undercuts the autonomy of certain individuals. Such conflicts are, I suspect, endemic to group representation, on questions ranging from whether to draw out or submerge a dissenting voice, to how to make an ultimate decision in light of the conflicting preferences of the members. It is important, therefore, to have a method of resolving these dilemmas.

Two such methods seem unacceptable. One alternative would simply, and automatically, favor individual autonomy over group needs (or vice versa). That response, however, would be at least in tension with the premise of this Article that both connection and autonomy should be honored. Moreover, if the issue is framed simply as a choice between the autonomy of one person and the autonomy of many (the dissenting minority as against the group's dominant majority), I do not understand why one person's autonomy is necessarily more valuable than many people's, nor why the wishes of many should always override the voice of a single individual.

A second alternative would escape the need to resolve these questions by giving the lawyer the prerogative to favor those group members — be they in the majority or the minority — whose position the lawyer feels is more just or more sensible. Although this rule is self evidently an authorization for lawyers' exercise of power over their clients, it cannot be rejected simply on that ground. The reality is that because legal services for disadvantaged people are so scarce, lawyers have little alternative but to exercise substantial discretion in choosing which cases they will take and which they will refuse. Certainly public interest lawyers regularly make decisions about the objectives they will pursue, and decline to take cases not fitting those objectives. Such practices can also be regarded as exercises of power over clients, who may be pressed to recast their grievances and concerns to fit the lawyers' mold.

Even assuming that we generally accept the propriety of this sort of pressure, however, that acceptance does not provide a sound rationale for lawyers' intervention in the decisionmaking process of their client groups so as to systematically favor those views they prefer over those they dislike. Lawyers' decisions to refuse cases not to their liking can be defended as expressions of the lawyers' own autonomy, and the resultant pressure on disadvantaged clients explained as a product of scarcity of legal services beyond the lawyers' power to rectify — but interfering with the client's deliberative processes does not fit easily with either of these defenses. If the lawyer is only prepared to take a case on particular terms, she should say so, but she should not then prevent those members of the client group who dislike those terms from having their say, or from having their views counted in the group's ultimate decisions. The lawyer who acts in these latter fashions is doing more than pressuring her clients; she is preventing them from thinking through their response to her pressure. I do not mean to argue that the lawyer must altogether abstain from steps that shape her clients' decisionmaking in ways they might not have chosen on their own. Interventions as blunt as silencing or not counting the views of some group members, however, constitute a drastic interference with those individuals' autonomy and with the essence of democratic group association as well, and they should rarely, if ever, be permissible.

Instead, I suggest a third alternative: that the lawyer should consider herself responsible for assuring a baseline of democratic and participative process within the group, but that beyond this baseline she generally should not override the arrangements evolved by the group itself. Concretely, in the context of identifying relevant considerations, this baseline might require the lawyer to encourage silent members, during the meeting, to speak their minds. If she felt that the leaders of the meeting were systematically refusing to call on some member, she might have to bring him into the discussion herself. But she would not have a mandate to make the group's processes "perfect"; often her role would be only to suggest, and not to insist upon, further refinements of the group members' ways of interacting. Rarely, if ever, would she have the right simply to usurp the role of the group's own leaders, for example by invoking her status as the lawyer to justify taking over the chairing of the group's discussion.

Id. at 1139-45. Other scholars have advocated that lawyers for groups should simply "facilitate" the implementation of group decisions rather than intervene in the heart of group affairs. Richard D. Marsico, *Working for Social Change and Preserving Client Autonomy: Is There a Role for "Facilitative" Lawyering?*, 1 Clinical L. Rev. 639 (1995). Who do you think is right? On the representation of community groups, see generally Paul Tremblay, *Counseling Community Groups*, 17 Clinical L. Rev. 389 (2010).

Consider Shauna Marshall's account of the accountability concerns implicated in the representation of tenants displaced by redevelopment in East Palo Alto.

> Susan . . . was the neighborhood's housing lawyer. At a macro level, Susan's goal was to help ensure that the community had a decent stock of affordable housing, particularly rental units. Some of her clients lived in large, dilapidated apartment buildings. One such building was located in one of the areas designated for redevelopment. Over the years Susan worked with and represented the tenants who lived in that building regarding issues of habitability. In fact, many of the tenants' habitability claims were still not completely settled and Susan was still actively representing them. Now, as part of the redevelopment plan, the city was going to acquire the building and have it torn down. In its place was going to be a shopping center with large warehouse retail outlets. Members of the City Council hoped the redevelopment project would bring employment opportunities to its residents along with badly needed tax revenues.
>
> The tenants living in the building scheduled for demolition were entitled to relocation benefits. In fact, Susan as well as Jamie had conducted educational sessions about a tenant's right to relocation benefits when his property is demolished as part of a redevelopment plan. Susan had even helped other tenants in other locations obtain relocation benefits. When, however, it was time for this large complex to be torn down, the city was strapped for cash. Fearing a fiscal crisis which might threaten the entire redevelopment project, the city wanted to pay the tenants their benefits in installments. Many of the tenants objected to payment over time and wanted the lump sum to which they were entitled. Moreover, they wanted "their" lawyer Susan to represent them in their attempts to obtain full payment.
>
> Susan, however, was concerned that the city did not have sufficient funds to pay these relocation benefits all at once. As she looked at the problem in the context of the larger community, she was not certain that she supported the tenants' objectives. But, these tenants had been her clients when she pursued habitability claims against their former, private landlord. In fact, some still were. Moreover, she had been a part of a public education program that informed them of their entitlement to full relocation payments. Could she now refuse to represent them because of her concerns for the city's financial health? After all, she was the only housing lawyer in town. What is her ethical obligation to these tenants, her clients? . . .
>
> [T]o whom does Susan owe her loyalty? Is it to the tenants being displaced by redevelopment or is it to the community which needs the completion of a successful redevelopment project? Can she divide her loyalties without violating her duty under the ethical codes to advocate zealously on behalf of her clients? What about her role at the tenant information sessions? Can she adequately shape the meeting so that she is just providing information and not giving out legal advice? Is that even her goal? Should it be? When do the attendees at the meeting turn into clients, expecting the cloak of privacy and confidentiality that accompanies that status? What obligations do those in attendance have to keep confidential the information they learn from other tenants, their neighbors?

Marshall, *Mission Impossible?*, *supra*, at 151-52. How would you answer these questions?

One other common role played by community lawyers is to educate community members about their legal rights in public education sessions. Consider Marshall's discussion of possible ethical concerns faced by the fictional lawyer "Susan" in this context:

Susan's concern about the confidentiality of her public education, self-help clinics stems in large part from her goals for those clinics. Susan's goals are many: to learn about the range of housing problems in the city; to impart information about housing laws; to teach clients to be their own and each other's advocates through self-help, lay lawyering strategies; and to build a community among tenants. To reach those goals, Susan knows that the clinics must create an environment where the tenants feel comfortable disclosing some personal information, discussing problems and helping one another. . . .

Rule 1.6 of the Model Rules of Professional Conduct prohibits attorneys from disclosing confidential information obtained while representing a client unless the client consents. The Rule, like Susan, attempts to promote trust and respect in the attorney-client relationship. . . . [A]lthough Susan can personally adhere to the Rule, what obligation do the attendees have to keep the contents of the sessions confidential? . . .

Susan's role at the public education self-help workshops is not that of agent or protector, but rather that of an educator, collaborator and facilitator of solutions. Although she too may want to foster loyalty and trust, she is doing so in order to build a community among the tenants and to foster cooperative, self-help lay advocacy. She is not developing the type of one-on-one relationship envisioned by the Model Rules. Her reasons for needing a trusting environment differ from those of the Rule and the Rule does not protect the type of relationship that Susan is fostering.

Clients who first arrive at the workshop, however, may have an expectation that Susan is their agent or protector; after all they have housing problems and she is the only lawyer in town. Susan, knowing that she is not providing the type of one-on-one representation that would give rise to the confidentiality protection afforded under the ethical rules, complies with her ethical obligations by informing the clients that they are not entering into an attorney-client relationship and that personal information given out at the meeting is not protected. Susan may add that she is aware that information shared at these sessions may be of a personal and sensitive nature and that she will not divulge information she learns to anyone. She may also suggest that the attendees do the same. But she is clear about reinforcing the notion that the traditional attorney client relationship is not being established at these sessions.

Once Susan gives her disclaimer, the participants' expectations should shift away from the conclusion that an attorney-client relationship is being created. In fact, under the "reasonable belief by the client" standard, one could safely argue that, following the explanation given by Susan, there is no expectation of the type of confidential communication inherent in an attorney-client relationship. The type of disclaimer given by Susan fits neatly within the case law: the attorney took affirmative steps to inform the attendees that statements made at the meeting were not protected and that the workshop was not the beginning of an attorney-client relationship.

The context in which the meeting takes place also negates the creation of an attorney-client relationship. The meetings are open, and no one-on-one relationships are created. Moreover, Susan points out that, if at the conclusion of the meeting she (or her law students) concludes that someone is in need of formal representation, that person will enter into a retainer agreement with the Law Project at a later time. Susan's disclaimer is consistent with the ethical rules; she is engaging in a public education, self-help group session which is not the type of representation protected under the Rule 1.6. The type of relationship that the Rule is designed to protect is not present at the public education, self-help sessions.

But does the story end here? Isn't it possible that the clients still feel that the attorney has some sort of fiduciary duty toward them? Do the clients believe that their communications, although shared among the meeting's members, will still not leave the legal services office?

Id. at 179-84. How would you answer these questions? Does Susan do enough to prevent establishing a lawyer-client relationship? Is this a situation in which the professional rules do not fit well with public interest lawyering? If so, how would you propose changing them?

3. Lawyering for Coalitions in Strategic Campaigns

Contemporary public interest lawyering sometimes moves beyond the representation of individual organizations, seeking instead to represent coalitions of groups in campaigns to achieve specific policy reforms. These campaigns often involve multidimensional advocacy in which lawyers are asked to play multiple roles in different venues in order to advance a campaign's goals. *See* Scott L. Cummings & Douglas NeJaime, *Lawyering for Marriage Equality*, 57 UCLA L. Rev. 1235, 1242 (2010). This approach to lawyering raises complex questions about how lawyers should relate to different stakeholders in coalitions. Scott L. Cummings, *The Accountability Problem in Public Interest Practice: Old Paradigms and New Directors, in* Lawyers in Practice: Ethical Decision Making in Context (Lynn Mather & Leslie Levin eds., 2012); *see also* Susan D. Bennett, *Creating a Client Consortium: Building Social Capital, Bridging Structural Holes*, 13 Clinical L. Rev. 67 (2005); Robin Golden, *Collaborative as Client: Lawyering for Effective Change*, 56 N.Y.L. Sch. L. Rev. 393 (2011-12). For a broad analysis of collaborative lawyering, see Ascanio Piomelli, *Appreciating Collaborative Lawyering*, 6 Clinical L. Rev. 427 (2000). We explore some of these cases in detail in Chapter 10. When you read them, think about how the lawyers might structure their client relationships in order to promote client accountability and avoid conflicts.

———————

After reviewing this material, do you think that public interest lawyers face unique ethical issues? Which situations do you find most challenging? What do you think are the best ways for lawyers to deal with the tension between client accountability and commitment to cause?

CHAPTER 8

EDUCATING PUBLIC INTEREST LAWYERS: OBSTACLES AND OPPORTUNITIES

I. INTRODUCTION

Public interest lawyering has long had a contested relationship with legal education. Law school is a necessary pathway to a public interest career and thus a rite of passage for all who aspire to deploy its lessons in the pursuit of social justice. But despite law school's unavoidable importance, it is often viewed as more of a hindrance to public interest lawyering than a helpmate. Deborah Kenn, Lawyering from the Heart 67-121 (2009); *see also* Jonathan Hafen, *Public Interest Law and Legal Education: What Role Should Law Schools Play in Meeting the Legal Crisis*, 2 B.U. Pub. Int. L.J. 7 (1992). This formulation overstates the case, but researchers have consistently shown that aspects of the conventional law school experience are in tension with sustaining public interest commitment. Indeed, law school — although it often purports to promote an ethic of public service — has often been charged with producing the opposite effect: undercutting public interest commitment as students are socialized (particularly in the first year) to "think like lawyers." Robert Granfield, Making Elite Lawyers: Visions of Law at Harvard and Beyond (1992); Elizabeth Mertz, The Language of Law School: Learning to "Think Like a Lawyer" (2007). The process of professional socialization has been claimed to promote a sort of "valuelessness" associated with the conventional "hired gun" conception of client representation: the notion that a lawyer should always advocate vigorously for her client's perspective and that there is no necessary "right or wrong," only stronger or weaker arguments, erodes the idealism with which public interest-minded law students enter the legal academy. *See, e.g.,* Henry Rose, *Law Schools Should Be About Justice Too*, 40 Clev. St. L. Rev. 443, 447 (1992). Socialization interacts with other features of law school — a competitive emphasis on the acquisition of private sector jobs, curricular inattention to social justice issues, a lack of role models, relatively fewer resources to facilitate public interest law placement, and increasing debt loads — to erode commitment to public interest causes.

Yet some students do, of course, "beat the odds" and persevere through law school to pursue public interest law careers. Stuart Scheingold & Austin Sarat, Something to Believe In: Politics, Professionalism, and Cause Lawyering 51 (2004). And although the evidence is not clear as to what factors matter the most in helping them to do so, law schools — for their part — are increasingly devoting greater resources and attention to both providing better training to aspiring public interest lawyers and trying to mitigate some of the financial risk. In short, there is an evolving institutional effort to contest public interest drift by buffering law students from the negative socialization effect of law school and training them to think (and act) like *public interest* lawyers. This chapter examines the pitfalls and promise of law school as the crucial pathway to public interest lawyering.

II. OBSTACLES: THE EDUCATIONAL CHALLENGE TO PUBLIC INTEREST LAW

Research has consistently shown the discrepancy between student idealism upon entering law school and placement in public interest jobs afterward. In his study of Harvard Law School students in the 1980s, Granfield found that over one-fourth entered law school with idealistic goals, which included helping others and promoting social justice. Granfield, *supra*, at 38. Other studies have found similar levels of idealism and commitment among entering students. *See* Robert V. Stover, Making It and Breaking It: The Fate of Public Interest Commitment During Law School (1989); Debra J. Schleef, Managing Elites: Professional Socialization in Law and Business Schools (2006). Even among recent law school graduates, who came of age in a political culture quite distinct from those in Granfield's study, "62 % reported that a 'desire to help individuals as a lawyer' or to 'change or improve society' had been 'important . . . goals in [their] decision to attend law school.'" Rebecca Sandefur & Jeffrey Selbin, *The Clinic Effect*, 16 Clinical L. Rev. 57, 91 (2009).

Yet there is a persistent gap between what motivates students upon entering law school and what they do upon graduation. Granfield's research at Harvard revealed that by the end of students' third year of law school, only 2 percent expressed a preference for legal aid jobs and only 5 percent for public interest jobs. Granfield, *supra*, at 48. After the JD, a longitudinal study tracking lawyers' careers starting in 2000, found that small numbers of new lawyers enter the public interest field: in 2002, 4.1 percent of new lawyers worked either in legal services/public defender or public interest jobs (another 16.5 percent were in government positions); the percentage decreased after seven years in practice to 2.8 percent. Ronit Dinovitzer et al., After the JD II: Second Results from a National Study of Legal Careers 27 (2009). These numbers are consistent with other findings. *See* NALP, Jobs & J.D.s: Employment and Salaries of New Law Graduates: Class of 1999 (2000).

Why does this happen? There are a number of theories, which we will explore in this section, none of which are necessarily exclusive. Before exploring them in depth, we frame the issues with the following excerpt in which renowned public interest lawyer and law professor Bill Quigley articulates some of the challenges law school poses to students who care deeply about social justice—and offers some advice for staying the course:

> "The first thing I lost in law school was the reason that I came." What a simple and powerful indictment of legal education and of our legal profession. It is also a caution to those of us who want to practice social justice lawyering.
>
> Many come to law school because they want in some way to help the elderly, children, people with disabilities, undernourished people around the world, victims of genocide, or victims of racism, economic injustice, religious persecution or gender discrimination.
>
> Unfortunately, the experience of law school and the legal profession often dilute the commitment to social justice lawyering.
>
> The repeated emphasis in law school on the subtleties of substantive law and many layers of procedure, usually discussed in the context of examples from business and traditional litigation, can grind down the idealism with which students first arrived. In fact, research shows that two-thirds of the students who enter law school with intentions of seeking a government or public-interest job do not end up employed in that work.
>
> It pains me to say it, but justice is a counter-cultural value in our legal profession. Because of that, you cannot be afraid to be different than others in law school or the profession—for unless you are, you cannot be a social justice lawyer.
>
> Those who practice social justice law are essentially swimming upstream while others are on their way down. Unless you are serious about your direction and the choices you make and the need for assistance, teamwork and renewal, you will likely grow tired and start floating along and end up going downstream with the rest. We all grow tired at points and lose our direction. The goal is to try to structure our lives and relationships in such a way that we can recognize when we get lost and be ready to try to reorient ourselves and start over.
>
> There are many legal highways available to people whose goal is to make a lot of money as a lawyer—that is a very mainstream, traditional goal and many have gone before to show the way and carefully tend the roads.
>
> For social justice lawyers, the path is more challenging. You have to leave the highway sending you on towards the traditional legal profession. You have to step away from most of the crowd and create a new path—one that will allow you to hold onto your dreams and hopes for being a lawyer of social justice.
>
> Your path has different markers than others. The traditional law school and professional marks of success are not good indicators for social justice advocates. Certainly, you hope for yourself what you hope for others—a good family, a home, good schools, a healthy life and enough to pay off those damn loans. Those are all achievable as a social justice lawyer, but they demand that you be more creative, flexible and patient than those for whom money is the main yardstick.
>
> Our profession certainly pays lip service to justice, and because we are lawyers this is often eloquent lip service, but that is the extent of it. At orientations, graduations, law days, swearing-in days and in some professional classes, you hear about justice being the core and foundation of this occupation. But everyone knows that justice work is not the essence of the legal profession. Our professional essence is money, and the overwhelming majority of legal work

consists of facilitating the transfer of money or resources from one group to another. A shamefully large part of our profession in fact consists of the opposite of justice — actually taking from the poor and giving to the rich or justifying some injustice like torture or tobacco or mass relocation or commercial exploitation of the weak by the strong. The actual message from law school and on throughout the entire legal career is that justice work, if done at all, is done in the margins or after the real legal work is done.

William P. Quigley, *Letter to a Law Student Interested in Social Justice*, 1 DePaul J. for Soc. Justice 7, 9-11 (2007). Quigley identifies three key elements of the law school experience that make the public interest path "more challenging": the dominant pedagogical approach, the overall institutional culture, and the financial sacrifices of public interest lawyering. We turn next to each of these features.

A. PEDAGOGY

1. Socialization: The Impact of Learning to "Think Like a Lawyer"

Research on the impact of law school on idealism has generally shown that there is an inverse relationship between the dominant mode of law school teaching — the vaunted case method in which students and professors analyze the text of legal opinions through a quasi-Socratic dialogue — and students' feelings of moral certitude and political engagement. *See* David Chavkin, *Training the Ed Sparers of Tomorrow: Integrating Health Law Theory and Practice*, 60 Brook. L. Rev. 314 (1994); Howard S. Erlanger & Douglas A. Klegon, *Socialization Effects of Professional School: The Law School Experience and Student Orientations to Public Interest Concerns*, 13 Law & Soc'y Rev.11 (1978); Howard Erlanger et al., *Law Student Idealism and Job Choice: Some New Data on an Old Question*, 30 Law & Soc'y Rev. 851 (1996); James C. Foster, *The "Cooling Out" of Law Students: Facilitating Market Cooptation of Future Lawyers*, 3 Law & Pol'y Q. 243 (1985); Lani Guinier et al., *Becoming Gentlemen: Women's Experience at One Ivy League Law School*, 143 U. Pa. L. Rev. 1 (1994); *see also* Richard D. Kahlenberg, Broken Contact: A Memoir of Harvard Law School (1992); *but see* James M. Hedegaard, *The Impact of Legal Education: An In-Depth Examination of Career-Relevant Interests, Attitudes, and Personality Traits Among First-Year Law Students*, 1979 Am. B. Found. Res. J. 791 (1979) (finding no evidence that students as a group were being "uniformly redirected toward a rather limited set of career paths").

Elizabeth Mertz's empirical study of the first year of law school suggests one reason for the decline of idealism: that the dominant pedagogical mode turns student attention from "a systemic or comprehensive consideration of social context and specificity" toward "more abstract categories and legal (rather than social) contexts." Mertz, *supra*, at 5. As a result, Mertz concludes, law school teaching in some cases "obscures very real social differences that are pertinent to making just decisions; it can also create an appearance of neutrality that hides the fact that U.S. law continues to enact social inequities and injustices." *Id.* The 2007 Carnegie Report on the state of American legal education reinforced this view, arguing that law school's "signature pedagogy" of case analysis had the "unintended consequence" of inadequately "developing the ethical and social dimensions of the profession." WILLIAM M. SULLIVAN ET AL., EDUCATING LAWYERS: PREPARATION FOR THE PROFESSION OF LAW 188 (2007).

It is precisely the illusion of neutrality fostered by the case method that some commentators have considered to be a pernicious force undercutting social activism. It is in this vein that Duncan Kennedy wrote his classic account of the first-year law school experience:

> The initial classroom experience sustains rather than dissipates ambivalence. The teachers are overwhelmingly white, male, and deadeningly straight and middle class in manner. The classroom is hierarchical with a vengeance, the teacher receiving a degree of deference and arousing fears that remind one of high school rather than college. The sense of autonomy one has in a lecture, with the rule that you must let teacher drone on without interruption balanced by the rule that teacher can't *do* anything to you, is gone. In its place is a demand for a pseudo-participation in which you struggle desperately, in front of a large audience, to read a mind determined to elude you. . . .
>
> The actual intellectual content of the law seems to consist of learning rules, what they are and why they have to be the way they are, while rooting for the occasional judge who seems willing to make them marginally more humane. The basic experience is of double surrender: to a passivizing class-room experience and to a passive attitude toward the content of the legal system.
>
> The first step toward this sense of the irrelevance of liberal or left thinking is the opposition in the first year curriculum between the technical, boring, difficult, obscure legal case, and the occasional case with outrageous facts and a piggish judicial opinion endorsing or tolerating the outrage. The first kind of case—call it a cold case—is a challenge to interest, understanding, even to wakefulness. It can be on any subject, so long as it is of no political or moral or emotional significance. Just to understand what happened and what's being said about it, you have to learn a lot of new terms, a little potted legal history, and lots of rules, none of which is carefully explained by the casebook or the teacher. It is difficult to figure out why the case is there in the first place, difficult to figure out whether one has grasped it, and difficult to anticipate what the teacher will ask and what one should respond.
>
> The other kind of case usually involves a sympathetic plaintiff, say an Appalachian farm family, and an unsympathetic defendant, say a coal company. On first reading, it appears that the coal company has screwed the farm family, say by renting their land for strip mining, with a promise to restore it to its original condition once the coal has been extracted, and then reneging on the promise. And the case should include a judicial opinion that does something like awarding a meaningless couple of hundred dollars to the farm family, rather than making the coal company do the restoration work.
>
> The point of the class discussion will be that your initial reaction of outrage is naive, non-legal, irrelevant to what you're supposed to be learning, and may be substantively wrong in the bargain. There are good reasons for the awful result, when you take a legal and logical view, as opposed to a knee-jerk passionate view, and if you can't muster those reasons, maybe you aren't cut out to be a lawyer.

Duncan Kennedy, *Legal Education in the Reproduction of Hierarchy*, 32 J. LEGAL EDUC. 591, 592-95 (1982). Does Kennedy's description resonate with your experience? Do you agree that the general law school pedagogical approach leads to pacification? A different way to look at the first-year experience is as a lesson in learning the master's tools in order to contest the master's rules. That is, by understanding the language and content of legal analysis, one will be better equipped to make persuasive arguments for the causes one believes in. Is this a more accurate description of law school from the point of view of aspiring public interest lawyers?

Anthony Kronman, in his noted examination of the "lost" lawyer-statesmen archetype of legal professionalism, argues that questioning one's assumptions (demanded by the case method) produces a salutary effect: forcing students to adopt a "judicial perspective" that analyzes problems from a vantage point of neutrality. From this point of view, students are asked to find solutions to problems that try to find a middle ground between conflicting positions and promote incremental reform. ANTHONY T. KRONMAN, THE LOST LAWYER: FAILING IDEALS OF THE LEGAL PROFESSION (1993). While Kennedy believes revolutionary thought and action are precursors to social change, Kronman believes that they are anathema to it. With whom do you agree? How does your theory of social change affect how you assess the value of the case method?

2. Inattention to Public Interest Law in the Traditional Curriculum

A related but distinct critique of law schools from a public interest perspective is that they do an inadequate job incorporating public interest themes into their curriculums. As Quigley notes, "There is far too little about justice in law school curriculum or in the legal profession. You will have to learn most of this on your own." Quigley, *supra*, at 13. Particularly in the first year of law school, engagement with public interest lawyering themes is crowded out by the traditional curriculum: "Private law remains the staple of the law school curriculum in the critical first year; that there are conspicuous efforts at reform illustrate how slow is the process of change." Daniel B. Rodriguez, *Foreword: Public Interest Lawyering and Law School Pedagogy*, 40 SAN DIEGO L. REV. 1, 2 (2003). When public interest issues are raised, they are often ancillary to the main thrust of the conversation or as an addendum to a case analysis otherwise devoid of social justice.

B. CULTURE AND INSTITUTIONAL SUPPORT

Beyond pedagogical style and course offerings, critics have pointed to the overall culture of law school as a negative influence on public interest-minded students. Scheingold and Sarat link the erosion of commitment that occurs as a result of the case method to institutional pressures to pursue private sector employment as the most professionally "prestigious":

> The most significant socializing force at work in law school turns out to be the social stratification, and prestige hierarchy, of the bar. Corporate practice sits atop the stratification and prestige hierarchy; everything else pales by comparison. The cognitive core of legal education, with its emphasis on the mastery of technical skills and the bracketing of moral commitment, prepares the way for students to succumb to the allure of the corporate law firm. The most important message that students are exposed to is to go where the money is. And, that is where most end up wanting to go.

Scheingold & Sarat, *supra*, at 67.

Law schools often send explicit and implicit institutional messages that reinforce this status hierarchy.

> Some law school placement offices steer students to law firm employment while marginalizing public service options. Students interested in law firm jobs receive generous amounts of visible institutional support buttressed by serious "wining and dining" inducements from law firms, while public interest students are largely on their own in identifying and pursuing hiring strategies. Without a community of support around them, public interest students need more institutional encouragement and support if they are to realize their career goals. This is unlikely to occur, however, so long as placement offices continue to refer to public interest employment as "nontraditional" career alternatives.
>
> Public interest students also routinely witness striking contrasts in the level of institutional support provided to students seeking post-graduate judicial clerkships from that provided to their own job searches. Law schools establish faculty clerkship committees that actively promote the value of clerkship opportunities and identify promising students in order to make sure that students consider judicial clerkships and receive needed institutional support. Faculty members readily accept these responsibilities, writing letters of recommendation on a strict timetable and contacting judges to promote the merits of promising students. These well-organized efforts reflect core institutional values that result in tangible benefits to clerkship applicants, including interested public interest students, while also serving the needs of the judiciary. They also demonstrate the positive impact that law schools can have on student choices when linking supportive resources to an institutional message that touts the enhanced value of certain post-graduate opportunities.
>
> At the same time, law schools sometimes convey a message to students that public interest work is less prestigious or academically rigorous than other types of post-graduate employment, especially law firm employment. Perhaps this message is most powerfully conveyed by the content of the mainstream law school curriculum where the institution's values are expressed most directly to students. As students select courses each semester, they readily understand which subjects are regarded as most essential to their education and which subjects are largely missing from the fabric of graded courses taught by distinguished faculty.

Louis S. Rulli, *Too Long Neglected: Expanding Curricular Support for Public Interest Lawyering*, 55 Clev. St. L. Rev. 547, 548-49 (2007). The competitive race among law schools to score high in the law school rankings game has generated additional challenges for public interest-minded students, whose schools structure curricula and career services to maximize the placement of graduates in high-paying private sector jobs. Have you experienced these types of messages at your law school? Are they more likely to be prevalent at the "elite" law schools, which might have stronger relationships with large, corporate law firms?

Even when law schools are not overtly lending their support to private sector job placement, the structure of the public interest law hiring market imposes additional stresses and burdens on public interest job seekers. There is a feeding frenzy over the "best" law firms among many students that reinforces the firms' elite position in the prestige hierarchy. As Scott Turow recalled in his classic account of his first year at Harvard Law School: "People go bananas about ZYX firm and XYZ firm. All this pressure begins to mount to take *any* job supposedly 'better' than another. You feel as though if you don't take the 'better' jobs then you're blowing all of the advantages built up by going to Harvard Law School." Scott Turow, One L 91 (1977). Scheingold and Sarat paint a similar picture when they recount the experience of another Harvard 1L, Richard Kahlenberg, who like Turow chronicled his law school experience:

> Consider, to begin with, the discouraging results of his efforts as a first-year student to secure summer work as a cause lawyer. "The day after Thanksgiving, I sent out fifty-three letters to public-interest groups in New York, Washington and Boston. . . . But nearly a month after sending out resumes, I became depressed. Most places didn't respond at all. Of those that did, some said they hired only 2Ls and 3Ls; some said that they would not hire until March; others that they would take only volunteers."
>
> Even more telling were the placement activities during Kahlenberg's third year. His job search went forward on two fronts — corporate and public service. With respect to the former, Kahlenberg was interviewed by and received offers from some of the leading firms in the country — including the prestigious Washington firms of Arnold & Porter and Covington & Burling. In the meantime, he was making virtually no headway on the other track: "In a wild failure of capitalism," he says, "I was faring much better with $70,000 law firm jobs than the $30,000 jobs on the Hill." Moreover, whereas the corporate firms had sought him out, his public service job search was conducted solely on his initiative and at his expense.

Scheingold & Sarat, *supra*, at 66-67 (*quoting* Richard Kahlenberg, Broken Contract: A Memoir of Harvard Law School 37, 190 (1992)).

Empirical evidence from the National Association of Law Placement suggests that this state of affairs persists. While the on-campus interview program is the source of most large law firm jobs, only 4 percent of public interest jobs are secured through that process. NALP, Jobs & J.D.s, *supra*. This means that public interest law aspirants, in contrast to their private sector counterparts, are much more likely to have to mount their own job searches — and to wait patiently until near the end of law school or even after graduation to obtain jobs. *Id.* For students who do not feel comfortable sitting by while their peers accept job offers early in their 3L year, the pressure to also pursue private sector options is strong.

C. DEBT

Over the past 20 years, law school tuition has increased much faster than the rate of inflation and faster than tuition at four-year colleges. "From 1989 to 2009, when college tuition rose by 71 percent, law school tuition shot up by 317 percent." David Segal, *Law School Economics: Ka-Ching*, N.Y. Times, July 16, 2011, §BU, at 1. Higher tuition has been driven by a number of trends, including declining state funding of public universities and the drive to invest in student and faculty recruitment and capital improvements that enhance law school rankings. *Id.* Increasing tuition, in turn, has caused a dramatic rise in average law school debt. Equal Justice Works, one of the leading national organizations dedicated to promoting public interest law careers, found that in "2002, the average amount borrowed in law school was $70,147 at a private school and $46,499 at a public school. In 2005, the average amount borrowed in law school [had] risen to $78,763 at a private school and $51,056 at a public school." Equal Justice Works, Financing the Future: Responses to the Rising Debt of Law Students 2 (2006). According to Philip Schrag and Charles Pruett, average law school debt increased further by 2009, to $100,000 for private schools and over $60,000 for public schools. Philip G. Schrag & Charles W. Pruett, *Coordinating Loan Repayment Assistance Programs with New Federal Legislation*, 60 J. Legal Educ. 583, 586 (2011). In addition, the percentage of law school graduates with student debt has risen sharply: from less than one-third in 1993 to two-thirds in 2004. Equal Justice Works, *supra*, at 2.

Yet while everyone agrees that debt has increased, there is significant disagreement about just how much of a barrier debt is to public interest careers. Equal Justice Works, for its part, has been a leading advocate of student debt relief, arguing that "debt stands between many law graduates and their desire to pursue public service careers." Equal Justice Works, *supra*, at iii. In a 2002 study, Equal Justice Works reported that 66 percent of third-year law students said that debt prevented them from considering public interest or government jobs. Equal Justice Works, From Paper Chase to Money Chase: Law School Debt Diverts Road to Public Service 6 (2002). The following year, an American Bar Association Commission concluded that "high student debt bars many law graduates from pursuing public service careers"; that "many law graduates who take public service legal jobs must leave after they gain two to three years legal experience"; and that "public service employers report serious difficulty recruiting and retaining lawyers." Am. Bar Ass'n, Lifting the Burden: Law Student Debt as a Barrier to Public Service (2003). As a result, the legal profession is "unable to promote and provide meaningful access to legal representation for all." *Id.*

Some researchers, however, have disputed the link between debt and career choice, emphasizing other factors—such as the disparity between private law firm and public interest salaries, or the availability of public interest jobs. At $38,500, average entry-level salaries of public interest lawyers are the lowest of any practice setting according to the After the JD research. Dinovitzer et al., *supra*, at 43. And the disparity between public interest and law firm salaries has grown significantly. In the early 1970s, the ratio of private firm to public interest salaries was 1.5:1. Neil K. Komesar & Burton A. Weisbrod, *The Public Interest Law Firm: A Behavioral Analysis, in* Public Interest Law: An Economic and Institutional Analysis, *supra*, at 80, 83. In 2004, the ratio of private firm (over 20 lawyers) to public interest salaries was roughly 3:1; the ratio of big firm (over 250) to public interest salaries was 3.6:1. Scott L. Cummings, *The Future of Public Interest Law*, 33 U. Ark. Little Rock L. Rev. 355, 359 (2011). And although the number of public interest jobs (in the nonprofit sector) relative to the entire bar has grown since the 1970s, the number remains small in absolute (approximately 14,000) and proportional terms (less than 1.5 percent of the total number of lawyers). *Id.* at 357.

Scholars have pointed to the disparity in salaries and the relative dearth of jobs as important factors steering students away from entering the public interest field. Data from the 1980s questioned the causal link between debt and public interest career choice. David Chambers, in a study of 1989 graduates from nine law schools, found that debt bore a weak relationship to job choice, and was less important than other factors, particularly student grades and the number of employers interviewing at the schools. David L. Chambers, *The Burdens of Educational Loans: The Impacts of Debt on Choice and Standards of Living for Students at Nine Law Schools*, 42 J. LEGAL EDUC. 187 (1992). Similarly, Lewis Kornhauser and Richard Revesz's study of NYU and Michigan law graduates in the late 1980s concluded that debt was less salient to job choice than student performance and the salary difference between private sector and public interest jobs. Lewis A. Kornhauser & Richard L. Revesz, *Legal Education and Entry into the Legal Profession: The Role of Race, Gender, and Educational Debt*, 70 N.Y.U. L. REV. 829 (1995). More recent studies have drawn similar conclusions. Christa McGill discounts the threat of debt to public interest careers, citing methodological problems (particularly low response rates) in the Equal Justice Works and other studies asserting a debt barrier. Christa McGill, *Educational Debt and Law Student Failure to Enter Public Service Careers: Bringing Empirical Data to Bear*, 31 LAW & SOC. INQUIRY 677, 680-81 (2006). Instead, her research found that market factors and motivation had more influence. For 2002 graduates, she concluded that the salary gap and the supply of public interest jobs were the most important factors influencing job choice. *Id.* at 692. For earlier graduates she studied "[t]he strongest influences on whether or not a student took a job in the public sector were (1) whether the student came into law school with that desire and (2) whether she worked in that setting in either summer between law school years, particularly the second summer." *Id.* at 702.

Do McGill's conclusions comport with your experiences? Note that the data she collected preceded the sharp spike in debt that occurred in the 2000s — and the decline in jobs after the 2008 recession. How do you think these changes might affect her conclusions? Do you think students would report different perceptions about the barrier that debt poses to low-paying public interest careers in light of the changed economic environment? Do you think they would actually act differently?

Note also that McGill discounts the impact of Loan Repayment Assistance Programs (LRAPs) on career choice. *Id.* at 690. This is consistent with another recent study analyzing data from the NYU School of Law. Erica Field's research found that students who were given tuition subsidies, which were repayable if the students did not go into public interest jobs upon graduation, were significantly more likely to enter public interest careers than recipients of LRAP assistance packages that were of identical value. Erica Field, *Educational Debt Burden and Career Choice: Evidence from a Financial Aid Experiment at NYU Law School*, 1 AM. ECON. J.: APPLIED ECON. 1 (2009). The study's conclusion was that requiring students to finance law school through debt led to irrational risk aversion that reduced the willingness to enter public interest jobs. Does this seem like a plausible explanation to you?

III. OPPORTUNITIES

As our discussion of LRAPs suggests, law schools have not sat idly by in the face of the challenges to public interest lawyering. To the contrary, many schools have mounted substantial institutional efforts to integrate public interest lawyering themes into the curriculum and to ease the financial and logistical impediments to pursuing public interest jobs upon graduation (and beyond). We may think of the institutional efforts in support of public interest lawyering as direct responses to the obstacles identified above. Thus, many law schools have confronted the central educational challenges to public interest careers—the signature case method pedagogy, the dominant culture, and increasing debt—by designing programs that attempt to minimize their negative effects: new public interest-oriented coursework, new programs that create alternative cultural norms that promote public interest work, and new financing options to alleviate the financial burden of law school. In this section, we examine these key institutional developments and ask what they mean for the future of public interest-centered legal education.

A. TEACHING PUBLIC INTEREST LAWYERING

Consider the following description of what a public interest pedagogy would include:

> There are three components of an educational agenda for exposing law students to the crisis in legal services and for inspiring them to take part in addressing the problem. First, law schools must make students aware of and sensitive to injustices in society and malfunctions in the legal system. Second, law schools must show students how law can be used to reform existing social arrangements and legal practice. Third, law schools must teach and motivate students to participate in the struggle for economic and social justice.

Stephen Wizner, *Can Law Schools Teach Students to Do Good? Legal Education and the Future of Legal Services for the Poor*, 3 N.Y. City L. Rev. 259, 263 (2000). Is this a good roadmap for educational reform? How likely do you think it is that law schools would adopt such an approach? What pressure might be brought to bear to support these changes and from whom? Keep these questions in mind as you read the following materials examining the current state of public interest-oriented legal education. What more can be done?

1. Curricular Innovations: Developing a Public Interest Pedagogy

Recall Quigley's assertion that law school will not teach the skills and approaches necessary to advance social justice. From his point of view, a law student committed to public interest advocacy must engage in a course of self-education:

> So how do you learn what the elderly, the working poor or the single moms think about these laws? It is not in the statute, nor the legislative history, nor the appellate decision. That is exactly the point. If you are interested in real social justice, you must seek out the voices of the people whose voices are not heard in the halls of Congress or in the marbled courtrooms.
>
> Keep your focus on who is suffering and ask why. Listen to the voices of the people rarely heard, and you will understand exactly where injustice flourishes.
>
> Second, look for the collateral beneficiaries. Qui bono? Who benefits from each law, and what are their interests? Why do you think that the minimum

wage stays stagnant for long periods of time while expenditures on medical assistance soar year after year?

This inquiry is particularly important since the poor and powerless — by definition — rarely have any say in the laws that apply to them.

"Follow the money," they say in police work. That is also good advice in examining legislation. Do not miss the big picture. You probably have a hunch that the rich own the world. Do you know the details of how much they actually own? You are a student of the law, you have learned the tools of investigation — you use these tools to find out. Then ask yourself: if the rich own so much, why are the laws assisting poor, elderly and disabled people, at home and abroad, structured in the way they are?

Third, carefully examine the real history of these laws. Push yourself to learn how these laws came into being. Learning this history will help you understand how change comes about. . . .

As part of your quest to learn the history of law and justice, learn about the heroic personalities involved in the social changes that prompted the changes in legislation. Biographies of people who struggled for social change are often excellent sources of inspiration.

Once you learn about the sheroes and heroes, push beyond these personalities and learn about the social movements that really pushed for revolutionary change. There is a strong tendency for outsiders to anoint one or more people as THE leaders or mothers or fathers of every social justice struggle. Unfortunately, that suggests that social change occurs only when these one-in-a-million leaders happen to be in the right place at the right time. That is false history. For example, as great as Dr. Martin Luther King, Jr. was, he was not the civil rights movement — he was a part of a very widespread and diverse and often competitive and conflicting set of local, regional, national and even international groups and organizations of people pushing for civil rights.

So, look for real histories about the social movements behind social change and legislation. See how they came about. You will again discover some of the methods used to bring about revolutionary social justice.

Fourth, look at the unstated implications of race, class and gender in each piece of the law. Also look carefully at the way laws interconnect into structures that limit particular groups of people. Race, gender and economic justice issues are present in every single piece of social legislation. They are usually not stated, but they are there. You must discover them and analyze them in order to be a part of the movements to challenge them.

The critique of law is actually a process of re-education — challenging unstated assumptions about law. This is also a lifelong process. I have been doing this work for more than 30 years and I still regularly make mistakes based on ignorance and lack of understanding. We all have much to learn. Real education is tough work, but it is also quite rewarding.

Quigley, *supra*, at 17-19.

Increasingly, law schools have sought to assist law students in this quest to learn about how law can contest injustice. There have long been innovators who have pushed a justice-oriented educational agenda, Howard S. Erlanger & Gabrielle Lessard, *Mobilizing Law Schools in Response to Poverty: A Report on Experiments in Progress*, 43 J. Legal Educ. 199 (1993); however, change over the past 20 years has occurred at a more rapid pace. This shift has occurred in response to student demand, but also to pressure from the organized bar, which has more assertively advocated for law school curricula that serve the interests of justice. For instance, the 1992 MacCrate Report, commissioned by the ABA to review the state of law school teaching, found that schools should design their curricula to promote core values, including "Promoting Justice, Fairness, and Morality," and working to "Ensure that Adequate Legal Services Are Provided to Those Who Cannot Afford to Pay." ABA Section of Legal Education and Admissions to the Bar, Legal Education and Professional Development: An Educational Continuum, Report of the Task Force on Law Schools and The Profession: Narrowing the Gap 213-15 (1992). Building on this conclusion, the Association of American Law School's Equal Justice Project also urged the curricular integration of themes to promote "commitment to the provision of legal services to underserved individuals, groups, and communities." AALS Equal Justice Project, Pursuing Equal Justice: Law Schools and the Provision of Legal Services 9 (2002).

These efforts have borne some fruit. According to the Equal Justice Works 2009 E-Guide to Public Service, there were over 50 schools that offered a combination of upper-division public interest courses, public interest-oriented clinics, and public interest field placements. Equal Justice Works, *2009 Guide to Law Schools*, at http://www.ejwguide.org/ (last visited Aug. 7, 2012). Many of these also indicated efforts to integrate public interest issues into the first-year curriculum. For instance, the Albany School of Law reported that "[f]aculty teaching traditional curriculum courses focus on public interest cases and issues as part of instruction." *Id.* In addition to this type of integration, CUNY also required a public interest course in the 1L year. *Id.* As this suggests, many law schools are trying harder to "infuse the curriculum with justice." Linda F. Smith, *Fostering Justice Throughout the Curriculum*, 18 Geo. J. on Poverty L. & Pol'y 427, 432 (2011).

Around the country, faculty have developed a number of specialized upper-division courses in public interest law. At the University of Pennsylvania Law School, for instance, faculty members have created a course called *Lawyering in the Public Interest*:

> The heart of the course is an examination of universal themes that confront all lawyers who engage in public interest advocacy and that transcend any one area of substantive practice. This is a *lawyering* course that is designed around the expectation that students have already gained some familiarity with the substantive law affecting their clients and that they have experienced, or will soon experience, common issues and problems that apply to all areas of public interest practice regardless of subject matter. It is our hope that through an examination of over-arching themes, students will teach each other substantive law and benefit collectively from individual practice experiences as they struggle to apply their own direct experience to a series of real and recurring problems in public interest practice.
>
> There are many common themes in public interest lawyering worthy of serious study, but time constraints permit us to select just a few each semester. Minimally, we try to integrate the following core topics into the syllabus: (1) client voice and autonomy, examining the inherent tension between intrinsic and instrumental goals; (2) scarcity of resources, exploring what it

means for the public interest lawyer and fundamental decisions about who will get the services of the public interest lawyer; (3) competing delivery service models, contrasting different models of legal advocacy involving individual representation, law reform, community lawyering, rebellious lawyering, legislative advocacy, and others, with critiques of different approaches; (4) third-party intrusions into the attorney-client relationship, reviewing congressional restrictions placed upon federally-funded legal services lawyers and discussing other types of influences or constraints imposed by public and private funders, the legal profession, and opponents; and (5) common funding mechanisms, looking comprehensively at both traditional and newer funding sources, such as governmental funding, interest on lawyers' trust accounts (IOLTA), user fees, and a variety of other potential funding sources that might hold promise for the future.

Rulli, *supra*, at 559-60.

Some schools have adopted quite different pedagogical models. Harvard, for instance, created a Summer Theory Institute in 2008 as a way of "combining reflection through social theory with the practice of public interest law." Nisha Agarwal & Jocelyn Simonson, *Thinking Like a Public Interest Lawyer: Theory, Practice, and Pedagogy*, 34 N.Y.U. Rev. L. & Soc. Change 455, 462 (2010). It brings together 12 to 14 law student fellows each summer to "read and discuss social theory in the context of their day-to-day experiences working for social change through law." *Id.* at 457. Consider the Institute's design:

During the Institute's first summer, the Fellows met with us for two hours each week. We assigned twenty- to thirty-page theoretical readings and asked them to submit a response paper before each session to assist the one or two Fellows who were leading discussion on the readings in a given week. However, it is there that any resemblance to the traditional law school seminar ends. The two-hour long "classes" were facilitated not by faculty members of the law school but by practicing lawyers. The Fellows were not sitting in a classroom but in the conference room of a public interest law office. There were no grades. And Fellows were not meeting in the middle of the day as part of a regular class schedule but in the evening, after a long day of practicing law. We emphasize these differences because they underscore the Institute's focus on eliminating the distance between reflection and practice — we wanted to show the Fellows that it is possible for theory to become a regular part of legal practice.

We put a great deal of thought into selecting the readings. On a micro level, our goal was to select twenty or thirty pages of text for each week that would loosely connect to a practice area from among those of the organizations at which the Fellows were interning. For example, for a week on "Immigrant Rights" we assigned two competing papers by Thomas Pogge and David Miller discussing theories of cosmopolitanism, neither of which reference contemporary debates on immigration. Instead, they present a philosophical conversation regarding the moral responsibility that the people of one place bear toward the people of another. On a macro level, we strove for variety. The thinkers we assigned, ranging from Kwame Anthony Appiah to bell hooks to Friedrich Hayek, reflected a variety of ideological and intellectual perspectives, as well as genders, races, and national and historical backgrounds. The decision to include conservative writers in the syllabus reflected our view that any kind of critical and social theoretical work, regardless of its political orientation, can help public interest practitioners develop their normative faculties. We also tried to provide balance in terms of the difficulty and accessibility of the texts, structuring the flow of materials so that there were not multiple weeks in a row with very dense readings.

More importantly, we excluded legal theory or works directly addressing the law. We deliberately did not assign any doctrinal theory, critical legal theory, critical race theory, or scholarship published by legal academics. We also did not assign the type of empirical social scientific research that legal realists new and old have argued is crucial to both the theory and practice of law. Instead, we focused on abstract texts that make arguments "about what is just, moral, good, and right"—works that, in Joseph Singer's words, can help law students finish the "because clause." We chose this particular type of reading, which we refer to as "social theory," because of the distinct impact it had on our thinking and practice as clinical law students and full-time public interest lawyers. We wanted to share this experience with the Fellows to demonstrate how engaging with texts that present provocative normative arguments with intellectual rigor and precision can challenge them to improve their thinking about the moral underpinnings of the practice they are entering.

Id. at 475-77. Does this course of reading seem more or less helpful than the approach described in the Lawyering in the Public Interest course offered at Penn Law School?

Teaching public interest lawyering may not only counteract public interest drift, but may also motivate students to embrace new concepts and forms of practice. Corey Shdaimah's account of legal services lawyers noted that some of her interview subjects had "read progressive lawyering literature" that supported the ideal of lawyers enhancing client autonomy—and tried to enact that role in their day-to-day practice. Corey S. Shdaimah, Negotiating Justice: Progressive Lawyering, Low-Income Clients, and the Quest for Social Change 68 (2009).

2. Clinics

Historically, it has been law school clinics that have led the movement for social justice-centered law school education. In this section, we look at two aspects of law school clinics: (1) as *producers* of public interest lawyers (i.e., their pedagogical impact); and (2) as *providers* of public interest law services (i.e., their political impact).

a. THE PEDAGOGICAL IMPACT OF CLINICAL EDUCATION

The clinical education movement began in the 1970s, in one sense, as the law school counterpart to public interest law. From its beginning, proponents of clinical education viewed it as advancing twin aims of skills training and social justice—the latter understood both in terms of using law school resources to affect surrounding communities and exposing students to social problems that would instill an ethic of public service. Margaret Martin Barry, Jon C. Dubin & Peter A. Joy, *Clinical Education for This Millennium: The Third Wave*, 7 Clinical L. Rev. 1, 13-14 (2000); *see also* Mark Spiegel, *An Essay on Clinical Education*, 34 UCLA L. Rev. 577, 590 (1987).

The claimed nexus between clinical education and social justice has not been without its challengers. As we saw in Chapter 6, William Simon in an early critique argued that the strong client-centered orientation of clinical education taught students to defer to their clients' wishes in such a way that disserved the public good since many students would go on to serve as counsel to more powerful clients (like corporations), in contexts in which their training would make them reluctant to contest clients' socially harmful positions. William H. Simon, *Homo Psychologicus: Notes on a New Legal Formalism*, 323 STAN. L. REV. 487 (1980). The notion of training for public service, however, has remained a central tenet of contemporary clinical education. *See, e.g.*, Douglas L. Colbert, *Clinical Professors' Professional Responsibility: Preparing Law Students to Embrace Pro Bono*, 18 GEO. J. ON POVERTY L. & POL'Y 309 (2011); Jon C. Dubin, *Clinical Design for Social Justice Imperatives*, 51 SMU L. REV. 1461 (1988); Larry R. Spain, *The Unfinished Agenda of Law Schools in Nurturing a Commitment to Pro Bono Legal Services by Law Students*, 72 UMKC L. REV. 477 (2003); Stephen Wizner, *The Law School Clinic: Legal Education in the Interest of Justice*, 70 FORDHAM L. REV. 1929 (2002).

Until recently, this tenet had not been empirically tested. The following excerpt reports on the findings of one study looking at the impact of clinical experiences on the career choices of newly minted lawyers.

REBECCA SANDEFUR & JEFFREY SELBIN, *THE CLINIC EFFECT*

16 CLINICAL L. REV. 57, 90-100 (2009)

To explore evidence of clinical training's contribution to the civic dimension of lawyer professionalism, we sought empirical indicators of whether law school graduates were "able and willing to join an enterprise of public service." Our analysis of new lawyers' behavior in the civic dimension of professionalism thus focuses on the work and volunteer activities of new lawyers. Lawyers may "provide public service through pro bono representation or professional or community activities," they may serve the public as employees of government, or they may work outside government in the public interest, "commit[ing] themselves and their legal skills to furthering a vision of the good society." To assess the relationship between participation in clinic during law school and the civic dimension of lawyer professionalism, we examine three different aspects of new lawyers' activities: pro bono service; participation in community, charitable, political advocacy and bar-related organizations; and public service employment.

In these analyses, we explore the potential influence of clinical training by comparing the experiences of three groups of new lawyers: (1) those who reported that clinical legal education was not helpful for making the transition to early work assignments as an attorney; (2) those who reported that clinical training was not applicable to their experience; and (3) those who reported that clinical education was helpful for making the transition to early work assignments as an attorney. We focus on these three groups of new lawyers for a substantive reason. To the extent that new lawyers are reporting faithfully on their law school experiences, distinguishing them in this way allows us to explore the contribution of two different aspects of clinical training experiences: whether someone was exposed to clinical training at all, and whether that exposure was a valued experience. . . .

The After the JD survey asked new lawyers to recollect their motivations for attending law school. Their responses thus represent their retrospective understanding of their own reasons for entering the profession. A majority of new lawyers reported that what might be termed "civic" motivations were important reasons for entering law. . . . Comparing lawyers who rated clinics as helpful versus not helpful revealed that their recollected motives for entering law were significantly different. Of lawyers who reported that clinical training had been helpful, 70% reported that a "desire to help individuals as a lawyer" or to "change or improve society" had been important reasons for entering law. By comparison, 56% of those who did not report on any clinical training said that they had entered law to change society or help individuals, while 51% of attorneys who did not rate clinic as helpful reported that these motivations had been important in their decision to attend law school. Thus, at least in their own recollection, new lawyers who experienced and appreciated clinical training were more likely to recall that they had entered law for what one might term "civic" reasons than were lawyers who did not receive the training or who did not find it helpful. . . .

1. Pro Bono Service

. . . Examining the relationship between clinical training experiences and pro bono service within groups of lawyers who reported similar motivations for entering law, there are no statistically significant differences. Among lawyers who recalled that they entered law to help individuals or change or improve society, 37% of those who reported that clinical training was not helpful did pro bono work, 41% of those who reported no clinical training did pro bono work, and 43% of those who reported that clinical training was helpful did pro bono work. Again it may appear as though helpful clinical training correlates with increased pro bono work, but these differences are not statistically significant. Among lawyers who recollected that they entered law for other reasons, 51% of those who reported clinical training was not helpful did pro bono work, 46% of those who reported no clinical training did pro bono work, and 48% of those who reported clinical training was helpful did pro bono work; as before, none of these differences is statistically significant. Given these data, we find no relationship between clinical training in law school and pro bono service by new attorneys in private practice and offices of internal counsel.

2. Civic Participation

. . . Overall, . . . 12% of respondents reported they were active participants or leaders in community organizations, 13% in charitable organizations, 3% in political advocacy groups and 13% in bar-related organizations. These rates of participation were similar among lawyers who reported different kinds of clinical experiences. Whether new lawyers reported that their clinical training had not been helpful, that they had not received clinical training, or that it had been helpful, there were no statistically significant differences in their likelihood of active participation in any of the four types of civic organizations.

On the other hand, lawyers' recollected motivations for entering law were significantly associated with their civic participation. Attorneys who reported that they had entered law to help individuals or change or improve society were more likely to be active in charitable, political advocacy and bar-related organizations. Fifteen percent of those who reported civic motivations for entering law were active in charitable organizations, in comparison with 11% of those who did not. Four percent of those who entered law for civic reasons were active in political advocacy organizations, in comparison with 2% of those who entered law for other reasons. Fifteen percent of those who entered law for civic reasons were active in bar organizations, in comparison with 12% of those who reported that they entered law for other reasons. A similar pattern appears for active participation in community organizations, but the difference is not statistically significant.

When we look among lawyers who reported similar reasons for entering law, the picture changes, but only a little. Controlling for recollected motivations, we do not see significant relationships between clinical experiences and different kinds of community participation, with a single exception. The exception is active participation in charitable organizations. Among new lawyers who recalled that they entered the profession to change society or help individuals, 13% of those who reported clinical training was not helpful were active in such organizations, 12% of those who reported no clinical training were active in charitable organizations, and 16% of those who found clinical training helpful were active in charitable organizations. The difference in participation between lawyers in the group who reported no clinical training and those who reported helpful clinical training is statistically significant. However, given the available data concerning civic participation as a whole, we find little evidence for a relationship between clinical training experiences and civic participation among new lawyers.

3. Public Service Employment

... Among those who reported that clinical training was not helpful, 11% were working in public service jobs. Among those who did not report on clinical training, 9% were working in public service jobs. But among those who rated their clinical training as helpful, 20% were working in such positions.

These differences are substantial and statistically significant. Early-career attorneys who found their clinical experience helpful were 82% $(= (.20 - .11)/. 11)$ more likely to be working in public service in their early careers than those who did not find it helpful. They were 122% $(= (.20 - .09)/.09)$ more likely to be working in public service than those who did not report on clinical experiences. Further analysis, however, reveals that the relationship between clinical experiences and public service employment is statistically significant for only some groups of lawyers.

As was the case with pro bono service and civic participation, lawyers' public service employment was significantly associated with their recollected motivations for entering law. New lawyers who recalled civic motivations for entering law were twice as likely to be working in public service jobs as those who did not (20% versus 10%). . . . [C]linical experiences are significantly associated with public service employment only for new lawyers who expressed civic motivations. Within this group of lawyers, those who found clinical training helpful were more than twice as likely to be working in public service jobs as those who did not report on clinical training or did not find clinic helpful (25% versus 12%). Among new lawyers who did not express civic motivations for entering law, 11% of those who did not find clinic helpful were working in public service jobs two years into their legal careers, 7% of those who reported no clinical training were working in public service employment, and 10% of such lawyers who found clinic helpful were doing so. None of these differences is statistically significant and thus there was no relationship between clinic experiences and public service work in this group of lawyers.

Only among new lawyers who report that they entered law to improve society or help individuals do we see evidence consistent with a "clinic effect." These lawyers are more likely to be in public service employment overall, and those who found clinic helpful are more than twice as likely to be working in public service employment than those who did not. This finding suggests the possibility of an accelerant effect, though it is not clear what is accelerating what. Clinical experiences may support or otherwise enable the public service work of people who are already more likely to do that work. Alternatively, clinical experiences may change the self-understandings of people who are helped into public service work by their clinical training. For example, a clinic graduate working in legal services may come to realize, post facto, that she entered the profession "to help individuals as a lawyer" or to "change or improve society" after all. Finally, people who entered law with civic motivations and take up public service work may give greater value to their clinical training because of its congruence with both their past motivations and their present employment. Probably, a mix of these processes occurs. With these data, it is not possible to determine precisely which processes are operating for which lawyers.

While not definitive, the available evidence is consistent with the presence of a "clinic effect" on public service employment. However, the relationship between clinical experiences and employment outcomes obtains only for some new lawyers: those who recollected that they came to law school wishing to "help individuals as a lawyer" or "change or improve society." What is not clear from the correlation between clinical experiences and public service employment is how any such effect might be created. In particular, it is not clear to what extent clinical training may affect what jobs students want or to what extent it affects the jobs they are able to get.

Does the fact that clinics appear to only increase the "civic dimension" of professionalism among those already inclined toward it argue for a different model of clinical education? That is, if clinics are not producing more public servants, should the emphasis shift from justice to skills? Note that some schools pursue clinical programming that is directly responsive to the training needs of private sector employers. *See, e.g.*, CENTER FOR THE STUDY OF APPLIED LEGAL EDUCATION, REPORT ON THE 2007-2008 SURVEY (reporting the percentage of law schools with the following types of live-client, in-house clinics: tax (4.1 percent), transactional (4.0 percent), intellectual property (1.9 percent), and securities (1.2 percent)).

b. THE POLITICAL IMPACT OF LAW SCHOOL CLINICS

Aside from their pedagogical impact, law school clinics also serve an important role as a provider of legal services to poor and other underrepresented clients. In many instances, they have been sites for "transformation"—if not of students, then of the communities they serve. Lucie E. White, *The Transformative Potential of Clinical Legal Education*, 35 OSGOODE HALL L.J. 603 (1997).

While transformative clinics have taken political risks to advance the interests of marginalized communities, they have inevitably courted controversy—and backlash. The controversy has come from two sources. One is external to the clinical movement itself and generally tracks conservative criticisms of the political aims of liberal public interest law. The following excerpt makes the case most strongly.

HEATHER MACDONALD, THIS *IS THE LEGAL MAINSTREAM?*

City Journal (Winter 2006)

To understand how politically one-sided law schools are, look no further than the law school "clinic." These campus law firms, faculty-supervised and student-staffed, have been engaging in left-wing litigation and political advocacy for 30 years. Though law schools claim that the clinics teach students the nuts and bolts of law practice, while providing crucial legal representation to poor people, in fact they routinely neither inculcate lawyering skills nor serve the poor. They do, however, offer the legal professoriate a way to engage in political activism—almost never of a conservative cast. If you wonder why law school profs invariably deem conservative jurists "out of the mainstream," a survey of the clinical universe makes clear what the academy's legal "mainstream" really means.

In the last few years alone, law school clinics have put the Berkeley, California, school system under judicial supervision for disciplining black and Hispanic students disproportionately to their population (yes, that's Berkeley, the most racially sensitive spot on earth); sued the New York Police Department for its conduct during the 2004 Republican National Convention; fought "gentrification" (read: economic revitalization) in "neighborhoods of color" in Boston, New Haven, and New York; sued the Bush administration for virtually every aspect of its conduct of the war on terror; and lobbied for more restrictive "tobacco control" laws.

Over their history, clinics can claim credit for making New Jersey pay for abortions for the poor; blocking job-providing industrial facilities; setting up needle exchanges for drug addicts in residential neighborhoods; forcing

Princeton's eating clubs to admit women; allowing female murderers to beat the rap by claiming "battered women's syndrome"; and preventing New Jersey libraries from ejecting foul-smelling vagrants who are disturbing library users.

Yet only a handful of law schools would have any interest in providing legal assistance to Shawna Spencer, an inner-city Chicagoan who hopes to turn her passion for shoes into a booming business. Already overextended on every possible credit line, Spencer couldn't afford an attorney to negotiate a lease for the shoe store she wanted to open. Fortunately, the University of Chicago Law School offers one of the few clinics to take struggling for-profit entrepreneurs as clients. "I couldn't have opened without my 'attorneys,'" Spencer says of the Chicago law students.

Had this energetic optimist been seeking government benefits or, better yet, had she struck a clinic director as a vehicle for litigating a new entitlement into existence, she could have had the pick of the law school elite to fight her case.

The history of the law school clinic explains why. A handful of clinics existed throughout the twentieth century, to give students hands-on experience of law practice. Drafting complaints and cross-examining witnesses can usefully supplement the traditional curriculum's emphasis on abstract legal doctrines. Having a real client, who usually presents himself as a muddle of contradictory desires, allegations, and denials, rather than as a neatly packaged cause of action, focuses the mind on how to use the law as a casebook rarely can. And the philanthropic justification for the early law school clinics — that they provided legal help to people who otherwise couldn't afford it — is unimpeachable.

But once the Ford Foundation started disbursing $12 million in 1968 to persuade law schools to make clinics part of their curriculum, the enterprise turned into a political battering ram. Clinics were the perfect embodiment of a radical new conception of lawyers and litigation that emerged in the 1960s — the lawyer as social-change agent. Up until that era, the entire law profession was seen as a form of public service, essential to a democracy. But now, as Attorney General Robert Kennedy urged in 1964, lawyers should fight "the problems of poverty, racial discrimination, and other great social ills." Henceforth, the noble, public-spirited attorneys would be those suing for the egalitarian transformation of society. Arthur Kinoy, the founder of clinical education at Rutgers, called for a new breed of lawyer: "people's lawyers — characterized by their compassion, competence and commitment to the cause of equal justice and positive social change." Note the implication: a solo practitioner who has spent his career helping the elderly draft wills or negotiating commercial leases for small-businessmen is not a "people's lawyer," nor are his clients "people." Ivy-educated activists like the late Harvard law professor Gary Bellow, however, lawyer for the Black Panthers and the intellectual patriarch of the clinical movement, are "people's lawyers."

Ford Foundation head McGeorge Bundy embraced this view and set the agenda for America's richest foundations when he declared in 1966 that law "must be an active, not a passive force. It is both urgent and right that the law should be affirmatively and imaginatively used against all forms of injustice." The foundation made sure that the tax code reflected this new hierarchy of virtue. Soon after launching the clinical revolution, Ford started agitating to make litigation a deductible charitable activity, *if* the litigation was in the "public interest"—a change that would help Ford spread activist lawyering throughout the country via federally subsidized "legal services" offices. After initially rejecting the demand, the IRS gave in.

No one can object to fighting discrimination and poverty. But the problem is that no one elected a Ford-funded "poverty lawyer" to create a new entitlement scheme. If that lawyer can find a judge who shares his passion for welfare, however, the two of them will put into law a significant new distribution of rights and resources that no voter or legislator ever approved.

And what if the activist philosophy of lawyering is wrong in its diagnosis of society's ills? Too bad: correcting its errors through the democratic process is extremely difficult. Sixties-era lawyering belonged to a larger revolution in thinking about the poor, and especially the minority poor. Gone was any reference to personal responsibility: to remark, for example, that dropping out of school, taking drugs, and having illegitimate children produce poverty was condemned as "blaming the victim." Eradicating poverty required massive changes in society, not in individual behavior. The activist lawyer would spearhead those changes by creating new court-enforceable rights and entitlements.

Unquestionably, racial discrimination, and the poverty that it fostered, were urgent problems when Robert Kennedy, McGeorge Bundy, and others issued their call for activist lawyering. But they all underestimated both America's ability to change and an individual's ability to better himself despite prejudice. Today, not only does virtually no major American institution discriminate against racial minorities; all fiercely compete with one another to admit or hire as many minorities as possible, using preferences and double standards to do so.

Yet law schools and their clinics hold firmly to the belief that discrimination remains a major factor holding back minorities. Columbia Law School's statement in support of clinical education is typical—and typically antique: clinics address the "legal problems that arise from poverty, racism, inequality, and political tyranny." And in language that would have seemed cutting-edge 40 years ago, Stephen Wizner, Yale's William O. Douglas Clinical Professor of Law, declares: "Representing groups in class actions, engaging in law reform litigation and supporting community organizing efforts are crucial to increasing the economic and political power of the poor." In other words, what lawyers can do for the poor is equally if not more important than what the poor can do for themselves.

Today's clinical landscape is a perfect place to evaluate what happens when lawyers decide that they are chosen to save society. "Some of us felt like kids in a candy shop: a public interest law firm funded by a law school with ready workers providing important client services," recall Yale's Wizner and Jane Aiken, a Washington University clinical professor of law. The law school clinics don't just take clients with obvious legal issues, such as criminal defendants or tenants facing an order of eviction. They take social problems—unruly students in school, for example—and turn them into legal ones. Florence Roisman, a housing rights activist at the Indiana University School of

Law, has inspired clinicians nationwide with her supremely self-confident call to arms: "If it offends your sense of justice, there's a cause of action." . . .

That leaves one final rationale for clinics: consciousness-raising. Though many clinics by now have left the poor far behind in their pursuit of Bush administration war criminals, say, or hapless state legislators trying to balance their budgets, others still aim to put students in contact with the disenfranchised and oppressed, to inspire a new generation of activist poverty lawyers. With almost Dickensian self-parody, the Harvard faculty touts clinics as a way to see "dimensions of social reality that must be experienced to be understood. . . . Exposure to the problems and the cultures of poverty, and to the intersection of those realities with legal rules and practice, deepens understanding of the legal system and its relation to the society at large."

Yale's legal-services clinic provided an especially up-close opportunity for such experiential learning. In the mid-1990s, the clinic wanted to stop a police plan to evict vagrants from the New Haven train station. Director Stephen Wizner advocated that the students spend the night with the vagrants: "We encouraged these students to act on their belief that in order to be 'lawyers' for the homeless people in the train station, lawyers [sic] needed to be present to argue against the proposed police action. The students ended up spending the night at the train station. Through their physical presence, and by appealing to the individual police officers as human beings, these students 'won' their 'case.' The people were allowed to sleep in the train station, rather than being driven out into the freezing cold streets of New Haven."

Wizner calls such "social justice" interventions "human learning." But what really did the Yale students learn in their night of solidarity, and why are only some kinds of experience with social reality of interest to clinic advocates? Doubtless the Yale students learned that it is less comfortable to spend the night in a train station than at home. But did they learn about the drug and alcohol addictions, mental illness, and social disaffiliation that keep vagrants on the street? Have they experienced the travails of social workers who cannot persuade vagrants to enter shelters? Did they bond with the maintenance men who must clean up the feces, urine, and discarded paraphernalia left by the "homeless"? Did they learn about the commuters who shun public transit for fear of being accosted by mentally ill drug addicts? And are they confident that they know how keeping the "homeless" in public spaces affects their "clients'" motivation to seek help? Do they consider how in-your-face public vagrancy weakens the viability of cities? . . .

Especially since clinical education is so expensive — the faculty-to-student ratio is orders of magnitude smaller than in large lecture courses — schools should either discontinue this pedagogically irrelevant subsidy to political agitation, or they should open clinics up to currently disfavored topics that would provide relevant practical training. Ending clinics is not likely: the ABA and the Association of American Law Schools are urging schools to give tenure-like rights, such as voting on new faculty hires, to clinical professors — a move that will only push the schools further leftward. All the more imperative, then, to broaden the range of clinical offerings.

If they were really serious about preparing students for their legal careers, every school would have a transactional clinic for small businesses. The vast majority of lawyers advise clients on business deals — negotiating contracts, setting up corporations and partnerships, trying to avoid legal and tax liabilities, and arranging securities offerings and registrations. As NYU's Martin Guggenheim acknowledges, "Students are entering a world where litigation is the least likely thing that they will do."

In grudging recognition of this reality, some law schools do offer transactional clinics, but most give priority to nonprofits. Harvard's Community Enterprise Project, for example, works chiefly with "community development" groups, while Yale's Housing and Community Development Clinic offers "consultation to community groups, particularly nonprofit organizations involved in affordable housing and economic development efforts." But getting a nonprofit up and running is far less complicated, and less pedagogically useful, than advising a for-profit venture.

The Institute for Justice runs perhaps the only exclusively for-profit business clinic in the country, at the University of Chicago. The law school at first assumed that the clinic would help businesses seek minority set-asides, recalls the Institute for Justice's director, Chip Mellor. "We said, 'That's a deal-breaker. We only do private sector advancement.' The Dean blinked, and said, 'Well, OK.' They had never thought anything to the contrary."

It is law school students, not professors, who are spearheading the creation of transactional clinics, and students are crowding into such clinics once they are created. The demand for such clinics is as high outside the school as in it. Struggling businesses, including those run by minority entrepreneurs, are hurting for lack of counsel, students have found. Dan Ehrlich, a second-year student at the University of St. Thomas School of Law in Minneapolis, has been leading the establishment of a business clinic there. "There is a *huge* need for such an enterprise," he says. The federal Small Business Administration offices in Minneapolis are overwhelmed with would-be entrepreneurs seeking assistance, he notes.

Just because such entrepreneurs hope to make a profit doesn't mean that they can afford legal counsel. "I opened up underfunded, and I've been working undercapitalized ever since," says Shawna Spencer, the shoe-maven client of the University of Chicago entrepreneurship clinic. "Every small business operates undercapitalized, because loans don't exist. We don't have money for marketing; we *definitely* don't have money to hire an attorney."

The possibility of launching future job-creators like Spencer, especially when they come from inner-city backgrounds, ought to fire up the "social justice" crowd. "The schools aren't looking at the bigger picture," Spencer says, when told that the University of Chicago entrepreneurship clinic is unique in helping only for-profit businesses. "A seamstress in a housing project doesn't know that she could become a renowned designer. When you're helping to realize someone's potential, you're creating less poverty."

Business clinics not only fit the "fighting poverty" rationale for clinics; they meet the experiential test as well. Working for a small business "deepens understanding of the legal system and its relation to the society at large," in the Harvard faculty formula. David Neil incorporated and tried to get licensing permits for a small moving company while enrolled in the University of Chicago's entrepreneurship clinic. "It was an eye-opener," Neil says. The owner needed to pay $1,000 in a nonrefundable fee just to apply for the permits. Such barriers to entry have a "chilling effect" on low-income entrepreneurs, Neil observed. "The experience taught me that the law is sometimes used to perpetuate the status quo," he says.

For schools interested in giving students hands-on training, representing the unrepresented, and providing "human learning," there is a world of clients and causes (however politically incorrect they may be) that meet every justification offered for the current one-sided array of clinics. Herewith some possible topics:

Representing small-businessmen, landlords, and property owners. The thicket of environmental law has grown so complex that "no one can stay out of trouble," according to former Natural Resources Defense Council litigator David Schoenbrod, author of *Saving Our Environment from Washington*. Unlike big businesses, small outfits have trouble affording lawyers to hack through those rules or to meet the EPA's onerous paperwork requirements. Providing them counsel would nicely balance the political bias of current environmental clinics and provide a real learning experience.

The country abounds with small landowners barred from developing their property because of zoning regulations or government eminent-domain actions. Only two clinics in the country defend such landowners—at George Mason's and Chapman's law schools—yet property rights and federalism cases pose cutting-edge constitutional-law issues.

Defending tenants against eviction is a law school staple. NYU's civil rights clinic is currently representing a tenant whom the landlord claims is "engaging in illegal drug activities in her apartment," according to the clinic catalog description. Certainly the tenant needs legal representation. But it would be equally useful for students to experience New York's housing court from the landlord's side, where getting rid of a dope-dealing tenant requires Herculean efforts against pro-tenant rules and judges. Numerous small landlords have scraped together just enough for a down payment on a two- or three-unit property, which they can pay off only by renting out the apartments that they are not occupying. When their tenants turn deadbeat or commit vandalism, their investment is at risk. "Human learning" in a small-landlords clinic might include surveying tenants in buildings where a resident drug trader is receiving free representation from another clinic. The "silent majority of tenants back landlords' efforts to get sleazeballs out, but they are afraid to talk because of retribution," says Carol Abrams, spokesman for New York's Housing Preservation and Development Department.

Defending the authority of school districts and teachers. Stanford's education law clinic just put the Berkeley, California, school district under court order for allegedly "discriminatorily" disciplining black and Latino students. The teachers will have to submit to "sensitivity training," and the schools will have to take corrective action to make sure that minorities are not being disciplined at rates disproportionate to their representation in the school population. (And if minorities really do cause disproportionate violence in the schools, too bad.) Students in a clinic dedicated to upholding school authority might shadow a principal in a district operating under a court-imposed consent decree, to experience the barriers to removing a disruptive student. Clinic students could also attend a classroom where the teacher must worry about whether his disciplinary decisions will be challenged as illegal and racist by pupils, lawyers, and judges.

Representing crime victims. The only crime victims currently on law schools' radar are domestic violence victims, but boy, do they get attention. Domestic violence clinics abound, taking a law-and-order stance that would be unthinkable for crimes where "gender" is not implicated. Many schools do offer a prosecution clinic to balance out their numerous criminal-defense clinics, but prosecutors famously give short shrift to victims' perspectives.

Victims' rights is ripe for the creative lawyering that transformed the legal universe in the 1960s. "There are many judges around the country who would be responsive to innovative arguments" in the field, says criminal-law theorist and Columbia Law School professor George Fletcher. But currently the only significant victims' rights clinic is at Arizona State University. Explains director Keli Luther: "Because there is so little case law in the field, students have to think outside the box. They're drafting motions that have never been written before." The clinic is experimenting with creative ways of seeking restitution, for example, such as filing liens on defendants' stolen stereos, cars, and jewelry.

Allowing students to work with victims would provide the sort of "human learning" that clinicians advocate. Seeing how crime affects families and communities would seem to be one of those "dimensions of social reality that must be experienced to be understood." And as for understanding the "intersection of realities with legal rules and practice," in the Harvard faculty's words, exposing students to victims of criminals who have escaped conviction thanks to defendants' rights rulings, or who have been assaulted by criminals out on early parole, surely would "deepen understanding of the legal system and its relation to the society at large."

Defending law officers. New York and other big cities host a cottage industry of suing cops for false arrest, whenever prosecutors decide not to file charges against an arrestee. A clinic could help police departments litigate such cases, rather than settle them, as they usually do, at considerable expense to taxpayers. Similarly, prisoners (often represented by clinics and fancy firms) sue prisons constantly, alleging various constitutional violations. Prison defense work would offer one of the best constitutional-law practices around, because the issues presented under the First, Eighth, and Fourteenth Amendments are so richly complex.

Supporting a colorblind America. Not a single civil rights clinic has pushed to end racial preferences, which would make the Constitution's promise of an America without color distinctions a reality. The targets for such an originalist civil rights clinic — one that would realize Martin Luther King's dream — are legion.

These examples center on litigation, unlike the law schools' current emphasis on policy advocacy, protest, and community organizing. But if the schools think they must provide advocacy experience, pro-life clinics could send students to state capitols to demand that parents be given a say over their children's abortion decisions. Clinics could organize inner-city residents to demand crime-free neighborhoods, whether through an end to the racial data collection mandates on police departments that discourage aggressive policing, or through tougher sentencing laws and parole conditions. Students could stuff envelopes for would-be entrepreneurs as they lobby for less confiscatory tax policies.

The proponents of social justice lawyering are unlikely to acknowledge any time soon that their revolution has triggered family breakdown, unleashed an epidemic of crime in inner-city neighborhoods, and burdened entrepreneurs with unnecessary regulations. At the very least, however, law schools should offer students the chance to question for themselves whether such lawyering is the best way to help society. Opening up clinics to radical perspectives on the benefits of limited government and personal responsibility would be a good place to start.

Do you agree that law school clinics are, in general, primarily focused on left-wing activism? Although most within clinical education would concede that it is dominated by faculty with politically liberal values, it is less clear that liberal advocacy (as opposed to more routine individual service cases) dominates the clinical docket—though the high-profile examples MacDonald highlights are not balanced out by similar successes for right-wing causes. Do you agree that clinics should be "devoid of politics" or, if not, more politically balanced? Is that even possible? Is it true that the issue areas identified by MacDonald for increased clinical investment—representing business owners, defending property rights, supporting school districts, defending crime victims and law enforcement officers, and advancing colorblindness—are underserved in the same ways that traditional clinical categories are? Note that this type of political criticism of clinics has generated recurrent attacks on clinics' autonomy. *See* Peter A. Joy, *Political Interference with Clinical Legal Education: Denying Access to Justice*, 74 Tul. L. Rev. 235 (1999) (discussing limitations on clinical practice imposed in Louisiana after Tulane's environmental law clinic took on a politically controversial case against a company seeking to build a chemical plant, which is discussed in more detail in Chapter 3).

The other controversy surrounding the political content of clinical education comes from within clinical legal education and relates to the appropriate political scope of clinical courses. Consider these opposing views:

Sameer M. Ashar, *Law Clinics and Collective Mobilization*

14 Clinical L. Rev. 355, 357-59, 389-94 (2008)

Poor people are not served well by the kinds of advocacy currently taught and reinforced in most law clinics. The canonical approaches to clinical legal education, which focus nearly exclusively on individual client empowerment, the transfer of a limited number of professional skills, and lawyer-led impact litigation and law reform, are not sufficient to sustain effective public interest practice. These approaches meet the experiential and service goals of law school clinics and reinforce the norms of conventional practice in the legal profession. However, they rely on a practice narrative that does not accurately portray the conditions that poor people face the resistance strategies that activist, organized groups deploy, or the new reality of public interest practice.

At the margins of the field, a growing number of law school clinics and innovative legal advocacy organizations are playing a key role in developing a new public interest practice, one informed by the critical poverty law scholarship of the past several decades. These lawyers and law students support and stimulate radical democratic resistance to market forces by developing litigation, legislative, and community education methods to advance collective mobilization. . . .

In the emerging alternative model of clinical legal education animated by collective mobilization that I espouse, political and social vision shape intake and pedagogy, rather than being shaped by them. As Gary Bellow says in the epigraph to this article, absent an affirmative political and social vision, even self-conscious practitioners reproduce the status quo. Programs that lack an explicit political and social vision conceal their implicit vision, with deleterious consequences for law students, clients, and communities. In this section, I document the approaches to case intake that my colleagues and I have taken and delineate the knowledge bases gained through this alternative clinical fieldwork. . . .

At the heart of this alternative approach is the conviction that clinics should select cases and projects that support the mobilization efforts of groups working to change the social order. Like all public interest practitioners, clinics should ask three questions of any proposed case or project: (1) whether it fits into a broader campaign for reform with other similarly situated clients; (2) whether the representation will help create or sustain some form of collective resistance; and (3) who will stand for (or work with) the population and its cause when students graduate and clinics move on to new cases and causes. With organizational partners, the legal case or project is part of a larger mobilization effort that continues after the case or project is complete.

In this section, I document methods by which my colleagues and I identified collective mobilization cases in New York, where there are active organizing networks in the areas of immigrant labor and deportation defense, and in Baltimore, where networks of immigrant organizing were just emerging when I was there in 2002-03. In each of these environments, we faced challenges in finding and collaborating with politicized collectives and in identifying legal cases and projects that were appropriate for a clinic docket. With a firsthand sense of the difficulty in constructing clinics with a collective mobilization mission, my goal in this article is not to discount or hide these difficulties but to argue that the extra time and effort put into intake based on an articulated political and social vision promise to make clinical legal education more relevant for social movements and a more effective training ground for public interest lawyers. . . .

In New York City, there are a significant number of worker centers organized by industry and along ethnic and racial lines. One such group with which we work at the CUNY Immigrant & Refugee Rights Clinic, the Restaurant Opportunities Center of New York (ROC-NY), organizes groups of workers in the high-end restaurant industry in the city. Union penetration in the industry is less than 1 percent. Wage and hour violations are endemic because of an unyielding supply of immigrant labor with limited market power vis-à-vis their employers. At the restaurants where the movers and shakers of the global economy meet, workers often receive 40 hours of pay for 50 to 80 hours of work. Additionally, the workplace is highly stratified by race and ethnicity, from Latinos in the "back of the house" to whites in the "front of the house,["] with Bangladeshis and other people of color stationed in between as runners and bussers.

ROC-NY analyzed the industry and carefully targets specific players in order to stimulate a positive ripple effect. The organization has limited resources with which to initiate organizing campaigns or enforce contracts with employers; instead, it relies on the power of groups of workers who band together to challenge their own working conditions. Individual employees complaining of bad work conditions are told by organizers to organize more of their co-workers. If they successfully draw more workers to the fight, they present the proposed campaign to the members of the organization, all veterans of past or ongoing campaigns at other restaurants. As part of a multi-faceted, overall strategy, the organization calls upon lawyers to file the legal grievances that will focus the campaign and mobilize courts and agencies against the bad employers.

With no shortage in New York City of employers committing wage and hour violations, the clinic could have a limitless supply of individual cases. However, we choose to use the clinic's scarce legal resources to support organizing and collective action for broader reform in an industry that has been shaped by accelerated migration and lowered labor standards and regulatory enforcement. The end result is that while we work on cases similar to that of a conventional public interest client-centered practice, our cases are linked to mobilization efforts that create the possibility of lasting change beyond the dollars won for an individual client.

The CUNY clinic has had a particularly successful record of collaboration with ROC-NY. We recently completed our second major campaign with the organization, focused on employment discrimination in the high-end sector of the industry, and recently began a third litigation campaign in August 2007. Student teams working with ROC-NY have also drafted a workers rights manual for distribution by the City's Department of Consumer Affairs to all restaurants, undertaken legal research for a pending bill in the New York City Council, and helped brainstorm legislative approaches to the problem of employment discrimination in the industry. In addition to ROC-NY and other more conventional legal groups, we have worked collaboratively with membership organizations in the following ways:

- New York ACORN is a chapter of the venerable national organization and a powerful constituent of a statewide labor-community electoral coalition. A clinic student had deep ties to the organization after a stint as an organizer in its Brooklyn office and lobbied for us to work collaboratively on an immigration-related project. Executive Director Bertha Lewis, with an eye toward expanded immigrant organizing, asked us to work on a report delineating the naturalization backlog in New York and comparing it to delays in other cities and regions.

- Andolan Organizing South Asian Workers was founded in 1998 by a former domestic worker from Bangladesh and uses litigation and direct action techniques to advance their campaigns. The organization has been a leading force against the abuse of the domestic workers of United Nations diplomats. The organization asked the clinic to represent an active member who worked as a domestic worker in federal wage and hour litigation against her former employers.

- Asociacion Tepeyac is composed of Mexican Catholic congregations in New York City. At the request of the New York Archdiocese, Jesuit Brother Joel Magallan Reyes was sent from Mexico to start a support network for the community in the city in 1997. Organizer and NYU law student Jared Bybee asked the clinic to represent five restaurant worker-members of the nascent organizing unit in state wage and hour litigation against their employer.

- Domestic Workers United was founded in 2000 as a collaboration of the predominantly Filipino Women Workers Unit of CAAAV Organizing Asian Communities and Andolan. The organization now also has bases of support in the Latino and Caribbean communities, has successfully lobbied for passage of a municipal law regulating employment agencies, and is currently campaigning for state legislation that would improve the terms and conditions of domestic work. The organization asked the clinic to represent a Latino member in federal wage and hour litigation against her former employer.

- Families for Freedom is a membership organization composed of the family members of current and former immigrant detainees. In addition to the work described in the next section, clinic students defended a member in deportation proceedings on the basis of prosecutorial discretion.

- Latin American Workers Center is a Brooklyn-based organization founded by Oscar Paredes in 1997. The clinic was asked to design and carry out a pro se small claims training program for members.

- New York Taxi Workers Alliance (NYTWA) organizes thousands of independent contractors and has mobilized two major taxi strikes in the last ten years. NYTWA is the first worker center to join the New York City Labor Council. The organization asked the clinic to undertake legal research for their fare increase and anti-GPS campaigns, as well as to interview organizers in cities across North America prior to the convening of the first "Internationale" of TWA chapters in March 2007.

- Queens Community House is a settlement house founded in 1974. ESL teacher and organizer Zoe Sullivan asked the clinic to create a workers'

rights training for ESL students that would lead to leadership development opportunities within the organization for Latino workers.

- The Workplace Project was founded in 1992 as an organizing center for
Central American immigrants in Hempstead, New York. The clinic filed
federal wage and hour litigation on behalf of a group of day laborers
against a contractor. Student teams are currently working with the
organization on the development of an immigration raid response
network.

Each of these relationships has resulted in effective work and important
outcomes, as well as some collaborations that have had limited effect. Because
we are engaged in a long-term exchange with these organizations, we learn
from both our successes and failures. Together with these organizations we
continually refine our ability to identify legal action that will advance organizing and mobilize necessary resources, from the clinic as well as elsewhere
within the profession. Student teams come to understand that our role must
sometimes include the formulation of legal options for our organizational
partners, as well as the identification and recruitment of other private sector
and public interest lawyers who might aid our partners in current and future
campaigns.

In the following response, Juliet Brodie defends the individual-service clinical model against Ashar's critique.

JULIET M. BRODIE, *LITTLE CASES ON THE MIDDLE GROUND: TEACHING SOCIAL JUSTICE LAWYERING IN NEIGHBORHOOD-BASED COMMUNITY LAWYERING CLINICS*

15 Clinical L. Rev. 333, 354-71 (2009)

I use examples from the neighborhood clinic I direct in East Palo Alto,
California, to illustrate how the goals of teaching and service can mutually
reinforce one another in a practice based on fundamental lawyering skills and
on the legal profession's obligation to serve the poor and provide access to
justice. In the neighborhood-based community lawyering model, the putative
"balancing act" between social justice and legal education can be reframed on
what I term the "middle ground" of social justice lawyering. Poised somewhere
between "service" and "impact," the neighborhood docket provides a volume
and variety of lawyering experiences that are rich with lessons for law students.

The Stanford Community Law Clinic ("SCLC") . . . operates out of its own
office, just over four miles from the law school campus, in the small city of East
Palo Alto, California. East Palo Alto is a storied municipality, the poor cousin to
Silicon Valley's string of well-to-do communities that run along the Peninsula
stretching from San Francisco to San Jose. . . . Predictably, legal services to the
city's residents are limited. The largest provider of legal services to low-income
people in the area is a private legal aid society that served about 1500 families
in the 2006-2007 fiscal year. With a few important exceptions, this society
generally limits its representation to advice and administrative advocacy.
In fact, SCLC is one of the only free legal services providers in the surrounding

area that offers full-scale representation in litigation in its three practice areas: housing, wage and hour, and criminal record expungement. As for volume, SCLC students conducted seventy-nine intake interviews in the 2007-2008 academic year, and the clinic went on to open individual representation cases for seventy (88%) of those prospective clients, evenly distributed across the three subject areas.

Without question, the mainstay of the caseload is individual representation in a litigation or adversarial administrative tribunal. In the housing context, it is likely to be eviction defense or representation of a tenant whose Section 8 subsidy is threatened with termination on the grounds of an alleged violation of the rules governing the subsidy program. All of the expungement cases are for individuals found to have clearance-eligible convictions. The typical wage and hour case is an individual worker — many day workers and, increasingly, restaurant workers — with unpaid wages and overtime. Each student maintains a caseload, typically with between four and six cases at any one time, with matters in each subject area.

Given the dominance of individual litigation matters, each clinic student engages in what most lawyers and clinicians would agree are fundamental (and traditional) lawyering skills, such as interviewing, counseling, research, investigation, negotiation, and dispute resolution. Using a traditional clinical pedagogical method, the individual representation cases are selected because they provide a scale of representation over which law students can be given primary responsibility. To that end, the docket is dominated by matters that are routine from a doctrinal point of view. Much of the work is what many experienced lawyers and law professors would call "basic"; SCLC students are not typically in the business of making new law. Unpredictable legal issues emerge in virtually every representation, but the relative legal simplicity of these small cases makes them well-suited for novice lawyers' first forays into lawyering. . . .

In addition to the individual representation cases, SCLC engages in various other community lawyering activities, all designed to leverage the social justice impact of the case work. These activities include community legal education workshops ("Know Your Rights"), morning strolls along the strip where day workers congregate to answer questions and distribute flyers, and attendance at community meetings where issues of concern to the low-income people of the mid-Peninsula are discussed. Additionally, clinic students have participated in legislative and quasi-legislative activities: working on a bill in the state legislature amending the provision prohibiting retaliation against workers who assert their labor rights; and, in a different forum, presenting public comments to the local housing authority on its screening of people with criminal histories who apply to the voucher program.

The SCLC practice reflects the broad values of community lawyering: practice for local low-income people on a community scale and with a flexibility and nimbleness that permit responding to that community's priorities and needs. While the practice is dominated by individual representation cases, the neighborhood-based practice and accompanying intellectual framing inject social justice effects and community lawyering values into every component of the SCLC practice, even those that could be described at first glance as "regnant." Every client, every case and every project are viewed as existing within a particular social, economic, and political context. These values are expressed through the neighborhood location, the responsiveness of the caseload, and the intellectual framing provided in the accompanying clinic seminar. . . .

This section turns to the defense against the critique that the kind of service cases dominant in a community lawyering docket is inadequately oriented to social justice outcomes and that its pedagogical preference for "student-appropriate" matters comes at too high a cost to justice. In mounting the defense, I take the long view. My point of reference is not only the social justice outcomes for clients and communities embodied in the actual casework of a neighborhood-based clinic. While that is of course vital, I refer also to the outcome of providing a new generation of lawyers with a vision of how to make working for social justice a defining part of their professional identity whether or not they hope to pursue it as a full-time vocation. I remain committed to the idea of balance — to the idea of maximizing social justice for clients, but also acknowledging the pedagogical mission of our institutions. I measure the social justice effectiveness of the work not only in terms of what the clinic students do in their clinical tour of duty but also what they are motivated and taught to do for the rest of their professional lives. . . .

A case selection model, such as that advanced by Sameer Ashar, which requires clients be part of a collective works a discriminating effect in case and client selection. Indeed, that is the point. If one's goal is to build up organizations of poor people, offering legal services only to members of those organizations is a good way to do it; it's a membership benefit that can boost recruitment and, thus, political power. Many leading social justice lawyers have explored this model, arguing that this incentivizing is an important way that lawyers can leverage their impact. This model has been promoted in opposition to the "first come-first served" model (which SCLC largely follows), which selects clients arbitrarily, perhaps favoring clients who know where the law office is, or who assess the risks of representation (say, against threats of retaliation or deportation) and conclude the risk is worth taking. Still, not all low-income people are politically motivated or activated. Not all clients are connected to "their progressive political and racial identifications" around which Ashar's clients expressly cohere. When one is committed to progressive social change, it is difficult to dispute that one should aspire to whatever model works the most leverage in the fight; however, when one's office is flooded with calls from individuals who are facing eviction, there is value in simply answering the call, without imposing a litmus test on the caller. . . .

Neighborhood-based clinics advance social justice for poor communities not only by virtue of the actual services delivered to clients and their communities, but also by providing a valuable educational environment in which future public interest lawyers can explore how to deliver that service to poor communities in the future. I address here the particular suitability of neighborhood-based clinics for public interest-minded students and articulate how the middle ground, neighborhood-based docket teaches essential lessons that such students can take forward into critical and reflective public interest careers. Because of their high volume of service cases, neighborhood-based clinics offer public interest students a breadth of exposure to poor people and law's involvement with them that can frame their future learning and practice in a unique and important way.

First, as described above, not all of us have abandoned the service docket as an important feature of public interest lawyering. Appreciating that it might not change the world, some students find their calling in serving the one tenant facing eviction next week, and will benefit from the opportunity do it in a reflective and critical manner in a clinical setting. Little in the law school curriculum is geared to those students, and this is one value that the neighborhood-based community lawyering clinic can serve.

But beyond this narrow career preparation, the neighborhood docket offers a unique environment in which aspiring public interest lawyers can gain their own, manageable version of key dramas and questions in social justice lawyering. The neighborhood-based scale of practice offers a terrain from which to address the following four topics crucial for today's public interest lawyers: (1) lawyering for the poor can be conceived as fundamentally different from lawyering for the non-poor, and there's an important academic-activist literature about the distinction, with implications for the core competencies of an effective poverty lawyer; (2) there has been an evolution of collective thinking about lawyering for the poor from concern about the power dynamics between attorney and client to a concern about collective social justice effects of the work (the so-called "lawyer domination problem"); (3) there are important questions one must engage about the role of one's own political conclusions and commitments with respect to those of the client community (is the "activist lawyer" more of a protagonist than a different kind of lawyer?); and, (4) there is a debate, perhaps tired, between "impact work" and "service work," and one must develop a personal frame through which to judge how and whether that debate still has traction.

Which model—Ashar's collective mobilization or Brodie's individual service—do you think is more defensible as a method of clinical education? As a matter of social change? How do you think each author would respond to MacDonald's critique of the left-leaning politics of contemporary clinical education?

B. PROMOTING A PUBLIC INTEREST CULTURE

1. Public Interest Programming: Communities of Resistance

While clinics have been important elements of law school since the early 1970s, the advent of public interest specializations and certificate programs is a more recent phenomenon, one that aspires to create public interest communities within law schools as an effective "oppositional strategy" to the dominant mode of socialization. GRANFIELD, *supra*, at 69; *see also* STOVER, *supra.* This kind of strategy was articulated in the 1980s by Costello, who suggested that the way to counteract public interest drift was to develop systematic programs "so that we lose fewer potential attorneys for the powerless." Jan C. Costello, *Training Lawyers for the Powerless: What Law Schools Should Do to Develop Public Interest Lawyers*, 10 Nova L.J. 431, 438 (1986). The core elements of her proposal were "designed to give law students (1) an opportunity to identify with powerless clients, (2) experience in the role of an attorney representing the powerless, (3) a realistic possibility of job placement after law school, and (4) temporary financial assistance to pursue their choice of a public interest law career." *Id.* at 438-39.

One method for counteracting the institutional pressures steering law students away from public interest careers is to make the law school experience more compatible with sustained public interest commitment. In 1966, Northeastern Law School was reopened as a new type of law school, one that aspired to be a law school for radicals. Granfield, *supra*, at 175.

> Energized by the spirit of the late 1960's, the New Left student movement, the feminist movement, and the establishment of the O.E.O. Legal Services program under the Johnson administration, the Law School sought to overcome the elitist and corporate orientation of most traditional law schools. The ideological role of the Law School was to be consistent with the values reflected by 1960's social activists; students would be trained for the goal of providing legal services to the poor, minorities, and oppressed social groups. . . . The ideological mission of the newly constituted Law School was to emphasize the progressive values of economic and social justice.

Id. at 173-74. One of the ways that Northeastern has sought to instantiate these values is through its "co-op" program in which every other semester students are required to engage in full-time employment related to their academic and career interests, often in the field of public interest law.

Other schools have instituted smaller scale efforts. The UCLA School of Law's Epstein Program in Public Interest Law and Policy (PILP) was one of the first public interest certificate programs. Established in 1997, the program was created against the backdrop of three developments that shaped its mission and design. Gary Blasi, *Creating a Program in Public Interest Law and Policy at a Public Law School: The UCLA Experiment, in* Educating for Justice: Social Values and Legal Education (Jeremy Cooper & Louise Trubek eds., 1997). The first development was the growing evidence of public interest drift, which argued for the creation of a "safe" space for public interest-minded students to forge bonds and resist the dominant law school socialization process. The second was academic ferment over different styles of public interest lawyering (see Chapter 6), which stimulated interest in how best to train students for the demands of new types of practice. Finally, in 1996 California voters passed Proposition 209, which amended the California Constitution to prohibit public institutions, like UCLA, from considering race, sex, or ethnicity in admissions decisions. The impact of Proposition 209 on minority admissions provoked efforts to create other lawful ways to promote diversity, such as focusing on socioeconomic disadvantage and alternative career visions.

The design of PILP reflects key elements of its founding principles. First, in order to respond to concerns about public interest drift, PILP admits 25 students per year through a separate admissions track (controlled by program faculty and students), which emphasizes past public service as a predictor of future public interest law practice. Admission to the program constitutes admission to the law school (subject to the approval of the law school admissions committee, which is rarely withheld). As part of its application, PILP asks students to describe (and document through references) the content and quality of their public interest activities, especially those that display qualities of "tenacity, idealism, and initiative that are particularly important for public interest lawyers who may forgo material incentives in their career." Richard L. Abel, *Choosing, Nurturing, Training and Placing Public Interest Law Students*, 70 FORDHAM L. REV. 1563, 1565 (2002).

To promote learning about innovative practice and link academic study to contemporary lawyering models, there are three major programmatic requirements: a special first-year lawyering skills section, a first-year not-for-credit introductory workshop, and a second-year problem-solving class. The courses are exclusive to PILP students on the theory that program-specific courses promote the creation of internal community, counteracting feelings of isolation and alienation that erode public interest law commitment. Finally, students are provided mentoring by upper-class students, faculty, staff, and alumnae/i, and have the opportunity to attend specially tailored colloquia.

In the following passage, Richard Abel, one of PILP's founders, reflects upon its theoretical and empirical foundations:

> Although many students are attracted to law by a desire to serve their own conceptions of the public interest, few ultimately do so. An obvious reason is the scarcity of public interest jobs. . . . Growing awareness of that fact undoubtedly contributes to declining public interest commitment during the three years of law school, but there are other causes. One may be public interest-minded students' increasing sense of isolation and alienation. These feelings may be less severe at the few schools where public interest is the dominant ideal (a proposition that could be tested). At other schools, public interest students eventually find each other, but their reluctance to speak in class (for fear of ridicule by fellow students and teachers), the division of the first-year class into sections (with little interaction among them), the overwhelming demands and anxieties of the first year (which discourage volunteer activity), and the lack of contact with upper-class students all obstruct solidarity.
>
> By identifying and bringing public interest students together from the outset, public interest programs may contribute to solidarity and mutual support. (It would be possible to test this hypothesis by comparing class participation and patterns of interaction among public interest students at schools with and without programs.) UCLA PILP, for instance, gives its students a separate lawyering skills section, which offers a "safe" place to exchange views. At the same time, because public interest students are politically self-conscious and opinionated (and because we tend to be most critical of those with whom we share common ground), such concentration may intensify internal friction, dividing the group and driving some to its margins or beyond. Furthermore, such programs accentuate the separation of public interest students from the rest of the

class. Those students who are uncomfortable with that heightened identification may drop out; outsiders with public interest goals may feel denigrated and abandon those aspirations. We could test these hypotheses by comparing changes in public interest commitment between students inside and outside programs and between schools with and without programs.

Robert Stover's excellent study of changes in law student aspirations documents the ways in which those initially attracted by public interest ends come to focus on means—lawyerly technique—forsaking public interest as intellectually less demanding than large firm practice. Students fear (with some justice) that overworked public interest lawyers do a poor job of preparing new recruits. By contrast, summer clerkships in large firms may solidify the conviction that they offer better training and superior opportunities to use hard-won legal skills. Students and lawyers may feel more concerned (and less guilty) about preserving and increasing their human capital than about maximizing their income. Just as law school is a default choice for many students primarily concerned with preserving or attaining middle class status and comforts, so large firm associateships offer them the best chance to continue to "keep their options open."

Public interest programs may counteract that process. Classes, colloquia and mentoring by upper-class students, faculty, staff and alumni can help to convince students that they can make a difference and that the work is challenging and rewarding. Many students report that volunteer activity, especially contact with clients and lawyers, powerfully sustains commitment. In the intensely individualistic and competitive law school environment, such activities allow students to work cooperatively and associate with those in other classes (and sometimes schools). They also foster interaction with public interest lawyers, providing role models and images of the satisfactions of public interest work. This is particularly important because law faculty offer role models that are either irrelevant (few students want to teach law) or antipathetic to public interest practice (federal clerkships and large firm practice). Students learn from doing public interest lawyering that it offers significant work, a reward that amply outweighs their sacrifices of money and professional status.

Fifty years ago law students did not seek jobs until Christmas of their third year and often obtained them through family contacts. Now job anxieties pervade all three years of law school, and the selection process relies on more impersonal factors. When public interest practice burgeoned with the rapid expansion of federally funded legal services and foundation-supported public interest firms in the 1970s, private practice paid new lawyers only about fifty percent more than public interest jobs. The ratio of starting salaries in elite New York law firms and the federal government rose from three to two in 1982 to more than five to two in 1990. Today the ratio can be as high as five to one and the disparity in summer salaries even greater ($25,000 to $4000). Because college and law school tuition have far outstripped inflation, a larger proportion of students come from poorer backgrounds, and loans have expanded while need-based scholarships have contracted, students graduate with a far greater debt burden, one that increased fifty percent in constant dollars just between 1982 and 1990. The combination of these factors produces the common credo that "I'm just going to the firm to pay off my debts." As Dr. Faustus found, however, it is hard to escape such entanglements. Few people find it attractive, or even possible, to take a salary cut of seventy-five percent or more in their thirties, just when they are assuming increased financial obligations for housing and children (or have simply become accustomed to material comforts). Although Kornhauser and Revesz found that loan repayment assistance programs have little or no effect on career choice, they also hypothesized that giving students already oriented toward public interest careers scholarships that have to be repaid only if they abandon these careers might strengthen such commitment.

In any market-based society, especially ours, money tends to be the most powerful signal of prestige. School teachers and social workers rightly complain that their derisory salaries — far lower than those paid for jobs requiring less training and inflicting less stress — signify disrespect. Studies have confirmed that status within the legal profession is inversely correlated with such variables as public service, representation of individual clients, and litigation in lower state courts — the core of public interest practice. Highly competitive post-graduate fellowships (Skadden, Open Society Institute, NAPIL, Echoing Green, for example) may be a partial antidote. Law schools also might structure loan forgiveness so that it honors public interest commitment as well as making it economically possible.

Abel, *supra*, at 1566-68. Are there specialized programs that create separate opportunities for students who want to pursue public interest work at your law school? If so, how do you perceive their effectiveness? What is the experience of students who are inclined toward public interest work but are not enrolled in the specialized program?

According to Equal Justice Works, there were 42 schools with public interest (or public interest-oriented) certificate programs as of 2009. EQUAL JUSTICE WORKS, *2009 Guide to Law Schools, supra.* The form and content of these programs vary across schools, but the motivation behind them is consistent: to formalize curricular and job-placement services for public interest law aspirants. Despite the growth of these programs, we still have little evidence that they actually work in contesting the erosion of public interest commitment and producing public interest lawyers. For instance, when Granfield reproduced his study of legal education at Northeastern — a law school founded explicitly upon an institutional commitment to political activism — the decline in public interest commitment was surprisingly similar to what he found at Harvard Law School despite the significant cultural differences. GRANFIELD, *supra*, at 185. Particularly in light of the Granfield study of Northeastern Law School — which was organized around social justice principles — is there any reason to think that smaller scale institutional efforts will be successful? If the major impediment to public interest careers is a scarcity of jobs, can specializations make a difference? Can they, for instance, promote entrepreneurial efforts by law students to pursue public interest careers via nontraditional routes? Or do they make promises that they cannot ultimately keep?

In addition to specialized curricular programs, there are other law school models for nurturing public interest commitment. The New England School of Law has a Center for Law and Social Responsibility (CLSR) dedicated "to the ideal of law as a means through which to achieve socially responsible goals." Russell Engler, *From the Margins to the Core: Integrating Public Service Legal Work into the Mainstream of Legal Education*, 40 NEW ENG. L. REV. 479, 490 (2006). The CLSR coordinates different educational activities that relate to social justice. "In keeping with this mission, the CLSR supports the faculty, students, and alumni classroom, scholarship, pro bono projects and other activities that study or otherwise address social problems that can be addressed through the law and those that are products of the inequities in the legal system itself." *Id.*

Law schools have made other investments in supporting students seeking public interest careers. Many schools have created specialized offices to assist students with public interest job searches. Harvard's Office of Public Interest Advising is one of the earliest and largest efforts in this regard, with a sizeable staff that, among other things, produces a regularly updated comprehensive guide to public interest employers. Harvard Law School, Serving the Public: A Job Search Guide, Vol. 1—USA (2009). One function of such offices is to assist students in finding public interest summer jobs, which studies (discussed above) suggest is an important factor predicting post-graduate public interest employment (as well as pro bono activity). NALP, The Significance of Summer Programs: Law Students and Legal Employers Report (2003); *see also* AALS, Learning to Serve (1999); Deborah L. Rhode, In the Interests of Justice: Reforming the Legal Profession (2000).

2. Pro Bono Programs

Over the past 20 years, many law schools have promoted pro bono service among students as a way to both enhance legal services to the poor and instill an ethic of public service among students. Deborah Rhode describes the history and impact of these efforts:

> Pro bono programs in law schools are a relatively recent development. Before the last two decades, students interested in law-related volunteer work generally had to identify service opportunities themselves. Schools provided little administrative support, and most exposure to public interest causes and low-income clients occurred in clinical courses, externships, or summer jobs. In the late 1980s, a growing number of faculty, administrators, and students, as well as bar leaders, began encouraging law schools to do more to promote public service. Tulane instituted the first law school pro bono requirement in 1987. Over the next 15 years, most law schools developed formal pro bono programs.
>
> Several initiatives encouraged that trend. In 1990, an association that later became Pro Bono Students American created a clearinghouse that began matching students with volunteer opportunities in public interest organizations. The association initially targeted students at its host institution, New York University School of Law, and then expanded to include students and organizations throughout the state, the nation, and the international community. In 1996, the ABA amended its accreditation standards to provide that every law school "should encourage its students to participate in pro bono activities and provide opportunities for them to do so." The revised standards also encouraged schools to address the obligations of faculty to the public, including participation in pro bono activities. In 1997, the Association of American Law Schools (AALS) appointed a Commission on Pro Bono and Public Service Opportunities in Law Schools. The Commission's Report and Recommendations helped lead to the creation of an AALS Section on Pro Bono and Public Service, and a follow-up AALS Pro Bono Project that provided technical support to individual schools. The section now has over 400 members. . . .

These initiatives were partly responsible for a dramatic increase in law school pro bono programs. Fifteen years after the first requirement was instituted, a survey of 147 ABA-accredited schools found that about a fifth of responding schools had instituted pro bono/public service requirements; about half (83 of 147) had developed formal, administratively supported voluntary programs, and about a quarter were relying on student groups to provide opportunities. Only about 10% of schools had no organized pro bono programs.

The scope and content of current programs vary considerably. Of schools that require service (30 of 147), about half have an hourly minimum, ranging from 20 to 70 hours, in placements for which students receive no academic credit or pay, or limited credit. A few of these requirements count nonlegal community service as well as legal work. Another half of the schools that mandate pro bono participation include internships, externships, and courses bearing credit. Some of these programs require that the work occur only in for-credit clinics. A few schools count classes in poverty law or independent student, and one includes nonlegal community service. . . .

Among the schools with formal voluntary pro bono programs (83 of 147), four-fifths have a referral system with a coordinator or group of coordinators. . . .

DEBORAH L. RHODE, PRO BONO IN PRINCIPLE AND PRACTICE 21-23 (2005). What have the impact of these programs been on post-graduate careers? Rhode provides data based on a survey of law graduates:

Fewer than a third of the overall sample reported that their objectives had changed during law school. . . . Most disturbingly, only a fifth (22%) indicated that positive law school experiences had encouraged involvement in pro bono service. . . . Of [those] who noted positive effects, a third mentioned law school culture; a fifth (22%) mentioned work or life experiences; and 15% cited personal beliefs and values. A smaller number identified opportunities to engage in pro bono or public service work in law school (4%) or financial support for such opportunities (7%).

Id. at 155-56. How do these results compare with Sandefur and Selbin's analysis of the "clinic effect"? What do they make you think about the utility of pro bono programs? If they don't promote pro bono service after law school, are they still justified as an effective means of enhancing pro bono activity during law school? Of providing needed services to under-represented clients?

C. FINANCING PUBLIC INTEREST LEGAL EDUCATION

As we discussed earlier, alleviating the debt burden is a key focus of law schools concerned about preserving the ability of graduates to pursue public interest careers. The development and expansion of law school LRAPs are designed to do just that by subsidizing loan repayment for law school graduates in public interest jobs earning low salaries. The number of LRAPs at law schools doubled, from 47 to 100, between 2000 and 2006. HEATHER JARVIS, EQUAL JUSTICE WORKS, FINANCING THE FUTURE: RESPONSES TO THE RISING DEBT OF LAW STUDENTS 6 (2d ed. 2005), *available at* http://www.equaljusticeworks.org/sites/default/files/financing-the-future2006.pdf (last visited Aug. 7, 2012). Yet considerable debate remains about their efficacy relative to other models of financing, particularly up-front scholarships.

Recent research suggests that the availability of LRAPs is an important factor in the choice to pursue public interest employment after law school. DINOVITZER ET AL., *supra*, at 72. Many law schools now have institutional LRAPs and Congress recently passed legislation creating a federal program that reduces loan payments and forgives certain loans after ten years in public service. In the following passage, the author of the federal legislation discusses these developments and what they mean for financing public interest careers:

> Beginning in the 1980s, some law schools responded by creating LRAPs through which the law schools themselves would subsidize loan repayments for graduates who took low-paying public service jobs. Typically, a law school would define eligibility criteria, income criteria, and levels of support. For example, a school might limit eligibility to graduates who worked for non-profit organizations, or it might also extend benefits to those who worked for government agencies. Income criteria further limited eligibility to those earning less than a specified amount of money. Typically, a school would set an amount below which the graduate qualified for the school's maximum support allowance, and then the school would gradually phase out the payments for graduates earning more than that level. A small number of schools with very substantial resources imposed few if any limitations based on their graduates' jobs, defining eligibility by low income alone. . . .
>
> By 2008, 76 of the nation's approximately 190 accredited law schools had functioning programs and were supporting 2,616 graduates with an average annual subsidy of $7,021. The total amount of money provided through the law school LRAP programs was $18,366,746. However, as in 2000, a few programs at schools with large endowments provided the bulk of the support. In fact, the same six schools that provided 70 percent of the funds in 2000 also provided 70 percent of the funds in 2008.
>
> Among the 76 programs, enormous variations could be seen in their eligibility criteria, income criteria, and levels of support. For example, while nearly all programs allowed benefits for graduates who became public defenders or staff attorneys at non-profit organizations, 13 did not cover prosecutors, 15 did not permit assistance for graduates in other types of government service, and only 24 supported graduates doing judicial clerkships. . . .
>
> The most striking differences among the programs involved the average level of loan repayment support provided to graduates in 2008. While the average amount overall was $7,021, the average level per school varied from $600 to $26,978. Twenty-two schools provided $3,000 or less, while 27 schools provided at least $5,000, 10 of them providing more than $8,000 on average. . . .
>
> [I]n 2007, Congress passed the College Cost Reduction and Access Act. The principal focus of legislators and the media, when this law was being debated, was on Title I, which halved the interest rates on government-guaranteed loans for undergraduate education. Two other provisions of the law, which received much less attention at the time, significantly reformed the way in which graduates could repay student loans, making expensive post-graduate education, including graduate and professional education, much more affordable for graduates with lower incomes. These two provisions established a system of "income-based repayment" (IBR) and created the federal Public Service Loan Forgiveness (PSLF) Program. . . .

A graduate with federally-guaranteed or federally-extended loans, and who would have to pay more on a "standard" ten-year repayment plan than under the IBR formula, may choose IBR instead and pay a percentage of her income each month instead of the often much larger amount that would otherwise be due. The required monthly payment is 1/12 of the annual payment, and the annual payment is 15 percent of the borrower's discretionary income, defined as the borrower's adjusted gross income (AGI) minus 150 percent of the federal poverty level for a family that is the size of the borrower's family. Because of the deduction from income for 150 percent of the federal poverty level, the formula in reality pegs the repayment obligation at about 10 percent of adjusted gross income (and less for those with large families). For a typical single law graduate with a total debt at graduation of $123,200 at 6.8 percent and an income of $50,000, this formula reduces the monthly repayment obligation during the first year from $1,417 (on a ten-year repayment plan) to $421. . . .

No public service is required for repayment of a loan through IBR. Eligibility to use the formula depends only on the source of the loan, the amount of debt, and the borrower's income. For lawyers in the private sector, this feature of the law became particularly important after the onset of the recession of 2008 and its resultant restructuring of the legal job market. Many graduates who before 2008 might have expected six-figure starting salaries have been unable to find work or have found themselves grateful to be employed at much lower wages. For these graduates, the IBR formula has been a huge relief, making it possible for them to make modest monthly payments and to avoid defaulting on their student loans. Making payments through IBR is better than utilizing forbearance and not making any payment at all, but, IBR is not a one size fits all program. Graduates should be made aware that when their payment amount is less than accruing interest, negative amortization may result.

The College Cost Reduction and Access Act is even more beneficial for graduates entering public service. They too can use IBR, but the benefits are much greater. Such graduates are eligible, through the federal government's Public Service Loan Forgiveness (PSLF) Program, to have the remaining debt forgiven after ten years, rather than twenty-five years. Because of the modest amount they will pay during that ten years (that is, about ten percent of adjusted gross income for ten years), a large fraction of their debt may be wiped out. For example, a single borrower who owes $123,200 when beginning repayment and spends ten years in public service, starting at $50,000 and receiving annual increases of 4 percent will pay, over the ten year period, a total of $62,111. At the end of the ten year period, the borrower will still owe $144,865 in principal and unpaid interest, and the federal government will forgive that entire amount.

The law defines eligible public service very broadly. All employment by any level of American government (federal, state, local, or tribal) qualifies, as does employment by any organization that is tax-exempt pursuant to Sec. 501(c)(3) of the Internal Revenue Code. Employment must be "full time," defined by the regulations as at least thirty hours per week unless the employer defines full-time employment to mean a larger number of hours. The ten years of public service need not be continuous; what the law actually requires is 120 monthly payments during months in which the borrower was employed by a public service organization. Therefore, a borrower may take parental leave or work for a non-qualifying organization for a period of time that does not count toward the 120 month count, and later return to public service and start counting the months again . . . . Although forgiveness of a debt is usually taxable income, forgiveness under PSLF is tax-free.

Schrag & Pruett, *supra*, at 587-93.

Commentators have raised some issues about the federal LRAP program and LRAPs more generally. With regard to the federal program, certain types of employment, such as low-paying private sector employment in public interest-oriented law firms or international work, do not qualify for forgiveness under the PSLF. One concern relates to graduates who move out of qualifying employment before their loans are retired under the federal program in order to move into another low-paying public interest-oriented job in the private or international sector. Doing so would eliminate the possibility of forgiveness (although the graduate could still take advantage of IRB over a longer 25-year period). Most law school programs would also not cover such students, leading to the anomaly that these types of graduates might be worse off under the federal program than if they had been covered by their law school's own LRAP. As Schrag and Pruett point out, law schools are trying to figure out the best ways of linking their institutional LRAPs to the federal programs, with some agreeing to pay the graduate IRB portion so long as graduates are in qualifying jobs. *Id*. at 598-611. However, despite the fact that the federal LRAP allows law schools to shift some of the cost of LRAP assistance to the federal government, it is not clear whether law schools will use the savings to support other types of public interest programming or divert it to other uses.

A persistent question, raised by the Field study of NYU law students discussed earlier, is whether up-front financial aid in the form of scholarships is more effective in promoting public interest careers than back-end assistance in the form of LRAPs. Perhaps the best known up-front program is NYU's Root-Tilden-Kern scholarship, which each year gives full tuition scholarships to 25 NYU School of Law students who show extraordinary public interest promise. Root-Tilden-Kern Public Interest Scholarships, http://www.law.nyu.edu/public interestlawcenter/financialassistance/scholarships/rootscholarship/index.htm (last visited Sept. 25, 2012). While the program has been successful in recruiting and graduating stellar public interest lawyers, it raises the issue of resource targeting. Root Scholars have a "moral obligation" to repay their scholarships if they leave public interest employment within ten years of graduation. (The law school reports that no one has ever reneged on this promise.) Yet, as other schools replicate the NYU program, there are mixed motives at play — including the desire on the part of law schools to recruit students with strong academic indicators for ranking purposes. Without an actual claw-back provision allowing schools to recoup scholarship money, scholarships may allow graduates to transition (debt-free) into the private sector. Moreover, to the extent that schools use public interest scholarships to recruit "high number" students for ranking purposes, the money may be given to students with weaker predictors of long-term public interest commitment. *See* McGill, *supra*, at 702 (noting that "[t]he higher a student's first-year law school grades, the less likely she was to enter" a government or public interest job). LRAPs do not provide the recruitment benefit that scholarships do, but subsidize students who actually take low-paying public interest jobs.

Some schools have tried other options. Most prominently, Harvard Law School announced a program in 2007 to waive third-year tuition to students who pledged to spend at least five years working for a public interest group or the government; the program was suspended two years later when the recession reduced the school's endowment and decimated the private employment market, contributing to significant oversubscription: "almost twice as many students as suspected signed up." Tamar Lewin, *Harvard Law School Suspends Program Giving Students Free Tuition*, N.Y. TIMES, Dec. 2, 2009, at A25. Some schools also provide their own post-graduate fellowships with public interest organizations. *See, e.g.,* MICHELE LORD ET AL., A PASSION FOR PUBLIC INTEREST LAW: AN ASSESSMENT OF THE NAPIL EQUAL JUSTICE FELLOWSHIP PROGRAM (2001).

Which programs do you think are most effective at ensuring that public interest students can pursue their career paths?

IV. MAKING GOOD: KEEPING THE PUBLIC PROMISE OF LEGAL EDUCATION

Public interest-minded students entering law school face a paradox. There are more resources than ever devoted to supporting their career choices, yet the barriers to realizing those choices have also in many ways become more serious, with increasing competition for fewer jobs, large salary disparities, and deeper debt. Institutional efforts to promote public interest law may counteract some of these barriers, but the pathway to public interest law is still one that requires determination and planning. Yet, as Deborah Kenn reminds us, for those who persevere, the rewards are great:

> For the courageous few, determined to pursue work that feeds their passionate hearts and not their wallets, creative ways to accommodate lives on public interest wages are found and flexible budgets and lifestyles are maintained. It *can* be done. Lawyers can graduate from law school with mountains of education debt and live comfortably, finding enormous reward and invaluable wealth in the work they love to wake up and go to each morning.

KENN, *supra*, at 121. For a series of profiles of lawyers who have forged their own paths in pursuing public interest careers, see ALAN B. MORRISON & DIANE T. CHIN, BEYOND THE BIG FIRM: PROFILES OF LAWYERS WHO WANT SOMETHING MORE (2007).

What do you think law schools can do — and do better — to make good on their promise to educate lawyers for public service? What programs do you think have the most potential to make the biggest impact on public interest career choice? What are the levers of reform for building more support and how would you go about mobilizing administrators, students, alumni/ae, and other stakeholders to create change?

CHAPTER 9

PUBLIC INTEREST LAWYERING IN GLOBAL PERSPECTIVE

I. INTRODUCTION

As with so many other areas of contemporary life, law has become increasingly globalized. In the commercial sphere, the globalization of legal practice is visible in the proliferation of global law firms, many working on behalf of multinational corporate clients attempting to manage complex interactions among legal systems at various levels (state, regional, and supranational). *See* Richard L. Abel, *Transnational Law Practice*, 44 CASE W. RES. L. REV. 737 (1994); David M. Trubek et al., *Global Restructuring and the Law: Studies of the Internationalization of Legal Fields and the Creation of Transnational Arenas*, 44 CASE W. RES. L. REV. 407 (1994). Public interest law has not escaped these globalizing tendencies, although its interaction with globalization has a distinctive character that requires analysis on its own terms. Scott L. Cummings & Louise Trubek, *Globalizing Public Interest Law*, 13 UCLA J. INT'L L. & FOREIGN AFF. 1 (2008). In this chapter, we look at global trends in public interest lawyering. Specifically, we ask what factors drive the development of public interest law around the world, what important similarities and differences exist across countries, and what the richness and variety of global practice teaches us about the use of law as a tool to promote social change and equality across societies. What do the experiences of lawyers in Brazil, Chile, China, Ghana, India, South Africa, Thailand, or Vietnam tell us about the possibilities for and constraints on "speaking law to power"? Richard Abel, *Speaking Law to Power: Occasions for Cause Lawyering, in* CAUSE LAWYERING: POLITICAL COMMITMENTS AND PROFESSIONAL RESPONSIBILITIES 69 (Austin Sarat & Stuart Scheingold eds., 1998) [hereinafter, Abel, *Speaking Law to Power*].

We start by noting the widespread interest in the use of law as a tool of social transformation around the world. There have, of course, long been lawyers across the globe engaged in the struggle for social transformation: Gandhi and Mandela being two of the most powerful examples. And there are important examples of U.S. public interest lawyers making global connections. For instance, the NAACP LDF and ACLU incorporated human rights claims in a number of civil rights cases during the 1940s and 1950s, while LDF lawyer Jack Greenberg helped to support the creation of South Africa's Legal Resources Centre on the LDF model. Lawyers from the Global South have, in turn, been important influences on U.S. practice, particularly in the promotion of "critical" approaches to lawyering (some of which are canvassed in Chapters 5 and 6) that emphasize non-litigation strategies and client empowerment. Stephen Ellmann, *Cause Lawyering in the Third World, in* CAUSE LAWYERING: POLITICAL COMMITMENTS AND PROFESSIONAL RESPONSIBILITIES 349, 359 (Austin Sarat & Stuart Scheingold eds., 1998).

But with growing interest in the globalization of law and the ease with which we can now learn about advocacy in other parts of the world, the global role of public interest law—and legal mobilization more broadly—has taken on more prominence. In some countries, lawyers are seen at the forefront of movements to promote democracy. *See* Austin Sarat & Stuart A. Scheingold, *State Transformation, Globalization, and the Possibilities of Cause Lawyering: An Introduction, in* CAUSE LAWYERING AND THE STATE IN A GLOBAL ERA 3 (Austin Sarat & Stuart Scheingold eds., 2001). There are indelible images from the Pakistani lawyers' movement protesting the ouster of the country's chief justice in 2007, and the dramatic 2012 escape of Chinese rights lawyer, Chen Guangcheng, who was imprisoned under house arrest after filing a class action challenging forced abortions. At the same time, scholarly work on legal mobilization around the world has intensified. Important research analyzes how lawyers have promoted political liberalism in both authoritarian and democratizing countries, how lawyers and activists use economic and social rights strategies to contest "radical poverty" in Africa, how lawyers and grassroots activists challenge the depredations of neoliberal globalization "from below," and how cause lawyering varies in relation to different configurations of state power. *See* CAUSE LAWYERING AND THE STATE IN A GLOBAL ERA 3 (Austin Sarat & Stuart Scheingold eds., 2001); FIGHTING FOR POLITICAL FREEDOM: COMPARATIVE STUDIES OF THE LEGAL COMPLEX AND POLITICAL LIBERALISM (Terence C. Halliday, Lucien Karpik & Malcolm Feeley eds., 2007); LAW AND GLOBALIZATION FROM BELOW: TOWARDS A NEW COSMOPOLITAN LEGALITY (Boaventura de Sousa Santos & Cesar A. Rodriguez-Garavito eds., 2005); STONES OF HOPE: HOW AFRICAN ACTIVISTS RECLAIM HUMAN RIGHTS TO CHALLENGE GLOBAL POVERTY (Lucie E. White & Jeremy Perelman eds., 2011). In addition to this research, there are other mechanisms that facilitate the circulation of information about what lawyers across the globe are doing to challenge power: lawyers engaged in social struggle are more networked because of enhanced technology; they engage in structured exchanges such as conferences; they study abroad and incorporate borrowed ideas into indigenous advocacy while sharing their experiences with others; and some may receive money from global funders to promote similar initiatives.

Public interest lawyers in the contemporary era should understand this new global terrain and be equipped with the skills to make a difference within it. Toward that end, this chapter examines what conditions make it possible to use law to challenge power across the globe, what institutions support such advocacy, and what strategies and tactics global lawyers use most effectively to make change.

An examination of public interest lawyering as a global phenomenon leads us back, in the first instance, to where we started: the contested definition of public interest law. Understanding "public interest law" from a global perspective is fraught with complexity since most lawyers around the world do not think of themselves as practicing under that label — and some (to the extent they think about it) may even define what they do in opposition to American conceptions of legal advocacy or the concept of political liberalism upon which it rests. Conversely, some examples of legal advocacy around the world may not fit comfortably with U.S. ideas of public interest practice — but may nonetheless be viewed as mobilizing law to advance social change. Therefore, our impulse to study and compare "public interest law" in an era of globalization must be framed as a project of drawing attention to similarities in advocacy styles and goals, while remaining acutely aware that legal advocacy approaches across (and even within) national borders have distinct sociopolitical meanings and histories that cannot be neatly related to the U.S. public interest law movement. Indeed, lawyers outside the United States may not only view the public interest law label as inapt but affirmatively *resist* it as contrary to their underlying goal, which is to counter the penetration of Northern institutions into their political, economic, and legal systems. In this sense, while the debate over the meaning of public interest law inside the United States often turns on left-right political ideology, the analogous contest outside its borders implicates the specter of imperialism. When looking at lawyering strategies across countries, we will therefore explore how the concept of "public interest law" itself has come to play an important role, while also comparing a broader range of legal mobilization strategies. *See* Michael W. McCann, Rights at Work: Pay Equity Reform and the Politics of Legal Mobilization (1994).

It is against this backdrop that this chapter explores public interest law from three different global vantage points. The first perspective takes note of the richness and diversity of legal mobilization around the world, and investigates the local contexts that promote and sustain this activity. The focus here is on the local drivers of legal mobilization and the distinctive nature of local practice. What roles do courts, social movements, the organized bar, and law schools (among other institutions and actors) play in creating the support structure for legal activism? How do lawyers seek out and exploit opportunities within widely divergent political systems — from heavily authoritarian to robustly democratic — to advance social justice causes? Our goal is to engage in comparison in order to understand the local forces propelling lawyers to pursue justice on their own national terms and then to identify patterns and draw contrasts. *See* Austin Sarat & Stuart A. Scheingold, *State Transformation, Globalization, and the Possibilities of Cause Lawyering: An Introduction*, in Cause Lawyering and the State in a Global Era, *supra*, at 3. What can we learn about the causes and consequences of legal mobilization from studying the efforts of courageous lawyers around the world who use law to contest state and private power?

We next explore how local efforts have interacted with, and been influenced by, global forces. This perspective, in contrast to the first, is explicitly transnational, in that we examine the relationship between local legal advocacy and global trends shaping its scope and content. How do global funding initiatives influence practice around the world? What use do local lawyers make of international institutions like the United Nations or regional courts? How do they deploy the discourse of human rights? How do they relate to global development projects, like irrigation in India or resource extraction in Africa? What other forms of transnational practice do they undertake? What influence do global networking and education abroad play in shaping local practice? In this section, we look at the role of the United States as an exporter of the public interest law concept, not because we believe that the United States is the normative center of the global public interest law movement, but rather because of its importance in providing examples of legal struggle, funding and technical assistance for global public interest initiatives, and educational opportunities for non-U.S. advocates. We also emphasize the role of other countries from the Global North and South in promoting the spread of ideas and institutions to advance legal mobilization that challenges extant power relations. This analysis leads us to discuss whether lessons from one country's experience can be disseminated to other nations, and how different social contexts may affect the viability, and transferability, of lawyering strategies.

We conclude by turning the lens inward and asking how the rest of the world has influenced the meaning and practice of public interest lawyering inside the United States. What we find is that the contemporary public interest law movement has become a profoundly globalized one in terms of the clients it serves, the venues in which its lawyers advocate, and the tactics that it deploys. While American-style public interest lawyering may once have played the role of global vanguard, it appears that its practitioners increasingly collaborate with and adopt strategies from their global counterparts.

II. THE PROMISE AND PERIL OF "PUBLIC INTEREST LAW" AROUND THE WORLD

Before comparing advocacy styles and systems, we confront the threshold issue of nomenclature. What role does the term "public interest law" play in understanding the range of legal mobilization activities around the world? As we discussed in Chapter 1, "public interest law" is a peculiarly American concept, albeit one with a contested meaning, which as a historical matter was derived from a particular set of institutional arrangements. These arrangements included "constitutional guarantees of individual rights and judicial independence, leadership from activist judges (particularly Supreme Court justices) who have been willing to use those constitutional provisions to transform society, and the rise of rights consciousness in popular culture," as well as a "support structure for legal mobilization, consisting of rights-advocacy organizations, rights-advocacy lawyers, and sources of financing, particularly government-supported financing." CHARLES R. EPP, THE RIGHTS REVOLUTION: LAWYERS, ACTIVISTS, AND SUPREME COURTS IN COMPARATIVE PERSPECTIVE 2-3 (1998). Over time, as we suggested in Chapter 1, the notion of what constitutes public interest law has grown beyond its court-centered origins, but some elements of judicial independence and professional autonomy for lawyers remain important ingredients.

Is it useful to refer to "public interest law" in analyzing global developments? On the one hand, the public interest law approach of seeking rights in court (and the institutional arrangements upon which it rests) has been deliberately spread and copied by lawyers around the world. Thus, it is important to ask how the project of transmitting public interest law has occurred and what its consequences have been. On the other hand, it is fair to suggest that much legal mobilization across the globe has little or nothing to do with the U.S. public interest law model, in terms of the way that non-U.S. lawyers understand their own activity and deploy law in struggle.

What do you think about the global role of public interest law? Is it a force for global progress? A tool of U.S. hegemony? A model that is simply inapt to other contexts or obscures what is distinctive about non-U.S. advocacy approaches?

In the 1980s, prominent Indian intellectual Upendra Baxi famously argued against India adopting the "public interest" label for legal rights advocacy ushered in by the judicial loosening of standing requirements to bring claims of constitutional violations, which he preferred to call social action litigation. Upendra Baxi, *Taking Suffering Seriously: Social Action Litigation in the Supreme Court of India*, 1985 Third World Legal Stud. 107. Baxi noted that "while labels can be borrowed, history cannot be. The [public interest litigation] represents for America a distinctive phase of socio-legal development for which there is no counterpart in India; and the salient characteristics of its birth, growth and, possibly, decay are also distinctive to American history." *Id.* at 110. Nonetheless, Baxi was pessimistic that lessons from the American model would be critically examined:

> [S]o great is the hold of colonial legal imagination that, in the last analysis, these lessons will be learned only after the attempts at transferring the success stories . . . have demonstrably failed. In the process, the appreciation of the vital political cultural differences between the two societies will be deferred; and a loose-minded importation of notions opposite to the circumstances of development in the United States will continue to obscure a genuine appreciation of the distinctive social and historical forces shaping, generally, the role of adjudication in India.

Id. at 110-11. Is Baxi correct to suggest that there is a political cost in adopting the lexicon and tactics of U.S. lawyering? What might the cost be?

Edwin Rekosh, writing in a different era about legal advocacy in the emerging democracies of Central and Eastern Europe, also strikes a cautionary tone, but notes the potential rhetorical and political benefits of the public interest rubric:

> As a normative framework, however, human rights continues to receive strong support among progressive civil society organizations in Central and Eastern Europe, most of whom still use the term to describe their goals and activities. But as an expression of the strategy and tactics employed, and as a means to address the constraints produced by problems of political development and

democratic governance, the term "human rights" has been less helpful, or at least confusing. Given the difficulty of resisting the slippage of these two semantic frames, normative and strategic/tactical, it became useful to coin a new term, public interest law, to refer to the strategies and tactics used to protect human rights and to pursue other elements of a progressive agenda within the developing structures of governance.

Edwin Rekosh, *Constructing Public Interest Law: Transnational Collaboration and Exchange in Central and Eastern Europe*, 13 UCLA J. INT'L L. & FOREIGN AFF. 55, 69 (2008). Do you agree with Rekosh or Baxi? Does the notion of "public interest law" create new space for legal struggle or does it impose American ideals and values where they do not belong?

As this debate underscores, the public interest law term can be both a political resource and liability to advocates in other countries. In the 1970s and 1980s, public interest law carried many positive global connotations as it was associated with important political struggles for disadvantaged groups in the United States, as we detailed in Chapter 2. The use of law in these struggles informed advocacy in other countries, such as South Africa. *See* RICHARD L. ABEL, POLITICS BY OTHER MEANS: LAW IN THE STRUGGLE AGAINST APARTHEID, 1980-1994 (1995). However, advocates and commentators also expressed a countervailing impulse to name the distinct cultural meaning of legal advocacy, as reflected in Baxi's commentary. This effort to both embrace and avoid the U.S. model suggests what Richard Abel called the "anxiety of influence":

> Concern about American influence is understandable in a post-Cold War world whose sole superpower is militarily and culturally hegemonic. . . . Dependence of any kind — on parents, teachers, governments, or charities for emotional support, material assistance, or intellectual guidance — tends to breed resentment. But influence is inescapable, absolute autonomy a mirage. There is little new under the sun. Successful social innovation depends on imitation as much as creativity. Japan borrowed much of its legal system from Germany, Turkey from Switzerland, Ethiopia from France. . . . If American law schools are attracting lawyers from all over the world today, earlier cohorts of future leaders from colonies and ex-colonies flocked to the European metropoles: Oxford, Cambridge, and London, Paris, Madrid, Lisbon, Berlin, and Moscow. Influence can flow in both directions: American legal academics have argued for the superiority of inquisitorial procedures. . . . [Research] reveal[s] many influences on public interest law besides the United States. Central Europe is far closer to Western Europe geographically, linguistically, economically, politically, historically, and culturally. The European Union is a strong magnet, and West European philanthropic and human rights organizations are at least as active as their American counterparts. Anger at the Bush administration's preemptive war in Iraq and unqualified support for Israel has inflamed anti-Americanism to levels not seen since the Vietnam War. Public interest lawyers, therefore, are right to be wary of influence, especially given the fundamental differences in both law and society. But they should not overreact by pursuing the chimera of wholly autonomous innovation.

Richard L. Abel, *The Globalization of Public Interest Law*, 13 UCLA J. INT'L L. & FOREIGN AFF. 295, 296-98 (2008).

Stephen Ellmann, writing about his research on global public interest law in the early 1990s, makes a different point about "influence," which is that the focus on U.S. transmission may obscure the contributions that lawyers in other countries make to each other and to the American public interest lawyering movement.

> In the field of cause lawyering in particular, Third World activists have played a very important part in rethinking the ways that law should be used. . . . The most important intellectual development may have been the development and embrace by many Third World lawyers of a conception of "alternative lawyering." "Alternative lawyering" is a somewhat capacious term, but in general it features an emphasis on working with and organizing community groups rather than simply taking a random set of individual cases; on de-emphasizing litigation in favor of other legal avenues, including interventions with executive agencies and use of alternative dispute resolution techniques; on enhancing clients' understanding of, and ability to use, the law through such steps as "legal literacy" education and paralegal training, while diminishing lawyers' aura of dominance; and most broadly on consciously aiming lawyers' (and clients') efforts toward achieving sweeping social change rather than merely reforming particular laws or increasing "access" to an otherwise unchanged system. . . .
>
> My sense is that the articulation of this distinctive perspective has been primarily the work of Third World figures. At the same time, even as a paradigm, alternative law thinking has analogs in the First World. Indeed, much of the "critical lawyering" literature of recent years offers comparably fundamental critiques of existing lawyering. One reason for this intersection may be that some First World lawyers themselves contributed to the development of alternative law thinking in the Third World. But another reason is that some First World lawyers have been learning from their counterparts in the Third World.

Stephen Ellmann, *Cause Lawyering in the Third World, in* Cause Lawyering: Political Commitments and Professional Responsibilities 349, 358-60 (Austin Sarat & Stuart Scheingold eds., 1998). Do you think U.S. public interest lawyers are insufficiently attentive to advocacy innovations abroad? If so, what could they do to improve their global awareness? Do you think it is important that U.S. lawyers focused on domestic issues know about global issues and strategies? Is the debate about the "anxiety of influence" important? Why?

Ellmann's framing of the "Third World" (a relic of the Cold War) has now largely been supplanted by talk of the "Global South," a term generally used to describe poor countries, mostly in the Southern Hemisphere, working toward different levels of economic development. As we will see, it is the relationship between groups and funders from the Global North (especially the United States) and the Global South that has provoked the most recent round of criticism of the "center-periphery" dynamic in which less wealthy countries are constructed as dependent and in need of Northern investment. It was a similar concern over the imperialistic "exportation" of U.S. style legal institutions in the postwar era that gave rise to the first critique of law as a tool for development. *See* David Trubek & Marc Galanter, *Scholars in Self-Estrangement: Some Reflections on the Crisis in Law and Development Studies in the United States*, 1974

Wis. L. Rev. 1062. The current era of development policy, powered as much by a search for economic as political influence, has reproduced concerns about the one-sided nature of the relationship between "donor" and "donee" countries. In the excerpt that follows, Colombian legal scholar Daniel Bonilla focuses on the costs of this relationship in the development of legal clinics. He argues that many of the North-South exchanges between clinicians are premised on a set of norms that foster subordination rather than cooperation. These norms include the "Production Well," in which "legal academia from the North is seen as creating original academic products, [while] legal academia from the South is considered solely as a weak reproduction of knowledge generated in the North"; the norm of "Protected Geographical Indication," which states that "all knowledge produced in the North is worthy of respect and recognition per se given the context from which it emerges"; and the norm of the "Effective Operator," which "indicates that academics from the North are much better trained to make effective and legitimate use of legal knowledge than academics from the South." Daniel Bonilla, *Legal Clinics in the Global North and South: Between Equality and Subordination—An Essay* (unpublished manuscript on file with authors, 2012). These norms, in turn, produce the following dynamic in the context of Northern "fact-finding missions," in which "a group composed of about five students and one professor from a clinic of the Global North establishes the general objective of drafting a human rights report on, for example, the violation of the rights of indigenous communities in the country of the South." *Id.*

> In these projects, the vulnerable population supposedly served and the partnering local clinics are often quickly relegated to the margins. In reality, the work becomes a means of ensuring that the members of the clinic in the North are enriched by the cultural experience and that its students develop the legal skills required to become competent professionals. Students of the clinic in the North generally return to their countries having accumulated personal and professional experiences that enhance their academic and cultural capital. In addition to gaining familiarity with a different culture and developing their professional skills, the visit makes them more attractive candidates for future employers. Their international experience makes them more competitive in the labor market.
>
> Similarly, these missions become an instrument for ensuring that members of the clinic in the North achieve greater professional visibility. Professors are personally enriched and accumulate a series of achievements that enhance or maintain their reputation within the academic community. The publication of reports contributes to making them more visible. The reports end up serving as the basis for academic articles published in journals in the Global North and thus expanding their resumes. However, the impact these projects have in solving the problems they examine is usually low. As I have indicated above, these reports are mainly a synthesis of existing local knowledge. They do not include facts not already known in the country where the project is developed or by specialists working on the issue. Similarly, because it is rare to follow the issue or advocacy efforts carried out long-term, the project soon passes into oblivion. The publication of the report and sometimes the performance of short-term advocacy work mark the completion of the project. The document becomes another achievement that the clinic in the North can show

its funders and colleagues. The institutional structures within which clinics usually work make it very difficult to do things differently. . . .

In many countries of the Global South, the money spent on travel and accommodation for eight people coming from a country such as the United States could easily be used to hire a full-time staff person for a year to coordinate the work of clinics in the North and South in defense of the interests and rights of the vulnerable population that the mission intends to serve, for example.

Id. Do you agree with Bonilla? What flows from his critique? Should U.S. public interest lawyers engage in collaborations with their counterparts in the Global South? If so, what should they look like? What should be the role of U.S. funders for public interest law abroad? Keep these questions in mind as we turn to the materials below on the role of globalization in shaping public interest lawyering.

III. LOCAL AND GLOBAL INFLUENCES ON "PUBLIC INTEREST LAW" AROUND THE WORLD

As the preceding discussion underscores, from a global perspective, there is no unitary "public interest law," but rather a range of practices, built upon different types of political systems and responding to different forms of political struggle, in which lawyers deploy law to influence power. Understanding these diverse practices requires a careful look into their history and development.

Using a comparative lens, there are three important sets of questions we might want to ask. First, what causes lawyers (and nonlawyers) in particular countries to mobilize law as a tool of social struggle? Drawing upon the U.S. experience, advocates must view law as having power to check governmental or private sector actors in a way that advances their cause. What types of institutions or ideologies make them think this is the case? Second, what factors influence the nature of the "public interest law" system in different countries? That is, what accounts for the existence of different institutional arrangements for administering legal aid to the poor, representing marginalized group interests, promoting human rights, and the like? What influences whether there is state, professional, and private sector support for these initiatives? Third, what impact do different types of legal mobilization strategies have on social outcomes such as equality and fairness?

In this part of the chapter, we raise these questions for consideration. We begin by suggesting that the answers are given neither by an exclusive focus on internal dynamics (strong endogeneity thesis) nor on external influences (strong exogeneity thesis). Rather, in each case, we would suspect to see an interplay of local and global forces that produce lawyering approaches and institutions (what we might call the dynamic thesis). Of course, the mix of these factors varies across countries and across time. Why and how they combine—and what space that combination creates for legal advocacy—is the interesting question.

Comparative research generally supports the dynamic thesis. In countries where law emerges as a tool for access to justice or broader political and social struggle, indigenous legal traditions and institutions mix with international influences to create systems that share some common elements, but also maintain unique local features. In their monumental study of worldwide "access to justice" initiatives in the 1970s, Mauro Cappelletti and Bryant Garth found that, although countries followed diverse trajectories, there were "basic trends and ideas" associated with "this world-wide creative effort," including the spread of legal aid, the promotion of alternative dispute resolution, the creation of specialized tribunals, and the development of group legal services plans. Mauro Cappelletti & Bryant Garth, *Access to Justice: The Worldwide Movement to Make Rights Effective: A General Report, in* Access to Justice, Vol. 1: A World Survey, Book I 3, 54-120 (Mauro Cappelletti & Bryant Garth eds., 1978). More recently, Po Jen Yap and Holning Lau examined public interest law across several Asian countries and found that "transnational public interest litigation trends have commingled with local dynamics" to produce "legal developments that cut across Asian jurisdictions," such as similar topical areas, multidimensional advocacy strategies, and homogenous actors, but also "developments that are unique to each of the jurisdictions studied." Po Jen Yap & Holning Lau, *Public Interest Litigation in Asia: An Overview, in* Public Interest Litigation in Asia 1 (Po Jen Yap & Holning Lau eds., 2011); *see also* Jayanth Kumar Krishnan, *Public Interest Litigation in Comparative Context*, 20 Buff. Pub. Int. L.J. 19 (2001-2002).

A. LOCAL FACTORS: WHAT ARE THE ROOTS OF LEGAL MOBILIZATION?

In order to distinguish between the internal (local) and external (global) factors influencing public interest law around the world, we start by probing more deeply into its distinctive country-specific roots. It is impossible to generalize from the experiences of different countries, each of which has a unique context that shapes precisely what it means to mobilize law for change and how one goes about it. However, we may begin to identify patterns. There are structural features that profoundly influence the ways that countries experience legal reform and the opportunities for advocacy that challenges the status quo. Some countries have experienced revolution; there are those with colonial histories and anticolonial movements; some have deep democratic traditions with liberal political governance structures while others are rigidly autocratic and nontransparent; still others are in transitional states, rapidly democratizing and modernizing their economies; social movements play different roles; some countries tolerate dissent more than others; legal professions are more or less organized and independent; legal education is more or less oriented toward social change. These are just some of the features that matter. What we offer in this section is an overview of some of the important internal factors that influence whether a culture of public interest law takes hold and, if so, what form it takes. Specifically, we explore the role of the following factors: the government system, social movements, civil society, the legal profession, and legal education.

1. Government System

That the type of government system would influence the opportunities for public interest lawyering seems self-evident. There are well-known differences in legal systems, with the civil-common law divide noted among scholars as forming an important difference in opportunities for legal challenges since civil law countries do not rely on judge-made law built upon precedent, which is the basis for much domestic public interest litigation. In addition, the legal foundations of different countries span a range of institutions, from Islam in countries such as Pakistan and Malaysia, to Socialism in countries like Vietnam and Myanmar. How lawyers might think of mobilizing law in those contexts must draw upon indigenous legal cultures.

Generally, in countries with strong democracies and a commitment to judicial independence, law is more likely to be seen by advocates as a viable tool to advance reform. In authoritarian countries with weak legal institutions and fear of reprisal for dissident activity, we would predict that lawyers may adopt less adversarial strategies on day-to-day matters — working within the system to promote incremental change — although we would also predict that there are moments when lawyers rise up and take significant risks to advance the democratic project. Thus, how lawyers pursue change and what type of institutional support they have to do so depends on the preexisting governmental framework, which ranges from highly open to highly repressive. Public interest lawyering in these contexts is about finding space in which to foster legal resistance to oppression and unfairness — and to enlarge that space over time.

In terms of the relationship between governmental structures and the nature of legal mobilization, the existence of constitutional frameworks, rights, and judicial independence are key factors promoting "public interest litigation." "In those countries adopting liberal democratic constitutional reforms, the availability of progressive legal rights, coupled with the development of judicial independence, has fostered domestic impact litigation strategies." Cummings & Trubek, *supra*, at 33. India, as referenced above, is the most well-known example.

> In the early 1980s a small number of judges and lawyers, seeking ways to actualize the Constitution's promises of justice — promises that were so starkly unrealized in practice — embarked on a series of unprecedented and electrifying initiatives. These included relaxation of requirements of standing, appointment of investigative commissions, appointment of lawyers as representatives of client groups, and a so-called "epistolary jurisdiction" in which judges took the initiative to respond proactively to grievances brought to their attention by third parties, letters, or newspaper accounts. Public interest litigation, or social action litigation, as these initiatives are now called, sought to use judicial power to protect excluded and powerless groups (such as prisoners, migrant laborers, and the environmentally susceptible) and to secure entitlements that were going unredeemed.

Marc Galanter & Jayanth K. Krishnan, *"Bread for the Poor": Access to Justice and the Rights of the Needy in India*, 55 Hastings L.J.789, 795 (2004).

Looking around the world, many other countries have had similar experiences. For instance, in his analysis of public interest litigation in Taiwan, Wen-Chen Chang links the rise of public interest litigation with democratization occurring in the 1980s and 1990s. Wen-Chen Chang, *Public Interest Litigation in Taiwan: Strategy for Law and Policy Changes in the Course of Democratization, in* Public Interest Litigation in Asia, *supra*, at 136, 138. In particular, he notes that a more liberal interpretation of rules permitting petitions to the Constitutional Court paved the way for "public interest groups [to] . . . strategically collaborate with various agents" to argue cases in front of the Court, as women's rights groups did successfully in the mid-1990s to win a legal change requiring gender equality in custody rules. *Id.* at 140, 143. A similar pattern is noted in Brazil. *See* Oscar Vilhena Vieira, *Public Interest Law: A Brazilian Perspective*, 13 UCLA J. Int'l L. & Foreign Aff. 219, 231-34 (2008).

One lesson from comparative study is that government institutions are not static. Over time, they may be more or less receptive to rights claims or other types of legal mobilization; indeed, successful rights advocacy may in certain situations provoke governmental recrimination (as occurred in the United States). In addition, different aspects of the political system may be more or less hospitable to social reformers. The following excerpt provides one example from Egypt, where rights mobilization achieved some success in the wake of the adoption of Egypt's constitution in the 1970s. But the government's response was not uniformly supportive of liberalization:

> The most aggressive group engaged in public interest litigation was the Centre for Human Rights Legal Aid (CHRLA), established by the young and forceful human rights activist, Hisham Mubarak, in 1994. CHRLA quickly became the most dynamic human rights organisation, initiating 500 cases in its first full year of operation, 1,323 cases in 1996, and 1,616 by 1997. CHRLA documented human rights abuses and used the cases that it sponsored to publicise the human rights situation. . . .
>
> By 1997, legal mobilisation had unquestionably become the dominant strategy for human rights defenders not only because of the opportunities that public interest litigation afforded, but also because of the myriad obstacles to mobilising a broad social movement under the Egyptian regime. Gasser 'Abd al-Raziq, director of the Centre for Human Rights Legal Aid explained that "in Egypt, where you have a relatively independent judiciary, the only way to promote reform is to have legal battles all the time. It's the only way that we can act as a force for change." A strong and independent judiciary was so central to the strategy of the human rights movement that activists institutionalised their support for judicial independence by founding the Arab Centre for the Independence of the Judiciary and the Legal Profession (ACIJLP). The ACIJLP set to work organising conferences and workshops that brought together legal scholars, opposition party members, human rights activists, important figures from the Lawyers' Syndicate and Judges' Association, and even justices from the Supreme Constitutional Court itself. The ACIJLP also began to issue annual reports on the state of the judiciary and legal profession, extensively documenting government harassment of lawyers and exposing the regime's interference in the normal functions of judicial institutions. Like other human rights groups, the ACIJLP established ties with international human rights organisations including the Lawyers' Committee for Human Rights in order to leverage international pressure on the Egyptian government.

Human rights activists engaged in public interest litigation also began to understand that *constitutional* litigation in the Supreme Constitutional Court was potentially the most effective avenue to challenge the regime. CHRLA's executive director, Gasser 'Abd al-Raziq recalled that "we were encouraged by [Chief Justice] 'Awad al-Murr's human rights language in both his formal rulings and in public statements. This encouraged us to have a dialogue with the Supreme Constitutional Court. CHRLA woke up to the idea that litigation in the SCC could allow us to actually change the laws and not just achieve justice in the immediate case at hand."

. . . CHRLA attorneys initiated a campaign systematically to challenge repressive legislation in the SCC starting in late 1997. Their first target was Law 35 of 1976, governing trade union elections. CHRLA initiated 50 cases in the administrative and civil courts, all with petitions to challenge the constitutionality of Law 35/1976 in the Supreme Constitutional Court. Ten of the 50 cases were successfully transferred, and within months the SCC issued its first verdict of unconstitutionality against Article 36 of the Law. CHRLA also successfully advanced three cases to the SCC challenging sections of the Penal Code concerning newspaper publication offences and three additional cases dealing with the Social Insurance Law. . . .

This brief review . . . illustrates how the new Supreme Constitutional Court provided institutional openings for political activists to challenge the state in ways that fundamentally transformed patterns of interaction between the state and society. For the first time since the 1952 military coup, political activists could credibly challenge the regime by simply initiating constitutional litigation, a process that required few financial resources and allowed activists to circumvent the highly restrictive, corporatist political framework. Most importantly, constitutional litigation enabled activists to challenge the regime without having to initiate a broad social movement, a task that is all but impossible in Egypt's highly restrictive political environment. . . .

Although the Supreme Constitutional Court took startlingly bold stands on most political issues, there were important limits to mobilisation through the courts. . . . At odds with its strong record of rights activism, the SCC ruled Egypt's Emergency State Security Courts constitutional and it has conspicuously delayed issuing a ruling on the constitutionality of civilian transfers to military courts. Given that Egypt has remained in a perpetual state of emergency for all but six months since 1967, the Emergency State Security Courts and, more recently, the military courts have effectively formed a parallel legal system with fewer procedural safeguards, serving as the ultimate regime check on challenges to its power.

Tamir Moustafa, *Mobilising the Law in an Authoritarian State: The Legal Complex in Contemporary Egypt, in* Fighting for Political Freedom, *supra*, at 193, 200-04. The Egypt experience, which now must be amended to include its 2011 revolution and the contentious aftermath, highlights the opportunities and risks presented by public interest litigation in authoritarian countries, in which dictators can respond to court decisions with reprisals and acts to limit the courts' power. Litigation is sometimes used in reaction to a politically oppressive regime, but there are correlated risks of backlash against judicial independence. Overall, in authoritarian countries without strong individual rights frameworks or in which courts are perceived as insufficiently independent from the executive, litigation strategies are less appealing and personally riskier. In such contexts, lawyers still may seek out ways to use the legal system to advance more incremental change. Consider Titi Liu's discussion of public interest litigation in China.

Titi M. Liu, *Transmission of Public Interest Law: A Chinese Case Study*

13 UCLA J. Int'l L. & Foreign Aff. 263, 286-90 (2008)

A Chinese plaintiff represents only himself because there are many obstacles to organizing plaintiffs into a collective lawsuit. While the Chinese civil procedure code does provide for representative lawsuits and the joining of lawsuits, resulting in lawsuits that are similar to a U.S. class action (these two different types of civil actions are referred to in Chinese collectively as group litigation (jituansusong)), in reality, Chinese courts are extremely reluctant to allow cases to proceed with a large group of plaintiffs. There are two key factors in explaining the court's reluctance. The first is that Chinese courts are extremely wary of getting involved in any disputes that might be political in nature. The larger the number of aggrieved parties involved, the more concerned the courts get that the plaintiffs may seek to exert social pressure on the courts through non-legal strategies, and that an adverse ruling to the plaintiffs may cause some kind of social unrest. A more pragmatic reason is that individual Chinese judges and entire courts are evaluated every year on workload in addition to other factors. By breaking up group litigation into individual cases, Chinese courts can artificially inflate their workload numbers. Chinese courts frequently will hold only one hearing and issue one short ruling for all of the individuals with similar issues of fact and law, so that they have minimized the actual workload while maximizing the number of cases they can take credit for having processed over any given period of time.

Even if a Chinese court were willing to take group litigation cases, public interest litigation lawyers find it logistically complicated and politically risky to attempt to organize significant numbers of individuals around an issue. Public interest litigation plaintiffs speak in terms of representing the public interest and mobilizing individuals, they do not seek to directly organize potential plaintiffs. Most public interest litigation plaintiffs do not even want to represent clients. They are concerned that by representing clients, they may run into conflicts of interest or potential cleavages may emerge between advocates and clients that could be exploited by opponents of the case. Luo Qiulin, a lawyer in the relatively small town of Hengyang in the central Chinese province of Hunan, brought a case that was widely heralded in press reports and by academics as China's first taxpayer public interest litigation. He worked closely with a village mayor, Jiang Shilin, to challenge the purchase of a luxury car by the township government, arguing that it violated standards for government procurement set out by the State Council and that the village mayor had standing to challenge the purchase because of income tax he paid to the township. Luo Qiulin thought Jiang Shilin was a principled and tough person, having worked with him in the past to successfully unseat a village mayor who had only won his seat after tampering with the election results. After a great deal of pressure was exerted on Jiang Shilin, Jiang disappeared into hiding and Luo Qiulin was unable to reach him in time to file the paperwork in order to appeal an initial decision by the court not to accept the case. Because any client could ultimately prove to be unreliable, Luo Qiulin has thus resolved to only represent himself in subsequent cases. Many other plaintiffs interviewed expressed similar sentiments. . . .

The ability of public interest litigation to achieve social impact through legal rulings is significantly constrained by a number of additional factors. One important factor is the role of the Chinese judiciary in the Chinese legal system. As a matter of law, Chinese courts are required to act "in accordance with the law, exercise judicial power independently and are not subject to interference by administrative organs, public organizations or individuals." However, the power of Chinese courts to interpret laws and to have those interpretations binding on the courts and other government institutions is extremely limited, even more so than in European civil law countries. Furthermore, the Chinese constitution sets out a unitary structure in which the courts, as any other government entity, are accountable to the people's congresses in the parallel level of government, and thus are subject to the dual leadership of the Party organizations, as well as supervision by higher level courts. Therefore, because local courts are dependent on local governments for funding and are subject to political oversight, they experience great difficulty deciding cases in an independent manner, especially in cases where entrenched local government or business interests are at stake, which is frequently the case in public interest litigation cases. . . .

Public interest litigation plaintiffs articulate an explicit objective of pushing the courts into acting on issues of social significance and therefore employ law-based and court-centric tactics. But they also seek to maximize the overall impact of the individual cases by using litigation to challenge government or corporate practices that adversely affect large numbers of people by mobilizing other social, administrative, and even political processes (including media reporting, administrative review, petitioning people's congresses, and letters and visits), to pressure the courts to rule in favor of the plaintiff and to pressure the defendants to change their practices, regardless of the court ruling.

Within the frame of common characteristics and tactics, public interest litigation cases can be separated into two main categories. In one type of case significant harm has been done to an individual, but due to the realities of Chinese legal culture, an individual suing is extremely unlikely to receive any significant relief. Plaintiffs who have initiated litigation have done so only to highlight the issue, in the hopes of changing future practice. One example of this type of case is employment discrimination cases. Until recently, although it was quite common for Chinese employers to refuse to hire workers due to residency, age, gender, appearance, and other characteristics, there had been no lawsuits challenging this practice. Plaintiffs who have challenged such practices have not sought compensation or a concrete remedy, such as employment, because Chinese law does not provide for such remedies. Instead, they have sought a change in future hiring practices. Although such a change is also difficult to achieve as a result of a court judgment, in some cases, plaintiffs have been successful due to the different forms of pressure brought to bear on defendants after discriminatory practices have been highlighted through litigation. . . .

In another type of case, plaintiffs bring cases in which the harm to a particular individual is relatively insignificant, having reversed the trajectory of converting a moral and ethical claim into a legal one. Plaintiffs identify technical violations of law and seek to argue that these violations harm a broader public interest, and that highly constrained courts should be operationalized to address these violations. By adopting such a strategy, these plaintiffs seek to identify legal issues that are somewhat technical and not politically contentious on the surface, and imbue them with greater social significance. Many of the cases in this category challenge administrative fee levies or price increases by monopoly utilities. Often the amount in controversy is negligible: less than a dollar. The plaintiff's goal is not merely to receive compensation for the fee levy or price increase, as such litigation would be economically inefficient, nor is it to claim compensation for everyone who had been similarly harmed. Instead, the goal is to pressure defendants and others similarly situated to change their policies and practices.

What is your reaction to these administrative law cases? Do they strike you as "public interest" cases? Do you think they are an effective means for advancing collective rights in an authoritarian context? What are the alternatives? We note that in jurisdictions without a strong judiciary, lawyering for change may be pursued through alternative, more grassroots channels, as noted by Ellmann, *supra*, in Latin America.

In addition to having created different opportunities for rights litigation, countries also develop different types of institutions to advance access to justice and support public interest law. Many countries have developed their own legal aid systems. *See* Cappelletti & Garth, *supra; see also* Richard L. Abel, *Law Without Politics: Legal Aid Under Advanced Capitalism*, 32 UCLA L. Rev. 474 (1985). In some places, governments have set up alternative dispute resolution systems to make legal decision making more accessible to ordinary people. For example, in India, as Marc Galanter and Jayanth Krishnan note, "people's courts," or Lok Adalats, which seek to resolve disputes in informal settings, have played an important, though complex, role promoting access to justice for the poor. Galanter & Krishnan, *supra*, at 801-03. In other places, the government may make investments in formal rights enforcement institutions. Consider Oscar Vieira's discussion of Brazil's Ministerio Público.

> The Ministério Público numbers around twelve thousand attorneys, both at federal and state levels. The structure of the Ministério Público follows the one adopted by the judiciary. The overwhelming majority of state and federal attorneys are still involved in ordinary criminal prosecution, or working on other branches of law, such as family, tax, bankruptcy, administrative, etc., as custos legis, writing memoranda to the courts in all these cases. Therefore only small fractions of this large number of legal professionals (promotores or procuradores) are directly responsible for the protection of fundamental rights. Within each state Ministério Público there is a division directly responsible for environmental issues, consumer rights or fundamental rights in general. The same is true at the federal level. Thus the number of members of the Ministério

Público working with public interest cases is in effect only hundreds rather than thousands.

Members of the Ministério Público have the legal obligation to keep their doors open to the public. They are also supposed to receive representações, or petitions, from civil society organizations and the public at large. In the last nineteen years of constitutional experience, members of the Ministério Público have become involved with several networks of public interest causes, mainly in the fields of environmental, consumer, children's and Native Indian rights. Most public interest cases that arrived in the Brazilian judiciary have passed through these channels. It is relevant to keep in mind, however, that members of the Ministério Público have full discretion to decide which public interest law cases they will bring to the judiciary. In this sense, civil society organizations do not control the agenda of the Ministério Público. The institution does not have the obligation to represent judicially the claims brought to its attention by civil society groups. It all depends on the relationship between the civil society and the members of the Ministério Público in the particular place and time. In the first years of the Constitution there was great enthusiasm about the potential of the Ministério Público to become the main representative of civil society organizations in the judiciary. This fact helps to explain why the great majority of civil society organizations abdicated from the task of organizing their own legal services to advance their causes. With the passing of time, this higher expectation of the role of the Ministério Público, as the defender per esselence of public interest, has been mitigated among civil society organizations. In fact there is no accountability mechanism by which civil society organizations could pressure members of the Ministério Público.

Vieira, *supra*, at 239-40. How would you compare the Ministério to the U.S. Department of Justice? Do you think that such a governmental agency can play a vanguard role in promoting the public interest? What political factors might influence its ability to do so?

2. Social Movements

The existence of social movements also profoundly influences the ways in which law is mobilized for change. Research from the United States shows that movements have been important to challenging dominant legal interpretations and developing ways to use law as leverage to advance social change goals. *See* William K. Eskridge, Jr., *Effects of Identity-Based Social Movements on Constitutional Law in the Twentieth Century,* 100 Mich. L. Rev. 2062 (2002); Michael W. McCann, *How Does Law Matter for Social Movements?, in* How Does Law Matter? 76 (Bryant G. Garth & Austin Sarat eds., 1998). Thus, the U.S. civil rights movement advanced a view of legal equality in the streets that fundamentally changed the way that courts and legislatures understood law on the books.

The interaction between movements, law making, institution building, and public interest career development is an important dynamic across the globe. *See, e.g.,* Frank Munger, *Cause Lawyers and Other Signs of Progress: Three Thai Narratives, in* The Paradox of Professionalism: Lawyers and the Possibility of Justice 243 (Scott L. Cummings ed., 2011). As the following example from Brazil suggests, the development of indigenous movements may create powerful social forces enlisting lawyers in struggles for political transformation.

MST (*Movimento sem Terra*), a movement of landless peasants, still very active in the Brazilian political scene today, was . . . a brainchild of the left and progressive religious groups. It emerged as a response to the strict limitations imposed by the military regime on social movements. In the early days MST based its activities on occupations of large farms in the interior of Brazil. In the late eighties and early nineties, MST created an in-house legal department to give support to its activities, and to protect its leaders who were systematically involved in confrontations with the police and landowners. The Catholic Church also fomented the creation of a network of radical lawyers, called RENAP, under the leadership of Jacques Alfonsin, Luiz Eduardo Greenhalg and Plínio the Arruda Sampaio. This network is still very active, and is responsible for the settlement of legal strategies and the provision of legal assistance to the MST movement all around Brazil. AJUP (*Apoio Jurídico Popular*), created by Miguel Presburger, a lawyer with a Marxist orientation, had strong links to MST, helping as an educational branch for grassroots lawyers acting far from the larger urban centers. The Human Rights sector of the MST produces publications, disseminates information, brings cases within the Brazilian judicial system, and also brings cases to the Inter-American Human Rights System. The creation of RENAP, and the establishment of in-house legal services at MST such as its Human Rights sector, represents the tip of the iceberg of numerous other grassroots legal services created in Brazil in the seventies and eighties to promote social rights such as housing, health services and others.

[A]nother important segment of the public interest legal movement that gained prominence before the 1988 Constitution is represented by the establishment of CUT (*Central Única dos Trabalhadores*), under the leadership of Luiz Inácio Lula da Silva, current President of the Republic, then President of the Union of Metal Workers, from São Bernado do Campo. CUT was a result of the fusion of several unions dominated by progressive sectors of the Catholic Church and the Communist Party. Their main objective was to overcome political and legal restrictions that prevented the free manifestation and organization of the labour forces at the end of the seventies. At the beginning of the decade the *Frente Nacional do Trabalho* (National Work Front), which had links to progressive Catholic leaders, organized a series of strikes at Perus, a community on the outskirts of São Paulo. These strikes set a new pattern of relationship between capital and unions. In the past, conflicts had been avoided by the submission of unions to the state. The Perus strikes set a new standard of labour independence in Brazil. The Frente Nacional do Trabalho was headed by Mario Carvalho de Jesus, and was composed of more than sixty labour lawyers who gave assistance to independent unions all over Brazil. Many of these lawyers contributed to the organization of an in-house legal department at the São Bernardo Union, and later at CUT. José Siqueira Neto, a young lawyer with communist sympathies, but not a member of the Brazilian Communist Party, became responsible for the organization of the Brazilian New Labour Movement, legal services. His first mission was to create a network of protection for union leaders. The second challenge was to organize elections at unions so that members of the New Labour Movement could have a chance to control new unions around Brazil. The third mission of the *coletivo jurídico* (legal collective) was to strategize over legal disputes taking place at the labour courts and to protect salaries against losses provoked by economic adjustment plans to control hyper-inflation. The experiences obtained during this period were crucial for the labour movement during the debates to establish the 1988 Constitution, and especially its chapter on labour rights.

Vieira, *supra*, at 223-30.

In addition to helping build legal institutions, social movements also deploy law in innovative ways to advance movement goals. In his case study of South Africa's Treatment Action Campaign, which sought the importation of cheap generic drugs to stem South Africa's HIV/AIDS crisis, William Forbath emphasizes the creative ways in which TAC linked a 2002 Constitutional Court Decision requiring the provision of "antiretroviral treatment in the public healthcare system to prevent mother-to-child transmission of HIV" with a broader political struggle to widely disseminate cheap drugs to those in need. William Forbath, *Cultural Transformation, Deep Institutional Reform, and ESR Practice, in* STONES OF HOPE, *supra,* at 51, 52. His conclusion summarizes the difference between TAC's approach to legal mobilization of economic and social rights (ESR) and the classic U.S. impact lawsuit paradigm:

> TAC made securing the constitutional social right to HIV/AIDS treatment the core of its efforts. Yet in contrast to the classic twentieth-century struggles for constitutional rights, constitutional *litigation* has played a subordinate, supporting role in TAC's work. In this supporting role, litigation and formal legal advocacy of ESR proved a good deal more valuable in bringing social rights to earth than many ESR scholars and activists believe possible. Because it put aside the court-centered model of rights advocacy in favor of a politics-centered model, TAC never made court victories the object of its campaigns; nor did it try to use the courts as the central arena for initiating or shaping pro-poor state policies. Instead, as we've seen, TAC used litigation in service of many-sided strategies to open up policy-making processes, to reshape programs and policies in democratic and pro-poor directions, and to prod government to implement them. In this context, ESR litigation and court victories provided invaluable political leverage and moral authority.
>
> Thus, the policy-shaping and policy-changing work of the 2002 Constitutional Court decision on [preventing mother-to-child transmission] was largely done outside the Court via pressure, protests, proposals, and alliances, with reformers inside government, before the litigation even got under way. What's more, TAC never brought to court its broader claim for a national ARVT plan in the public health system. Instead, TAC chose the public political sphere as the arena for pressing the case for the social right to adequate healthcare for HIV/AIDS: holding workshops and conferences; preparing studies and proposals; monitoring government's performance at local, provincial, and national levels; educating the lay public; and at the same time, building a social movement, staging dramatic public protests and demonstrations, and several times resorting to civil disobedience to dramatize the government's death-dealing failure to develop and then implement a responsible program.

Id. at 87. How does Forbath's description of ESR advocacy in the TAC campaign compare to the discussion of "community lawyering" from Chapter 6? Also, consider how it relates to the "multidimensional advocacy" approach discussed later in Chapter 10.

3. Civil Society

Outside of the social movement sector, the existence and strength of civil society organizations capable of providing access to justice or mobilizing law for change is an important element of a country's legal system. The development of indigenous nongovernmental organizations (NGOs) with sustainable funding strengthens the ability of lawyers in those organizations to advance the interests of less powerful social groups. Funding, of course, is the crucial element and, as we saw in Chapter 4, it is difficult to rely on one source, particularly the government. Even in countries with strong histories of legal aid — the United Kingdom, for example — funding has been cut over the past two decades as it has in the United States. *See* Deborah James & Evan Killick, *Empathy and Expertise: Case Workers and Immigration/Asylum Applicants in London*, 37 Law & Soc. Inquiry 430, 437-38 (2012). In many countries without internal sources of support, external funding is fundamental to public interest lawyering, which we will see later in this chapter.

4. The Legal Profession

The strength and independence of lawyers, and the degree to which they feel empowered to criticize the government and powerful private actors, further influences the type and nature of legal mobilization from country to country. Sometimes this is reflected in the power of professional associations, which can facilitate cause lawyering in a number of ways. First, by maintaining the authority to regulate the profession and discipline its members, professional associations can insulate lawyers from repression by the state. Abel, *Speaking Law to Power*, *supra*, at 98. Second, professional associations may be important in supporting the delivery of legal services to underrepresented groups. *Id*. Yet Abel argues that the record of professional associations in promoting public interest law is mixed.

> Lawyers (like everyone) sometimes seem better able to perceive injustice at a distance than at home. Most professional associations champion "neutral" process values, but a few are openly partisan: compare the American Civil Liberties Union with the National Lawyers Guild, the Lawyers Committee for Civil Rights under Law with the Lawyers Constitutional Defense Committee (all in the United States), Justice with the Haldane Society (in the United Kingdom), Lawyers for Human Rights with the National Association of Democratic Lawyers and the Black Lawyers Association (in South Africa), the International Commission of Jurists with La Ligue des Droits de l'Homme, the International Juridical Association, and the International Association of Democratic Lawyers (in the world arena). Professional associations have a spotty record of resisting threats to the rule of law. Bar associations did not stand up to McCarthyism in the United States, the German occupation in France, or fascism in Italy or Brazil. Nevertheless, professional bodies in Ghana, Malaysia, and the Occupied Territories of Israel have threatened to strike in support of the judiciary, and Egyptian lawyers have resisted the state attack on lawyers who represent religious fundamentalists.

Id. at 98-99.

As Abel notes elsewhere in his analysis, lawyers may take the strongest (and most self-interested) stand for the independence of legal institutions when they are threatened by state repression. In Malaysia in the 1980s, lawyers demonstrated in front of Parliament against proposed legislation that would have imposed greater regulation on lawyers and limited judicial review. Daniel Lev,

Lawyers' Causes in Indonesia and Malaysia, in CAUSE LAWYERING: POLITICAL COMMITMENTS AND PROFESSIONAL RESPONSIBILITIES, *supra* at, 431, 444-45. In 2009, lawyers in Pakistan flooded the streets to protest the ouster of Chief Justice Iftikhar Muhammad Chaudry by then-president General Pervez Musharraf—ultimately winning Chaudry's reinstatement. Note, *The Pakistani Lawyers' Movement and the Popular Currency of Judicial Power*, 123 HARV. L. REV. 1705, 1712 (2010). Yet the role of lawyers as a vanguard for the rule of law is complicated. It is one thing for lawyers to promote their own independence from the government, quite another to fight for broader democratic principles. For example, some commentators expressed surprise when many younger members of the Pakistani lawyers' movement demonstrated *in support of* a man accused of assassinating—in the name of the Prophet Muhammad—the governor of Punjab for criticizing Islamic blasphemy laws. For these lawyers, their support for judicial independence did not extend so far as to reject the tenets of Islamic law. Carlotta Gall, *Pakistan Faces a Divide of Age on Muslim Law*, N.Y. TIMES, Jan. 10, 2011, at A1.

In general, what type of support would you expect lawyers to provide for legal advocacy that challenges existing governmental, religious, or corporate institutions? What *should* we expect?

5. Legal Education

How lawyers are trained affects their interest in and ability to use law as a tool for change. As Abel puts it: "The willingness and capacity of lawyers to represent controversial clients or causes may vary with their training. An academic education in law may foster greater independence than an apprenticeship. Entry barriers also affect the number and backgrounds of those who qualify and consequently the cost of legal services." Abel, *Speaking Law to Power*, *supra*, at 96. What type of legal education do you think best equips lawyers with the tools and ideas to engage in public interest law? What countries would you think best provide such training?

In the United States, Legal Realists promoted the idea of law as a flexible policy tool and law students are generally taught to think about the ways in which law is made, whether it is normatively justified, and how to change it. The approach to law training in other countries varies in ways that create different opportunities for and impediments to legal mobilization. Particularly in countries where legal education is highly formalistic, focused on the narrow application of doctrine, training for more transformative uses of law is limited. Stephen Meili raises some of these limitations in the following excerpt on Latin America:

> Lack of support for cause lawyering at law schools in Argentina and Brazil has also spurred many cause lawyers to seek alternative means of working for democratic change. Legal education in both countries is very traditional, emphasizing memorization of the legal codes, with little emphasis on legal theory, the role of law in society, or the interconnectedness of law, politics, and economics. Clinical programs, where law students receive school credit for working on actual cases (usually of the public interest variety), are rare.
>
> According to Celso Campilongo, a professor at the University of Sao Paulo: "Law schools have been conservative and do not support the alternative law

movement. This could be the remains of the aristocratic makeup of the legal population. The traditional educational training is very technical; the graduate should come out knowing how to manipulate the codes, etc. The more innovative practices of the law demand much more than this; they demand an understanding of social reality, of sociological aspects, etc. [Graduates] should be able to take the manipulation of the codes and fit it into the broader sociological aspects."

Similarly, Martin Bohmer, a University of Buenos Aires law professor who is attempting to formulate a public interest-oriented exchange program with Yale Law School, observes that law school in Argentina is "pretty much professors speaking and students taking notes," without any discussion. "There is very little critical thinking about the law." He says that there is simply no institutional support for public interest work at law schools, since they "are controlled by conservative professors and lawyers." Bohmer links the authoritarian nature of Argentina's law schools with the country's authoritarian public discourse, in which there is very little room for discussion or dissent: "There is very little critical thinking about the law; so there is a linkage between the way we teach law and public discourse." Julio Garcia of CISALP believes that the reason for the lack of support for public interest work is that it is interpreted by the power structure as a criticism of the legal system.

Stephen Meili, *Cause Lawyers and Social Movements: A Comparative Perspective on Democratic Change in Argentina and Brazil, in* Cause Lawyering: Political Commitments and Professional Responsibilities, *supra*, 487, 498-99. How can public interest practice emerge in countries that do not have well-resourced law schools? In nations such as Indonesia, NGOs sometimes provide an alternative training ground for lawyers who wish to pursue public interest practice. Yves Dezalay & Bryant G. Garth, Asian Legal Revivals: Lawyers in the Shadow of Empire 226 (2010). Promoting greater policy flexibility and practical knowledge has been a major focus of global legal education reform movements, which we turn to in the next section.

B. GLOBAL FACTORS: "PUBLIC INTEREST LAW" BEYOND BORDERS

While we have established the pre-existence and sustained development of indigenously derived legal advocacy strategies, it is also the case that legal mobilization in the global age extends beyond borders and, in many places, has been influenced by public interest advocacy models from the United States and other countries with well-known public interest law traditions. This section therefore looks specifically at the *transnational* dimension of public interest lawyering, focusing on both why and how lawyers move beyond their own nation-states to advance causes and how "public interest law" as we understand it in the United States has traveled to other countries. In both instances, we highlight the forces promoting transnational practice and examine their consequences.

1. Economic Development

One important development over the past 30 years has been the linkage between public interest law and global development policy emanating from the North. In the first so-called law and development movement that emerged in the 1960s, the United States sought to export law to promote modernization in developing countries — part of the United States's Cold War effort to extend its sphere of influence. Major sponsors of the law and development movement included the U.S. Agency of International Development (USAID) and the Ford Foundation, which established the International Legal Center in 1966 with a $3 million grant to provide legal assistance to developing countries. It was believed that by exporting the policy-oriented approach to law from America, foreign officials would be given the tools to reorient economic systems in a way that could spur modernization. Law and development proponents argued that the modernization of economic rules would then "spill over" to enhance democratic values and ensure individual rights. David M. Trubek, *The "Rule of Law" in Development Assistance: Past, Present, and Future, in* THE NEW LAW AND ECONOMIC DEVELOPMENT: A CRITICAL APPRAISAL 74, 77 (David M. Trubek & Alvaro Santos eds., 2006). Because the goal was the transformation of legal culture, the central target of reform was legal education, which was to be reoriented to emphasize pragmatic problem solving, equipping lawyers to embrace policy-sensitive uses of law. American law professors were therefore key proponents of law and development, enlisted to transmit the U.S. method of legal education to targeted countries. During the 1960s, major law and development projects were launched in Asia, Africa, and Latin America. However, this approach fell out of favor in the 1970s as it came to be viewed as a form of U.S. legal imperialism. *See* Trubek & Galanter, *supra.*

The reemergence and reorientation of development policy in the 1980s around the goal of open markets (often referred to as the "Washington Consensus" or "neoliberalism") influenced the globalization of public interest law. The neoliberal vision, instituted under President Ronald Reagan and extended after the fall of the Berlin Wall, sought to bring developing countries and those transitioning from Soviet rule into the sphere of market integration and was touted by its architects as fueling global economic growth. However, critics pointed to neoliberalism's association with economic inequality and instability. These concerns with neoliberalism led to a reformulation of development policy during the 1990s toward a modified open markets approach under the auspices of Rule of Law reform, which recognized the prevalence of market failure and reconceptualized development as not merely about growth but also about freedom. The Rule of Law movement attempted to respond to the critiques of neoliberalism by tempering the excesses of open markets with appropriate regulation and an emphasis on democratic rights. Its goals were reframed in terms of "good governance," which combined market liberalization with strong rights enforcement and political accountability.

The advent of the Rule of Law movement facilitated the globalization of public interest law in several ways. Significantly, it operated to connect public interest law explicitly to international development aims. In order to promote the twin goals of rights enforcement and political accountability, Northern donors turned to public interest law as a tool to counter government power and increase access to justice. Beginning in the 1990s, major foundations — such as the Open Society Institute and Ford Foundation — as well as governmental and international agencies — such as USAID and the United Nations — began to make significant investments in supporting public interest law programs, particularly access to justice (legal aid and pro bono) and clinical legal education, in diverse countries across the globe, including Bangladesh, Bulgaria, Cambodia, China, Hungary, Liberia, Mongolia, Poland, and Russia. In this way, the lexicon of public interest law, which remained the *lingua franca* of the international funding community, was exported into countries with distinct traditions.

In addition, the growing power of international financial institutions — such as the World Bank, International Monetary Fund (IMF), and World Trade Organization (WTO) — to set global trade and investment rules prompted lawyers to use transnational advocacy strategies to contest their influence. In doing so, lawyers and activists developed two main strategies: (1) entering international financial institutions directly in order to challenge their internal decision making processes as excluding and injuring local communities; and (2) mounting local and transnational campaigns to resist the impact of international development policies and practices.

Particularly as the World Bank, IMF, and WTO gained influence in defining the global rules of the marketplace during the 1980s and 1990s, the impact on local economies and indigenous practices grew more pronounced. In exchange for development financing or greater trading rights, many developing countries agreed to austerity and privatization programs that resulted in curtailed social spending. In response, some lawyers and activists sought to challenge the decision making that had produced these policies in the first instance by creating a process for people affected by finance and trade decisions to submit formal complaints. This advocacy succeeded in creating a modest level of administrative review within the World Bank and WTO, but no significant change in institutional practice. Cummings & Trubek, *supra*, at 20-21.

Other groups tried to advocate at the national level to force politicians to resist internationally imposed policy changes that would negatively affect the poor. In Tanzania, for example, a coalition of women's rights organizations engaged in local lobbying, public education, and mass demonstrations to challenge cuts to economic and social services mandated by the World Bank. Their short-term focus was on

> reforming the policy and budget frameworks so as to provide quality public social and economic services for poor groups and women, to eliminate user fees [for health and education] and to bring back subsidies for small-scale farmers. The long-term emphasis was on advocating for a reduced role of [international financial institutions] and other donors in policy and financial management of the nation's economy, and the greater participation of the poor and disempowered.

Mary Rusimbi & Marjorie Mbilinyi, *Political and Legal Struggles over Resources and Democracy: Experiences with Gender Budgeting in Tanzania, in* LAW AND GLOBALIZATION FROM BELOW, *supra*, at 283, 296.

Lawyers and activists in other places have sought to combine local legal and political campaigns with international advocacy to create explicitly transnational movements to challenge internationally financed development projects. One of the most famous examples comes from India.

BALAKRISHNAN RAJAGOPAL, *LIMITS OF LAW IN COUNTER-HEGEMONIC GLOBALIZATION: THE INDIAN SUPREME COURT AND THE NARMADA VALLEY STRUGGLE*

Law and Globalization from Below: Towards a New Cosmopolitan Legality 183, 191-210 (Boaventura de Sousa Santos & César A. Rodríguez-Garavito eds., 2005)

The Narmada River is India's fifth-longest river and one of the last major rivers to be dammed. The desire to build dams across the Narmada River, a westward-flowing river in the middle of India that crosses three state boundaries (Madhya Pradesh, Maharashtra, and Gujarat), in order to harness its water for drinking, irrigation, and power, had existed at least since the 1940s. . . .

The projects were transnationalized from their conception. The World Bank sent its first mission in late 1979 to Gujarat and helped to get US$10 million from the United Nations Development Program (UNDP) for the basic planning of the projects. . . .

[Local NGO] Arch-Vahini and other NGOs moved the Supreme Court for the first time in 1985. Although the government of Gujarat stated in the proceedings that encroachers had no rights, the court issued an interim injunction against displacement. Independently of this, another group, the Narmada Dharangrasta Samiti, had filed legal challenges to land acquisition at the local courts in Maharashtra, but without success. Despite this brief involvement of the courts in the struggle against displacement, they remained marginal. The injunctions had not been against construction of the dam per se, and the courts never grappled with the question of what rights the so-called encroachers actually had under Indian law. As a result, the construction of the dams continued even as Arch-Vahini and other groups managed to extract a progressive policy on resettle-ment and rehabilitation from the government of Gujarat in 1987, ensuring a minimum of five acres of land for land owners and extending its package to encroachers as well. However, this policy was constantly breached. Thus, until 1988, the focus of domestic mobilization remained largely on obtaining better terms of resettlement and rehabilitation for the displaced people in the valley, and the access to courts was a notable but not a particularly significant part of this mobilization.

The groups working on resettlement and rehabilitation had better success at the international level. An alliance between Arch-Vahini and Oxfam UK led to the formation of a transnational campaign focused on the role of the World Bank in the project. The World Bank also came under pressure from NGOs like Survival International, which charged that India was violating the rights of tribal people under International Labour Organization (ILO) Convention No. 107, to which it was a party, due to the dam construction. In 1986, NGOs petitioned the ILO's Committee of Experts to investigate possible violations of Convention No. 107 relating to the rights of indigenous peoples. That led to a warning from the Committee of Experts to the World Bank and the Indian government which acknowledged their duty to comply with the Convention. Although the World Bank pressured the Gujarat government to improve its package for the displaced people, in the end it signed the loan agreement in 1985 with the government. Put differently, the Narmada Valley struggle had some limited impact on the international legal rules and institutions concerning resettlement and on the World Bank. Domestic policy on resettlement in Gujarat was formally changed due to the struggle but implementation on the ground remained very poor.

On the environmental front, there were major encounters between the Narmada Valley struggle and the law. In the late 1980s, a new transnational environmental coalition emerged and used the political opportunities provided by the World Bank's own 1984 guidelines as well as emerging norms of international environmental law, for the struggle in the valley. At the core of this coalition was a domestic social movement, the NBA. The NBA was formed in 1989, as a social movement of affected communities, domestic NGOs, and individuals drawn from all over India but consisting mainly of the Narmada Dharangrast Samiti from Maharashtra, the Narmada Ghati Navnirman Samiti from Madhya Pradesh, and the Narmada Asargrastha Sangharsh Samiti from Gujarat.

A successful international campaign led by the NBA, with the participation of NGOs drawn from several countries from Europe. North America, and Japan, forced the World Bank to commission an unprecedented independent review of the dam projects in 1991 which found that the World Bank had failed to comply with its own guidelines. Meanwhile, domestic agitations in the valley intensified and confrontations with the state increased as the state pursued more and more aggressive tactics to counter the successes of the Narmada Valley movement. The construction of the Sardar Sarover dam had continued as there had been no injunction against it. The Gujarat state in particular, began treating the dam construction as part of an ideology of cultural nationalism, and branding all opponents as "enemies of Gujarat." In 1989, Gujarat politicians from across various party lines criticized the dam critics as anti-national agents of foreign interests and adopted a resolution in the state assembly supporting the project. A sophisticated media campaign was launched by the proponents of the dam, led by Sardar Sarover Nigam Limited. Meanwhile, the NBA had intensified mass resistance through direct action in the valley, and the goal of the struggle had changed at this stage to demand a comprehensive reevaluation of the whole project, not just better terms of resettlement and rehabilitation. Thus, the goal of the struggle in the valley had shifted from a focus on resettlement to a comprehensive questioning of the whole project through confrontation and mass action from 1988 to 1991.

Between 1991 and 1994, the Narmada Valley struggle became even more internationalized as well as more judicialized. The independent review team, appointed by the World Bank, concluded in its report in June 1992 that the project was "flawed" and that the World Bank should "step back" from the project. Citing hostility in the valley and local opposition to the project, the report also stated that "progress will be impossible except as a result of unacceptable practices." As a result, the World Bank worked out a face-saving formula with the Indian government whereby the Indian government would announce that it was asking the World Bank to cancel the remaining US$170 million of the US$450 million loan and that it would complete the project on its own. This was announced in March 1993.

Despite this success at the international level, the situation in the valley was grim and the NBA and its allies were taking recourse to courts in desperation. A flurry of legal action followed. As early as 1990, the villages that were scheduled to be submerged were beginning to be cleared in Maharashtra. The submergence and the displacement were challenged in the Bombay High Court in 1990, which restrained the government from forcible evictions which it had, in an earlier case, eloquently declared as unconstitutional. Despite this, the construction of the Sardar Sarover dam proceeded apace, even as forced evictions and agitations continued. . . .

The NBA filed a petition before the Supreme Court in May 1994, challenging the Sardar Sarover project on many grounds, calling for a comprehensive review of the project, and prayed for a court order stopping all construction and displacement until such a review was done. This petition was admitted by the court as a form of public interest litigation by a bench which had a pro-human rights, liberal character. . . .

Protests in the valley continued in late 1994, with the affected people engaging in various forms of direct political action such as dhamas and indefinite fasts. In the light of these developments, and in view of the Supreme Court proceedings, the [Narmada Control Authority (NCA)] decided to suspend the river bed construction of the dam in December 1994. In May 1995, the Supreme Court confirmed this decision through a stay order on further construction of the dam. The NBA's struggle in the valley seemed to have achieved victory, but it would prove to be fleeting.

Even as the river bed construction of the dam was suspended formally by the NCA and the Supreme Court, the construction continued on the ground in violation of these orders. To contest this, the NBA organized a massive march on Delhi in late 1995 which resulted in suspension of the construction work. . . .

Meanwhile, the Supreme Court refused to lift the stay order against the construction of the dam in a hearing in August 1996, and expressed its concern over human rights violations, especially relating to resettlement and rehabilitation. . . .

During 1996, the struggle in the valley also began to transform itself. As the construction of the dam had stopped, the NBA began to focus on positive reconstruction rather than confrontation, and it began to branch off into national and global political action. In 1996, the NBA took the lead in establishing the National Alliance of Peoples' Movements (NAPM), an umbrella of like-minded peoples' movements and trade unions from all over India, and also contributed to the formation of the World Commission on Dams in 1998. But even as the NBA was notching up victories abroad, it was facing trouble back home. For reasons that can only be guessed at, from 1998, the Supreme Court began to dispense with the need to decide the jurisdictional question which it had assigned to a constitution bench in 1997. It also limited itself to the resettlement and rehabilitation question, though it had previously asked counsel for the states and the federal government to be prepared to argue all aspects relating to the project. Thus, the NBA's hope that the court would order a comprehensive review of the whole project, and that the constitution bench would set important legal precedent for settling disputes over large projects and peoples' rights, had been dashed. . . .

After the hearings were concluded, the final order of the Supreme Court came on October 18, 2000, landing like a bombshell on the NBA. In its order, the court (a) allowed the construction of the dam to proceed up to ninety meters (which the Relief and Rehabilitation Sub-Group of the NCA had already allowed) and announced that the priority was to complete the construction of the dam as soon as possible; (b) ordered that further raising of the height of the dam will be pari passu with the implementation of rehabilitation and environmental measures and after clearance by the Relief and Rehabilitation Sub-Group and the Environmental Sub-Group of the NCA at every additional five meters; and (c) ordered the states concerned to comply with the decisions of the NCA, particularly relating to land acquisition and rehabilitation, and asked the NCA to prepare an action plan in this regard. The decision of the court left no doubt that the final decision-making authority belonged to the political arena, and declared that in case the Review Committee of the NCA could not decide any issue, it shall be referred to the Prime Minister, whose decision shall be final. It was clear that completing the construction of the dam was more important to the court than the social and environmental costs it imposed. The court also extolled the virtues of large dams.

Thus the decision by the NBA to approach the Supreme Court had backfired, as many within the NBA itself had feared. . . .

What lessons do you draw about transnational advocacy from the Narmada case? Did the advocates have options other than turning to the Indian Supreme Court? What power, if any, did the transnational phase of the struggle provide to the local movement?

In general, what are the best legal options for challenging global development policies that harm poor communities? Does lawyering make a difference at all? Do you think that challenging international institutions directly can work or are they too remote and powerful? If so, what other viable options exist?

2. Human Rights

As the discussion of development highlights, the emergence of global governance institutions has exerted a powerful influence on the globalization of law, which has operated both to foster inequality and provide tools to contest it (another example of a global legal institution is the International Criminal Court in The Hague). One of the main legal tools in the struggle for global justice has been the development of a powerful set of human rights institutions that have been used to promote greater respect for individual rights and democratization, and also to challenge some of the local impacts of global development policy.

The human rights movement has been important in shaping global legal advocacy by providing a source of supranational law that advocates can use to pressure change in domestic systems without strong legal institutions. MARGARET E. KECK & KATHRYN SIKKINK, ACTIVISTS BEYOND BORDERS: ADVOCACY NETWORKS IN INTERNATIONAL POLITICS (1998). The human rights movement emerged as a way to challenge the power and legitimacy of authoritarian governments from the outside. South Africa's human rights movement in the 1980s was one of the earliest and most powerful examples. *See* ABEL, POLITICS BY OTHER MEANS, *supra*. During the same period, human rights were mobilized in South America by various pro-democracy groups challenging military-backed dictatorships that emerged in the postcolonial period. *See* Hugo Frühling, *From Dictatorship to Democracy: Law and Social Change in the Andean Region and the Southern Cone of South America, in* MANY ROADS TO JUSTICE: THE LAW RELATED WORK OF FORD FOUNDATION GRANTEES AROUND THE WORLD 55, 57-61 (Mary McClymont & Stephen Golub eds., 2000). In this context, human rights advocates challenged the abuses of dictatorships supported by the U.S. government during the Cold War era. Yves Dezalay & Bryant G. Garth, *Constructing Law Out of Power: Investing in Human Rights as an Alternative Political Strategy, in* CAUSE LAWYERING AND THE STATE IN A GLOBAL ERA 354, 360-61 (Austin Sarat & Stuart Scheingold eds., 2001).

After the fall of the Berlin Wall and the end of the Cold War, the human rights movement grew in a new direction, challenging the open markets agenda of international financial institutions and global capital:

> [T]ransnational activists, in collaboration with public interest law groups, began to assert human rights as an international public law counterweight to the private law regime advanced under the open markets agenda. Thus, the move was to build up and radiate out human rights as a credible systemic alternative to neoliberal governance, which demanded the diminution of state regulatory and social welfare protections as a quid pro quo for international investment. As suggested by the transnational campaigns around labor standards, the environment, and indigenous rights, activists raised human rights in venues such as the NAFTA side labor agreement, ILO, Inter-American Commission on Human Rights, and United Nations to provide legal foundation for their challenges to the impact of deregulation and privatization on local populations. This occurred both through the formal assertion of claims in dispute resolution bodies and through the formulation of human rights policy, as in the case of the United Nations Declaration on Indigenous Peoples. Because it responded to the problems of economic insecurity and displacement, this use of human rights spotlighted the importance of economic and social rights in the open markets regime.

Cummings & Trubek, *supra*, at 25-26. For more about economic and social rights campaigns, see STONES OF HOPE, *supra*.

The struggle of the U'wa people in Colombia against the oil drilling of Occidental Petroleum (Oxy) in their native land provides a compelling example of the use of human rights to resist economic exploitation and illustrates another type of transnational advocacy campaign:

CÉSAR A. RODRÍGUEZ-GARAVITO & LUIS CARLOS ARENAS, *INDIGENOUS RIGHTS, TRANSNATIONAL ACTIVISM, AND LEGAL MOBILIZATION: THE STRUGGLE OF THE U'WA PEOPLE IN COLOMBIA*

Law and Globalization from Below: Towards a New Cosmopolitan Legality 241, 248-58 (Boaventura de Sousa Santos & César A. Rodríguez-Garavito eds., 2005)

The U'wa (a name that means "people who think, people who know how to speak") currently occupy a swath of land of approximately 60,000 hectares in northeastern Colombia. However, their ancestral territory is considerably larger, encompassing areas of several Colombian provinces and extending to the western part of Venezuela. . . .

[I]n the early 1990s, encouraged by the recognition of indigenous rights in the 1991 Constitution, the U'wa and the national indigenous movement (through ONIC [the National Indigenous Organization of Colombia]) resumed the campaign for their right to live together in a unified reservation in a portion of their ancestral territory.

It was at the height of this two-decade-long struggle in 1992 that Oxy entered the scene, eventually prompting the internationalization and judicialization of the case. Upon signing a joint venture agreement with Colombia's oil company (Ecopetrol) and Shell to exploit a drill site (called Samore Bloc) that partially overlapped with the U'wa homeland, Oxy applied for a license from Colombia's environmental authorities in May 1992. At around the same time, Oxy began geological testing on the site through a contractor.

These developments prompted the first U'wa declaration against Oxy, released in March 1993. In it, the U'wa announced their opposition to any kind of oil exploration or exploitation in their territories. . . .

[The Colombian Ombudsman's Office then filed two suits on behalf of the U'Wa, one in the Constitutional Court, arguing that the issuance of Oxy's license had violated the U'Wa's constitutional right to participate in the process, and one in the highest administrative court, the Council of State, focusing on the violation of national laws. Although the Constitutional Court ruled in the U'Wa's favor, the Council of State held that Colombia was not required to negotiate with the U'Wa prior to issuing a license for oil drilling. The administrative ruling was viewed as undercutting the constitutional one and channeling efforts away from the courts.]

[T]he transnationalization of the U'wa struggle rook place simultaneously through political and juridical routes. Reacting quickly to the outcome of the judicial impasse in Colombia, the transnational advocacy network (TAN) that had been assembling pursued two strategies. On the one hand, in May 1997, the Amazon Coalition, a US-based environmentalist NGO, invited U'wa and ONIC leaders on a speaking tour of several US cities. The presentation of the case by U'wa leader Berito Kubaru'wa helped establish direct relations with transnational activists and NGOs that would prove instrumental in future phases of the campaign. On the other hand, while in Washington, DC on the same trip, Berito Kubaru'wa and the head of ONIC submitted a formal complaint against the Colombian government before the Inter-American Commission of Human Rights. Drafted by experts from transnational litigation-oriented NGOs (the Earth Legal Defense Fund, the Center for Justice and International Law, and the Colombian Commission of jurists), the complaint added a regional layer to the protracted legal battle of the U'wa.

After the first visit of the U'wa to the US, the membership and activities of the TAN grew exponentially. Turned into icons of indigenous resistance against environmental degradation and ethnocide Berito Kubaru'wa and other U'wa spokespeople have since split their time between work in their community and participation in multiple international fora. The number of U'wa international tours at the height of the campaign between 1997 and 2000 (seven in the US seven in Europe, and many more in Latin America) illustrates the dynamism of the transnational campaign.

The TAN's membership and strategies are highly heterogeneous. In the US, the key organizations have been Rain Forest Action Network (RAN) and Amazon Watch, as well as the coalition of NGOs that established the U'wa Defense Project to serve as a coordinating node for the campaign. To put pressure on Oxy to withdraw from U'wa territory, US activists have pursued numerous strategies and forms of direct action. They have included negative publicity campaigns in visible media outlets such as the *New York Times,* the award of the US$100,000 Goldman Environmental Prize in 1998 to the U'wa, well-attended rallies against presidential candidate Al Gore (who has long-standing ties with Oxy) during the 2000 campaign, protests at Oxy's shareholders' meetings, and the targeting of Oxy's main institutional investor, mutual fund conglomerate Fidelity Investments, and demonstrations and direct actions at over seventy-five locations in the US, Japan, and the UK.

Acción Ecológica, a transnational environmentalist NGO based in Ecuador, coordinated the Latin American and European branches of the TAN. Through Oilwatch (a transnational coalition focusing on creating direct grass-roots links among communities harmed by oil exploration), Acción Ecológica sponsored a trip by Colombian indigenous Senator Lorenzo Muelas to Nigeria in 1999, as well as a subsequent trip by Muelas and Berito Kubaru'wa to the land of the Ecuadorian Secoya, an indigenous community affected by Oxy's drilling in their territory. In Europe, activism by TAN members including the Italian Green Party and London's Reclaim the Streets led to the decision of the Spanish government to award the U'wa the Bartolome de las Casas Prize for their role in the defense of indigenous rights.

Thus integrated into the global justice movement, the U'wa case has been featured prominently at several events, from the rallies against the World Bank in Washington in 2000 to the 2004 Social Forum of the Americas in Quito and the annual World Social Forum. In a "boomerang effect," the new strength that such an outbreak of transnational solidarity infused into the movement shifted the correlation of forces at the local scale in the next round of confrontation between the U'wa, Oxy, and the Colombian government. From this point on, the local, national, and international threads of the conflict would become woven together in an intricate pattern that exposes the complexity, potential, and limits of political contention and legal mobilization across borders. . . .

It would take an unexpected turn of events to change the course of the case. During its annual shareholders' meeting on May 3, 2001, Oxy announced that it was returning oil concessions on U'wa land to the Colombian government and abandoning its plans to drill in the region. Although Oxy declared that it was withdrawing because it had found no oil in the area, the decision probably had more to do with the persistence of the four-year transnational campaign in support of the U'wa and the risk it represented for Oxy's corporate image.

As the U'wa example highlights, the creation of regional human rights institutions have offered a new forum for legal mobilization. These regional bodies have played an important role in both spreading public interest law and shaping new types of legal mobilization that combine international and national law elements:

> The development of public interest law has also been influenced by the interaction between local institutions and regional human rights systems. Brazil's ratification of the American Convention on Human Rights in 1992 and subsequent acceptance of the jurisdiction of the Inter-American Court of Human Rights prompted organizations to use the regional human rights system more aggressively. [An example is] the creation of Justiça Global, an organization dedicated to using the human rights system to bring to justice to those abused by the military regime. In a similar vein, the Artigo 1 project of Brazil's Conectas, started in 2001, works on human rights impact cases in areas such as juvenile detention. Although its main focus is on enforcing constitutional and treaty-based human rights in domestic courts, it also uses the regional human rights system, as it did in 2005 when it filed a case in the Inter-American Court on behalf of 4000 adolescent detainees in Sao Paulo for inhumane treatment. In a parallel development, [commentators highlight] the importance of the admission of Central and Eastern European countries into the Council of Europe, which administers European human rights treaties, on public interest law's institutional development. Admission requires that member countries ratify the European Convention on Human Rights and accept jurisdiction of the European Court of Human Rights, which has strong human rights precedent. As a result, public interest groups have been drawn to the European Court of Human Rights as a potentially sympathetic venue for litigation. However, admission to the Council has also had the effect of stimulating domestic impact litigation: because the Court has an exhaustion of domestic remedies requirement, legal groups have been pushed to develop strategic litigation in national courts first, thereby reinforcing the model of domestic public interest law. . . .

Cummings & Trubek, *supra*, at 32-35. As this suggests, legal mobilization strategies around the world combine international and national law approaches in flexible ways in order to advance social justice goals. In this sense, legal mobilization transcends the labels of international human rights or domestic public interest law, integrating the two in new and innovative ways to pursue change through law.

As lawyers pursue change across borders, what ethical problems might they face? Lawyers practicing in public interest contexts across national boundaries may have to consider the challenges of qualifying for practice in multiple jurisdictions or attempting to follow distinct, and perhaps conflicting, rules from different ethics regimes.

3. Funding

As with the U.S. public interest experience, philanthropic foundations, mostly from the global North, have been key players in the global public interest law movement. Foundations have promoted the dissemination of public interest law around the world as a tool of democratic resistance to authoritarianism and as a means to empower politically marginalized groups.

Global philanthropic organizations such as the Ford Foundation and the Open Society Institute have played dominant roles in the diffusion of public interest law. Their role has encompassed fostering information exchange and implementing programs. In terms of information exchange, both funders have sponsored important conferences designed to bring together activist lawyers from different countries to compare practices and trade ideas. In the early 1990s, Ford sponsored a conference called Public Interest Law Around the World that connected American lawyers with their counterparts from eighteen countries in Africa, Asia, and Latin America. . . .

Global foundations have also spurred programmatic changes as well. As democratic state-building became the focal point of development efforts around the world, the funding emphasis shifted toward strengthening organizational capacity to promote practices associated with the American public interest law system: impact litigation, legal aid, pro bono, and clinical legal education. This can be seen in Ford's funding priorities across a number of nations. For instance, after focusing on human rights during the period of authoritarian rule in South America, Ford returned to the region in 1995 to support incipient public interest law programs under the banner of "democratic governance." As part of a broader effort to foster judicial independence and operationalize new constitutional provisions, domestically focused litigation — patterned on the U.S. impact litigation model — became a major funding priority. Ford's portfolio thus began to focus on ensuring governmental accountability through domestic legal channels, supporting groups like Colombia's FUNDEPUBLICO, which filed class actions to stem official corruption, and Argentina's Centro de Estudios Legales y Sociales, which also litigated cases to force the government to meet domestic mandates, like the provision of health services.

Similar investments have been made to support the development of legal aid. For instance, in 1997, Ford funded the creation of the Public Interest Law Initiative at Columbia University to focus on building public interest law systems in Central and Eastern Europe. The organization . . . has provided technical assistance in the implementation of access to justice programs in Poland and Bulgaria, and is undertaking research and providing programmatic support in connection with initiatives in the Balkans and Russia. Similarly, Ford has played an important role in supporting legal aid in China, providing resources to the state-run China Centre for Legal Aid, which was created in 1996. In addition, Ford has supported Chinese nongovernmental legal aid programs based at universities and run by liberal elites who rely on small staffs to help litigate cases in specific substantive areas, like women's rights and the environment. . . .

Reflecting the diversity of funding sources, government agencies and international institutions have also played key funding roles in globalizing public interest law — with funding targets that reflect their own priorities. For instance, balancing the twin goals of open markets and human rights has been the main thrust of the USAID and World Bank-funded Central and Eastern European Law Initiative of the ABA, which has sponsored refugee, prisoner, and women's rights clinics in Europe, the former Soviet republics, and South Asia. . . . In Central and Eastern Europe, while Ford, the Open Society Institute, and other major U.S.-based funders like Rockefeller have been strong supporters of public interest law, the European Union ("EU") has also played an important role in funding human rights programs to help countries meet Rule of Law objectives as pre-conditions to EU accession; in addition, legal aid was included in a checklist of reforms for enlarging the EU and thus received EU development assistance. In North America after NAFTA, the Mexican government has become a supporter of U.S. immigrant rights programs, reflecting concern about the treatment of its citizens, whose work in the United States generates significant remittances to México each year.

Cummings & Trubek, *supra*, at 28-32.

Although these funding relationships raise concerns about the power of funders to shape public interest law strategies in less powerful countries, Ellmann observes that the relationships between "First World" funders and NGOs can actually be cooperative and symbiotic, with the grantees even teaching grantors to accept and support new ideas and activities. Ellmann, *supra*, at 357. Do you think funding from the United States and other powerful nations acts to promote or limit advocacy in other countries? What are the costs and benefits? How do these funding issues compare to concerns about the relation between funding and autonomy for domestic public interest law groups, discussed in Chapter 4?

In describing the development of legal aid in China, Titi Liu notes that foreign assistance facilitated but did not ultimately determine the shape of the program, which has both a state and nonstate element.

> In the years leading up to the promulgation of the Regulations on Legal Aid, there was significant donor activity that educated the National Legal Aid Center, the organization charged by the Ministry of Justice with formulating legal aid policy, about legal aid systems in other countries. The primary funders were bilateral and multilateral donors including United Nations Development Program, Canadian International Development Agency, and the Royal Netherlands government; and the form of cooperation was joint research, exchanges, and study visits. In each instance the Chinese counterpart was the Ministry of Justice Legal Aid Center. These activities included study visits to the United States, Canada, the Netherlands, Hong Kong, and the United Kingdom. Translations of legal aid regulations from those countries were also completed. . . .
>
> [D]espite significant foreign assistance by Western bilateral and multilateral donors in drafting the Regulations, the final form of legal aid as defined by the Regulations does not closely resemble the regulations of any foreign jurisdiction that was studied. Government actors virtually monopolize the provision of legal aid, including having the power to assign private lawyers and law firms to cases with minimal compensation. The scope of the types of individuals and cases that qualify for legal aid is very narrow, and there are no effective remedies for denial of legal aid by governmental actors. The legal aid regulations allow the state to claim it is strengthening the legal system, alleviating poverty, and addressing inequality without creating any significant rights for potential legal aid clients. The norm-setting potential of governmental legal aid is minimal. Because of the heavy reliance on private lawyers who handle on average one legal aid case per year, the governmental legal aid centers do not build up

specialized expertise on the issues that economically disadvantaged clients face. In addition, the high degree to which these governmental legal aid centers are embedded within state institutions makes the highlighting of problems within those very institutions highly problematic. . . .

Although the process of developing legal aid regulations was heavily dominated by the state and its interests, and resulted in legal aid centers which were institutionally embedded within the Ministry of Justice administrative structure, other types of legal aid services developed in parallel to the formal governmental legal aid structure. . . .

Since the early 1990s, a small number of non-governmental organization ("NGO") centers have been established by individuals who are recognized as leading thinkers with respect to a particular field of law highly relevant to vulnerable groups. Based at universities or research centers, they rely heavily on part-time and volunteer staff at these institutions having a high degree of specialized expertise. These centers focus on a relatively small set of issues such as gender equality, environmental protection, and criminal legal aid, and engage in advocacy and research in addition to direct representation on the issue.

The domestic actors who established non-governmental legal aid centers were mostly liberal reformers who sought to closely emulate public interest lawyers in other countries, with a particular interest in the United States. They all received their initial funding from Ford and continue to receive core funding from Ford while also diversifying their funding sources to other international funders. They were exposed to American public interest lawyers through various study visits, conferences, and exchanges, and developed a form of litigation that closely tracks the American impact litigation model, using individual cases to highlight systemic issues. While the civil law system makes it difficult for an individual case to have systemic legal impact, the Centers typically choose cases in which individuals seek to challenge abusive practices by local governments or large corporations, whether domestic or international. Center staff then attempt to use advocacy through the media, local people's congress, and other channels to highlight the underlying social justice issue and advocate for change.

The existing space for civil society groups to represent the interests of different constituencies is very limited. There are many restrictions on the establishment of non-governmental organizations in China, and as a result, most of these organizations are informal centers within universities or research centers and are not formally registered. While nonetheless subject to some oversight by their host state-funded institutions, a relative degree of financial and institutional independence from the state enables these legal aid organizations to develop litigation and advocacy strategies that highlight inadequacies in the existing legal system with respect to the protection of the rights of vulnerable groups. In sharp contrast to the governmental legal aid centers, which focus on individual cases, these quasi-NGO centers tend to be oriented towards promoting policy changes around a particular issue.

Liu, *supra*, at 263, 275-81. Based on Liu's description, how do you think the source of funding (inside or outside of China) affects the potential for funded organizations to undertake transformative work—however you might define it?

As Liu's discussion of the more globally oriented NGO legal aid groups suggests, the spread of the U.S. public interest law model has raised questions about whether it can be effectively "transplanted" to new locations with different systems and traditions. Noga Morag-Levine, examining the development of an Israeli environmental advocacy group based on the U.S. model, suggests that such groups are only successful when they are connected to local constituencies and adapt to the reality of local politics. Noga Morag-Levine, *The Politics of Imported Rights: Transplantation and Transformation in an Israeli Environmental Cause-Lawyering Organization, in* CAUSE LAWYERING, *supra,* at 334. Under what conditions do you think the "importation" of public interest models works best — if at all?

One additional example of "transplantation" involves efforts by some U.S. funders to promote pro bono outside of the United States. Consider how pro bono was adapted to the local context in Brazil. In the early 1990s, as Brazil opened up its economy to encourage more international trade and outside investment, its legal profession restricted international law firms' access to the legal market to promote opportunities for itself.

> . . . As law firms were increasingly viewed as important actors in the economic scene, they also had to show commitment to social responsibility, which meant, primarily, undertaking pro bono work. The idea of promoting pro bono is also a consequence of the exchange of clients and personnel with international law firms in the North, and the influence of a new generation of Brazilian law students that started to be trained in American universities. So, although there was a long tradition of involvement of the legal profession with voluntary services and public interest law in the Brazilian legal profession, a new rubric began to be used to designate these services.
>
> Under such conditions, and with the support of the Ford Foundation in Rio de Janeiro, Conectas Direitos Humanos formed a group of top São Paulo lawyers to organize a pro bono initiative in Brazil. Public Counsel, a pro bono organization based in Los Angeles, was of great help in establishing the initiative. The Instituto Pro Bono (IPB) was created in 2001, but faced severe criticism from the local Bar. The ethical committee of the São Paulo section of the Bar questioned some of the founding members, accusing them of promoting unfair competition and co-opting clients. Following a large debate, pro bono activities were regulated through very strict rules in the state of São Paulo. The reaction of the Bar to IPB's creation shows a complete shift of the Bar regarding the role of the legal profession vis-à-vis the poor and disadvantaged. Its Ethical Code of 1930 established free services to the poor as an obligation. Now, following the impoverishment of large portions of the legal profession, the Bar began to view its mission as the protector of market spaces for the legal profession.
>
> Today Instituto Pro Bono mobilizes over 400 attorneys from São Paulo's major law firms that volunteer their time and expertise in support of civil society organizations, and consequently helps a broad range of human rights and public interest causes. IPB works on three major fronts. First, it acts as a clearinghouse for pro bono opportunities. The program has an open door policy for NGOs seeking legal assistance. The IPB team receives the requests from civil society organizations, checks the potential beneficiaries, and frames the cases. After this initial procedure, IPB makes the request available to its network of volunteer lawyers. IPB's experience shows that in less than 12 hours a lawyer will volunteer to take the case. Rare are the circumstances when IPB does not receive an immediate and positive response from the legal profession.

> Even though the Brazilian legal experience has produced several public interest initiatives throughout its history, there is still some skepticism about whether private lawyers from the corporate world are fit to represent human rights and public interest cases. Therefore, most of the requests IPB receives from NGOs for pro bono legal assistance deal with internal administrative, tax or labor concerns, rather than the use of legal strategies to advance their missions and the interests of their constituents.

Vieira, *supra*, at 256-58. As Vieira notes, the response of the local Brazilian bar to the advent of pro bono was not uniformly positive since some elements of the bar viewed pro bono as potentially undercutting the market for paid work at the low-end of the income scale. Thus, as a compromise, the São Paulo State Bar Association permitted pro bono representation only for NGOs; it remains illegal to provide free legal services directly to individuals. As this underscores, attempts to transplant foreign practices must confront and adapt to internal political realities. Given this fact, do you think that it makes sense for Northern sponsors to attempt to "export" concepts like pro bono?

4. Legal Profession

As the Brazilian example highlights, the legal profession may play a role in both promoting and limiting certain types of public interest law. In addition, as the legal profession becomes more globalized, we see globally oriented corporate firms in countries around the world serving an elite global corporate clientele in ways that may influence the development of public interest law systems in their countries. One provocative analysis views the role of globally oriented corporate lawyers as crucial to the rise of public interest law. In this view, domestic lawyers seek to serve global corporate clients as a way to build their own political and economic position within the domestic field of state power; in so doing, they import global rules and practices as part of facilitating the link between their countries and global capital. This process of "modernization" on the corporate side then produces spillover effects that operate to promote the rise of legally oriented NGOs working on policies associated with globalization (like environmental protection) or the domestic Rule of Law (like legal aid). Yves Dezalay & Bryant G. Garth, *Corporate Law Firms, NGOs, and Issues of Legitimacy for a Global Legal Order*, 80 Fordham L. Rev. 2309, 2311-12 (2012). Public interest law-type activities, in this account, grow to give legitimacy to the Rule of Law, so it is not just seen as vehicle for corporate exploitation. In this project, corporate lawyers play key roles. *See* Dezalay & Garth, *supra*, at 217. Their professional status offers relative economic stability and connection to centers of political power, and this has positioned corporate law firms to provide funding and staffing for the establishment of legal aid offices. *Id.* at 220-22. The emergence of issue-focused NGOs is more complicated, since some of them engage in work opposing official government policies, but even here they sometimes benefit from their connections to the legal elite. *Id.* at 223. These types of groups soften the harshest impacts of economic globalization and thus are important for the legitimacy of the legal modernization project.

Do you agree that corporate law and public interest law are inextricably linked in this way? That corporate lawyers are essential to the promotion of public interest law?

5. Networks

Another aspect of transnational advocacy is the development of cross-border networks as a vehicle to launch and sustain global campaigns, share strategies and tactics, or to build professional networks of solidarity and friendship. As the following excerpt highlights, these networks are not primarily North-South, as in the case of funding, but rather can have regional dimensions:

> Cause lawyers in Latin America articulate two principle reasons for forming or participating in cause-lawyering networks: the need to exchange information with other cause lawyers, advocates, and affected groups; and to attempt to alter the behavior of domestic decision makers who would otherwise ignore their demands. Comments from individual cause lawyers are illustrative. According to Soraya Long, of the human rights organization CODEUCA (Commission for Human Rights in Central America) in Costa Rica, the major benefit of linkages with cause lawyers active in other advocacy groups is what she terms "retroalimentacion," or nourishment: By working with and sharing information and strategies with each other, cause lawyers give and receive support for their causes. In addition, the notoriety created by regional and international linkages has allowed cause-lawyering organizations to mount successful human rights campaigns; i.e., they have used international pressure and publicity to influence government officials in their own countries.

Stephen Meili, *Latin American Cause-Lawyering Networks, in* Cause Lawyering and the State in a Global Era, *supra*, at 307, 312.

6. Legal Education

Law schools, in both rich and poor nations, have been crucial to facilitating the cross-border circulation of legal elites, who learn social change theories and techniques from their counterparts around the world. The circulation has occurred in both directions, with lawyers from developing and transitional countries taking graduate degrees in the United States and U.S. lawyers studying abroad. American LL.M. programs have provided important linkages between the U.S. public interest community and foreign lawyers, who capitalize on American training and contacts to support the development of public interest systems in their home countries. One direct effort to train foreign public interest lawyers was NYU's LL.M. program in Public Service Law, which was started in 1998 under the auspices of the Global Public Service Law Project to examine global public interest models and promote cross-cultural collaboration and training. Though the program suspended operations in 2006 for lack of funding, it succeeded during its tenure in producing graduates who returned to public interest law positions in Africa, East Timor, the Philippines, and Argentina. Since 1993, Georgetown's law school has sponsored a Leadership and Advocacy for Women in Africa program that provides an LL.M. to African lawyers committed to returning to their countries to advocate for women's rights; the program includes academic training, a six-month internship with a D.C.-area public interest or governmental organization, and public interest seminars designed to expose students to U.S. public interest methodologies. Harvard also has provided significant training opportunities for foreign lawyers, who may take both masters and Ph.D-level degrees. Although Harvard's track is focused on academic rather than practice-based training, it has nonetheless fostered exchange of public interest law theories and methodologies.

Information exchange has also occurred as the result of U.S. lawyers spending time in foreign law schools seeking to develop new programs and curricula around public interest law. A focus of these exchanges has been to provide support for clinical legal education. In addition to short-term exchange programs funded by major foundations, some U.S. clinicians have engaged in more intensive study through the Fulbright program, which has supported clinicians working to expand and deepen clinical education curricula abroad. In an effort to formalize global information exchange among progressive academics, the Global Alliance for Justice Education was founded in the late 1990s to facilitate the network of clinical and practice-oriented law school professors from around the world interested in promoting social justice pedagogy. Partly as a result of such exchanges, some law schools in the Global South have themselves been important sites for the incubation and practice of public interest law. *See* EDUCATING FOR JUSTICE: SOCIAL VALUES AND LEGAL EDUCATION (Jeremy Cooper & Louise G. Trubek eds., 2007); THE GLOBAL CLINICAL MOVEMENT: EDUCATING LAWYERS FOR SOCIAL JUSTICE (Frank Bloch ed., 2010); Richard J. Wilson, *Three Law School Clinics in Chile, 1970–2000: Innovation, Resistance and Conformity in the Global South*, 8 CLINICAL L. REV. 515, 555-56 (2002); *see also* Stephen Golub, *From the Village to the University: Legal Activism in Bangladesh, in* MANY ROADS TO JUSTICE: THE LAW-RELATED WORK OF FORD FOUNDATION GRANTEES AROUND THE WORLD, *supra* note 27, at 127, 144-45 (detailing Ford's clinical initiative in Bangladesh). Note here, however, the critique of these types of exchanges as promoting a vision of clinics in the Global South dependent on Northern patrons. *See* Bonilla, *supra.*

In addition to faculty exchanges, law school clinics have directly facilitated the connections between law students from around the world who have come together to work collaboratively on social justice projects — sharing insights and learning strategies from one another. Perhaps one of the best examples is Making Rights Real: The Ghana Project at Harvard Law School, through which students work with Ghanian organizations that "focus on the human rights dimensions of Ghana's health policies and practices. . . . Each year, [Harvard Law School] students work with law students from the University of Ghana and Ghanaian community partners to plan and realize Winter term fieldwork, which seek to make the nation's health care system work for all." Harvard Law School, Making Rights Real: The Ghana Project, at http://www.law.harvard.edu/academics/clinical/clinics/ghana.html (last visited Aug. 7. 2012). These and other projects promote the two-way exchange of advocacy ideas and may create a sense of enduring global connection between lawyers from the North and South committed to social justice.

IV. HOW GLOBALIZATION HAS INFLUENCED AMERICAN PUBLIC INTEREST LAW

In the context of international exchange, U.S public interest law has also become inevitably more globalized. The following discussion examines how U.S. public interest law has been influenced by globalization and what impact it has had on lawyering practices.

A. INTERNATIONAL FEATURES OF U.S. PUBLIC INTEREST LAW

Historically, as we have seen, U.S. public interest law was primarily a domestic affair. Now, however, American practice is marked by a number of international features that connect it to the types of advocacy we have just reviewed from around the world. Why has this happened and what are the consequences?

There have been "three defining transnational processes of the modern public interest era" that have "internationalized" U.S. public interest practice:

> (1) the increasing magnitude and changing composition of immigration (bringing in new *clients*), (2) the development and expansion of free market policies and institutions (extending transnational economic *arenas* within which advocacy takes place), and (3) the rise of the international human rights movement (stimulating the importation of new *norms*). . . . [E]ach of these processes has contributed to institutional revisions within the U.S. public interest system: the rise of *immigrant rights* as a distinctive category of public interest practice, the emergence of *transnational advocacy* as a response to the impact of free market policies abroad, and the movement to promote *domestic human rights* both as a way to resist free market policies at home and to defend civil rights and civil liberties in the face of domestic conservatism and antiterrorism.

Cummings, *The Internationalization of Public Interest Law*, 57 DUKE L.J. 891, 896 (2008). This section describes each of these changes in turn.

1. The Rise of Immigrant Rights

U.S. public interest lawyers have always found immigrant clients on the front lines of practice. Yet there have been profound changes since the 1980s. Specifically, there has been a *quantitative* increase in immigration to the United States, combined with a *qualitative* change in both its pattern (more geographically dispersed) and composition (more undocumented entrants). A key aspect of recent migration patterns is the influx of undocumented immigrants, mostly from Mexico, who entered the United States seeking work. As we discussed in Chapter 2, beginning in the 1990s, this trend powered a new wave of immigrant rights advocacy focused on workplace abuse (in contrast to the early orientation of immigration work around political asylum claims, largely from Central American asylum seekers). The dilemma of immigrant rights advocates in this new environment was to figure out how to assert legal protections for a class of noncitizens defined by their "illegality."

2. Advocacy Outside the United States

In addition to serving noncitizen clients inside the United States, American public interest lawyers have also taken the struggle for social justice outside U.S. borders. From a lawyering perspective, the key question is what levers exist for regulating global capital in the absence of global government to impose rules and sanctions. Consider the following excerpt, which describes efforts by U.S. public interest lawyers to promote corporate accountability in the global marketplace and to regulate regional economic activity through trade agreements.

SCOTT L. CUMMINGS, *THE INTERNATIONALIZATION OF PUBLIC INTEREST LAW*

57 Duke L.J. 891, 950-57 (2008)

[T]he outflow of U.S. corporations in search of investment opportunities and low-cost production locales extends it to developing countries abroad. This inside-out movement further challenges domestic legality—not by importing legally degraded labor, as is the case with immigration—but by exporting U.S. corporate activity to deregulated geographic spaces where it escapes the full force of U.S. law. Within these new arenas of U.S. economic activity, the main focus of public interest law becomes upgrading systems of legal governance and regulatory enforcement outside of U.S. borders. . . . Thus, transnational economic activity shapes new forms of transnational advocacy, with public interest lawyers following market activity across U.S. borders into regional and global economic arenas. . . .

For U.S. public interest lawyers, the move toward regional market integration, punctuated by NAFTA [the North American Free Trade Agreement], has focused attention on the unique relationship between the United States and México, which is defined by a gulf in economic and regulatory circumstances that prompts in-migration by Mexicans seeking jobs and out-migration by U.S. companies seeking low-cost labor and a less stringent regulatory environment. . . .

Corporate access to cheap Mexican labor has been the driving force—and major battlefield—of regional market integration. Its symbol is the Mexican maquila program, which has permitted foreign-owned assembly plants to import unfinished goods duty free to the border region, process them using cheap Mexican labor, and then export the final products to the United States with duties imposed only on labor's value added. Despite its opposition to the maquila program as it evolved after its creation in 1965, U.S. organized labor retained an isolationist stance toward México through the 1980s, driven by its staunch opposition to the emerging NAFTA movement and its deep skepticism of the official Mexican union, the pro-integration Confederación de Trabajadores Mexicanos (CTM). The passage of NAFTA in 1994 altered the terrain in two ways that created new opportunities for public interest advocacy focused on transnational workers' rights.

First, NAFTA sparked the formation of new transnational labor networks, composed of progressive unions, like the Mexican Frente Auténtico del Trabajo (FAT), and grassroots organizations, such as the San Antonio-based Coalition for Justice in the Maquiladoras (CJM), that came together to address cross-border grievances. In addition, NAFTA had the effect of internationalizing domestic labor disputes under a side labor agreement that permitted private parties to challenge their home country's failure to enforce domestic labor laws in venues set up within foreign member states. Though the agreement lacked hard enforcement mechanisms, its unique structure did create the potential for political pressure to complement organizing campaigns: successful petitions could be used to provoke high-level "ministerial consultations" about labor violations, outside expert reviews, and — in limited cases — arbitration of disputes.

Because the structure of the side labor process required workers to object to their own government's labor violations by filing a complaint in another member country's National Administrative Office (NAO), it encouraged the formation of transnational networks to execute submissions. On the Mexican side, this meant enlisting U.S. legal groups to bring Mexican grievances to the U.S. NAO — a dynamic that, in turn, drew U.S. groups across the border in support of Mexican labor struggles, which coalesced around two main issues within the maquila sector.

The first wave of Mexican complaints centered on the official system for state certification of union representation, which critics charged was biased in favor of unions affiliated with the CTM and effectively excluded the certification of independent unions, like those allied with the FAT. The D.C.-based International Labor Rights Fund (ILRF), started in the 1980s to monitor labor standards under international trade agreements, emerged as a key organization in these campaigns, providing legal support for petitions challenging Mexican labor practices. In one of the earliest petitions, filed in 1994 by the ILRF and CJM against Sony, workers alleged that local labor boards illegally denied an independent union's request for official registration. Though the independent union did not achieve victory on the Sony plant floor, the United States issued a strong condemnation of Mexican practice and recommended ministerial consultations, which labor activists used to publicly criticize the labor certification process. Three years later, the ILRF helped to file another challenge to the certification system, singling out the labor board for bias and delay that harmed an independent organizing drive at the Han Young truck assembly plant. The U.S. response this time was even stronger, citing the fact that only one independent union existed in the entire maquila sector and charging the local board with imposing obstacles to independent labor organizing in a manner that "is not consistent with Mexico's obligation to effectively enforce its labor laws."

The positive reception given to the petitions around independent union certification prompted advocates to pursue a parallel set of NAFTA complaints focused on workplace conditions, particularly health and safety issues. While attempting to redress health problems within the maquilas, these petitions also sought to test the side labor process: unlike the independent union complaints, petitions alleging health and safety violations were technically open to review by a committee of outside experts — and even arbitration. As with the independent union organizing drive, the health and safety campaign was forged by the ILRF, which in 1997 charged México with permitting maquiladoras to impose illegal pregnancy screening on female job applicants. In response, the Mexican government launched an outreach campaign on antidiscrimination laws and a number of U.S. companies discontinued the screening practice. CJM coordinated the most systematic and well-documented health and safety petition in 2000 on behalf of workers at two U.S.-owned plants who placed leather covers on steering wheels and gear shifts and suffered from a range of musculoskeletal disorders. This petition represented the first drafted with U.S. law school clinics as legal counsel: the International Human Rights Clinic at St. Mary's School of Law in San Antonio helped to prepare the submission, as did the Columbia Law School International Human Rights Clinic. Despite the optimism generated by the NAO's aggressive handling of the case, the transition from the relatively labor-friendly NAO under the Clinton administration to the more hostile Bush NAO thwarted the effort to appeal health and safety claims up the NAFTA system, and signaled a new era of diminished interest in the side labor process as a vehicle for reforming Mexican labor practices.

What does the NAFTA story teach about the levers for lawyers to influence corporate activity abroad? In a context in which U.S. based companies move to Mexico specifically to take advantage of lower working standards, is it even appropriate for U.S. lawyers to pursue cases against them? What other mechanisms do you think are available?

3. Bringing Human Rights Home

For U.S. public interest lawyers, the interest in "bringing human rights home" represents the optimism of the international human rights movement, but also a pragmatic acknowledgment of the limits of domestic law to produce political change at home. The picture of American public interest lawyers — who a generation ago championed the transformation of domestic law for progressive ends — now turning to human rights as a master frame for social change highlights the contrasting fortunes of public interest law at home and its human rights counterpart abroad. It also suggests the strong influence of changing U.S. policy on the circuitous path of human rights domestication. Whereas the international human rights system promoted in the Cold War era was, in part, a way to *export* American-style public interest law to activists in foreign countries resisting authoritarian regimes, the current U.S. human rights movement represents an effort by public interest lawyers to *import* the very norms and methods built through international struggle to contest what they view as the erosion of domestic legal standards resulting from new American policy imperatives: market integration, conservatism, and the War on Terror.

It has been suggested that several factors have promoted domestic human rights advocacy: the creation of institutional opportunities for advocacy within international institutions like the United Nations and Inter-American Human Rights systems; key financial backing from the Ford Foundation, Open Society Institute, and other foundations; the vision of individual leaders and power of growing educational (particularly clinical) opportunities for human rights advocacy; and the creation and extension of U.S. human rights networks. Cummings, *supra*, at 970-92.

Consider the following effort to use human rights as a tool for domestic struggle in the context of U.S. welfare policy. As discussed in earlier chapters, with President Clinton's support, Congress adopted comprehensive welfare legislation in 1996 that resulted in a reduction in the number of people entitled to benefits and a corresponding increase in the number of people living in poverty. In response to the cuts, antipoverty advocacy groups engaged in a range of traditional and nontraditional tactics—including a human rights campaign—to challenge the welfare reform law and call public attention to the real damage it had done.

THE FORD FOUNDATION, CLOSE TO HOME: CASE STUDIES OF HUMAN RIGHTS WORK IN THE UNITED STATES

26-31 (2004)

The Poor People's Economic Human Rights Campaign, a network of grass-roots anti-poverty organizations, was formed in 1997 as a response to welfare reform. . . . Its membership is made up primarily of those who are living in poverty or on welfare. Spearheaded by the Kensington Welfare Rights Union, a Philadelphia-based advocacy organization, the campaign chose the Universal Declaration of Human Rights to show that U.S. welfare policies often violate human rights. As part of this effort, organizations under the umbrella of the rights campaign began gathering testimony from their constituents who felt the effects of welfare reform legislation on their lives. These testimonies were collected in hopes of using an international human rights mechanism or body to hold the U.S. government accountable for these violations of economic rights.

Enter Cathy Albisa, the director of the U.S. Program at The Center for Economic and Social Rights . . . who . . . would play a key role in devising a legal strategy to counter the new welfare policies using human rights.

The Brooklyn-based Center for Economic and Social Rights . . . focuses on strengthening the capacity of U.S.-based anti-poverty activists to use human rights. "The methodology we've adopted at the center is not supposed to create a detached legal project," said Albisa. By supporting grassroots initiatives throughout the country, the center helps link local organizers' efforts directly to international human rights standards and mechanisms and provides resources and training along the way. "We support people who do campaigns. We do trainings with activists and lawyers, do documentation, write reports, and share information with various human rights bodies. We come in and figure out together how best to support their existing work."

In the U.S. courts, public welfare benefits have been determined to be "a privilege" and not a "right." Because U.S. law imposes no governmental duty to ensure social and economic rights, many lawyers allied with the poor people's campaign, including prominent civil rights lawyer Peter Weiss, were intrigued by the idea of using an international mechanism to hold the U.S. government accountable for protecting these rights. After several years and numerous setbacks, their goal was finally realized. . . .

In July 2003, Albisa, along with Monica Leggett, a young mother of three in West Virginia who had reached her lifetime limit on benefits, the Poor People's

Economic Human Rights Campaign and others, filed a petition with the Inter-American Commission on Human Rights, specifically challenging the reform law's five-year lifetime limit on receiving benefits. It was the first petition of its kind to charge the U.S. government with economic human rights violations and the first to challenge U.S. welfare policy before an international human rights body. For the petitioners, however, preparing for the filing had been a bumpy road.

In deciding to file the petition with the IACHR, The Poor People's Economic Human Rights Campaign activists and attorneys were looking for a legal process to emphasize the U.S. government's obligation under international human rights law to end poverty. Several practical factors also made IACHR the right choice: its legal format is flexible regarding admissible evidence, the commission holds hearings where both parties are required to attend and the U.S. government had historically responded to commission requests. Also, unlike other human rights bodies based overseas, the commission headquarters are located in Washington, D.C.; organizers with The Poor People's Economic Human Rights Campaign wanted to file the petition just ahead of a month-long protest march in August 2003 commemorating the 35th anniversary of The Reverend Martin Luther King, Jr.'s Poor People's Campaign.

An earlier version of the petition was first filed in October 1999, but then withdrawn for procedural reasons. Over the next several years, Albisa shepherded it through many drafts as it traveled with her while she worked at several different human rights institutions. The original petition was a broad challenge to the welfare reform legislation. Based on an assertion of the right to social welfare and security, the petition called the reform law a retreat from government responsibility to ensure economic rights. The petition specifically attacked the legislation's work requirements, arbitrary time limits, and denial of benefits to immigrants and convicted felons as economic human rights violations.

In early 1999, Albisa and the other attorneys on the legal team were having difficulty identifying welfare recipients who would be willing to be named as petitioners. Given their general state of economic instability, welfare recipients were hard to find, and even harder to keep track of in an on-going manner. Attorneys also encountered problems in establishing a causal relationship between the harm the person was experiencing and the actual economic rights violation. It was easier to establish harm by invoking broader poverty statistics than proving an individual's circumstances were a direct result of the welfare law. These hurdles meant that the original petition was filed mostly by non-governmental organizations that represented welfare recipients, rather than by the recipients themselves.

In April 2000, the IACHR sent Albisa a letter saying that in order for the petition to be accepted petitioners needed to be individually named victims who were being affected by the violations and whose domestic legal remedies for obtaining or retaining benefits had been exhausted. After reconsidering their strategy, the legal team and the activists decided in late 2001 to narrow its focus to a specific population of the poor that had lost its benefits due to the 1996 welfare law reform. And one of its provisions—the five-year lifetime limit on benefits—was beginning to impact significant numbers of welfare recipients.

The five-year ban was playing out in dramatic fashion in West Virginia. One of the poorest states in the country, almost 18 percent of its population lives below the poverty line compared with 11 percent nationwide. Poverty in the state is particularly stark among households headed by females, with 36 percent living below the poverty line compared to 26 percent nationwide. On Dec. 9, 2002, the West Virginia Supreme Court decided that "regression" of welfare benefits was constitutionally permissible and let stand the state's implementation of the lifetime limit on benefits. . . .

Despite the historic nature of filing an economic human rights petition against the United States, Albisa had to confront the skepticism she and others felt about using the international human rights framework to tackle domestic social justice issues. "In the long run, no use of any legal standard alone is enough to make change. Whatever kind of law it is won't work unless there is a depth of support in the culture for the change," she said. Albisa and other U.S. human rights activists and advocates had to be realistic about applying the higher standards of governmental responsibility articulated in international human rights instruments to a domestic legal system that is unacquainted with and unwelcoming to such challenges.

The IACHR petition strategy has several limitations. The petition process itself is very slow. The commission can sometimes take years to issue a final report. A recent report issued by the commission in July 2002 on indigenous peoples' land rights was based on a petition filed in 1993. . . . More important, the commission has no enforcement power and the U.S. government often disputes or ignores its findings. As the welfare-reform petition shows, the IAC's emphasis on individual victims often requires a narrowly focused complaint that fails to capture the largest number of victims or those most affected by the violations. Finally, international human right mechanisms often seem "foreign" to U.S. activists, who are not always convinced of their effectiveness. Albisa encountered this element of "foreignness" in her search for petitioners. She said that antipoverty organizations were "happy to do what they could to help out," but when she asked them how the human rights approach would be helpful to them "they drew a blank," she said.

In spite of these obstacles, the on-going petition effort has several important benefits. First, attorneys and advocates from the international human rights community have a direct link to the individuals actually experiencing violations of economic rights. The IACHR petition strategy allows these two U.S. communities—international human rights attorneys and advocates and grassroots anti-poverty activists—to work in tandem, doing what each does best. The result is a "common strategy to end poverty, rather than to tinker with the system to alleviate it," Albisa said. Second, the petition process is educating grassroots activists about the value of human rights standards and international human rights mechanisms. Grassroots organizers with The Poor People's Economic Human Rights Campaign as well as attorneys point to the petition and the filing process as a way to "concretize public education efforts," Albisa said. "We use the petition as an example of how it all works, as an example of what economic rights are, as an example of what regression is and as an example of how human rights mechanisms can help," said Albisa.

Finally, during the search for petitioners, current and former welfare recipients have been introduced to international human rights standards and in some cases become involved directly with anti-poverty grassroots organizing in their areas. Albisa described such an instance when she spoke with a woman directly affected by the drug-felony ban. "When I first talked to her about being a petitioner she said 'no' because she wasn't emotionally ready. When she was ready, she also started working directly with the Kensington Welfare Rights Union and now works in their office part-time, goes to demonstrations with them and is very involved. She was homeless until a few months ago. The Kensington Welfare Rights Union helped her get housing."

Do you think it was useful for the advocates to promote human rights in this context? What did they accomplish by doing so? Do you think there are any downsides to using human rights language and strategies in the domestic context? Is there any difference between human rights advocacy in the United States and abroad? Should there be?

Compare the welfare rights story with this summary of death penalty advocacy:

> The major effort to import human rights into domestic racial justice practice has been around racial bias in the criminal justice system. The administration of the death penalty, in particular, has been subject to systematic efforts to bring human rights to bear, reflecting both the strong anti-death penalty orientation of international treaties and the distinct historical trajectory of U.S. death penalty litigation, which was marked by early failure in the Supreme Court to invalidate the death penalty on the ground of racial discrimination. The limit on domestic redress, coupled with the building international movement to restrict the death penalty, spurred U.S. advocates, including those in the NAACP LDF's Capital Defense Project, to create networks with international human rights groups and European abolitionists. Beginning in the 1980s, advocates mounted a campaign to challenge the juvenile death penalty that combined human rights advocacy, organizing, and traditional litigation. At the Inter-American Commission, lawyers brought a series of petitions challenging U.S. juvenile death penalty practice, all of which resulted in findings that the United States violated the right to life set forth in the American Declaration. This Commission litigation complemented human rights organizing against the juvenile death penalty, coordinated primarily by the National Coalition to Abolish the Death Penalty, which worked to build political support at the UN level by providing testimony and materials to UN monitoring bodies. In the United States, the legal campaign culminated in Roper v. Simmons, in which the Supreme Court struck down the juvenile death penalty, referencing an amicus brief condemning the practice on international law grounds filed by Human Rights Advocates.

Cummings, *supra*, at 993-95. Do you think the human rights frame helped here?

B. GLOBAL IMPACT ON U.S. ADVOCACY

The engagement by public interest lawyers with international forces has had a number of domestic impacts. One question involves the degree to which lawyers have adopted different advocacy approaches in the face of greater global exchange. The following excerpt suggests three ways in which lawyers' tactics have been influenced by global engagement.

SCOTT L. CUMMINGS, *THE INTERNATIONALIZATION OF PUBLIC INTEREST LAW*
_____

57 Duke L.J. 891, 1015-23 (2008)

In contrast to the traditional focus on litigation, lawyering in the international sphere readily incorporates nonlegal techniques — organizing, policy advocacy, and publicity — to advance goals. The emphasis on multifaceted advocacy over narrow legal representation is a product of both strategic necessity and tactical innovation. To the degree that public interest lawyers find domestic courts inhospitable, alternative strategies are a must: as lawyers move into what they view as more receptive fora, such as the human rights system, traditional strategies do not apply with the same force, and nontraditional techniques, such as lobbying and reporting, are required. And even in contexts in which domestic courts are technically available, the perception of their limited effectiveness prompts lawyers to supplement legal with nonlegal strategies. An important example of this within the immigrant rights field is the emergence of worker centers that combine legal, organizing, and policy advocacy to respond to immigrant labor abuse, which advocates see as resistant to conventional rights enforcement strategies. The complex nature of transnational problems, which cut across multiple jurisdictional boundaries, also invites flexible responses. In the environmental context, in particular, the transnational scope of environmental harm causes lawyers to approach problems from the perspective of an advocacy campaign rather than a legal case. . . .

The current wave of international practice also challenges the claim that the pursuit of legal rights necessarily co-opts transformative political action. As the domestic human rights and immigrant rights movements highlight, lawyers are both sensitive to the potential political risks of rights strategies and skillful in deploying rights in flexible and pragmatic ways to leverage short-term policy gains and stimulate long-term political mobilization. Thus, rights are not simply viewed as claims to be invoked in court, but are also seen as resources to help frame policy demands and motivate grassroots action. . . .

Tactical decisions — *how* to advocate — are framed by locational decisions — *where* to advocate. It is often the case that a lack of alternative options dictates the locus of advocacy. Yet the move into different venues is not simply a matter of lawyers being pushed out of domestic fora. Instead, groups may choose to enter international venues out of an effort to influence international decisionmaking processes that impact client constituencies. In addition, international venues offer alternative platforms from which to assert political pressure for domestic gain. This polycentrism invites lawyers to move into multiple arenas, where they are required to calculate strategic costs and benefits, weighing which venues offer the greatest possibilities for politically meaningful intervention.

In undertaking this calculus, lawyers balance aims of enforceability, legitimacy, and publicity. The question of enforceability implicates debates about "hard" versus "soft" law strategies and their relative merits. Do lawyers turn to venues that have the capacity to issue directives that are binding on state and private actors and have clearly defined methods of enforcement ("hard" law)? Or do they opt for venues that lack mechanisms for directly constraining action, but nonetheless establish norms and offer opportunities for participation that promote negotiation and flexible compliance standards ("soft" law)?

Public interest lawyers operating on the global stage resist this either-or dichotomy, looking instead for ways to enlist both hard and soft law systems in mutually reinforcing ways. Advocacy around workers' rights offers one perspective on this dynamic. Where venues offer the potential for legal enforceability, lawyers take advantage of them to bring workers' rights claims. Domestically, lawyers have therefore invested heavily in wage-and-hour enforcement actions for immigrant workers, while the potential for enforceability has also drawn lawyers to use the [Alien Tort Statute] in federal courts to pursue transnational labor claims against offending corporations. Outside of U.S. courts, however, opportunities for hard enforcement are sharply curtailed. Engagement in soft law regimes is therefore increasingly common. But even when advocates enter soft law venues, it is not always the case that they do so simply with an eye toward leveraging political pressure. Rather, some groups have also sought to "harden" soft law systems by expanding the possibilities for legal enforcement from within. Engagement in soft law venues may therefore reflect not just a commitment to flexibility, but also an effort to *transform the venues themselves*.

Advocacy within the NAFTA side labor agreement, which provides a soft monitoring and reporting system, suggests this type of effort. Though labor advocates have used the NAFTA process as a venue to raise public awareness about labor abuse, their early efforts were also designed as test cases to push the system in the direction of greater enforceability. In particular, the early maquiladora labor cases on health and safety issues saw advocates pushing to see how far the United States would go in pressing for outside expert review and arbitration, which are technically available under the agreement. This effort failed, in part because of the transition from the Clinton to Bush administration, but it reflected an effort to promote greater enforcement within the system, rather than simply a commitment to its soft law orientation. . . .

Enforceability, however, is not the only metric for evaluating engagement with international venues. To the degree that the choice of venue is made to advance a political cause, a central question is how venue selection may impact the *audience* advocates seek to influence. At times, that audience may be a group's own constituency, which the group seeks to mobilize by using an international decision to publicize a cause and galvanize grassroots action. For example, when the Center for Economic and Social Rights filed its 2003 Inter-American petition challenging the international legality of welfare reform, it was timed to coincide with a march planned to commemorate Martin Luther King Jr.'s Poor People's Campaign. Thus, the goal was partly to use the media attention generated by the petition to draw people to the march. In addition, the petition sought to reframe the issue of welfare reform in human rights terms as part of a coordinated effort to promote grassroots education about human rights among the welfare population and raise awareness about the antipoverty organizing efforts of the Philadelphia-based Kensington Welfare Rights Union and the Poor People's Economic Human Rights Campaign that it led. Again, the aim was to produce publicity that would bring community members into the campaign's organizing fold.

In other contexts, venue selection is designed to put pressure on an identified set of corporate or political decisionmakers. There, the strategy is to use a venue's authority to spotlight wrongdoing and legitimate grievances, bringing negative publicity to bear in an effort to force decisionmakers to take remedial action. In the case of corporate wrongdoing, the choice of venue is often designed to elicit a negative reaction from consumers or investors. . . .

———————

Do you think that public interest lawyering in the United States is becoming more like the legal mobilization strategies abroad that we've read about in this chapter? Why or why not? Is there such thing as global public interest lawyering?

PART **IV**

EPILOGUE

Chapter 10: New Directions, Ongoing Challenges

10

NEW DIRECTIONS, ONGOING CHALLENGES

I. INTRODUCTION

This concluding chapter examines how public interest lawyers continue to adapt and redefine their practices to make a difference in the evolving world in which they work. It asks how these lawyers, confronting the contemporary political terrain—with persistent and evolving forms of inequality and oppression—understand the possibilities of their advocacy and develop strategies to promote change in the face of significant obstacles and strong opposition. It thus explores new directions that public interest lawyers are forging—and the ongoing challenges they face.

The chapter begins by briefly revisiting central concerns about public interest lawyering that we have seen throughout the book—mainly, that it can be unaccountable to communities and ineffective in producing enduring change. It then offers two case studies of legal campaigns that seek to advance different types of systemic reform in the contemporary environment. The first is the multidimensional advocacy campaign to establish the statewide right of same-sex couples to marry in California; the second is a local campaign by labor, environmental, and community groups to stop the opening of a Wal-Mart big-box store in Los Angeles. These campaigns represent only one type of contemporary public interest practice—movement lawyering for systemic reform—but highlight important theoretical and empirical themes in the broader field.

As you read these case studies, consider the following questions. How do the lawyers in these campaigns think about and attempt to address concerns about accountability and effectiveness? How, if at all, do these efforts differ from others we have explored in this book? Do you think that the approaches of lawyers in these studies offer models for lawyers who are planning public interest law campaigns in other fields? What do they teach us about how to evaluate the success of such campaigns? Finally, what do they tell us about the ongoing challenges that public interest lawyers face? Picking up on this last question, we conclude by considering some of the central challenges to public interest lawyering as the movement, launched a half-century ago, confronts its next phase.

II. THE LIMITS OF PUBLIC INTEREST LAW

Although the very concept of public interest lawyering optimistically asserts the power to change, practitioners and commentators—both inside and outside the movement—have long noted its problems and limits. As we have explored throughout the book, concerns about public interest law have centered on questions about legitimacy and accountability, on the one hand, and effectiveness, on the other. This section briefly reviews these arguments in order to frame the case studies that follow.

Recall that from a systemic perspective, there are two basic criticisms of public interest lawyering—one focused on legitimacy costs and the other on the potential disjuncture between lawyer goals and client interests. With respect to legitimacy concerns, critics have argued that in a democracy it is inappropriate for lawyers to accomplish social change through litigation. *See* David Luban, Lawyers and Justice: An Ethical Study 303 (1988). They describe such practices as "social engineering" through the courts, which can undermine the majoritarian political process. The accountability concern is that public interest lawyers can be unresponsive to the constituencies they purport to represent, making crucial political and tactical decisions to advance a cause that are not based on input from—and, in extreme cases, may even be inconsistent with the interests of—the affected class. In this vein, recall Derrick Bell's argument that public interest lawyers may sacrifice the best interests of their clients in order to serve the broader cause they seek to support. Derrick A. Bell, Jr., *Serving Two Masters: Integration Ideals and Client Interests in School Desegregation Litigation*, 85 Yale L.J. 470 (1976).

Each of these concerns presumes, in different ways, that public interest lawyering *is effective* in promoting social reform—the worry is that its effectiveness comes at too high a price. In contrast, other critics have argued just the opposite—that public interest law practice does not advance change in meaningful, sustainable, and effective ways. As we have seen, there are multiple clusters of efficacy concerns. One focuses on the practical limits of rights claims in general and litigation in particular. These limits are based on factors such as the individualistic nature of rights, the inability of courts to enforce their own orders, and the administrative discretion of bureaucrats responsible for implementing reforms. *See* Joel F. Handler, Social Movements and the Legal System: A Theory of Law Reform and Social Change 18-22 (1978); Gerald N. Rosenberg, The Hollow Hope: Can Courts Bring About Social Change? 10-21 (2d ed. 2008) [hereinafter, Rosenberg, Hollow Hope]; Stuart A. Scheingold, The Politics of Rights: Lawyers, Public Policy, and Political Change 5-7 (2d ed. 2004).

Another set of concerns focuses on how law may undercut social movements. Reform litigation that succeeds in establishing new legal principles through Supreme Court decisions or other publicized changes in the law can also produce a backlash by those who disagree with the outcomes, diminishing the initial gains achieved. *See, e.g.*, Michael J. Klarman, Brown *and* Lawrence (*and* Goodridge), 104 Mich. L. Rev. 431 (2005) [hereinafter, Klarman, Goodridge]; Michael J. Klarman, *How* Brown *Changed Race Relations: The Backlash Thesis*, 81 J. Am. Hist. 81 (1994); Gerald N. Rosenberg, *Saul Alinsky and the*

Litigation Campaign to Win the Right to Same-Sex Marriage, 42 J. Marshall L. Rev. 643, 643 (2009). For example, some of the major constitutional criminal procedure decisions of the 1960s not only created new rights for persons accused of crimes, but also changed the landscape of the national political debate about crime and acted as a lightning rod for a new law and order agenda that proved politically powerful for the Republican Party. Samuel Walker, In Defense of American Liberties: A History of the ACLU 252 (1990). Similarly, some observers attribute the intensity, solidification, and effectiveness of the anti-abortion movement to the Court's decision in *Roe v. Wade*, which served as a call to action for those opposed to legal abortion. *But see* Linda Greenhouse & Reva B. Siegel, *Before (and After)* Roe v. Wade*: New Questions About Backlash*, 120 Yale L.J. 2028, 2086 (2011) (noting that the anti-abortion movement was growing in power prior to *Roe* in opposition to state laws permitting abortion); Thomas M. Keck, *Beyond Backlash: Assessing the Impact of Judicial Decisions on LGBT Rights*, 43 Law & Soc'y Rev. 151, 152 (2009) (questioning the backlash thesis in the same-sex marriage context). Moreover, prioritizing litigation can drain limited resources from other social reform campaigns, thus undermining potentially more effective and sustainable mobilization efforts. *See, e.g.,* Michael W. McCann, Taking Reform Seriously: Perspectives on Public Interest Liberalism 200 (1986); Rosenberg, *supra*, at 423. The discourse of liberal rights can also limit the transformative imagination of movements and thus circumscribe what they can accomplish.

Finally, there are concerns that public interest law can be detrimental not only to causes, but also to the clients it purports to serve, for example, by offering false hope that diminishes the urgency that people feel about investing in other forms of social change work. Scheingold, *supra*, at 6, 91, 204; Orly Lobel, *The Paradox of Extralegal Activism: Critical Legal Consciousness and Transformative Politics*, 120 Harv. L. Rev. 937, 939 (2007). Radical critics suggest that an individual, case-centered, rights-based litigation approach legitimizes and perpetuates the existing social order in ways that counteract real social progress. Peter Gabel & Paul Harris, *Building Power and Breaking Images: Critical Legal Theory and the Practice of Law*, 11 N.Y.U. Rev. L. & Soc. Change 369, 375 (1983) ("an excessive preoccupation with 'rights-consciousness' tends in the long run to reinforce alienation and powerlessness, because the appeal to rights inherently affirms that the source of social power resides in the State rather than in the people themselves."); *see also* Scheingold, *supra*, at 204 (arguing that law inherently sustains the status quo, first, because of its close connection to the "dominant configurations of power," and second, because in its "ideological incarnation," it encourages faith in the political system by presenting it as "beneficent and adaptable"). In addition, public interest lawyers simply may not fully understand the negative consequences that can sometimes befall clients engaged in controversial cases, such as the commitment of time and other resources and the potential for retaliation or alienation from their communities.

How should we understand these concerns in the context of contemporary public interest practice? Note that much of the criticism of public interest lawyers is based on accounts of social change litigation from the mid- to late-twentieth century. *See* Alan K. Chen, *Rights Lawyer Essentialism and the*

Next Generation of Rights Critics, 111 Mich. L. Rev. ___ (forthcoming 2013). Yet as we have seen (both domestically and globally), many public interest lawyers now adopt a complex, multidimensional approach to addressing social problems—one that combines traditional tools like litigation with other tactics and mobilizes communities to create reform and take a more central role in addressing the problems they face. How do contemporary public interest lawyers think of and respond to the concerns raised above? Do their practices mitigate or reproduce the problems of accountability and effectiveness? What new challenges do public interest lawyers face?

III. NEW DIRECTIONS: STORIES FROM THE FIELD

The new stories of public interest lawyering come out of different substantive areas, respond to distinct political opportunities and constraints, and reflect a range of strategic and tactical approaches. There is a rich and growing literature that describes and analyzes sophisticated campaigns for social change, highlighting the many roles law can play both domestically and around the world. *See, e.g.,* Cause Lawyers and Social Movements (Austin Sarat & Stuart Scheingold eds., 2006); Fighting for Political Freedom: Comparative Studies of the Legal Complex and Political Liberalism (Terence C. Halliday, Lucien Karpik & Malcolm M. Feeley eds., 2007); Jennifer Gordon, Suburban Sweatshops: The Fight for Immigrant Rights (2005); Law and Globalization from Below: Towards a Cosmopolitan Legality (Boaventura de Sousa Santos & César A. Rodriguez-Garavito eds., 2005); Michael W. McCann, Rights at Work: Pay Equity Reform and the Politics of Legal Mobilization (1994). As this work illustrates, careful case studies of law and social change campaigns can provide rich descriptive accounts of the strategic and tactical decisions that lawyers and other movement leaders have to make and whether those decisions prove effective, what barriers arise, which institutional settings are the battlegrounds for the campaign and why, how groups collaborate and work against opponents to reach their desired goals, and what happens in the aftermath of even a successful campaign. From this vantage point, we can examine campaigns in great detail and extrapolate from those accounts in ways that may help to inform future efforts and identify important factors for assessing what makes a campaign successful.

In this section, we offer two different stories of contemporary public interest advocacy. The stories by no means represent the range of legal activism that characterizes contemporary practice, but are illustrative of distinct approaches and are useful lenses through which to reexamine the field's central questions. The first case study comes out of the campaign for marriage equality in California, where public interest lawyers have pursued a more top-down reform strategy (led by lawyers) across multiple policy domains (primarily at the state level) on behalf of a diverse constituency of same-sex couples. The second involves the pursuit of better conditions for low-wage workers, in which lawyers represent a community-labor coalition (relatively strong, but organizationally complex) to advance policy reform from the bottom up—in the sense that the community-based client group (not its lawyers) is driving the policy reform strategy, which takes place in the local legislative arena. As you read these stories, ask yourself how they compare to other examples of public interest lawyering you have encountered in this book or in your own experience. How do they respond to the critiques above? What do they tell us about the future direction of public interest lawyering?

A. THE MARRIAGE EQUALITY MOVEMENT

The movement to establish the right of same-sex couples to marry has been one of the most prominent social movement struggles in recent times. As this book goes to press, six states, plus the District of Columbia, have legalized same-sex marriage; thirty states have banned it, either by statute or state constitutional amendment. The issue may be resolved in the United States Supreme Court, where a case from California challenging that state's ban, *Perry v. Brown*, is now on appeal.

Debate about the strategy to advance same-sex marriage has centered on the role of litigation and backlash. Critics such as Gerald Rosenberg have argued that litigation has undermined progress toward the recognition of same-sex marriage in ways analogous to what he contends were the failures of school desegregation and abortion rights litigation campaigns. Specifically, Rosenberg claims that state court decisions on same-sex marriage and relationship recognition in Massachusetts, Hawaii, and Vermont have provoked a national backlash that has undermined the movement. He lays blame on movement lawyers, claiming that "[s]ame-sex marriage proponents had not built a successful movement that could persuade their fellow citizens to support their cause and pressure political leaders to change the law. Without such a movement behind them, winning these court cases sparked an enormous backlash. Lawyers confused a judicial pronouncement of rights with the attainment of those rights. The battle for same-sex marriage would have been better served if they had never brought litigation, or had lost their cases." Gerald N. Rosenberg, *Courting Disaster: Looking for Change in All the Wrong Places*, 54 Drake L. Rev. 795, 813 (2006) [hereinafter Rosenberg, *Courting Disaster*]. Similarly, in Michael Klarman's view, watershed cases promoting relationship equality for gays and lesbians, such as *Lawrence v. Texas* and *Goodridge v. Dep't of Public Health*, led to significant and effective backlash, including the adoption of constitutional amendments in 13 states limiting marriage to heterosexual couples; the mobilization of the Christian right and other social conservatives to increase turnout in the 2004 presidential election in numbers that may have actually changed the election's outcome; a similar mobilization affecting turnout and results in key states where there were closely contested U.S. Senate races, helping Republicans increase their Senate majority; and the bolstering of confidence for conservative activists to continue their efforts to contest marriage equality. Klarman, Goodridge, *supra*, at 466-72; *but see* Michael Klarman, *Marriage Equality: Are Lawsuits the Best Way?*, Harv. L. Bull., Summer 2009, at 7, 9 (stating that litigation may have had some impact in advancing marriage reform).

Against this backdrop, we turn to a case study of how movement lawyers have sought to advance the right to marry for same-sex couples in California.

Scott L. Cumming & Douglas NeJaime, *Lawyering for Marriage Equality*, 57 UCLA L. Rev. 1235 (2010) [hereinafter, Cummings & NeJaime]. To understand the role that lawyers and litigation have played in the marriage equality movement, it is useful to trace the complex series of events that led to the current state of affairs. The early phase of the movement was marked by a first wave of unsuccessful litigation challenging restrictions on same-sex marriage in the 1970s and early 1980s. These cases were not the product of a strategic approach by movement lawyers, but were initiated by private lawyers. In fact, gay rights organizations were just beginning to emerge at this point. There was an early, internal debate among movement lawyers about whether marriage equality was essential to gay rights or whether marriage should not be the ultimate goal for same-sex couples because it was too narrowly defined, did not recognize other non-traditional relationships, and was steeped in gender stereotypes. In 1986, when the Supreme Court decided *Bowers v. Hardwick*, denying constitutional protection for same-sex adult couples to engage in private, consensual sexual conduct, the movement retreated from marriage equality as a priority. *Bowers* was also a signal that federal impact litigation to seek marriage equality was not likely to be a successful short-run strategy. Instead, movement lawyers emphasized efforts to overturn state sodomy laws through state law claims brought in state courts. Cummings & NeJaime, *supra*, at 1248-50. Lawyers and activists also pursued domestic partnership and other relationship recognition laws at the state and local level.

On the heels of spirited intra-movement debate over whether to pursue marriage, movement lawyers collectively decided not to pursue marriage litigation. While some were motivated by normative commitments rejecting marriage as a movement goal, others had strategic reasons — fearful of precisely the type of backlash that critics anticipated. However, that did not stop private efforts to do so. In Hawaii, a private attorney represented same-sex couples in a case that resulted in the Hawaii Supreme Court's decision in *Baehr v. Lewin*, 852 P.2d 44 (Haw. 1993), which held that Hawaii's restriction against same-sex marriage constituted a sex-based classification that must be justified by a compelling governmental interest. Before the trial court ultimately concluded that the state could not meet the strict scrutiny standard required under state constitutional law, a backlash formed. Hawaii voters enacted a state constitutional amendment reserving the determination of marriage to the state legislature, which adhered to a same-sex marriage ban. As part of the political compromise to put that initiative on the ballot, however, the state legislature also adopted a law that opened up limited rights and legal benefits to same-sex couples. Cummings & NeJaime, *supra*, at 1249-50.

The reverberations from the Hawaii marriage equality case reached California and had two immediate repercussions. First, it mobilized marriage equality opponents, who began efforts, parallel to those that led to the enactment of the federal Defense of Marriage Act (DOMA), to push through a state law banning the state from recognizing the unions of same-sex couples who were married in other states where such marriages were legal. Second, the events in Hawaii led movement lawyers in leading LGBT rights organizations to undertake a careful evaluation of their strategic options.

To develop a long term-strategy, leaders from a range of organizations came together to discuss the best approach to advancing the marriage equality cause. "The tactical decision to deemphasize marriage and avoid courts was devised by a group of leading LGBT rights lawyers in California. Lawyers affiliated with the key LGBT legal organizations—Lambda Legal, NCLR [the National Center for Lesbian Rights], and the ACLU—combined elite academic credentials with deep experience in the LGBT movement." *Id.* at 1253. This group decided to pursue a legislative campaign to enact a California domestic partnership law. The lawyers engaged in a broader discussion of the merits of long-term marriage equality litigation, but opted not to pursue litigation in California out of backlash concerns. Instead, movement lawyers decided to target marriage litigation in states that had more favorable conditions: strong LGBT legal protections in other contexts (like antidiscrimination law), sympathetic public opinion, a receptive judiciary, and a state constitution that was difficult to amend in the event of a judicial victory. California did not present hospitable conditions for litigation, particularly because state supreme court justices were subject to reconfirmation elections (which had resulted in the removal of three liberal justices in the 1980s in an effort led by conservative activists) and because California law made it relatively easy to amend the state constitution through ballot initiative. *Id.*

Movement lawyers thus pursued a legislative strategy to confer on domestic partners rights similar to those attached to marriage, such as rights to hospital visitation, insurance proceeds and government benefits, and adoption and inheritance. California legislators introduced bills to extend some rights to domestic partners, which included both same-sex and different-sex unmarried couples (such as seniors). In 1999, Governor Gray Davis signed AB 26, California's first domestic partnership law, which extended modest rights to hospital visitation and health benefits to partners of government employees.

Even this incremental success mobilized marriage equality opponents, who viewed it as a movement toward full marriage equality. In response to AB 26, marriage opponents placed on the ballot an initiative labeled Proposition 22, which sought to amend state law to prohibit the recognition of same-sex marriage. While California law already limited marriage to a relationship between a man and woman, another state law provision recognized marriages from outside the state as valid. Thus, the principal effect of Proposition 22 was to prevent California from recognizing same-sex marriages from other states. After an expensive and hard-fought political campaign, the measure was enacted by a wide margin in 2000, thus imposing a statutory ban on the recognition of same-sex marriage in California.

As with any major setback in a social movement, the enactment of Proposition 22 provoked a robust dialogue among marriage equality supporters about future strategy. Some were radicalized, viewing Proposition 22 as a sign that the movement lawyers' incrementalist legislative approach had failed—and that a more assertive legal strategy was necessary. Others believed that Proposition 22 underscored the power of same-sex marriage opponents to mobilize, which they argued would also occur (and perhaps even be more likely to occur) in response to an aggressive litigation approach. Against the backdrop of this debate, movement leaders had to decide whether to challenge Proposition 22 in court. They opted not to, based on a determination that their chance of success was limited and that Proposition 22's practical impact was likely small, since same-sex marriage was not at that time recognized in any other state. Lawyers were also not certain that Proposition 22 would even operate as a legal bar to a future California law recognizing same-sex marriage.

In the aftermath of the Proposition 22 campaign, marriage equality activists determined that they needed a stronger political organization. As with any coalition, there was some concern that there was not a sufficiently strong and centralized leadership structure to facilitate and coordinate supporting organizations and individuals. Equality California emerged as the newly energized political arm of the movement, emphasizing public education and legislative advocacy in the continued pursuit of comprehensive domestic partnership benefits as a step toward same-sex marriage. Spurred by the group's efforts, California enacted important legislation that expanded the rights of domestic partners to include the right to adopt a partner's children, substitute medical decision making when a partner became incapacitated, take leave to care for a partner with health issues, sue for a partner's wrongful death, and inherit a partner's property. In a signature achievement built on years of struggle, movement leaders ultimately won the enactment of AB 205, a comprehensive domestic partnership benefits act giving same-sex couples all of the rights and privileges of marriage (without the title), which the governor signed in 2003.

During this same period, movement lawyers continued to explore the possibility of a litigation strategy to achieve marriage equality. In 2003, movement leaders and academics met at UCLA as the California Marriage Litigation Roundtable to consider a range of factors bearing on a possible frontal legal challenge to California's marriage ban — including case theory, precedent, possible forums, judicial profiles, the likelihood of success on the legal merits, and the potential for reversal by statewide initiative. Once again, the group determined that it was not the right time to bring marriage litigation, primarily because advocates feared the likely backlash through the state ballot initiative process and were not confident they could defend a favorable court decision against such a challenge. After extensive discussion, the group concluded that an affirmative marriage case should not be considered until 2006 at the earliest.

Movement lawyers then turned their attention to defending AB 205, the domestic partnership law, which was immediately challenged by conservative groups in court on the theory that it violated Proposition 22. Opponents had briefly considered a ballot initiative to repeal AB 205, but did not view that as having a high chance of success. Equality California and some domestic partners who had registered under the act were allowed to intervene in the litigation to help the State defend the law. The California appellate court ultimately rejected the challenge, agreeing with marriage equality proponents that the language of Proposition 22 was limited to banning marriage recognition, not to precluding the enactment of domestic partnership — an issue that was not put to the voters in the initiative process. *See Knight v. Superior Court*, 26 Cal. Rptr. 3d 687 (Ct. App. 2005). Thus, although they had lost the fight to defeat Proposition 22 in the first instance, movement lawyers prevailed in their defense of the domestic partnership law in court on arguments rooted in popular democracy.

The next stage of the campaign centered on what to do in the wake of two 2003 cases: the Supreme Court's decision in *Lawrence v. Texas*, 539 U.S. 558 (2003), invalidating the state's anti-sodomy law as a violation of the Fourteenth Amendment's Due Process Clause, and the Massachusetts Supreme Judicial Court's decision in *Goodridge v. Dep't of Public Health*, 798 N.E.2d 941 (Mass. 2003), which held that same-sex couples had the right to marry under the Massachusetts Constitution. With these two victories propelling the movement forward, some activists believed that the time was ripe to advance a same-sex marriage bill in the California legislature. But there were concerns about whether this would succeed with an upcoming presidential election, in which same-sex marriage would be used as a wedge issue. However, the debate was cut dramatically short by San Francisco Mayor Gavin Newsom's decision (based on his own interpretation of the California Constitution in light of *Goodridge*) that same-sex couples could marry. In early 2004, he ordered the county clerk to begin issuing marriage licenses to same-sex couples in San Francisco. Newsom's move was met with mixed reaction among marriage equality supporters, who believed that Newsom was substantively correct but worried that his actions would trigger an immediate counter-movement. Some movement leaders tried to dissuade Newsom from carrying out his plan, but he persisted.

Marriage equality supporters were thus forced to decide how to respond to Newsom's actions. After much debate, movement lawyers determined that they could be most effective running a public education effort to help defend Newsom's decision. In addition, they anticipated an inevitable legal challenge to Newsom's order. What followed was two lawsuits by conservative organizations seeking to invalidate Newsom's order on the ground that it was beyond local government authority to issue marriage licenses to same-sex couples. Marriage equality groups intervened to join the city in defending the order. The San Francisco City Attorney filed a cross-complaint directly raising the issue of whether the California marriage law was unconstitutional. Other litigation ensued, all of which was consolidated into one case titled *In re Marriage Cases*. As recounted below, there were a number of important strategic decisions about how best to present the constitutional arguments against the California marriage law and whether and how to introduce a record that would support the strongest constitutional claims. In the end, the California Supreme Court issued a landmark ruling in 2008 declaring that the state law limiting marriage to a man and a woman violated the state constitution on both due process and equal protection grounds. *In re Marriage Cases*, 183 P.3d 384, 400-01 (Cal. 2008).

As movement lawyers had predicted, the struggle immediately returned to the political arena, where marriage equality opponents launched a campaign to pass a ballot initiative, Proposition 8, to overturn the California Supreme Court's ruling. In November 2008, California voters approved Proposition 8 in a close election, 52 percent to 48 percent, and *In re Marriage Cases* was overturned.

As a result, marriage equality supporters were placed in the position they had long sought to avoid and were forced to reassess their options in the face of a devastating electoral loss. While the enactment of Proposition 8 provoked widespread protest at the local and national levels, there was no obvious path to respond to the initiative. Movement lawyers brought a lawsuit to challenge the process by which Proposition 8 was adopted, arguing that because it "revised" rather than "amended" the state constitution it needed to be approved by two-thirds of the legislature before it could be submitted to voters. However, in *Strauss v. Horton*, 207 P.3d 48 (Cal. 2009), the state supreme court rejected that challenge. In one bright spot in the opinion for marriage equality supporters, the court in *Strauss* ruled that Proposition 8 did not affect the marriages that had occurred prior to its enactment. The California legislature then enacted SB 54, which required that California recognize same-sex marriages performed in other states prior to the date on which Proposition 8 was enacted. But the broader validation of Proposition 8 refocused attention on whether the time had come to consider a federal court challenge to the constitutionality of the same-sex marriage ban — a challenge that would possibly set a national precedent vindicating marriage equality or deal it a profound legal blow. The stakes were high.

Movement lawyers did not change their view about which path to take. Before Proposition 8 was enacted, they had issued a statement discouraging a federal lawsuit in the event that the measure was approved. After Proposition 8 passed, the pressure to file such a challenge mounted, but the consensus of movement lawyers was that it was not the right time to bring such a case. Yet they could not stop private lawyers from going to court, which is precisely what happened in 2009 when a group called American Foundation for Equal Rights (AFER) retained lawyers to file *Perry v. Schwarzenegger*, a case on behalf of same-sex couples challenging Proposition 8 on federal constitutional grounds. The lead attorney in the case is Ted Olson, an elite private law firm lawyer with strong ties to the Republican Party who was the Solicitor General of the United States under President George W. Bush. His co-counsel is David Boies, an equally prominent lawyer affiliated with the Democratic Party. For an excellent account of the decision leading up to the filing of the case, see Margaret Talbot, *A Risky Proposal*, The New Yorker, Jan. 18, 2010, at 40.

Though Olson consulted with some LGBT rights attorneys before the suit was filed, movement leaders claimed to have not learned of its actual filing until it was publicly announced. Having not made the initial decision to file, movement lawyers found themselves in a difficult position. They could try to intervene, they could participate as amicus curiae, or they could file a separate, parallel suit. They initially decided to participate as amici, but that position changed over an important tactical point. Though the trial judge had indicated that he felt it was necessary to hold a trial and develop an evidentiary record, Olson and his team resisted a trial, viewing the challenge to Proposition 8 as purely a matter of constitutional law. At that point, movement lawyers sought to intervene in the case, but Olson's team vigorously opposed the motion on the basis that there would be too many lawyers trying to control the course of the plaintiffs' case. The trial court rejected the motion to intervene and limited the movement lawyers to participating as amici. However, the pressure on the plaintiffs' team from the advocates' motion, as well as a successful motion to intervene by the City of San Francisco, whose attorneys also supported the need for a strong trial record, moved the case toward trial. At that point, the movement lawyers tried to support the plaintiffs' case by helping to provide background information and identify strong expert witnesses, and by using their amicus role to help steer the court to a narrow ruling that would be less subject to attack. The trial judge ruled after a full trial that Proposition 8 was unconstitutional because it violated both the Due Process Clause and the Equal Protection Clause of the Fourteenth Amendment. 704 F. Supp. 2d 921 (N.D. Cal. 2010). The Ninth Circuit Court of Appeals affirmed the trial court's decision on equal protection grounds. *Perry v. Brown*, 671 F.3d 1052 (9th Cir. 2012), *reh'g en banc denied*, 681 F.3d 1065 (9th Cir. 2012). At the time this book went to print, a petition from the supporters of Proposition 8 for grant of review by the Supreme Court was pending.

The complex, and still ongoing, course of the California marriage equality campaign highlights important features of contemporary public interest practice. The authors of the case study summarize their findings as follows:

> The California campaign is framed by three overarching dynamics. The first is movement lawyers' resistance to affirmative litigation and the influence of external events and countermovement actors in ultimately drawing lawyers into court to challenge the marriage ban. In California, the legal rights campaign to establish marriage equality through judicial decree began, paradoxically, as an effort by LGBT rights advocates to pursue a legislative strategy. The second related dynamic is LGBT rights advocates' deliberate attempt to coordinate their efforts across the litigation, legislative, and organizing domains. Throughout the campaign, lawyers not only pursued multiple avenues of reform, but did so with an eye toward how advocacy in one arena would impact advocacy in another. Third, the record of policy achievements in support of same-sex relationships was substantial: from no laws recognizing same-sex couples in the late 1990s to comprehensive domestic partnership in 2005 to some legally recognized marriages by 2010. It is true that by the end of the decade, Proposition 8 and the federal challenge to it overshadowed these developments, but this occurred over the objection of movement lawyers—not because of them.

Cummings & NeJaime, *supra*, at 1247-48.

B. THE CAMPAIGN AGAINST BIG-BOX RETAILERS

In 2003, a coalition of labor unions, community and workers' rights organizations, environmental activists, and other groups formed a campaign to stop Wal-Mart from locating one of its big-box "Supercenter"[1] stores in Inglewood, California—a working-class, largely African-American city in Los Angeles County. The coalition's central concerns with the planned siting were typical of those in other areas of the country where communities have objected to the building of big-box stores. While these stores offer jobs to the local community and savings to consumers, they do so in part by paying workers low wages enabled by their opposition to unionization. More broadly, the

---

1. Supercenters are Wal-Mart retail stores that are especially large and are able to combine under one roof a grocery operation as well as a full complement of retail products.

opening of big-box stores with nonunionized grocery workers has long been viewed as an existential threat to unionized grocery workers in traditional grocery store chains—thus provoking the resistance of union leaders. Yet the fact that big-box stores offer some benefits to low- and middle-income consumers often divides communities over whether they provide a net gain despite the costs to workers. The following summary is drawn from a case study of the Wal-Mart site fight. *See* Scott L. Cummings, *Law in the Labor Movement's Challenge to Wal-Mart: A Case Study of the Inglewood Site Fight*, 95 CAL. L. REV. 1927 (2007) [hereinafter, Cummings, *Wal-Mart*].

The Inglewood campaign took place against the backdrop of the declining power of labor unions at the national level over the past half-century. This decline has been attributed to a number of factors. These include significant restrictions on federal labor law rights and lax enforcement of protections for workers that undercuts unionization drives. Unions have also faced internal challenges, including what some observers have viewed as a bloated bureaucratic structure that has focused too heavily on collective bargaining and politics, rather than mobilizing workers from the bottom up. At the same time, dramatic changes in the global economy have eased employers' ability to ship jobs overseas, reducing unions' bargaining power. Domestically, the movement toward increasing labor flexibility, such as hiring more part-time and contract workers, has also eroded organized labor's power.

In this environment, the United Food and Commercial Workers union (UFCW), which represents retail and grocery workers nationally, has been unsuccessful in trying to organize Wal-Mart employees despite several attempts. In addition to facing the same broader challenges to unions just described, the UFCW has confronted specific obstacles in its efforts to unionize Wal-Mart. These include Wal-Mart's internal policies, which have emphasized employing part-time workers who are less likely to organize because of detachment and vulnerability; Wal-Mart's early focus on opening stores in "right to work" states, making it harder to organize; and the company's vigilant maintenance of an anti-union culture. UFCW has also lacked a strong national strategy for organizing Wal-Mart workers and the resources to fight Wal-Mart's substantial efforts at preventing unions from forming.

Confronted by these barriers, activists who objected to Wal-Mart's plans for the Inglewood site looked for an effective alternative to traditional union organizing.

> In the face of the challenges to traditional unionism, labor leaders in the Wal-Mart context have followed a broader arc of movement activism . . . turning away from the traditional paradigm of federally supervised union organizing and toward an alternative model emphasizing local coalition building and policy reform designed to increase union density in targeted industries. This turn to localism responds to three central features of the contemporary field of labor activism. First, it targets non-exportable industries tied to local economies—either because they offer inherently immobile services, have fiscal ties to local governments, or gain economic benefits through association with larger regional economies—that offer key opportunities for union organizing. Second, it takes strategic advantage of the spatial configuration of political power, de-emphasizing advocacy within the now more conservative federal

government and instead building political alliances with progressive big-city officials who possess the political will to advance regulation on behalf of their low-wage worker constituents. Finally, labor's local strategy provides it with distinct legal levers for advancing union organizing goals that are unavailable at the federal level.

Id. at 1942.

Following this strategy, the campaign to limit Wal-Mart big-box stores began with an effort to lobby the state legislature to enact legislation banning them from locating in California. The legislature passed the act, but the governor vetoed it. Labor leaders then looked to the local level, where they hoped to persuade city governments to adopt policies that would either ban big-box stores or strengthen the rights of employees through living wage ordinances that might ameliorate the stores' negative impact. The UFCW took the early lead on the campaign, working with the Los Angeles Alliance for a New Economy (LAANE), one of a small but growing number of local organizations that work to mobilize organized labor and community- and faith-based groups around issues of economic justice.

The coalition's next step was to advocate for a local ordinance banning big-box stores. The Inglewood city council initially passed the law, but then repealed it in the face of pressure from Wal-Mart, which threatened to sue the city to invalidate the ordinance as having been improperly enacted. The UFCW responded by focusing on electoral work, helping unseat an incumbent pro-Wal-Mart city council member and thus tipping the power on the city council to Wal-Mart opponents ready to revisit a local ban.

Wal-Mart then went on the offensive, creating a front group called the Citizens Committee to Welcome Wal-Mart to Inglewood, which gathered enough signatures to place an initiative titled "Measure 04-A" on the local ballot. If passed, Measure 04-A would have mandated Supercenter development uses on the precise site that Wal-Mart owned and had targeted for its store — thus bypassing the typical city land use approval and environmental review process. In response, LAANE spearheaded the formation of the Coalition for a Better Inglewood (CBI), made up of local residents, sympathetic public officials, local union members, and representatives from community-based religious and economic justice groups.

The fight over Measure 04-A illustrates the complexity of ballot initiative fights. Wal-Mart launched a sophisticated public relations campaign to persuade Inglewood voters that they would benefit from new jobs and sales tax revenues generated by the Supercenter. Though it lacked the finances to compete on par with Wal-Mart, CBI worked with a political consulting firm to disseminate information that provided a counter-narrative — one that showed that Wal-Mart's entry into low-income communities tended to adversely affect local business and suppress wages and benefits. When polling data showed that CBI's message was not influencing voters' views, the coalition changed strategy to emphasize that Wal-Mart was circumventing the regular legal process for approving development and used heavy grassroots outreach efforts to get that message into the community. The final piece of the election strategy was an aggressive get-out-the-vote campaign to generate high turnout among those voters likely to oppose Measure 04-A.

Parallel to this organizing strategy was a legal strategy that examined a variety of possible responses to the initiative. Strategists considered litigation challenges to the measure that would either get it removed from the ballot or invalidate it if enacted. Lawyers contemplated the possibility of challenging the measure on the ground that it circumvented local government control over land use planning and environmental review. Another factor in developing a legal strategy was that California provides strong protection to ballot initiatives (which are sometimes proposed by progressive groups as well), making a legal challenge to enjoin the vote both difficult and potentially harmful in the long run. LAANE formed a large legal team to consider all legal theories that might be used to defeat Measure 04-A in court, ultimately opting to file a pre-election challenge to keep the initiative off the ballot. This effort was unsuccessful, but generated publicity that may have had positive effects for the campaign by underscoring the message that Wal-Mart was not playing by the normal rules. The legal team then turned to planning a post-election suit to invalidate Measure 04-A.

In the end, the success of the grassroots campaign rendered a post-election lawsuit moot as Inglewood voters defeated Measure 04-A by a decisive margin. It was Wal-Mart's first ballot-box defeat and an embarrassing setback in the company's Southern California expansion plans, particularly in light of the fact that Wal-Mart had spent over $1 million to secure the initiative's passage.

The momentum from the campaign carried over to the enactment of innovative citywide Superstore Ordinances—first in Los Angeles, then in Inglewood—that made any future effort by Wal-Mart to open a Supercenter more difficult. After Measure 04-A was defeated, coalition leaders debated the wisdom of again trying to pursue a total ban of big-box stores, which was likely to trigger a lawsuit. They ultimately decided to mobilize behind a less rigid big-box ordinance focused on compelling companies that wanted to locate big-box retail stores in the community to first conduct a cost-benefit analysis to evaluate the potential adverse economic effects (similar to the process of environmental review). UFCW and LAANE lawyers and staff members took the lead in coordinating with the Los Angeles City Attorney's Office to draft the new ordinance. LAANE's outside lawyer produced and circulated drafts based on policy input from staff and then made revisions based on feedback from the groups; she also testified and prepared other community members to testify at a Los Angeles city council hearing to build a strong public record for the ordinance. LAANE staff and the UFCW's general counsel managed the process of educating council members and coordinating community input. Despite early hostility, Wal-Mart eventually accepted the ordinance once it became clear that it had the overwhelming support of the city council. In August 2004, after roughly three months of negotiations, Los Angeles passed the nation's first Superstores Ordinance requiring an economic impact analysis demonstrating the absence of adverse economic impacts prior to big-box approval. A similar ordinance was enacted in Inglewood two years later.

The Inglewood case study illustrates the complexity and fluidity of contemporary advocacy, which in that campaign included: an initially successful legislative initiative (big-box store ban) that was met with strong opposition and repeal; a focus on electoral politics to build a more sympathetic city council; a defensive legislative campaign (opposing Measure 04-A) that employed a targeted public education effort as well as a conventional get-out-the-vote drive; a preventative litigation campaign (with the anticipation of a post-election challenge as a backstop tactic); and a post-election legislative effort to both forestall future big-box developments and position the community to gain economic benefits should a site be approved. As a coda, despite this success, the issue of Wal-Mart entering the Los Angeles area remains very much alive and indeed has become a central labor issue once again with the 2012 announcement by Wal-Mart that it had acquired a site and gained city approval to open a store in Los Angeles's historic Chinatown.

IV. LESSONS

What do these stories teach us about contemporary advocacy? In this section, we place the case studies in context, identifying a set of themes that may be useful to (aspiring and actual) public interest lawyers and scholars of law and social movements. We offer two vantage points, one strategic and the other evaluative. First, the case studies provide a window into the strategic and tactical choices made by movement lawyers. What do you think about those choices? How were they made? Do you think they were sound? Second, the studies allow us to reconsider how to measure the success of social movements in relation to the strategic and tactical choices made by activists and lawyers. We have presented examples of social change campaigns that employed multi-tiered tactical approaches integrating affirmative and defensive litigation, legislative work, public education initiatives, and other mobilization efforts. These campaigns had many successes, but also setbacks; their leaders often made effective strategic decisions, but sometimes miscalculated. In this section we ask: What impact did the legal advocacy in the marriage equality and big-box context have on outcomes? How did lawyers address accountability concerns? Did they succeed?

A. OPPORTUNITY STRUCTURE AND POWER ANALYSIS

No social change campaign writes on a blank slate. As public interest lawyers approach a campaign, they must take inventory of the social, political, legal, and cultural context in which it is planned and conducted. In so doing, they evaluate the existing political opportunity structure in order to identify the best route to move power to achieve their political goals. What factors do — or should — public interest lawyers consider in developing their approach?

1. Rights Regime and Movement Goals

At the outset of a social change campaign, lawyers and activists may undertake an analysis of how the extant rights regime relates to their constituents. Do members of the group seeking reform lack formal legal rights or suffer from the non- or under-enforcement of existing rights? If no formal rights exist, how can they best be acquired? Or is it even "rights" that the constituents want? If not, what are the desired goals and how can they most effectively be reached? If formal rights exist, but are unenforced, what are the reasons for the lack of enforcement? And which institutions (government, nonprofits, private actors) or individuals can best undertake the job of enforcement? Are there barriers to the potential agents of enforcement carrying out such action? Are there structural impediments (e.g., lack of funding, cumbersome administrative bureaucracies) to enforcing rights even if the political will to enforce them exists?

In the context of the California marriage equality campaign, the existing legal framework was inimical to movement goals, which thus focused advocates squarely on changing the law — as well as cultural attitudes — regarding same-sex relationship rights. Same-sex couples who wanted to marry clearly lacked the formal legal right to do so. On the positive side of the legal analysis was the fact that during the course of the campaign the U.S. Supreme Court announced that the Fourteenth Amendment's Due Process Clause provided constitutional protection for same-sex couples to engage in consensual sexual conduct in the privacy of their homes. *Lawrence v. Texas*, 539 U.S. 558 (2003). Also relevant were positive judicial decisions, including the Massachusetts Supreme Judicial Court's recognition of the legal right of same-sex couples to marry and the Vermont Supreme Court's finding that same-sex couples must be given the state-law rights and benefits of marriage even if through a nonmarital recognition regime. Another important aspect of the legal background was the powerful counter-movement, in part sparked by the decisions in these other states. Opponents of marriage equality had already won the passage of DOMA and parallel laws in many states denying the recognition of out-of-state same-sex marriages. At the same time, there were an increasing number of state laws recognizing a range of rights for domestic partners, making those relationships more like marriage, although still not equivalent.

The legal background for the Wal-Mart campaign was quite different. Labor rights activists opposed to the siting of the Wal-Mart Supercenter in Inglewood first considered federal labor law. Recall that one of the initial goals of the campaign was not to ban Wal-Mart per se, but to leverage control over the siting decision into stronger rights for Wal-Mart employees to improve their working conditions. One way to protect those rights would have been to unionize Wal-Mart workers. But campaign organizers knew that enforcement of federal labor law rights was not likely to effectively address the problem. Although the National Labor Relations Act created a legal framework for collective bargaining, judicial and administrative decisions, combined with weak enforcement, undercut its utility for unions. In addition, Wal-Mart's policies and anti-union practices made it a particularly difficult target of unionization.

Outside the Inglewood site fight context, labor advocates had used strategic lawsuits to hold Wal-Mart to its obligation to comply with wage-and-hour and antidiscrimination law.

> In the Wal-Mart context, litigation has been used as an important technique to ensure compliance with minimum labor standards — a weapon for exposing

intrafirm violations, challenging illegal labor practices, and holding the company to account. Litigation has obvious limits from a labor perspective, since the goal of labor activism is typically to use the collective power of workers to raise standards above the legally mandated floor. However, strategic lawsuits targeted at Wal-Mart labor violations could have a systemic impact to the degree that Wal-Mart's pricing structure requires it to cut legal corners to maintain its low labor costs. . . . [W]ell-known lawsuits have alleged that Wal-Mart fails to provide state-mandated meal breaks, forces employees to work off-the-clock, violates child labor laws by requiring minors to work too many hours, and contracts with janitorial services that employ undocumented immigrant workers who are denied minimum wage and overtime. To the extent that such litigation can enforce legal baselines that are systematically flouted, Wal-Mart may be forced to reevaluate its pricing and wage policies to ensure ongoing legal compliance. In addition, advocates can coordinate impact cases with a media strategy to publicize wrongdoing in a way that raises the visibility of labor abuse and increases public pressure to reform. Labor unions have generally supported these lawsuits, publicizing them as examples of Wal-Mart's systematic mistreatment of workers.

Cummings, *Wal-Mart, supra*, at 1946-47.

However, a lawsuit to enforce workers' employment rights was not available in the Inglewood context because the campaign sought to influence workplace practices prospectively—and such suits typically provide relief for retroactive harm. In general, employee rights suits also had the downside of requiring piecemeal enforcement rather than providing a comprehensive strategy to negotiate enhanced labor rights for all employees. Lawyers could seek to gain broader leverage over Wal-Mart employment policies through a large-scale class action—and, before the Inglewood campaign began, a team of public interest lawyers had filed such a lawsuit on behalf of over one million female Wal-Mart workers who claimed they were denied promotions and paid less than their male counterparts. However, after a decade of litigation, the U.S. Supreme Court declined to certify the class on the ground that it did not involve common questions of law since the employment decisions at issue were individualized and not the result of an overall policy. *See Wal-Mart Stores, Inc. v. Dukes*, ___ U.S. ___, 131 S. Ct. 2541 (2011).

Given the limits of federal labor and employment law, advocates in the Wal-Mart campaign turned to consider the potential of state and local law to advance their goals. In order to advance labor rights, leaders of the campaign thus looked beyond labor law to see if they could gain leverage through state and local environmental, zoning, and land use regulations to stop Wal-Mart's development or at least condition it on changes to Wal-Mart's workplace practices. Toward this end, coalition leaders assessed how they could use existing land use law to address the potential negative impacts of a Supercenter (such as the closure of local businesses), while ultimately crafting a new land use law (the Superstores Ordinance) that conditioned big-box store approval on a careful evaluation of its economic impact. In this way, advocates creatively used non-labor rights regimes to advance core labor goals in the face of weak federal labor law.

2. Political Background

Leaders of the marriage equality movement were deeply conscious of the volatile politics of same-sex marriage. From the outset, in their consideration of whether to pursue marriage litigation, movement lawyers evaluated the degree to which there was sufficient political support in the state to defeat any popular initiative that might overturn a positive state court decision. Moreover, they were sensitive to the fact that they had support from some important elite members of the political establishment, who could help advance a legislative agenda. Working with officials who were politically accountable required sensitivity to their focus on re-election. For example, Governor Gray Davis asked advocates not to push high-profile LGBT issues during the year leading up to his re-election campaign. This commitment came with a quid pro quo: in exchange for helping the governor to be re-elected, advocates secured Davis's commitment to support comprehensive domestic partnership legislation in his second term. Cummings & NeJaime, *supra*, at 1265.

In the Wal-Mart case, the political context offered a different set of opportunities and challenges. A statewide restriction seemed unlikely given organized labor's earlier unsuccessful effort to secure a big-box ban. And Wal-Mart's choice of Inglewood as a separately incorporated city was deliberately designed to avoid having to go through Los Angeles's more pro-labor city government for approval. Cummings, *Wal-Mart, supra*, at 1956. Moreover, "the identity of Inglewood as an African American working class city was an important feature, which played into Wal-Mart's broader strategy of exploiting tensions between black leaders and organized labor — with its disreputable history of racial discrimination — in order to swing community members in favor of proposed stores." *Id.* Inglewood was also politically diverse. Some Inglewood city council members initially expressed opposition to the Wal-Mart siting and labor activists were thus able to generate sufficient political support to get the city to enact an ordinance banning big-box stores. *Id.* at 1958. But the tide shifted rapidly after Wal-Mart threatened litigation challenging the ordinance as having been improperly enacted under local law and the city council swiftly repealed it. Movement leaders then turned their attention to running a candidate against one of the Inglewood council members who was a Wal-Mart supporter, ultimately tipping the balance of power on the city council back to the anti-Wal-Mart members. *Id.* at 1958-59. As this underscores, leaders viewed political strategies (gaining a sympathetic city council majority) as deeply intertwined with their grassroots and legal strategy (thwarting Measure 04-A and passing the Superstores Ordinance).

3. Social Context

For social reform to advance and take effect, changing popular opinion and cultural attitudes is perhaps even more important than changing formal law and policy. *See, e.g.*, ROSENBERG, HOLLOW HOPE, *supra*, at 415; Thomas B. Stoddard, *Bleeding Heart: Reflections on Using the Law to Make Social Change*, 72 N.Y.U. L.

Rev. 967, 978 (1997). Cultural change is key to the sustainability of social change. At the same time, trying to overcome embedded cultural norms is one of the greatest challenges for reformers.

The cultural context of the marriage equality movement was complex. At one level, there was deep polarization and hostility. The nation was profoundly divided over the issue of same-sex marriage. Organized social conservative opposition to same-sex marriage remained powerful, as reflected in the large number of states that had passed statutes or constitutional amendments banning marriage between same-sex partners. In addition, the pursuit of same-sex marriage through courts — like other highly charged social issues in the so-called culture war — appeared vulnerable to the conservative critique of the anti-democratic nature of judicially mandated reforms. *See, e.g., Romer v. Evans*, 517 U.S. 620, 652 (1996) (Scalia, J., dissenting) ("I think it no business of the courts (as opposed to the political branches) to take sides in this culture war."). At the same time, movement leaders could feel some confidence in other cultural shifts that signaled more positive views about same-sex couples. For instance, there was clear evidence that younger people were more supportive of the right of same-sex couples to marry. Andrew Gelman, Jeffrey Lax & Justin Phillips, *Over Time, a Gay Marriage Groundswell*, N.Y. Times, Aug. 22, 2010, at WK3. And there were some positive legal trends suggesting that attitudes were changing. An increasing number of states and private employers had begun to recognize benefits for domestic partners, including those in gay and lesbian relationships. Even before *Lawrence*, 40 states had either repealed their consensual sodomy laws or had them invalidated by state court decisions. Sheldon Bernard Lyke, Lawrence *as an Eighth Amendment Case: Sodomy and the Evolving Standards of Decency*, 15 Wm. & Mary J. Women & L. 633, 657-58 tbl. 1, 660-61 tbl. 3 (2009).

In the Wal-Mart campaign, movement leaders confronted a cultural landscape marked by the diminishing power and popularity of national labor unions. Institutionally, Wal-Mart's strong corporate culture was defined by hostility to unionism, which was portrayed as inimical to Wal-Mart's narrative about the employer-employee relationship as rooted in family and community values. Wal-Mart had also developed significant consumer loyalty in low-income and middle-class communities by offering easy access to goods with low prices, which created potential tensions between the interests of consumers and workers. Furthermore, Wal-Mart had been able to garner support from African-American leaders suspicious of unions and eager to see development (particularly grocery stores) in disinvested areas, thus exposing divisions between organized labor and certain civil rights groups. *Id.* at 1956.

B. MULTIDIMENSIONAL STRATEGIES

Most public interest lawyers no longer operate in a single forum or use a single mode of advocacy. These lawyers develop campaigns on parallel tracks, including litigation, policy and legislative advocacy, community and public education, media advocacy, and international or transnational advocacy. As a result of critical scholarship, as well as changes in the composition of the bench, litigation is now increasingly de-centered and no longer presumed to be the

preeminent strategy for social change. Nonetheless, our organizational partners, already engaged in other mobilization and advocacy efforts, seek counsel
to file cases before many different kinds of courts and agencies. These organizations are opportunistic and develop their campaigns through as many means
as possible. They understand that each legal and political advocacy method is
contingent and ineffectual in isolation.

> Sameer M. Ashar, *Law Clinics and Collective Mobilization*, 14 Clinical L. Rev. 355,
> 399 (2008).

One hallmark of the approach taken in each campaign is the employment of
a variety of tactical options to advance social reform. This model of multidimen-
sional advocacy has been adopted more broadly. *See* Po Jen Yap & Holning Lau,
Public Interest Litigation in Asia: An Overview, in Public Interest Litigation in Asia 1, 5
(Po Jen Yap & Holning Lau eds., 2011); Ford Foundation, Close to Home: Case
Studies of Human Rights Work in the United States 13 (2004); Michael McCann &
Helena Silverstein, *Rethinking Law's "Allurements": A Relational Analysis of Social
Movement Lawyers in the United States, in* Cause Lawyering: Political Commitments
and Professional Responsibilities 261 (Austin Sarat & Stuart Scheingold eds., 1998).
Within it, public interest lawyers move beyond a litigation-centric focus to
embrace other approaches to social change (canvassed in Chapter 5), including
legislative and policy advocacy, community organizing (including community
economic development), and public education and media work. The lawyers
evaluate which of these tactics are optimal for particular facets of a social change
campaign. Moreover, they seek to understand how these tactics interact with
one another and how they can be mutually reinforcing as part of a comprehensive mobilization strategy that addresses many of the critiques of the traditional
model of public interest practice.

1. Evaluating and Deploying Multiple Tactics

The crux of the standard critique of public interest lawyering is that it too
heavily emphasizes affirmative litigation to the exclusion of other forms of
advocacy and mobilization. To some degree, these critiques were overstated
even at the time they were first articulated. Accounts of earlier phases of public
interest practice demonstrate that it was not limited to advocacy in court. *See,
e.g.,* Handler, *supra,* at 3. Law reform activity was never simply about achieving
splashy judicial decisions, but also was designed to promote consciousness-raising and enhance movement legitimacy by using the legal system "as a vehicle to
make clients and the community aware of goals and issues." *Id.* Stuart Scheingold, best known as a thoughtful critic of public interest litigation, articulated
what he styled "the politics of rights," which offered an alternative vision of
public interest practice that viewed litigation not as an isolated tactic, but as an
element of advocacy that could spur mobilization. As he argued:

> Rights are no more than a political resource which can be deployed, primarily
> through litigation, to spark hopes and indignation. Rights can contribute to
> political activation and organization, thus planting and nurturing the seeds of
> mobilization. . . . Mobilization thus emerges from this perspective as the strat-
> egy, litigation as a contributory tactic, and rights as a source of leverage. With

mobilization as the centerpiece, it is immediately clear that legal tactics cannot be judged in isolation. Their utility is derived from mobilization and cannot transcend the opportunities inherent in that strategy. Moreover, effective mobilization is surely not the automatic consequence of deploying rights. So far, all that has been established is that legal tactics can make a contribution to mobilization.

Scheingold, *supra*, at 204-05; *see also* Scott L. Cummings & Deborah L. Rhode, *Public Interest Litigation: Insights from Theory and Practice*, 36 Fordham Urb. L.J. 603, 609 (2009) (noting that recent "research sees law as politics by another name, and links courtroom battles to political mobilization and community organizing. In these accounts, litigation is shaped by clients and community activists and the objective is political transformation, not doctrinal victory.").

Moreover, it is worth underscoring that earlier versions of public interest litigation were not viewed in isolation. *See* Tomiko Brown-Nagin, Courage to Dissent: Atlanta and the Long History of the Civil Rights Movement (2011); Kenneth W. Mack, *Rethinking Civil Rights Lawyering and Politics in the Era Before Brown*, 115 Yale L.J. 256 (2005). Rather, such work was envisioned as part of a larger, organic enterprise within a social movement that was closely related to other events and strategies. Consider Professor Tushnet's analysis of the NAACP's school desegregation litigation campaign.

> The NAACP's litigation effort illustrates the dimensions of litigation as a social process. A group of people discover that they agree that something is wrong. They formulate their grievance in light of what they have learned over the course of their lives. They discuss matters with their lawyers, and the grievance may be reshaped. They present their claims, and discover that a remedy will not be immediately forthcoming, and that the remedy may provide some of them with what they want while depriving others of what they may already have. Their opponents respond, sometimes by settling the dispute, sometimes by changing their behavior to make it harder for the plaintiffs to win. However the courts respond to a lawsuit, the problem is not resolved. Settlements and decrees must be enforced. Often the locus of controversy shifts from the courts to the legislatures, as prevailing plaintiffs seek more effective relief, or as losing plaintiffs seek to get some relief from someone. Thus the social process of litigation begins well before a lawsuit is filed and ends well after a judgment is entered.

Mark V. Tushnet, The NAACP's Legal Strategy Against Segregated Education, 1925-1950 143-44 (2d ed. 2005); *see also* Michael McCann, Rights at Work, *supra*; Robert L. Rabin, *Lawyers for Social Change: Perspectives on Public Interest Law*, 28 Stan. L. Rev. 210-24 (1976).

Even to the extent that the litigation-centric focus of public interest lawyers carries force as a retroactive critique, there may have been good reasons for public interest lawyers to pursue it *at the time.*

> In a political moment in which radical progressive social transformation seemed possible, and in an intellectual moment in which the limitations of court-led social change strategies were not fully appreciated, it was understandable that a radical vision of the just society would be used as the metric of success against which public interest law's achievements would be judged.

However, in retrospect, it seems unfair to measure public interest law's impact by the gap between where we are and where we would ultimately like to be, rather than by the distance between where we are and where we started—a distance traveled in the face of implacable political opposition triggered not simply by public interest law but by the collective efforts of progressive political movements. Particularly if we begin from the premise that courts are constrained in their ability to produce change, we might ask whether public interest lawyers have effectively leveraged the judiciary's power to advance progressive causes—incrementally, but forward nonetheless—rather than judging success on the basis of fully and faithfully implemented judicial decisions.

Scott L. Cummings, *The Pursuit of Legal Rights—and Beyond*, 59 UCLA L. Rev. 506, 554 (2012). As this suggests, in the early phase of the public interest law movement, liberal public interest litigation was attractive precisely because courts were more receptive to large public law cases and judges were typically more willing to engage in activist decision making to implement social reform. HANDLER, *supra*, 1-2. When those conditions change, public interest advocacy changes with it.

The case studies summarized in this chapter illustrate the impact of this change and lawyers' response to it. In each case, lawyers viewed litigation tactics not in isolation, but as part of a comprehensive set of tools that are useful in advancing social reform. This understanding has sometimes been described as "tactical pluralism." *See* Barbara L. Bezdek, *Alinsky's Prescription: Democracy Alongside Law*, 42 J. MARSHALL L. REV. 723, 748 (2009); Cummings, *Wal-Mart, supra*, at 1932. Contemporary movement leaders examine the potential range of tactics and evaluate the benefits and risks of each against the background factors discussed above (and in the manner described in Chapter 5).

For example, in each campaign, lawyers were willing and able to design campaigns that incorporated lobbying for legislative reform. This occurred in a creative and pro-active way, seeking to establish new rights or legal duties, and in a defensive manner, fighting against the enactment of regressive legislation. In the marriage equality campaign, for example, litigation initially took a back seat to legislative reform tactics and public education. As described above, movement leaders in California specifically avoided litigation at the outset because they had doubts about the likelihood of success and feared political backlash even if they won. In this sense, they were being responsive to the criticisms of Rosenberg and others about the need to establish broader public acceptance through political mobilization before judicial decisions could be meaningful. ROSENBERG, HOLLOW HOPE, *supra*. "LGBT movement lawyers prioritized a nonlitigation strategy over litigation, and conceptualized litigation as a tactic that succeeds only when it works in conjunction with other techniques—specifically, legislative advocacy and public education." Cummings & NeJaime, *supra*, at 1312. Thus, the California marriage equality campaign started out with a strategy to incrementally expand rights for domestic partners through state legislation.

Public education also played a large role in these campaigns, suggesting that contemporary public interest lawyers consider such work to be central to their mission. Marriage equality advocates in California effectively employed public education both affirmatively and in response to some of the setbacks or unanticipated events their campaign faced. For example, after San Francisco announced it was granting marriage licenses to same-sex couples in 2004, movement leaders selected Del Martin and Phyllis Lyon, a lesbian couple who had been together for 50 years, as the first couple to get married as a symbol of the type of loving and committed relationships the law would recognize. *Id.* at 1278-79. In doing so, advocates sought to "shape media coverage by highlighting the marriage of Del and Phyllis, and then using the fact that four thousand same-sex couples had been married [in San Francisco following the Newsom decision] without event to argue that there was no threat to marriage as an institution." *Id.* at 1311. This approach was designed to show the human side of the legal battle as a way of diminishing political resistance to marriage equality—to underscore that gay and lesbian couples, many of whom already had children together, were simply people trying to form families.

Community organizing was also an essential element of the marriage equality campaign. Following voters' enactment of Proposition 8, which overruled the California Supreme Court decision protecting same-sex marriage, there were widespread public demonstrations. Many of these were coordinated by movement lawyers as they considered their next tactical options. "The passage of Proposition 8 unleashed a wave of protests both within California and around the country, many of which were facilitated by activists on social networking sites like Facebook. Join the Impact, a group created immediately after the passage of Proposition 8, established a website used to coordinate a National Day of Protest on November 15 that saw hundreds of thousands of protesters turn out across the country." *Id.* at 1296.

As the case study authors observe, lawyers in the marriage equality campaign were sophisticated and broad-minded in their approaches.

> LGBT rights lawyers in California appreciated the relationship between litigation and nonlitigation strategies and made decisions based on how to maximize overall success. They understood that court-centered disputes constitute one of the many ways in which ongoing social conflicts play out. Accordingly, they did not look to courts as saviors, but rather saw them as just one of the many players in the marriage equality movement. Similarly, they viewed litigation as just one tactic in their repertoire, seizing upon the dynamic relationship among courts, other governmental branches, elites, and the public.

Id. at 1317.

The Wal-Mart campaign, too, illustrates tactical pluralism and a problem-solving approach to social reform. The lawyers and other organizers in that effort neither relied on litigation nor discarded it completely. Rather, litigation was "[d]eployed as part of a broader repertoire" from which they could choose. Cummings, *Wal-Mart, supra*, at 1985.

The story of the Wal-Mart site fight shows that activists and lawyers conceived of the effort to mobilize the community to participate in the land use planning process as a major part of the campaign. Lawyers advised community leaders about the possibility of seeking an amendment to local land use laws to address concerns with big-box stores, and helped mobilize them to participate in the land use process to either block the development or negotiate community benefits as a condition of site approval. The latter approach grew out of strategies coalition members had used to promote community participation in the approval of local development deals as a way to secure community benefits. Overall, the lawyers working on the campaign shared the goal of empowering community groups to directly engage in the process of advocating for more accountable development projects. *Id.* at 1986-87.

Toward this end, lawyers in the Wal-Mart campaign collaborated with activists on a range of advocacy efforts, including advancing legislation, coordinating public relations, and mobilizing grassroots support. *Id.* at 1988. The main legislative work involved drafting, negotiating, and lobbying in support of the Superstores Ordinances in Los Angeles and Inglewood, which amended land use laws to require big-box developers to evaluate and potentially ameliorate their stores' negative economic impacts on the local community. *Id.* at 1948-50. Lawyers also collaborated with coalition members on political strategy in response to Measure 04-A, the ballot initiative that would have bypassed normal land use processes in approving the big-box site. Coalition members conducted a public relations outreach campaign, first to show the negative impact Wal-Mart stores could have on the community, and later, to persuade voters that Wal-Mart was circumventing the ordinary process for development approval by abusing the initiative process. The coalition also worked to promote voter turnout as the election approached. Organizers deployed outreach techniques that included public presentations about Wal-Mart, phone banks, press conferences, and other media and community education efforts. *Id.* at 1962.

2. Tactical Synergies

As the case studies reveal, lawyers working on multifaceted social change campaigns are attentive to the dynamic relationship among different tactical options they employ. That is, advocates execute tactical options with an eye toward how one tactic may influence the success of another. Both the California marriage equality battle and the Wal-Mart site fight illustrate how lawyers view tactics such as litigation, lobbying, organizing, and public education not in insolation, but as mutually reinforcing components of an overall strategic enterprise.

First, when lawyers in both cases invoked litigation, they explicitly considered how their litigation choices would affect legislative, public education, and other mobilization efforts. Marriage equality lawyers, for example, viewed litigation as a tactic that not only had value in its own right, but also could be used to further legislative and public education agendas. In individual cases concerning rights of domestic partners, movement lawyers used litigation to publicly display the human toll of laws denying rights to same-sex partners in order to generate support for legislative change. For example, they highlighted the unjust denial of wrongful death benefits to same-sex partners in a high-profile case on behalf of a woman whose partner was mauled to death by a dog. Cummings & NeJaime, *supra*, at 1263-64. Similarly, litigation for victim compensation benefits on behalf of the gay partner of a man killed in the World Trade Center attack on 9/11 not only advanced the client's interests, but also drew support for the passage of a state law providing inheritance rights to same-sex partners. *Id.* at 1264. Cases such as these were important in establishing greater support for expanded state law rights for domestic partners and building a political base that would support legislative reform. Movement lawyers selected and litigated them with a clear eye toward how they could reinforce and build their legislative strategy and advance the movement's overarching goal of expanding the relationship rights of same-sex couples.

Important decisions such as the selection of lead plaintiffs in litigation also had important public education implications. Once litigation became inevitable because of the challenge to Mayor Newsom's issuance of marriage licenses to same-sex couples, movement lawyers tried to broaden the public's view of gay and lesbian couples in the selection of plaintiffs who would serve as the public face of the lawsuits. For example, in *Woo v. Lockyer*, lawyers sought to select plaintiffs who would be more broadly reflective of the state's gay population than the stereotyped version of the white, urban gay male. This was, at bottom, a litigation decision — but one made with the public education campaign and the development of public support in mind.

Additionally, litigation in the marriage equality movement was used to defend crucial legislative victories. In one important example, lawyers intervened to defend the enactment of the domestic partnership bill, AB 205, from a lawsuit by social conservative interest groups. *Id.* at 1314-15.

In the Wal-Mart campaign, litigation was also understood and strategically deployed in relation to other tactics. The pre-election challenge to Measure 04-A was a key example. Although lawyers were skeptical about the judiciary's willingness to interfere with the electoral process, they decided to pursue the lawsuit nonetheless. Cummings, *Wal-Mart, supra*, at 1967. Their decision did not simply involve a calculation of whether they could prevail in court.

> [T]he legal team ultimately agreed to pursue a pre-election challenge for two reasons. First, the lawyers and LAANE agreed that they should take advantage of the outside chance to succeed on the merits to shut the initiative down. In fact, LAANE was concerned about its ability to win the election outright and thus viewed litigation as perhaps its best chance of ultimately gaining victory in Inglewood. Second, LAANE believed that even if the lawsuit proved unsuccessful, it could serve beneficial purposes. An early filing would put Wal-Mart on notice that, even if it won the election, it would face a strong legal challenge that would at the very least tie up the plan in court for some time. Moreover, LAANE viewed the lawsuit as a way of generating additional media visibility and grassroots momentum for its voter mobilization efforts. Toward this end, [coalition attorney] Margo Feinberg was able to persuade California Attorney General Bill Lockyer to issue a letter raising legal concerns about the initiative just before the filing of the lawsuit. Thus, even if the lawsuit did not prevent the election from going forward, LAANE and the broader coalition believed that the publicity it created would amplify its central argument: that Wal-Mart was attempting to place itself "above the law."

Id. at 1967-68. As it turned out, the lawyers' predictions were correct. A California court ruled against their pre-election challenge, yet the coalition ultimately concluded that the court ruling was important in helping grassroots organizing efforts and calling national attention to the campaign. *Id.* at 1969, 1986. Coalition lawyers then turned their attention to mapping out a post-election legal challenge to the initiative, but that proved unnecessary when Inglewood voters defeated Wal-Mart's initiative to approve the necessary zoning changes—aided, in part, by the anti-Wal-Mart publicity generated by the first suit.

As this example suggests, lawsuits that fail in the short term can nevertheless lead to longer-term wins. Some scholars have argued that public interest lawyers may capitalize on litigation losses by using them to help shape a movement or organization's identity, particularly for groups that are relatively new to the social change arena. *See* Douglas NeJaime, *Winning Through Losing*, 96 Iowa L. Rev. 941, 972-83 (2011). Advocates may also use a courtroom loss as a catalyst to mobilize their constituent groups into political action. *Id.* at 983-88. Both of these effects can have substantial benefits for a movement's efforts to educate the public about its cause and to generate active support in the community for legislative reform, fundraising, and community organizing. As Doug NeJaime points out, losing litigation can also redirect movements in productive ways. For example, a litigation loss in federal court may usefully refocus movement strategy on state courts, as occurred in the wake of the Supreme Court's decision in *Bowers v. Hardwick*, when LGBT lawyers invested in state court litigation to overturn laws banning consensual same-sex sexual conduct. *Id.* at 989-98. Major litigation losses can also have a generative effect on reform by other government institutions, primarily legislatures. Movement lawyers can use their lack of courtroom success to appeal to political actors to provide legislative relief from the social problems they seek to address. *Id.* at 998-1002. Finally, of course, sophisticated advocates can use a litigation loss as a way of educating the general public and garnering sympathy and broader support for social reform efforts. *Id.* at 1002-11; *but see* Catherine Albiston, *The Dark Side of Litigation as a Social Movement Strategy*, 96 Iowa L. Rev. Bulletin 61 (2011) (arguing that litigation, without regard to outcome, can have a de-radicalizing effect and reshape social movements in undesirable ways that push in the direction of maintaining the status quo).

Just as litigation may affect other movement tactics, it is also the case that other tactics—legislative advocacy, public education, and others—may influence litigation, or anticipated future litigation. In the case studies, lawyers anticipated this relationship and planned advocacy efforts to reinforce litigation aims. For example, though the California marriage equality movement started as a campaign emphasizing legislative reform through expansion of domestic partnership rights, the coordinators of the legislative strategy anticipated that marriage litigation might occur down the road. Accordingly, movement lawyers constructed their legislative strategy for domestic partnership with an eye toward building a record that might eventually help future litigators succeed. This was no easy task. The short-term goal was to make substantial legislative advances toward recognition of rights for partners in committed same-sex relationships, such as hospital visitation and medical decision making. At the same time, such legislation had to be crafted in a way that was sensitive to the legal arguments that would be made in the event of future marriage litigation.

Movement lawyers pursued a legislative strategy mindful of the prospect of future marriage litigation, carefully creating a record that would aid such litigation when it occurred. There were two facets to this strategy. First, in the context of domestic partnership, lawyers made sure that the legislative record supported the potential legal arguments that the state did not have any legitimate interests in withholding marriage from same-sex couples, and that such a denial was based on animus. In according same-sex couples all the rights and benefits of marriage, the comprehensive domestic partnership law emphasized the prevalence of discrimination against same-sex couples while affirming the legitimacy and value of same-sex-couple-headed families. The law also clearly (and deliberately) demonstrated that domestic partnership remained an institution separate from, and inferior to, marriage. This put movement lawyers in a strong position during the [state supreme court] Marriage Cases, allowing them to argue that domestic partnership was separate and unequal, but that full-blown marriage for same-sex couples was, in a sense, only a small—albeit crucially important—step for the courts to take.

The second facet of the legislative strategy—advancing a marriage bill—was ultimately unsuccessful, but also showed how lawyers viewed the interplay between legislation and litigation. In the wake of the Newsom decision, it became clear to movement lawyers that it would be valuable to have married same-sex couples in California in order to show that "the sky didn't fall." This would be helpful in making the constitutional case that there was no harm in same-sex marriage and thus any exclusion based on sexual orientation was irrational.

Cummings & NeJaime, *supra*, at 1313-14.

3. Multidimensionality Across Public Interest Practice

As the following excerpt suggests, the efforts of lawyers in the case studies to integrate legal and nonlegal tactics in a broader multidimensional advocacy approach are consistent with evidence from other public interest contexts.

Empirical research on public interest lawyers suggests that they often view their work as complementing and contributing to political mobilization. McCann and Helena Silverstein's study of the pay-equity and animal rights movements found that lawyers generally did not view lawsuits as "ends in themselves" and were "committed to encouraging, enhancing, and supplementing" movement activity. Similarly, Ann Southworth's study of civil rights and poverty lawyers found that both groups saw litigation as part of multidimensional strategies. Many perceived lawsuits as "political assets" that could provoke legislative reform, discourage future wrongdoing, and mobilize community participation. In the same vein, Cummings' project on low-wage worker advocacy in Los Angeles has examined lawyers who view legal advocacy as part of a comprehensive campaign that deploys multiple strategies to advance local policy reforms to strengthen labor rights.

Rhode's recent empirical study of prominent public interest organizations confirms that their leaders generally recognize the need to think strategically and to pursue multiple approaches. Litigation remains important, but it is used strategically in tandem with other initiatives. Some 90% of leading public interest legal organizations bring impact cases, and nearly half devote at least 50% of their efforts to such work. These lawsuits often attempt to maximize effectiveness by targeting practices that require systemic reform. Objectives apart from winning can be critical, such as making a public record, raising awareness, or imposing sufficient costs and delays that will force defendants to adopt more socially responsible practices. Many leaders stress the need to maintain litigation as a "credible threat," but also to avoid a "scattergun" approach that would "spread [resources] too thin" for structural change.

Cummings & Rhode, *supra*, at 611-12.

C. INSTITUTIONAL TARGETS

Public interest lawyers' decisions about the best tactical choices (*how* to advocate) are deeply shaped by the opportunities and constraints afforded by different institutional settings (*where* to advocate). As the case studies underscore, contemporary campaigns operate across a range of institutional settings in pursuit of reform, including legislative and regulatory bodies at the federal, state, and local levels, as well as adjudicative forums for dispute resolution. In short, public interest lawyers seek to exploit advocacy opportunities for advancing their cause wherever the institutional context seems most promising.

In the California marriage equality campaign, the institutional choice was initially framed by the movement lawyers' assessment of judicial risk. They considered the fact that, despite important LGBT rights victories in the Supreme Court in *Romer v. Evans* and *Lawrence v. Texas*, most observers doubted that the Court would go so far as to recognize a constitutional right of same-sex couples to marry. And the California state supreme court, though potentially receptive to same-sex marriage, was still risky because of the ease with which California voters could (and ultimately did) overturn a judicial decision that voters perceived as getting "too far ahead" of public opinion. The state legislature, in contrast, was a relatively progressive forum for expanding the rights of same-sex couples. Finally, for much of the campaign, California's governor was not only supportive of LGBT rights, but also had actively campaigned on that issue.

Nonetheless, as the California case suggests, even the most well-thought-out choice of institutional targets does not mean that leaders can either control the choice of forum or mitigate the potential for backlash. Despite movement lawyers' best efforts, they were eventually dragged into litigation initiated by same-sex marriage opponents in the wake of San Francisco's issuance of marriage licenses. As this underscores, organizations opposed to marriage equality mobilized themselves as much in response to *political* progress toward marriage equality as they did in response to the California Supreme Court's marriage decision. This dynamic—opponents pushing back against gains achieved in any institutional setting—was consistent with the experience in states such as Maine, where the state legislature adopted a same-sex marriage law, only to have it overturned by the state's voters. Thus, "the different institutional postures of the initial legalization did not determine the ultimate outcomes." Cummings & NeJaime, *supra*, at 1325.

In the Wal-Mart campaign, labor and community advocates focused initially on public education and legislative reform, in part because there was no obvious litigation option to bar Wal-Mart from locating a Supercenter in Ingle-wood. Movement leaders first pursued a big-box ban in the state legislature and the Inglewood city council to no avail. Thus thwarted, the Inglewood coalition was forced into a local site fight, in which the land use planning process became the setting for what was primarily a labor rights struggle.

> The opportunity to challenge Wal-Mart at the local level stems from the ple-nary power of cities to control land use planning for the public welfare, which gives them broad discretion over the process of granting development entitle-ments and codifying general land use plans. Developers generally must go through a local planning commission to obtain key discretionary land use approvals, such as zoning variances and conditional use permits, which the City Council must then approve. The structure of the entitlements process permits well-organized opposition groups with strong political connections to delay or even deny key approvals based on legitimate land use concerns, such as limiting sprawl or preventing incompatible uses. Accordingly, politi-cally influential labor groups can lobby governmental officials to deny land use approvals for Wal-Mart Supercenters, which frequently need zoning changes or amendments to a city's general land use plan to accommodate their massive sites.
>
> Another key legal lever in the site fight process is embedded in the process of environmental clearance for development projects. In California, this process centers on the California Environmental Quality Act (CEQA), which requires that a public agency, such as a city's planning commission, evaluate the envi-ronmental impact of projects before issuing discretionary development approvals or providing public subsidies. If the public agency determines that the project may have a significant environmental impact, an environmental impact report (EIR) must be prepared and circulated for public comment. The final approval of a project may be challenged in court on the grounds that it does not meet the substantive and procedural requirements of CEQA, forcing the agency to repeat the EIR process. Though it is not possible to defeat a project on the grounds of a defective EIR, it is possible to cause costly delays and build additional pressure on local officials to vote against a project if the negative environmental impacts appear to be substantial.

Cummings, *Wal-Mart, supra*, at 1963-64. Movement leaders in the Inglewood case sought to use these processes to gain leverage for their opposition to Wal-Mart either to stop the siting or negotiate improvements to workplace condi-tions. In the end, it was precisely Wal-Mart's disinclination to pick those fights that prompted them to try to circumvent the land use approval process with Measure 04-A—a decision that ultimately backfired. This suggests that both sides in deeply contested campaigns attempt to maneuver themselves into the most favorable institutional venues—while trying to block their opponents from gaining the same advantage.

D. ADAPTABILITY

Movement lawyers in all types of campaigns must anticipate and adapt to the setbacks that inevitably arise. This has always been the case, though to the degree that the public interest and broader political field is defined by sophisticated movement/counter-movement organizational dynamics, strategic flexibility becomes even more significant. What the case studies suggest is that the contemporary field of social struggle is highly mobilized on all sides; any advance by movement lawyers and activists is met by responses from counter-movements. Public interest lawyers and their allies must therefore anticipate responses and adapt to changed circumstances. In addition, the number of individual and institutional actors involved and the inability to foresee or forestall all moves by interested parties (as the movement lawyers in California were unable to prevent AFER's filing of a federal lawsuit challenging Proposition 8) makes the social change arena increasingly complex. In this context, a crucial aspect of public interest lawyering is anticipating opponents' moves if possible and changing course when necessary.

1. Backlash

As we have seen, some critics of public interest litigation have claimed that it can do more harm than good. Court-ordered reforms, even by the U.S. Supreme Court, are often illusory or short-lived. And, what is potentially more damaging, they can result in backlash from those opposed to a dramatic shift in the law. In Rosenberg's view, litigation under many conditions is counterproductive, resulting in "two steps forward, one step back." ROSENBERG, *supra*, at 368. He and other critics attribute backlash to naive reliance on the courts by movement lawyers. However, the blameworthiness of movement lawyers for these decisions presupposes that bringing impact litigation was a conscious decision on their part — which, as we have seen, is not always the case.

Because of the dynamics and complexity of social movements, public interest lawyers are not always in control of decisions regarding litigation and other tactical options. Rather, they are frequently drawn into litigation reluctantly in reaction to other events or acts, including litigation brought by other parties. Instead of sitting on the sidelines, public interest lawyers in this posture may try to intervene and influence the litigation even if they would prefer that it had never been brought.

Concerns about backlash were central to the marriage equality movement from the earliest stages. Indeed, the initial decision to not pursue marriage equality through litigation was driven by movement lawyers' strong perception of backlash risk. This perception was based on the experience at that point, which significantly included the backlash against the Hawaii Supreme Court's 1993 decision in *Baehr v. Lewin*, 852 P.2d 44 (Haw. 1993), in which voters quickly enacted a constitutional amendment authorizing its legislature to prohibit same-sex marriage.[2] As indicated earlier, backlash concerns were also based on a close analysis of California voters' views on same-sex marriage

---

2. Since the time the case study was published, there has been at least one concrete illustration that fears about backlash against the judiciary are not unfounded. In *Varnum v. Brien*, 763 N.W.2d 862 (Iowa 2009), the Iowa Supreme Court held that state laws banning same-sex marriage violated the state constitution. In November 2010, Iowa voters recalled three state supreme court justices who had voted to strike down the state marriage laws. A.G. Sulzberger, *Ouster of Iowa Judges Sends Signal to Bench*, N.Y. TIMES, Nov. 4, 2010, at A1.

and the likelihood that a state court victory would be reversed via ballot initiative. Fueled by these concerns, movement lawyers pursued the legislative route to expand rights for domestic partners in order to minimize risk of backlash. However, they found that despite their efforts to avoid litigation on the constitutional validity of same-sex marriage, opponents nonetheless drew them into court, ultimately forcing a resolution of the issue in the California Supreme Court's *In re Marriage Cases*, which was sparked by lawsuits brought by religious conservatives. In this context, rather than preempting backlash, lawyers come to think of their work as dealing with its inevitability. In reflecting on the California marriage equality campaign, the case study authors conclude as follows:

> Litigation plays an important, but not decisive, strategic role: It is part of an overall arsenal that includes legislative advocacy and public education, and it is always undertaken in the context of a careful analysis of the likely political consequences and how they might be addressed. Opposition is constant and sophisticated, so that there is never a clear "win," only moves that are certain to be countered. In this sense, the model of lawyering in the marriage equality context is not one of avoiding backlash, but managing its inevitable onset by influencing its form and intensity.

Cummings & NeJaime, *supra*, at 1329.

2. Events Beyond Public Interest Lawyers' Control

The diversity of stakeholders—not all of whom agree about strategic and tactical priorities—further complicates social change campaigns. As suggested above, parties that are sympathetic to the substantive goals of movement leaders, though not in sync with their strategic priorities, may trigger unanticipated events that lead lawyers to situations they did not expect or want. And, as we have suggested, movement opponents are always on the lookout for opportunities to wrest control of the issue. The case studies provide several illustrations of how this may occur.

First, powerful actors not directly involved in a social movement may take actions that disrupt the planned strategy of a campaign. In the marriage equality campaign, the most important instance of this was Mayor Newsom's unexpected decision to order the San Francisco clerk to start issuing marriage licenses to same-sex couples. Newsom's decision, motivated by both his sincere views and political considerations, was made without consulting leaders in the LGBT movement, though he did notify them before he made his public announcement. Movement lawyers first tried to dissuade him from going forward because of concerns about the political fallout. Once it was clear that Newsom was not going to change his mind, however, they altered course to seize the opportunity for public education about same-sex marriage, while also offering Newsom support in the form of talking points about marriage litigation and other issues that would help him address the media. Thus, lawyers adapted to this unanticipated move to maximize its public education potential as well as to defend its substance.

Second, as we've seen, litigation may be initiated by lawyers outside of— and sometimes in spite of—movement lawyer control. Lawsuits can be brought by private lawyers with pro-movement sympathies (often to the dismay of movement lawyers) or by opponents. In either situation, the choice for movement lawyers is the same: to sit out or intervene. Recall that in the heat of the Proposition 8 campaign, movement leaders publicly argued that turning to the federal court would not be the optimal strategy should the initiative pass. Nonetheless, shortly after the election, elite private lawyers Ted Olson and David Boies filed *Perry v. Schwarzenegger* (now pending on appeal to the Supreme Court as *Hollingsworth v. Perry*), on behalf of same-sex couples challenging the federal constitutionality of Proposition 8. The case was filed after consultation with movement lawyers but without their support.

The challenge for movement lawyers at that point was to figure out what role they should play in the *Perry* litigation. Though they initially determined that they should not intervene and would participate only as amici, they changed their decision (as described earlier) over a disagreement about the decision by Olson's team not to ask for a trial. While Olson viewed the matter as one that could be decided as a purely legal question, movement lawyers had spent years establishing the factual basis for many of the issues that would inevitably arise, such as the history of marriage, historical discrimination against gays and lesbians, and the extent to which gays and lesbians could protect themselves in the political process, and the empirical validity of any state interest in prohibiting same-sex couples from marrying. Against that backdrop, movement lawyers did not want the let the opportunity to develop a full factual record pass.

Although their effort to intervene was rejected, the San Francisco City Attorney was granted intervenor status and helped to secure a full evidentiary hearing. Thereafter, movement lawyers reengaged the Olson team, providing them with background information and helping them identify expert witnesses for trial. They continued to work as amici to help shape the legal issues to give the court an opportunity to rule against Proposition 8 on narrow grounds, which they hoped would protect a successful decision on appeal. The work of movement lawyers in the context of this epic federal litigation — which they had spent much of their professional lives trying to prevent — underscores the importance of recalibrating and persevering in the face of complex and dynamic social change processes.

In the Inglewood campaign, Wal-Mart's decision to put Measure 04-A on the city ballot caught everyone off guard. Recall that if approved, Measure 04-A would have amended local land use and zoning laws to create a special zone for the site that would "mandate the project's exact physical site plan and leasable space, its sewage and energy requirements, its transportation plan, its signage, and even its landscape design — all without having to go through the typical city land use approval and environmental review process." Cummings, *Wal-Mart, supra*, at 1959. In a measure designed to lock in the approval, the initiative also included a provision that would nullify any competing ballot initiative that was adopted with fewer votes than Measure 04-A, and would require a two-thirds vote to repeal measure 04-A (which itself only had to be approved by a majority vote). *Id.* at 1959-60. This tactic forced the coalition to adapt its overall strategy to defeat Measure 04-A, putting them on the defensive and refocusing its resources on legal, public education, and electoral strategies around the ballot initiative. In the end, the coalition was able to turn the surprise of Measure 04-A to its advantage — portraying it as a usurpation of power and convincing Inglewood residents to vote it down.

E. COLLABORATION

Never depend upon institutions or government to solve any problem. All social movements are founded by, guided by, motivated and seen through by the passion of individuals.

Margaret Mead[3]

The success of social movements is to a large degree dependent upon effective collaboration among organizations and the individuals who lead them. This is not always easy to accomplish given the stakes involved, the natural desire to seek credit for one's organization in social reform victories, the differences in available resources and access to policy makers and courts, and the egos of leaders and public officials.

As we have seen throughout this book, social change campaigns often involve a large and diverse set of actors whose interactions and conflicts shape the campaigns' trajectory. When law is used as a reform tool, lawyers with relevant experience and a range of skills and subject matter expertise are called upon to participate. How these lawyers relate to other actors is a key factor shaping the scope and nature of cross-disciplinary collaborations. These relations are influenced by many factors, including the backgrounds of the lawyers and other stakeholders, and how they all understand and seek to advance collaborative values and multidimensional practice.

Both of these case studies reveal the challenges to and benefits of collaboration. In the marriage equality context, the movement was made up a range of groups, including LGBT rights legal organizations, public policy groups like Equality California, university-based programs, progressive faith-based groups, civil rights organizations focused on non-LGBT issues but supportive of the cause, and sympathetic public officials and private stakeholders. From the outset, substantive differences of opinion about the validity of marriage as a movement goal created divisions. Some members of the LGBT community viewed domestic partnership as a desirable end in itself, rather than a "stepping stone" to same-sex marriage. They did not view marriage as normatively desirable or strategically helpful to advancing the goal of creating space for alternative family arrangements. Others viewed marriage equality as the ultimate civil rights objective for same-sex couples.

There were differences in background and approach. LGBT rights lawyers were elite-educated and well credentialed, which allowed them to gain influence in setting the agenda and making tactical decisions. The national movement for marriage equality overall was highly legalized, which reinforced the privileged position of lawyers as movement decision makers. That was a

---

3. David Suzuki & Holly Dressel, From Naked Ape to Superspecies: Humanity and the Global Eco-Crisis 347 (2d ed. 2004).

benefit in many respects, since it brought the movement a high level of specialized skill, experience, and knowledge that produced significant victories, such as the *Goodridge* decision in Massachusetts. However, it may also have limited the movement's field of political vision in ways that marginalized competing interests in promoting non-marital relationship recognition regimes. Thus, "a distinct criticism of the movement [has been] that the focus on achieving marriage as a legal right—waged by relatively well-off, mostly white, elite-educated lawyers in relatively well-resourced organizations—may have had the effect of de-radicalizing the movement and narrowing the field of possible alternatives within the broader arena of LGBT activism." Cummings & NeJaime, *supra*, at 1327. Yet in the effort to achieve the right to marry, movement lawyers worked in a highly collaborative fashion with political strategists, organizers, media relations experts, and other nonlawyers dedicated to the cause. To advance legislation, they relied on the expertise of the Equality California staff, which had the relations in the state legislature and knew how to mobilize votes for pro-LGBT bills. There were setbacks along the way, but these often produced stronger institutional leadership and collaboration over time. For instance, after the failed campaign against Proposition 22 (which created a statutory bar to recognition of same-sex marriage), there were concerns about the lack of strong political leadership to carry out statewide coordination. This resulted in the reorganization of Equality California as the central public education and legislative advocacy arm of the movement.

Over the course of the campaign, movement lawyers coordinated with grassroots groups to mobilize against Proposition 8 and protest the California court decision upholding its validity. Throughout the decades-long campaign, lawyers were also attentive to working with media specialists to promote their message and change public opinion. Collaboration with research institutes was another important element of the movement's overall strategy. The Williams Institute at the UCLA School of Law, a national research institute devoted to examining issues of sexual orientation law and policy, was an important resource for valuable empirical data at various stages of the legislative and legal campaign. The Williams Institute was also a source of credibility outside the movement because of its commitment to objective research that did not simply toe the movement line. *Id.* at 1316. It also served as an important intermediary that facilitated discussions among movement leaders about strategic options and the tradeoffs of pursuing a litigation campaign. *Id.* at 1269-70. In addition to these enduring partnerships, other collaborations were more ad hoc and strategic. During the advocacy for early domestic partnership legislation in California, for example, advocates built a bridge to senior citizens' groups for support because unmarried senior couples would benefit from the extension of some domestic partnership rights in the same way as same-sex couples. This had the strategic benefit of mobilizing another powerful constituency in favor of the bill—thus helping to win lawmakers' votes by making domestic partnership not only about gays and lesbians. *Id.* at 1259.

As this analysis suggests, although the marriage equality movement is associated with top-down litigation efforts driven by movement lawyers, it has progressed in a more collaborative fashion — with multiple stakeholders pursuing different advocacy paths and often contesting the normative centrality of marriage. Yet, as the case study highlights, collaboration is a fragile enterprise. In the most recent phase of the movement, the interest group AFER, along with non-movement lawyers Olson and Boies, have wrested control from the main movement organizations and taken a high-stakes gamble on the Supreme Court. The decision by the *Perry* lawyers to pursue the fundamental right to marry in the Supreme Court — despite winning a ruling on narrower, state-specific (and therefore, some believe, less legally vulnerable) grounds at the Ninth Circuit — may result in a monumental victory that changes the course of marriage equality advocacy in the United States. If it does not, critics will wonder whether the *Perry* team was seduced by the "myth of rights" to break ranks with movement strategy for an ill-advised judicial long shot — bringing the conversation back to the question of whether collaborative decision making and advocacy results in more effective social reform.

The Wal-Mart campaign also illustrates the power and perils of collaboration. The Inglewood mobilization was built on the premise that there is power in bringing together diverse groups around the same goal. To challenge Wal-Mart's big-box plans, leaders from LAANE and the UFCW helped to create the Coalition for a Better Inglewood (CBI), bringing together Inglewood residents, public officials, union members, and a range of organizations with a stake in the outcome, including ACORN and the progressive faith-based group, Clergy and Laity United for Economic Justice. The goal of the coalition was to present a broad and unified front against Wal-Mart and to leverage the connections of different elements of the coalition to advance the cause. Throughout the campaign different member groups played important roles educating community members, coordinating media relations, turning out voters in the election on Measure 04-A, charting legal strategy, and lobbying for the Superstores Ordinances.

Yet coalitions, built upon the convergence of diverse interests, are complex and sometimes fragile entities. Like any broad-based institutional decision-making structure, members disagree and divisions may occur. Such divisions may be actively exploited by opponents. As discussed earlier, Wal-Mart has sought to weaken coalitions of community, labor, and environmental groups that oppose it by creating ties with African-American groups (e.g., making donations to the NAACP), while promoting initiatives to attract environmentalists (e.g., building "green" stores) and building community support (e.g., providing grants to community-based small businesses). Cummings, *Wal-Mart, supra*, at 1990-91.

Divisions within coalitions can also arise from differences among constituent groups about goals and strategy, which can create challenges for the lawyers seeking to represent them. For lawyers in the Wal-Mart campaign,

> there were complexities involved in representing both a multi-organizational coalition (CBI) and the lead organizing group (LAANE) within the same case. Group representation raises difficult questions about who speaks for the group, but here those questions were exacerbated to the degree that CBI itself was an amalgam of several groups that operated with a range of organizational formality and endowed with very different resources. Thus, on the one hand, CBI was composed of representatives from LAANE and the UFCW, who

brought critical financial and organizational resources; on the other, CBI contained more loosely constituted resident and faith-based groups that lent credibility and authenticity, but did not have the same decision-making clout. This created inherent questions of governance and authority to make decisions on behalf of the entire coalition. . . .

Id. at 1994.

How lawyers approach these issues may affect the sustained viability of the coalition and thus the ultimate success of the campaign. In the Inglewood case, the lawyers generally sought to address the potential for conflict by letting constituent groups hash out decisions on their own and then taking their instructions from the coalition's representatives. Although not without complication, this was designed to allow the coalition to come to decisions on its own terms in ways that would strengthen its bonds. The coalition's lawyers were personally committed to a client-centered approach that valued the full participation of community members and groups in the coalition's decision-making process, which further supported the goal of inter-organizational collaboration. *Id.* at 1992-93.

F. SUSTAINABILITY

Social change efforts do not end, they just change — as the struggle moves into different institutional domains, changes tone, or comes to address different issues. Examples from materials throughout this book underscore this central lesson: civil rights lawyers' victory in *Brown v. Board of Education* did not achieve immediate desegregation of public schools (and arguably still has not); *Roe v. Wade* affirmed a woman's constitutional right to choose to terminate a pre-viability pregnancy, yet abortion rights advocates have spent the more than three decades since *Roe* battling against well-organized counter-movement efforts to lobby for legislation imposing increased restrictions on women's access to abortion, defending such legislation from lawsuits, and urging the Court to overturn *Roe*; more recently, the victory obtained by gun rights advocates in *District of Columbia v. Heller* marked what will no doubt prove to be the beginning of an ongoing struggle to define the scope of permissible government regulation of firearms. These examples suggest that one element of a "successful" social change effort is simply its ability to sustain itself over time against changing legal, political, and social conditions, and in the face of persistent opposition. With that in mind, we turn back to our case studies to examine some of the features that may affect their sustainability.

One element of sustainability may be rooted in the very concept of multi-dimensional advocacy. That is, to the extent that efforts are coordinated across multiple institutional domains (courts, legislatures, media) using a range of tactics (litigation, policy advocacy, organizing, public education, and public relations), advocacy may be more resilient in the face of challenges. Thus, the marriage equality campaign has grown stronger despite significant losses around the country in part owing to its leaders' skillful combination of mutually reinforcing tactics, their sensitivity to the need for holding crucial constituent groups together, and multi-forum advocacy that has helped them adapt to counter-movement efforts and unexpected events that disrupt the campaign.

Advocates' ability to "shift scales" — going from the national to state to local level (and back) — may also promote sustainability. The Inglewood campaign directs attention to the reciprocal nature of national and local organizing campaigns. Local activism can respond to the limits of national-level efforts (in the Wal-Mart case, the failure of federal labor law). Such local efforts can benefit from national resources and strategic assistance (such as the support of national groups like Good Jobs First). Local campaigns, in turn, can feed their experience and resources back to national organizations (like the labor-backed Partnership for Working Families), which disseminate successful models to other communities, where they can be deployed and adapted to local conditions. This dynamic national-local feedback can strengthen and extend social change efforts across jurisdictions. Within these networks, lawyers who develop expertise in one local campaign — for instance, by drafting model legislation — can serve as a valuable resource to national groups coordinating with activists elsewhere. In this way, local experimentation can help sustain support for a cause from the bottom up by building successful precedent, offering inspiration, and diffusing expertise that can be adapted to distinct political contexts.

In this process, policy victories can — sometimes — actually protect advocacy gains and promote long-term movement sustainability. The Superstores Ordinances in Los Angeles and Inglewood offer a case in point. Remember that these ordinances require proposed big-box developers to conduct a comprehensive analysis of their proposed stores' economic impact on the community (local workers, consumers, other local businesses, tax revenues, etc.) as a condition of securing land use approval. The laws alter the ex ante bargaining position of developers and community groups by making developers show that they will do no harm and giving community groups the opportunity to demand concessions to ameliorate negative impacts — such as agreements to pay employees a living wage as a condition of being awarded development permits. *Id.* at 1981-82. The laws also make it less likely that Wal-Mart will incur the cost of attempting to site a big-box store within these jurisdictions in the first instance. In fact, since the ordinances were passed, Wal-Mart has not sought to open a store in the big-box format. This not only affects local communities, but also advances the labor movement to the extent that unionized groceries are shielded from Wal-Mart's nonunion competition. And indeed, in the aftermath of the Wal-Mart campaign, Southern California grocery chains struck a favorable collective bargaining agreement that area unions hailed as a victory for grocery workers and the broader labor movement. In this sense, the local site fight contributed to building the Los Angeles labor movement.

The technical features of the Superstores Ordinances may also promote their long-term effectiveness. Instead of mandating that big-box retailers pay workers at a specified living wage level and provide designated benefits, the ordinances set up a process for information exchange and negotiation — consistent with the "new governance" regulatory approaches that we studied in Chapter 5. *See* Charles F. Sabel & William H. Simon, *Destabilization Rights: How Public Law Litigation Succeeds*, 117 Harv. L. Rev. 1015, 1019 (2004); William H. Simon, *Solving Problems vs. Claiming Rights: The Pragmatist Challenge to Legal Liberalism*, 46 Wm. & Mary L. Rev. 127, 181, 193, 198 (2004). Because they avoid top-down mandates in favor of flexible benchmarks, proponents suggest that they may promote more effective and sustainable policy outcomes since disputes over the economic impact of development projects can be evaluated and negotiated on a case-by-case basis in light of distinct circumstances. In addition, they provide a framework for sustained participation by community groups that avoids the necessity of a costly site fight each time they may oppose a big-box store.

V. CONTINUING CHALLENGES

Although these case studies reveal the transformative possibilities of legal reform campaigns, they also underscore the continuing challenges that public interest lawyers face. These challenges include sustained institutional resistance to law reform efforts; intra-coalition conflicts on the inside of movements and the potency of counter-movements on the outside; ongoing barriers to funding public interest practice; and the ingrained limits of traditional legal education to nurture and train public interest lawyers. In the end, we would expect public interest lawyering to always be an uphill battle — challenging the established structures of power is never easy and never over. It is a persistent struggle that changes and adapts. The hallmark of public interest lawyering, then, is a recognition that the fight never ends, success is never complete, but that the struggle must nonetheless constantly be joined — and rejoined. Courage and perseverance in the face of powerful opposition thus defines public interest lawyering. In this sense, understanding the challenges that the work confronts and how best to respond is not simply a point of academic concern — it is essential to the movement's success going forward.

In this spirit we conclude with two different perspectives on the challenges that confront public interest lawyers at this juncture in the movement's history. Deborah Rhode focuses attention on organizational challenges, particularly the need for funding, and highlights the specific political constraints; Louise Trubek concludes by identifying barriers to the completion of public interest law's "unfinished projects."

DEBORAH L. RHODE, *PUBLIC INTEREST LAW: THE MOVEMENT AT MIDLIFE*

60 Stan. L. Rev. 2027, 2042-46 (2008)

[L]eaders of public interest organizations are also acutely aware of the limitations of their achievements and the major challenges that remain. The fundamental problem involves resources. Direct service providers and human rights organizations face the most obvious and painful reminders of the overwhelming demand and limited capacity to meet it. Brooklyn Legal Services is forever "putting a thumb in the dyke;" the vast majority of needs of disabled, homeless, and immigrant populations remain unserved. "Bailing with a thimble" is how Gen Fujioka, director of the Asian Law Caucus, described a similar experience. Restrictions on legal service programs and attorneys' fees have left only a tiny number of lawyers available to handle prisoners' rights cases for 2.3 million incarcerated individuals. Human Rights Watch has only two staff members in areas of Asia that account for a quarter of the world's population.

Although liberal public interest leaders often described opposing conservative organizations as "well-heeled," the heads of those groups tended to see themselves as financial underdogs. Leaders of the Center for Equal Opportunity, the Criminal Justice Legal Foundation, the Heritage Foundation, and Mountain States Legal Foundation, all perceived far more resources on the other side.

Even the richest organizations, environmental groups with $75 to $80 million in annual budgets, confronted major funding constraints, given the global dimensions of the challenges and the financial incentives of opponents. Natural Resources Defense Council President Beinecke acknowledged that her organization was better off than others in terms of "public and financial support, but the scale of the [environmental] problem is so much greater and the lack of a national strategy on issues like global warming is [more] appalling." Fred Krupp, president of the Environmental Defense Fund, similarly noted that because reform on the dimensions needed has broad economic effects, the political opposition has often been exceptionally intense and "the legislative strategies need to be unusually powerful, as do the resources to . . . execute them."

Other limitations involved the inadequacies of litigation, particularly given the increasingly conservative climate in judicial decision making. A long-standing critique of "cause lawyering" is that it places too much faith in lawsuits and diverts energy from the political strategies that are necessary to secure long-term social change. Many leaders shared those concerns, and noted that "victory in the courts does not necessarily mean victory in practice." As counter-majoritarian institutions, courts lack the legitimacy, expertise, and enforcement resources sometimes necessary for meaningful institutional reform. Doctrinal change without a political base to support it is vulnerable to chronic noncompliance, public backlash, statutory reversal, or judicial retrenchment. It is, as surveyed leaders generally recognized, impossible to "create policy," "change attitudes," or "build a movement" solely through litigation. Lawyers in this, as in other studies, have ample experience with rights gone wrong—litigation strategies that yielded only temporary victories or counterproductive consequences. The lesson that leaders like Buck Parker of Earth Justice have drawn is that organizations also need to have educational programs, lobbying strength, and "staying power" to monitor agency and industry practices. As Ralph Nader once summed it up: "You have to deal with the adversary on all the fronts on which the adversary deals with you."

Yet such strategies, in turn, require a level of financial and popular support that many groups find difficult to marshal. Part of the reason public interest groups have relied heavily on lawsuits is because they can sometimes mobilize such support and because other options are less available. Courts may not always be the most effective dispute resolution forums, but they are often the most accessible; they are open as of right and can force more economically or politically powerful parties to the bargaining table. As research on social movements makes clear, lawsuits can help frame problems as injustices, identify perpetrators and responses, and reinforce a sense of collective identity, all of which build a political base for reform. In this, as in other surveys, leaders were under no illusions about the relative limitations of litigation, but they were equally realistic about their challenges in other policy arenas.

The challenges varied across substantive areas. The ability of gays and lesbians to pass for straight "enables individuals to avoid homophobia but undercuts their collective ability to challenge it." The public often sees Asians as the "model minority," and their relative economic success obscures the serious problems of poor and undocumented immigrants. Children might be "cuter and more sympathetic" than other groups, but they don't have the votes or money necessary for political leverage. Nor do undocumented immigrants, whose diversity in backgrounds and languages and hostile reception among large segments of the public complicate efforts by advocacy organizations. Groups representing poor communities often confront a public "exhausted by their plight." As noted earlier, civil rights and women's rights organizations are also hobbled by cultural complacency, and Americans' conviction that "we've solved that." Conservative groups feel that their issues are not "sexy," and fail to get sympathetic coverage in the press. Lawyers working on technology and individual rights emphasize their unique challenge in framing cases that would be compelling to the average American. It is "difficult to come up with a picture like belching smokestacks or kids with AIDS"; "peoples' eyes glaze over" when technology is at issue, even though it raises serious privacy and free speech concerns.

Robert Bernstein, director of the Bazelon Center for Mental Health Law, summarized the situation: "Everyone says the group they represent is worst off." In his view, however, "our [group] is. It is still fine to ridicule the crazy and psychotic." There were, however, other contenders for the "worst-off" title. Civil liberties' leaders acknowledged that "these are tough times for all liberal public interest organizations," but believed that it was hardest for their groups because it was easier to "ratchet up public fears" on security-related issues. Brian Stevenson of Equal Justice Initiative argued that prisoners, especially death penalty defendants, are "uniquely disempowered" and despised. Steven Bright of the Southern Center for Human Rights agreed, but added, "I didn't really know what unpopular was before I began representing sex offenders as well."

A final group of challenges that public interest leaders identified are more within their control. One concern involves the fragmentation of groups and splintering of their efforts. Too often individual organizations have "worked in silos," in isolation or in competition for resources and recognition. As subsequent discussion indicates, although most leaders reported a fair degree of collaboration, many also acknowledged competitive pressures that get in the way. Another concern involves expertise. Some leaders noted the disconnect between the skill set required for effective lawyering and that required for effective management. "Why didn't I go to business school?" was one direc-tor's question. Barbara Arnwine, director of the Lawyers' Committee for Civil Rights, put it bluntly: most public interest organizations "are not good at leadership development." Nor, according to some leaders, have their organiza-tions mastered the marketing skills necessary for effective public communica-tion. Only one leader, however, raised a concern often voiced by conservative critics, that public interest groups speak from a "too narrow" and "sometimes dogmatic" ideological perspective. On the whole, the picture that emerged was of a diverse, self-critical community, proud of its achievements but conscious of its challenges and the diverse strategies necessary to address them.

Louise G. Trubek, *Public Interest Law: Facing the Problems of Maturity*

33 U. Ark. Little Rock L. Rev. 417, 424-33 (2011)

A. Unfinished Projects: Inequality in Society and Limits of the Regulatory Process

Although the institutional project [of public interest law] can be deemed a success, two goals for public interest law envisioned in the 1970s have not fully been met and the sector faces two unfinished projects. First, income and resource inequalities within American society are increasing. Such inequalities are evident in the growing number of poor people, the increasing plight of the middle class, and the lack of legal resources for poor and moderate income people. Second, the regulatory process still has limited success in problem-solving for the public good. The recent recession, replete with the failures in the housing and financial markets and the contentious health care reform debate, indicate the continuing limits of administrative processes.

1. Income and Resource Inequalities: The Poor and Middle Class

Reducing poverty and creating a more equitable society were integral goals of the public interest founding decade. . . .

Today, the situation for the poor and moderate income people is grim. In September 2010, the U.S. Census Bureau reported that the number of people living in poverty increased for the third consecutive year, from 39.8 million people in 2008 to 43.6 million people in 2009. This estimate — 43.6 million people or 14.3% of the American population — was the highest in 51 years of data collection. The Bureau further noted that the increase in the overall pov-erty rate was "larger than the increase in the poverty rate during the November 1973 to March 1975 recession" but "smaller than the increase in the poverty rates associated with the January 1980 to July 1980 and July 1981 to November 1982 combined recessions."

In a recent op-ed piece, *New York Times* writer Bob Herbert noted that disabled or elderly low-income people are losing access to medical, rehabilita-tive, or other health services through budget cuts or increased service fees. "Look out the window[,]" Herbert observed. "More and more Americans are being left behind in an economy that is being divided ever more starkly between the haves and the have-nots." In July, Edward Luce of the *Financial*

Times discussed how middle class America is suffering at the hands of the "median wage stagnation"—also known as the "Great Stagnation"—in which "the annual incomes of the bottom 90 per cent of US families have been essentially flat since 1973—having risen by only 10 per cent in real terms over the past 37 years." In comparison, the incomes of the top 1% have tripled in the same amount of time. Luce noted that a majority of Americans now "expect their children to be worse off than they are." Some blame the stagnation on globalization while others point to the "conservative backlash" and the decline of unions starting with the Reagan era. Less than 10% of private sector workers belong to a union.

While public interest lawyers have continued to do anti-poverty work and the absolute number of poverty lawyers has increased, the percentage of lawyers in the overall public interest sector doing poverty work has declined. In the 1970s, almost-two thirds of all the lawyers in the public interest sector broadly defined worked on poverty issues. Today, using the same definitions, the percentage of poverty lawyers has fallen below 50% of the total, while the absolute number of people in poverty and the percentage of the population below the poverty line have increased.

2. The Limits of the Regulatory Process: The Need for Expanded Participation and Problem Solving

Reform of the regulatory process was one of the goals of the public interest law enterprise. In the period of the 1960s and 1970s there was an explosion of national legislation for consumer protection and environmental betterment. The War on Poverty provided a rich framework of laws that could substantially reduce inequality. The founding public interest lawyers believed that successful implementation of these laws would occur only through participation of under-organized groups at the agency and community level.

Today the financial and housing markets are in severe difficulty, based in part on inadequate regulatory oversight. The new health care legislation is mired in controversy over the role and breadth of government agencies in charge of the reforms. Richard Stewart in a recent article refers to the situation as "regulatory administrative fatigue." He states that the traditional method of "command and control" regulation is no longer viable due to increased complexity and rapid growth of technology. In addition to complexity and technology, there is contestation at the national level on the value of government [intervention]. He states that "participatory interest group approach" model for regulation can no longer be relied on as effective or efficient to meet the regulatory and political demands of the current time. . . .

4. From a Participant in the U.S. Legalist Democracy to a Participant Around the World

The 1970s public interest lawyers had a clear vision. They viewed themselves as reformist participants in a flawed but fixable democratic, market-based polity. They utilized respectable economic theories to support their claim for the participation of diffuse and subordinated groups in government decision-making. This participation was the route toward a more equitable and efficient national political economy. They expanded on the older concept of the lawyer as statesmen. The new concept was the lawyer as a key actor in the emerging new economic protections for the consumers and environment and as the protector of the economically impoverished and victims of racial and gender discrimination.

This clear vision is much harder to achieve today. Within the United States there is little agreement on a single overarching theory of how to achieve equality and equity. Despite substantial economic growth, inequality has grown, and the gap between rich and poor continues. Trying to solve these problems through better interest-group representation in administrative agencies seems naïve. The clear line between public action and private initiatives is eroding. Moreover, the public interest lawyers face a world where the clear demarcations of the nation-state are hard to see. Internationalization has affected domestic practice. Poverty lawyers face immigration as a crucial element in U.S. poverty. They also see the outsourcing of jobs to other countries. Both these challenges require knowledge of foreign laws and treaties and transnational links and networks.

There are examples of how U.S. lawyers are using international laws and networks as opportunities to assist American workers. Beth Lyon documents how US anti-poverty activists use international strategies to benefit immigrant worker movements in the United States. These include "'broadcasting' domestic violations to international entities, international law formation, and importing international standards into domestic advocacy." The emergence of human rights, including economic and social rights in the global arena, allows a greater range of tools that can be employed within the United States. . . . While promising, all these initiatives seem very fragile and preliminary. This is due in part to the newness of globalization and the difficulties of figuring out how to govern in a global world.

What is your reaction to these challenges? How significant are they? Are there others that the authors miss? What do you think the biggest challenges are facing public interest law students and lawyers? How does it vary by political context (liberal versus conservative), substantive area, and even location around the globe?

TABLE OF CASES

INDEX